HISPANIC ARTS *and* ETHNOHISTORY *in the* SOUTHWEST

A Spanish Colonial Arts Society Book

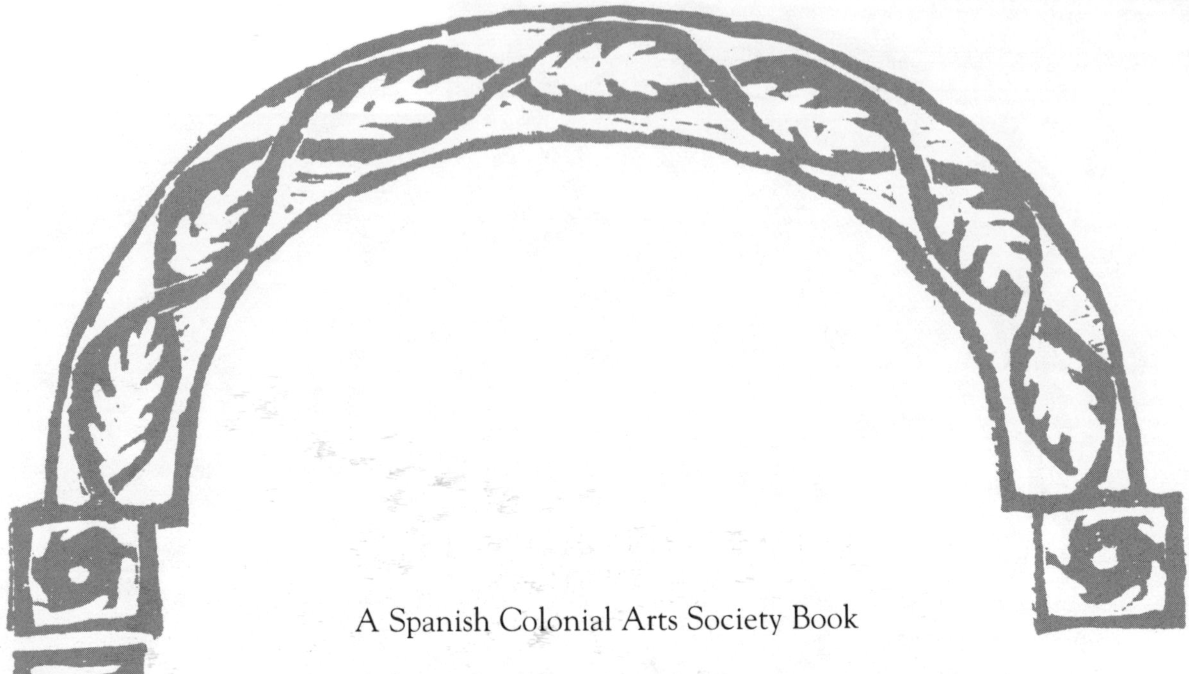

A Spanish Colonial Arts Society Book

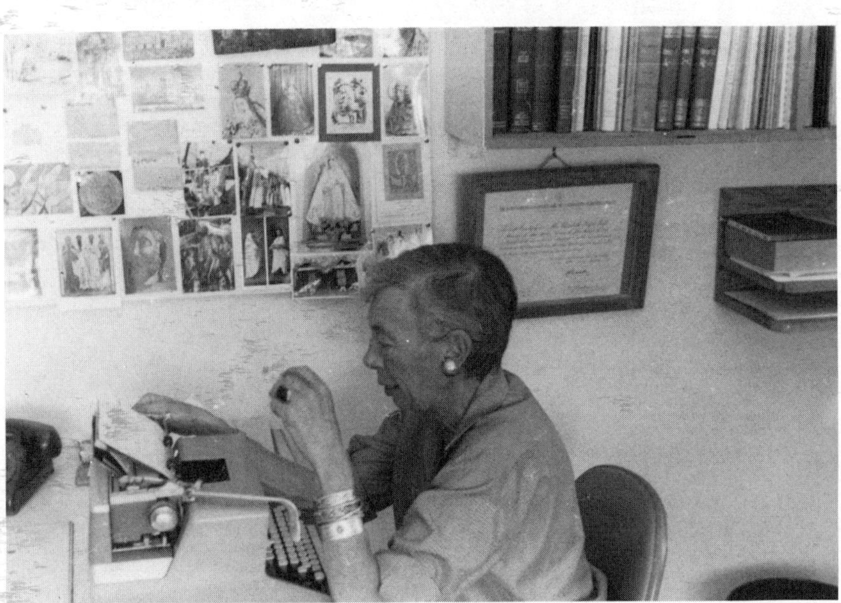

Photo by Richard B. Stark

E. Boyd (1903-1974)

University of New Mexico Press · Albuquerque, New Mexico

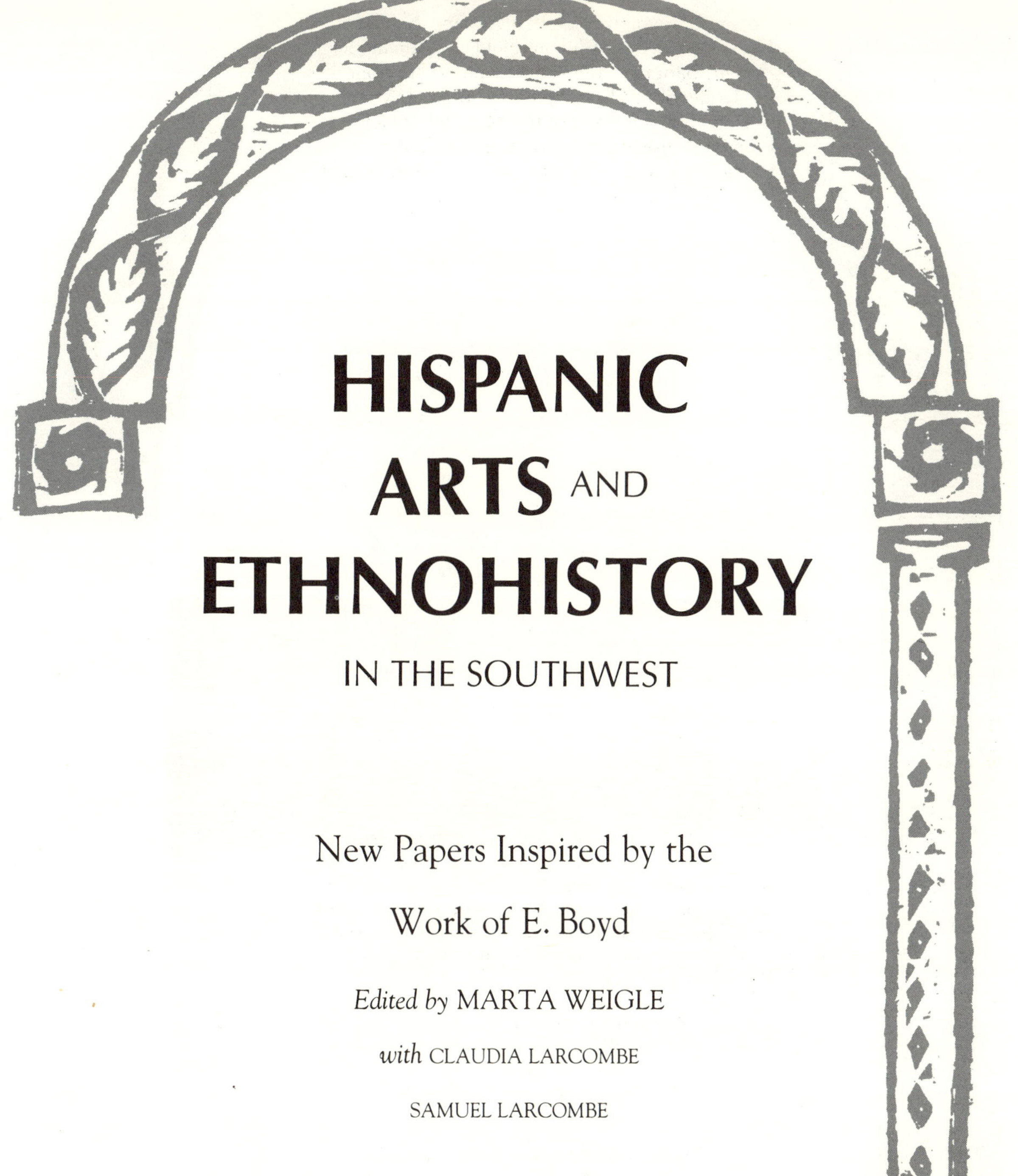

HISPANIC ARTS AND ETHNOHISTORY IN THE SOUTHWEST

New Papers Inspired by the Work of E. Boyd

Edited by MARTA WEIGLE

with CLAUDIA LARCOMBE

SAMUEL LARCOMBE

Ancient City Press · Santa Fe, New Mexico

Cover photograph by Robert Nugent, Santa Fe. It was designed by William Field of William Field Design, Santa Fe. Items in the photo are from the Collections of the Spanish Colonial Arts Society, Inc., on loan to the Museum of New Mexico, Museum of International Folk Art, Santa Fe. Woodcut title by Barbara Whitehead of Whitehead & Whitehead, Austin, Texas.

Second Printing

International Standard Book Number:
0-941270-13-0 (paperback)
0-941270-14-9 (case bound)
Library of Congress Catalogue Number:
82-74221

Designed by Whitehead & Whitehead
Austin, Texas
Typesetting by Business Graphics, Inc.
Albuquerque, New Mexico
Printed in the United States of America by
Inter-Collegiate Press
Shawnee Mission, Kansas

CONTENTS

PREFACE

E. BOYD WAS AN INTERNATIONALLY RECOGNIZED AUTHORITY on Spanish colonial arts and crafts in the Southwest. She began her career as an artist and art historian. After working on the *Portfolio of Spanish Colonial Design* for the New Mexico Federal Art Project in the 1930s, she directed her skills and training, both in New Mexico and at the Los Angeles County Museum in California, toward the research and conservation of Hispanic material culture. For nearly twenty-five years, E. Boyd served as Curator (later Curator Emeritus) of Spanish Colonial Art at the Museum of New Mexico in Santa Fe. She documented, conserved, and analyzed countless examples of Spanish colonial religious and domestic arts and crafts for that museum and for museums throughout the country. This lifework culminated in her monumental *Popular Arts of Spanish New Mexico,* published shortly before her death in 1974.

A pioneer scholar in the best sense, E. Boyd was an imaginative, exacting, and prolific worker who set high standards in all her work and by personal example. She was generous with her knowledge, and that generosity has provided inspiration to the twenty-three individuals who have contributed their own new work to this collection. Each has been deeply influenced by her professionally, and most were fortunate to have known her personally as well.

The essays have been divided into sections on E. Boyd, on Hispanic arts in the Southwest, on preservation, and on Hispano ethnohistory. A bibliography of E. Boyd's work precedes the bibliography of sources cited in the papers. The diversity and depth of these papers attest to E. Boyd's broad, longstanding commitment to the preservation and interpretation of Hispanic culture in New Mexico and throughout Spanish America.

The Spanish Colonial Arts Society was begun in 1925 by Santa Fe writer Mary Austin and artist Frank G. Applegate to help preserve traditional Spanish colonial arts within New Mexico and to encourage artisans. E. Boyd was instrumental in its revitalization during the early 1950s. The sale of this book benefits the Spanish Colonial Arts Society, Inc., and will help carry forward Boyd's work, assuring the continuation of society efforts to preserve traditional Spanish arts and crafts for New Mexico.

Generous contributions from the Spanish Colonial Arts Society, Inc., its members, and friends of E. Boyd have made possible the publication of this volume. Society members William Field, Alan C. Vedder, and Ann Vedder have supported the project throughout, as have the staffs and associates of the two presses, Ancient City Press and the University of New Mexico Press. Our colleagues whose work appears herein have responded promptly and graciously to the endeavor, and we are very grateful to them. This is truly a collective tribute to E. Boyd, and all contributions have been given in the same spirit which she brought to the task of preserving and understanding Hispanic arts and ethnohistory in the Southwest.

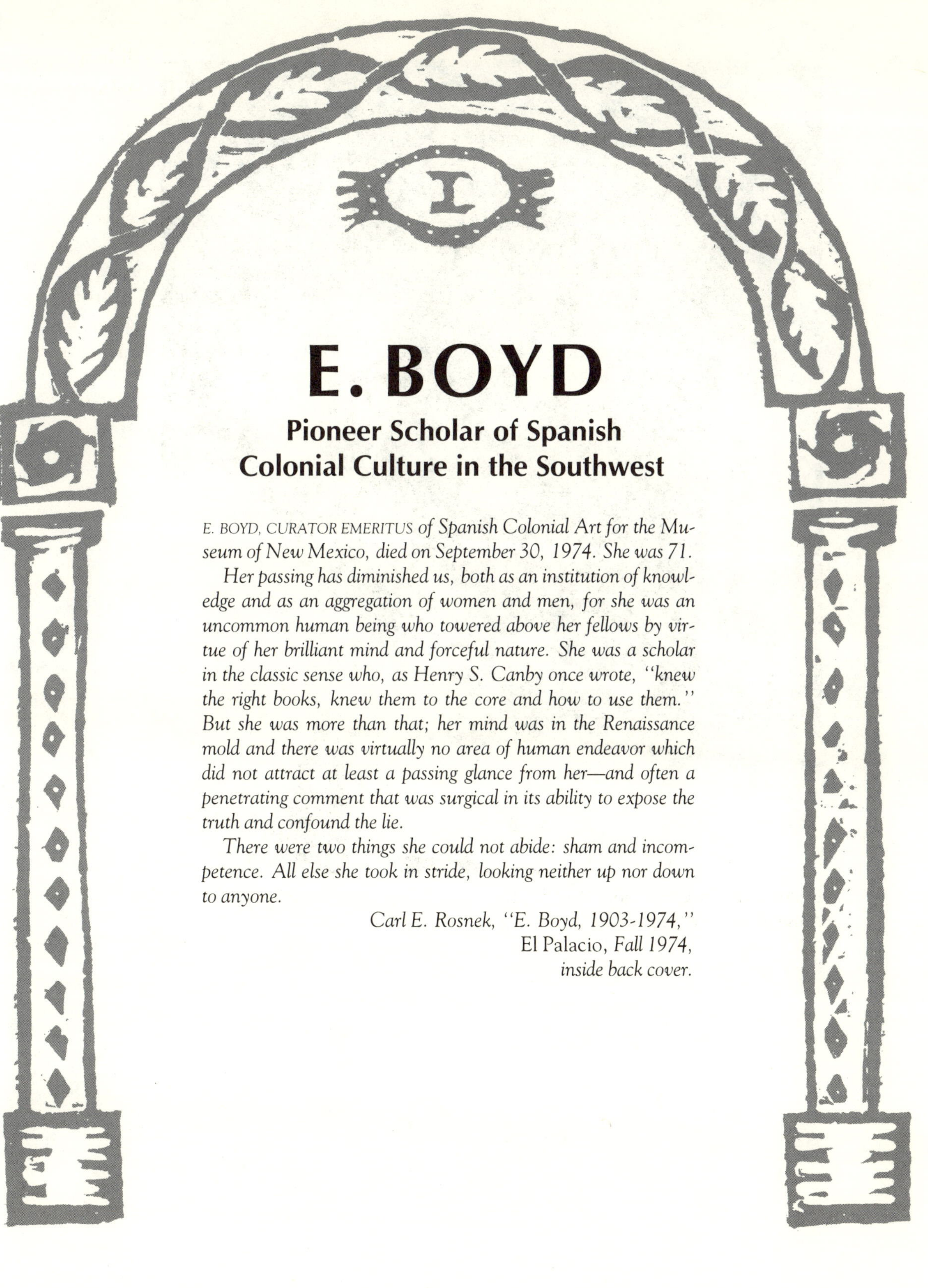

E. BOYD

Pioneer Scholar of Spanish Colonial Culture in the Southwest

E. BOYD, CURATOR EMERITUS *of Spanish Colonial Art for the Museum of New Mexico, died on September 30, 1974. She was 71.*

Her passing has diminished us, both as an institution of knowledge and as an aggregation of women and men, for she was an uncommon human being who towered above her fellows by virtue of her brilliant mind and forceful nature. She was a scholar in the classic sense who, as Henry S. Canby once wrote, "knew the right books, knew them to the core and how to use them." But she was more than that; her mind was in the Renaissance mold and there was virtually no area of human endeavor which did not attract at least a passing glance from her—and often a penetrating comment that was surgical in its ability to expose the truth and confound the lie.

There were two things she could not abide: sham and incompetence. All else she took in stride, looking neither up nor down to anyone.

Carl E. Rosnek, "E. Boyd, 1903-1974,"
El Palacio, *Fall 1974,*
inside back cover.

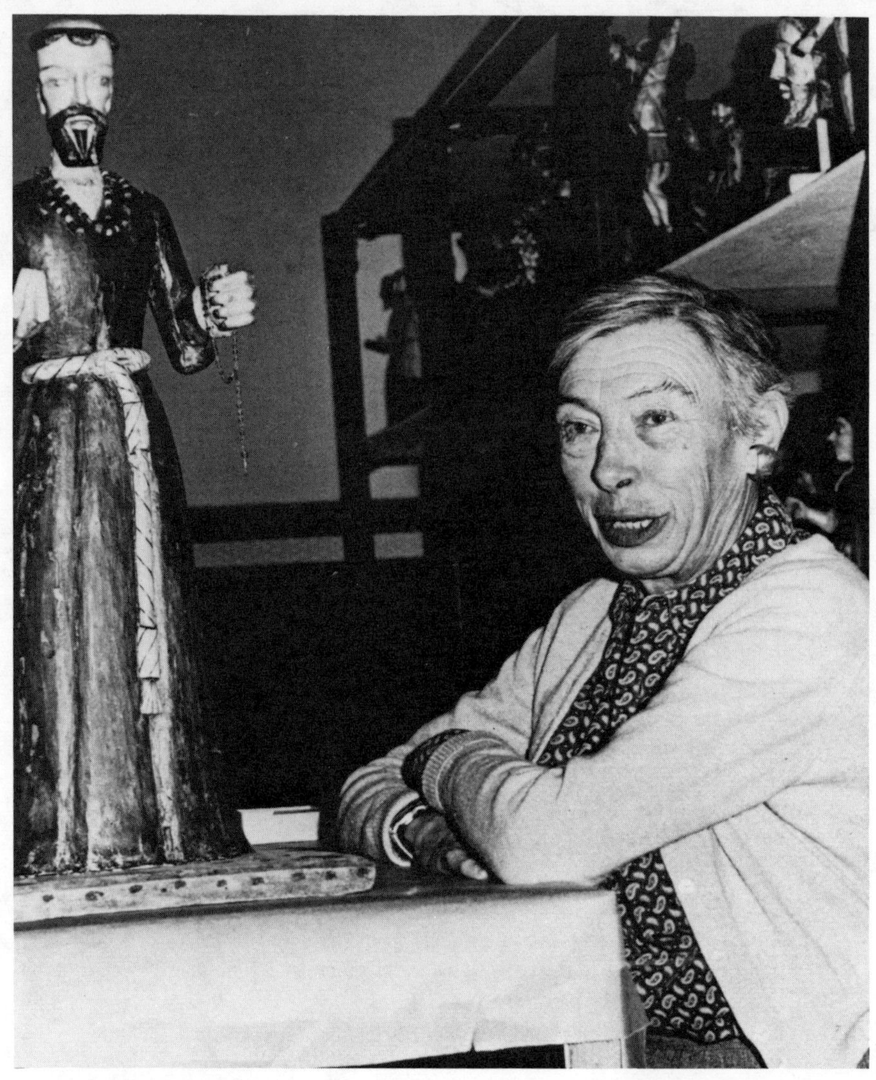

E. Boyd. (Photo Collections, No. 50818, Museum of New Mexico.)

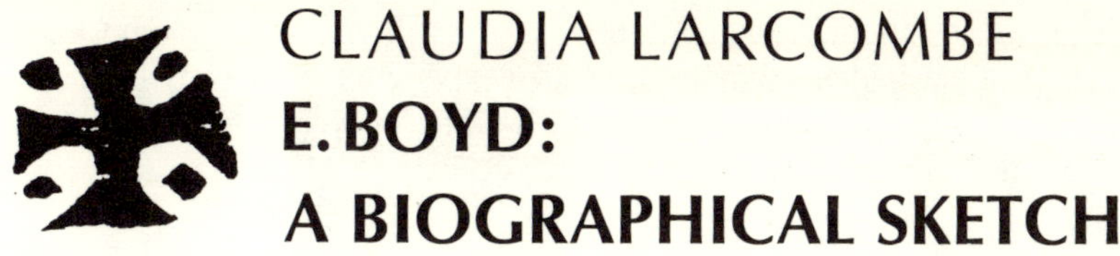

CLAUDIA LARCOMBE

E. BOYD: A BIOGRAPHICAL SKETCH

ELIZABETH BOYD WHITE, daughter of Susan and Edward White, was born in Philadelphia, Pennsylvania, on September 23, 1903. Known as E. Boyd, she became the internationally recognized authority on the Spanish colonial art of New Mexico. During her younger years, she received training both as a fine artist and as an art historian; later on, she called on this training, as well as on her powers of observation and her skills in research, to begin the scholarly study of the material culture of Hispanic New Mexico. Although interest in this indigenous art was expressed (and collections of it amassed) before E. Boyd came to New Mexico in 1929, little was known about it.

A great part of her scholarly work concerned religious art. *Santos,* which are holy figures, either flat *(retablos)* or carved in the round *(bultos),* were often found in poor condition, unsigned by their makers. E. Boyd took on the tasks of classifying these santos by maker; of listening to folklore about their makers *(santeros)*; of following up those stories with careful research into the records of church inventories; of using the results of scientific tests to determine what the santos were made of; of restoring the sometimes badly damaged objects; and of collecting examples of Hispanic material culture and making them available to the public through the Museum of New Mexico in Santa Fe.

As an expert, E. Boyd was often interviewed. She would be horrified when her interviewer's first question would be aimed at discovering what the "E." in her name stood for. She never accepted the idea that her use of an initial as part of her name was of interest to anyone. Colleagues and correspondents learned quickly not to show much curiosity about her name and her private life, but she did explain to one person that "Eboyd" had been a childhood nickname. Known as E. Boyd Van Cleve, and then as E. Boyd Hall in the 1930s, she began to sign her art work "E. Boyd," explaining then that:

> There is no sex in art, so why should one sign their work as a man or woman? And if a woman, why in her chosen career, should she be obliged to change her name just because she has chosen to marry? A man's work is not so branded

> by his marriage, so why should a woman's be? . . . It is absurd for a woman to have to label herself married or single. If her added experience means anything to her it means that she will paint better; or be a better lawyer, or doctor, or teacher, for her life is enriched. (Cassidy 1938: 28)

Her friends called her E.

This article is about her life, and especially how she became such an expert on Spanish colonial material culture. During her last years, she rarely mentioned personal anecdotes unless they had direct bearing on the subject at hand; she was more interested in discussing her work than herself. That is not to say that she was not perfectly capable of carrying on a conversation on more general topics, unwilling to express a strong opinion on some subject, or disinterested in the doings of other people, but she was very private. In keeping with what seemed her own preference, I shall focus on the events of her life that involved her work, including only enough personal information to enliven her for the reader.[1]

E. Boyd never accumulated the diplomas and degrees now thought to be proof of a good education, but she did have a fair amount of schooling. After completing the eleventh grade at the Phoebee Anna Thorne School for Girls, a progressive institution associated with Bryn Mawr College, she attended the Pennsylvania Academy of Fine Arts in Philadelphia for four years. A two-year study of schools and periods of art at the Ecole de la Grande Chaumier in Paris followed; she focused on the Byzantine, Romanesque, and French early Gothic periods. Later, she said that she had learned far more about art from life than she ever did in school, indeed, that "one must know life before one can know or understand art" (Cassidy 1938: 28). While in France, she worked in Paris doing advertisements for the couturier Paul Poirot and designing needlepoint handbags.

It was in France that she married Frank Andrews and bore an infant who lived only a few months. The couple soon returned to Philadelphia, where E. Boyd did "anything from hand-painted valance boards, folding screens, or book jackets to lamp shades."[2] In 1929, she and her husband came to Santa Fe for a three-month visit.

The Santa Fe in which the couple arrived had a population of about 11,400, mostly Hispanic. The chamber of commerce advertised the city for its healthful climate, its evidence of three distinct cultures, and its small but active colony of artists and writers. With wandering, unpaved streets, a distinctive architecture, clear air and cool summers, the city combined a foreign ambience with a physical atmosphere ideal for the cure of tuberculosis sufferers. The surrounding countryside provided intriguing scenes for artists and a wealth of ruins for archaeologists. According to Charles Barrows,[3] who first stayed in Santa Fe in 1928, the city was then run by the artists and writers, and although some members of that group could be accused of having exploited the Hispanic and Indian cultures, they certainly helped to maintain and even to re-create the area's old traditions. E. Boyd later credited this group, along with the archaeologists and health seekers, with the discovery of and a new appreciation for the New Mexican Hispanic religious art that had been created in the eighteenth and nineteenth centuries.

The marriage of Frank Andrews and E. Boyd broke up in the Southwest; they returned to the East and were divorced. After recovering from a serious illness that kept her in Pennsylvania for several months, E. Boyd returned to Santa Fe alone. During the 1930s, she worked at a number of jobs, painted in watercolors, was married and divorced at least twice more, and developed a deep interest in the material remains of the Hispanic culture of the preceding centuries. She also kept working on her art all through that decade (Anonymous 1936*a:* 101, 1936*c:* 53, Cunningham 1937: 64; Anonymous 1940).

In 1933, E. Boyd joined with several other artists in a group called the Rio Grande Painters, with the common goal of displaying their work and the common hope of selling some of it even though the Depression was deepening (Anonymous 1934*a,* 1934*b*). At that time there were no private galleries in Santa Fe, although the Fine Arts Museum did show the work of local artists. The Rio Grande Painters intended to establish a permanent gallery to exhibit the work of living artists, and, indeed, did open a gallery in October 1935. The group wanted to develop a public interest in art and resolved, along with maintaining their gallery, to provide scholarships where possible and to help educate children about art, offering prize competitions and free criticism for them. Always cooperative rather than competitive, E. Boyd was willing to do such tedious chores for the group as arranging a traveling exhibition of their work and writing the text for a pamphlet about them. Although a critical success, the traveling show was not remunerative, and by 1936 the group had disbanded, with some members returning to the East and others finding jobs in Santa Fe.

E. Boyd found a local job with the Federal Art Project (FAP) of the Works Progress Administration. Although the earlier arts projects of the Depression years had hired artists on the basis of competition, the FAP guidelines required that 90 percent of the artists engaged be qualified as relief recipients. The project in New Mexico was supervised by R. Vernon Hunter, an artist himself, who hired his impoverished colleagues. E. Boyd's job, which she reported to be in line with her interests, was as a watercolorist and research artist for the *Portfolio of Spanish Colonial Design in New Mexico* (Anonymous 1936*b,* 1936*d:* 93). Two hundred copies, begun in 1937, were completed by August 1, 1938 (McDonald 1969: 437, 456).

The *Portfolio* was a forerunner of and contributor to the national Index of American Design, both of which were established to record information on and the appearance of objects—among them furniture, pottery, metalwork, and textiles—produced by Americans of European descent. (It was assumed that ethnologists and archaeologists were already recording Native American artifacts.) Among the goals set for the project was to find (assuming they existed) the roots of American design, a task made difficult because of the European influences on American art and the disparity between, for example, Shaker and Hispanic understandings of form and color. The index was meant to be a rich source of material to industrial and commercial researchers, enabling them to design domestic and business products of truly American derivation.

The artists employed by the project made watercolor renderings, which are now housed in the National Gallery of Art in Washington, D.C. In some states, copies were made of the renderings and distributed in portfolios. In New Mexico, project artists concentrated on making renderings of the religious art and the decorated practical objects made by Hispanic New Mexicans. Although much of this art had been destroyed or had disappeared from New Mexico by the 1930s because of church disapproval and the increasing availability of cheap mass-produced religious art, there was still some remaining. The archbishop of Santa Fe, Rudolph A. Gerken, gave permission for the artists to enter the old churches to study what was left, but church records, still untranslated from Spanish, were not made available to the workers. There had been very little published on the arts and crafts of the region, and the few works in print were sadly lacking in dates, maker's names, and materials used. Donald Bear, the regional director of the FAP in Denver, wrote in his "Introductory Note" to the *Portfolio:*

> At present some attempt is being made to solve these questions through chemical analyses of the color and scientific determination of the age of the wood. However, at this time, little more than a few experimental notes are available. (Federal Art Project of New Mexico 1937–1938: 9)

E. Boyd wrote the text for the *Portfolio,* relying heavily on historic sources to describe the conditions under which the art was produced. Among the problems involved in the study of santos was determining what saints they originally represented. This determination was often complicated because of the custom among pious New Mexicans of giving the saints new clothes or repainting the old ones, with the subsequent loss through the years of identifying attributes. As yet, there had been no attempts to identify santeros, though some pieces could be assigned to the work of one person. Although E. Boyd was able, through historical data, to give rough dates for many bultos and retablos, she wrote:

> There is no reference available to date, no exact dates set. Local tradition labels these pieces "very old"—further information is buried with an older generation. (Federal Art Project of New Mexico 1937–1938: 16)

Although two hundred copies of the *Portfolio of Spanish Colonial Design* were published and distributed in 1938, unfortunately, most of them were re-called because the publication had not been cleared with the director's office in Washington. Thus, there are few copies available today. A definite interest in regional Hispanic art had been sparked, however, and though thefts and forgeries resulted, the objects and the tradition behind them benefited, at last, from serious study and careful preservation.

In an interview for the *WPA Reporter,* E. Boyd reported her own feelings toward what she was doing for the project:

> Since living here, I have become deeply interested in the study of religious carvings and paintings in the territory, of which there is much material, and little or no informations available. The more consideration the work involves the more I am convinced there should be a complete record made of this type of art. This should be done as soon as possible, as valuable pieces are constantly being sold out of the district, and others destroyed by fire, water, theft, and neglect. The materials are fragile, and have already had hard treatment. It has been a privilege to work on the present Spanish-Colonial art portfolio for the WPA, as it is directly in line with the research in which I am interested.[4]

E. Boyd soon took her own advice and became the leading recordmaker for "this type of art." She expanded the research she had begun for the *Portfolio,* and in 1946 her first book, *Saints & Saintmakers of New Mexico,* designed by Merle Armitage, was published by the Laboratory of Anthropology in Santa Fe.

That publication was the first truly scholarly and well-researched book on santos. Maurice Ries wrote in his introduction to it:

> Once having read this book, you will discover that you are an authority on the subject of *santos.* That is because the book is the most authoritative, the most complete, thing of its kind. (Boyd 1946: 1)

Using a test group of santos, E. Boyd was able to begin to identify some of the santeros, on the basis of style and local folk wisdom. From this work she concluded that the religious art of New Mexico had been produced by relatively few men. However, she soon discovered that her careful research for the book was being superseded quickly by new research, and that her writings contained errors. Cady Wells, a nationally recognized artist whose own collection had been used as part of the test group, remarked about one such discovery in a 1947 letter to E. Boyd:

> Willard came in at the end of our conference. With that excited, eager calamitous look he said, "The most awful thing has happened." When I asked. "We have discovered (?) direct evidence proving that oil paints were used prior to—(a date I can't remember) which makes that part of E. Boyd's book all wrong." In so many words I said, "So what?" He seemed to think it would upset you and I told him he ought to know you better or to know anyone better who had written the first authoritative book on ANYTHING. I said forgodsake what's research and don't you expect to find something new that changes something old all the time.[5]

Although it is unlikely that E. Boyd found great pleasure in being confronted with anything that contradicted what she had written, she continually accepted and incorporated new evidence into her work. Unwilling to popularize further what was misleading in *Saints & Saintmakers,* she refused to have it reprinted. Not until her second book was published in 1974, did the demand for the first decrease.

During the late 1940s, E. Boyd moved to Los Angeles where there were more jobs. She worked first as an assistant to the owner of the Hispano-American Bookstore and then for the Los Angeles County Museum, starting there as a research librarian and, in 1950, becoming the museum's registrar. Her earlier study was useful to her in her after-hours work as an art critic for *Arts and Architecture* magazine.

Recognized in California as an expert on the Spanish colonial art of New Mexico, she gave at least two talks on the subject. In a newspaper interview before one of them, she commented:

> My interest in Spanish Colonial art is due partly to its artistic appeal and also to the fact that it is the one single school of art that is completely indigenous to the United States and not imported with the exception of Indian art of course.[6]

In the same period she began writing articles on individual santos for the Museum of New Mexico's periodical, *El Palacio;* she also completed a pamphlet for the Southern Methodist University Press entitled *The Literature of Santos* (1950*a*).

For many years she had advised her friend Cady Wells on his substantial collection of santos and had also catalogued it for him. In 1951, he decided to give his collection to a worthy institution. He considered, among others, the National Gallery of Art in Washington, D.C., and the Taylor Museum in Colorado Springs, Colorado, but finally decided on the Museum of New Mexico in Santa Fe. His concern that the collection be adequately and knowledgeably cared for led him to make several stipulations in the gift agreement. Two of those stipulations were that the museum set up a separate department of Spanish colonial art and that it hire a curator of whom he approved. Knowing and appreciating E. Boyd's work in the field, he recommended her for the job. The director of the museum, Boaz Long, replied to Wells that the museum could accept some of his stipulations, but he clearly stated that an outsider could not be allowed to influence personnel decisions. After making that statement Long agreed that E. Boyd would be excellent for the job. She began work for the museum in 1952.

By this time, she was already recognized as an authority on New Mexican Spanish colonial art, having pioneered the study of santos, written about them, restored them, and catalogued collections of them. E. Boyd knew not only her curatorial subject but also many Santa Feans who were interested in Spanish colonial art. Always more interested in the job at hand—in this case protecting and preserving Spanish colonial art—than in her own fame, she was skilled at getting others interested and involved in projects she favored. Aware that the by then inactive Spanish Colonial Arts Society, which had been formed in 1925 and incorporated in 1929, was incorporated only until 1979, she took it upon herself to "reanimate the society in 1952." This was not an easy task; first it involved finding members of the original group and convincing them that the newly interested people "were not a rival society nor [did they have] dishonest intentions."[7] Then old board members had to be asked to resign, notices had to be published in the newspaper, and new volunteers found to supplement the membership. The reactivated society was then able to collect money as a nonprofit organization and to spend it on Spanish colonial art and restoration. The importance of this becomes more evident when one realizes that, in the early years, the museum's Spanish colonial art department was appropriated only two hundred dollars a year for new acquisitions and that, since the society's holdings were housed at the museum, the department was able to use a much larger collection for research and exhibition. In part through the help of the Spanish Colonial Arts Society, E. Boyd was able to build a substantial collection of santos for the museum.

The society's original purpose was to preserve old examples of Spanish colonial art and to foster new productions of the same type of work. In 1965, the society-sponsored Spanish Market was reactivated to encourage native craftspeople to make traditional objects by providing them with a sales outlet. The Spanish Market continues to grow in popularity, and some of its participants remember E. Boyd's help in getting them started. She would show them pieces in the museum collection, explain how they were made, and urge them to make the same sorts of crafts. Max Roybal from Santa Fe,[8] a santero for many years, was a neighbor and a friend of E. Boyd. In the early 1950s he told E. Boyd he had decided to stop making santos; her reply was simply "no." He continues to work as a santero today.

E. Boyd's job as a curator also involved caring for the collection of santos. Some of them had been spruced up over the years to make them look newer and more appropriate to the worship of which they were part; others were in terrible condition. E. Boyd first experimented with the restoration of santos in the late 1930s when she and her husband, Edward T. Hall, could afford only rather battered examples of the art. As her knowledge increased, so did her restoration skills, and she was called on to repair and reclaim on numerous occasions—notably, in the church at Laguna Pueblo, New Mexico, in 1950 and at the San Miguel Chapel in Santa Fe in 1955.

Since her workload was great, she asked others for help with the collection. She discovered Alan C. Vedder's interest after he bought an adobe house in Santa Fe and thought he should have a retablo to hang in it. He went to a dealer in town and found a santo that he liked. But, fearing that he may not have chosen an authentic piece, he arranged to take it home and try it on his walls. Vedder had heard that E. Boyd, then at the Fine Arts Museum, was the expert in santos, so he took his retablo directly to the museum to ask her advice. She pulled from the collection three other pieces of the same subject and laid them out so that he could compare them. He immediately saw that his was different, and after some examination, he and E. Boyd concluded that his had been overpainted, so he returned it to the dealer and on E. Boyd's advice bought another from a more reputable source. She recognized that he had a good eye for santos, because of his quick recognition that the one he had brought in was unlike the others she showed him, and she asked him to volunteer one day a week at the museum to help with restoration. He did so for some time and was eventually employed by the museum as a conservator.

Another time, when E. Boyd was setting up an exhibit of a New Mexico chapel, she noticed that the bulto of the Virgin that she intended to use looked rather shabby, and so in traditional New Mexican fashion she decided to provide it with a new dress. Recollecting that her friend Jane Ivancovich from Tucson, Arizona, was an accomplished needleworker, E. Boyd asked her to make the new dress. Having accepted the job, Mrs. Ivancovich had to travel to Santa Fe to finish the job, because it was necessary to sew the dress, piece by piece, onto the rigid bulto.

The Spanish colonial art department contained more than santos. Colonial New Mexicans had had to be self-sufficient, and the museum's collection included examples of many other objects. E. Boyd had written about crafts other than religious art for the *Portfolio,* but her main interest and expertise concerned santos. As she continued to work at the museum, however, she increased her study of other colonial crafts, and in 1959 the Museum of International Folk Art published her booklet, *Popular Arts of Colonial New Mexico,* in which she wrote about architecture, textiles, furniture, and, of course, santos.

At about the same time, she began work that would greatly expand the material skimmed in the booklet and would replace *Saints & Saintmakers,* which remained, in spite of its mistakes, the authoritative work on santos. *Popular Arts of Spanish New Mexico,* the result of her new studies, was not published until 1974. Several factors combined to make progress on the new book so slow, among them her job at the museum, which took a great deal of time, especially during the summers when she would spend hours showing one visitor after another the holdings of her department. The job also involved writing catalogues, lecturing, and setting up exhibits. More important, she was still doing pioneer research work and supposedly completed sections needed constant revision because of new information. Merle Clark, who was the editor for museum publications, remembers editing sections of the book only to have them re-called because E. Boyd wanted to incorporate the results of some new findings. Although his work was frustrating, Clark had a good professional relationship with E. Boyd, and when he was laid off from the museum staff in 1966 as a budget-cutting measure, she was furious and withdrew the book completely. Only the constant urging of friends like Clark and Bobby Berg convinced her to finish the manuscript and allow it to be published. It came out, shortly before her death, in the spring of 1974.

Interestingly, she titled the book *Popular Arts . . .* rather than using the more common term *folk* to describe the art of Spanish New Mexico. When asked about this, she replied:

> Folk, folk, folk: nasty old German word—I hate it. "Popular" is from the Latin, all the way back to classical days, and Latin is the source of Spanish and popular is like populace; the people.[9]

E. Boyd held strong opinions, and although she would at times recognize that they were not grounded in careful consideration, she was happy to admit to them. She did not seem to mind ignorance if it was offered innocently, but she was quick to condemn anyone who tried to mask ignorance with pretense. She could be intimidating and knew it without completely understanding why. She wrote to George Holzapfel in 1968:

> The other funny thing is that I find I scare many people without even trying—when I ask my old friends why so-and-so puts his or her head in bucket around me I am told "he—she—is frightened to death of you"—the old bark perhaps—or lack of toleration for stupidity.[10]

That lack of toleration probably gained her as many friends as enemies. In any case, she was not a person to elicit disinterest. Her opinions ranged widely—from a dislike of mini skirts to scathing contempt for people she considered professionally inept. Her ethics were as strong as her opinions, and she had little patience with anyone whose own ethics seemed questionable. She did not expect everyone to share her interests, but she did expect them to be treated with respect.

She also enjoyed pleasures. In the same 1968 letter to George Holzapfel she wrote:

> The other "hot" topic of cigarettes I am weary of hearing about—am still doing same despite propaganda—as it is one of the few things left that I ever enjoyed—(my work and bourbon being the others).[11]

Putting work in the same category as cigarettes and bourbon may seem a denigration, but possibly the three may have been grouped together as all being necessary and calming habits. In any case, E. Boyd would have hated our analyzing or taking much interest in her personal preferences, so enough.

As a museum employee, E. Boyd acquired pieces for the museum, found information about them, and made both the pieces and the information available to the public. In Santa Fe, where her department was located, first at the Fine Arts Museum and then at the Museum of International Folk Art, she was able to increase public understanding with exhibitions and, more widely, with publications, lectures, and displays. In 1963, she traveled to Washington, D.C., and set up a display of a New Mexican room at the

Smithsonian Institution, and in 1961 Alan Vedder went to Bath, England, to help the museum there with a show of New Mexican objects.

When the Cultural Properties Review Committee, charged with the listing and preservation of historic sites in New Mexico, was established in 1968, E. Boyd was made its advisor, and, as part of this group, she helped to evaluate sites in the state. She wrote the recommendations for the Plaza del Cerro in Chimayó for the state historic plan in 1971. One member of the committee, George Pearl, recognized that she was well versed in the studies that surrounded her own and enjoyed testing her knowledge. Hoping to stump her, he brought six Latin American silver spoons to a meeting of the committee and placed them at her seat. She took a look at them and named the place and date, within two years, of their origin.

Although her expertise could make her abrupt when confronted with foolish suppositions, she was also a kind woman. Myra Ellen Jenkins, who was the state historian and sat on the Cultural Properties Review Committee in the early 1970s, remembers a trip that members of the group made to see a village church. Claiming to remember who kept the key to the church, E. Boyd went in search of it while the others waited, and waited, and waited. After what seemed a long time they went in search of her and discovered her in the house of an old Spanish-speaking woman, helping the woman to fill in forms in English for assistance with her sewage. Caught in this kindness, she looked at the others and said gruffly, "Well, it's too late to see the church anyway."

In spite of her abruptness and her distaste for stupidity, E. Boyd considered it her duty to help people who had questions about her subject regardless of whether they were smart, or well-informed, or recognized scholars. Her files at the Museum of International Folk Art were filled with requests for information, sometimes about only one possibly interesting piece. Carefully filed with them were copies of her replies. To some people, she gave information; to others, who wanted more specific services, she had to explain that, as a museum employee, she could neither make appraisals (though she could suggest people who could) nor accept any money for her help. One suspects that her answers were not entirely due to good nature: she had a tough, practical understanding of how one finds out about long-forgotten items that might add to a museum's collection or simply to the record of a subject. Of course, she had a strong sense of herself as a public servant and of what she considered to be a public good—learning about and making available to people what rightfully belongs to them.

Among her correspondence were letters from established scholars and students in her field and in adjoining fields. Again, recognizing cooperation as the best way to increase knowledge, she worked with colleagues to clarify and expand on information, while helping students to clear away the debris of misinformation about their particular concerns so that they could continue to develop sound bases for them.

As she would have hoped, scholars have continued to advance knowledge in the field to which she devoted most of her life, and, as those who knew her would have expected, her influence remains powerful even today, some eight years after her death. Alan Vedder remembers meeting Kate Peck Kent in the parking lot at the Laboratory of Anthropology. She asked him what he was working on, and he replied that he was finishing his book on furniture (1977). She was curious to know if he intended to thank E. Boyd in his introduction. He told her that, indeed, he intended to write that the book itself could not have been written without her help and added that he was very indebted to her. Kate Peck Kent replied, "Isn't that true of all of us?"

NOTES

1. Much of what I have learned about E. Boyd has been due to the willingness of her friends and colleagues to talk with and write to me about her. Consequently I would like to thank Richard Ahlborn, Kay Baisden, Charles Barrows, Merle Clark, Edward T. Hall, Jane Ivancovich, Myra Ellen Jenkins, Dr. and Mrs. Pál Kelemen, George Pearl, Max Roybal, Ann Vedder, and Alan Vedder for their help.
2. *Rio Grande Painters,* unidentified pamphlet in the E. Boyd Collection, New Mexico State Records Center and Archives, Santa Fe (hereafter NMSRC).
3. Personal communication from Charles Barrows, 1978.
4. Joy Yeck, "New Mexico WPA Art Program Includes E. Boyd Hall Doing Important Work," *The Reporter,* Works Progress Administration for New Mexico, April 1936, p. 8. Copy in E. Boyd Collection, NMSRC.
5. Cady Wells to E. Boyd, 12 March 1947. E. Boyd Collection, NMSRC.
6. "Expert Will Speak Today on New Mexico Santos," unidentified newspaper clipping, E. Boyd Collection, NMSRC.
7. E. Boyd to Dr. and Mrs. Pál Kelemen, 14 July 1954.
8. Personal communication from Max Roybal, 1981.
9. Telephone conversation between E. Boyd and Samuel Larcombe, 14 May 1974.
10. E. Boyd to George Holzapfel, 3 October 1968. E. Boyd Collection, NMSRC.
11. Ibid.

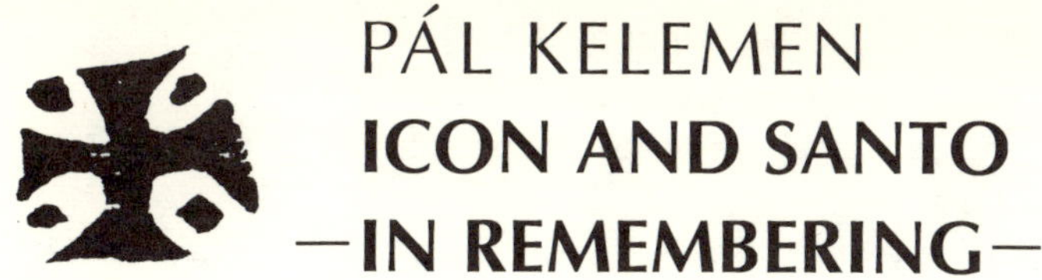

PÁL KELEMEN

ICON AND SANTO —IN REMEMBERING—

IT IS CALLED THE ATCHISON, TOPEKA AND SANTA FE Railway System. But the tracks swerve away from the old Spanish colonial town, and the train stops at Lamy. My wife and I took a car at the station for the eighteen-mile drive. In the autumn of 1936, they had just finished building a wing at the hotel, La Fonda. Although not all the rooms were furnished, we were lucky to have been given quarters there that enjoyed a certain quiet and were away from the noisy elevator. After helping to arrange our belongings, I hurried down to the street to see something of the city before dusk fell. I stood on the main plaza in front of the Old Palacio. It was decayed, its paint flaking; the protruding ends of the *vigas* (ceiling logs) looked like petrified sponges. Few other buildings were built in the local style. Some showed the taste of the East, some that of the bazaar.

Soon I was in open country, conscious that pre-Columbian life once thrived here, that the soil kept secrets of a sunken civilization. My breath grew heavy in the unaccustomed altitude. My eyes wandered into the flat, extended view. In the thin air, a strange quietness floated over all, and the ragged edges of the Sangre de Cristo range looked in the distance like a granite curtain, shutting out the rest of the world. A year before I had sat on our terrace in Florence, Italy, taking in the sunset as it lit the cupola of the Duomo, the Giotto tower, and the weather-beaten crenellations of the Palazzo Vecchio. The distance was very great, and the difference was vehement.

This was only my second contact with the realties of the pre-Colombian world, hitherto known only from books, photographs, and objects lined up on the sober shelves of museums. And it showed me a very different aspect from that unrolled before us three years earlier in Yucatán and the high Valley of Mexico. Would I, a European, be able to present in acceptable form the aesthetic side of this vast pre-Columbian civilization?

Next day we went to meet Edgar Lee Hewett, director of the Museum of New Mexico, in his modest and shabby room attached to the original Palace building. He took us around. The patio had gravel walks. The exhibits showed the lack of money and of time to work with them. The floorboards were cracked in a number of places and uneven along the walls. The spirit that emanated from the adobe walls and from the cranky tired doors could not be defined, but I began to feel the atmosphere of history, like everyone here who has eyes and ears.

Dr. Hewett held the degree of Docteur ès Lettres from Geneva, Switzerland, equivalent to the American Ph.D. He expressed ideas that I did not hear from anyone on the eastern seaboard. For him, archaeology was a living study and belonged to the humanities as interpreted in Europe. He felt uncomfortable with the term *anthropology.* His horizon was wide; he had recently returned from a visit to South America with its diverse cultures.

He took us to Saint Francis Cathedral. While the pseudo-Gothic exterior and interior seemed incongruous to the ambience, a surprise met our eyes when he led us to a small curtained opening. There, buried vertically, mortared against the wall, stood a tall, carved stone retable. Bishop Lamy had had it transferred from the crumbling colonial military chapel to his new structure but a successor had evidently held it unsuitable and had incarcerated it behind a more "modern" altar.

Another deep impression came when we saw gifts of santos and bultos stored in disorder in a back closet of the museum. Those painted panels and statues, standing in perpetual dusk, had a power of communication that was startling.

At the nearby Laboratory of Anthropology we found acquaintances from our stay in Yucatán and Mexico (1933), for the Carnegie people gathered here during the rainy season when they could not do field work at Chichén Itzá. There was Karl Ruppert, with whom we had shared the sensational arrival of a kerosene-regulated refrigerator at the former Thompson hacienda, for there was no electricity at Chichén. Under a full moon floating in the steel-blue tropical sky, Sylvanus G. Morley had played Beethoven's fifth symphony on his record player in the Ball Court, to demonstrate the remarkable acoustics of the place. A. V. Kidder, *spiritus rector* of Southwestern archaeology, was visiting the laboratory at Santa Fe. With him, we watched lambs being loaded onto trucks for shipment from the famous Kelley ranch—a spectacle that brought out the lighter side of that warmly human personality. And with him and Dr. Hewett, we were drawn into the discussion of where to place an organ that had been donated recently for the Saint Francis auditorium in the Fine Arts Museum.

J. Eric S. Thompson (later, Sir Eric), Cambridge University graduate, was the only other "foreigner" among the Americans. A close friendship developed between our families. Our visits to their rented home with its adobe walls and small windows remain vivid in memory. Eric's collection of Southwestern rugs and mantles revealed the same discriminating taste that the Maya epigrapher brought to his profession.

A new impulse to involvement came at the Laboratory of Anthropology, from an exquisite collection of colonial silver and from shelf upon shelf of vintage Southwestern weaving, of workmanship and design that today have long been diluted by commercialism. There also I saw for the first time the extended charts of dendrochronology, tree-ring dating, pinned along the walls.

By daytime the plaza at Santa Fe showed a cross section of the three types of population—Indian, Hispanic, and Anglo—easily identified by the variety of clothing, an ever-moving kaleidoscope. But evenings, Santa Fe retired within its shuttered houses. The one motion-picture theater offered a continuous show. We usually went quite late and sat in one of the "loges" at the back in spacious rocking chairs. The audience gradually drifted away; sometimes we were the only ones left. When the picture reached the point where we came in, we rose to go, and had not reached the velvet-curtained entrance when the projection stopped and the hall went dark except for the single bare emergency bulb.

The artistic talent of the Indian had long been appreciated and indeed turned to account. But it was not before 1933, at the urging of Hewett, that the Indian Bureau in Washington agreed to establish a department of painting in the Santa Fe Indian School. There, led by the talented Dorothy Dunn, the children produced, largely in watercolor and similar material, ingenious paintings of fairy-tale quality drawn from their own lives and legends: bareback riders hunting antelope with bow and arrow, Apache fighting Comanche on horseback, an evening feast around golden embers where the immobility of the figures was enhanced by the black background (Dunn 1968). When the artist of the feast picture, a girl, was asked why the black paper, she answered simply, "It was at night." Not until driving west one night across the plain and coming upon such a group, did we recognize the realism of her painting. There was nothing for the firelight to reflect on but the colorful costumes, and the figures stood out startlingly in the blackness.

At dinner with Dr. Hewett, our discussions touched many subjects. He suggested that we settle in New Mexico; he thought that a European could best emphasize the aesthetic side of both pre-Columbian and Spanish colonial civilization, so miserably neglected. Also, he advised us on further trips.

At Pueblo Bonito, New Mexico, Paul Reiter explained the intricacies of that magnificent structure, built by "savages." There was so much water on the floor of Canyon de Chelly that we could not ford it. But at Mesa Verde, Colorado, though the season was over, we received permission from the National Park Service to rent a cabin for two days. We breakfasted at the rangers' quarters on flapjacks dealt out by the dozen on the surface of a huge wood stove. A ranger took us over the complex. We climbed ladders, tested foot- and handholds in the cliff walls, knelt to examine the ingenious use of backroom crevices, photographing—unhampered by the barriers that nowadays control the ruthless crowds.

In Tucson, Arizona, we came upon an impressively large colonial crucifix neglected in the open vestibule of the cathedral, dusty, attacked by heat, and streaked over with pigeon droppings. On a road that was just a sandy strip full of potholes and stones that scattered under the car's tires, we reached the mission church of San Xavier del Bac (Ahlborn 1974). The main entrance was boarded over. The place was attended only by Father Chinn, who welcomed the rare visitors to the mission. He gave us a tastefully printed booklet, which was all he could afford.

By that time we had become aware of the great variety in Spanish colonial art. In Santa Barbara, California, we photographed the mission church facade with its patina of age; after an earthquake it had to be rebuilt—not by careful craftsmen but by masons putting stone on cement, stone on cement. We spent Christmas of 1936 there. Even though we were far from our home, the candelit altar, the aroma of incense, and the familiar carols of choir and organ brought us some of the mood of Holy Night.

At Berkeley, California, we found amphitheater, stadium, and Greek theater, but art history was being taught in a shack with a roof of corrugated iron. I was permitted to browse among the uncatalogued pre-Columbian Peruvian pottery from the Max Uhle collection and chose some to be photographed. Dr. Alfred L. Kroeber encouraged my project and offered sound advice; on an afternoon at his home, Dr. Robert H. Lowie played Viennese light music on the piano with the verve and clarity that characterized his professional discussions.

Fifteen years later, on a transcontinental lecture tour in 1951, we came again to Santa Fe; Bertha Dutton drove us from Lamy in her car. Many changes were noticeable. The comfort and practicality of the local building style had been recognized. The unique stone retable of Nuestra Señora de la Luz was effectively placed in the church of El Cristo Rey, a new building but designed in good Pueblo style (Kelemen 1954). Unfortunately, the central part of the altar frontal with Saint Anthony, three-quarters of which had survived, was not incorporated; nor was a section of the surrounding border—later used for a time as a mail drop (Boyd 1974: 74).

Boaz Long was director of the Museum of New Mexico at that time. On various diplomatic posts in Latin America, he had already shown lively interest in the art and architecture of the Spanish colonies. He deplored the financial stress of the struggling museum, the upkeep of which was deprecated by an indifferent state government.

It was then that we came into contact with E. Boyd. From the first it was clear that as curator of Spanish colonial art—a position recently created—she was the right person in the right place. She had had experience at the County Museum of Los Angeles. Her talent for clear and intelligent writing was already evident in her publications. That she was also an experienced painter with an unerring eye was invaluable to her work. We kept up correspondence with her during the years and received very valuable information. To mention only one case, when I was supervising the restoration of the paintings and writing the catalogue for an exhibit of Peruvian colonial painting at the Brooklyn Museum (Kelemen 1971), she wrote:

> March 13, 1971
>
> Apropos of your comment on *tela* vs. other supports for painting: I ran into that some years ago in regard to colonial canvases from New Spain. Many sent here for missions were painted on *ixtle,* made from maguey fibers and of the quality of burlap bags. In fact, the industry in the colonial period actually was more engaged in making gunnysacks or porters' sacking for all sorts of commodities than in making artists' canvas.
>
> Occasionally we find a piece of really strong, solid, hand-spun and woven linen canvas which is no proof that the art work on the face was necessarily of equally fine quality.

Her enthusiasm sharpened my interest in the unique art expression of this region. I began to realize how different it is from any other—even folk art—that we had seen elsewhere in our travels over the Americas.

Life in those distant corners behind the back of God was hard and exacting. Although the Franciscans, concerned about their brethren in those wild regions, sent what they could, from Querétaro and later from Zacatecas, of beautifying as well as practical material, the thirteen years of Indian destruction had made away with much of the religious paraphernalia that had been imported from Mexico, even from Europe, before the 1680 Pueblo uprising (Adams 1944; Scholes and Adams 1952). Bad weather, impassable roads, and Indian attacks often disrupted traffic, and the shortage of basic utilitarian items wrought grave hardship on the striving little communities. Replacements, when they did arrive, were often inadequate and of mixed quality. More and more requisites had to be made by local craftsmen. Not only were the materials at hand different from those available from Mexico but the local craftsmen had little artistic tradition. It was natural that the interior as well as the exterior of their churches developed a distinctive New Mexican style. Local talent came to expression, bringing forth the folklore of isolated and neglected communities with a power of its own.

On a way that led across mountain ridges and narrow valleys, one came to the village of Las Trampas, New Mexico, with mud houses as if grown out of the ground and an old church that looked against the wooded slopes like a stage design for some religious play of bygone days (Hewett and Fisher 1943; Sanford 1950). Inside, the ceiling was supported on wooden vigas with carved corbels; old paintings adorned the walls; and a wooden latticed construction served as a communion rail. The altar screen with its straight vertical and horizontal divisions was in the tradition of New Mexican churches. Whether carved, painted on wood, or visible in the remaining murals, the style of the religious figures had its own flavor. The cross-shaped wooden chandelier with its candles and a cord on which to raise and lower it was like those in medieval churches.

As we stood on the plaza, the houses mute and immobile in the hard midday sun that leaves no shadow, I had to think of distant centuries and lands where life regulated religion and religion sustained life. In the dramatic setting of the oracle at Delphi, Greece, one feels why the site was holy. In the little chapel at Assisi, Italy, the spirit of Saint Francis lingers. At Berea, near Thessalonica, Greece, Saint Paul preached in a low-ceilinged room obscured among farm buildings. The windows are bare slits; in the dusk some pallid icons lean against the wall, although a sober daylight shines outside. The walls are smudged by the smoke from oil lamps and candles and permeated by the smell of cold incense. And at one end, there is a fragment of a mural, a very fine Christ as judge, the Pantocrator. Its transcendental beauty ennobles the place.

In 1925 I had been in Spain for a long stay, searching for the reason why I did not find El Greco an entirely Spanish painter and could not pigeonhole him among the Venetians (Kelemen 1961). In 1954, I turned again to that old project. Trying to visualize the ambience in which he developed into a master painter, I went to Crete and later to Macedonia and to other regions that had been overwhelmed in his time by the Ottoman Empire. In the lands in which Christianity once had triumphed, the splendid mosaics in the churches had been plastered over, if not destroyed; the Christian inhabitants were oppressed, both in their religious and civil life. Their faith alone sustained them. Forbidden to congregate in numbers, they hid their places of worship among farm buildings, in their fields, or in some unfrequented wood. In a tiny church in a Cretan ravine once serviced by Orthodox monks, in a family chapel in Macedonia inconspicuous among fields of grain, I felt the religious mystique that I sometimes experienced in New Mexico. There also such oratories preserved a kind of primal Christianity seldom apparent in sumptuous modern churches, neon-lit and resounding with electric-driven organ music.

The conditions under which the Orthodox peasant lived through four hundred years of Turkish occupation have something in common with the Spanish colonial settlers of New Mexico in those perilous decades. Both Christian communities lived under constant danger and stress, whether from Turk or Indian. For them, the burgeoning Baroque had little meaning. Whether icon or santo, there was a standstill in their religious art. In vain had Crete in the sixteenth century belonged to the Venice of Giorgione, Titian, Tintoretto, and Veronese: the chapels of the Orthodox remained unchanged. In vain was New Mexico held by a thread, however thin, to the sumptuous life of Mexico City, Puebla, and the other silver-rich towns that flaunted large canvases with biblical legends, brilliant in tone and framed in heavy gold. In the perilous existence, Eastern Orthodox artisan and New Mexican santero clung to the fixed tradition that kept their hope alive. For them, studied perspective, three dimensionality, coloristic bravura, freedom of movement and of drapery held little interest.

Saint Luke, one of the four Evangelists and secretary to Saint Paul on his many missionary jouneys, was a medical man. According to legend, he painted the first image of the Virgin and Child, and thus, in a way he was the first santero. As a result of his two vocations, he is the patron of doctors and painters.

The icon represented in Figure 1 comes from a monastery church in Montenegro and is dated from the second half of the seventeenth century. The saint is depicted in biblical robes. Small jars of pigment and other utensils of rather illusory purpose are set before him. The table, his seat, and his footstool are in Byzantine tradition, as are the stylized folds of his robe. There is

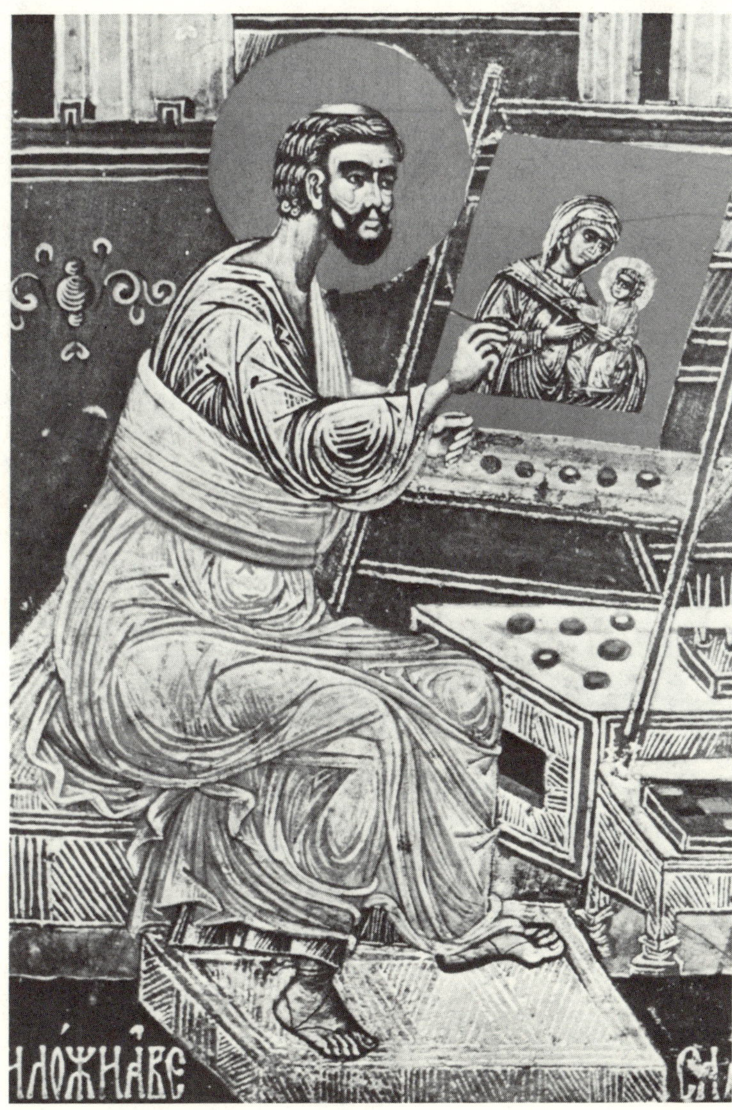

FIGURE 1
Saint Luke painting the Virgin and Child. Icon, Montenegro. (From the Kelemen Archive.)

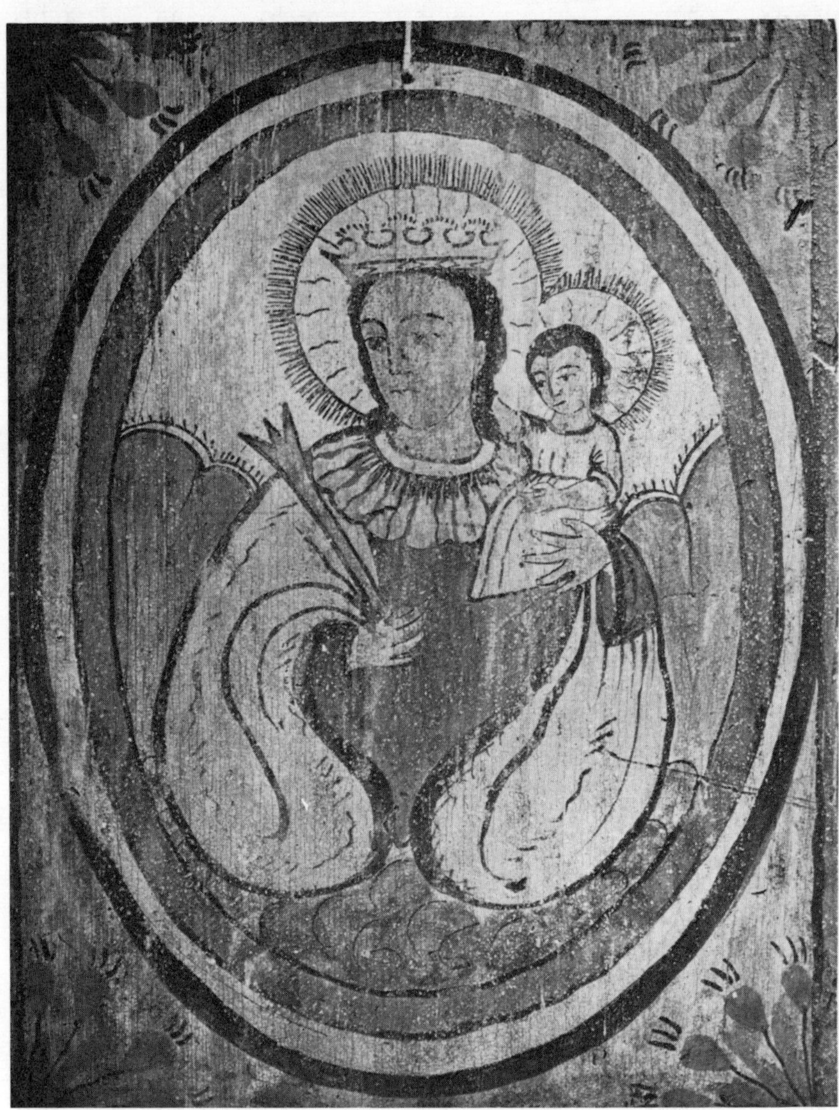

FIGURE 2
Our Lady of Refuge. Retablo, New Mexico. (After E. Boyd 1974:383; Collections of the Museum of International Folk Art, Museum of New Mexico, Santa Fe.)

no attempt at foreshortening. The easel on which his painting is placed is oversized, to emphasize the importance of the action. His painting has a plain gold background. The entire representation illustrates how the strict traditions of the icon survived into later centuries.

Similarly, the santero of New Mexico worked with little worldly decoration. In Figure 2, the folds of the Virgin's mantle are conventionalized to parallel the curve of the oval frame. The image of Our Lady of Refuge appears always as a bust. The original painting is said to be the work of a Jesuit in Italy early in the eighteenth century. A copy appears in Mexico somewhat later as a gift to the Apostolic College of Guadalupe in Zacatecas, and in this aspect the Virgin became patroness of the missions connected with that institution (Garcia Gutierrez 1946*a*).

In the mosaic from a Byzantine church in Nicaea, Turkey (Fig. 3), dating from around the sixth century, the Mother of God stands on a dais in splendid austerity with the Child on her arm, in a pose that continued through the centuries. The Virgin's feet are invisible, as prescribed since earliest times. The gaze is straightforward. Each figure has its individuality, but the inner relationship is evident. Mosaic work was general during the glory of Byzantine art. As the empire declined and the advancing Turks took more and more land, the icon became the perpetuating idiom of the religious tradition.

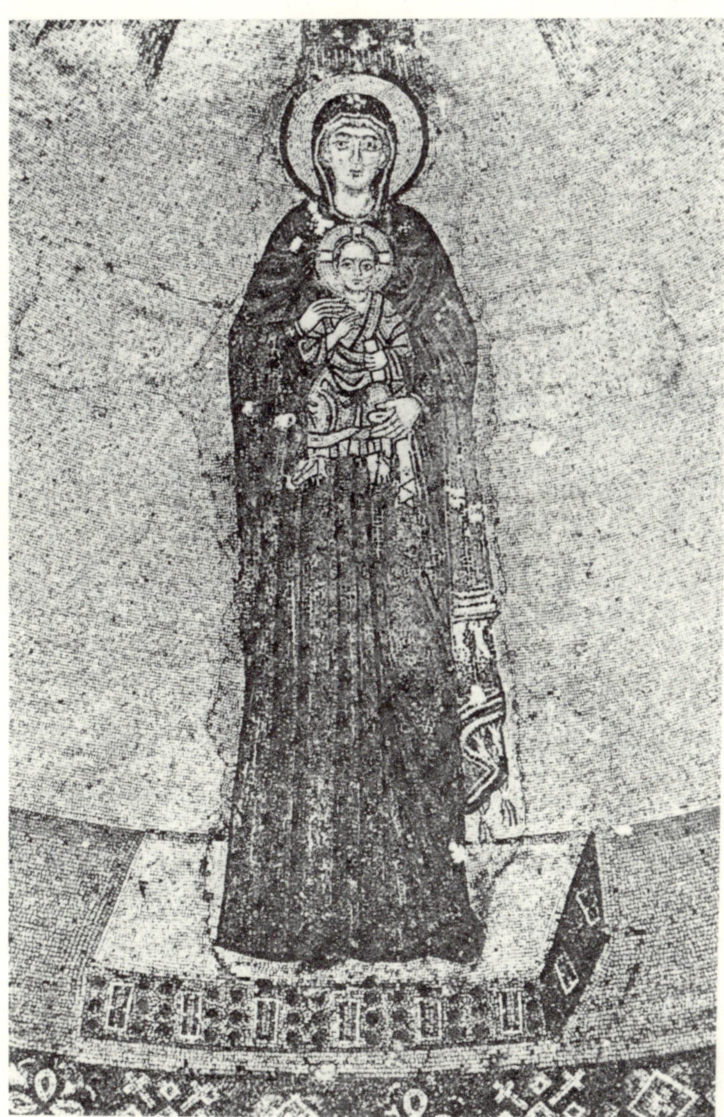

FIGURE 3
Virgin and Child. Byzantine mosaic, Turkey. (From the Kelemen Archive.)

The New Mexican bulto of Our Lady of the Rosary (Fig. 4) has a certain parallel with the Byzantine example in the elongation of the figure. This too is mounted on a dais and the feet covered. In spite of its small size (twenty-five inches), the figure has dignity and a certain monumentality. The piece is said to be the work of José Rafael Aragón (ca. 1796–1862), one of the greatest santeros.

This aspect of the Virgin is connected with a vision of St. Dominic. Her cult, with its lay sponsorship, reached maximum fervor with the development of the American colonies. As patroness of the Royal Armada, she guarded the galleons that sailed between Cádiz, Spain, and America and between Acapulco, Mexico, and Manila in the Philippines.

The New Mexican bulto reminds one of the paintings frequently seen in South America: miraculous statues enshrined—mannequins dressed in richly brocaded, voluminous gowns, characterized by loops of pearls and gold lace. Although in a much more modest version, the New Mexican Rosario also has the three-field flowered decoration on her conical skirt between horizontal loops of white. The crescent moon, symbol of the Virgin, is there in miniature at the hem of her garment. Otherwise, the usual attributes have disappeared. The extended right hand probably carried a scepter crowned with roses or the rosary, her gift to Dominic. The Christ Child, originally held on her left arm, was lost during a traveling exhibition in 1944 (Wroth 1982: 158).

In the figure of Isavrios, a Byzantine saint (Fig. 5), part of an eleventh-

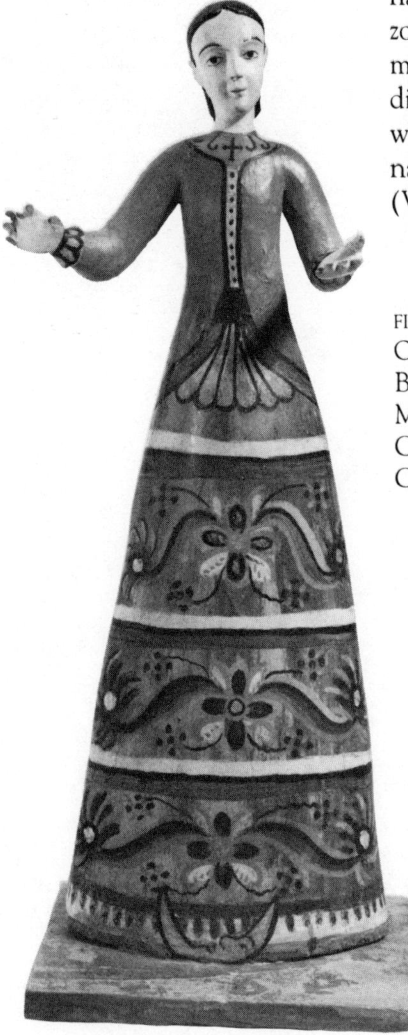

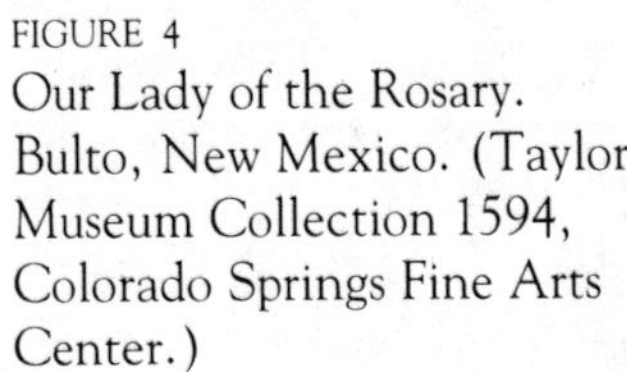

FIGURE 4
Our Lady of the Rosary. Bulto, New Mexico. (Taylor Museum Collection 1594, Colorado Springs Fine Arts Center.)

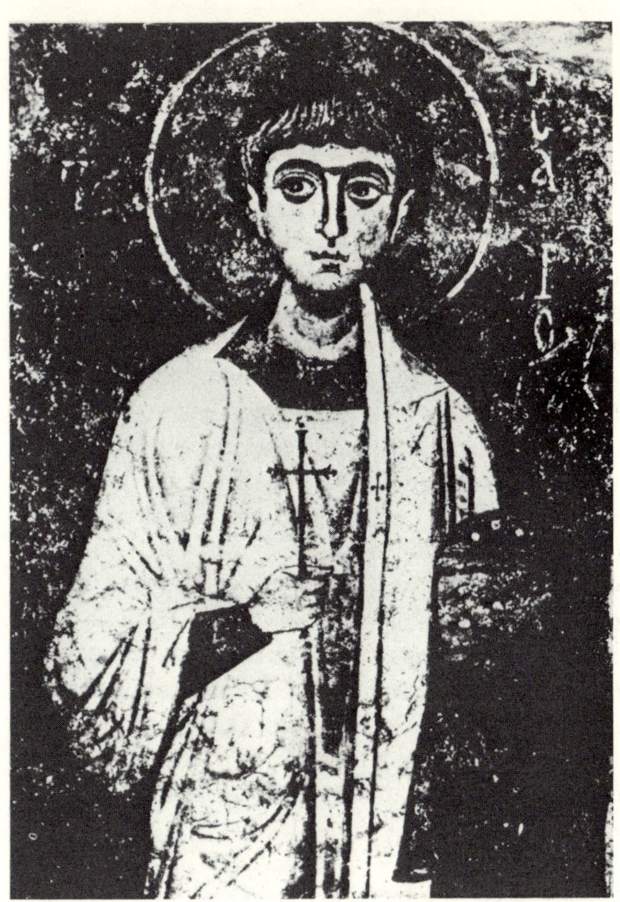

FIGURE 5
Isavrios, Byzantine saint. Icon, Greece. (From the Kelemen Archive.)

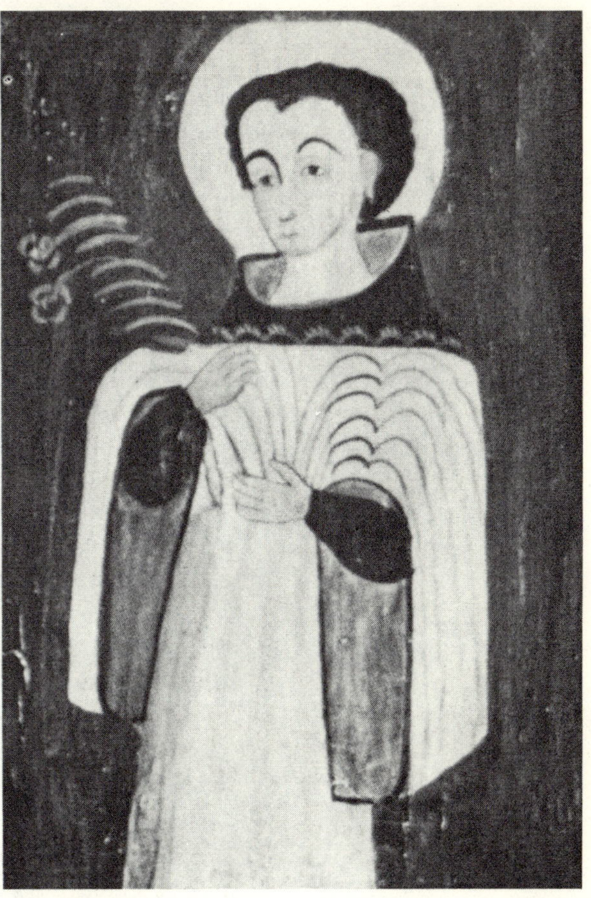

FIGURE 6
Aloysius Gonzaga, Jesuit saint. Retablo, New Mexico. (From the Kelemen Archive.)

century mural from Strip, Macedonia, again the immobility of stance and the economy, as well as the assurance of line in the garments, are notable. A few deftly applied lines, especially around the sleeve, break and lighten the spread of white surface on his garment and lead the eye to the face and the broad halo. The gaze is focused on infinity. He is remote but alert and authoritative.

The garb of the New Mexican santo (Fig. 6) also enjoys a certain linear decoration, echoed in the almost abstracted palm branch. He too stands without gesture, and the hands are underemphasized in the effective, painterly accenting of face and the dominant nimbus.

In the suburb of Zacatecas known as Guadalupe, the Franciscans kept a powerful *colegio* from which missionaries went out to the frontiers (Kelemen

1951). A charming version of Saint Luke painting the Virgin is carved on the stone portal of the college church (Fig. 7). The saint holds a palette in his hand, the pigments marked by colored stones that glisten in the light. His picture presents a slender young woman enveloped in radiance. Her robe falls in simple folds. Her eyes are obsidian. This is the Virgin of Guadalupe, as the santero painted her and as she appears, sometimes guarded by cherubs, throughout Mexico. So she was depicted in Mexican tiles on the doorway of the Guadalupe church in old Santa Fe, a building that served as spiritual and social center of the pre-Anglo society (Workers of the Writers' Program 1940:208).

Very different, however, is the original image of the Virgin of Guadalupe, venerated at the great Hieronymite monastery of Guadalupe, near Caceres in the state of Estremadura in Spain and said actually to be the work of Saint Luke. She is represented with scepter and crown, with the Son on her arm. Both figures are cone-shaped, stiff in robes of brocade studded with jewels.[2]

The Spanish Guadalupe appears in the New World as well. According to a rather picaresque history, a copy of the original statue was brought from Spain to the village of Pacasmayo near Trujillo, Peru, in the sixteenth century, where a shrine was erected to her and where miraculous cures came to pass. Even the viceroy of Peru, Francisco de Toledo, visited there. By the early seventeenth century, the original modest building had changed into an imposing complex maintained by the Hieronymite order, which flourished for nearly two hundred years (Vargas Ugarte 1931).

Venerated throughout Mexico, the New World Guadalupe began its career as a painting of a lily-slender woman alone, without the Child. The ancient Spanish Guadalupe, cone-shaped in sumptuous robes and laden with ornaments, with her Son on her arm, was transplanted to the New World as a statue and serves as forerunner of a number of holy images, especially in South America.

Most of the saints we encounter in the Orthodox world—Charalambos, Cyril, Demetrios—do not occur in Spanish colonial America. There, we find Isidro, Cayetano, Nepomuceno, often reflecting the predeliction of the individual missionary (Garcia Gutierrez 1946*b*). As in all folk art, the attributes of particular figures are often interchanged or omitted as the craftsman is individually inclined, and exact identification is therefore sometimes hazy.

Painters of the Renaissance and the Baroque in Western Europe and in the Americas south of the Rio Grande directed their talent and imagination to subjects that displayed their coloristic virtuosity, their daring designs, their command of anatomy and perspective and often depicted trance and frenzy. In the need to preserve the faith, the style of the highly sophisticated artist of the Byzantine world was crystallized in later icons. The santero of New Mexico started with a small iconographical vocabulary and held to it.

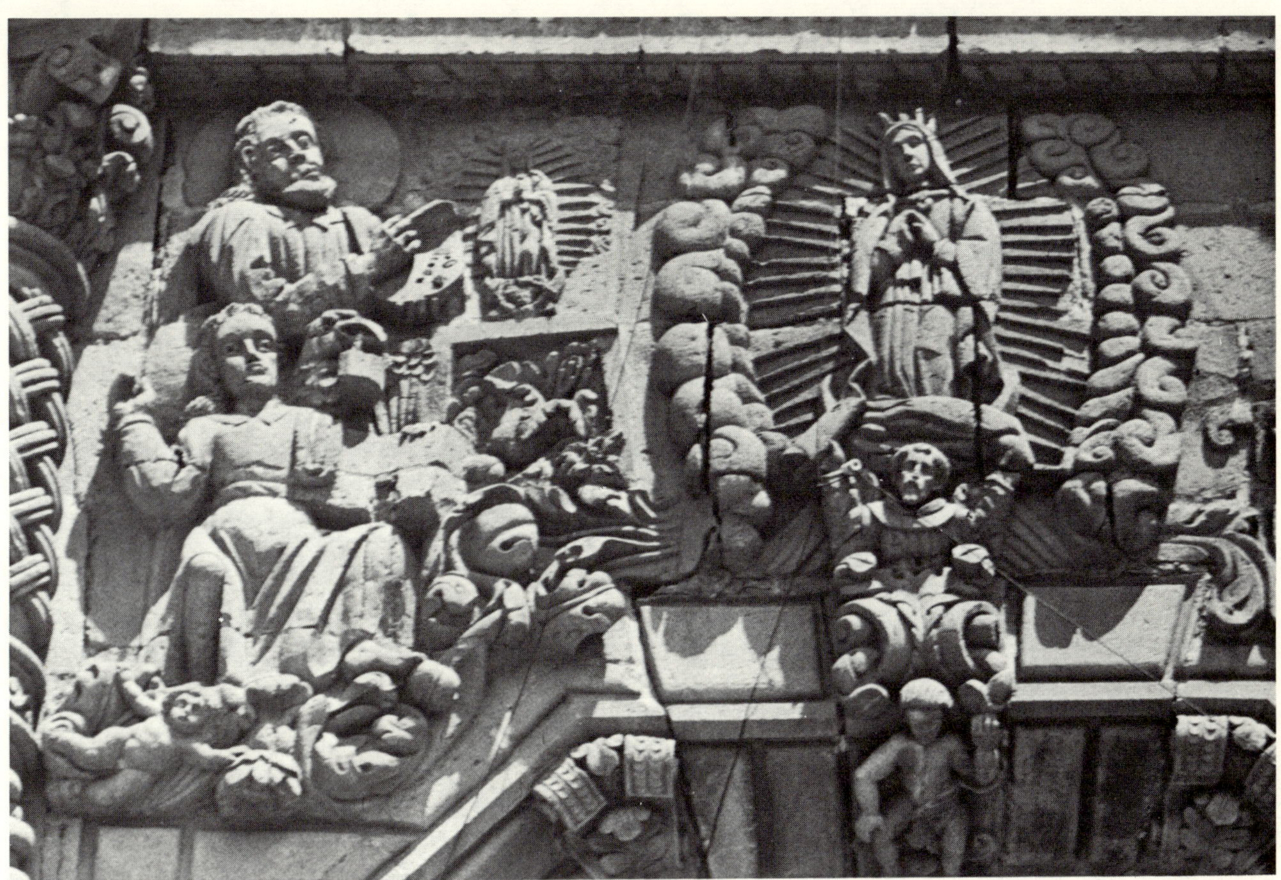

FIGURE 7
Saint Luke painting the Virgin and Child. Sculpture, Guadalupe-Zacatecas, Mexico. (Photograph by Elisabeth Z. Kelemen.)

Therefore, the retablos and bultos remain more or less unchanged from their inception to the age of commercialization and soulless imitation. Icons and santos were not intended as realistic images, but to betoken mediators of divine beneficence.

Today, it is difficult to come by a fine old santo, and the same is true of icons in the Eastern Orthodox world. When I asked a friend in Athens how I could acquire a fine old icon, he smilingly replied: "You either inherit or steal one."

"*La nostalgie n'est plus ce qu'elle était,*" says a French writer. My nostalgia is not of that type. I remember with gratitude my first teacher of art history at the Royal Hungarian University in Budapest (1911). His slide projections stopped with Delacroix and Courbet. The large black-and-white glass slides were lit by electric arc light and cooled by running water behind them.

And the jovial Swiss, Heinrich Wölfflin in Munich, who sat on the windowsill in the university corridor and talked to me of the Baroque of the Habsburgs.

And tea with the Berensons at I Tatti, overlooking the Arno valley, discussing the reliability of color in those early illustrations.

And meeting E. Boyd for the first time in that dark room with the bare cement floor, lit by one naked bulb hanging on a cord. Retablos and bultos stood on shelves and on the floor, interspersed with painter's equipment and closed and open books wherever there was room. From the look in her eyes, a communication in a few words, one recognized a person working with fierce enthusiasm, talent, and strength. As we left, we knew that we had met a remarkable human being impossible to forget.

She is not forgotten.

NOTES

1. Personal discussion with Francisco de la Maza, Mexico, D.F., January 1954.

2. The Hieronymite order was widely spread in mid-sixteenth-century Europe, with more than fifty-five establishments. That at Yuste, west of Toledo, Spain, became especially notable because the Emperor Charles V spent his last years there (1557–1558). The Royal Monastery of Guadalupe was among the most spectacular, the focus of pilgrimages to the miraculous statue of the Virgin Mary and Child. Another much-praised monastery functioned in Granada. There, the main retable in the Capilla Mayor is still to be seen, with ten rows of polychrome and gilded figures. However, when Philip II lavished funds that would have gone elsewhere on the construction of his Escorial, nearly all other foundations of the order suffered. Even the Royal Monastery of Guadalupe fell into neglect, and the nineteenth-century secularization of the order was the final blow. Now, a project is afoot to restore it, at least to some extent (Archivo Español de Arte, No. 168. Madrid, 1969).

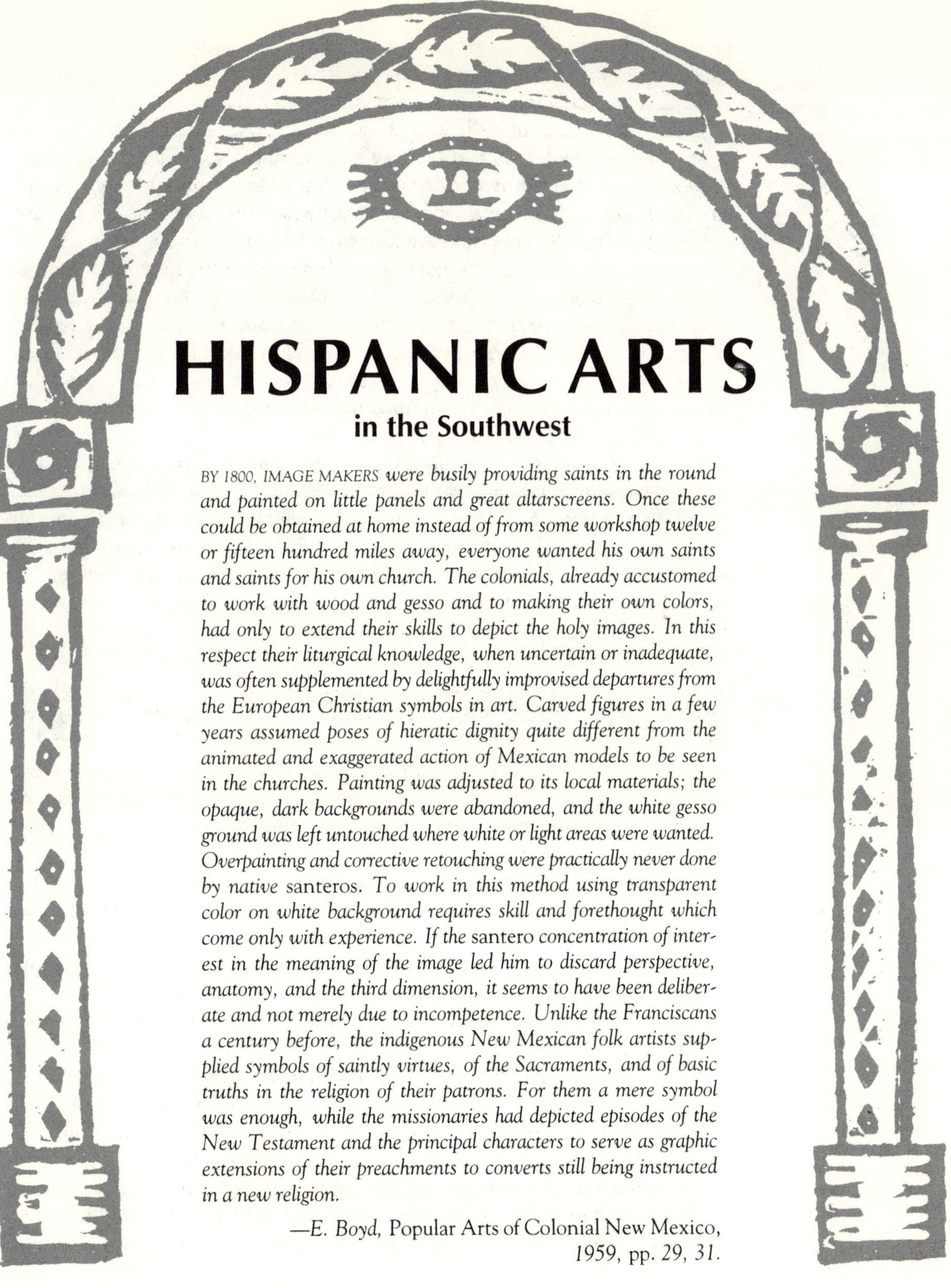

HISPANIC ARTS

in the Southwest

BY 1800, IMAGE MAKERS were busily providing saints in the round and painted on little panels and great altarscreens. Once these could be obtained at home instead of from some workshop twelve or fifteen hundred miles away, everyone wanted his own saints and saints for his own church. The colonials, already accustomed to work with wood and gesso and to making their own colors, had only to extend their skills to depict the holy images. In this respect their liturgical knowledge, when uncertain or inadequate, was often supplemented by delightfully improvised departures from the European Christian symbols in art. Carved figures in a few years assumed poses of hieratic dignity quite different from the animated and exaggerated action of Mexican models to be seen in the churches. Painting was adjusted to its local materials; the opaque, dark backgrounds were abandoned, and the white gesso ground was left untouched where white or light areas were wanted. Overpainting and corrective retouching were practically never done by native santeros. *To work in this method using transparent color on white background requires skill and forethought which come only with experience. If the* santero *concentration of interest in the meaning of the image led him to discard perspective, anatomy, and the third dimension, it seems to have been deliberate and not merely due to incompetence. Unlike the Franciscans a century before, the indigenous New Mexican folk artists supplied symbols of saintly virtues, of the Sacraments, and of basic truths in the religion of their patrons. For them a mere symbol was enough, while the missionaries had depicted episodes of the New Testament and the principal characters to serve as graphic extensions of their preachments to converts still being instructed in a new religion.*

—*E. Boyd,* Popular Arts of Colonial New Mexico, *1959,* pp. *29, 31.*

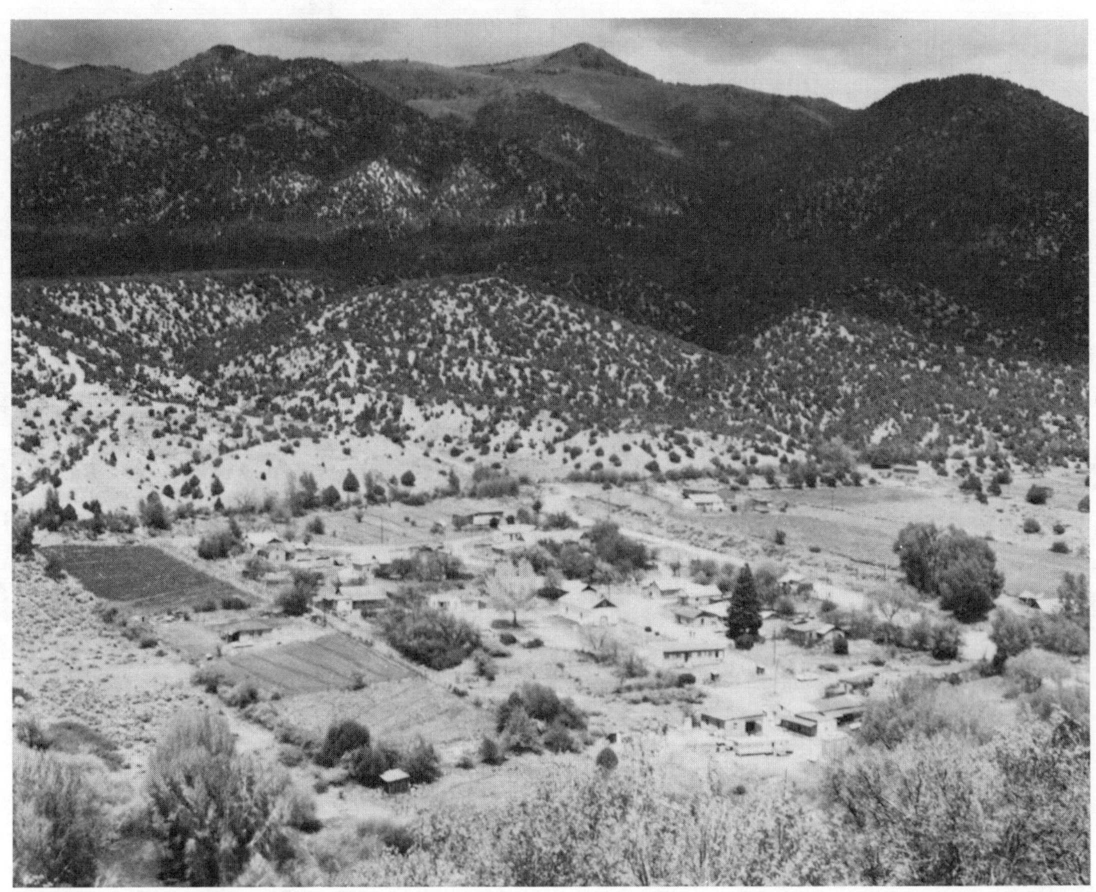

The mountain village of
Valdez, New Mexico.

BAINBRIDGE BUNTING
THOMAS R. LYONS
MARGIL LYONS

PENITENTE BROTHERHOOD MORADAS AND THEIR ARCHITECTURE

Two short years after retiring as professor of art at the University of New Mexico, Bainbridge Bunting died of a heart attack. In numerous publications on the art and architecture of New Mexico, he had revealed over and over his love for his adopted home. The present collabororative effort was begun in the early 1970s while we (Thomas and Margil Lyons) were in the midst of an extensive survey to locate and record on film as many moradas as possible before their abandonment or conversion to different uses. It was our task to secure, wherever possible, permission from the local Brothers to allow Bain's students to make measured drawings of the structures and associated features. Some of these drawings are with *Historic New Mexican Buildings: A Collection of Measured Drawings,* edited by Bainbridge Bunting, in the Fine Arts Library at the University of New Mexico, Albuquerque, and some are in the collection of the Albuquerque Museum. This work progressed for some eight years and resulted in the present paper, a joint effort with Bunting taking major responsibility for the architecture section.[1]

IN THE MOUNTAINOUS AREAS of northern New Mexico and southern Colorado are numerous small towns and villages that have supported and in many cases continue to support chapters or *moradas* of the Penitente Brotherhood and one or more of their meetinghouses, also called *moradas.* (The word *morada* comes from the Spanish verb *morar,* "to dwell," "to reside," or "to sojourn.") The buildings are the locus for worship during Holy Week and on various saints' days. Individual chapters, independent entities that are sometimes joined loosely with other moradas in the area, supervise such observances and organize mutual welfare benefits at times of crisis throughout the year.

The Penitente Brotherhood, known variously as La Fraternidad or La Cofradía de Nuestro Padre Jesús Nazareno, is composed exclusively of male Catholics, predominantly men of Hispanic ancestry. Although best known in the past for the expression of religious fervor through public and private penitential activities, from its inception in the late 1700s until the present day (Chávez 1954*b*; Weigle 1976; Woodward 1974) La Fraternidad has been an important source of social integration and cohesion during times of quiescence and stress.[2] The Brothers of La Fraternidad pray for health, for bountiful crops, for aid in leading an exemplary life, for friends and relatives, for the living and the dead, for soldiers away from home; in a word, for all who may benefit from their heavenly petitions. Guided in all their observances by strict *reglas,* or rules, that serve to heighten the participants' awareness and understanding of the deity, Brothers' religious views are not necessarily espoused but certainly acknowledged by all members of Hispano village society as part of their cultural heritage.

Moradas provided, and to a limited extent still provide, both spiritual and temporal leadership in the community (Kutsche and Gallegos 1979; Weigle and Lyons 1982). In the nineteenth century, they served as a means of maintaining law and order through the impress of religious sanctions during periods when connections with both secular and ecclesiastical authorities of Spain, Mexico, or the United States were minimal and tenuous. Perhaps of greatest significance was the fact that La Fraternidad remained a fortress of cultural identity when the Hispanic settlers and natives were faced with Indian incursions and later with the more culturally destructive forces of the dominant Anglo-American society. Nonmembers—neighbors and outsiders, whether men, women or children—were and are invited to participate in the *rosarios* (rosaries), *velorios* (wakes), stations of the cross, patron-saint days, and other observances of the Brotherhood, and they too may receive charitable benefits from the morada.

Leadership among the Brothers *(Hermanos)* is not conferred by formal preparation and dictum ("Thou art a priest forever according to the order of Melchizedek") as in a priestly hierarchy, but is earned by virtue of individual ability and dedication. The morada's highest office, that of *Hermano Mayor* or Elder Brother, is elective. Once elected, the Hermano Mayor usually retains his position for an extended period of time, often until his death or until he is no longer capable of carrying out his considerable responsibilities. Other officers (Weigle 1976: 146–48) are usually appointed by the Hermano Mayor and are directly responsible to him for the proper performance of their administrative, charitable, and spiritual duties.

In the later 1800s, La Fraternidad began to develop organizations beyond the local morada. *Concilios* (councils) within and across county and state lines were organized in the late nineteenth and early twentieth centuries (Weigle 1976: 121–38). In more recent years (1934–1947), Miguel Archibeque of Santa Fe and M. Santos Melendez of Mora worked to establish a *Concilio Supremo* (Supreme Council) of numerous moradas scattered throughout northern New Mexico and Colorado. The establishment of such a council was crucial to their efforts to secure recognition by the American Catholic church, to incorporate the activities of La Fraternidad within that sanctioning group, and to be governed officially as a Catholic confraternity. In 1947 the Concilio Supremo was recognized by Archbishop Edwin V. Byrne of Santa Fe, with Archibeque elected the first *Hermano Supremo Arzobispal* (Chief Episcopal Brother). It should be made clear, however, that not all moradas were persuaded to relinquish their independence and to be reincorporated into the mainstream of Anglo-American Catholicism. Still, both Concilio Supremo moradas and independent chapters attempt to preserve culturally meaningful and distinctive social forms and religious beliefs and practices. Consequently, La Fraternidad exerts a strong ethnic appeal that has no messianic element but does possess nativistic elements expressed in the predominantly Hispanic membership, language, art, architecture, and traditional Hispanic Catholicism.

LA FRATERNIDAD TODAY

La Fraternidad traditionally has drawn its members from the Hispano male Catholic population of villages and rural communities. Female auxiliaries *(auxiliadoras)* with ties only to the local morada support and minister to the Hermanos during times of secluded prayer and sacrifices. These pious women, who are often wives and relatives of the Brothers, are sometimes referred to as Veronicas, Carmelitas, or Terceras and are reported to practice some devotions and penances separately from the males (Weigle 1976: 144–46). In addition, some chapters are known to have male auxiliaries who provide the Hermanos with various services throughout the year but are not themselves considered novices, initiates, or fully participating members.

Although Hermanos presently reside in both urban and rural communities, most live and work in small villages and rural areas. Perhaps no more than 5 percent of the total membership reside in an urban environment, which in any case is not the ideal locale for fostering the growth and vigor of La Fraternidad. Only a few contemporary moradas function in an urban setting; most are concentrated in the valleys of the southern Rocky Mountains of northern New Mexico and southern Colorado. The highest density of active chapters in New Mexico is in Taos and Mora counties, where life is not entirely agrarian but where communities are small with day-wage employment, small ranching, and relief rolls being the primary means of subsistence.

Since the end of World War II, Hispano village life has changed drastically. Emigration to urban centers, particularly among the younger community members, has taken place on a large scale. Radio and television, highway improvements, and greater availability of motor transportation have increased familiarity and contact with predominantly Anglo communities. Even rural members' occupations are more varied than in the past, when most village men farmed, ranched, or hired out as herders. The emphasis on agrarian life has been diluted with wage opportunities on the railroad, in highway construction and maintenance, and in urban communities.

Many Brothers have found employment in places like Albuquerque, Santa Fe, and Los Alamos, and some have moved to their place of work. Members who live in cities but remain active in rural chapters have a much greater occupational diversity and more varied social roles. They include equipment salesmen, post-office employees, seminarians, laborers, retirees, federal and state government employees, store owners, and so on. Among them are men with active leadership roles in community and veteran affairs. In this manner, many chapters have suffered some loss of membership, since it is not always possible to maintain active ties with the morada of initiation, though some Brothers have managed to retain their commitment. The late Hermano Supremo Arzobispal, M. Santos Melendez, for example, lived and worked in Albuquerque but maintained active ties with his home morada in the Mora Valley.

Recruiting by the Hermanos is not as a rule through proselytizing or membership drives. Rather it is a passive method whereby an interested Catholic male may ask to be considered for membership in a specific morada. There is no fixed age limit; boys of about twelve years of age may express a desire to join the Brotherhood and can be considered for membership. Consequently, some moradas boast a mix of ages from youths to mature and older men. In others, membership has been reduced to only a few elderly Hermanos, who must soon disband for lack of new recruits able to carry on the ceremonial activities and the work of maintaining the morada structure itself.

Señor B. F., who was until recently an active member and an official of the Concilio Supremo of La Fraternidad and who in the course of his duties visited most of the member chapters in New Mexico and Colorado, kept records which showed that in 1970 there were approximately 1,530 members affiliated with some 125 chapters in the Concilio Supremo. Our fieldwork sampling of chapters indicates that approximately 80 more moradas, with an estimated membership of some 1,000 souls, are no longer Concilio members, or perhaps never were. The total census, then, amounts at this time to approximately 2,530 Brothers in over 200 moradas.

GEOGRAPHIC DISTRIBUTION OF LA FRATERNIDAD

Eighteenth-century Spanish settlements clustered in the Rio Grande Valley roughly between Belen and Tomé in the south and Taos in the north. This original area was expanded eastward to Mora, Tecolote, and Anton Chico, southward to Socorro, westward to Cebolleta, Jémez Springs, and Vallecitos, and northward to Arroyo Seco, Arroyo Hondo, and the San Luis Valley of southern Colorado in the first decades of the nineteenth century. Formally organized moradas are still found in many of these core and outlying communities.

Field investigations have pinpointed the distribution of moradas. Today, active chapters exist from a small village about fifty miles south of Albuquerque, New Mexico, to the area around Pueblo, Colorado, and in the northern San Luis Valley. A Denver chapter has been organized by Hermanos who came to that city from various communities to the south. In 1972, an active morada stood in grand isolation some thirty miles northeast of Tucumcari, New Mexico. To the west, the morada at the village of San Mateo has been active before and since Charles F. Lummis's 1888 visit (Lummis 1966; Mayfield 1925; Woodward 1974). Not far to the east of Bloomfield, New Mexico, a group of Hermanos have recently reestablished a chapter near the site of an old morada destroyed by a flood of the San Juan River in 1927.

La Fraternidad previously extended over a much larger area than it does today. In the village of Doña Ana in southern New Mexico, the rounded sanctuary of a small morada has been incorporated into a house block and is used as a private chapel (Fig. 1). Mrs. María Vasquez of Doña Ana told us that when she was a small girl her grandmother talked about the morada and the Hermanos who used it. Woodward (1974: 21) reports moradas in the Piños Altos Mountains of southwestern New Mexico and in Clapham, on the northeastern plains of Union County, New Mexico. Lamb (1968) describes a "Penitente cemetery" near Lincoln, in the southeastern part of the state. Presumably this was once used by a local chapter of Hermanos as well as by other residents of the area.

We have heard as yet unconfirmed reports of moradas in St. Johns, eastern Arizona, and in southeastern Utah. Diligent inquiry in Arizona towns like Winslow and Flagstaff has not yielded so much as a memory of former Brotherhood activity in the vicinity, but it is too early to draw any conclusions; La Fraternidad may indeed have reached this area of the Southwest.[3]

During the twentieth century, there has been a marked migration of Hispanos from the southern Rocky Mountain area. Men have sought work as herders, railroad and farm laborers, construction workers, and industrial plant employees in Montana, Wyoming, California, and other states. Migrating Hermanos probably set up temporary or permanent chapters like the Denver morada, and further research may well reveal congregations of Brothers in other urban and rural areas outside northern New Mexico and southern Colorado. On the other hand, several Hermanos have told us about Brothers who live in California and Colorado and yet return to their moradas of initiation each year for *Semana Santa* (Holy Week).

MORADA ARCHITECTURE

Tangible evidence of La Fraternidad's persistent adaptability is found in the location and form of their moradas, most of which were built after 1821. Faced with what was for the most part a largely unsympathetic clergy (whether Mexican, French, or American) and with insensitive Anglo cultural attitudes, the Brothers responded by utilizing indigenous domestic architectural styles and modified familiar ecclesiastical architectural forms. When necessary, the morada was removed from the village to provide the secluded facilities that members required.

Despite a well-defined local meaning and specialized function, then, moradas vary considerably in appearance, location, and relationship to other structures in the community. Moradas are found within occupied villages, on their outskirts, and in total isolation—deep in a forest, or valley, or on lonely, windswept plains. Although certain buildings may seem to resemble small Catholic churches, others look more like a simple dwelling or storage shed. Such architectural variety exhibits differences in the size and wealth of the groups sponsoring the structures, in the materials available to them, and in the building technologies current at the time. The lack of identifiable location or architectural form also reflects the loose organization of Brotherhood chapters and La Fraternidad's uneven relations with the church historically.

Not all religious structures too small to serve as churches are moradas. There is a long tradition in New Mexico of families constructing *oratorios* (chapels) for private use. These may stand alone, be semidetached, or form an integral part of a large house. Examples of the first type are the Santuario at Chimayó, with construction (1815–1816) sponsored by Bernardo Abeyta (Borhegyi 1953), and the picturesque chapel that once stood in the complex of houses belonging to the Duran family in Talpa (Wroth 1979). The Ortega family oratory on Plaza del Cerro in Chimayó is semidetached (Anonymous 1971: 80, 85; Bunting 1974: 6, 27). There are numerous records of private oratories within mansions of the eighteenth and nineteenth centuries; two notable examples are found at the Ortiz hacienda in Galisteo and the Armijo house on Rio Grande Boulevard in Albuquerque (DeWitt 1978: 35). Except for Abeyta, the other families did not have Brotherhood associations. On the other hand, in recent decades there have been several instances of a chapel owned by an individual but erected by him explicitly for use as a morada (examples exist in Lower Colonias–Pine and in the Atrisco area of Albuquerque). We should also note two instances of a room or rooms set aside for use as a morada within a private dwelling, an arrangement found in the Sanchez house in Tijeras (partly burned in 1972 and later demolished during highway construction) and in the old Flores house at Villanueva (now abandoned).

Another point of variation is the way in which the morada is related to the parish or mission church. The arrangement of buildings may imply something about the relationship of the Brotherhood to the official church structure. Customarily the morada was placed some distance from the church building, but, in the case of Las Trampas, for example, this was not so (Boyd 1974: 334, 459; Bunting 1970; Leyba 1933). Here the morada was contiguous with the church fabric, though lacking an interior communication with it (Fig.

2). Sometime between 1961 and 1967, however, the morada was physically detached from the church building by the demolition of a small connecting storeroom (Fig. 3).

Such propinquity recalls chapels of the Third Order of Saint Francis in some European and Latin American communities, and it brings up the matter of the relationship of the Brotherhood to the Third Order, still a controversial question (see, for example, Chávez 1954*b*; Fisher 1941; Weigle 1976). Only one chapel belonging to the Third Order remains in New Mexico, that at Santa Cruz, built in 1798 (Adams and Chávez 1956: 75; Boyd 1974: 447, 449; Kubler 1940: 103). Reasonably large and connected with the parish church in such a way as to form a kind of transept, the Santa Cruz chapel is totally unlike the morada at Las Trampas, which is domestic in scale and appearance. The paucity of moradas attached to churches need not be taken as evidence for or against the Franciscan origin of the Brotherhood; it may simply be due to the strained relations between the Brothers and the church hierarchy in New Mexico after 1850. Those cases where a morada was attached to a church might be explained in several ways: a date before 1850, an unusual rapport between the local priest and the Hermanos, or the absence of a priest assigned to the community on a regular basis.

In some instances, it is possible to identify a morada at a glance; in others recognition may be difficult. This is because of the wide range of architectural forms the building can take and because the Penitente Brotherhood has no interest in public recognition. Indeed, in the face of past sensational publicity, the group has preferred to remain quite circumspect.

While there is no single feature by which a morada can be recognized, several characteristics may be present. Identification is secure only when a combination of these is found.

1. Generally the morada is remote from the parish church, often on the outskirts of the community where privacy can be insured for such religious observances as are conducted outdoors.
2. The morada is often adjacent to a cemetery (Figs. 4 and 5). This may be the cemetery officially designated for the whole community, as at Truchas where the original parish church building was too closed in by secular structures for an adjoining graveyard. At Llano de San Juan (Fig. 6), however, the morada has its own cemetery in addition to another not more than one hundred yards away next to the church (Bunting 1974: 75).
3. A processional path, the *Via Crucis* or Way of the Cross, is often discernible (Fig. 7). Of varying lengths, these paths are sometimes curving, sometimes straight and broad and marked by borders, almost as if bladed by a road grader, as indeed they sometimes are. In other places, the Via Crucis is distinguishable only because of a change in vegetation. Always, however, the Via Crucis terminates in the *Calvario,* which is generally on higher ground. The Brothers move along this route, stopping at the fourteen stations of the

cross for prayer and penance (Fisher 1958). These stations are designated by small crosses of wood or metal; these crosses are staked in the ground during the ceremonies but are stored inside most of the time (Fig. 8).

4. Often a large cross, which may be as much as six or eight feet tall, is present (Fig. 9). This can be located at the Calvario, at the beginning of the Via Crucis, or in front of the morada. At the Calvario, there are sometimes three crosses, the central one being larger than the others. In a different arrangement at La Puente, the three large crosses are separated: one for the Calvario, another at the opposite end of the Via Crucis, the third in front of the morada.

Such crosses are often painted white and are sometimes elaborated with subsidiary arms (Figs. 10 and 11). Occasionally the arms are arranged in such a way as to suggest three crosses in one, as at Truchas (Fig. 12) and Rodarte (Bunting 1974: 76). In addition to these stationary crosses, one may also find carrying crosses *(maderos)* of large dimensions leaning against the morada wall (Figs. 13 and 14). Used by Hermanos during religious observances, maderos can be identified by the way one side of the stem is worn down from being dragged along the ground. More frequently, however, such objects are stored inside.

5. Since a chapter can function under one or more roofs, several buildings may be associated to form a morada. Examples in which the chapel *(oratorio)* is in one building and the meeting and storage rooms are housed in another are found at Cuba, San Luis, and La Madera (Figs. 9 and 15). At Rodarte, the chapel and the meeting room form one edifice with storage in a separate log structure (Fig. 16).

6. There is but one privy, usually a two-seater, although one with five seats exists at Taos (Fig. 27). A single privy distinguishes a morada from other religious buildings, which maintain two separate facilities.

In addition to these characteristics, which are more related to the emplacement of a morada than to its architectural appearance, several other points, each subject to wide variation, may be mentioned. Sometimes moradas are equipped with a bell. This can be mounted in a freestanding wooden rack as seen near San José and San Ysidro (Figs. 17 and 18). More often, the belfrey takes the form of a small wooden tower perched on the roof ridge, either at one end or in the middle (Figs. 19 and 20). On a flat roof as at Taos, the bell is usually situated near the chapel (Fig. 21), but at Abiquiú, it sits on a masonry buttress attached to the apse (Figs. 22 and 23). Sometimes the wooden frame is sheathed with sheets of corrugated iron (Fig. 24).

Perhaps the most incisive generalization one can make about the external appearance of a morada concerns the paucity of windows. This is particularly true of older examples. Frequently any windows are boarded over or are provided with shutters (Figs. 16, 23, and 25).

The floor plan of a morada admits considerable variation. Although moradas of one room are known (Bartolo Baca and Cochiti), this is exceptional, and a two-room unit is generally minimal. Depending on the size and wealth of a chapter, a morada can be more elaborate, but only Taos, with five, is known to have more than four rooms (Fig. 27).

The building can vary in shape from a straight line of rooms to L- and cross shapes. The most common linear solution resembles the arrangement of a typical early New Mexican house (Figs. 25 and 26). Although the L-shape arrangement can also be found in homes, the way this shape is used in a morada is usually closer to that of a small church in which the sacristy forms the small arm (Figs. 28 and 29). Chimayó has the only morada with a cross shape (Fig. 30).

The most important room in a morada, the oratorio, is subject to the greatest architectural variation. While most chapels are of simple rectangular plan, a small but important group of moradas articulates the altar end with a small polygonal, semicircular, or rectangular bay. An interesting treatment is provided by the two moradas at Abiquiú (Ahlborn 1968), where the converging walls of each sanctuary are further accented by a heavy buttress that supports a belfrey (Figs. 22, 23, and 31). Converging walls without the projecting belfrey, an arrangement found in many New Mexican churches, are found in several moradas of intermediate date (Gallinas, Sapello, Newkirk) and in three late examples (Albuquerque, Manuelitas, Los Ojos). Round ends were employed by Hermanos for the lower morada at Arroyo Hondo (Shalkop 1969: 16, 27), at Llano de San Juan (Fig. 8), and at Upper Rociada (Fig. 32). By no means as numerous as those with polygonal shape, this rounded termination was also used for a few small churches presumably erected during the latter part of the nineteenth century, as at Vadito and Placitas (Bunting 1974: 74).

If several types of building materials have been used in the construction of a particular morada, the one considered the finest will be used for the chapel. In the valley of the Mora River in northern New Mexico, for example, the chapel of the abandoned morada is of adobe, while the meeting and storage rooms have log walls (Fig. 33). At Villanueva, the chapel is stone (with mud mortar), the *cocina* (kitchen) of wood frame and stucco. The distinction may be only a matter of whitewash, paint, or cement plaster, but where a difference exists, the chapel is the more finished or better constructed. For example, the interior walls of two rooms at Watrous are left rough, while those of the chapel are plastered. Similarly, the chapel ceiling may have a somewhat better finish: logs adzed to a rectangular shape rather than left round (Arroyo Hondo), a layer of *manta* (cotton cloth) stretched below the beams (Sapello), or decoration in some manner such as stars painted on a blue ceiling (Chimayó).

The oratory is located to insure privacy. Although it is frequently provided with direct access to the outside, one never has to pass through the oratory to reach another room. While an opening generally connects the chapel with other rooms, in a few instances there is no inside connection

(Watrous, Talpa, Veguita), and sometimes chapels occupy a separate building altogether (Figs. 9 and 15). For privacy, a chapel is also apt to have few windows, which are almost invariably equipped with shutters or drawn curtains. Windows in old buildings are usually small (fifteen or eighteen inches square) and may be closed with a solid shutter. The chapel at Watrous has no windows at all.

Heating is important since most Brotherhood groups are situated in high country with elevations of five thousand to seventy-five hundred feet. The only source of heat in early times, of course, was the fireplace *(fogón)* (Figs. 34, 35, and 49). Later, when iron stoves became available, they were preferred because of their greater efficiency, and in some instances the old fogón was removed. In early moradas, a hearth was always part of the meeting room and sometimes of the records room, when those were present, but early Brothers appear to have dispensed with heat in the chapel. Thus the older morada at Abiquiú had two fireplaces in the meeting room but none in the chapel (Ahlborn 1968: 131, 136), and Arroyo Hondo had fireplaces in the meeting and records rooms but none in the chapel (Bunting 1964: 55, 60, 61). Brothers apparently relented later because certain chapels are now heated. The absence of heat in early places of meditation and worship may have been an aspect of the Brotherhood practice of mortifying the body as a means of penance and spiritual purification.

The interiors of early oratorios were undoubtedly quite plain. The floors were of packed earth, usually covered with *jerga,* a home-woven carpet (Boyd 1974: 181–87), although more modern establishments boast boards or linoleum and sometimes a rug in front of the altar. No adobe *bancos* (benches) have been found in the oratorios of older moradas, possibly in deference to the Brothers' practice of austerity, although these were provided in meeting rooms. Today, however, wooden benches or even pews (inherited from remodeled parish churches) are admissible (Fig. 36). Some moradas are still too remote from power lines to have installed electricity, but a good many now have it.

The altar end of an oratorio is ordinarily differentiated from the rest of the chapel by a step, rail, lattice-work "arch," or cloth valance hung from the ceiling (Figs. 36, 37, and 38). Crowded onto the altar is an assortment of statues, candles, crosses, and other religious objects owned by the chapter. By contrast, the walls are relatively bare, and the windows are curtained, even though outside shutters usually cover the openings.

Altars vary too. At Valdez, the altar table was formed by an adzed log running the width of the room and embedded in lateral walls much as a storage shelf in an early house. Sometimes the altar is an ordinary table covered with cloth, but most chapels have homemade altars constructed of finished boards, often with an elevated rear shelf for the crucifix (Fig. 39). Occasionally one finds a more elaborate, conventional altar, probably inherited from the local parish church when the latter was remodeled and apt to be overscaled for the chapel (Figs. 37 and 40).

Many bultos are placed on or adjacent to the altar table. The central image is usually an antique and fairly large *Cristo* (Christ on the Cross), but sometimes many smaller versions of the same subject may be placed on the table or hung on the wall behind. These are often paired for size. In addition, medium-sized figures of Mary or other saints may also share the table with candlesticks or oil lamps, glass cups containing votive candles, and vases with paper or plastic flowers. To these are added religious medals of various sizes and materials with perhaps a snapshot or two left as *ex votos.* Larger statues stand on the floor beside the altar. Grouped with these are one or two large candelabra constructed of two-by-fours with at least one standard supporting a satin banner inscribed with the chapter's name or representing Veronica's veil (Figs. 37, 38, and 41).

By far the most numerous among these statues is the Christ on the Cross (Fig. 42). Many of these figures are provided with actual clothing. Three Cristos obtained from a morada in 1961 and now in the collection at the Museum of Albuquerque were dressed in three layers of satin or lace garments (Figs. 43 and 44). Sometimes the clothing disguises the fact that the figure has been broken from age or use. Certain chapters own so many crucifixes that they overflow the chapel to the walls of the meeting room. Additional representations of Christ may include the Man of Sorrows, the Interred Christ *(Cristo enterro,* that is, the figure laid in a coffin as in Figure 45), and Christ at the Column. He is also present as the Child with Mary, in the Holy Family, as the Santo Niño de Atocha, or in the arms of Joseph or of a saint like Anthony of Padua. Mary too is well represented, especially in the roles of intercessor and Woman of Sorrows. Saints account for a smaller portion of a morada's bulto population. Their selection appears to depend on the patron of the morada or of the community in which it is located.

In all, the statues may run into the dozens, in a wide assortment of materials and sizes. Modern figures in plastic, plaster, and metal alloys are venerated alongside old bultos of great emotional force and aesthetic value. To the Hermanos who own these figures, the subject matter and personal associations are more important than the bulto's age, aesthetic worth, or monetary value.

Retablos are also found on the altar and side walls of the chapel. These range from rare works by early santeros to Spanish colonial engravings and nineteenth-century colored lithographs to recent purchases from religious art stores. They may be plain wooden panels, pictures enclosed in charming old tin *nichos,* or in frames straight from the dime store.[4]

If a morada contains only two rooms, the second will house all functions other than worship; if there are more than two, the second is reserved as the place of meeting. In Abiquiú, this room is called the sacristy (Ahlborn 1968:

137); in Veguita, *el sepulcro.* During Holy Week, when the Brothers are in continuous attendance at the morada from Wednesday to Saturday, they wait in the meeting room when not engaged in prayer, rites, or processions, and there they partake of food prepared in the cocina or brought in from the homes of members or auxiliaries. As at Arroyo Hondo (Bunting 1964: 61), the chief architectural feature of this room is the fireplace, which is often equipped with a shelf on which pots of food can be kept warm (Fig. 35). In the older morada at Abiquiú, this room has small fireplaces in opposite corners, a custom frequently followed in large rooms of early New Mexico homes (Fig. 31). A banco may run around the wall of this room, and fenestration is more ample than in the oratorio. There is usually an outside entry.

On Saturday, at the end of their Holy Week vigils, processions, and penitential exercises, the Brothers bathe and refresh themselves. In many instances, galvanized washtubs are provided for this ablution. Both moradas in Abiquiú have built-in basins, the older constructed of wood with mud plaster, the newer of cement. A wooden tub with an ingenious outside wooden drain survives at Mora. One from Ensenada is hollowed from a log (Fig. 48). The Abiquiú basins are situated in the meeting room (sacristy), which is heated by a fireplace or stove. In Ensenada, a wooden partition screened the bathing area from the rest of the meeting room, indicating a desire for privacy that a fourth room would have provided. If a morada had an additional room with a fireplace, as at Arroyo Hondo, it is possible that ablutions were performed there rather than in the meeting room.

The third and fourth rooms, where they exist, vary in size. One is needed for storage and can be either a connecting room or a detached building. In such a room are kept the small stations of the cross, the carrying crosses, the ladder, the equipment used in penitential exercises, and various instruments to make noise such as ratchets *(matracas),* chains, iron sheets, and drums. If the room is large, flagellation may have been practiced in it, to judge from the bloodstains present on the ceiling of the old Arroyo Hondo morada. In keeping with its storage or penitential functions, this room has minimal fenestration and no fireplace.

The last room may have been used for records, *el escritorio,* to judge from the desk and papers still in place as late as 1961 in the then abandoned upper morada at Arroyo Hondo (Fig. 49). It was next to a fireplace and may also have been used for bathing, though it lacked a stationary basin. The morada at Taos is quite exceptional in having five rooms, but two of these, built in 1902 and 1938, merely duplicate an original kitchen and dining room. Indeed, these additions were abandoned in the 1950s when the Brothers reoccupied the old quarters (Fig. 27).

THE ARCHITECTURAL HISTORY OF MORADAS

Despite variations in morada design and appearance caused by differences in size, affluence of the chapters, and available building materials, it is possible in a general way to identify three periods of construction: early (prior to 1900), middle (1900–1940), and late (1940 to present). Since there are very few firm dates, this approximate chronology must be deduced from internal evidence based on the appearance of the morada and on the building technology employed.

The loose, largely autonomous organization of chapters in the early years means that there is no center for Brotherhood records, and building accounts in rural New Mexico are almost nonexistent. Because of the reluctance of members to discuss Fraternidad matters with outsiders, historical information that might have been transmitted orally has gone unrecorded, and in recent years chapters have been disinclined to permit core borings to be made in roof beams as a means of obtaining tree-ring dates. Although it is likely that additional building facts and dates of morada will turn up from time to time in unexpected contexts, setting out deliberately to find them is a futile task. Recorded or even reasonably substantiated dates are therefore few:

1852–1856	Arroyo Hondo, upper morada
1900	Abiquiú, south morada
1922	Cleveland, west morada
1929	Albuquerque
1932	Lower Colonias–Pine
1975	Mora

Nevertheless, it is possible to draw a hypothetical picture of an early morada. As several historians have observed (Ahlborn 1968: 130; Kubler 1940: viii), the architectural character of a morada was somewhere between a house and a church, although closer to the former. As was standard in early New Mexican construction, the roof was flat, and the level of the edifice's several rooms was determined by the contours of the building site. Thus the morada's silhouette might be stepped in a way that emphasized both the modular quality of its composition and its close relation to the setting (Figs. 19, 21, and 50). This handsome characteristic has sometimes been obscured when for practical purposes a gable roof of metal was added to an old structure (Fig. 25).

Windows were small and few in number, emphasizing the building's compact, sculptured appearance. Exterior surfaces were almost always plastered with adobe, the only material available in the earliest days. All this related a morada to its environment and produced an architecture that was organic in the true sense of the word. However, the appearance of a morada was subject to change as the technology of the region evolved under the impact of improved transportation.

Information can be derived from an examination of the materials and methods employed in the construction of any building. In remote areas of New Mexico, where roads were poor and transportation difficult, early structures were limited to materials in the immediate neighborhood. Despite its prevalence, adobe brick is not the only material used for morada walls. In some areas, nature provides a good ledge stone, which, laid with adobe mortar, makes a handsome, stable wall. Particularly fine stone moradas are seen at Upper Rociada and south of Santa Rosa (Figs. 32 and 50). In areas where timber is plentiful, log construction is used. More often the members are laid horizontally, but they can also be set vertically (Figs. 51 and 52). This latter form of construction, seen in the sacrisity of a morada north of El Rito (Fig. 54) and known as *jacal* (Bunting 1976: 13, 85, 101), anchors one end of the log in a trench and fits the top into a grooved plate at the eave line.

Structures built in recent decades or erected earlier in communities located near railroads were less restricted in their choice of material. At Monero (Fig. 60) and at Blanco in northwest New Mexico, Brothers availed themselves of used railroad ties. In the past half-century, conventional wood-frame construction with two-by-four studs covered with cement plaster or plasterboard has replaced earlier methods and materials for the repair or construction of moradas.

A nice record of the changing choice of materials can be seen in a village some distance south of Albuquerque where the original morada of about 1895 was adobe, as was the meeting room added in 1932. A new oratorio was constructed of concrete blocks in 1960, while in 1970 a bathroom was built of wood frame covered on the inside with sheetrock and on the outside with cement plaster (Fig. 53). During the last stage, a slightly pitched composition roof was added to the whole edifice. To the north, in a morada near Mora, a new wood-stud oratorio in 1975 replaced the old adobe edifice, which was demolished (Fig. 54).

The most useful clues for dating are found in the various ways builders shaped the timber used in construction. Although wood was always plentiful, means of sawing it into boards were not available until after 1848, when the first steam-powered sawmill was brought into the area. Prior to that it was easier to shape heavy planks than thin boards when splitting a log. Thus, suitable material for doors or architectural trim was scarce in early times. For this reason, it is probable that some openings between rooms had no doors, as still seen in the Talpa morada (Fig. 4), although openings may have been provided with doors subsequently.

In the interests of privacy, however, the oratorio did have a door. A splendid early example is the low, rather clumsy interior door to the chapel in Arroyo Hondo (Fig. 55). The stock from which it is constructed is some 2½ inches thick; the panels are 1¼ inches thick. Its height, less than five feet, is impossibly low by present standards, and it hinges on wooden pintels, extensions of a vertical stile that fit into sockets in both the lintel and the sill. Although the morada was erected in 1852–1856, this door continues building practices of the colonial period (Bunting 1964: 5–6, 56–57; 1976: 69–71).

A later form of door from the morada at Picurís, dating probably between 1880 and 1910, has milled boards, window glass, and metal hinges. The use of more workable wood and better shaping tools is also indicated by the lighter weight, better fit, and the application of decorative moldings to the door formerly found at the Las Trampas morada (Fig. 56). Several moradas have two-ply doors with one layer of boards set vertically and the other diagonally. An even simpler door made only of vertical boards was probably used for interior openings and was built on location. Sometimes a painted cross or one worked out in moldings was added as embellishment (Fig. 57). Unfortunately for the picturesque quality of a morada, five-panel factory doors began to supersede homemade products as soon as transportation limitations were removed, and these have now given way to hollow-core doors.

Roofing is another indication of date, since important changes have occurred in this area. Early moradas had flat roofs covered with earth, a method utilized by the Spanish colonists but extending back to the earliest constructions of the Indians. This roof was a combination of logs spanning a room covered by a secondary system of poles placed at right angles with four or more inches of earth above these. Usually the logs were only peeled, but in special cases they might be adzed to a rectangular shape, as in the upper morada at Arroyo Hondo (Bunting 1964: 7, 59; 1976: 25, 65). The secondary covering consisted of contiguous poles, round or split, two or so inches in diameter. Such construction was outmoded after sawmills began to produce one-inch boarding and squared beams, a change nicely illustrated in the two moradas of otherwise rather similar design at Abiquiú, the second as late as 1900 (Ahlborn 1968). The presence of milled lumber in the roof cannot be conclusive proof of a late date, however, because of the periodic need for roof replacement or repair, as several dates penciled on the ceilings at Arroyo Hondo indicate. Similarly, all early moradas undoubtedly had floors of packed earth, but in many instances wooden floors have been added, especially in the important rooms.

Boards produced by sawmills were also employed to construct gabled roofs, which were simply added above the old flat ones. Laid on an incline and lapped or covered with battens, the boards of the roof shed moisture while the older earth covering provided insulation (Figs. 15, 33, and 58). Corrugated iron was not available in New Mexico before the arrival of the railroads in 1879, and in remote areas, this material was not much used for another forty or fifty years because of difficulties in local transportation. Thus, most of the "tin" roofs one sees on moradas postdate 1920, and some examples have been added since 1965 (Figs. 28 and 59). Another form of metal roofing, called terneplate, which comes in smaller panels, was also used after the Civil War (Fig. 50).

Fenestration also furnishes a useful indication of age (Bunting 1964: 5; 1976). Prior to 1848, window glass was all but unknown in New Mexico. A common method for closing a window opening was with a solid wooden shutter, an example of which remains at Valdez. When glass became available, especially after the completion of the railroad, both old and new buildings were equipped with glazed windows. At that time, the size of the opening might be enlarged, especially in an adobe building where it was easy to cut through the soft material. This appears to have been the case at San Ysidro and Taos, where openings in the chapel and meeting rooms have a decidedly horizontal and untraditional proportion (Figs. 18 and 21). Windows added between the wars were generally six-pane, double-hung, factory-produced, wooden sash. After World War II, metal casements were popular, and since 1970, the preference has been for sliding aluminum sash.

Another useful index of change is the manner of heating. The earliest form was the fogón, which was generally situated in a corner (Figs. 34 and 49). Similar to those in homes, these fireplaces were small but efficient; if more heat were needed a second fogón was added in another corner, as seen in the meeting room of the older morada at Abiquiú. Unusual because of its size and its bell-shaped hood is the fogón in the meeting room at Arroyo Hondo (Fig. 35). When iron stoves became available, they superseded the fireplace, and an even more recent innovation has been an oil drum modified to serve as a stove (Fig. 60).

The new stoves are used more liberally than were fireplaces, as can be seen by their present use in the previously unheated chapel at Abiquiú. To make way for a new heater, the old fogón was sometimes demolished. An ingenious contrivance for heating is found where the metal drum, placed horizontally instead of vertically as is usual, was inserted in an earlier adobe fireplace in order to utilize the existing adobe chimney (Fig. 61). A number of chapters have even installed cook stoves. One very modern one now has a fully equipped kitchen, complete with butane stove and water heater, as well as hot showers and flush toilets.

Although the chronological changes in building practices in New Mexico are relatively easy to identify, it should be borne in mind that dating by this means can be complicated by one or more stages of remodeling. Thus, for the visitor and architect, the most interesting moradas from a visual and historical point of view are the oldest ones and their subsequent development. Two textbook examples are the upper morada at Arroyo Hondo and the one at Taos.

Although abandoned in the middle 1950s, the Arroyo Hondo structure remained in almost unchanged form long enough to be measured and photographed in 1961 (Figs. 15, 35, 49, 55, and 62). Its history can also be traced with reasonable completeness. Erected between 1852 and 1855, as we know from land-transaction records in the Taos courthouse, the morada illustrates the kind of building program the Brotherhood undertook at the time it was going underground in the face of opposition from Bishop Lamy and the official church hierarchy (Weigle 1976: 52–57). Intermediate changes that cannot be dated exactly were the enlargement of glass windows and the installation of wooden floors in the chapel and meeting room. It is possible that the wooden altar still in place in 1961 was added at the same time. Roof repairs in the large storage room are recorded in the form of penciled inscriptions that bear the dates 1909, 1911, and 1938, as well as workmen's names (Bunting 1964: 55). By 1960, surviving members of the chapter were too old to take part in the strenuous religious observances and to make needed structural repairs, so the edifice was sold the next year to be remodeled and enlarged as a private residence.

The morada just east of the village core of Taos is even larger and more picturesque (Figs. 21 and 27). The setting is austere and isolated, a low rise on a vast plain of sagebrush. Well over one hundred yards in the direction of Taos Mountain, which forms an impressive backdrop, is a large white cross, the Calvario at the end of the Via Crucis. The morada roof is flat, but it steps down as three rooms in succession conform to the sloping site. Walls are mud plaster, corners worn and rounded, and the windows are few, small, and closed with solid shutters, all of which enhances the compact, sculptural quality of the building.

Although the last surviving Brothers, both over eighty, think the morada dates back to the early nineteenth century, no one has been able to determine exactly when it was constructed. The morada has grown and changed with the chapter. It has been enlarged twice, in 1902 and 1938, and various improvements have been made from time to time. Wooden floors were added in the chapel, and when the parish church of Taos was demolished some years ago following a fire, an arched door and frame from that building were salvaged to serve as the door to the morada chapel. Three rooms have served as kitchen at different times. In 1977, the last two Hermanos sold the morada to the Kit Carson Foundation of Taos, which will repair and stabilize the structure, provide better security, and maintain the building as a historic site.

From the foregoing it is obvious that the Brotherhood morada did not develop a fixed or recognizable architectural form. Midway between a church and a dwelling, some moradas resemble one building type, some the other. But, just as the appearance of both churches and dwellings in New Mexico changed during the last decades of the nineteenth and the early years of the twentieth centuries when better tools and commercially finished lumber became available or as window glass and corrugated iron roofing came into use with improved transportation facilities, so too morada design changed. Furthermore, structures owned by active chapters have been constantly subject to remodeling. Thus the addition in recent years of pitched roofs or the covering of adobe walls with cement plaster have materially changed the appearance of even the oldest moradas.

We are fortunate that at least one morada, among the oldest and largest of all, has been acquired by a foundation that has stabilized the building and is dedicated to preserving it as nearly as possible in its traditional form. Thus, in the future, it will continue to remind us of the important and unique role the Hermanos de la Cofradía de Nuestro Padre Jesús Nazareno played in New Mexico society.

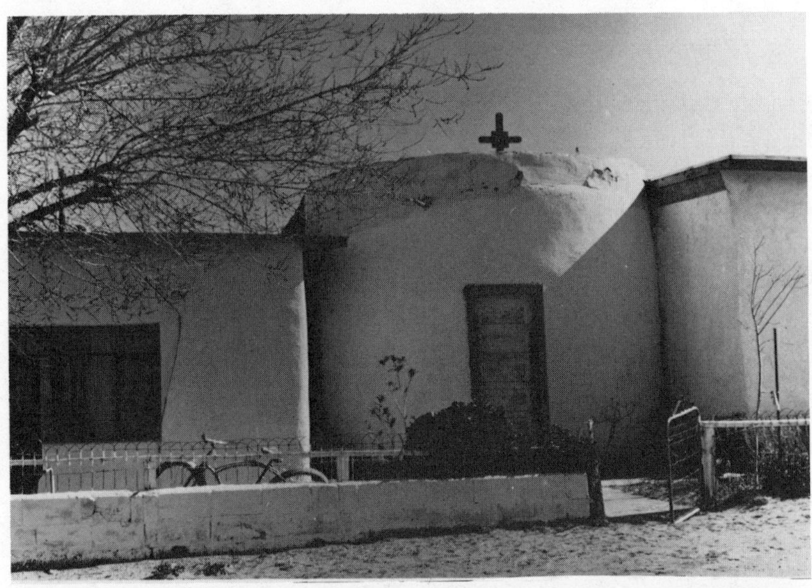

FIGURE 1
Morada sanctuary now used as a private chapel. Doña Ana, New Mexico.

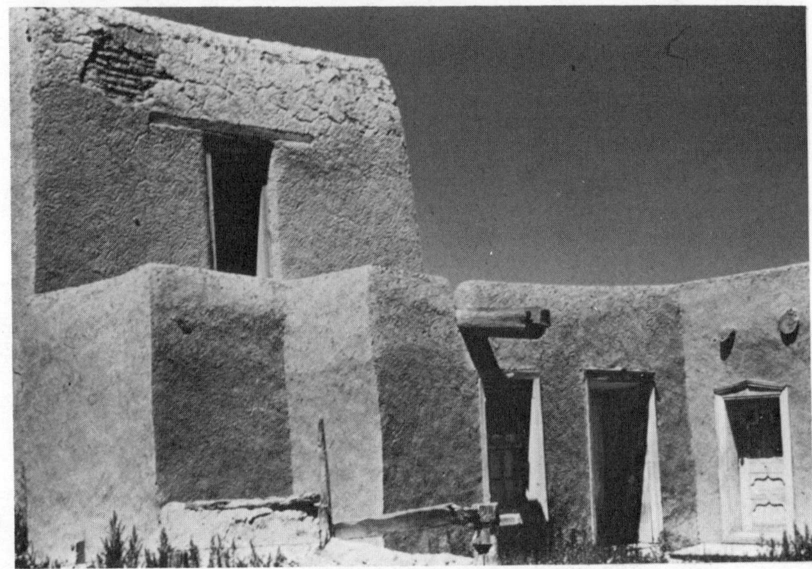

FIGURE 2
The only example known in recent times of a connected church and morada as it appeared in 1961. The entrance on the right, though now filled with a modern door, survives. The room(s) between it and the transept of the church have been removed. Las Trampas, New Mexico.

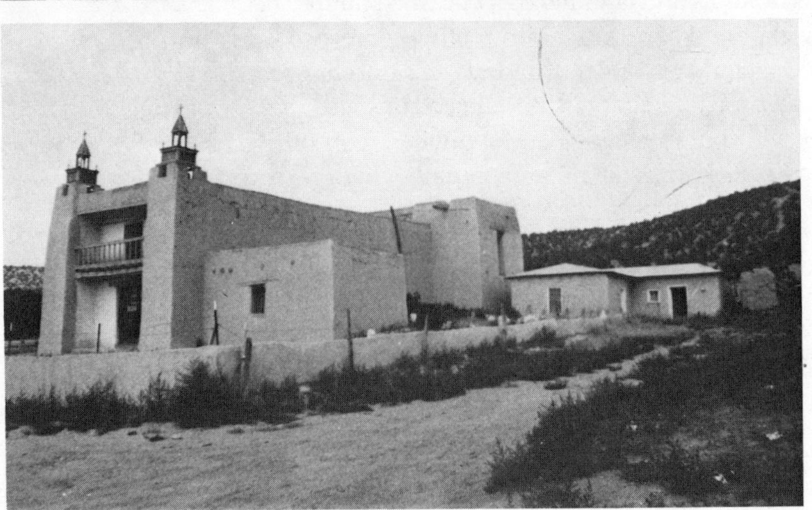

FIGURE 3
Las Trampas in 1969 with the morada completely detached from the church but with a new roof and an ell added on the right.

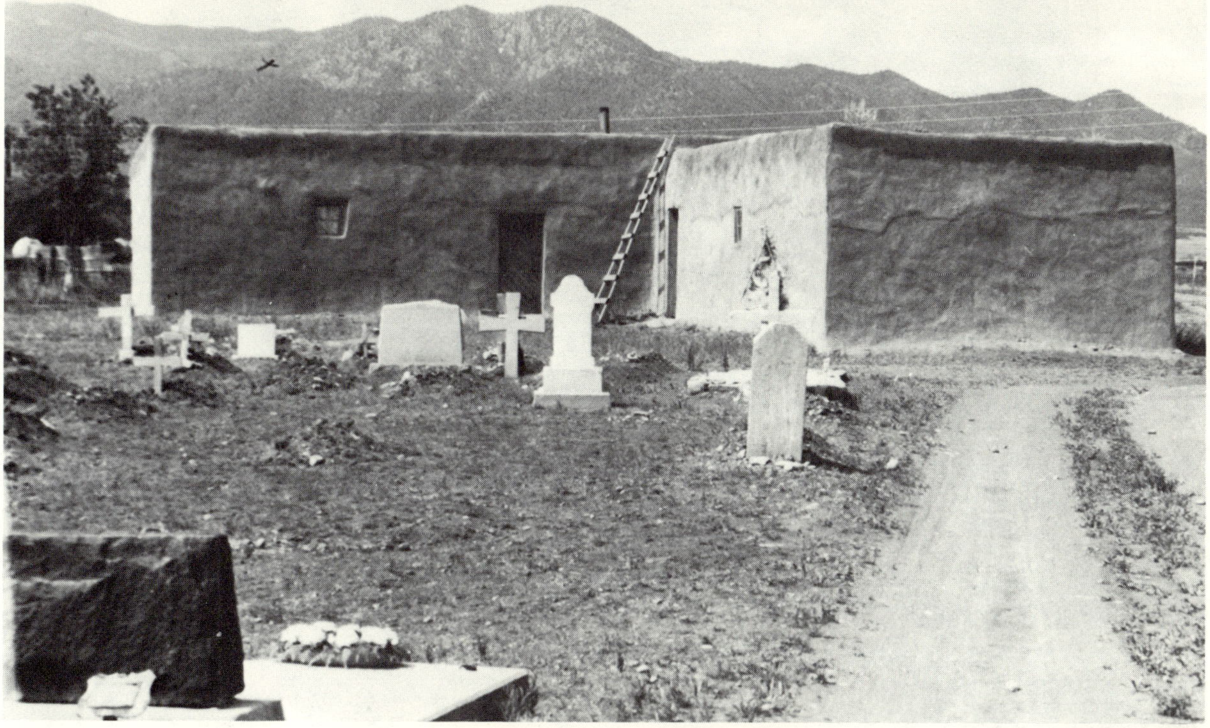

FIGURE 4
A little-changed example of an early morada surrounded by a cemetery and retaining the flat roof, very small windows, and interior openings without doors. Talpa, New Mexico.

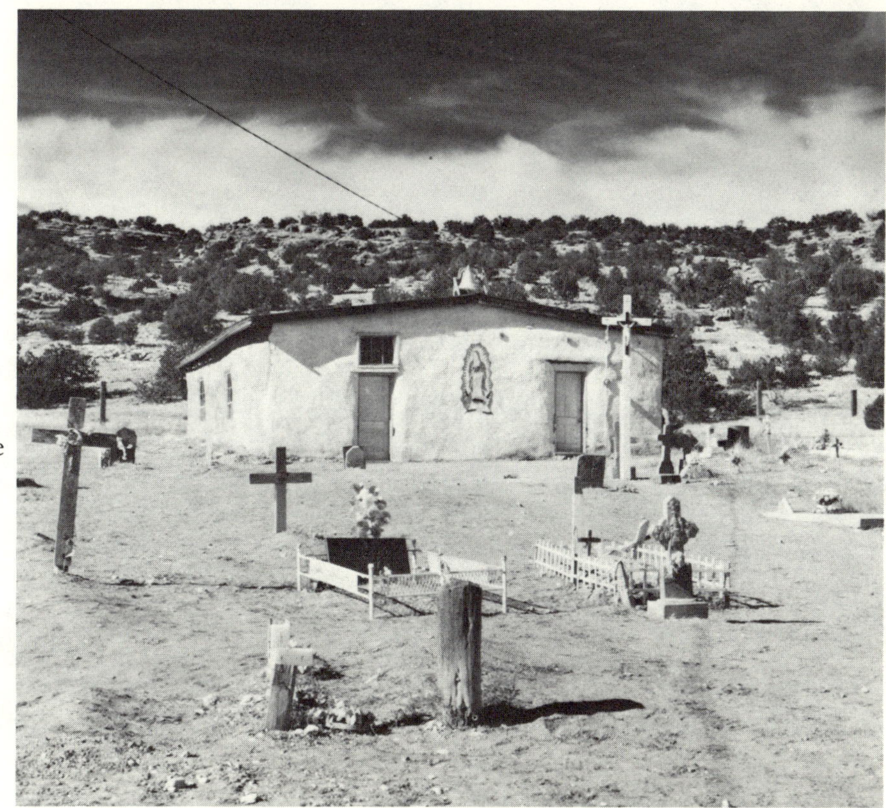

FIGURE 5
One door enters the oratorio, the other the meeting room. The large white cross that stands before the morada has a smaller superimposed cross and figure. The slightly pitched roof is probably original. Near Grants, New Mexico.

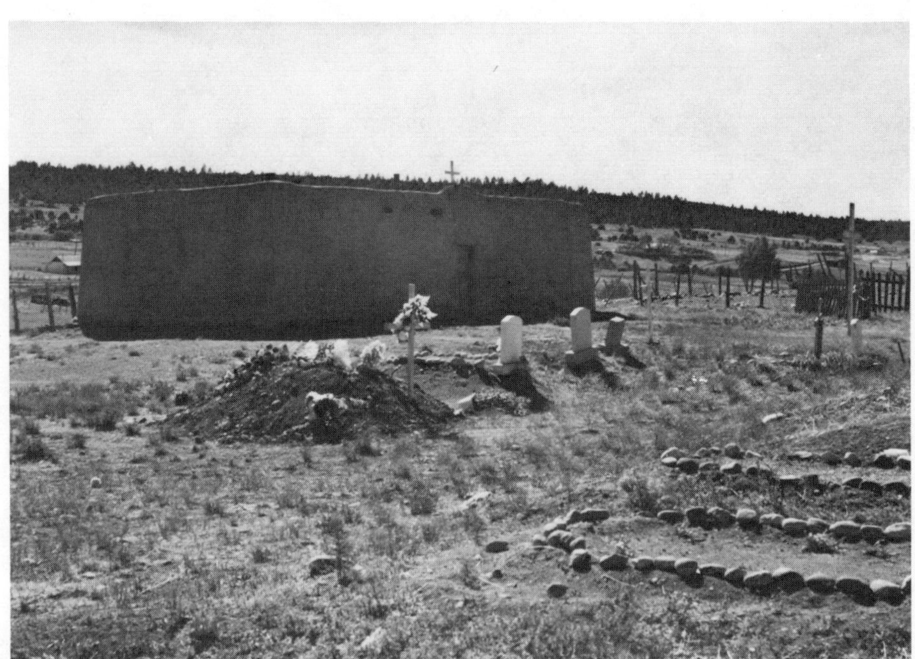

FIGURE 6
The morada with its cemetery, which still contains a number of graves with elaborate wooden crosses and fencing, is distinct from the parish church with its cemetery. The building has a round-ended oratorio. Llano de San Juan, New Mexico.

FIGURE 7
This Via Crucis, which is some one hundred yards from the morada, is unusually straight and appears to have been leveled by machine. The Calvario stands in the foreground. Near Las Vegas, New Mexico.

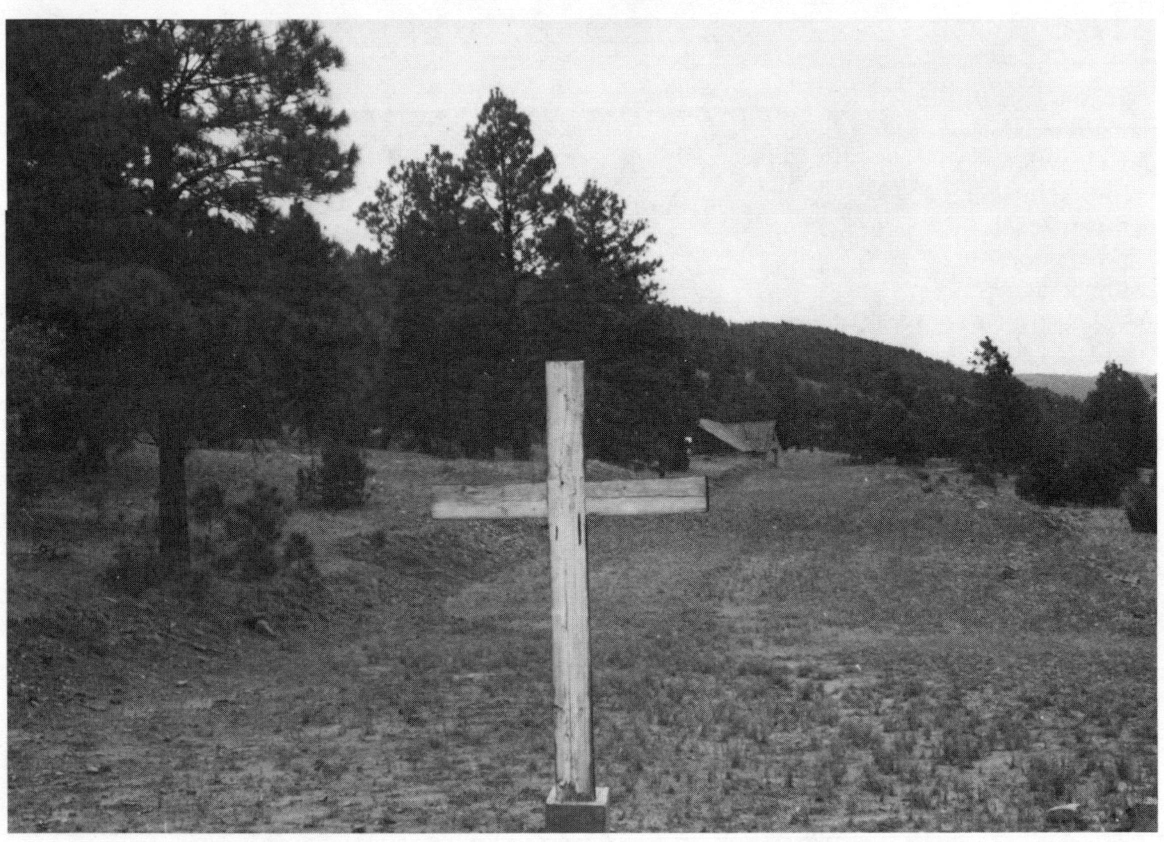

FIGURE 8
Placing the stations of the cross (here made of metal) along the Via Crucis prior to services. Near Villanueva, New Mexico.

FIGURE 9
The large cross some ten feet tall stands in the cemetery in front of the morada. The building to the left contains the meeting room and storage area. Near Cuba, New Mexico.

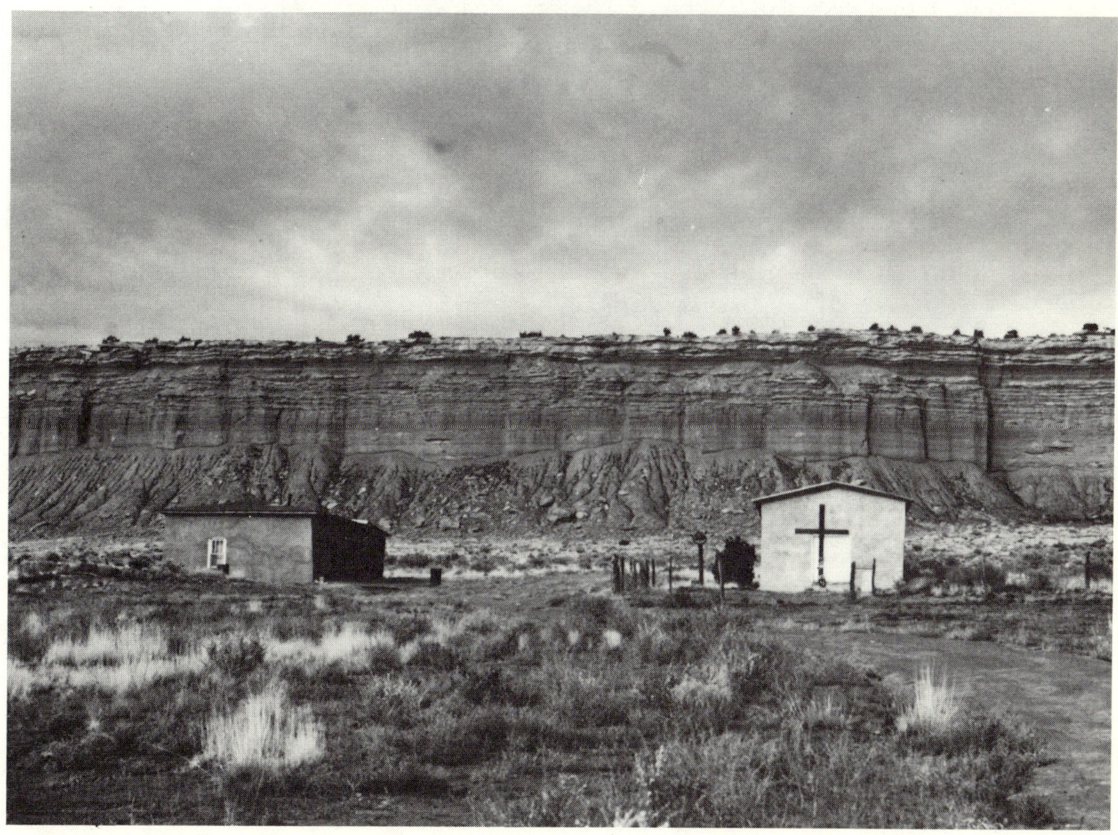

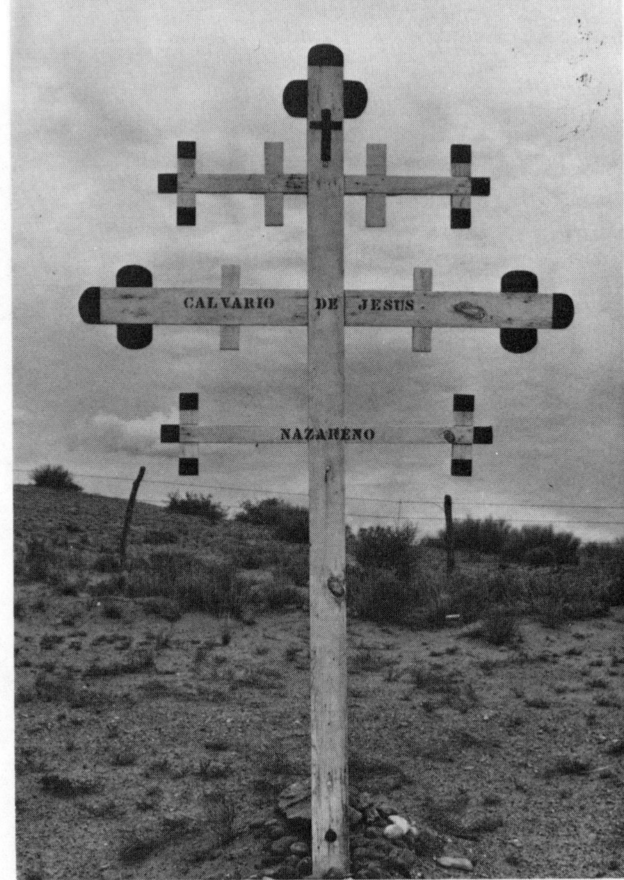

FIGURE 10
Ten feet high, this is the most elaborate morada cross that survives. The Calvario stands at the far end of the Via Crucis. South of Albuquerque, New Mexico.

FIGURE 11
The large cross composed of thirteen small crosses is attached to the facade above the door to the oratorio. The cross atop the belfrey resembles those sometimes placed as headstones in a *camposanto* (cemetery). Near Mora, New Mexico.

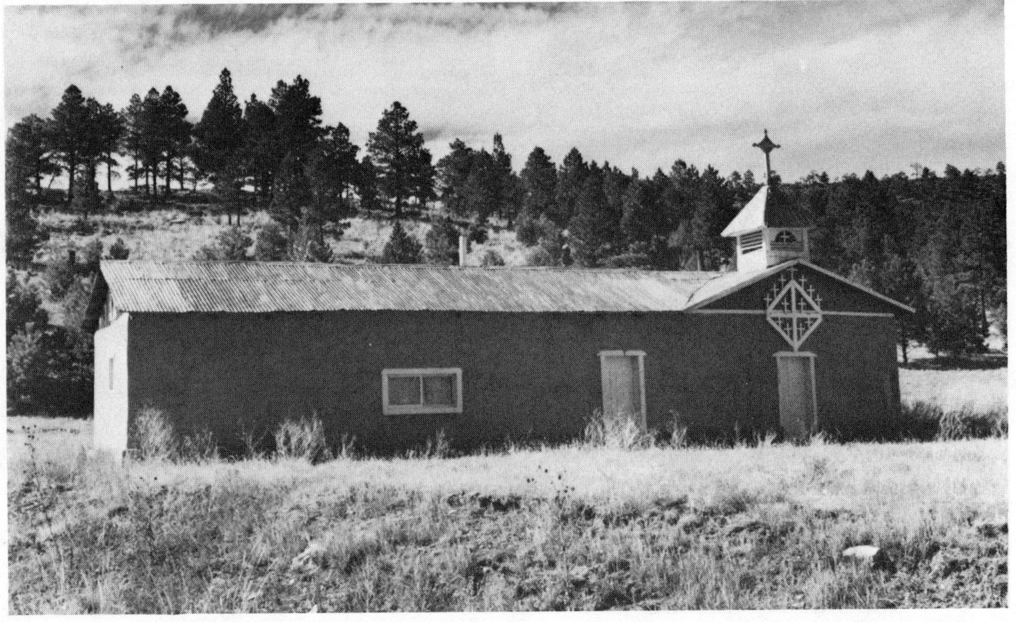

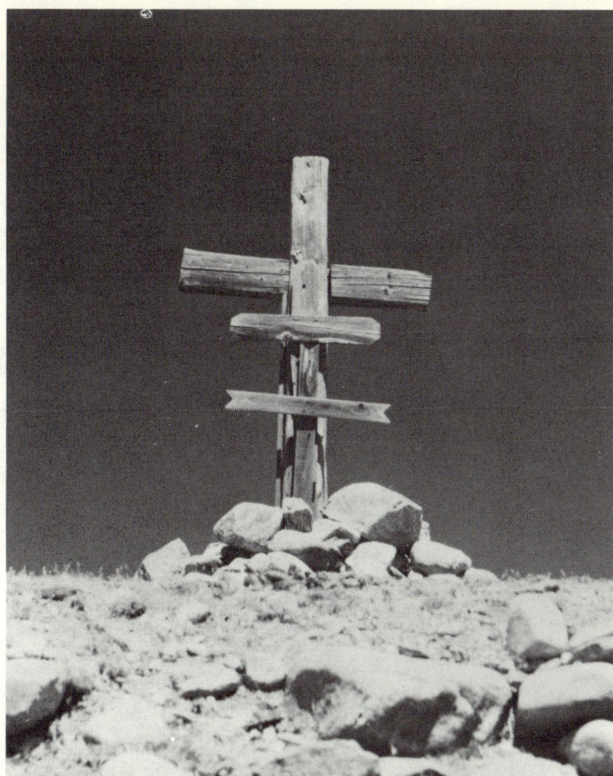

FIGURE 12
This large composition of three superimposed crosses is not directly related to the morada but stands near the high road at the southern entrance to the village. Truchas, New Mexico.

FIGURE 13
Maderos, large carrying crosses that members of La Fraternidad drag to the Calvario at the end of the Via Crucis during the Holy Week penitential observances.

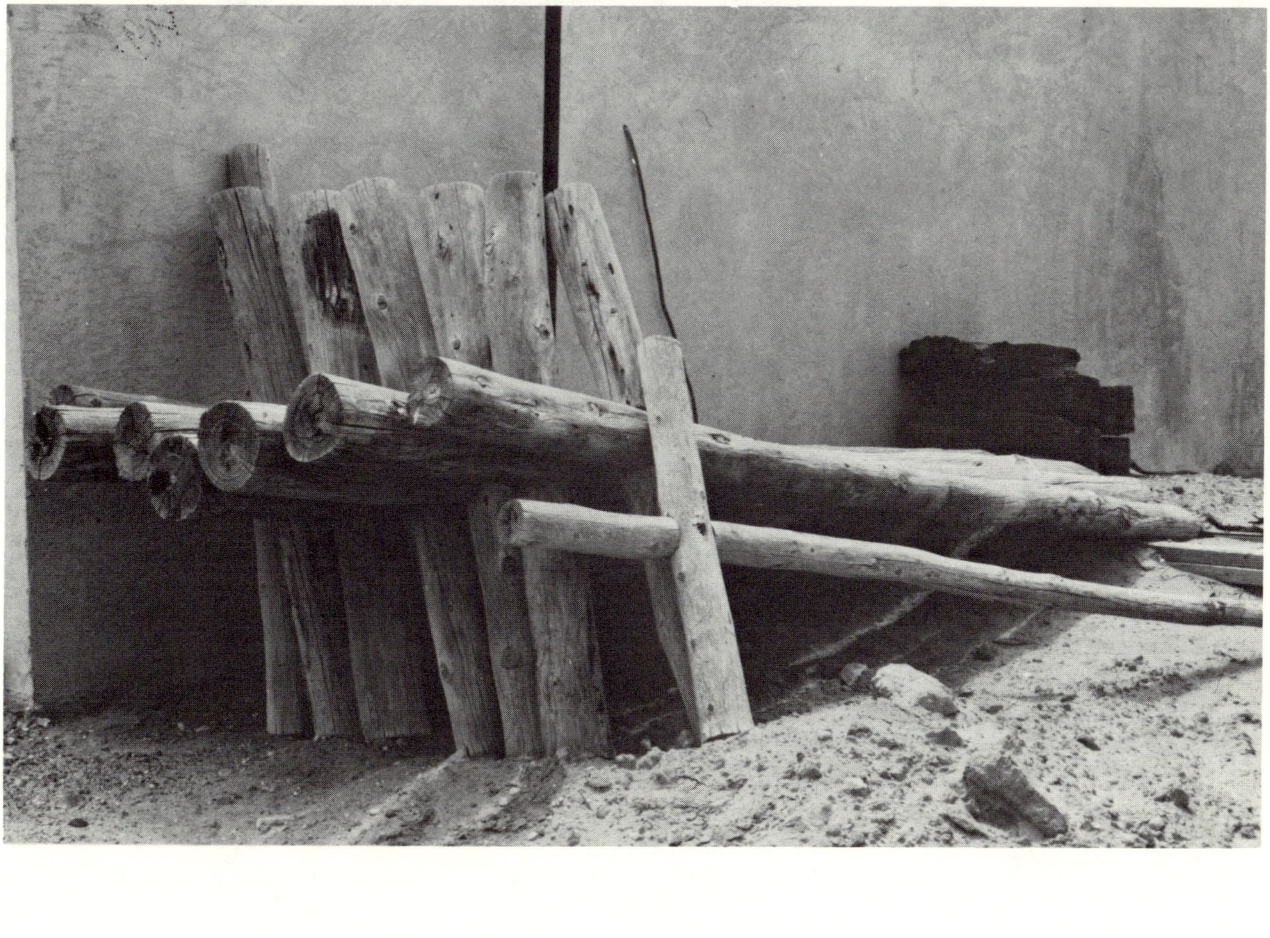

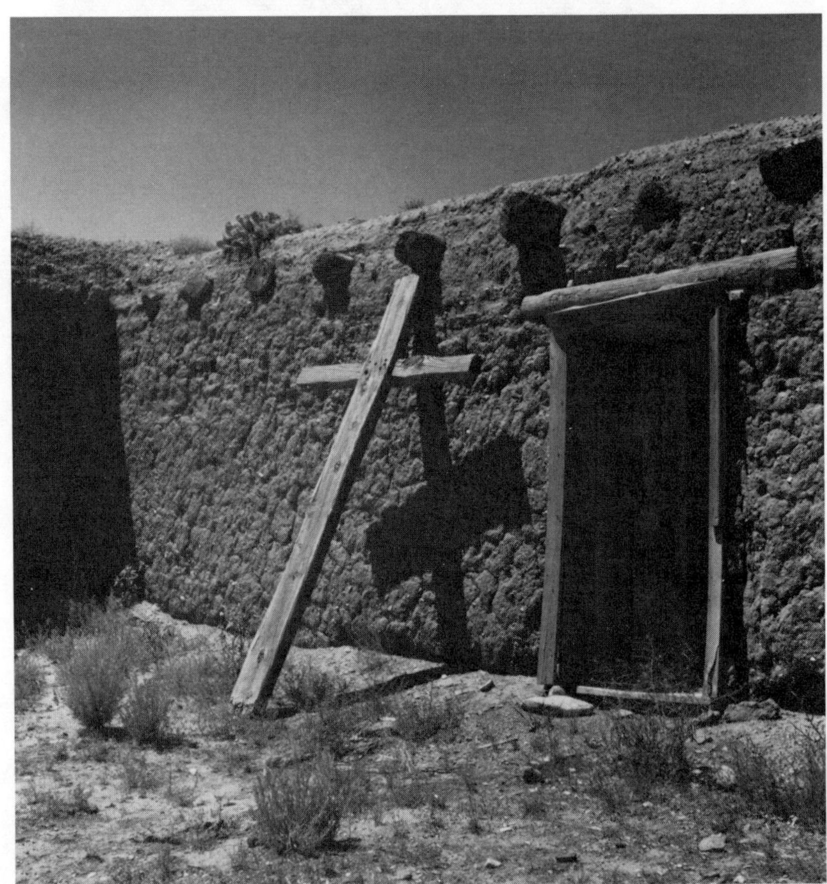

FIGURE 14
This large cross probably stood in front of the morada when this chapter was still active. Arroyo Hondo, New Mexico.

FIGURE 15
This abandoned morada consisted of an oratorio on the left and the meeting and storage building on the right. The former, with its corrugated iron roof and complex shape, is undoubtedly more recent than the decaying structure with the board-on-board roof. Cuba, New Mexico.

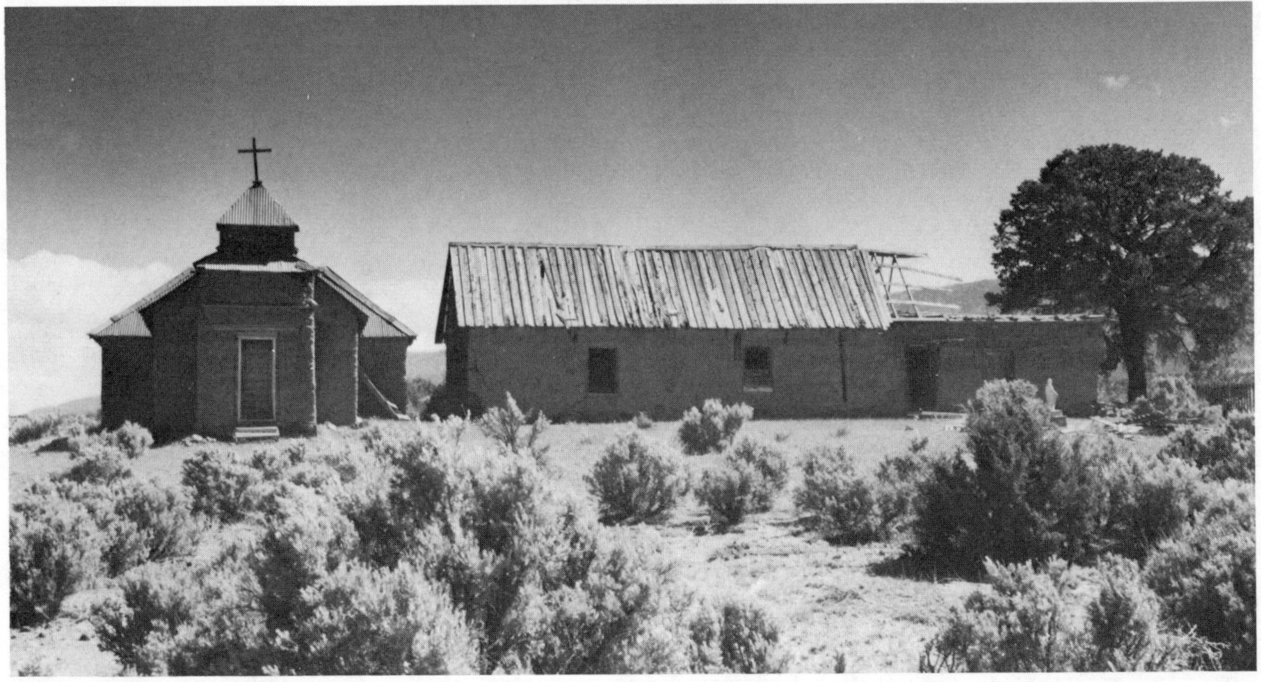

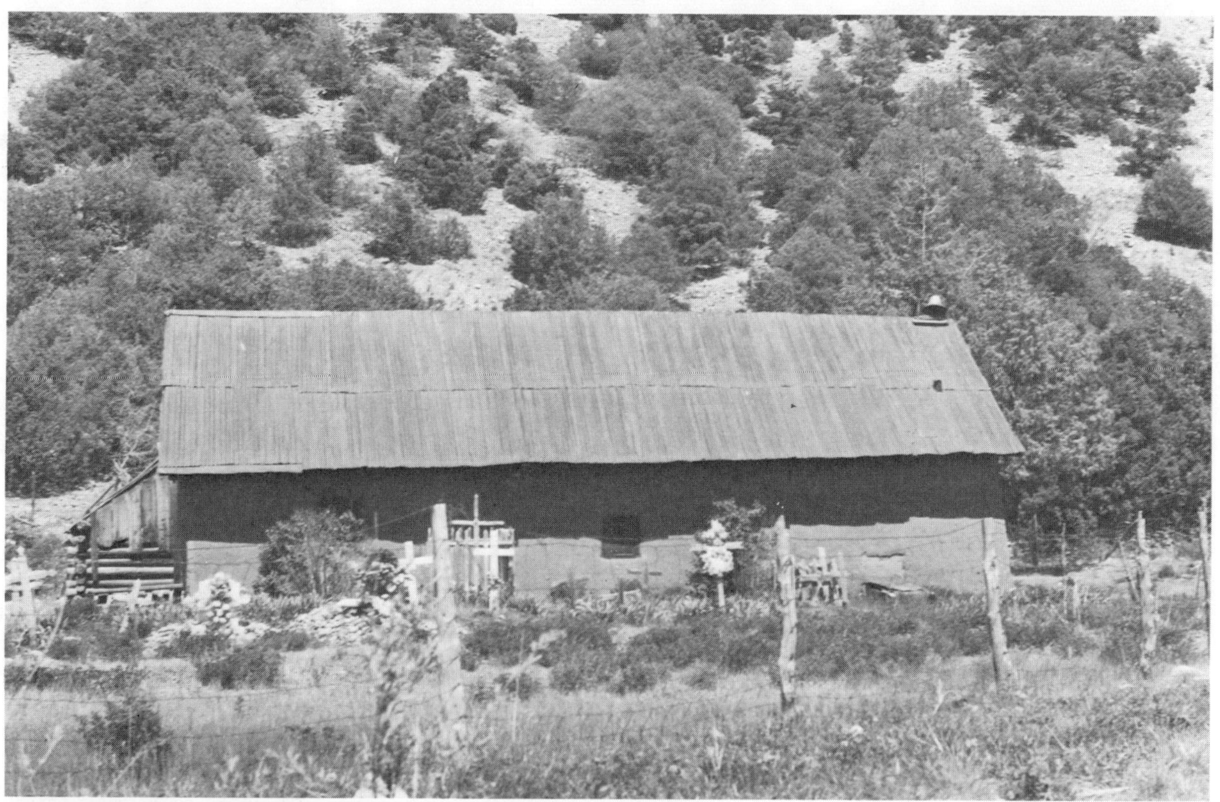

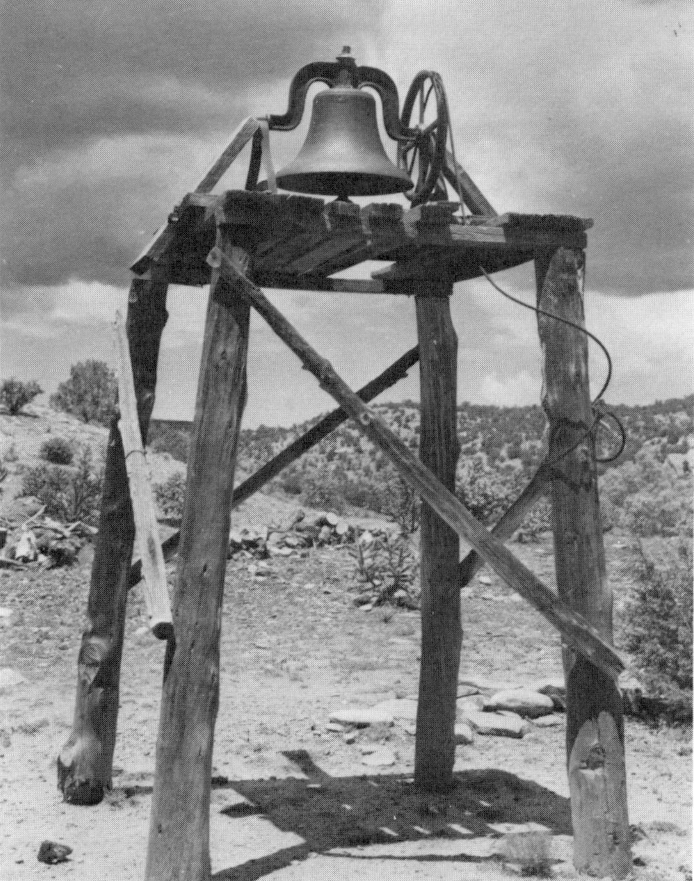

FIGURE 16
Situated in a small graveyard above the level of the irrigation ditch, this morada consists of a chapel and meeting room in the iron-roofed structure and a detached storeroom of logs behind it. Rodarte, New Mexico.

FIGURE 17
Freestanding bell tower. Bells such as this became common in New Mexico after the arrival of the railroad. At a morada on the Pecos River, New Mexico.

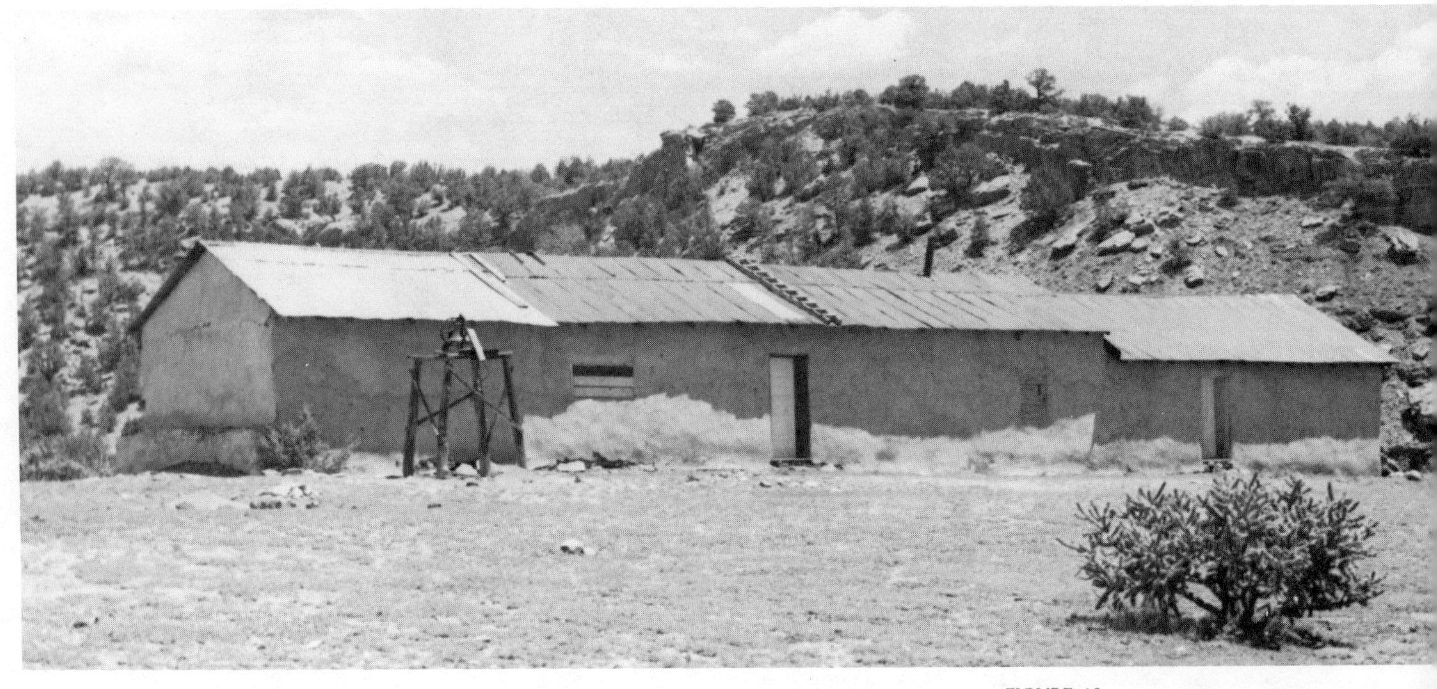

FIGURE 18
The long, linear plan of this morada contains the chapel in the lower section near the large cross. The middle section with a stovepipe is the meeting room, while storage undoubtedly occupies the left end with its wide, modern window. San Ysidro, New Mexico.

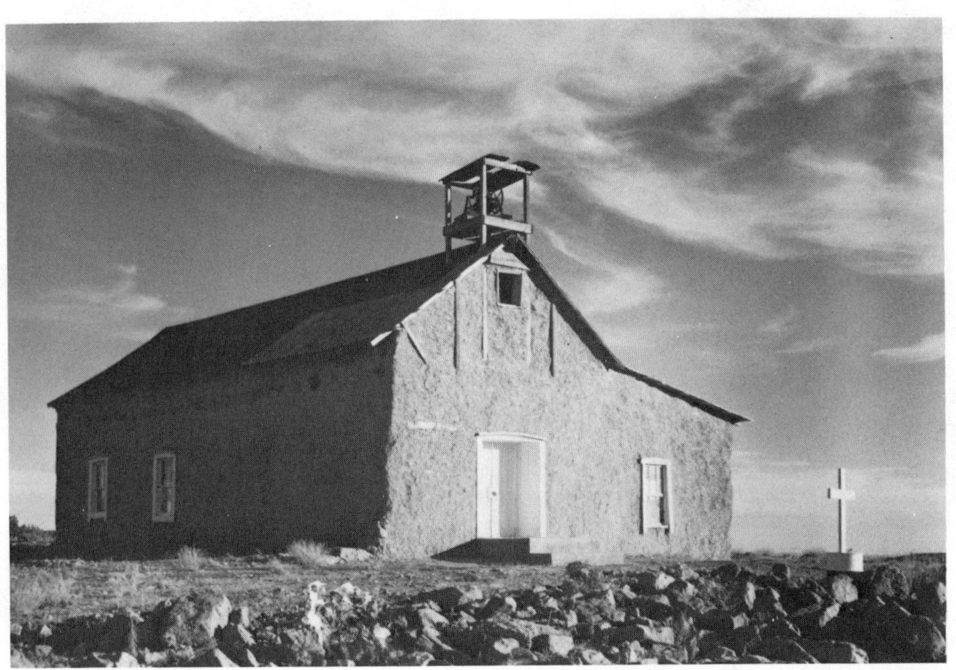

FIGURE 19
This morada, probably of the early twentieth century, has a fine entrance with territorial trim. The belfrey in all probability once had more elaborate trim. Village at foot of Mount Taylor, New Mexico.

FIGURE 20
A typical linear-plan morada with the very small window and belfrey indicating the oratorio at the right end, the meeting room with one door in the center, and the storeroom and second door on the left end. The buttress is of later construction, added when the wall began to lean outward. Near Mora, New Mexico.

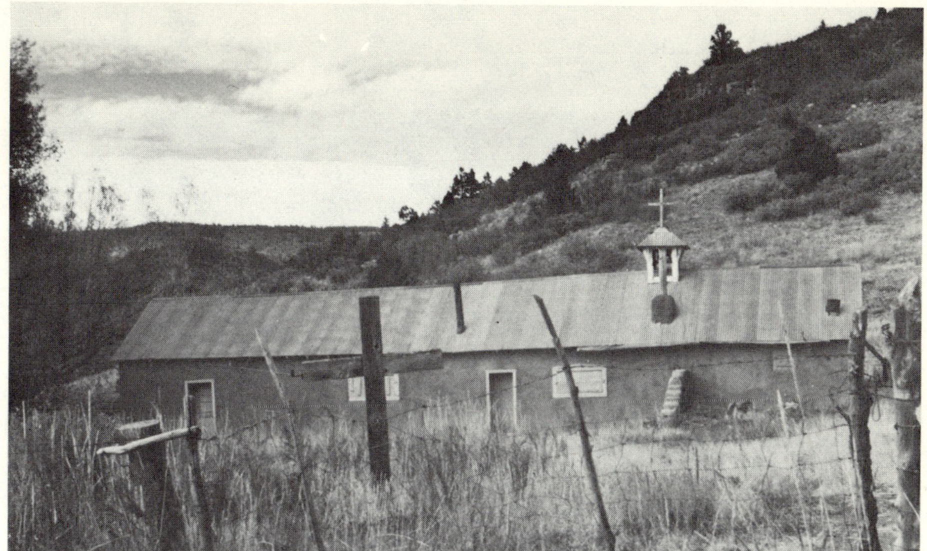

FIGURE 21
The largest surviving morada, this structure has a small rectangular apse extending from the chapel on the left (see Fig. 27). Each room is on a different level; the large window of horizontal proportions and the buttresses are late additions. West elevation; Taos, New Mexico.

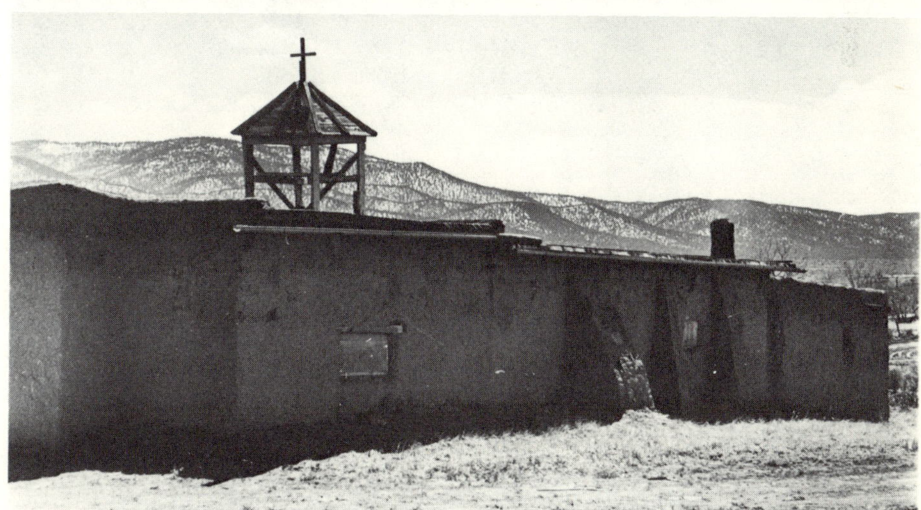

FIGURE 22
One of the most picturesque Brotherhood structures in the state. The apse of the oratorio has a polygonal plan; the solid-stone bell tower attached to it was undoubtedly added later. The modern morada at the Rancho de las Golondrinas open-air museum village in La Cienega was copied from this structure. South morada; Abiquiú, New Mexico.

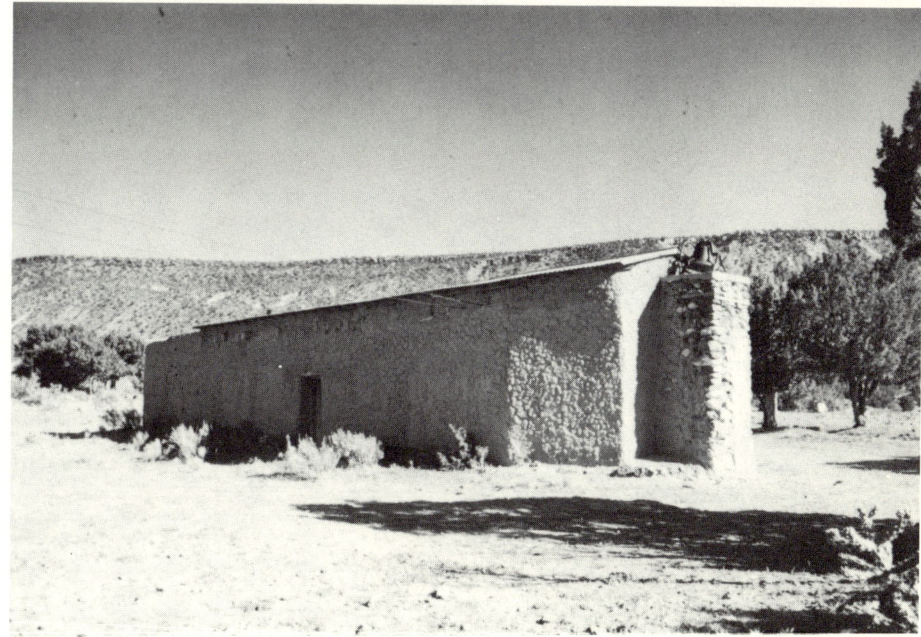

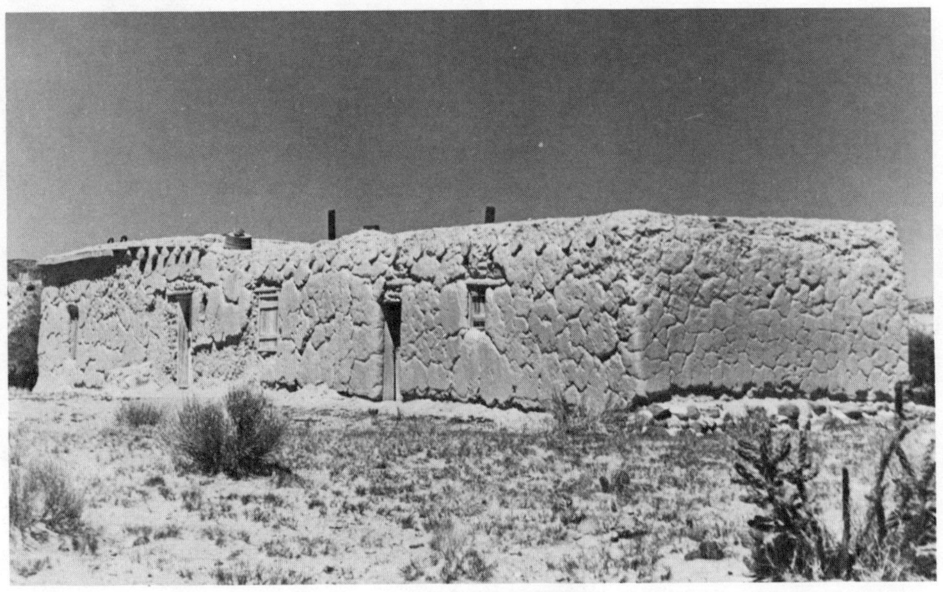

FIGURE 23
One of the oldest known moradas in the state. East morada; Abiquiú, New Mexico.

FIGURE 24
This morada, which stands within the village, contains the community graveyard because the original church was hedged in by houses. Several elaborate wooden grave markers are preserved in it. Truchas, New Mexico.

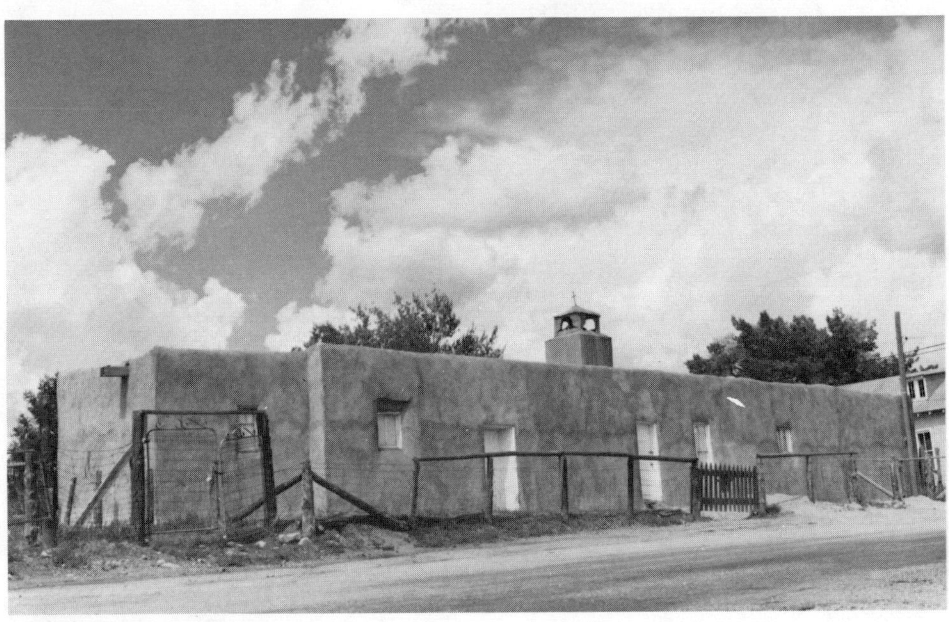

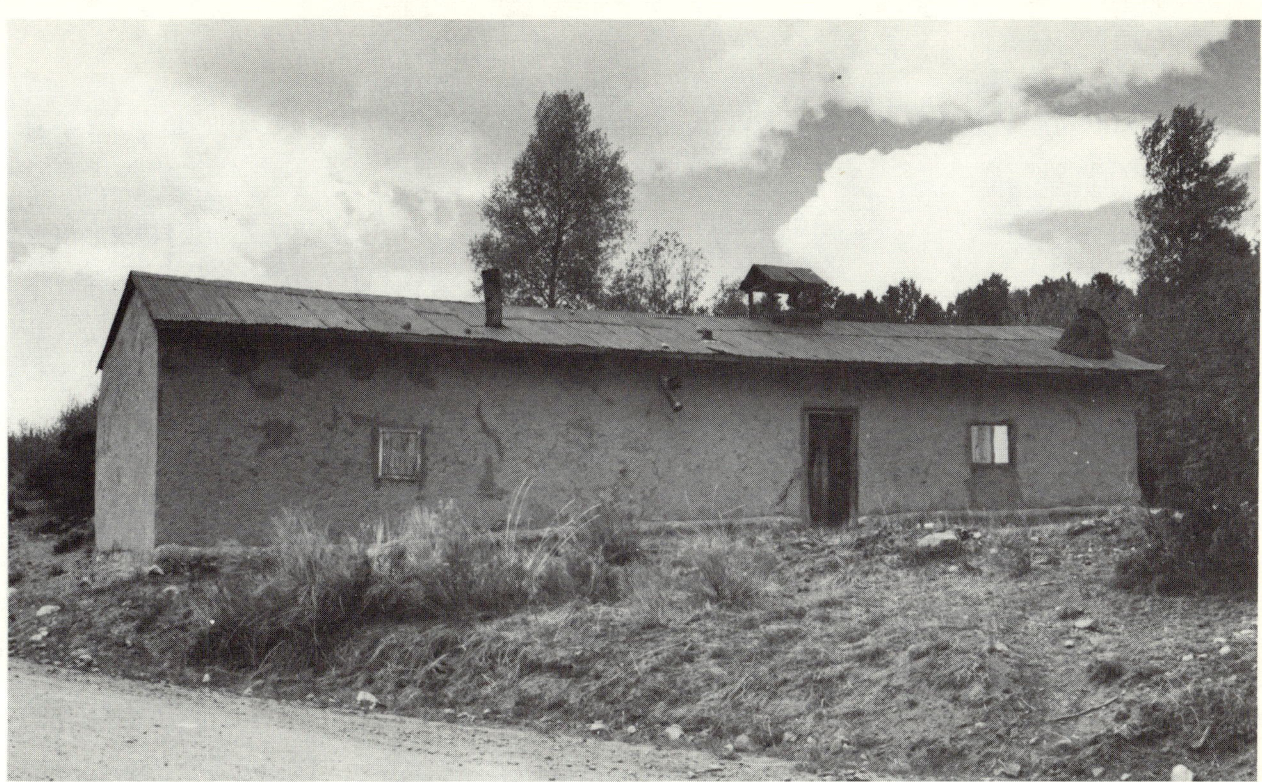

FIGURE 25
Built on sloping land, each room is on a different level, but the stepped profile of the building was obscured when a corrugated iron roof was added, probably in the 1920s. Valdez, New Mexico.

FIGURE 26
Floor plan of the morada in Valdez, New Mexico.

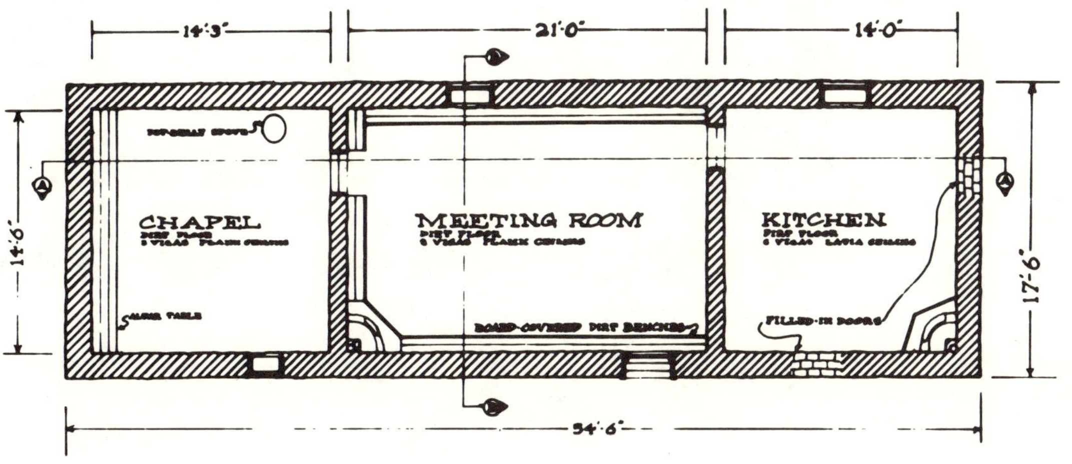

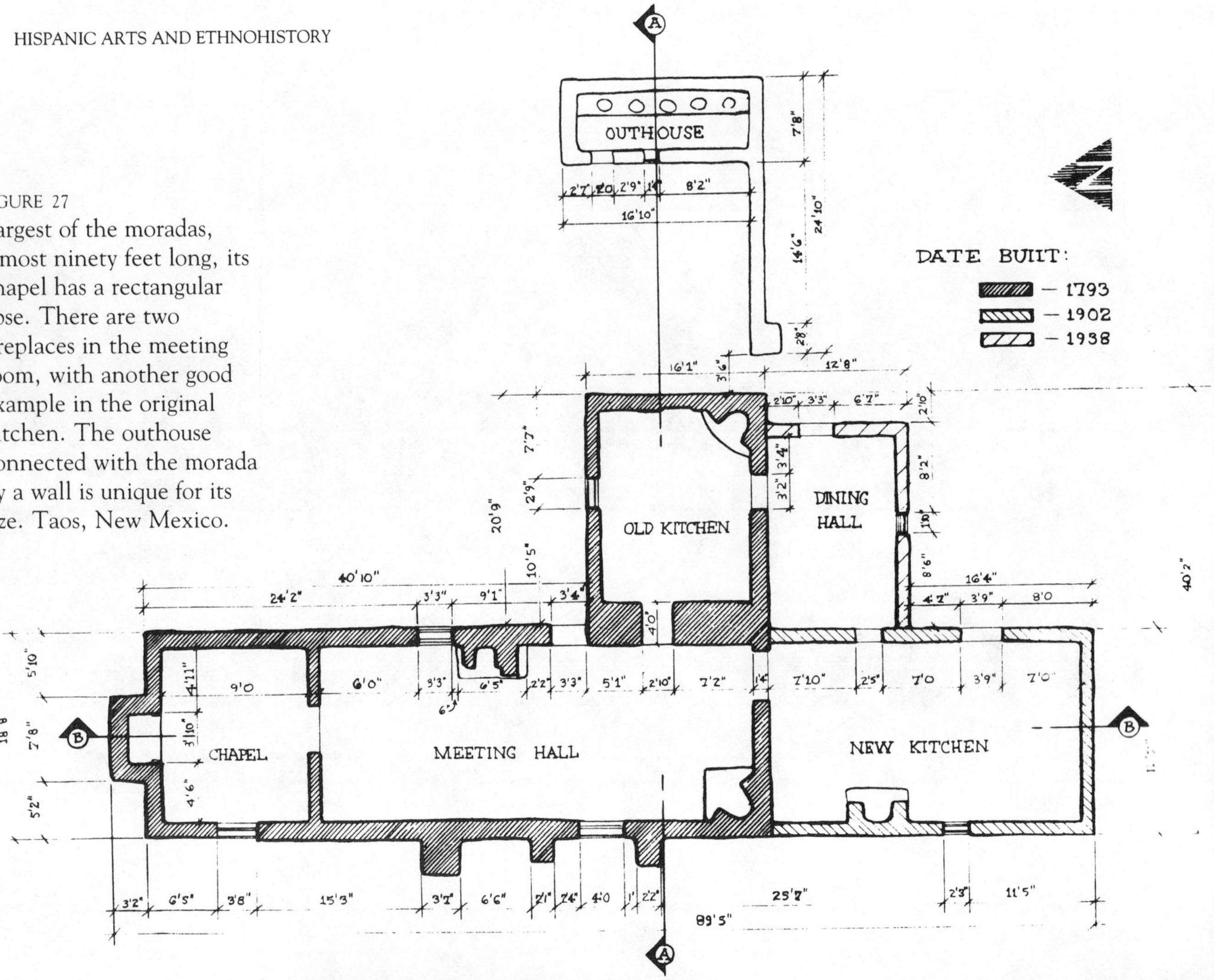

FIGURE 27
Largest of the moradas, almost ninety feet long, its chapel has a rectangular apse. There are two fireplaces in the meeting room, with another good example in the original kitchen. The outhouse connected with the morada by a wall is unique for its size. Taos, New Mexico.

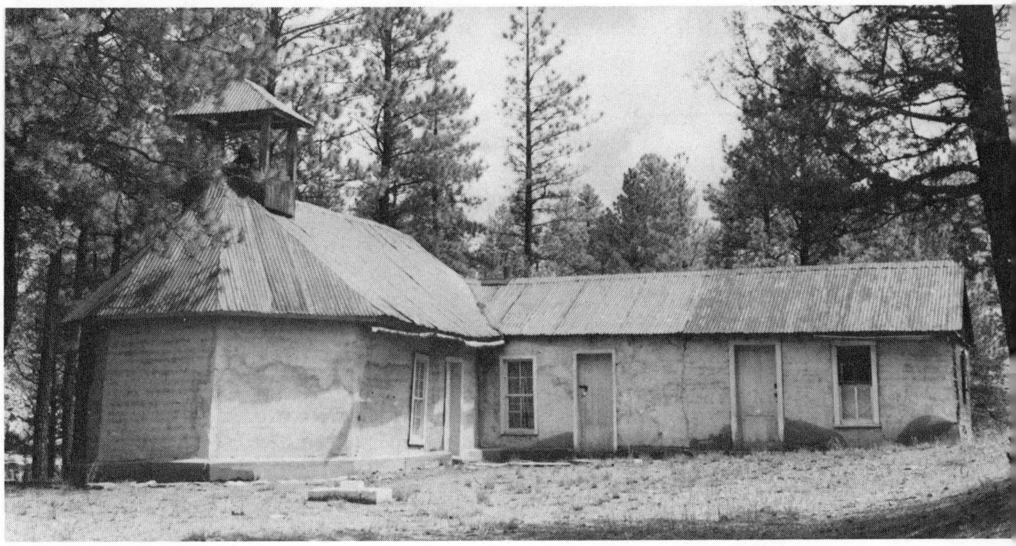

FIGURE 28
Constructed of logs with a large polygonal-ended chapel and iron roof, this morada is one of the more churchly in appearance. Gallinas Canyon, New Mexico.

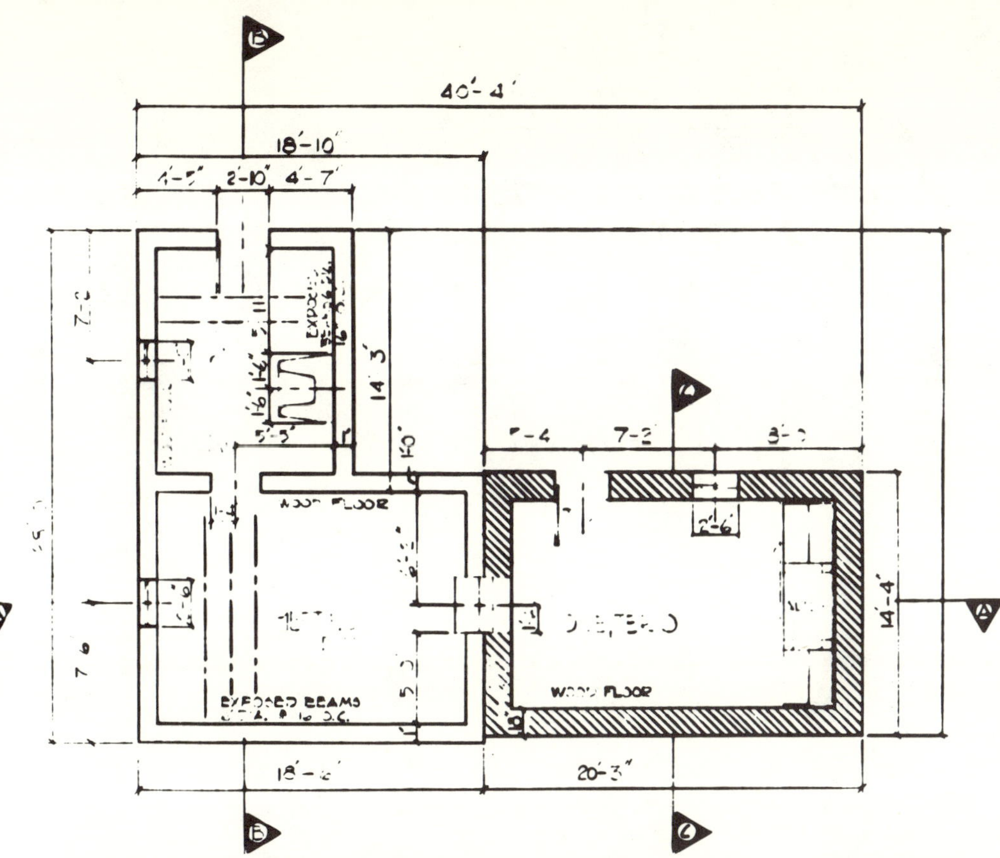

FIGURE 29
Located on a hillside, the adobe chapel is several steps higher than the meeting room and kitchen, which are constructed of logs. The board-on-board roof is seen in Figure 58. Cleveland, New Mexico.

FIGURE 30
The large size, regular shape, and corrugated iron roof, which appears to be original, indicate this is a middle-period structure. A fixed cross stands before the entrance; carrying crosses are stored in the bushes behind the structure. Near Chimayó, New Mexico.

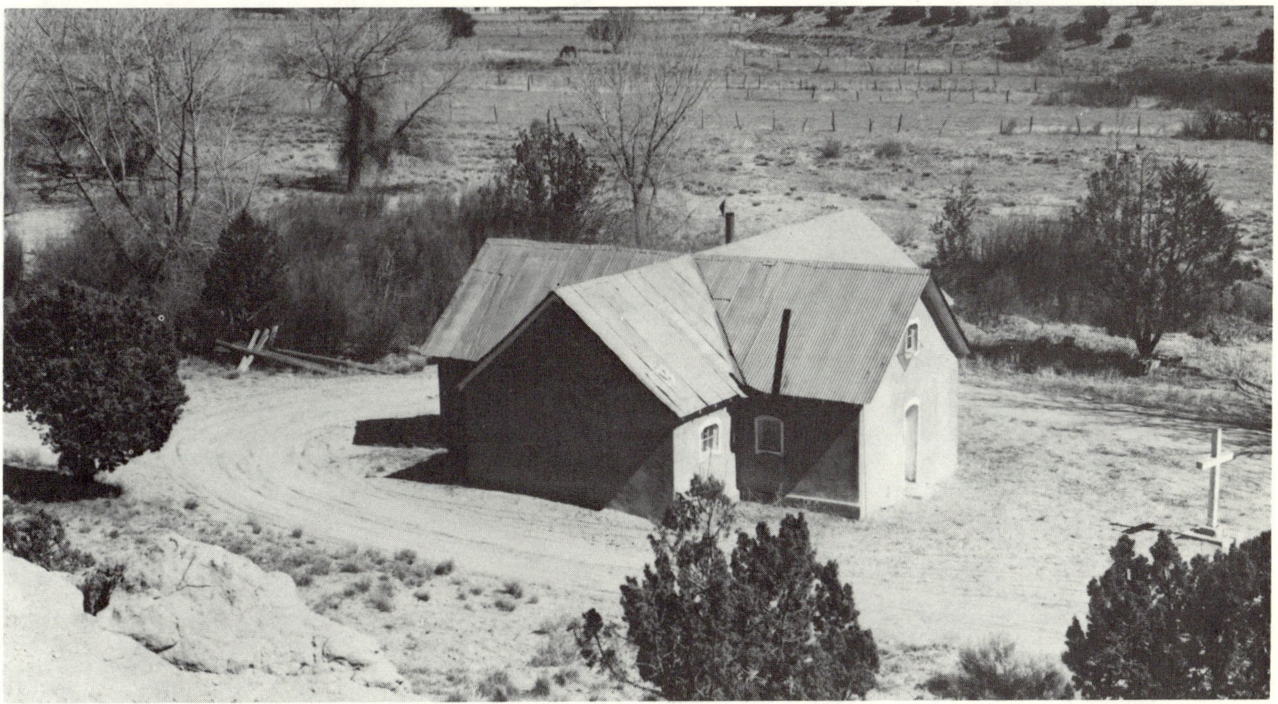

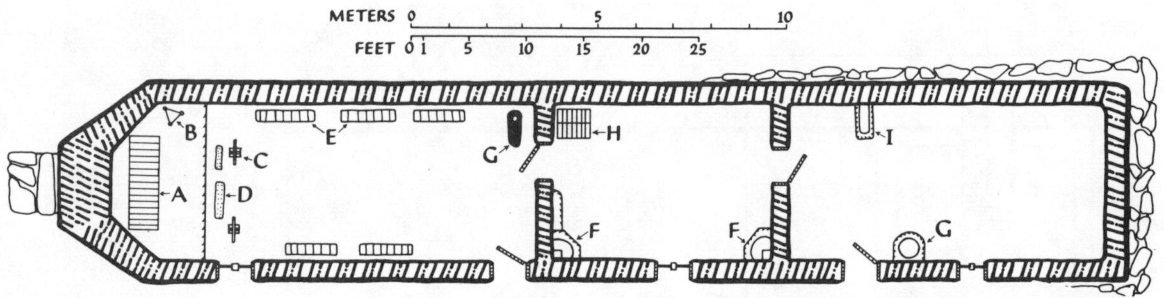

A=altar; B=standard; C=candelabra; D=sandbox; E=benches; F=fireplace; G=stove; H=chest; I=tub.

FIGURE 31
This plan, Richard Ahlborn's (*bottom* in 1968: 131), illustrates an early morada from the nineteenth century. Of particular interest are the solid base for the belfrey at one end of the oratorio, the two fireplaces in the meeting room, and the permanent basin for cleansing after completion of the ceremonies. East morada; Abiquiú, New Mexico.

FIGURE 32
An unusual morada constructed of stone with a round-ended apse, L-shaped storeroom, and corrugated iron roof. Upper Rociada, New Mexico.

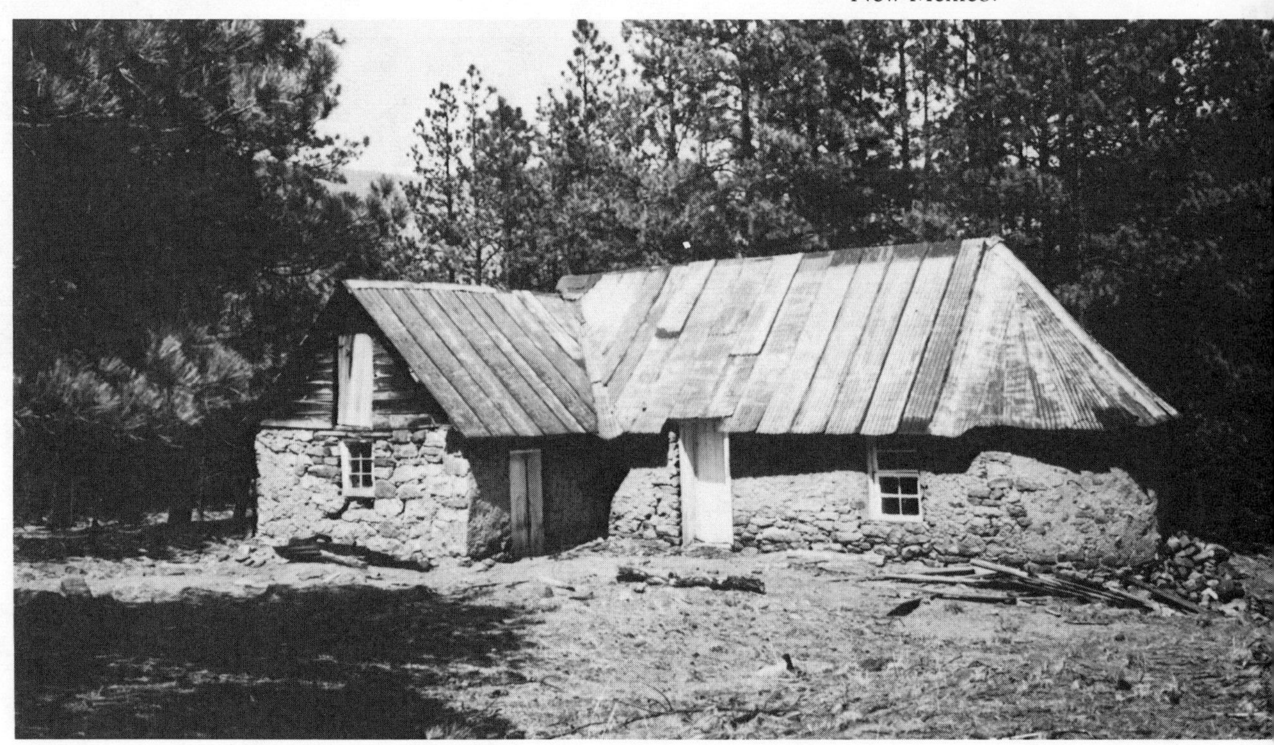

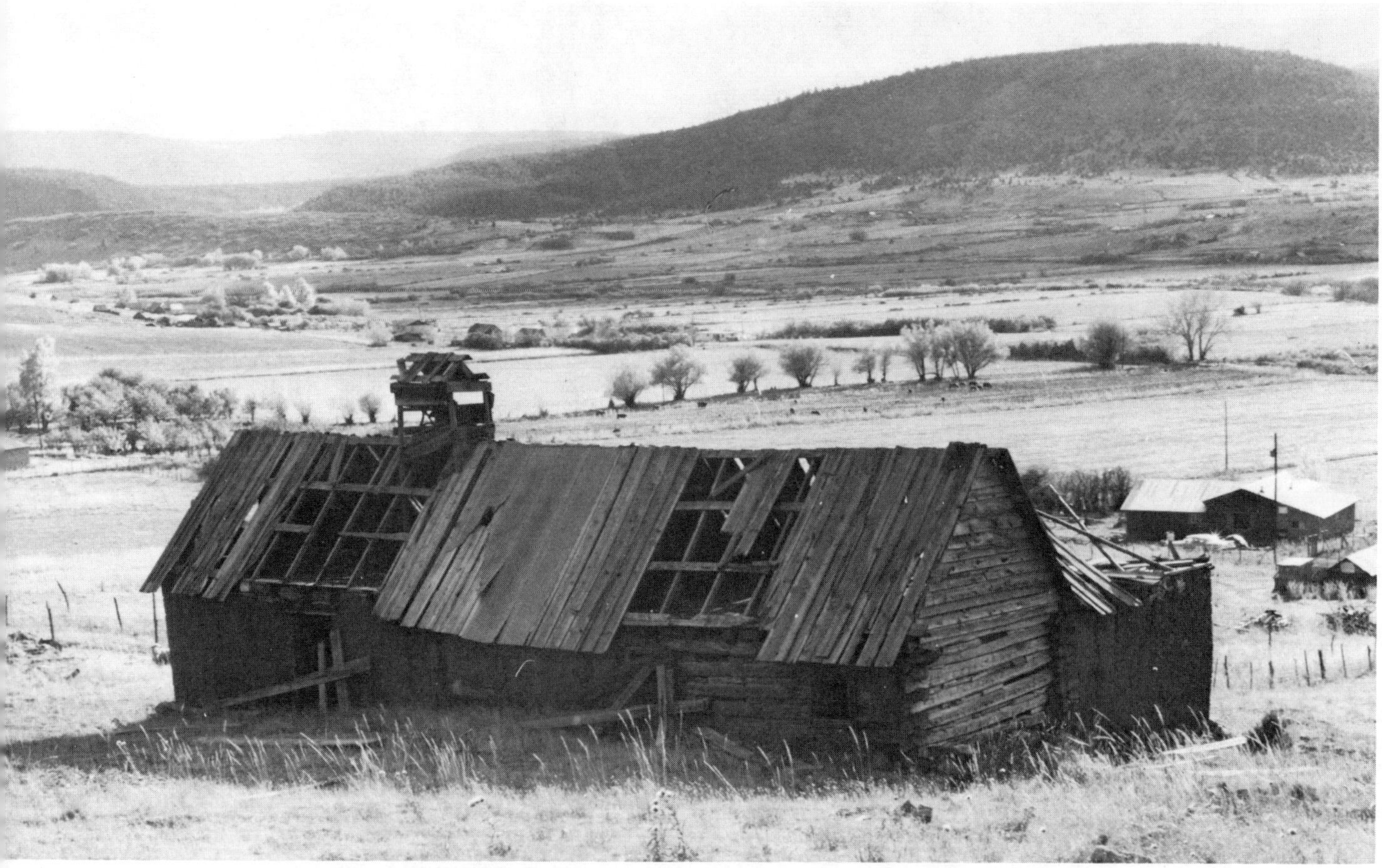

FIGURE 33
Constructed of adobe (chapel) and logs (meeting and storeroom), this abandoned morada had a board-on-board roof common for dwellings in the Mora Valley.

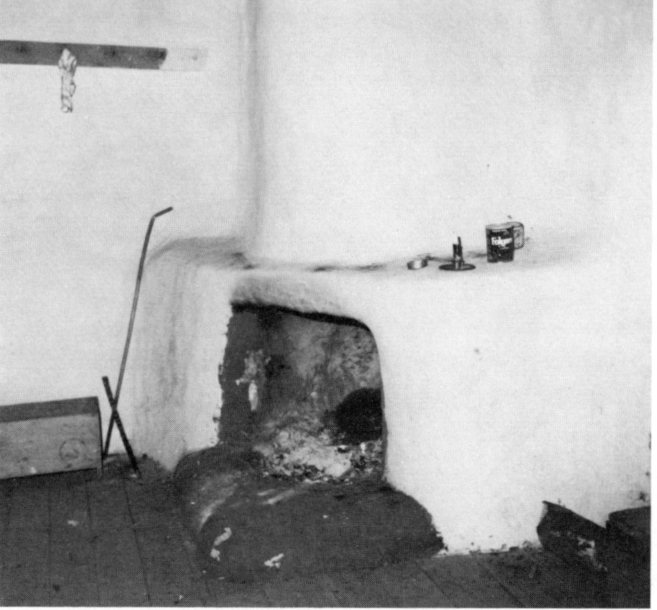

FIGURE 34
The unusual size of this fogón indicates that it was situated in the meeting room. Its awkward shape suggests a relatively recent date.

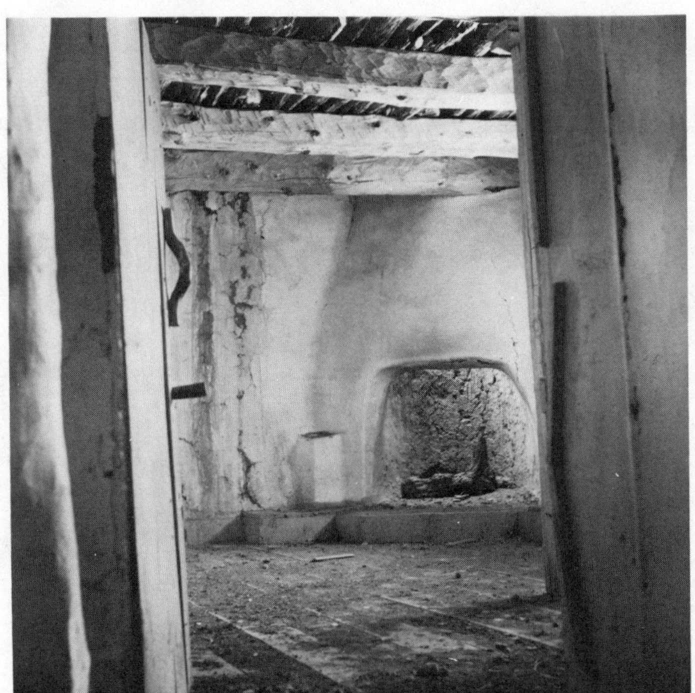

FIGURE 35
The meeting room of this important morada is dignified by the unusually large fogón with adjacent warming shelves, a board floor, and vigas roughly adzed to a rectangular shape. The batten door has a handle and latch made of wood. Arroyo Hondo, New Mexico. (Photograph by Jack Boucher, Historic American Building Survey.)

FIGURE 36
Oratorio with a bulto-laden altar. The stations of the cross and the pews were undoubtedly discards from a parish church.

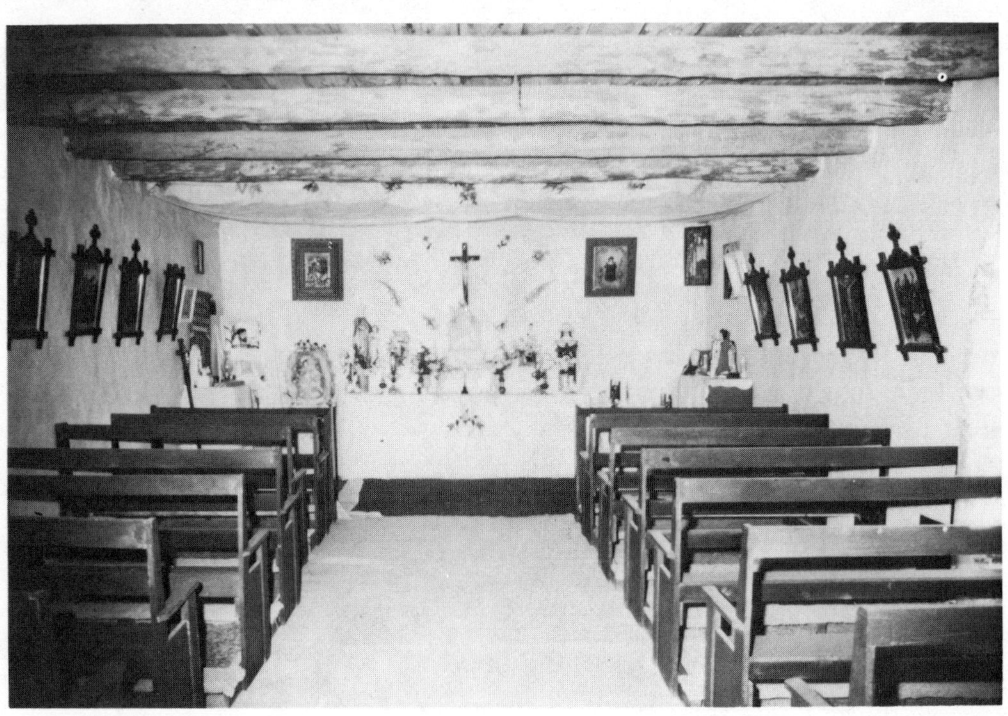

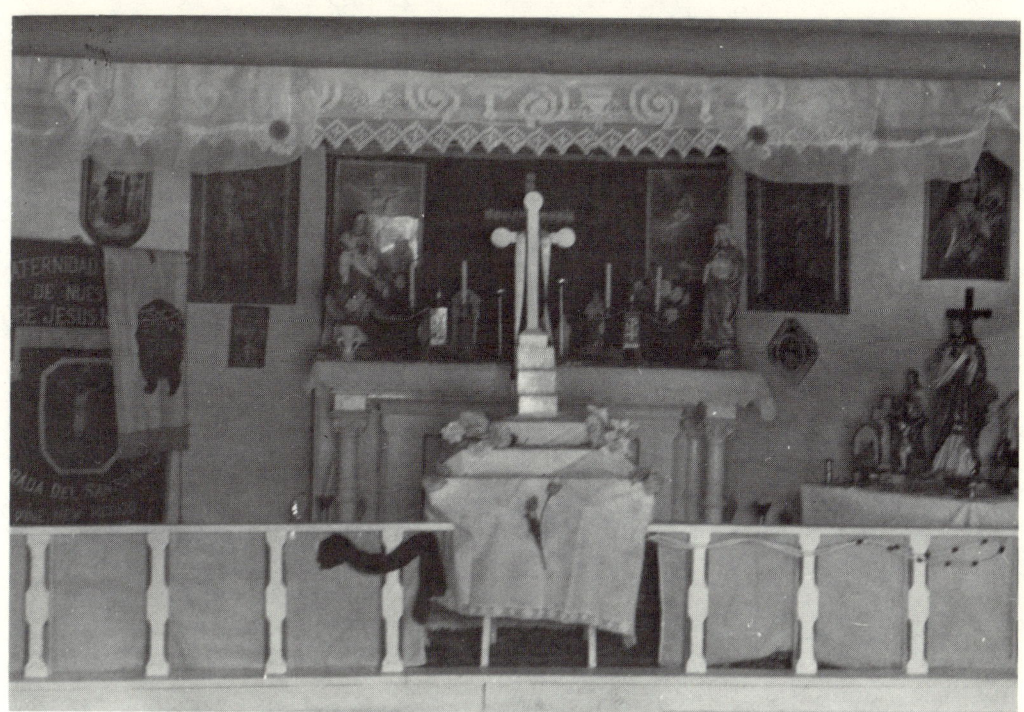

FIGURE 37
This altar in a functioning morada is separated from the oratorio by a raised step, railing, and embroidered valance suspended from the roof beams. Bultos and santos crowd the rear wall and altar table (obtained from a church), while a standard with a Veronica's veil image stands to the left.

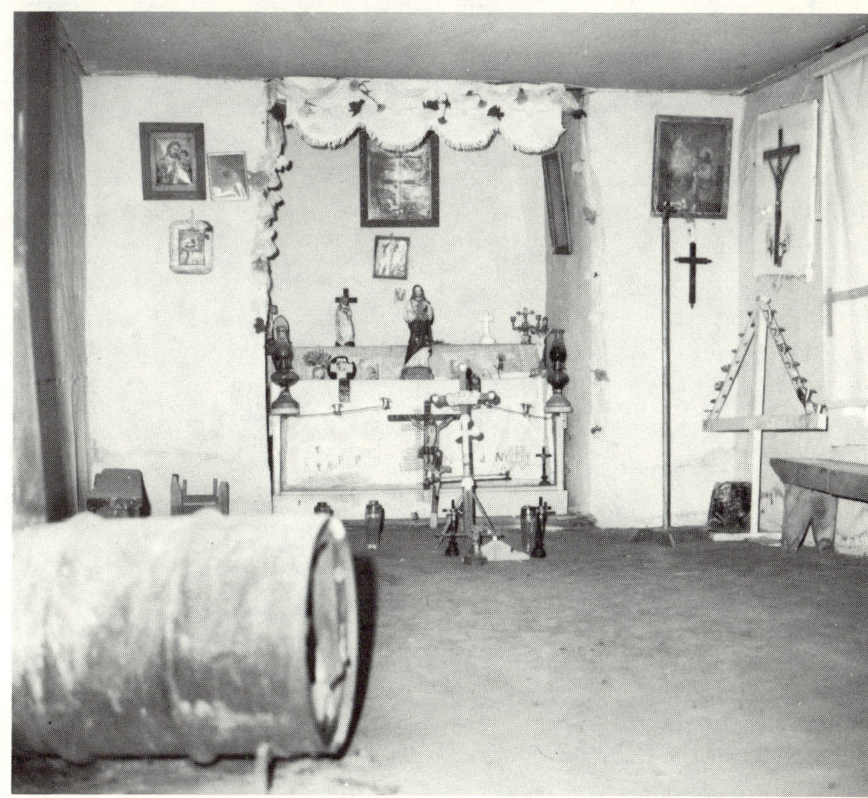

FIGURE 38
Oratorio with a rectangular apse, a typical triangular-shaped candelabrum made of two-by-fours, and an oil-drum stove.

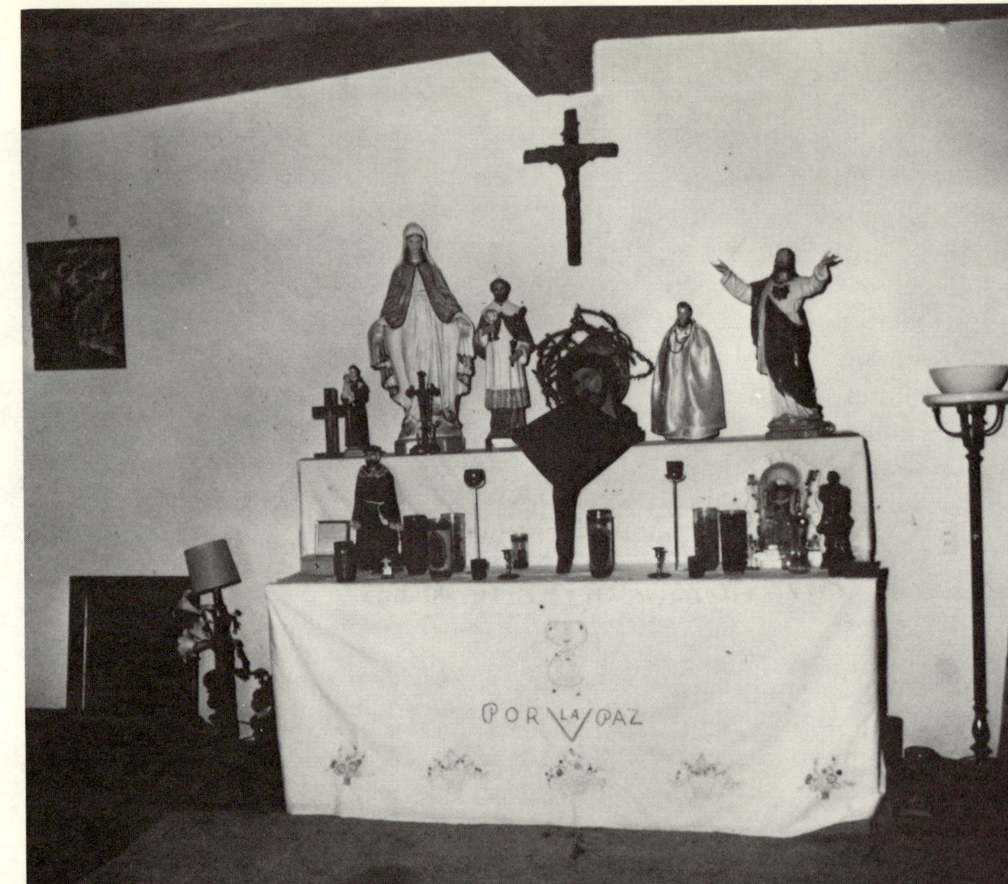

FIGURE 39
Morada altar with an elevated rear shelf.

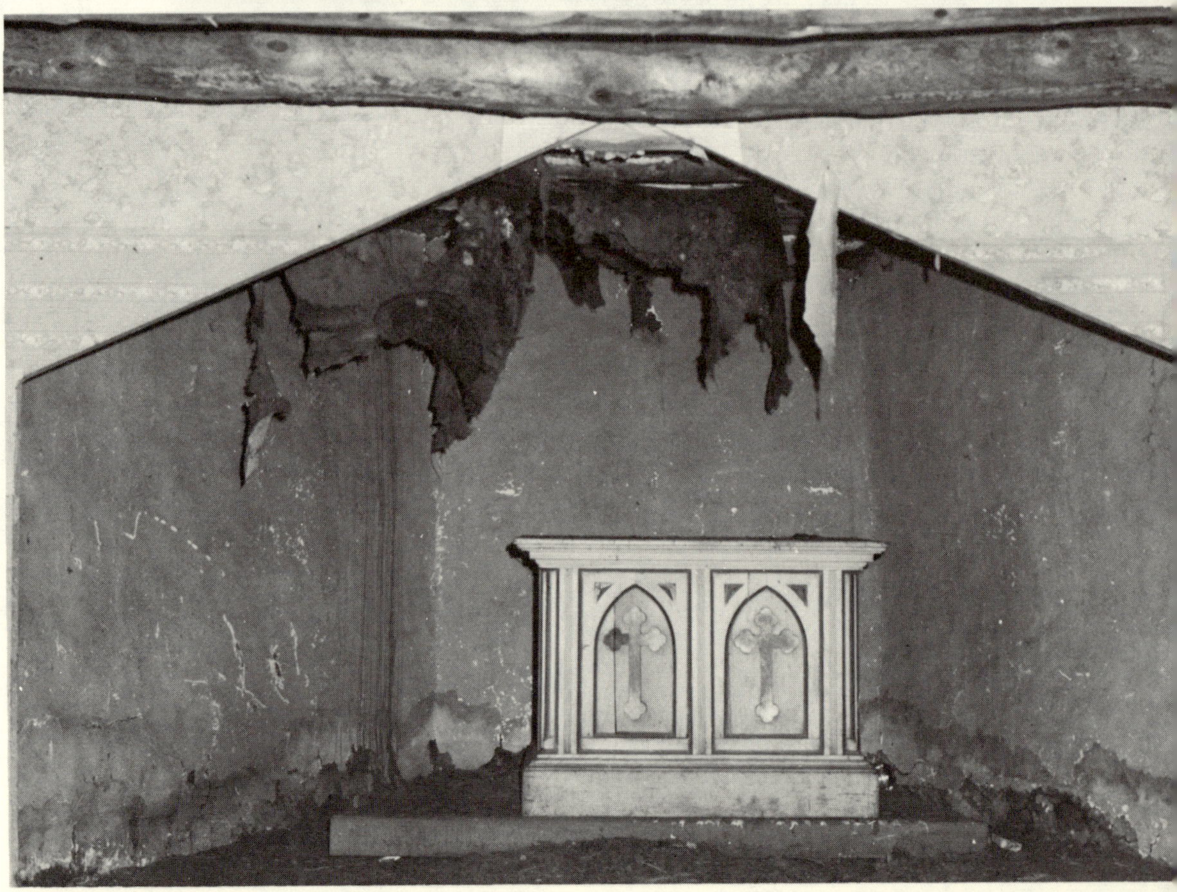

FIGURE 40
Altar of abandoned morada near Sapello. The more finished altar table was undoubtedly brought from a parish church. The shredded fabric hanging from the ceiling is coarse cotton cloth once painted white, which protected the altar from dirt filtering through the wooden roof.

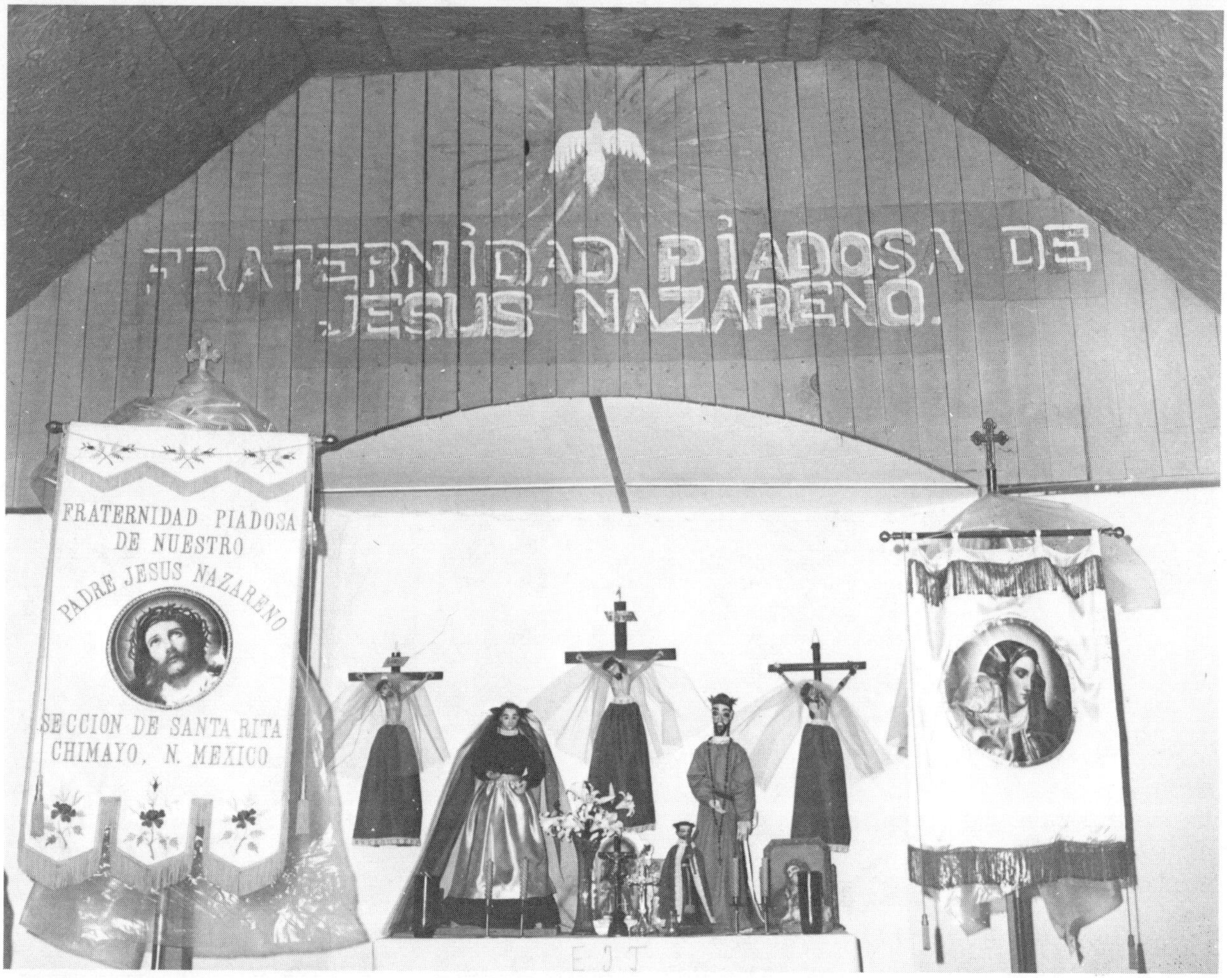

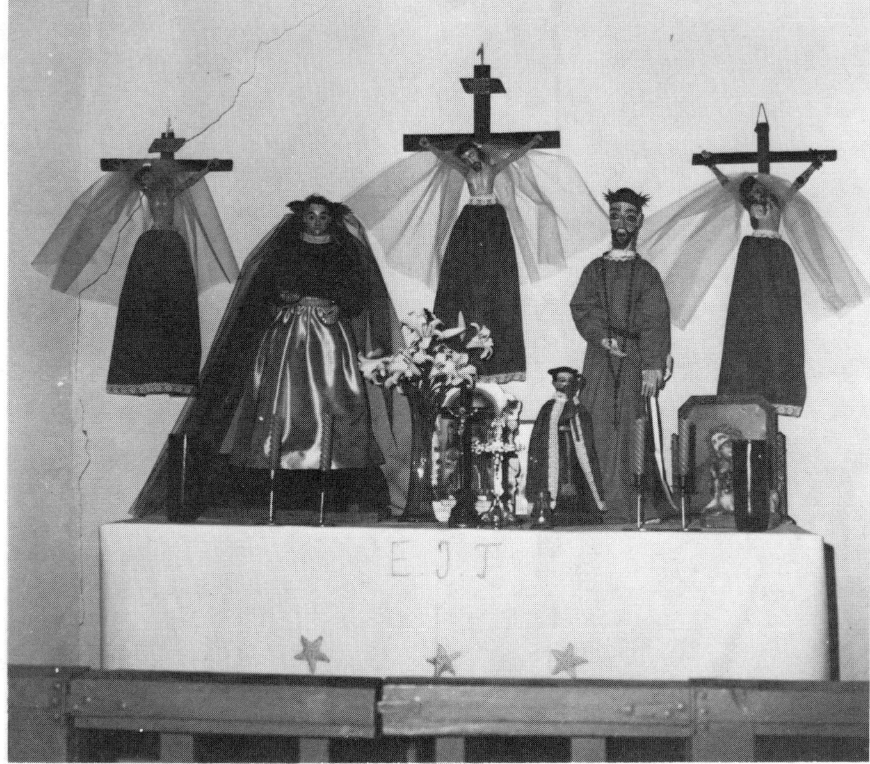

FIGURE 41
Unusually elaborate oratorio with a decorated wooden proscenium and two satin standards.

FIGURE 42
Close-up of Figure 41, showing fine nineteenth-century bultos swathed in skirts and dresses.

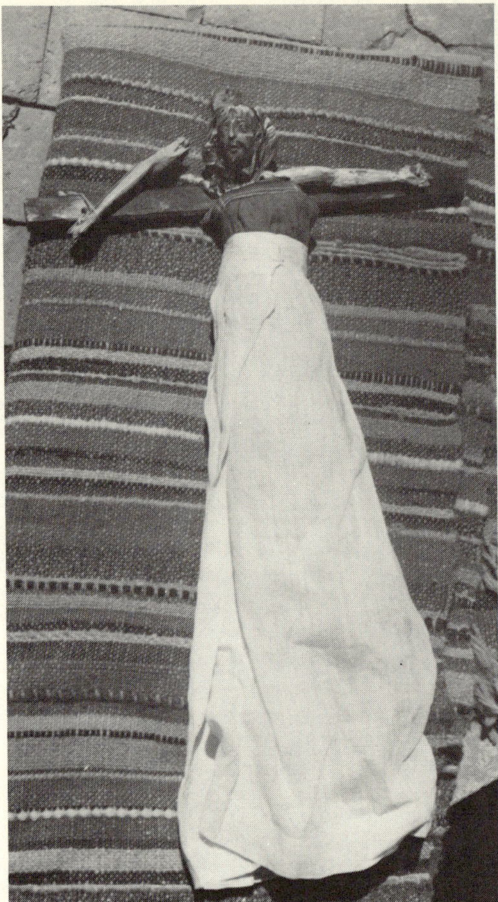
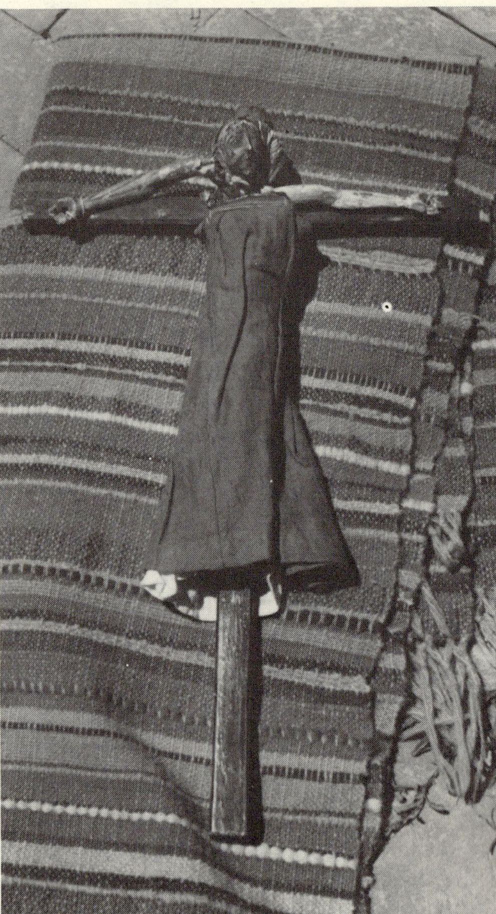
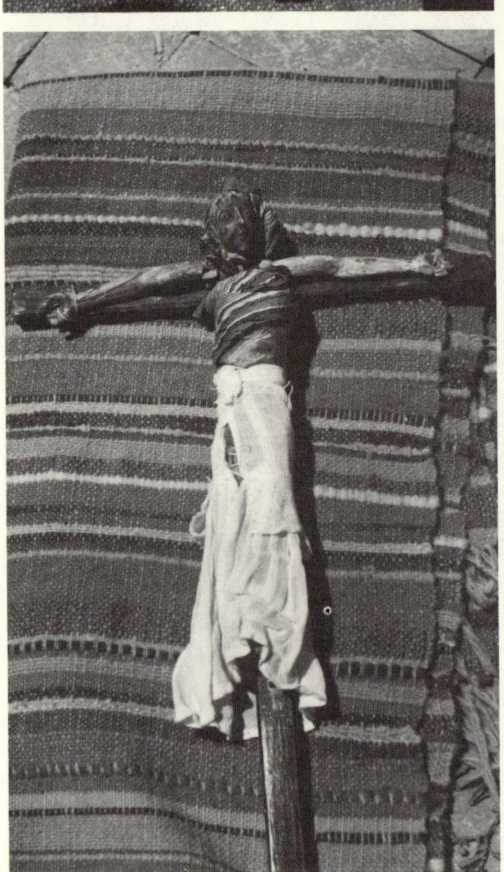
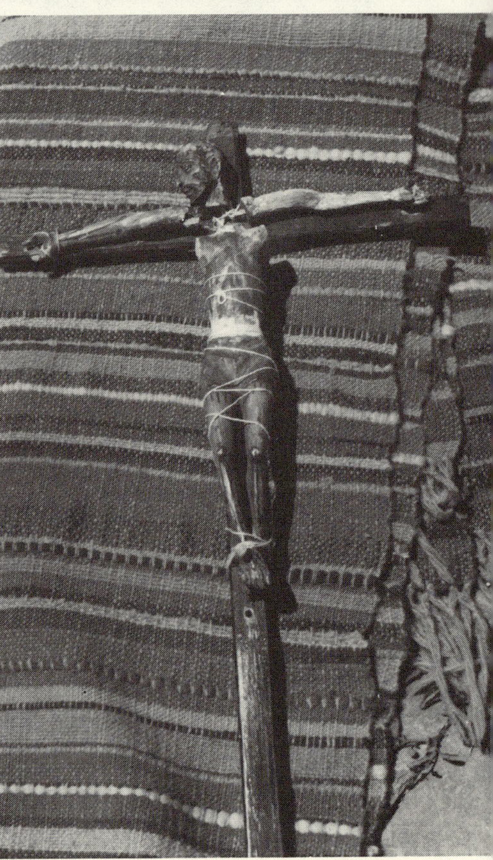

FIGURES 43 and 44
Small crucifix about nine inches high. It was wrapped in three layers of clothing that helped to hold the broken figure together. (Museum of Albuquerque Collection.)

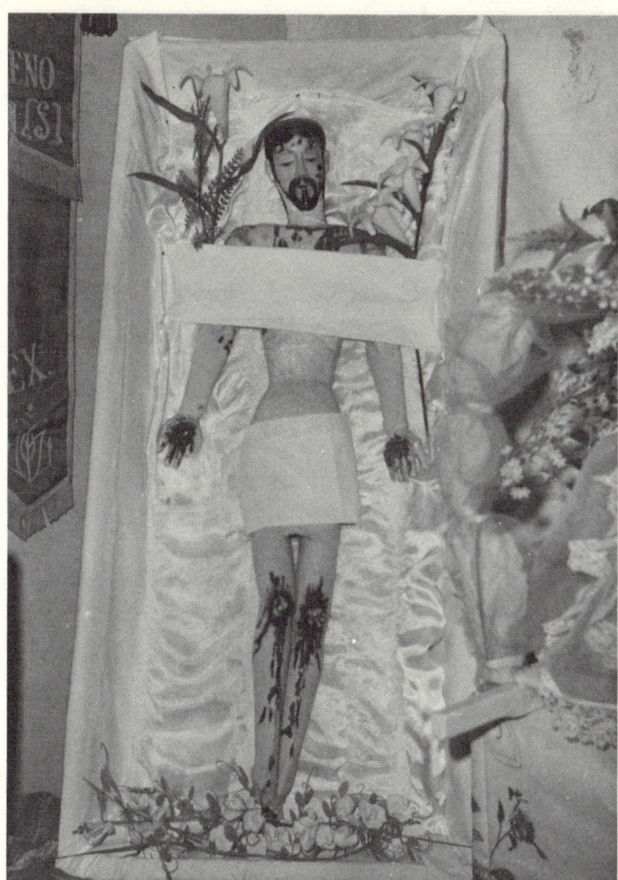

FIGURE 45
Cristo enterro, the interred Christ, with movable arms that permitted the figure to be attached to a cross or laid in a coffin as shown here.

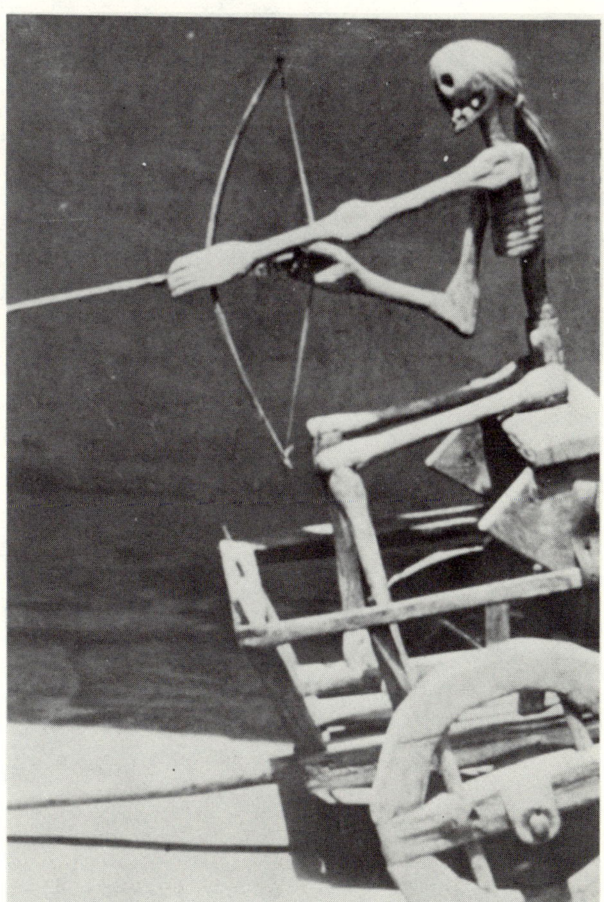

FIGURE 46
La Muerte, the figure of Death, shown as a skeleton about to shoot an arrow and seated in a cart that was drawn by penitents in Lenten processions. The figure is usually crowned and often had mica set in the eye sockets.

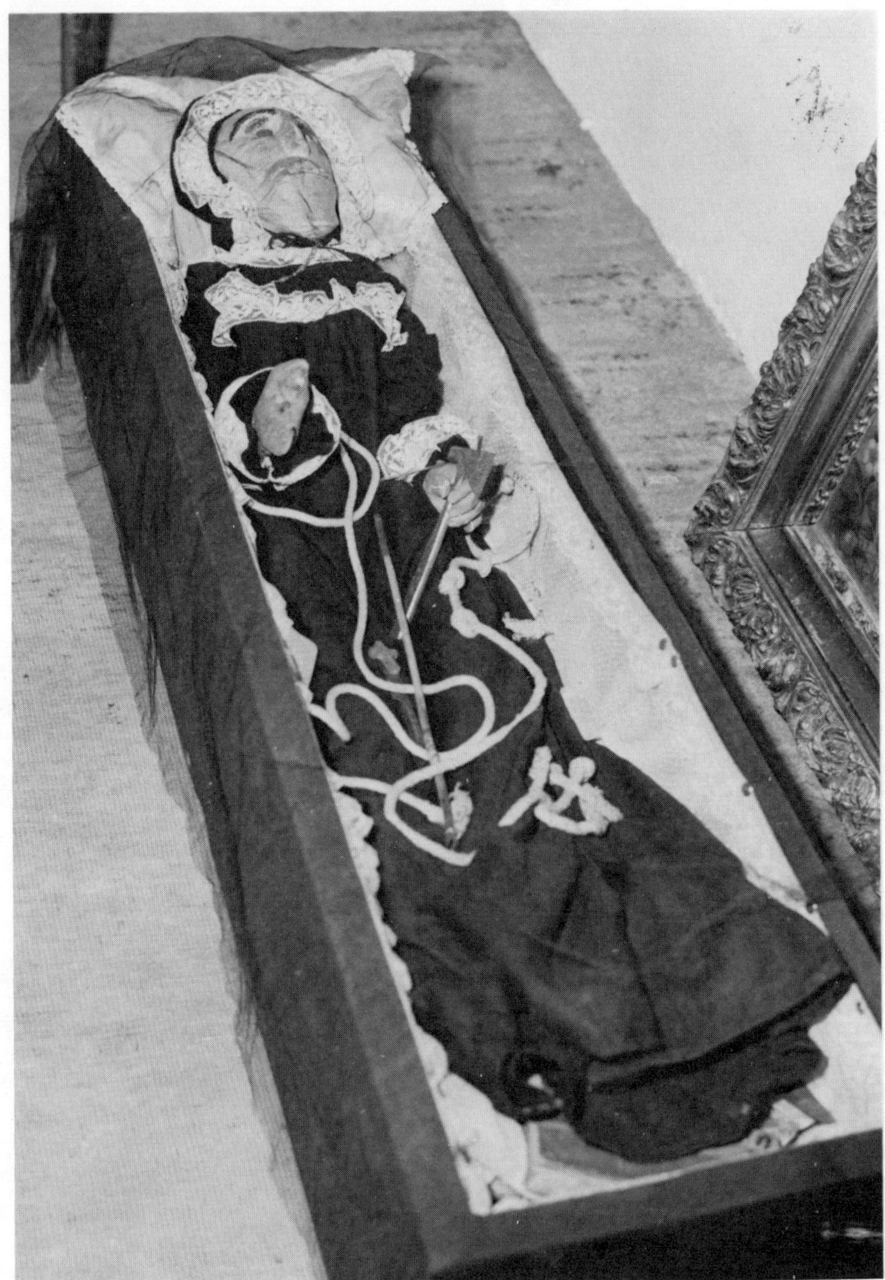

FIGURE 47
Doña Sebastiana, another type of death figure, clothed and laid in a coffin.

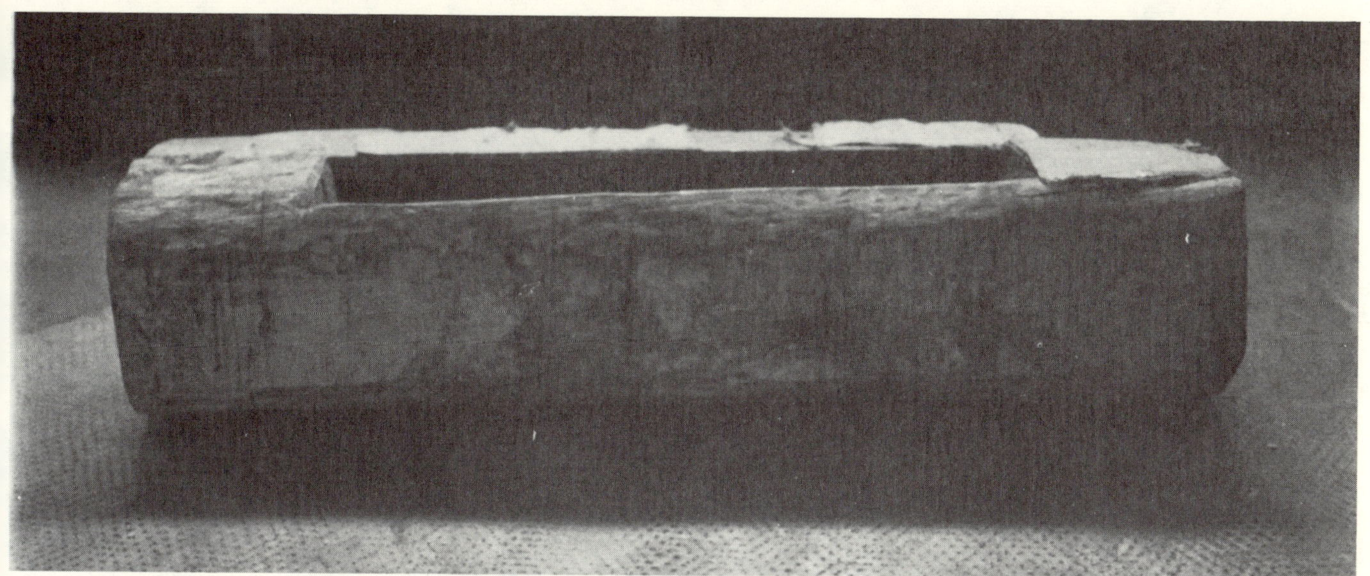

FIGURE 48
Tub for ablutions at the conclusion of penitential exercises. This tub, formed from a hollowed log, is seventy-six inches long. (Museum of Albuquerque Collection.)

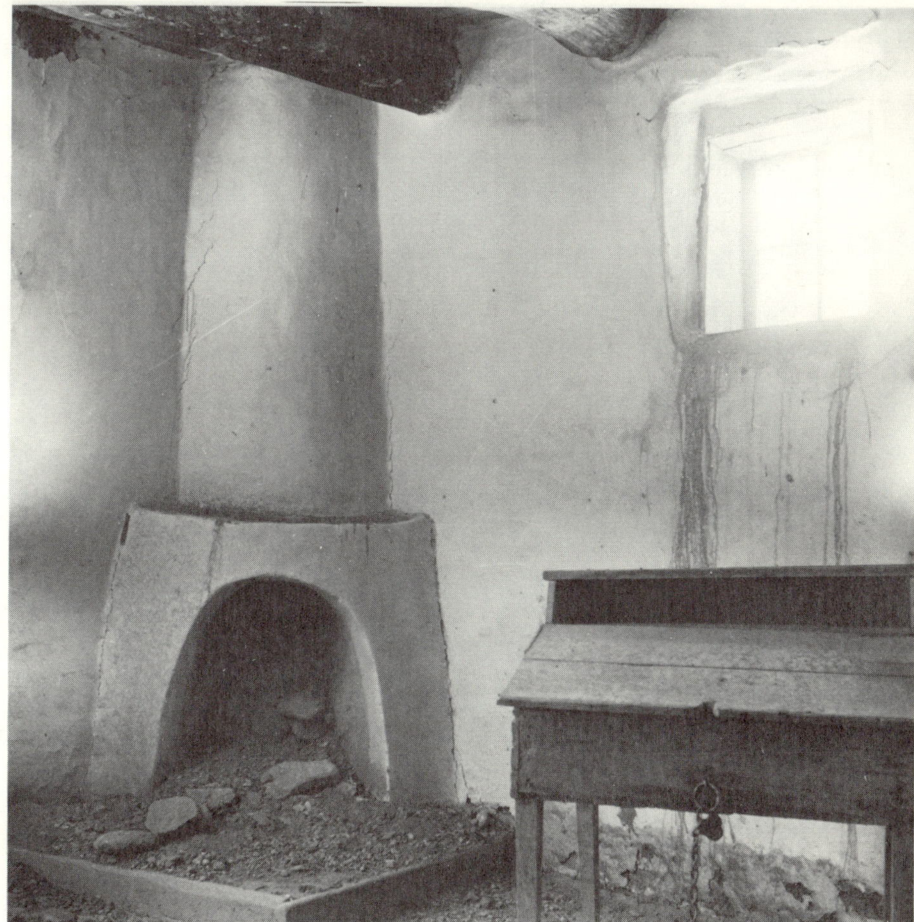

FIGURE 49
El escritorio, the records room of an abandoned morada in Arroyo Hondo. The small corner fireplace on a low hearth is typical of those found in colonial New Mexican dwellings. The desk was crudely made of commercially finished lumber.

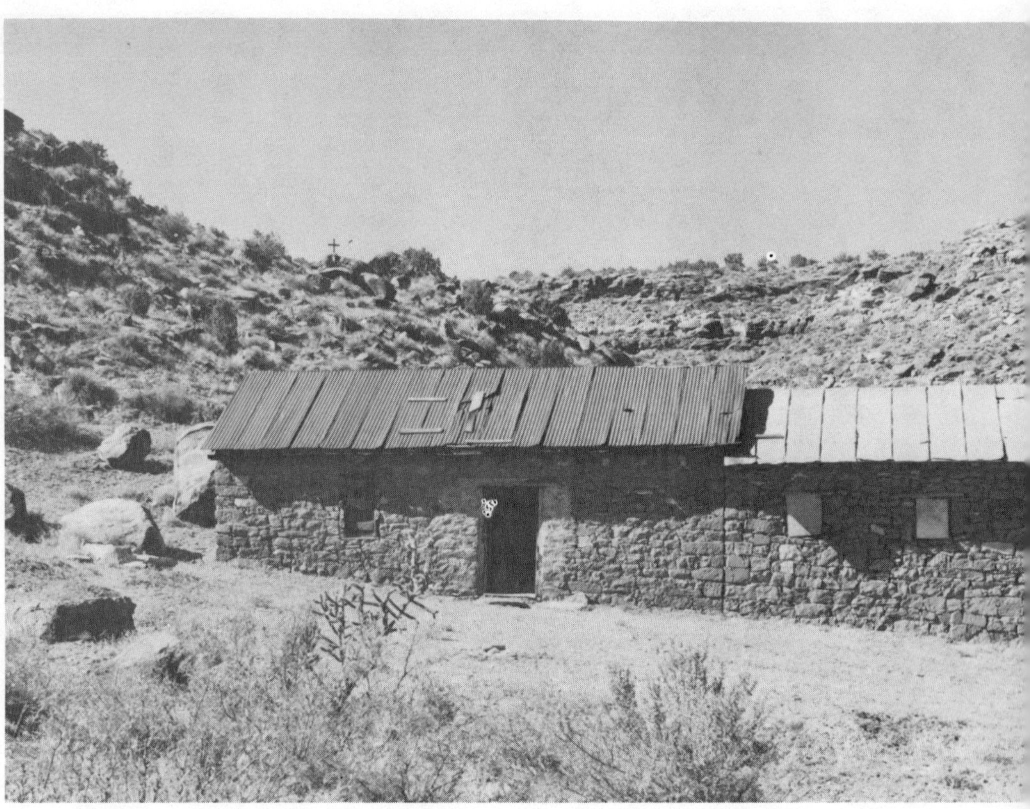

FIGURE 50
This stone morada was obviously built in two sections. The chapel at the right is undoubtedly older because of the terneplate roof. The Calvario can be seen on the rocky hill in the distance. South of Santa Rosa, New Mexico.

FIGURE 51
Squared timbers were obviously used for the original oratorio at the left. Its door was blocked when the meeting room of unshaped logs was added. North of El Rito, New Mexico.

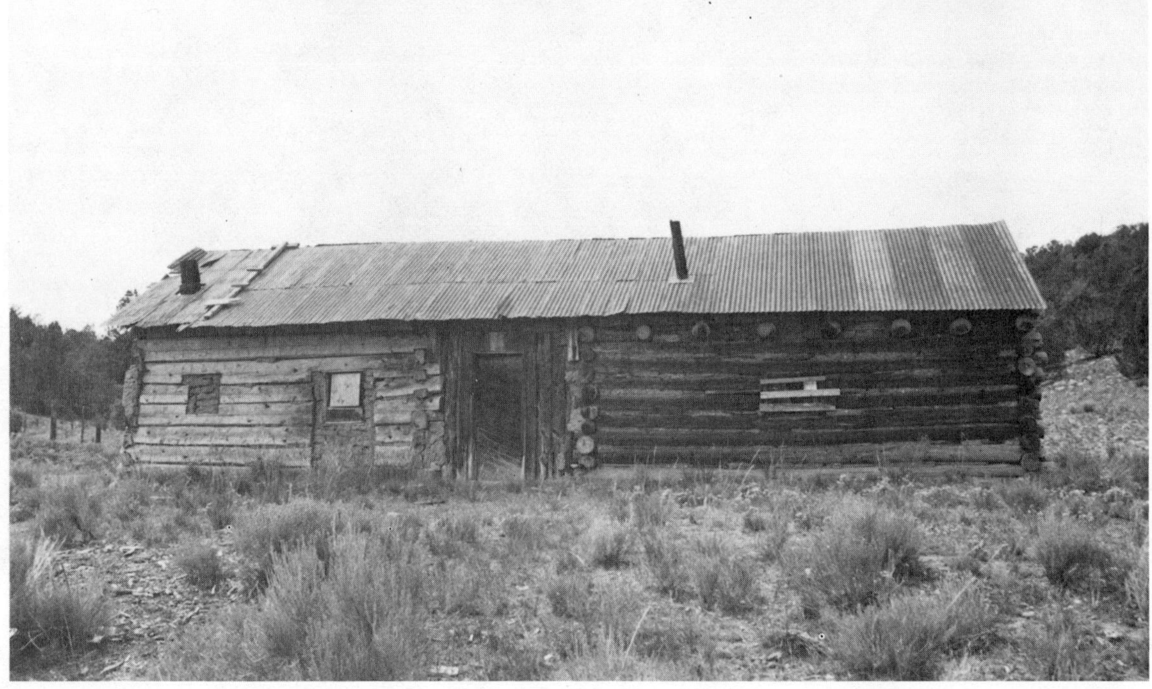

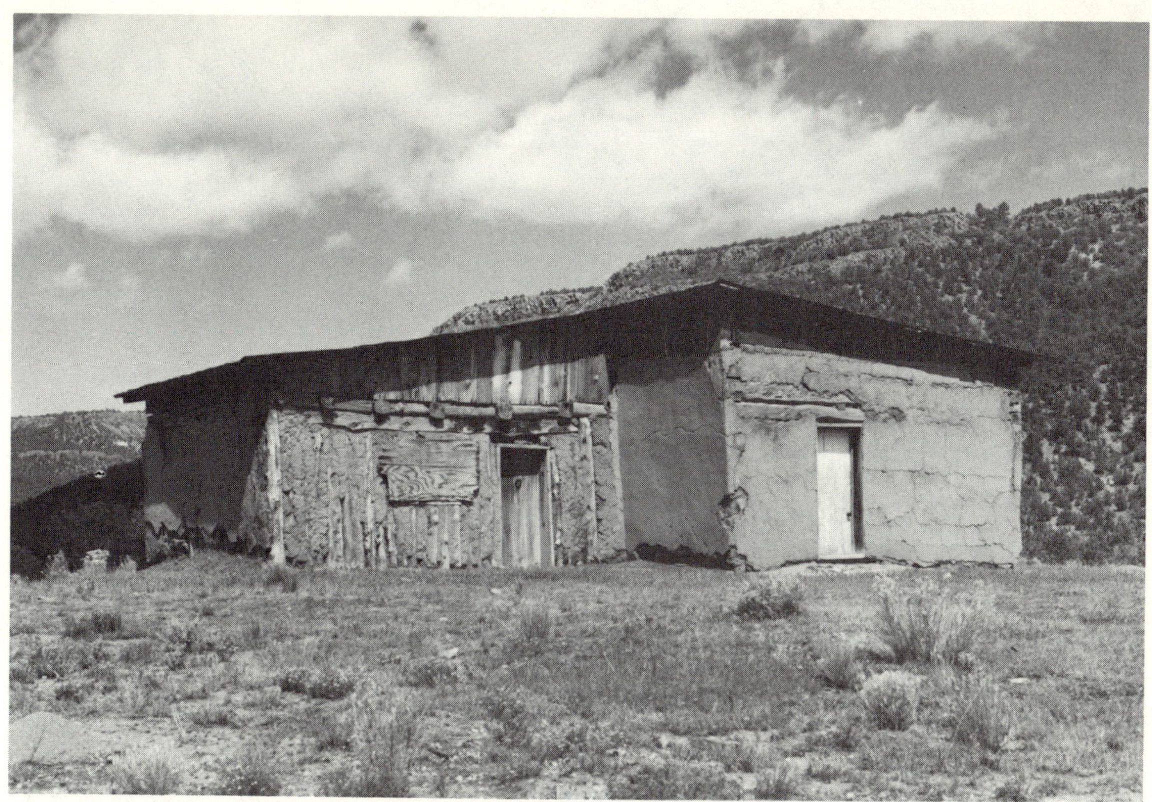

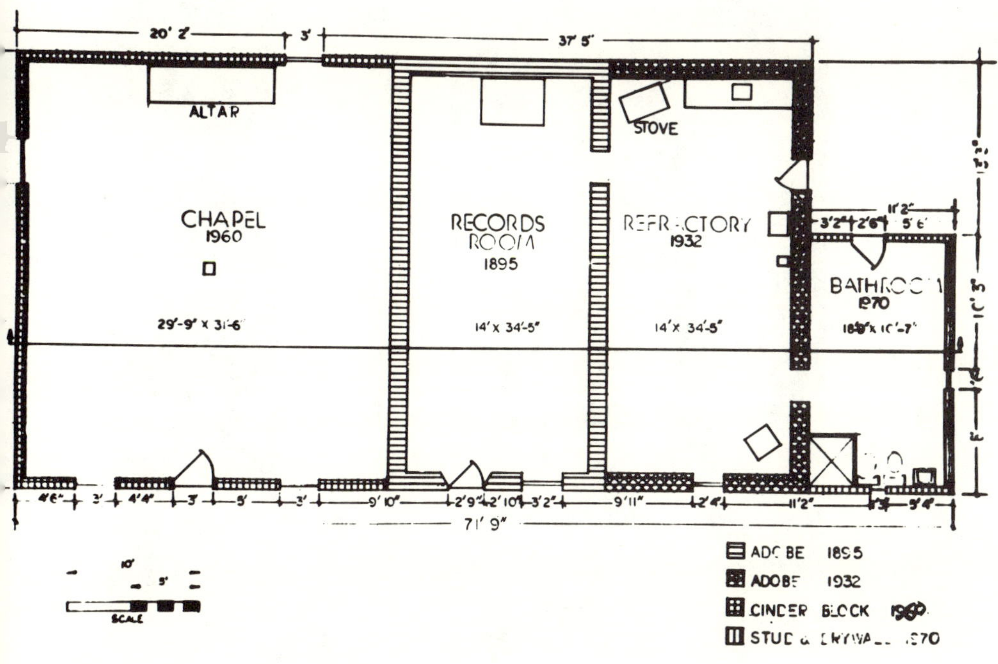

FIGURE 52
The whole morada is constructed of logs, although all surfaces were originally plastered with adobe. The chapel on the right used roughly squared logs laid horizontally; the meeting room is of jacal construction with logs set upright. North of El Rito, New Mexico.

FIGURE 53
The history of this morada constructed in four stages is unusually complete. South of Albuquerque, New Mexico.

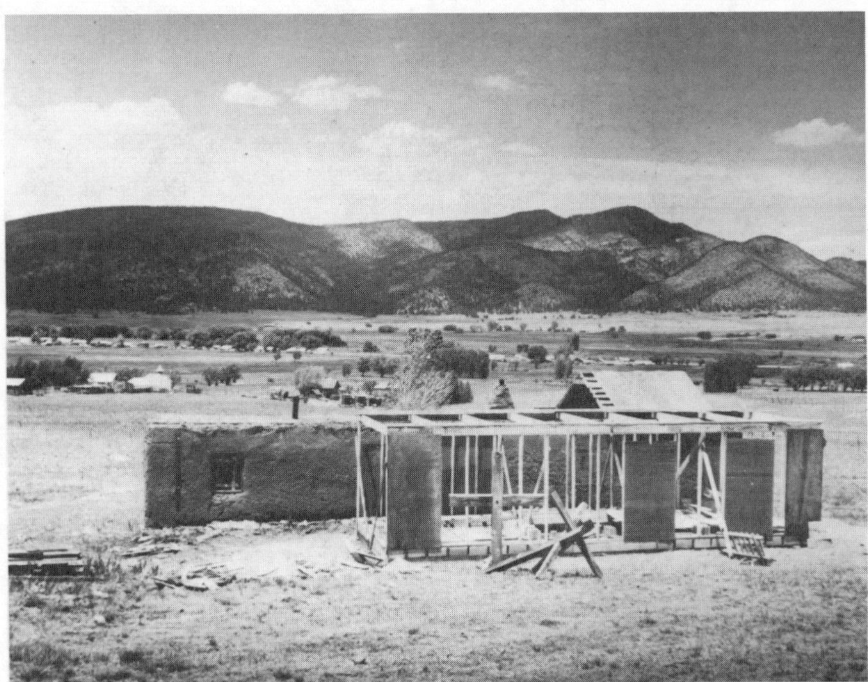

FIGURE 54
The small new morada was constructed in 1975, after which the old adobe building behind it was demolished. Near Mora, New Mexico.

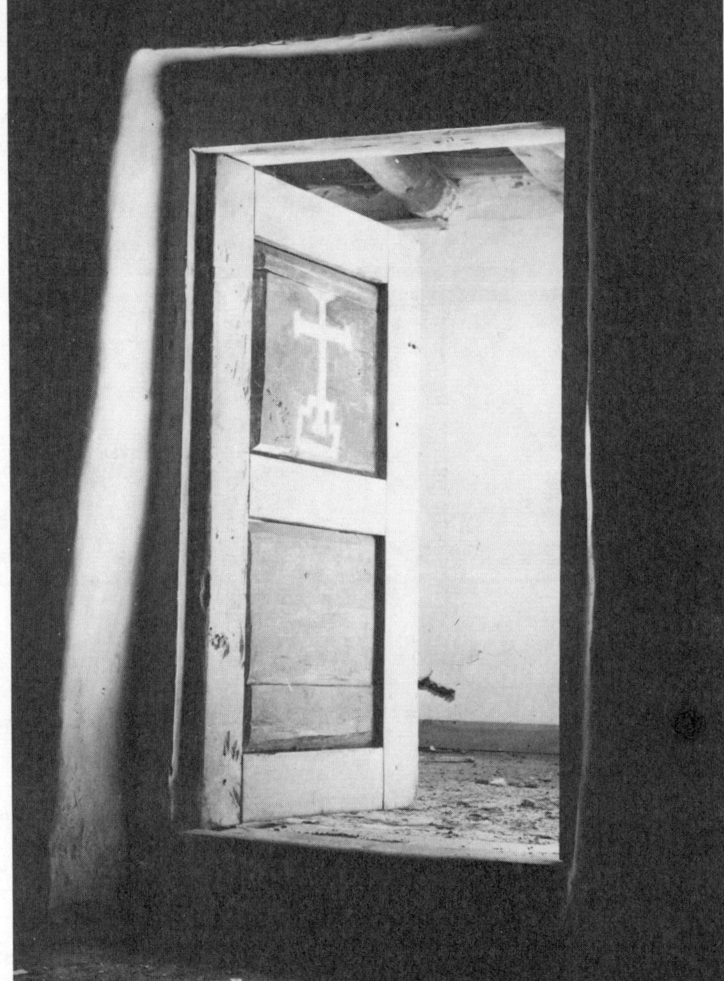

FIGURE 55
The door to the chapel of the abandoned morada in Arroyo Hondo dates from 1852–1856. Of extremely heavy members and less than five feet high, the door hinges on wooden pintels set into the sill and lintel. (Photograph by Jack Boucher, Historic American Building Survey.)

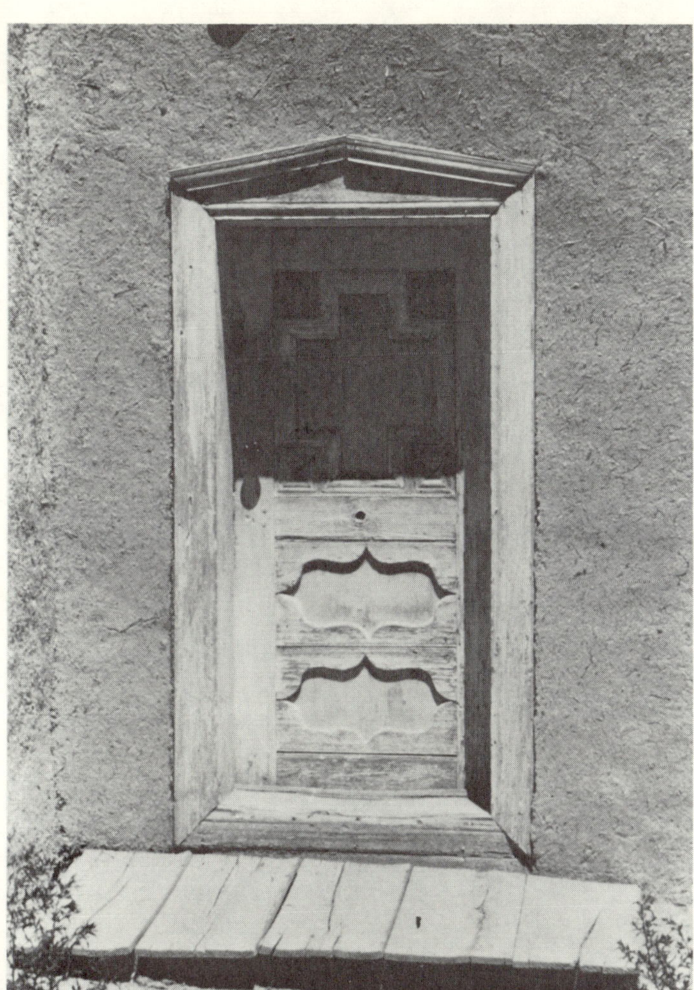

FIGURE 56
This door with curved linear designs and mitered panels is typical of wood work done in the last decade of the nineteenth century in northern New Mexico. Unfortunately, it disappeared when the morada was remodeled in the 1960s. Las Trampas, New Mexico.

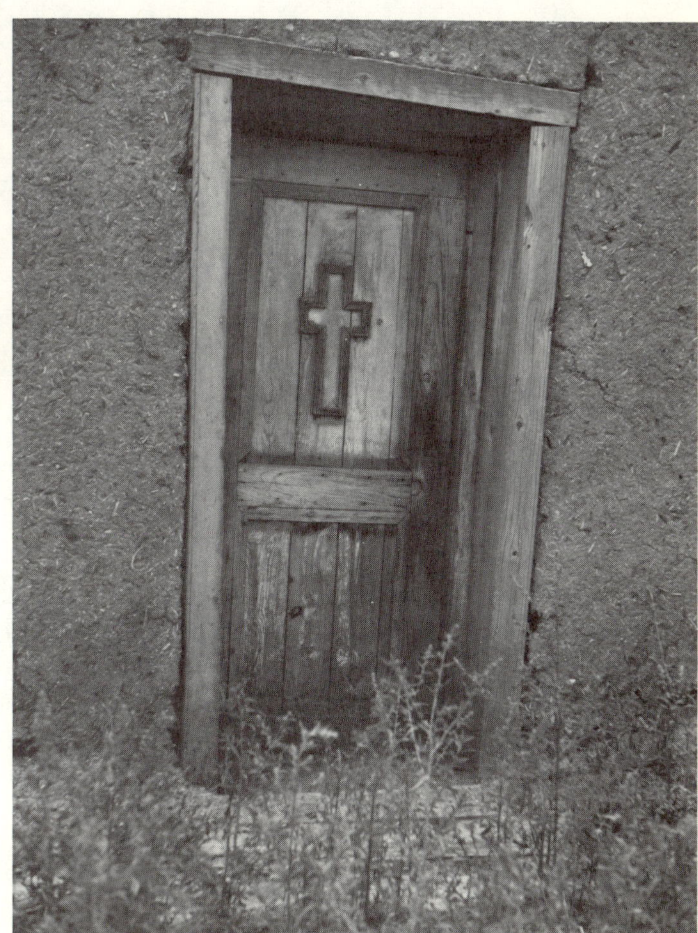

FIGURE 57
The cross design on this morada door is made from hand-planed moldings applied to a batten-and-frame door. Llano de San Juan, New Mexico.

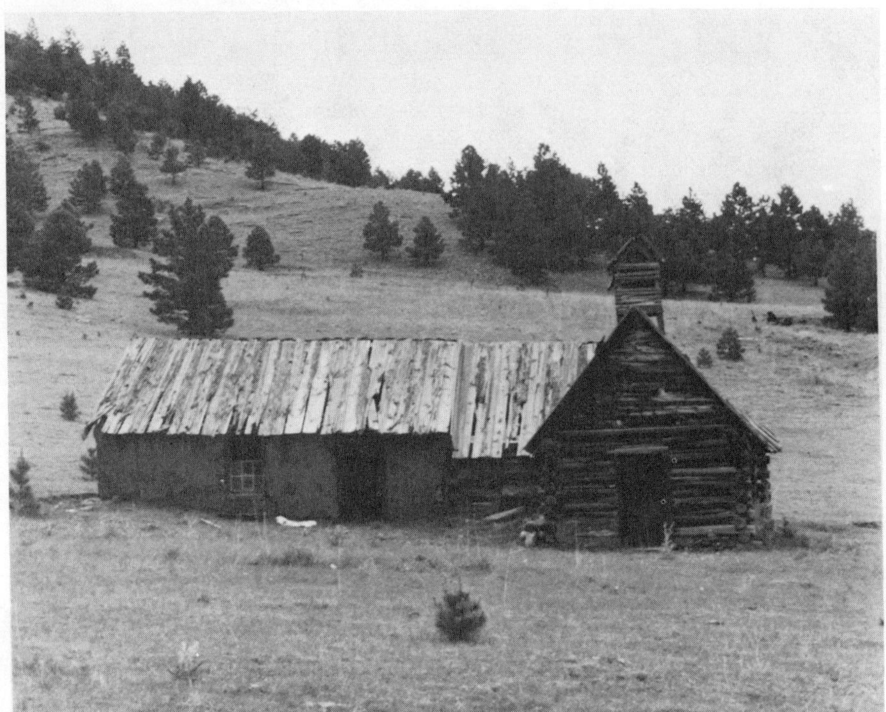

FIGURE 58
An adobe chapel *(left)*, log kitchen, and meeting room with a board-on-board roof are built on a hillside. The plan is shown in Figure 31. Cleveland, New Mexico.

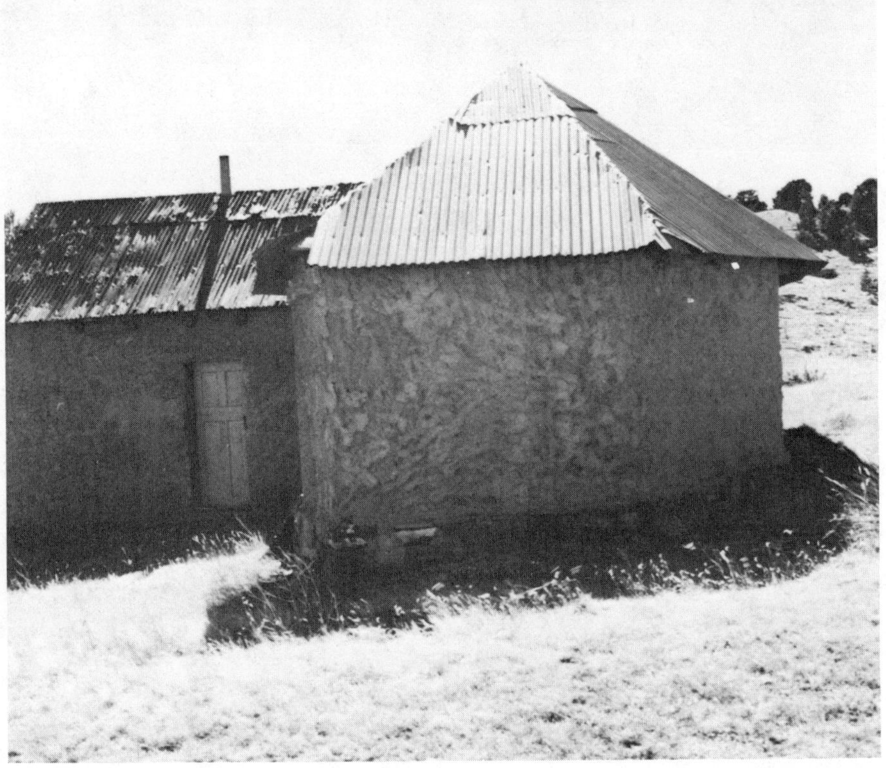

FIGURE 59
An L-shaped morada whose chapel has a polygonal end plan and a corrugated iron roof. Near Las Vegas, New Mexico.

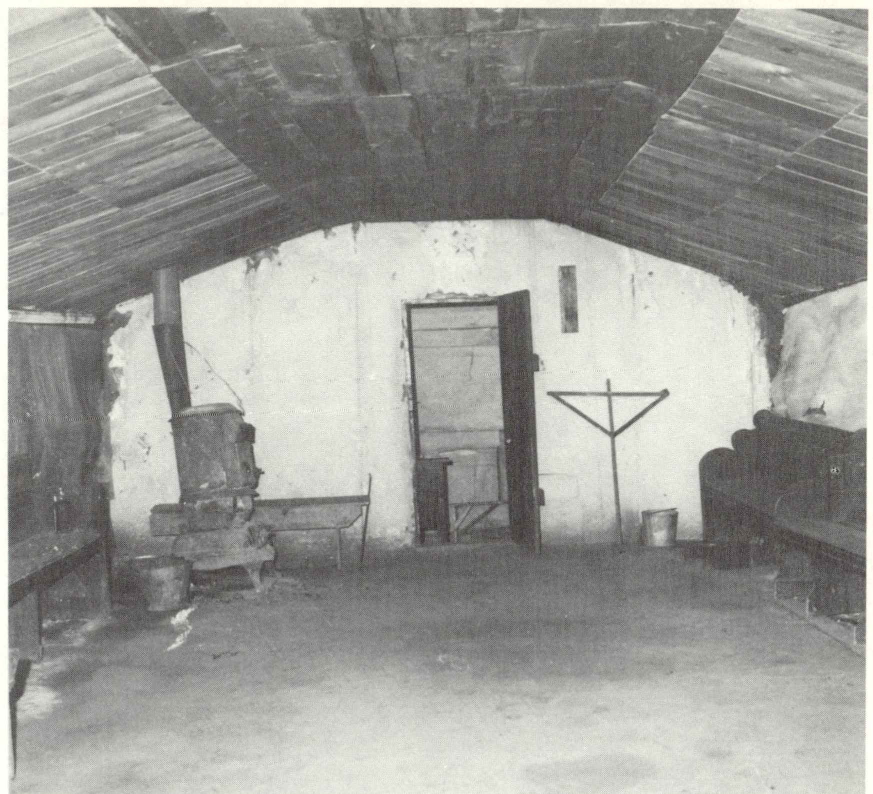

FIGURE 60
Meeting room of a morada with an old iron stove. The slanted roof is obviously original. Monero, New Mexico.

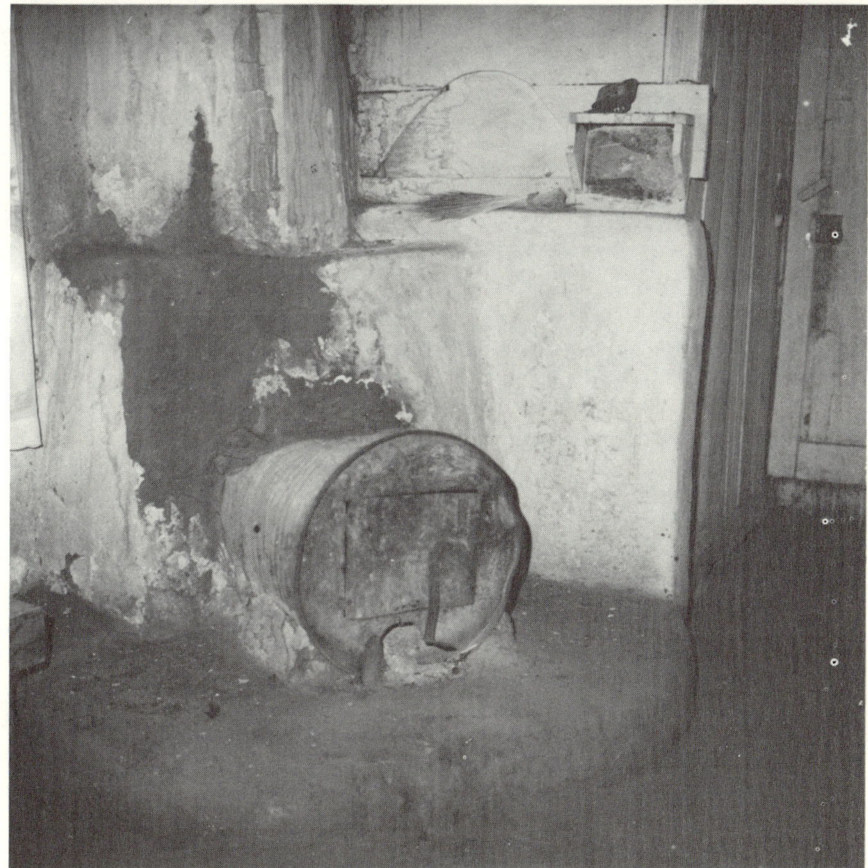

FIGURE 61
Oil-drum heater improvised by inserting the drum into the opening of the older corner fireplace. The old flue serves the new heater.

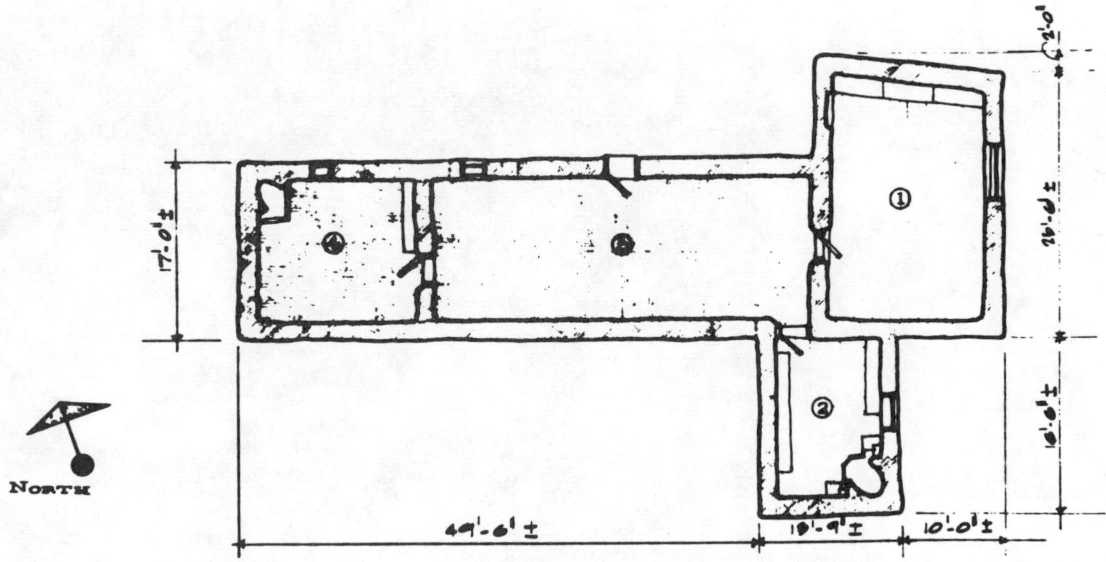

FIGURE 62
Room 3 served for storage and also, to judge from bloodstains on the ceiling, for flagellation. Room 4 may have served for ablutions. Arroyo Hondo, New Mexico.

ROOM	CEILING		FLOOR
① CHAPEL	10'-2" HIGH	PLANK	PLANK
② MEETING RM.	7'-4" HIGH	CEDROS	PLANK
③ COMMUNITY RM.	9'-4" HIGH	PLANK	PACKED DIRT
④ RECORDS RM.	9'-4" HIGH	PLANK	PACKED DIRT

NOTES

1. This study has been financed in part with federal funds from the Heritage Conservation and Recreation Service, U.S. Department of the Interior, and administered by the Historic Preservation Bureau, State Planning Division, Department of Finance and Administration. However, the contents and opinions do not necessarily reflect the views or policies of the Department of the Interior, the Bureau, Division or Department of Finance and Administration, nor does the mention of trade names or commercial products constitute endorsement or recommendation by the above-named agencies.

Field work for this project was generously supported by the Museum of Albuquerque and the American Philosophical Society. Their help contributed not only to this paper and to several other planned ones but also to the collection of morada furnishings for future display and study. Marta Weigle, James Ebert, and Rosalie Fanale all read the manuscript and offered many useful and usable suggestions. Numerous students in Bainbridge Bunting's classes in the history of architecture at the University of New Mexico provided measured drawings of moradas used as figures in the text. Hermanos in various chapters have been most cooperative in helping us obtain so much of the information contained in this essay. Their wish is to remain unnamed for fear of unwelcome intrusion and idle, unsympathetic curiosity.

2. The Brotherhood's origins have posed a perplexing problem, with some scholars suggesting they were a transformation of the Third Order of Saint Francis in New Mexico (e.g., Boyd 1974: 440–41, 446; Fisher 1941) and others, notably Chávez (1954*b*), claiming that they can be traced to Sevillian penitential confraternities. We support the hypothesis that La Fraternidad was not the result of a simple metamorphosis of the Third Order into a folk-religious brotherhood but a developed amalgam of Iberian cultural traditions and singular adaptive responses to the new socioecological setting in northern New Mexico.

Whereas the Third Order was and is composed of members of both sexes, La Fraternidad is exclusively a male organization. Membership qualifications can and do change for corporate groups, but there has been no explanation put forward, nor does one come readily to mind, to explain female exclusion during the presumed time of transformation during the late 1700s and early 1800s. On the other hand, it is clear from Foster's account of *cofradías, gremios,* and *hermandades* in Spain and Mexico (1953) that membership was strictly male in these organizations, which developed in Spain as early as the latter part of the twelfth century and which were still viable and presumably influenced New World society as late as the eighteenth century. Given Spanish penitential history and tradition, one might expect to find similar practices and similar but not necessarily identical organizations in former Spanish colonies, as is indeed the case in Mexico, Panama, Colombia, Argentina, the Philippines, New Mexico, and undoubtedly other areas that could be identified with diligent research and travel.

The New Mexican Fraternidad developed as an organization unique in its combination of locality, organizational structure, functions, adaptive responses, and antecedent elements. Its origin cannot be ascribed simplistically to a single preexistent religious sodality. Rather, it derived from a complex of Hispanic social and religious elements realigned to the local environment as a logical response to shifting temporal and spiritual needs in a frontier situation.

3. Penitential practices, though not necessarily formal orders such as La Fraternidad, are reported in many Spanish colonial areas such as Mexico, Panama, Colombia, Argentina, and the Philippines. E. Boyd (1950*b*) has recorded such an instance at San Gabriel, California, in 1852. In this century, we are acquainted with such observances, for example, in Tucson, Arizona, where we have seen men and women make pilgrimages or walk on their knees across the hot sand of the Arizona desert between Tucson and the San Xavier Mission about nine miles to the south. Archbishop James P. Davis, formerly of the Archdiocese of Santa Fe, related a story of such penitential practices to us. During his early ministry as a parish priest in Arizona, a man came to the rectory with a burden of cactus strapped to his back and chest. The penitent had made a private vow to carry this excruciating load from morning until sundown but found the suffering unbearable and so had come to beg dispensation from the promise he had made. The young priest took the afflicted man into the church sanctuary and, with appropriate prayer and ceremony, dispensed him from the balance of his obligation.

4. An invaluable, detailed inventory of the contents of both moradas at Abiquiú was made by Richard E. Ahlborn in 1967 (Ahlborn 1968: 123–67); also see Shalkop (1969) for Arroyo Hondo.

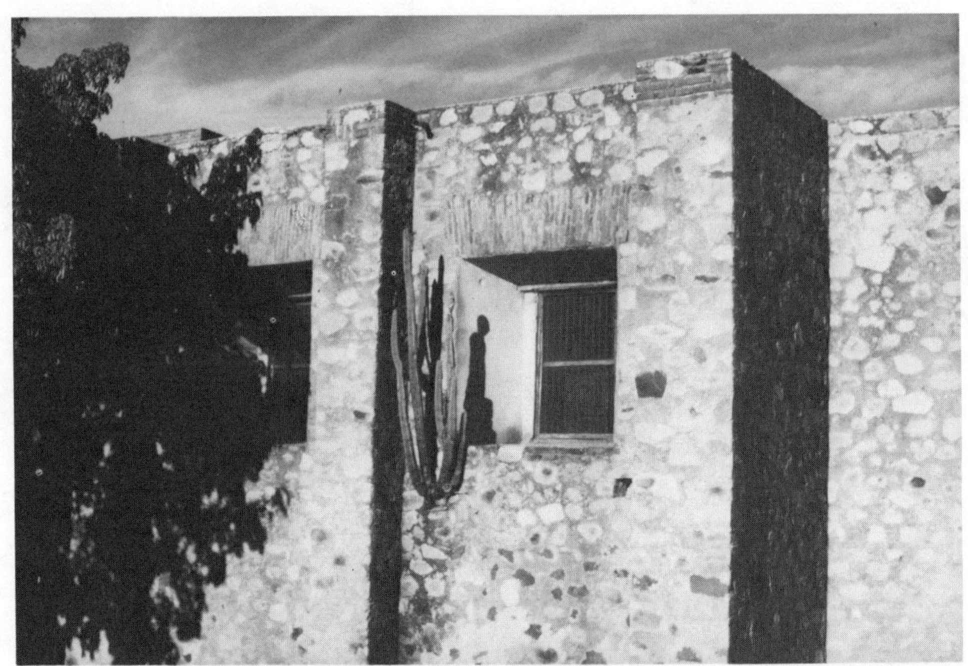

FIGURE 1
Organ pipe cactus growing out of the stone wall of the church at Aduana, Sonora, Mexico, casts a shadow of Our Lady of Valvanera on the side of a splayed window jamb. November 1979. (B. L. Fontana photograph.)

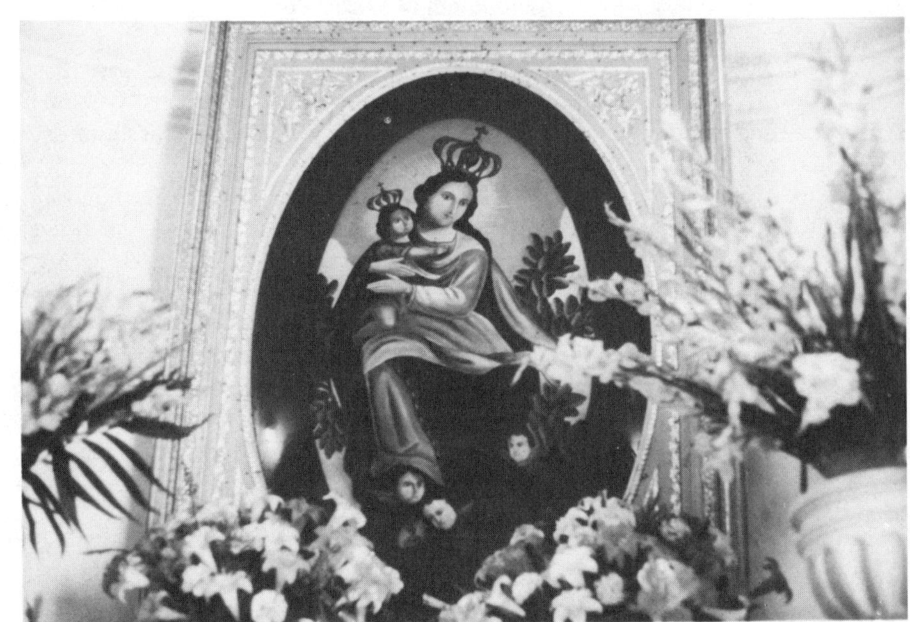

FIGURE 2
Oil painting of Our Lady of Valvanera in the Church of Aduana, Sonora, Mexico. November 1979. (B. L. Fontana photograph.)

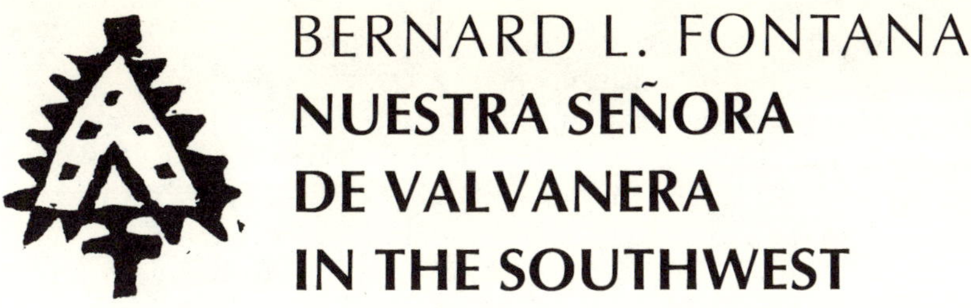

BERNARD L. FONTANA

NUESTRA SEÑORA DE VALVANERA IN THE SOUTHWEST

"Who was Balvanera?"

The question was simple enough. The voice at the other end of the phone was that of a reporter for the *Arizona Republic,* a Phoenix newspaper with the largest daily circulation in the state. He, like me, was going to southern Sonora, Mexico, for the annual Fiesta de Nuestra Señora de Balvanera (more generally spelled Valvanera), and he wanted to know something about the lady in whose honor the celebration was being held. A logical inquiry, but I didn't have the answer. Now, however, I do. More or less. And this essay is the result.[1]

THE FOOTHILLS OF THE SIERRA MADRE OCCIDENTAL lying between Alamos in southern Sonora and the agriculturally rich flatlands between the rivers Mayo and Fuerte mark the joining together of thorn forest and vegetation characteristic of the Sonoran desert. Spikes and thorns greet hiker and horseman alike. Here and there, however, the monotonous spread of inhospitable plants is broken by trails, dirt roads, isolated households, and small clusters of homes. A thirty-three-mile stretch of two-lane highway joins Navojoa, a large city on Mexico's West Coast Highway 15, and Alamos, a large town in the center of a former silver-mining district with roots in the seventeenth century. And elsewhere in the hills are great scars where rocks from beneath the earth have been dragged and tumbled downslope as a by-product of man's dreams of mineral riches.

Nestled in the foothills of such scars as these, about five miles west of Alamos, is Aduana, a tiny settlement whose ruined and abandoned structures speak clearly of its bygone wealth and grandeur. A few homes continue in use, and at one edge of town there is a handsome stone church facing a plaza. The church is dedicated to Nuestra Señora Balvanera. Historian Rachel French tells the story:

> La Aduana, another of the early camps . . ., became the center of the rich-

> est mines in the [Alamos] district. Discovered in 1683, there is an interesting story in connection with the Aduana mines.
>
> According to tradition, Indians passing through the country saw a beautiful maiden on top of a tall cactus. Much to their surprise, when they again looked up she had vanished. Then, on glancing at the ground where one of the rocks had been dislodged, they saw an outcropping of silver ore. Surely, the Indians believed, this was a heaven-sent miracle. The lovely maiden had shown them where to find the silver. So firm was their belief in this miraculous apparition that they later built a church on the very site. In the girl's honor they named the church Nuestra Señora de Balvanere. As if to lend credence to the natives' belief, a giant cactus grew out of a side wall of the church, ten or twelve feet above the ground. The cactus is there today for all to see. [Fig. 1]
>
> Despite the fact that the Catholic Church has never officially recognized the miracle, in 1737 the Bishop of Nueva Vizcaya ordered that the annual Fiesta of Nuestra Señora de Balvanere be celebrated on the 21st of November rather than the 8th of September to allow the faithful to make the trek from Alamos to Aduana unhindered by September's flood waters. Aduana is almost deserted today, but on November 21st of each year it returns to life with the coming of thousands of pilgrims paying homage to the "Virgin of Balvanere" (French 1962: 3).

The Aduana Valvanera is ahistorical. She is represented in the church by both an oil painting and by a statue some fourteen inches tall kept within a glass cabinet within another glass cabinet. No one knows the age of either the painting or the statue; they have "always been here." No one is sure when the church was built, but it is "very old." It was clear, too, that such questions in the mind of the *sacristana* (female sexton), who had spent her entire life in Aduana and who was probably in her sixties, were of no relevance. The absolute and relative ages of statue, painting, and church mattered not a whit. Our Lady of Valvanera is not so much a creature of Aduana's past as of its present. She is the subject of a living devotion rather than the object of historical interest.

The oil painting (Fig. 2) hanging at the rear of the church above what would have been the main altar in pre–Vatican II times shows a crowned Valvanera seated in a nopal, or prickly pear cactus, holding a crowned Christ Child on her left knee. The heads of four cherubs are at her feet. It is an oval painting some five feet from top to bottom, set in a gilded rectangular frame. The painting had been sent to an artist in Guaymas or Hermosillo about 1970 for cleaning and repair, and it appears that the "restorer" overpainted the entire original, though I was unable to examine it close at hand.

Neither was it possible to examine the statue except at a respectful distance. The sacristana opened the glass door of the outer cabinet to make it possible to take a somewhat blurred photograph, but she would not open that of the inner one. Valvanera is a doll-like figure fully clothed *(de vestir)* in untreated (that is, unwaxed) garments; only the hair, head, and hands could be seen. Her head and hands were flesh color *(encarnación)*; her light brown hair appeared to be human hair. She used both hands to hold the crowned Christ Child—an even smaller doll figure—on her left side. Like the Virgin in the painting, she wore a red dress and a blue cape; unlike that in the painting, she was standing rather than seated. There was no cactus nor were there other symbols with her that would clearly identify her as Aduana's Valvanera. The importance of her crimson dress was indicated by the fact that several persons at the fiesta were wearing red *habitos* (robes) in fulfillment of a *manda* (vow).

Why Our Lady of "Balvanere," "Balbanera," "Valbanera," "Balvanera," or "Valvanera," as the name is perhaps most generally spelled? I asked this question in 1979 during the November fiesta in Aduana. No one with whom I spoke—priest, pilgrim, or sacristana—had any idea; that had always been the name. Our Lady of Valvanera was theirs and theirs alone. No one had heard of her presence anywhere else in the world, whether in Mexico City or Spain. And the northwestern Mexican devotion to her is sufficiently strong that "Valvanera" is not an unusual name for Sonoran girls.

But, unknown to the people of Aduana and to the thousands of hope-filled pilgrims—both Indians and mestizos—who make their way to the church each year, there is another Nuestra Señora de Valvanera, though this one traditionally resides in a tree rather than in a cactus. The Benedictine monastery that enshrines her image, a wooden statue carved possibly as early as the tenth century (Fig. 3), is nestled in the mountains of the Rioja district not far from Najera and Logroño in northern Spain. She is the patroness of Rioja and Cameros, and since at least the fifteenth century, she has been the object of pilgrimage and the raison d'être of a cult with a large following. The shrine of Valvanera was included in a 1530 list of the twelve major shrines of Spain compiled by Italian humanist Lucio Marineo Siculo (Christian 1981: 205). As recently as 1951 the brotherhood of the Caballeros de Santa María de Valvanera was formed in Spain (Pérez Alonso 1971: 241–42).

Like all good legends, that concerning Spain's Lady of Valvanera has many versions. When those from various published sources have been combined, the story unfolds something like this:

The statue of Our Lady of Valvanera was carved by Saint Luke. It was brought to Spain in the first century A.D. and taken to the rugged mountain-and-canyon wilderness in the vicinity of what is now called Valvanera. In the fourth century, Saint Athanasius and a group of fellow Christian ascetics took up abode in the many caves of this region and began a special devotion to the statue, which by then was attributed with special powers. A sanctuary was erected to house the image.

At the time of the Moorish occupation of the Iberian peninsula, a man whose name was Arturo took the image to protect it and secreted it in the hollow of a live oak. No sooner was the statue placed in the hollow than the bark grew over the hole to conceal Our Lady.

The area where all this happened is bisected by a stream referred to in a document dated A.D. 1016 as the *rivus Vallevenaria,* or Valvanera River. The term itself may have as its root the word *venas,* which in Spanish can refer either to veins of ore or to the porcelain shells carried by pilgrims returning from the shrine of Santiago at Compostela. It is also possible the name derives from *Vallis-veniae,* or "Valley of Forgiveness" or "Valley of Indulgences," a reference to the fact that a pilgrim visiting the shrine would receive an indulgence from God. More likely, however, Valvanera is from *vallis-venationis,* Latin for "Valley of Wild Game," an allusion to the abundance of game animals in the region (Anonymous 1928: 853; Pérez Alonso 1971: 37–40).

Regardless of etymology, in the beginning of the tenth century a priest named Dominico de Brieva arrived at Valvanera in the company of 106 hermits. They had been attracted there because of stories they had heard of one Nuño Oñez. Oñez had been a thief and murderer who, like many fellow criminals, used the relatively inaccessible Valvanera region as a hideout. One day, as he was about to rob a kneeling farmer who was praying to the Virgin Mary, he was stricken by such an intense attack of contrition that he retired to the life of a Christian hermit. It was word of this miraculous conversion from a life of sin to one of penitence that attracted Father Dominico and his followers.

One night Oñez had a vision in which he saw the statue of Our Lady of Valvanera in her live oak. Further, the tree was a honey tree, a beehive. It

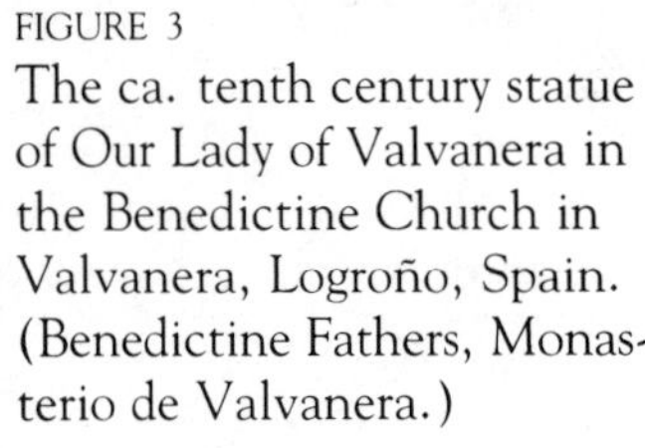

FIGURE 3
The ca. tenth century statue of Our Lady of Valvanera in the Benedictine Church in Valvanera, Logroño, Spain. (Benedictine Fathers, Monasterio de Valvanera.)

was situated on a hill; water flowed forth from a spring near the tree. The next day Oñez told Father Dominico of his vision, and the two of them set out to find the image's hiding place. At last they came to the top of a hill where they spotted a live oak that housed a swarm of bees and near whose base there was a spring of fresh water. They chopped the tree open and removed the statue from its sanctuary (Anonymous 1929; Roschini 1964: 587; and Sánchez Pérez 1943: 422–24).

In A.D. 1063, the care of the shrine for Nuestra Señora de Valvanera was turned over to the Benedictine friars. They planted vineyards, raised hogs and merino sheep, and built beehives for making honey. They used the income from these industries to build a large monastery, the sanctuary of which holds the venerated wooden statue. In time, the kings of Aragon and Castile made Our Lady of Valvanera their special protector. Queen Isabel made a personal visit to the shrine in 1482, and in 1592 King Philip II sent a friend to Valvanera to pray to Our Lady in his behalf. It has been said, although not documented, that the flagship of the fleet of Christopher Columbus was not merely the *Santa María,* but the *Santa María de Valvanera* (Anonymous 1929; Kelemen 1977: 58; Pérez Alonso 1971: 299).

During a French invasion in 1809, the Valvanera monastery was burned down, but the sanctuary with its image was spared. Benedictines rebuilt the monastery between 1820 and 1824 but were expelled in 1835. The statue was moved temporarily to Brieva in 1839; the Benedictines returned in 1883; and in 1885 the image was returned to her original home. Except for being removed for occasional processions, she has remained in the Benedictine church to this day (1982) (Anonymous 1929; Pérez Alonso 1971).

Although it is impossible to say precisely when the statue of Nuestra Señora de Valvanera was carved, the story of Saint Luke aside, in a Gothic book of the ninth century there is a portrait of the wife of Ordoño I of Galicia who lived in the mid-ninth century. The portrait shows her seated on a throne above four dogs, symbols of fidelity. There is said to be a marked resemblance between this portrait and the statue of Our Lady of Valvanera (Anonymous 1929).

Whoever the immediate model may have been, Spain's original Valvanera is a classic Romanesque statue. She is of the whole genre of Mother and Child enthroned, the *sedes sapientiae,* the seat or throne of wisdom. This style reached its peak in the twelfth century, but its origins are much earlier (see Forsyth 1972 for a detailed discussion). Valvanera, as in classic throne-of-wisdom depictions, sits rigidly upright, her thighs at right angles to her body and her lower legs at right angles to her thighs. She is seated on a triumphal chair formed of four stylized eagles as can be discerned by their beaks and claws. She holds the barefooted Christ Child with her right hand on her right lap; her left hand now holds an apple or pomegranate (what it held originally is unknown). She is forty-three inches in height, not counting her removable crown (Pérez Alonso 1971: 43–45).

The devotion to Our Lady of Valvanera spread throughout most of Spain's possessions in the New World by the end of the sixteenth century. There are numerous churches dedicated to her in Colombia, Peru, Puerto Rico, Costa Rica, and Cuba (Pérez Alonso 1971: 299–318). In Argentina, she is the patroness of the Iglesia de Nuestra Señora de Balvanera in Buenos Aires, built between 1799 and 1810. There are two bultos of her and the Christ Child in this church (Fig. 4), where she is also depicted in a stained-glass window (Fig. 5) seated in front of the hollow tree (Luqui Lagleyze 1981: 157–62). A sixteen-page *Novena de Ntra. Señora de Balvanera* was published in Buenos Aires in 1943.

The cult of Valvanera is said to have been instituted in Mexico City dur-

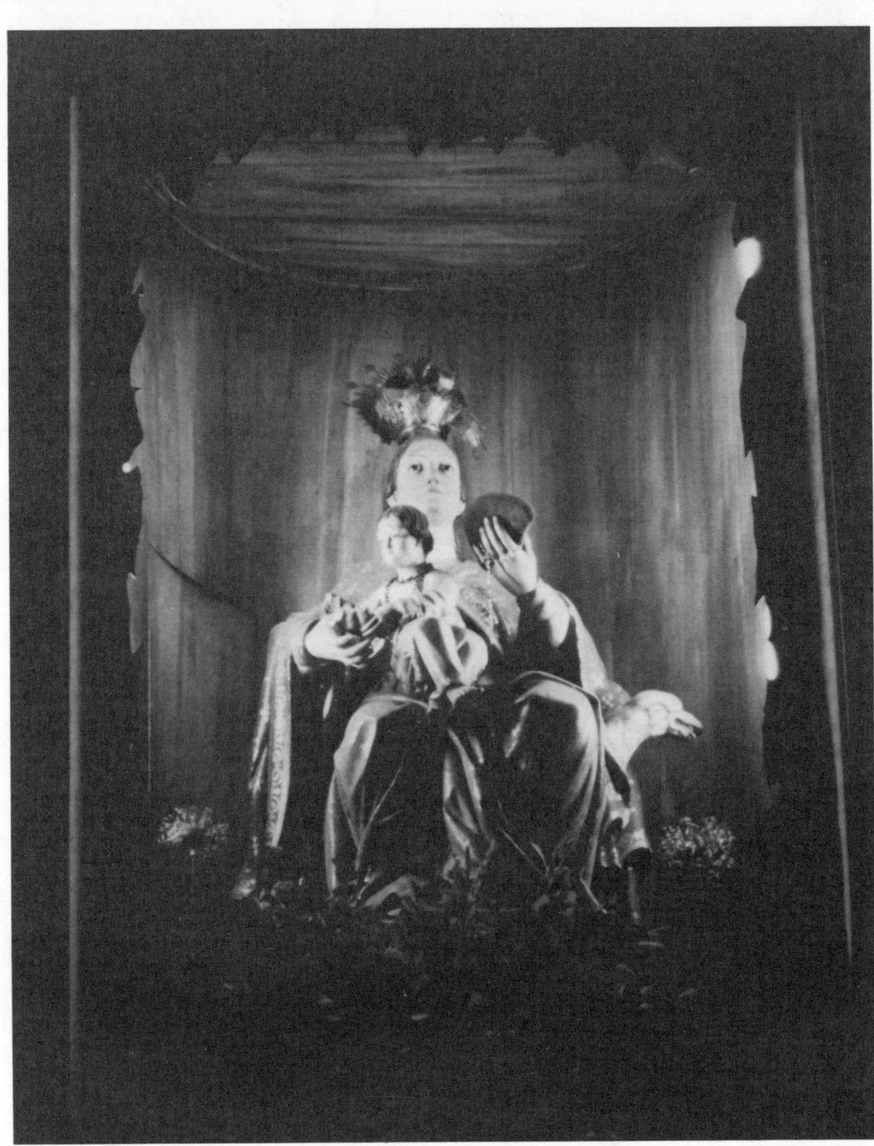

FIGURE 4
Our Lady of Valvanera in her tree-trunk niche above the main altar of the Church of Nuestra Señora de Balvanera, Buenos Aires, Argentina. January 1982. (Giancarlo Puppo photograph.)

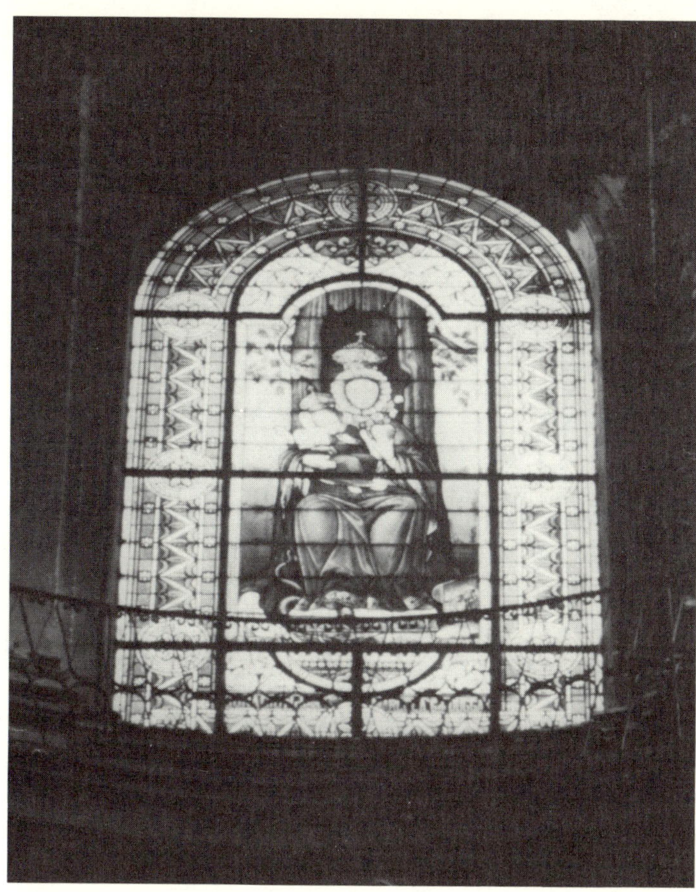

FIGURE 5
Our Lady of Valvanera in a stained glass window in the Church of Nuestra Señora de Balvanera, Buenos Aires, Argentina. January 1982. (Giancarlo Puppo photograph.)

ing the first half of the seventeenth century by Don Francisco Manso de Zúñiga, member of an illustrious Rioja family and a devotee of Our Lady. He was archbishop of Mexico from 1627 to 1636, and he is credited with having begun construction on the Iglesia de Nuestra Señora de Balbanera (Barnes et al. 1981: 115; Pérez Alonso 1971: 307–8). Manuel Toussaint (1967: 191) tells us that the church, with its tile-covered Mudejar bell tower, was completed in 1673.

Sometime after the Mexican Revolution of 1810, the church was taken over by Maronites, members of a Syrian-Lebanese religious order devoted to San Maro. A colony of Syrian-Lebanese Catholics had moved into the neighborhood, now Mexico City's garment district, where they remain to this day. The sculpture of the Virgin of Valvanera that had been in the church was destroyed, and she is represented there now by a large painting hanging above the old main altar.[2]

Since Nuestra Señora de Valvanera was well known in Mexico City in the seventeenth century, it would be easy to conclude that it was from there that the devotion to her came to Aduana. However, one of the most powerful and wealthy figures of early eighteenth-century Alamos and vicinity was

Francisco Elías Gonzáles de Zayas. In 1729, a marriage took place at Alamos between him and María Agueda Campoy, older sister of the Jesuit scholar José Rafael Campoy. The Elías Gonzáles family became owners of two large silver mines and of a large hacienda, and their progeny later intermarried with members of the Almada family, famous in the late eighteenth- and nineteenth-century history of Alamos and Sonora. What is noteworthy is that Francisco Elías Gonzáles de Zayas was a native of the Rioja district in Spain, the homeland of Nuestra Señora de Valvanera. It was very probably he or his descendants who were ultimately responsible for the stone church at Aduana, the statue, the painting, and the devotion, although that is merely an educated guess (Almada 1952: 239; Miles 1962: 11; Stagg 1978: 4).

When Bishop Pedro Tamarón y Romeral visited Aduana in 1760, the Valvanera church was in place—very probably the one that is there today in altered form (Roca 1967: 345). Never a mission, it has always been cared for by secular clergy. The three bells in the bell tower, one of which is dedicated to Nuestra Señora de Balvanera, are dated 1806, 182[0] or 2[1], and 1837. According to historian Francisco Almada (1952: 13), the mines around Aduana were exhausted by 1842.

It is impossible to say how old the organ pipe cactus *(Lemaireocereus thurberi)* is that grows on the outside of the nave wall of the church. It is a large, fully mature plant, however, one that gets at least some water from a drainpipe on the roof directly above it. That the painting in the church shows the Virgin seated on a prickly pear (species *Opuntia)* rather than an organ pipe is of no concern to anyone at Aduana. It is miraculous enough that such a large columnar cactus should take root in the mortared interstices of a stone wall. And what is even more miraculous is the fact that each late afternoon and evening the sinking sun throws the shadow of the organ pipe onto the splayed jamb of the nave window and that the shadow is in the shape of a throne-of-wisdom figure like the original in northern Spain! (Figs. 1 and 3)

Although the New World Valvanera seems to have made a nearly complete transformation only in Aduana in southern Sonora, where the tree has become a cactus and where, like the more famous Guadalupe, she has become a purely native phenomenon complete with her own version of an origin legend and her own miracles, she occurs elsewhere in the Southwest. For reasons that may never be fully explained, she is carved in bas-relief on the upper tier of the stone retable now in the Church of Cristo Rey in Santa Fe, New Mexico (Fig. 6). In this carved depiction, Valvanera holds the Christ Child on her right lap as she is seated in the hollow of a tree. She holds a heart-shaped apple or pear in her left hand as well as what appears to be a lily. The carving is almost an exact copy of the painting of Nuestra Señora de Valvanera as it appears in her church on Calles Valvanera and Uruguay in Mexico City, the church said to have been completed in 1673.

The Santa Fe retable was carved in 1761 by an unknown artist who was sponsored in his efforts by New Mexico's governor Antón Marín del Valle.

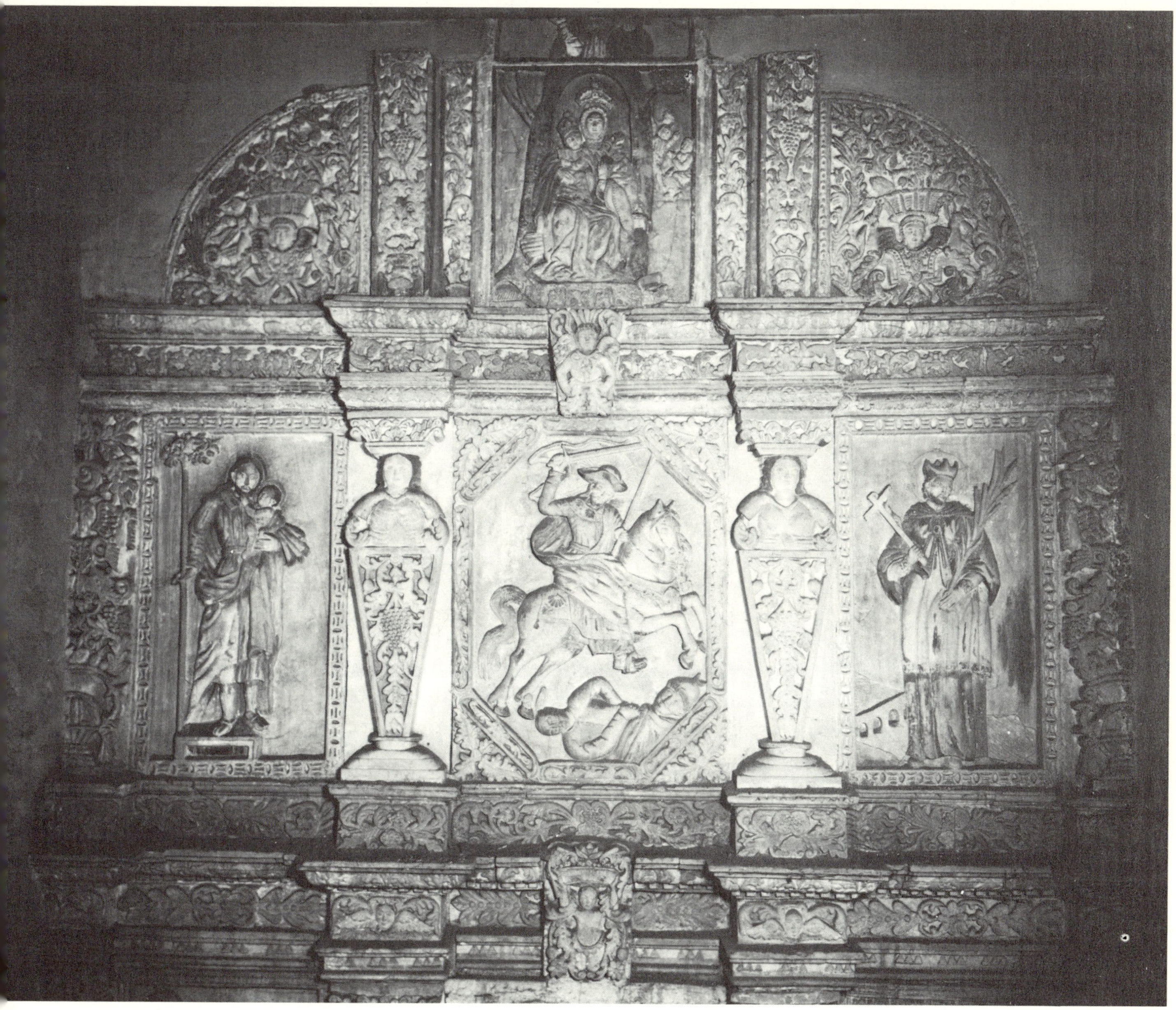

FIGURE 6
Upper two tiers of the 1761 stone retable in the Church of Cristo Rey, Santa Fe, New Mexico. (Elisabeth Kelemen photograph.)

It is unusual in several respects. Pál Kelemen (1954: 249) has remarked: "Our Lady of Valvanera was a favorite of the Benedictine order; it is astonishing to find her in Santa Fe, which was exclusively Franciscan territory, with occasional Jesuit influences." The altarpiece is dedicated to Our Lady of Light, and it is extraordinary to find two representations of the Virgin on a single retable. And E. Boyd (1974: 162) has pointed out that until 1760 there was in New Mexico no tradition of stone altarpieces, but after 1761 and the Lady of Light retable, all subsequent wooden altar screens were influenced by it. Given the virtual identity between the Mexico City painting and the Santa Fe carving of Valvanera, it would seem fair to suggest that the anonymous stone sculptor was brought to Santa Fe, probably from Mexico City, for this specific task.[3]

A painting of Nuestra Señora de Valvanera (Fig. 7), or one at least identified as such by E. Boyd, is on a wooden panel now part of the collections of the Taylor Museum of Colorado Springs, Colorado (Wroth 1982: 145). It is attributed to the santero José Rafael Aragón (ca. 1796–1862) of Santa Fe and Llano Quemado (Córdova), New Mexico. Boyd (1974: 392–407) has written extensively concerning him. His Valvanera painting shows Our Lady holding the Christ Child on her right lap rather than on her left as in the stone retable.

Finally, Nuestra Señora de Valvanera continues to arrive in the Southwest, although more as matter of art than of religious devotion. A 1765 painting of her by Mexican artist Miguel Cabrera, much like that in the Mexico City church and on the Santa Fe retable, is now on loan to the Denver Art Museum. It had hung originally in the Valvanera chapel in the church of San Francisco in Mexico City (Stroessner 1981). An eighteenth-century oil painting of her that originated in Colombia is now in a private collection in southern Arizona. It was displayed in 1976 at the Tucson Museum of Art (1976: No. 29).

The Benedictine friars of Rioja who continue to watch over their tenth-century image of Our Lady of Valvanera will doubtless be pleased to know that devotion to her is alive and well, both in pilgrimage and art, in what those of us living north of the Mexico–United States boundary refer to as the Greater Southwest. She has taken root in the arid soil of northwestern Mexico and the southwestern United States, a lasting reminder of our ancient Hispanic heritage.

NOTES

1. As a complete novice in the field of art history and as a total stranger to the subject of Mariology, I have become greatly indebted to many people in the course of trying to answer the question, "Who was Balvanera?" I have also become more

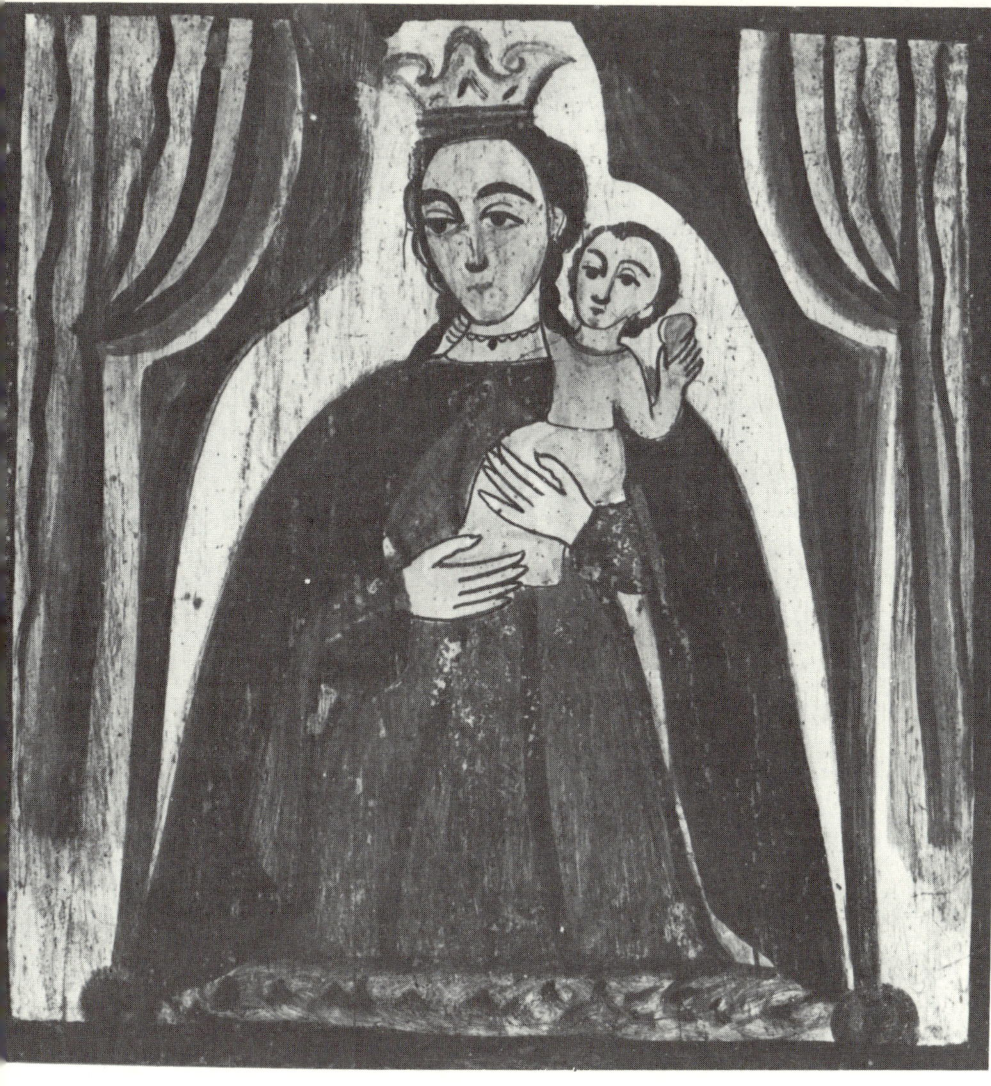

FIGURE 7
Nuestra Señora de Valvanera, painted panel by José Rafael Aragón (ca. 1796–1862), of Santa Fe and Llano Quemado (Córdova), New Mexico. (Taylor Museum Collection 3847, Colorado Springs Fine Arts Center.)

awe-stricken than before about the incredible abilities and knowledge of the late E. Boyd.

Most especially I wish to thank Pál and Elisabeth Kelemen for their encouragement, advice, leads, and photographs. Tucson art historian Gloria Giffords visited the Valvanera church in Mexico City and made available her notes and photographs; architect Giancarlo Puppo of Buenos Aires, Argentina, supplied me with similar materials concerning that city's Valvanera. Tom Naylor and Father Charles Polzer, S.J., of Tucson paid a 1981 visit to the Benedictine monastery of Valvanera in Spain at my urging, and they brought back much valuable information as well as a full bottle of fine brandy made by those good friars under the Valvanera label. William Wroth of the Taylor Museum lent a large helping hand, and in ways both big and small, so did Kieran McCarty, O.F.M., of the University of Arizona, and Norman Neuerburg of Los Angeles, California, a specialist in Spanish colonial art and architectural history. I am further indebted to Darley Gordon of Alamos, Mexico; to Mary Malaby of Tucson; to John Kessell of Albuquerque, New Mexico; and to Cabot Sedgwick of Nogales, Arizona. I thank all of you and apologize for my mistakes and errors in interpretation.

2. Personal communication from Gloria Kay Giffords (1982) and also see Pérez Alonso (1971: 308).

3. The 1761 retable has been the object of considerable attention by art historians, and a good deal has been written on the subject, notably by Boyd (1974: 58, 59, 60, 109, 162, 167, 268); Kelemen (1954, 1977: 54–61); and von Wuthenau (1935).

MARTA WEIGLE

"SOME NEW MEXICO GRANDMOTHERS": A NOTE ON THE WPA WRITERS' PROGRAM IN NEW MEXICO

> Storytelling was looked forward to on winter nights. All the family, big and little gathered around the fire-place, and by the light of a kerosene lamp, or ocote wood "pitch" would shell corn, or the women sewed, while some grandmother or neighbor viejita "Old woman" told stories until time for bed. The beds were made down on the floor. The colcons "Matress *[sic]*" were stuffed with wool, and folded on bancos against the wall in the day time. At night they were layed on the floor.
>
> The stories that were told by these grandmothers were religious ones. About Santos, and the miracles they use *[sic]* to perform. And about brujas "Witches", and those who had been embrujada "bewitched."
>
> —Annette Hesch Thorp, "Stories," 17 December 1940, p. 1.

BETWEEN SEPTEMBER 1940 AND JULY 1941, WPA writer Annette Hesch Thorp listened to and recorded such stories, together with the life histories of their tellers, and submitted colloquial and descriptive pieces to the Santa Fe office of the Work Projects Administration's Writers' Program, headed by Charles Ethrige Minton. When he took over the newly reorganized New Mexico Federal Writers' Project from Aileen Nusbaum in September 1939, Minton's primary task was to oversee completion of the long-delayed state guide, *New Mexico: A Guide to the Colorful State,* finally published by Hastings House, New York, in August 1940.[1] Freed of this chore, he had initiated a number of smaller projects by fall 1940.

In a November 7, 1940, letter to national Writers' Program director John D. Newsom, Minton detailed twelve fledgling endeavors, four dealing solely with Hispano culture in northern New Mexico:

1. *Las Placitas.* Field writer Lou Sage Batchen had collected folklore and ethnohistory from these communities in the foothills of the Sandia Mountains. Minton revised Batchen's collection and submitted a three-hundred-page illustrated manuscript to Washington on November 6, 1941. This was returned on January 27, 1942, as a "fascinating and unusual work," ineffectively

presented, which probably could not be published "due to war condition." A children's book adapting the Placitas material, *Before Your Time,* was also planned but was never even begun.[2]

2. *Deep Village, the Story of Córdova, New Mexico.* By November 1940, Lorin W. Brown, who had submitted Córdova folklife manuscripts since 1936, was working on the nationally sponsored History of Grazing project. Thus, Minton claimed, "although there is enough material for a small book on Cordova, we should like to round it out with other material of a certain kind, which probably cannot be done until the grazing study is much further along than it is now." In a letter of May 27, 1941, he noted that the manuscript "should be rounded out with something about the children for two reasons: a) because it is lacking in that kind of material; b) because the book is not large enough as it stands." By the status report of November 13, 1941, Brown was at work on the nationally instigated *Hands That Built America* volume. He left the Writers' Program soon after, and the first draft of *Deep Village* was never finished and sent to Washington (Brown 1978: 19–29, 259–64).

3. *Alabados* (and other materials on folk religion) *from Taos County.* Apparently these were to be a compilation of the hymns, prayers, and accounts of village and Penitente Brotherhood worship collected by Reyes N. Martínez, primarily in Arroyo Hondo. Martínez had been on the New Mexico Federal Writers' Project and then in the Writers' Program since 1936 but was given an eighteen months' furlough on May 27, 1941, when Minton wrote that "we have not received all the material we should like to have on this, but if the worker does not return, and nothing is added, it will still be possible to publish a booklet whenever I can get to it and get it ready" (Weigle with Powell 1982: 68, 69–70, 71–72).[3]

4. *Some New Mexico Grandmothers.* "We have wanted to get the life stories of several of the old crones in the villages before it was too late. Several of them have died, and they are going fast. However, there are still some of them alive whose memory is adequate and who are still able to furnish material about their long life, together with folk lore of various kinds. . . . We believe this book will be of national interest if we can get what we want, but it will be a year or more before we shall know whether we have enough material of the kind we want to justify national publication." The widowed Annette Hesch Thorp, then of Box 104, Santa Fe, New Mexico, qualified for the job and was hired to do the interviews.

Annette Hesch's Austrian father was a sheep rancher near Palma, New Mexico, but it was from her Irish mother's side that she had acquired the nickname "Blarney" (Thorp with Clark 1941: photo opposite p. 64). She married N. Howard (Jack) Thorp in 1903. A composer and collector of cowboy songs and stories from the earliest days of their marriage and before, Mr. Thorp was later employed by both the New Mexico Federal Writers' Project and the Writers' Program until his death at age seventy-three on June 4, 1940. Most of Jack Thorp's submissions concerned cowboy life and lore, but

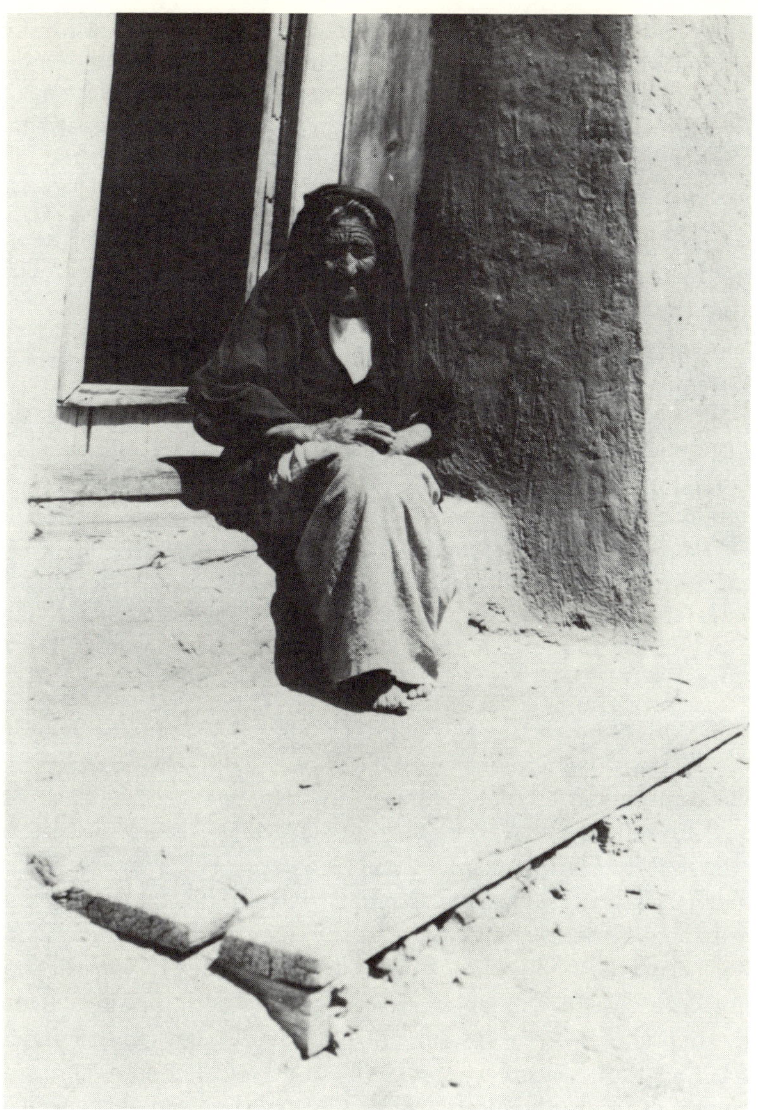

FIGURE 1
Unidentified old woman. (Photo Collections, No. 43740, Museum of New Mexico.)

several described Hispano folklife, for example, one from November 11, 1937, which was entitled "A Wedding Feast" and was "taken from Annettes Thorp's collection of New Mexico, Folklore *[sic]*." Mrs. Thorp apparently used this collection and her knowledge of Spanish and Hispanic New Mexicans when she joined the Writers' Program soon after her husband's death. The couple had been impoverished, and she had relief status on the program.

From her first extant submission, a reconstructed conversation with eighty-year-old Catalina Viareal, Annette Thorp clearly tried to fill the job the way Minton envisioned it in his letter of November 7, 1940:

> This is very slow work, for it means many visits for the most meager results and copious immaterial conversations and strayings from the point in order to get

> the outline, as well as any stories about the early days. All this is in fluent idiomatic Spanish, the interviewer being an elderly woman who is sympathetic and interested; also she is free to go to any locality where the material can be obtained. She must spend hours getting acquainted and establishing a friendly relationship, getting behind walls of reserve and suspicion and establishing a kindly free exchange.

At least one side of this "kindly free exchange" is seen in the opening paragraphs of two early, less polished pieces, transcribed below without change from the originals:

> There was no respect for the old any more, and she was muy vieja. "Very old." She did not like the way young people behaved now days. When she was young, children always said. Si Señora, or No Señora. Now if you speak to them, they answer. Si, No or what do you want. Said Cesaria Gallegos, who lives with her son Antonio, and his wife. (No. 4, 23 September 1940)
>
> Women think they work now days. Pero no, they don't know what work is. The Americano's have made it so easy for them now. They would die if they had to work like she did when she was young, and strong. Said Chana. A very old woman who lives in the country with her granddaughter. (No. 5, 8 October 1940)

This colloquial, conversational style grew more impersonal and straightforwardly narrative and descriptive as Thorp gained experience.

Thorp submitted manuscripts of some three to six pages almost every week, but she must have worked slowly. On May 27, 1941, Minton reported to Newsom that "we continue to receive copy on ["Some New Mexico Grandmothers"] from the worker assigned to it, but it is far from being ready, since only about one-fourth or more of the material has been collected." On July 24, he notified Newsom of new cuts in the state Writers' Program, including "the elderly woman who has been gathering material for the Grandmothers book . . . [who was] cancelled out because she had managed to scrape together $200 toward a down payment on a little house, after nine months of great sacrifice and denial." Minton's final mention of the proposed volume, which was to have included photographs, was a bitter note in a letter to Newsom dated November 13, 1941:

> Almost half of this material was in when the writer who was working on it received her 403 [notice of termination] because she had managed to save $200 toward a down payment on a little adobe house. The possession of this vast wealth made her ineligible for WPA employment, so nothing further has been done with this exceptionally interesting material.

Nevertheless, some effort was made, probably after Thorp's tenure, to refine and disguise her pieces and to assemble them into a book (Nos. 16 and 22). Thorp's rewritten life stories apparently were to have followed Lorin W. Brown's accounts of Tía Lupe, Guadalupe Martínez—wise woman,

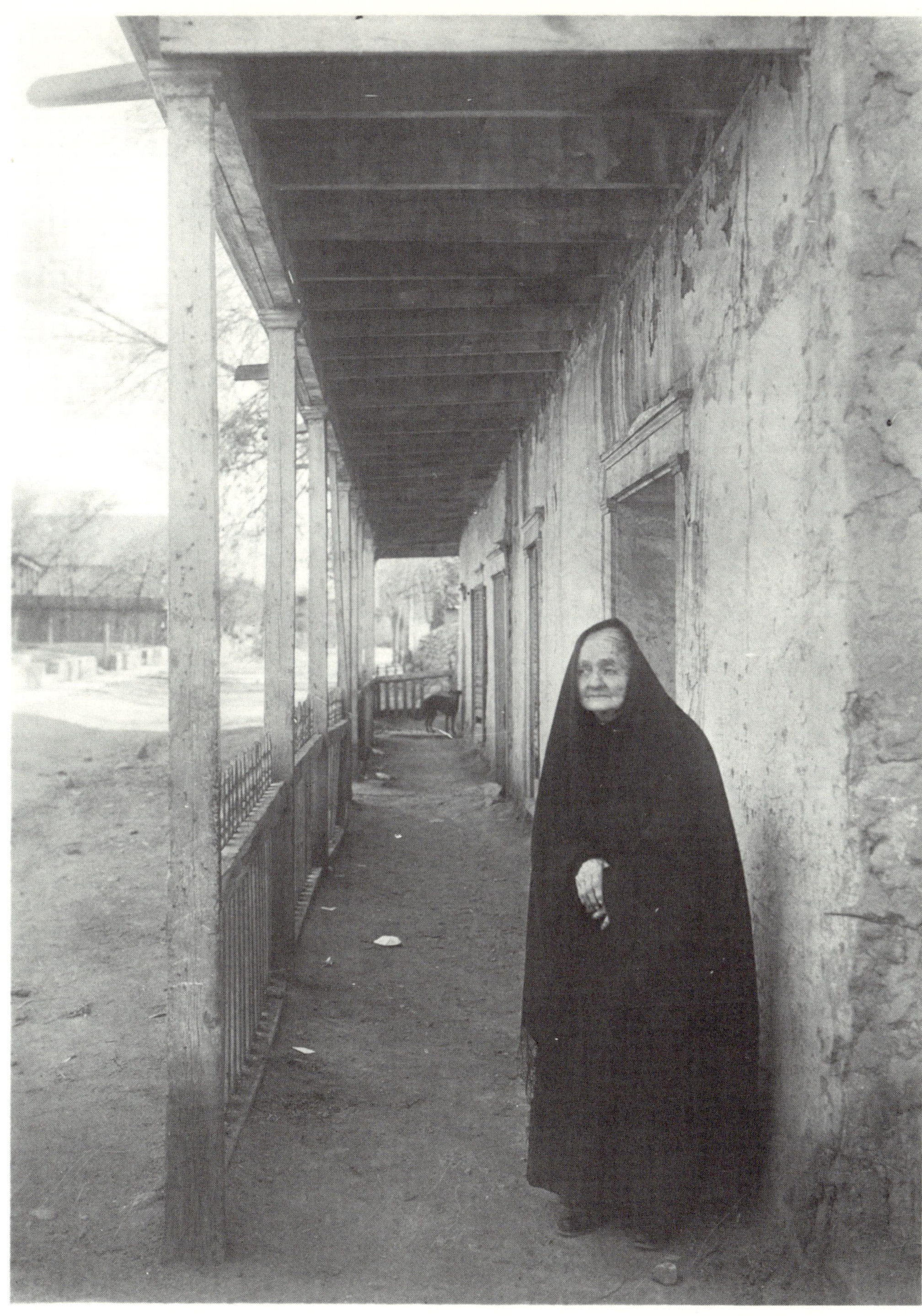

FIGURE 2
Unidentified old woman at the corner of Shelby and Water Streets, Santa Fe. Photo by T. Harmon Parkhurst. (Photo Collections, No. 14022, Museum of New Mexico.)

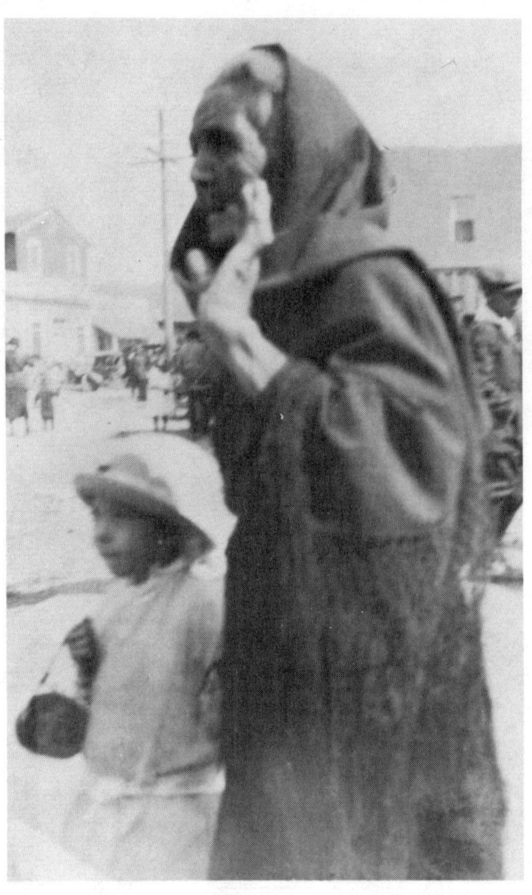

FIGURE 3
Unidentified old woman and child. (Photo Collections, No. 42241, Museum of New Mexico.)

storyteller, and keeper of the church and its santos in Córdova, New Mexico,[4] and possibly other Córdovans, but such a manuscript never was sent to Washington. Until recently, unfortunately, the voices of all these "New Mexico Grandmothers" have been stilled and almost forgotten. For, as grandmother Tita observed (No. 18, 1 October 1940, p. 5):

> Yes she has always lived in the little three room house her mother left her. She does not like the way things are now days, but thinks old times were better. Why, nowdays, the Mexicano's want to be Americano's, and the Americano's want to be Mexicano's.

NOTES

1. Research for this paper was sponsored by a National Endowment for the Humanities grant, "Governmental Support of the Arts in New Mexico, 1933–1943" (RS-00056-79-0589), to Weigle (co-director for the verbal arts) and William Wroth (co-director for the visual arts). Both Mary Powell and Lois Vermilya-Weslowski served as Weigle's research assistants during part of the project. This

grant made it possible to expand and correct earlier "Notes on Federal Project Number One and the Federal Writers' Project in New Mexico" (in Brown 1978: 239–52). For a brief updated history of the FWP and the Writers' Program in New Mexico, see Weigle with Powell 1982 and Weigle and Fiore 1982: 50–56, 68–70, 128. Administrative documents are found in Record Group No. 69: "Records of the Work Projects Administration," National Archives, Washington, D.C. Because these sources are not yet readily accessible in New Mexico, exact citations will not be given.

2. Minton did not rework Batchen's material again until he wrote *Juan of Santo Niño: An Authentic Account of Pioneer Life in New Mexico, 1863–1864* (1973). Selections from Batchen's original submissions were published in *Las Placitas: Historical Facts and Legends* (1972).

3. Between 1936 and 1941, Martínez submitted about 364 items, among them handwritten texts and translations for some 90 *alabados* and 12 *oraciones*. There are also sixteen or more pieces on village religious customs, perhaps half dealing with the Penitente Brotherhood. Most of his handwritten work is in the Library of Congress, Manuscript Division, Washington, D.C. Also see, for example, Anonymous 1975; Shalkop 1969; and three folklife books by Martínez's sister, Cleofas M. Jaramillo (1941, 1942, 1955).

4. An anonymous, edited account of "Tía Lupe" and her stories, done on the same typewriter and in format identical with "Some of Tía Lupe's Contemporaries: True Stories of Some New Mexico Grandmothers," is numbered pp. 96–116 (Brown 1978: 129–46, 264–No. 116). Apparently none of the rich folktales told to Bright Lynn between 1937 and 1938 by Guadalupe Baca de Gallegos, a grand old lady of West Las Vegas, New Mexico, were planned for inclusion with Tía Lupe and her contemporaries (Weigle 1980–1981).

INVENTORY OF ANNETTE HESCH THORP'S WRITERS' PROGRAM MANUSCRIPTS

The manuscript's title is followed by a brief description of its contents, the informant, number of pages, and date(s) of submission and processing. *MNM* followed by an identifying number refers to vertical files in the Museum of New Mexico, History Library, Santa Fe. *NMSRC* identifies materials in the New Mexico State Records Center and Archives, Santa Fe, where WPA documents are stored by file (first title) and folder (second title). Some NMSRC records are simply filed by number, referring to designated B.C. numbers assigned by Gilberto Benito Córdova in his limited pioneer inventory, *Bibliography of Unpublished Materials Pertaining to Hispanic Culture in the New Mexico WPA Writers' Files* (1972).

1. "Amalia." Life history, anecdotes about miserly woman who lived alone by the river in Albuquerque and was reputed to be quite wealthy in real estate. Amalia Lucero (ca. seventy) was the daughter of Juan Lucero and Rufina Montoya of Corrales, likewise rich but miserly. Told by Albuquerquean Vicenta (seventy-six or seventy-

eight), daughter of Juan José Sanchez and Juanita Chávez. 4 pp., 6-17-41; 5 pp., 6-24-41; 6 pp., 7-1-41. MNM 5-5-53 No. 7.

2. "Casorio's 'Weddings.' " Customs from courtship through the *prendorio* ("receiving the bride") to the wedding day. 5 pp., 12-10-40. MNM 5-5-52 No. 67. (Also see N. Howard Thorp, "A Wedding Feast," 4 pp., 11-11-37, MNM 5-5-23, which begins: "Taken from Annettes Thorp's collection of New Mexico, Folklore, is this discription of an elaborate wedding feast, celebrating nuptials of a young couple of wealthy Mexicans, held on one of the old ranches *[sic].*")

3. "Catalina Viareal." Conversations with Catalina (ca. eighty), daughter of Antonio Viareal and María Vigil, of Alcalde. Planting customs and land *partido* ("shares"); description of her house; legend told by her grandmother about *El Santo Niño de Las Buenas Obras* ("The Holy Child of Good Deeds") who appeared in the placita. 5 pp., 9-17-40. MNM 5-5-52 No. 68.

4. "Cesaria Gallegos." Conversation with Cesaria (ca. one hundred), daughter of Vicente Ortega and Dolores López of Agua Fria and widow of Antonio Gallegos. Food preparation; piñon gathering; "Mexican remedies"; popular beliefs about Friday activities. 4 pp., 9-23-40. NMSRC Cultural History II: Frontier Stories. (Reprinted in Weigle with Powell 1982: 73–74.)

5. "Chana." Conversation at Jacona with Chana (Cresenciana) Atencio (ca. ninety), daughter of Policarpio Montoya and Antonia Valencia (both "born and raised in El Sombrio in La Canada de la Santa Cruz") of El Santo Niño on the Santa Cruz River and widow of Manuel Atencio. Life history; adobe plastering; food preparation; respect of young for old; beliefs about *animas* ("souls of purgatory"); *descansos* (roadside crosses); Santiago day dances and *corrida del gallo;* extensive materials on fall *mielero* ("molasses") dances; molasses cooking, use, and trading; planting customs; *Salinas* ("salt lakes") trips; position and activities of *Resador,* who usually learned prayers, hymns, and lay rites from his father; four stanzas (Spanish and English) of *La Alba* ("Song of Dawn"); *ollas* (pots); *bailes* (dances). 3 pp., 10-8-40; 3 pp., 10-15-40; 4 pp., 10-22-40; 4 pp., 10-29-40; 4 pp., 11-5-40; 5 pp., 12-3-40 [was to have been continued]. MNM 5-5-52 No. 71.

6. "The Curandera" [continued as "Remedios"]. General description of curer-midwives' activities and various *remedios; plateros* who made copper bracelets and silver rings called *anillos de corimiento* ("neuralgia rings"); *mal ojo* ("evil eye") in children. 4 pp., 11-19-40; 4 pp., 11-26-40. MNM 5-5-52 No. 70.

7. "Fabiana: Witch Story." Village woman bewitched *(maleficio)* by stranger Fabiana ("about middle age, but very dark and ugly"), diagnosed by hot springs, cured by old Pueblo Indian woman; husband's cows bewitched, and he kills Fabiana while she is an owl. Told by Juliana Martínez (seventy or seventy-two) of Agua Fria. 3 pp., 4-1-41; 5 pp., 4-8-41. MNM 5-5-52 No. 69.

8. "Lina." Conversation with Lina (Marcelina), widow of Tiofilo Garcia, born and raised in Pojoaque by aunt, Josefa Vigil, after parents' death. Life history; descriptions of *misa de cabo de año* ("mass on first anniversary of a death"); cleaning, baking; godparents *(comadre* and *compadre)*; saints' days *(fiestas)*; aunt's legend about San Pedro's cure of woman some sixty to sixty-five years earlier. 3 pp., 12-31-40; 3 pp., 1-7-41; 3 pp., 1-14-41; 3 pp., undated; 3 pp., 2-4-41. MNM 5-5-52 No. 74. [Apparently missing: B.C. 537, " 'Lina'—A number of baptismal traditions are

described," 1-21-40, MNM, 616 words; also listed under "File of Annette H. Thorp" as "Lina. More about god-parents' duties."]

9. "Manuela." Life history of Manuela, daughter of Liandro Chávez and Juana Padilla of Galisteo, whose father would not let her marry. At age sixty-three, she finally married Donicio Aragón and moved to town. Told by Albuquerquean Vicenta (seventy-six or seventy-eight), daughter of Juan José Sanchez and Juanita Chávez. 5 pp., 5-20-41; 6 pp., 5-27-41; 6 pp., 6-3-41. MNM 5-5-52 No. 72.

10. "Nuestra Señora del Rosario." Legend about her patronage of travelers on freight trains to Mexico. Handwritten note: "Part of Chana material, to be included in part about stories around the fireside. These were told to Mrs. Thorp by Antonia Vigil of San Ildefonso, who died about 10 years ago." 2 pp., 12-30-40. MNM 5-5-52 No. 73.

11. "Partera. 'Midwife.' " Story of midwife Candelaria, an older single woman who raised the baby of a woman who died in childbirth. Told by Marcelina, who heard it from her aunt, Josefa Vigil of Pojoaque. 5 pp., 3-18-41. MNM 5-5-53 No. 8.

12. "Parteras. 'Midwife.' " Beliefs and practices of Juana Romero, who attended Lina's children's births. Told by Marcelina (sixty-eight), niece of Josefa Vigil of Pojoaque. Typescripts with extensive ink editing: 3 pp., 2-25-41; 4 pp., 3-4-41; 4 pp., 3-1-40; 5 pp. rev. typescripts of these. MNM 5-5-53 No. 8.

13. "The pie and the plate (A witch story)." Legend of girl bewitched by a neighbor woman and healed by male Indian "*arbolario* ('Witchdoctor')." 3 pp., undated. MNM 5-5-53 No. 6.

14. "Remedios." Ten healing herbs and their uses. From Marcelina (sixty-eight), niece of Josefa Vigil of Pojoaque. 4 pp., 3-25-41. MNM 5-5-53 No. 3.

15. "Satan and the Girl. Story." Legend. "This story was told to young girls by their grandmothers, as a warning of what might happen to them if they talked to, or went out with boys." Told by Juliana Martínez (seventy or seventy-two) of Agua Fria. 2 pp., 4-1-41. MNM 5-5-53 No. 4.

16. "Some New Mexico Grandmothers: Chapter on Parteras." Prefinal revision No. 1 (see No. 12 above). 8 pp., 3-17-41. NMSRC 538 [B.C. 538].

17. "Stories." Storytelling by old women; witch beliefs. 2 pp., 12-17-40. MNM 5-5-53 No. 5. (First page reprinted in Weigle with Powell 1982: 73.)

18. "Tita." Conversation with Manuelita (Tita) Romero—mother Natalia Urioste, father unknown—about her "sad life." Raised by "Martin El cojo, 'The lame one' and his wife Gregoria," who knew *remedios;* accounts of *maleficio* ("witchcraft"), including her late husband Lino. 5 pp., 10-1-40. MNM 5-5-52 No. 75.

19. "Velorio." Penitente Brotherhood beliefs and rites surrounding sickness, death, wakes, and burial. Account from Barbarita Nieto (daughter of Luis Chávez and Manuela Gallegos) of Cedar Grove in the San Pedro Mountains about her Penitente husband Merejildo Nieto's death. 5 pp., 2-11-41, 2 pp. with note on the "Mortaja. 'Shroud.' " and pure salt for religious ceremonies, 2-25-41. MNM 5-5-53 No. 2.

20. "Vicenta." Conversation with Vicenta Sanchez (seventy-six or seventy-eight) of Albuquerque—daughter of Juan José Sanchez and Juanita Chávez, granddaughter of Moises and Francisca Chávez, all of Peña Blanca. Family history and legends; customs on Sundays and feast days; children's games; cheese making; wine making; *colchas* ("bedspreads"); Holy Week exchange of food; story about buffalo hunters

and woman who went on a hunt, told by her grandmother—with handwritten note: "This is an early instance, usually thought to be of very recent occurrence, when the wife went out to provide for her family while the husband stayed home." 6 pp., 4-15-41; 4 pp., 4-22-41; 4 pp., 4-29-41; 4pp., 5-6-41; 5 pp., 5-13-41. MNM 5-5-53 No. 1.

21. "Witch Stories. The story of a headache." Woman bewitched by neighbor woman, cured by her son breaking the neighbor's clay figures. Handwritten note: "Part of Chana's biography, to be included in section that mentions story telling. Told to Mrs. Thorp by Antonia Vigil of San Ildefonso, who died about 10 years ago." 2 pp., undated. NMSRC 539 [B.C. 539].

22. Anonymous. "Some of Tía Lupe's Contemporaries: True Stories of Some New Mexico Grandmothers," final edited version of various items above. Cover plus pp. 234–311, undated. NMSRC 17 [B.C. 17]. Contents:

a. "Lina," pp. 234–60. Introduces Marcelina as "born and raised near Tía Lupe." Combines Nos. 6, 8 (including B.C. 537), 11, 12 (16), 14.

b. "Amalia Ceferino," pp. 261–69. From No. 1. (B.C. 1.)

c. "Manuela Gonzales," pp. 270–78. From No. 9. (B.C. 11.)

d. "Vicenta Montoya," pp. 279–93. From No. 20. (B.C. 22.)

e. "Barbarita Naranjo," pp. 294–300. From No. 19, including "Note on *Mortajas.*" (B.C. 4)

f. "Tita," pp. 301–4. From No. 18. (B.C. 21.)

g. "Catalina Padilla," pp. 305–7. From No. 4. (B.C. 5.)

h. "Antonia Ortega," pp. 308–11. From No. 3. (B.C. 3.)

CHARLES L. BRIGGS

A CONVERSATION WITH SAINT ISIDORE: THE TEACHINGS OF THE ELDERS

IN 1972, WITH THE ACTIVE ENCOURAGEMENT of E. Boyd, I began a study of the wood carvers of Córdova, New Mexico, especially the López family.[1] Although only nineteen years old and a sophomore in college, my youth and inexperience turned into great assets in Córdova. I spoke Spanish, but I lacked the knowledge and practical experience requisite to being considered a full-fledged adult in the community. Accordingly, the Lópezes and another family informally adopted me and set about the difficult task of teaching me what it meant to be a Córdovan. They involved me in activities like gardening, cutting firewood, wood carving, singing, and dancing. Of equal importance, however, were the many hours we spent discussing the wisdom of *los viejitos de antes,* "the elders of bygone days." Fortunately, I was able to tape-record quite a number of these pedagogical dialogues, and the transcripts are most telling with respect to what these Córdovan elders wished to teach me and how they conducted their "classes."

The following transcript was among the most provocative. The conversation provides a striking illustration of the sort of knowledge that *Mexicanos*[2] deem crucial to comprehending the role of a given saint. It took place a few weeks into my first major field stay in Córdova.

The two elders, whom I shall call Guadalupe and Manuel, called me *hijo,* "son," and I addressed them as *mamá,* "mother," and *papá,* "father." As one of the principal *rezadores* or prayer leaders in the community, Manuel was especially concerned with teaching me central Hispanic moral and religious tenets. We were sitting at their kitchen table as we spoke, and Manuel was selecting *alabados,* "hymns,"[3] from one of his hand-copied notebooks, then singing them and explaining their significance. Having long been fascinated with Saint Isidore, I asked him to sing the hymn that venerates this saint.

MANUEL:
Esta es la tonada:
San Isidro labrador
patrón de los labradores
liberta nuestro sembrado
de langostias y temblores.

MANUEL:
This is the melody:
Saint Isidore the husbandman
Patron of husbandmen
Free our fields
From locusts and storms.

Y luego dijo
Por el gran merecimiento
con que te adoró el Senti *[sic]*
liberta nuestro sembrado
San Isidro labrador.

Por el sudor y trabajo
con que fuistes fatigado
San Isidro Labrador
liberta nuestro sembrado.
Y dice la verdad, ¿no?
CLB:
Yah, yo creo.
MANUEL:
Oh sí. En aquellos tiempos este
San Isidro, lo traiban en la labor.
Digo que aquellos tiempos estaban
muy secos, y cuando sacaban este,
este San Isidro y a San Antonio
de Padua que está aquí en la
capilla pa' 'lla, por los labores
'onde había frijoles y trigos,
todo all'
en la . . ., pa' 'lla en la
sierra. Y al momento se venía
el agua. Por ahora—
GUADALUPE:
Tenían los velorios allá en
un tapectio.
MANUEL:
Sí, velorios. Y ahora no hay
quien saque un imagen de esos
a pasearlo en la labor, no. Y
no más saca úno este imagen muy
milagroso y San Antonio, y al
ratito, mire, está el agua
(bate las manos).
Llenaron los frijolares asina.
Trigo; vino una cuarta al
espiga. Asina de larga, de
aquí donde está el pajón pa'
'rriba. Y, y . . ., 'ta mi
papá era vivo. Y venía y me
decía, "A ver, mi 'jito," cuando
estaba [?] madurando, "agarrate

And then he said
By the great merit
With which you worshipped the Lord
Free our fields
Saint Isidore the husbandman.

By the sweat and toil
Which had fatigued you
Saint Isidore the husbandman
Free our fields.
And he tells the truth, doesn't he?
CLB:
Yeah, I think so.
MANUEL:
Oh yes. In those days this
Saint Isidore, they took him out
into the fields. I say that it
was very dry in those days, and
when they took Saint Isidore and
Saint Anthony of Padua, who is here
in the chapel, up there, through
the fields, where there were
beans and wheat, everything up
in the . . ., up there in the
mountains. And the rain came
right away. By now—
GUADALUPE:
They held the wakes there in a
little enclosure.
MANUEL:
Yes, wakes. And now nobody
would take one of these images
around the fields. And a person
just takes out this very
miraculous image and that of
Saint Anthony, and, look, the rain
comes very quickly *(claps hands)*.
They filled the beanfields
like this. Wheat; each spike
produced a handful. It was this
long from the stalk here
to the top. And, and . . ., my
father was still alive. And he would
come and say to me, "Let's
see, son," when it was [?] ripening,

una espiga." Y la agarraba, estaba madura, ves, y lo hacía asina *(triando el trigo en las palmas)*. Y luego soplaba que saliera la paja. Arriba de un puño de trigo de pura, pura espiga. Y ahora no. Así son las espigitas. ¿Qué será? No tiene fé alguno. No tiene fé, no tiene esperanza de que, de que Dios le puede dar de la nada. Y por eso compusieron este alabado. Y no más llegaban cantándolo all', hacían un velorio en la noche. Iba mucha gente, all' cenabamos. Y otro día lo traiban *a pie*. No, no caballo, no, nada, puro *work, work* pa' 'ca.

CLB:
¿Y velaron a San Isidro?

MANUEL:
Sí, sí. Y allá donde estaba, iba mucha gente. Pues, si no hubo lluvia el mismo día, para otro día. ¡Se plantaban las lluvias! Y aquí hubieron unos velorios [?]. Y dice all' en el alabado, que más que pise el hombre la mata, con el poder de Dios *(castañetea los dedos)* se endereza pa' 'ribba.

Y antes [?] la gente le pisaba asina. Muchos hombres dicen asina, "Oh, que no lo pisen, que no se levanta." La poca fé. All' lo dice, poca fé el hombre.

CLB:
¿Cuándo era la última vez que rezaron el velorio de San Isidro?

MANUEL:

"get a spike." And he would get it, it was ripe you see, and he would go like this *(threshing the wheat between his palms)*. And then he would blow off the chaff. More than a handful of the pure, pure grain of the wheat. But no more. The spikes are like this. What could it be? Nobody has faith. People don't have faith, they don't believe that God can give them anything. And that's why they composed this alabado. And when they would arrive there, singing it, they would hold a wake in the night. A lot of people used to go, and we used to eat up there. And the next day they would bring it on foot, not on horseback, no, nothing, just work, work back here.

CLB:
And they held a wake for Saint Isidore?

MANUEL:
Yes, yes. And a lot of people used to go up there. Well, if the rain didn't come that same day, [it came] the next day. The rains sure came! And there used to be such wakes here [?]. And it says there in the alabado, that even though man may step on the plants, through the power of God *(snaps fingers)* they straighten out. And before [?] the people used to step on them like this. Many men say, "Oh, don't step on them, they won't come up." So little faith. There it says, man has little faith.

CLB:
When was the last time that they prayed the wake for Saint Isidore?

MANUEL:

Uh, hace yo creo como, ¿cuántos
años? Como, desde mil novecientos,
yo creo, treintai—
GUADALUPE:
Treintaidos.
MANUEL:
Ocho, ¿no? O treintaidos?
GUADALUPE:
Yah.
MANUEL:
Yah. De all' pa' 'ca no, ves.
No hay fé, se acaba la fé.
Muchos dicen, "Oh, yo no siembro
porque se seca." Pero no.
La voluntad de mi Dios dice
claro, a los arcobispos all' en
su evangelio, que dice mi Señor
Jesucristo en su evangelio que
no, no sea hombre de poca fé.
Que tire su semilla, para que
levante y que lo asista. Ye de all'
vivirá el pecador, vive el hombre,
dice. Y es verdad. Y ahora
no quiere sembrar nadie, no más
¿sabes qué? Alfalfa, pa' 'l
caballo, por la vaca. Pues no más.
De modo que está muy diferente a
aquellos tiempos. Y luego a ver
lo que dice aquí:
Porque estás [comisionado][4]
por patrón de la labor
liberta nuestro sembrado
San Isidro labrador.

Porque fuistes anunciado
  Lo anunciaron a él, ve
de Dios por trabajador
liberta nuestro sembrado
San Isidro labrador.

Por el gran merecimiento
que cautivastes el terreno
liberta nuestro sembrado
San Isidro labrador.

Uh, it's been about, how many years?
About, since nineteen, I think,
thirty—
GUADALUPE:
Thirty-two.
MANUEL:
Eight, right? Or thirty-two?
GUADALUPE:
Yeah.
MANUEL:
Yeah. Since then no, you see. There
is no faith, the faith is
lost. Many say, "Oh, I don't
plant because it dries up." But
no. The will of my God clearly
says, to his archbishops in his
gospel, that my Lord Jesus Christ
says in his gospel
not to be a man of little faith.
Throw your seeds, so that they
will come up, and take care of
them. And that's how the sinner will
live, how man lives, he says. And it's true.
And now nobody wants to plant, [they
plant] only, you know what? Alfalfa,
for the horse, for the cow.
That's all. So it's very different
from those days. So let's see what
it says here:
Because you are [commissioned][4]
As the patron of farmwork
Deliver our fields
Saint Isidore the husbandman.

Because you were called
  They called him you see.
By God as a worker
Deliver our fields
Saint Isidore the husbandman.

By the great merit
With which you cultivated the land
Free our fields
Saint Isidore the husbandman.

Por el temor que causastes
a tu devoción por tu
  honora
liberta nuestro sembrado
San Isidro labrador.
  ¡Muy largo!
CLB:
  Yah. Muy bonito.
MANUEL:
Del ladrón acostumbrado
y sin temor al Señor
  El lo hacía de todo corazón,
  ve.
liberta nuestro sembrado
San Isidro labrador

Pues el Señor te escogió
como patrón de la labor
temiendo las opidemias *[sic]*
  Ese es la opidemia que venga
  un granizo, y que no tema
  del opidemia, dice.
CLB:
  No.
MANUEL:
  Sí. Tener fé, ¿ve?
CLB:
  Yah.
MANUEL:
San Isidro labrador.

Pues el Señor se determinó
Por el gran merecimiento
Te mandó un mal vecino
  Ve, el mal vecino es como
  si esté yo y usted, fueramos,
  y vivieramos cerquita.
  Y él huyó del vecino, a ver
  lo que dice all'. El no
  quiso estar viviendo, era
  un mal vecino, ve

San Isidro labrador.

Tempestades y granizo

By the fear which you caused
To your devotion for the sake of
  your honor
Free our fields
Saint Isidore the husbandman.
  [This hymn is] so long!
CLB:
  Yeah. Very beautiful.
MANUEL:
Accustomed to thieves
And without fearing the Lord
  He did it with all his heart,
  you see.
Free our fields.
Saint Isidore the husbandman.

Well, the Lord chose you
As the patron of farmwork
Fearing plagues
  The plague is a hailstorm,
  and he doesn't fear a
  plague, it says.
CLB:
  No.
MANUEL:
  Yes. To have faith, you see?
CLB:
  Yeah.
MANUEL:
Saint Isidore the husbandman.

Well, the Lord determined
Because of [your] great merit
He sent you a bad neighbor
  You see, a bad neighbor is
  as if you and I were, if we
  lived very close. And he
  flew from the neighbor, see
  what it says there. He didn't
  want to be living [there],
  he was a bad neighbor,
  you see
Saint Isidore the husbandman.

Storms and hail

All' lo va diciendo, ve.
CLB:
Yah.
MANUEL:
Que daña nuestra labor
liberta nuestro sembrado
San Isidro labrador.

Por ti esperemos ser felices
Y llevar cosecha en unión
Mira que, ¡este santo sí está
milagroso!
Por tu misercordia
San Isidro labrador.

Por ti esperemos Señor
El le dice San Isidro a
mi Señor Jesucristo
Esperemos tu bendición
Y llevar cosecha en unión
San Isidro labrador.
Un imagen muy milagroso. Y
Dios, y fue mandado por Dios,
¿ve?
Adios mi santo glorioso
patrón de la labor
liberta nuestra sembrado
San Isidro labrador.

Adios mi Padre querido
Asina le dice San Isidro
a mi Señor Jesucristo
patrón de la labor
liberta nuestro sembrado
San Isidro labrador.

Adios mi santo glorioso
cortesano del Señor
hasta el año venidero
San Isidro labrador.

All' le dice a mi Señor
Jesucristo, mi Señor Jesucristo
le dice a él, que hasta el año
que no viene otra vez, el año
venidero. Pero mira, que estudia
de este santo milagroso.

There it is telling it, you see.
CLB:
Yeah.
MANUEL:
Which damage our fields
Free our crops
Saint Isidore the husbandman.

Through you we hope to be happy
And to bring in the harvest in harmony
Look, this saint certainly
is miraculous!
By your great mercy
Saint Isidore the husbandman.

We wait for you, Lord
Saint Isidore says to
My Lord Jesus Christ
We await your blessing
And bring a good harvest
Saint Isidore the husbandman.
A very miraculous image. And
he was sent by God, you
see?
Farewell, my glorious saint
Patron of farmwork
Free our fields
Saint Isidore the husbandman.

Good-bye, my dear Lord
This is what Saint Isidore
says to my Lord Jesus Christ
Patron of farmwork
Free our fields
Saint Isidore the husbandman.

Farewell, my glorious saint
Courtier of the Lord
Until the coming year
Saint Isidore the husbandman.

There he says to my Lord Jesus
Christ, my Lord Jesus Christ
says to him, that he won't come
again for a year, until the
following year. But look, what an
understanding of this miraculous

Y él no temió, él no tuvo desconfianza de granizos ni de tempesdades. El le dice, sin miedo, le dice mi Señor Jesucristo, a ver que, que correspondía él. A ver si él tenía poca fé o tenía mucha fé, en las creencias que mi Señor Jesucristo le daba de los cielos, ve. Dirigirle que visitara todas las labores, para que lloviera y pa' que viniera fruto. ¿Es mucho no?

saint. And he wasn't afraid, he didn't fear hailstorms or tempests. He says to him without fear, my Lord Jesus Christ says to him, to see how he measured up. To see if he had little faith or had a great deal of faith in the beliefs which my Lord Jesus Christ had given him from Heaven, you see. To direct him to visit all the field, so that it would rain and so that they would bear fruit. That's really something, isn't it?.

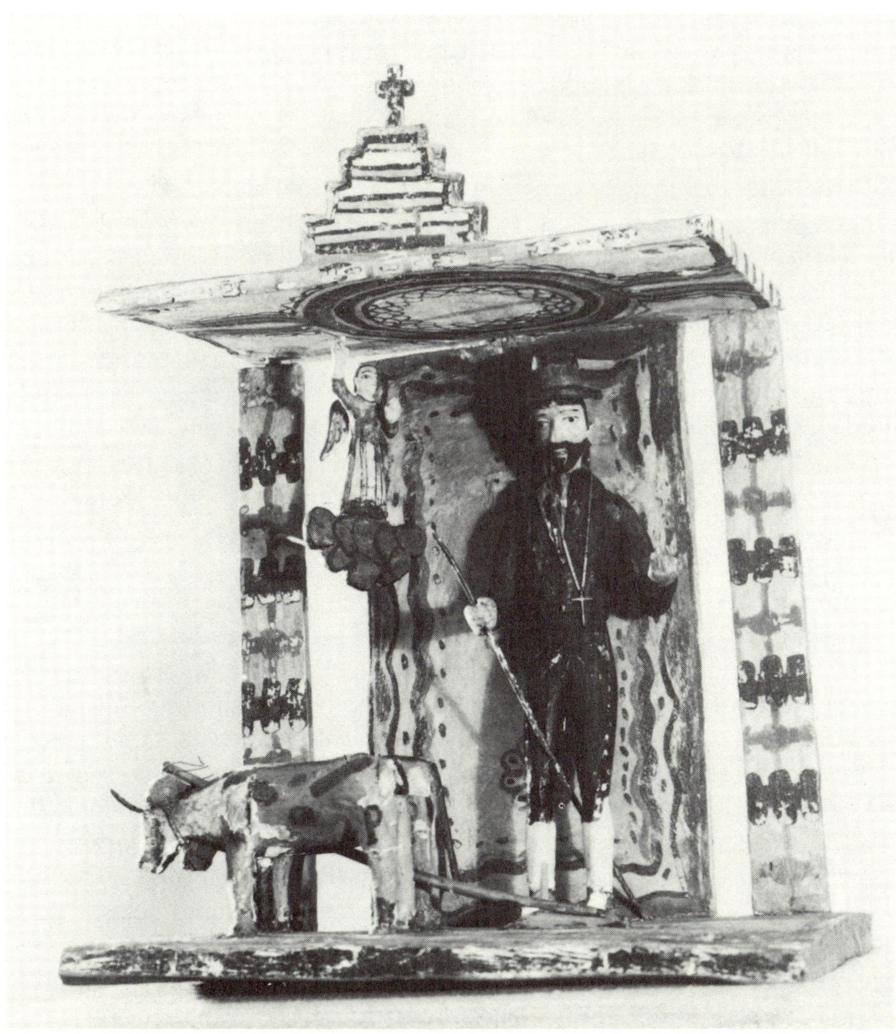

FIGURE 1
Saint Isidore with angel and oxen in wooden niche. Polychrome wood, nineteenth century. Height from base to top of cross, 1'3". (Taylor Museum Collection 1244, Colorado Springs Fine Arts Center.)

The first thing that should be noted about Manuel's intonation of the hymn for Saint Isidore is that he was not simply *performing* it, he was *teaching* it to me. His short parenthetical remarks (for example, lines 7, 16, 129, 147–48, and so on) and his long stretches of exegesis distinguish this pedagogically oriented usage from the simple presentation of the hymn as a supplication to Saint Isidore. It is not hard to see that Manuel and Guadalupe were trying to impart some broader and more fundamental concepts to me while Manuel was complying with my request to sing the hymn.

Manuel's central concern in the conversation was to convince me that the Córdovans' present-day situation contrasts sharply with that of their ancestors, *los viejitos de antes,* "the elders of bygone days." Thus he begins in lines 16–122 to draw out the implications of Saint Isidore traditions for this more general point. Córdovans used to be monetarily poor; the semiarid climate was no more conducive to farming in bygone days than it is now. But the people had a deep faith in God's compassion and in the ability of Saint Isidore to intercede on their behalf. This religiosity was reflected, it is said, in bountiful harvests. Manuel notes that these days people have so little faith that they refuse even to plant, because they assume that their crops will wither and die.

Manuel cites one major example of the manner in which Córdovans used to seek God's blessing and Saint Isidore's intercession: by celebrating Saint Isidore's feast day. The wake began after vespers on May 14, the eve of the saint's day.[5] All the villagers would gather at the community chapel, where Saint Isidore's image was placed on a freshly decorated processional platform. Saint Anthony of Padua, the patron of both chapel and community, was similarly honored. A procession then formed, and the group descended the hillside, crossed the Quemado valley, and ascended approximately three miles to the upland dry farms at Las Joyas. The journey was punctuated by the rhythm of chanted prayers and of the melodious hymn for Saint Isidore.

Upon reaching Las Joyas, the image was taken from the platform and laid in a green bower. Córdovans who owned fields at Las Joyas would take turns preparing the bower and hosting the wake on their land. The normally early-retiring farmers then began an all-night vigil. The darkness around the image was broken only by a line of candles. Two or more rezadores sang the many stanzas of the hymns, and the people intoned the chorus. This devotional concentration was broken only by a communal meal served at midnight.

The end of the wake was signaled when the face of Saint Isidore's image was illuminated by the first rays of direct sunlight. A procession immediately formed around the image, and the saint was carried on the platform at the head of the crowd across all of the Las Joyas fields, down the trail to the beginning of the Quemado valley and through each of the valley fields. Upon reaching the plaza the image was returned to its place in the chapel, and the populace dispersed. Most would reassemble at nightfall for an all-night dance.

The wake thus unified the villagers through their faith in God, their re-

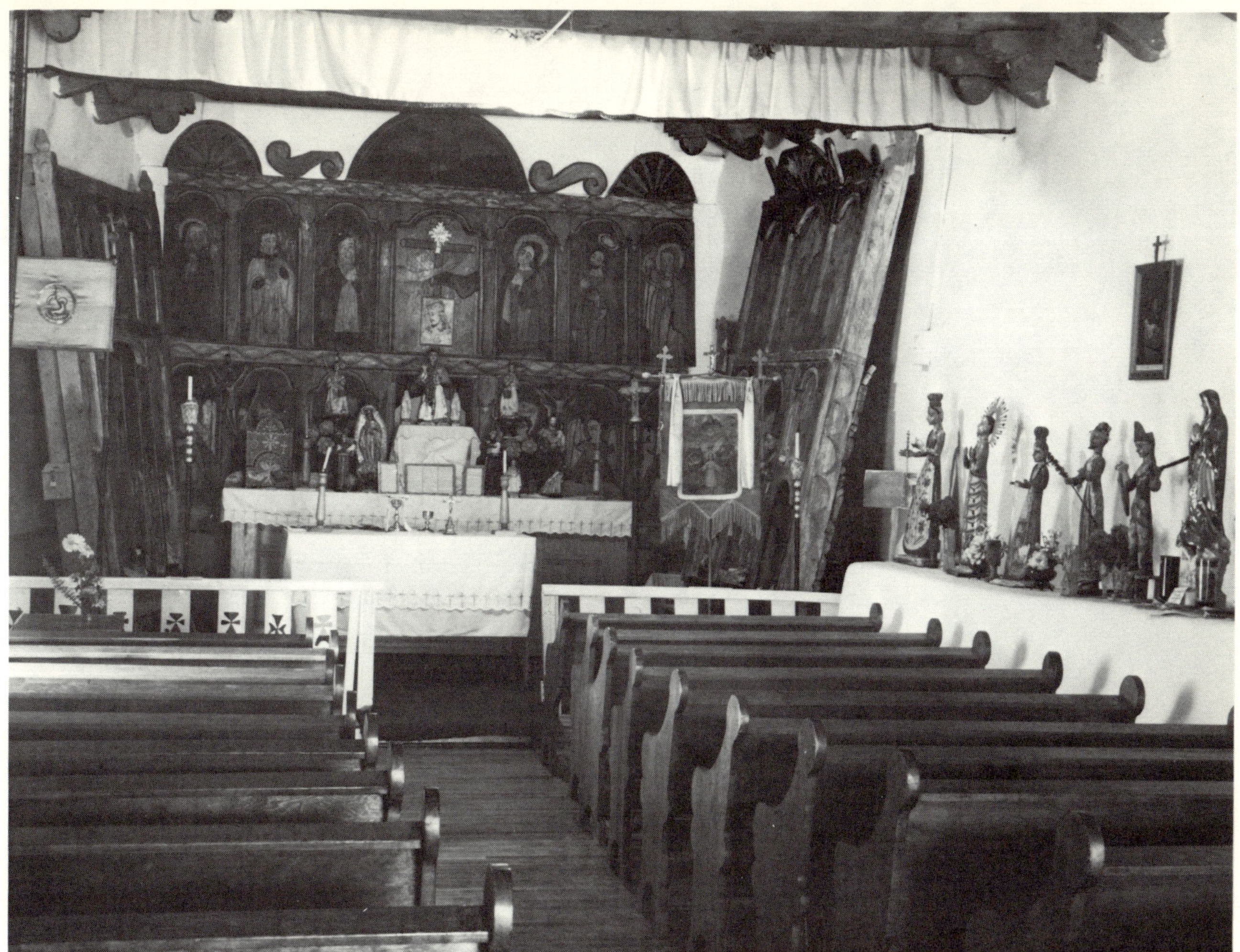

FIGURE 2
Interior of San Antonio de Padua del Pueblo Quemado Chapel. Córdova, New Mexico, 1976. (Photo by Charles L. Briggs.)

spect for Saint Isidore, and their desire to obtain an abundant harvest. Manuel notes that Saint Isidore responded quickly to the villagers' petitions, since "if the rain didn't come that day, [it came] the next day." An additional sign of faith was provided by the farmers' willingness to allow the procession to trample the young plants, believing God would renew them.

However, residents note that Córdova, like all communities, is not immune to discord. A popular legend about Saint Isidore reflects this concern, and Manuel recounted it in another of our conversations:

> Saint Isidore was very manly *[muy hombrote]*, a very good farmer *[ranchero]*, and he adored our Lord a great deal. One time it was Sunday, and his wife made him work. Once he was working, the Lord spoke to him, telling him that

> as it was Sunday he should not work. Saint Isidore responded that he had to work. The voice then said that if Saint Isidore didn't stop working, God would send hail. But Saint Isidore said that he wasn't afraid of hail, and that he was going to keep working. Then the voice spoke to him again, and said if he didn't stop working, God was going to send him a plague of locusts. But Saint Isidore was not afraid, and he kept on working. Then the same voice spoke to him again, saying that if he didn't leave his work, God would send him a bad neighbor. Saint Isidore replied that this he couldn't stand, so he left his work and went to mass. When he returned from mass his wife was not angry, because an angel had planted his fields.

Note that the fear of a bad neighbor induced Saint Isidore to place devotion to God over agricultural duty. The farmers accordingly ask the saint in lines 185–86 of the hymn to help them *llevar cosecha en unión,* a reference not simply to romantic and metaphorical unity in harvesting the crops. The farmers used to join together to reap the community's crops, visiting each field

FIGURE 3
View of the Quemado Valley from the east. (Photo by Charles L. Briggs.)

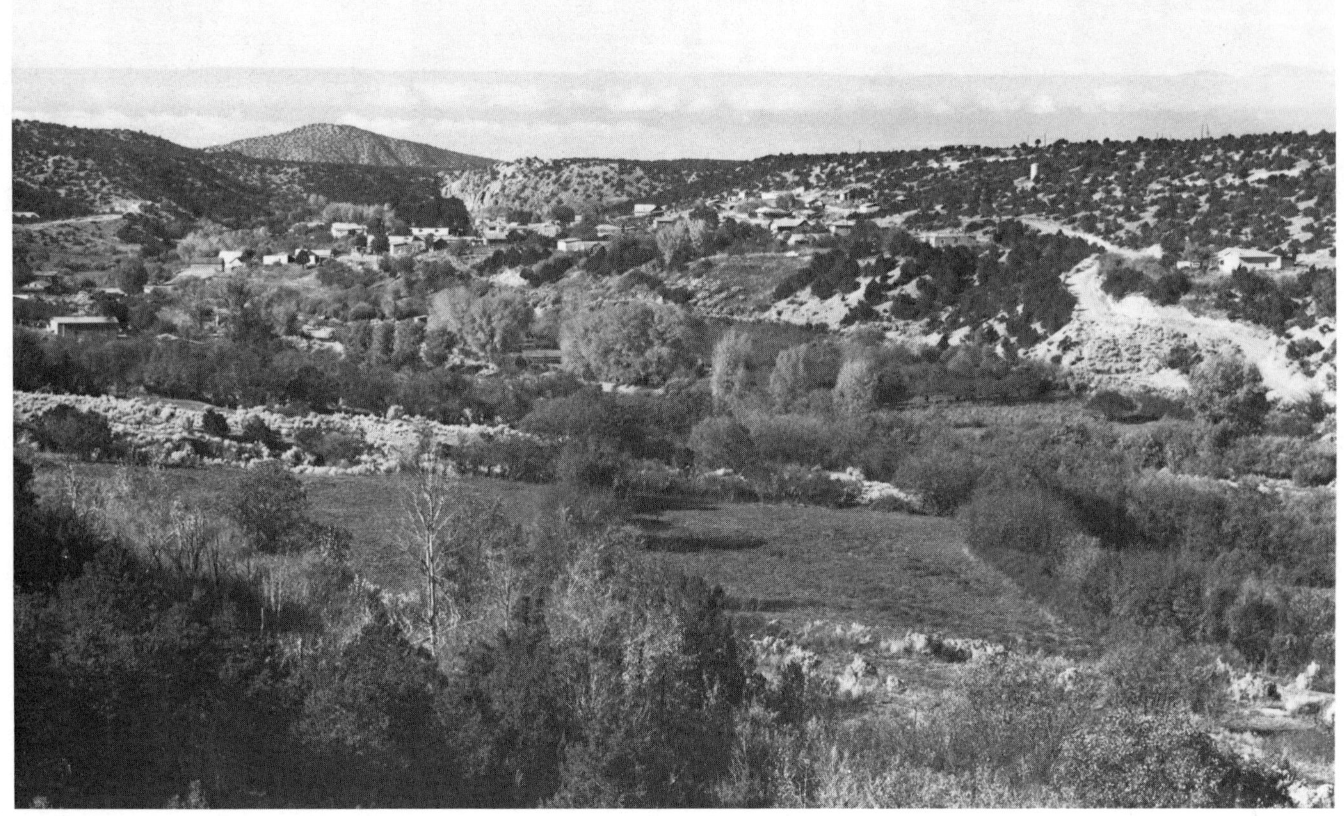

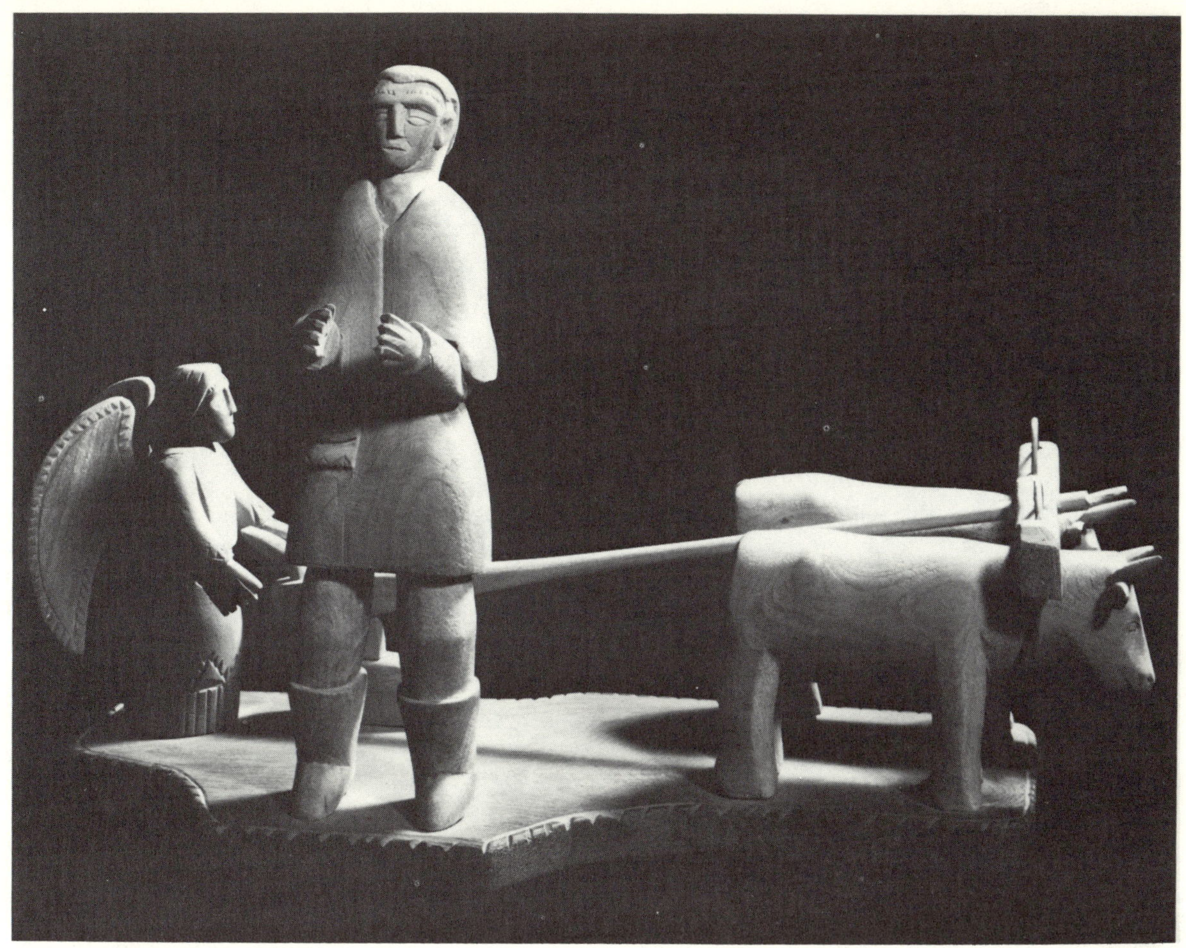

FIGURE 4
Saint Isidore with angel and oxen, carved by George López, Córdova, New Mexico, 1949. Height of St. Isidore, 11"; of angel, 5.5"; base, 14.3" x 7.5". (From a private collection; photo by Charles L. Briggs.)

in succession. Saint Isidore too brings out this unification theme in a new way in lines 191–96 by using the first person plural in asking for God's blessing ("we wait for you, Lord / we await your blessing").

In conclusion, two features of this text bear special consideration. First, Manuel's remarks provide a striking illustration of the elders' ability to reveal central cultural values in the course of explicating almost any particular subject. Manuel underscores the importance of religious belief and a corporatistic spirit to the Mexicanos' former way of life. Although these values are hardly synonymous with the so-called Puritan work ethic, they are equally far from the passivity and fatalism so often attributed to persons of Mexican descent.[6] Manuel clearly notes that such faith is expressed through the rigorous labor that the farmer must generate in *anticipation* of God's assistance.

Second, Manuel's explication of the text provides us with a sense of why Córdovans still sing this hymn. Córdova is no longer primarily a farming community. Lost access to upland grazing areas and increasing needs for cash income have forced most residents to work for wages in Los Alamos and elsewhere.[7] As Guadalupe and Manuel state, the diminishing importance of agriculture was reflected in the abandonment of the wake for Saint Isidore after 1932. Why, then, do Córdovans still tell the legend and sing the hymn for the saint? The answer lies not only in the nature of these texts but also in their role in community life.

The significance of the hymn and the legend is not exhausted by their use in promoting agricultural success, and they are not exclusively tied to the wake. Forty years after the last Córdovan enactment of the wake, Manuel and Guadalupe used this text (along with many others) to teach me about the saint, Córdova's past, and what it means to be Mexicano. They used it to convey a strong sense of what it was to be a *ranchero,* a hardworking farmer-rancher. Their words clearly showed that even if Córdovans now work for wages, the values and sentiments expressed by the rancheros of bygone days continue to provide a raison d'être for their descendants. In other words, each invocation of hymn and legend articulates the raconteur or vocalist's identification with Mexicano values and his or her commitment to preserving an important cultural heritage.

The continued viability of these texts points to their open, creative character. On the one hand, they are relatively conventionalized, having been handed down from person to person and from generation to generation. On the other, the same hymn or tale can be used in a variety of social settings to address a multitude of specific concerns. Thus they stand, so to speak, with one foot in the world of the elders of bygone days and the other in the details of everyday contemporary life.

Images of saints, which have been carved in Córdova for well over a century, possess this "bridging" capacity too. Statues were produced for fellow Mexicanos in the nineteenth century and for Anglo-American tourists and art lovers in the twentieth. They have also been readopted as central symbols of Mexicano ethnicity in the last two decades (Briggs 1980).

Such images, hymns, and legends about Saint Isidore and numbers of his fellows, together with other vehicles for cultural expression, have exhibited the Mexicanos' remarkable ability to bring a strong sense of the past to bear on rapidly changing present circumstances. All such arts suggest some important ways in which these Mexicanos have been able to maintain their ethnic identity in the face of strong assimilative pressures. This is surely one of the most striking of the many messages that can be gleaned from Guadalupe and Manuel's teachings.

NOTES

1. I acknowledge a profound debt to E. Boyd, who labored for decades to further our understanding of how Hispanic New Mexicans express their religious beliefs in artistic form. She did not write herself out of her work, often mentioning her own role in the research process when she described artists and images. I chose to relate one of my own attempts to learn about the saints in order to pay tribute to this aspect of her work.

I am greatly indebted to my student, Sieneh Wolf, for transcribing the interview with Guadalupe and Manuel. I would like to thank Marta Weigle for inviting me to contribute to this volume and for encouraging me to focus on a transcription of a taped interview. Acknowledgment is also due Gilberto Benito Córdova, Juanita Córdova, Paul Kutsche, and Edward H. Spicer, who advised me during the time of my initial research. The Museum of International Folk Art (Museum of New Mexico, Santa Fe)and the International Folk Art Foundation provided logistical and financial support, respectively.

2. *Mexicanos* are descendants of primarily Spanish and Mexican citizens who settled in what is now New Mexico and southern Colorado during the seventeenth, eighteenth, and nineteenth centuries. My preference for this term over its many competitors (Spanish-Americans, Hispanos, Mexican-Americans, and so on) springs from the fact that it is the expression most commonly used by Córdovans in reference to their ethnic group.

3. I have used the term *alabado* here simply because it appears in the conversation. Manuel noted on another occasion that hymns that do not describe the Passion of Christ, and this includes "Saint Isidore Husbandman," are best referred to, if one wishes to be precise, as *alabanzas.* On the alabado/alabanza distinction, see Robb 1980: 612–13.

4. Manuel actually misread *comisionado,* which appears here in his notebook, as *comenzando,* "beginning." His eyesight was failing rapidly at the time, and he occasionally had to be prompted by either Guadalupe or myself when he could not discern a word or phrase.

5. This description is drawn from Lorin W. Brown (Anonymous 1941; Brown 1978: 185–87, 193) and from my own field work in Córdova. Also see Briggs 1980: 182–86, 1981*a.*

6. See Octavio Ignacio Romano-V. (1968) for a critique of social-scientific stereotypes of Mexican-American values.

7. See Harper et al. (1943) and Soil Conservation Service (1937) for the effects of land loss on Mexicanos in northern New Mexico. My dissertation (Briggs 1981*a)* describes these effects on Córdovans.

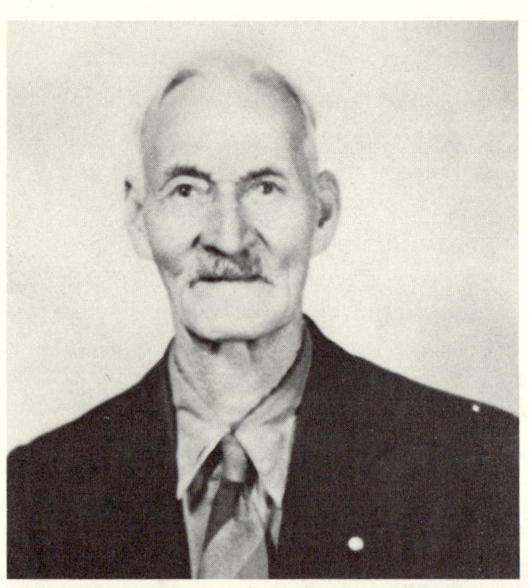

FIGURE 1
Luís Montoya of Cerro, New Mexico.

FIGURE 2
Graveyard at Cerro, New Mexico.

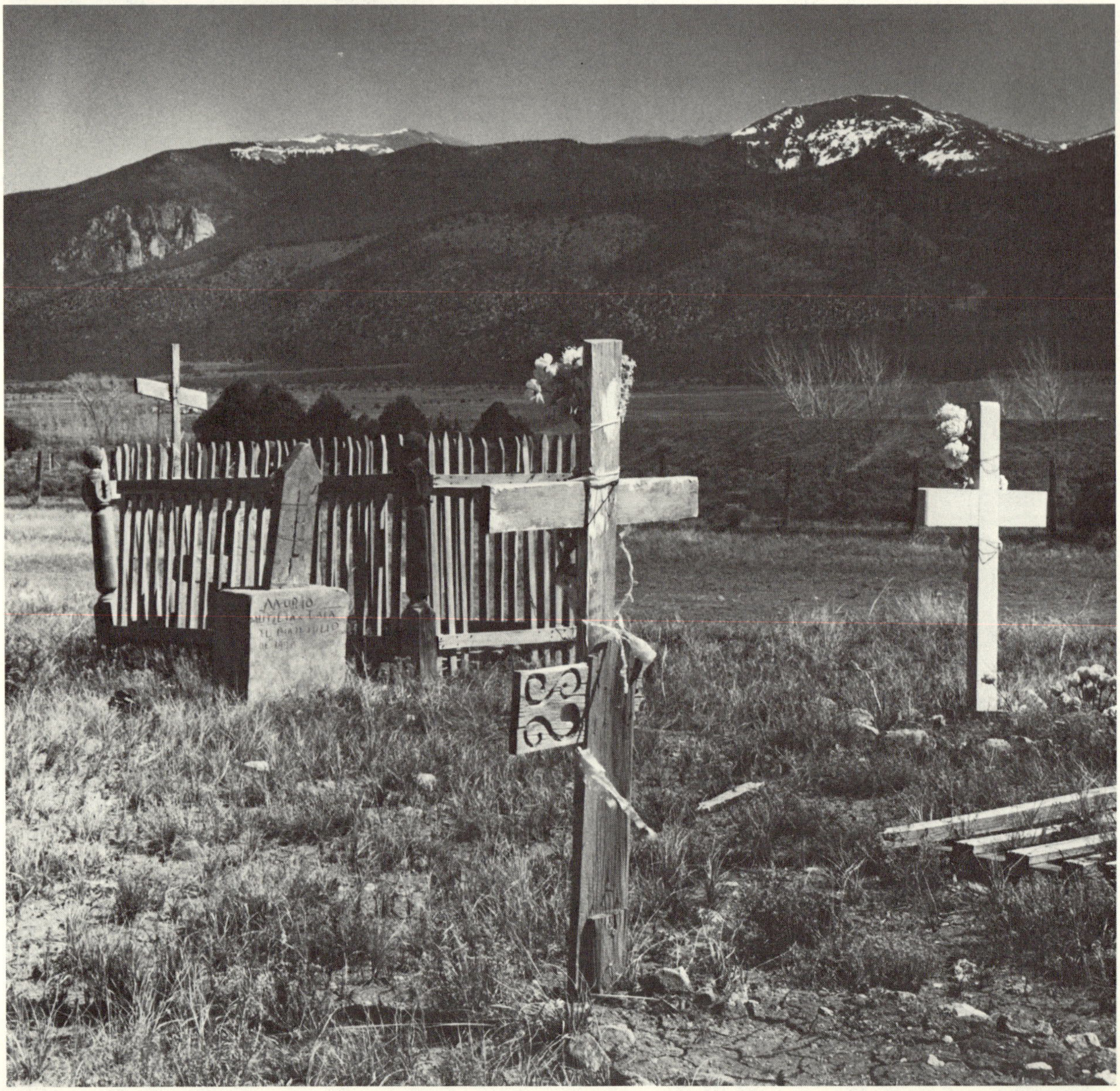

RICHARD B. STARK

NOTES ON A SEARCH FOR ANTECEDENTS OF NEW MEXICAN ALABADO MUSIC

THE "BOOK" DISCUSSED HERE is the last in a series of four that resulted from my studies of certain music that exists (or recently existed) among the Spanish-speaking people of New Mexico. Unlike the others—*Music of the Spanish Folk Plays in New Mexico* (1969), *Juegos infantiles cantados en Nuevo México* (1973), and *Music of the "Bailes" in New Mexico* (1978*b*)—this book is not yet in print. It does, however, have a title—*Music of the Alabados in New Mexico*—and it is fresh in my mind as I have recently returned from Spain, where I sought the roots of this music.

The New Mexican sources of this book-to-be are disc recordings made in 1940 at Cerro, New Mexico, by Juan B. Rael, then professor of romance languages at Stanford University and a native of the nearby village of Arroyo Hondo, New Mexico (Rael 1951: 19). Rael was interested primarily in the texts of these religious hymns, a genre of New Mexican Hispanic folklore closely associated with the lay religious brothers known as Los Hermanos Penitentes or the Brothers of Our Father Jesus. My main interest is in the music itself.

Alabados (from the Spanish verb *alabar,* "to praise") are still sung in New Mexico today, and several collections of them have been tape-recorded in the last twenty years. None, to my ear, are as interesting musically as Rael's early recordings from Cerro. These were sung by two men, Luís Montoya, then age seventy, and Ricardo Archuleta, then age seventy-two. Both are now deceased, but in 1969 I was able to interview several members of Montoya's family who were still living in Cerro (Stark 1978*a:* 1).

A daughter-in-law, Pina Montoya, spoke affectionately of Luís Montoya. She especially remembered him as "muy católico" (very Catholic, deeply devout) and "muy alto" (very tall, well over six feet). He was a Penitente Brother who helped people in the community during times of crisis and who was known for singing alabados. A good reader with a sound understanding of Spanish, he was born in Los Sauces (The Willows), a tiny village in southern Colorado. He thought his parents came from Spain but either did not know precisely or did not divulge this information within Mrs. Montoya's hearing, although her memory may have failed her. A photograph of Montoya shows a tall man with a strong, square jaw and prominent nose.

When first I heard Luís Montoya on recording singing alabados such as "*Buenos días, paloma blanca*" (Stark 1978*a:* 1, band 6; Rael 1951: 95–96, 145), "*Al pie de este santo altar*" (Stark 1978*a:* 1, band 1; Rael 1951: 23–24, 139), and "*Dividido el corazón*" (Stark 1978*a:* 1, band 4; Rael 1951: 21–23, 139), I knew that this music was unlike other Spanish New Mexican music I had heard. Except possibly for a fragment or two, the other Spanish New Mexican songs were always in major or minor keys, in easily recognizable meters, and tonally conceived, that is, outlining simple tonic, dominant, subdominant harmony. But these alabados were sometimes modal, difficult to determine metrically but probably for the most part in three beats to a measure, and not often suggestive of tonal harmony. Most obviously different was the inclusion of simple ornamentation, akin in the most general sense to that found in much folk music of southern Spain. The singing was in a high range, and often the voice shook in a little sob, which the Spanish in Spain call *trino.* [1]

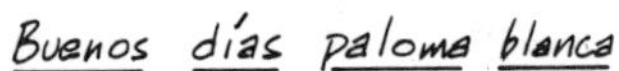

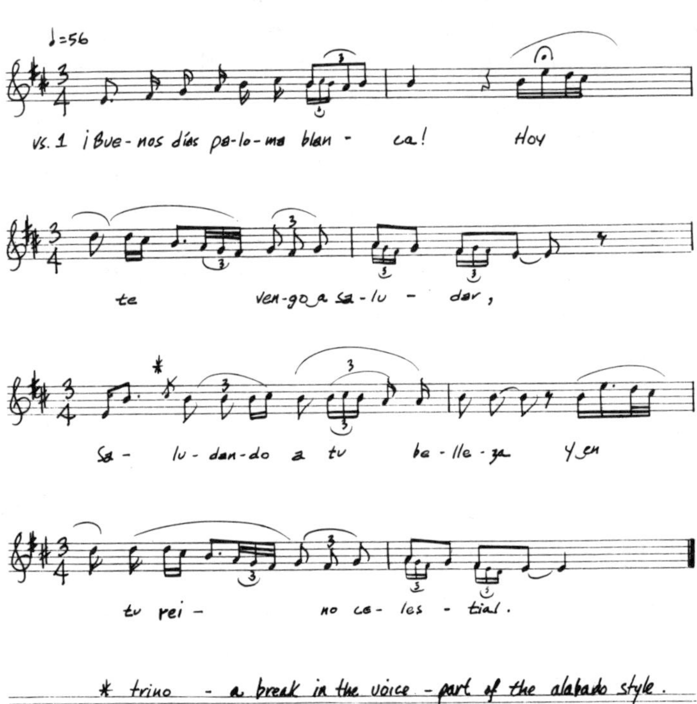

The search was on. Where did these songs come from, and how did they come to be in the little village of Cerro, New Mexico?

Knowledgeable people offered suggestions about where I might look for sources of this music. The first was Luís Gonzáles Robles of the Instituto de Cultura Hispánica in Madrid, not a musician but a man with a vast knowledge of Spanish life, who heard me sing several alabados at a meeting of the International Institute of Iberian Colonial Art in Santa Fe, New Mexico. He claimed that the alabados that I had sung were Sephardic, from the Spanish Jews—not the texts, of course, but the music—and also told me that there was a large collection of such songs from Rhodes and Turkey in the institute's library at Madrid.

This was an exciting idea. Was there really any connection between the Spanish colonists of New Mexico and the Spanish Jews, both emigrants from sixteenth-century Spain? Did they share a common musical tradition carried in their memories so that one could find similar music in Cerro, New Mexico, and in Sephardic communities in Turkey?

Alas, except for some minor details of ornamentation, the Madrid collection—*Coplas Sefardies* by Alberto Hemsi (published in separate volumes from 1932 through 1973)—did not contain any music that was at all like the alabado. But I could not really be sure that there was no connection because Hemsi was not a scholar and did not document his findings except to cite the places where he found the songs ("Smyrna" and "communities of Anatolia," for example) and to state that he had started collecting them in 1932. He has transformed the songs into recital pieces with piano accompaniment, and who knows what he has done to the melodies.

While something of a disappointment, this collection could not receive a definite "no," and the search continued, this time to the library of the Instituto de Estudios Hebraicos in Madrid, where there were other collections of Sephardic music but nothing that looked promising. The institute's director was impressed with a recent book, *Judeo-Spanish Traditional Ballads from Jerusalem* (1972), by Israel J. Katz of Columbia University. He gave me Katz's address, and I sent him some transcriptions of alabados. These interested him, but he reserved any comments on Sephardic connections until he could have an opportunity to hear them on tape recordings.

Then I journeyed to Córdova and to the synagogue there. Everything of Jewish life is gone except the small, beautiful building and a striking statue of the Jewish philosopher Moses Maimonides, which is nearby. Toledo, formerly another great Jewish center, yielded nothing, and I had a dramatic realization of how complete had been the expulsion of the Jews by the kings of Castile. But the tantalizing question remained: Are there common remnants of sixteenth-century Spain in the memories of both Jews and Christians, who left the country carrying with them the same language and musical heritage?

The next person to help was Lincoln Bunce Spiess, professor emeritus of

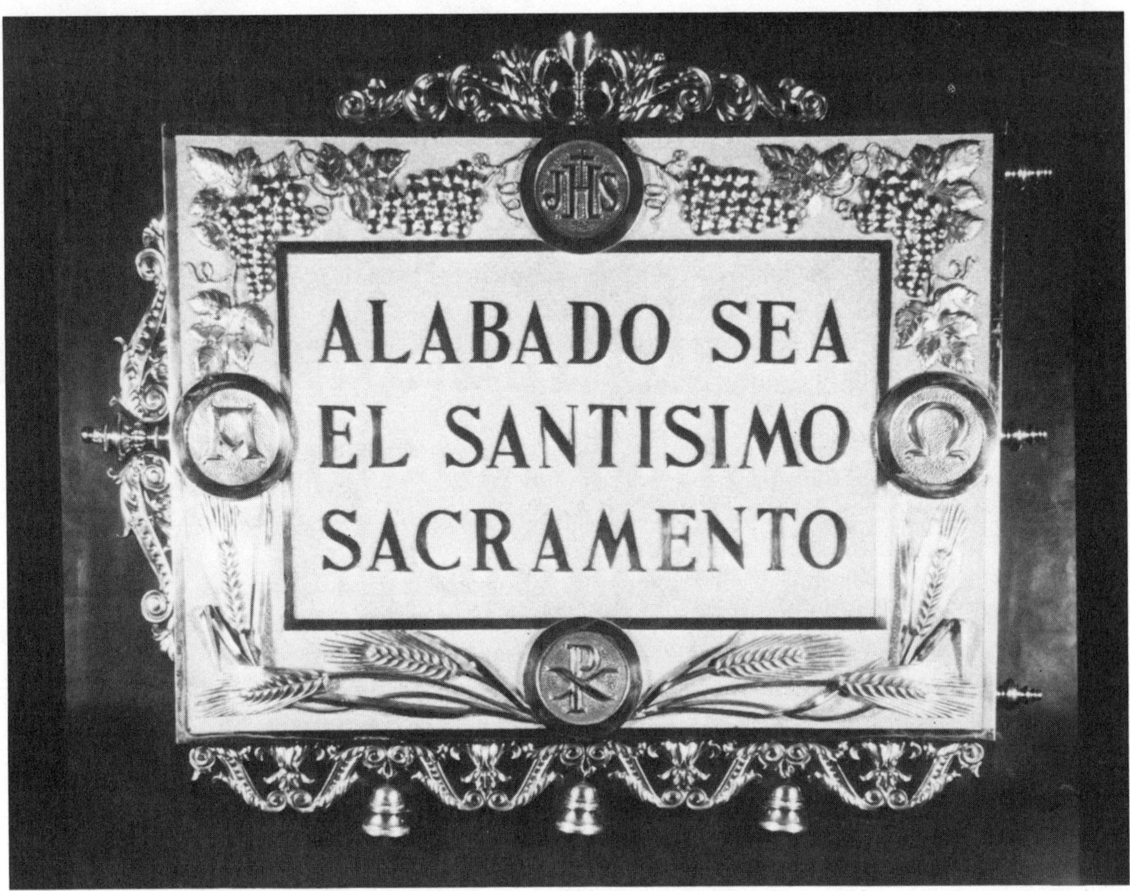

FIGURE 3
Standard from the Penitente chapter house of San Roque, Seville, Spain. First seen in the Museo de Los Venerables, Barrio Santa Cruz. (Photograph by Richard B. Stark.)

music at Washington University in St. Louis, Missouri, a musicologist, medievalist, and frequent visitor to New Mexico. Spiess had become interested in discovering the kind of music that had been performed in the mission churches of New Mexico (see, for example, Spiess 1964, 1965). He talked with me about an intuition of his: that there might have been a Spanish counterpart to the Italian *laudi spirituali.* There was no great movement in thirteenth-century Italy akin to that of the troubadours in France who wrote and sang of courtly love and other worldly interests. Rather the Italian mode was penitential, inspired by Saint Francis of Assisi. The laudi spirituali were folk hymns sung by religious congregations within the churches or by bands of flagellants who paraded through the streets mortifying their bodies to rid their souls of sin. Spiess thought that these hymns might, in spirit and text, be very much like the New Mexican alabados.

A connection seemed possible: Isabel la Católica, being a member of the Third Order of Saint Francis, appointed Franciscans to be the official mis-

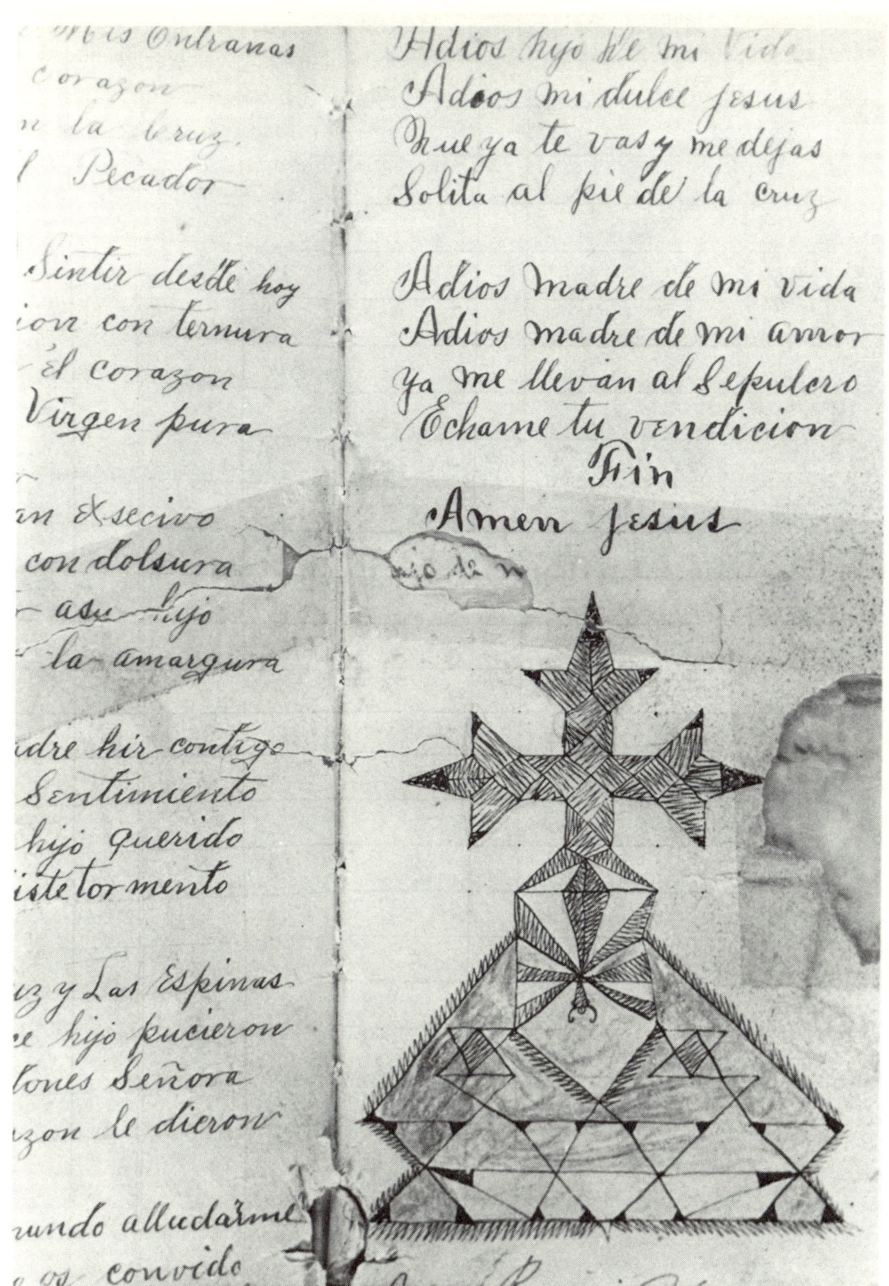
Entranas
corazon
n la cruz
l Pecador

Sintir desde hoy
ion con ternura
el corazon
Virgen pura

an Exsecivo
con dolsura
asi hijo
la amargura

adre hir contigo
Sentimiento
hijo querido
iste tormento

z y Las Espinas
e hijo pucieron
lones Señora
zon le dieron

undo alludarme
os convido

Adios hijo de mi vida
Adios mi dulce jesus
Que ya te vas y me dejas
Solita al pie de la cruz

Adios madre de mi vida
Adios madre de mi amor
ya me llevan al Sepulcro
Echame tu vendicion
Fin
Amen jesus

FIGURE 4
From José Rosario Herrera's *cuaderno* (notebook) of alabado texts. Late nineteenth century, from the Chama River Valley, New Mexico. (Collections of the Museum of International Folk Art, Museum of New Mexico, Santa Fe.)

sionaries to the New World, and thus, for two centuries, Franciscans ministered to the Spanish communities in northern New Mexico. But that was so long ago. Could there have been a body of spiritual songs deriving from the Italian laudi spirituali, known to the Franciscans from their monasteries in Spain, and brought with them to the New World? I proceeded to look for some evidence of this.

At the cathedral in Seville's Biblioteca Colombina, a library of books collected by the son of "el gran Almirante Cristóbal Colón," which includes a large collection of music from all over Europe, I found some Italian laudi. However, they were in four parts—soprano, alto, tenor, and bass—rather than being simple monophonic music, and they appeared to be the type that developed in sixteenth-century Italy into a kind of spiritual madrigal, unlike the primitive congregational song I was seeking.

I also visited San Angel in Seville, once the most important Franciscan center in Spain, the headquarters that supplied the missionaries for the New World. During the sixteenth and seventeenth centuries, it included almost the entire central part of Seville, plus eight other *conventos.* Today, however, San Angel is a small mission of twenty brothers housed in a small convento. The brother with whom I talked, a historian and musicologist, had never heard anything like the alabados I sang for him, nor indeed even of New Mexico itself!

At the monastery of La Rábida, where Columbus planned his voyage to the Indies, the librarian thought we might find some reference to music sung at the monastery. But, he explained, the library had been burned in 1936 during the Civil War and had been ransacked previously by the French and by revolutions in Spain. The library was pitifully small, with no manuscripts and only standard printed books of the kind one could pick up in any bookstore. I found the same situation in several other Franciscan monasteries. Still, the search should continue for some relationship between the alabado and the laudi spirituali, and, curiously enough, I have just learned of a collection of Italian laudi published in Rome (Liuzzi 1935) that may be helpful.

A third person who helped in the search was Fray Angélico Chávez of Santa Fe, New Mexico, a Franciscan, historian, and poet. In a 1973 letter to me in Spain, he wrote: "I am still convinced that the Alabados come from within the Cante Hondo of southern Spain, as the resemblances are too compelling in nasal wail etc. between them and the gypsy songs of unrequited love, or comments on fate."

I was spending considerable time in Seville, making it the center for my search in the south. It had been the port city through which the early colonists coming to the New World passed, a city rich in culture, with Roman ruins, evidence of Moorish influence everywhere, and the picturesque old Jewish section, now called Barrio Santa Cruz, where I lived. There is also a profusion of penitential confraternities and brotherhoods. I met several Penitentes, went with them to their meeting places, which were rooms within their parish churches, saw their rule books, and learned of their benevolent work among the poor.

The person who proved the most knowledgeable about the confraternities and their customs and history was Juan Infante Galán, author of books on folklore and *periodista* (journalist) for the newspaper *ABC.* I asked if there were some music uniquely associated with the *cofradías.* He immediately answered, "the saeta," a type of song within the genre *cante hondo.* I had heard saetas sung during Holy Week in Seville and wondered if it were possible that these richly ornate, passionate songs to the figures of Christ and the Virgin could be related to the simple New Mexican alabado.

Musical transcriptions of saetas were almost impossible to make because of their improvisatory character and lack of regular metrical groupings. However, in Madrid, the expert on Spanish folk music at Radio Nacional de España, Arcadio de Larrea, told me that the saetas one hears now throughout southern Spain (Andalucía) during Holy Week are not worth hearing—"*no valen nada*"—being so heavily influenced by flamenco music on the radio and television. He showed me what the traditional saeta, which can still be heard on occasion, looked like. Having the same general structure and simple ornamentation, it appeared to resemble the alabado "*Tened piedad, Dios mío*" (Rael 1951: 84–86, 143; Stark 1978*a:* 1, band 5)—which, incidentally, is one of the few obviously tonal alabados.

Arcadio Larrea's scheme for a Saeta from Andalucia

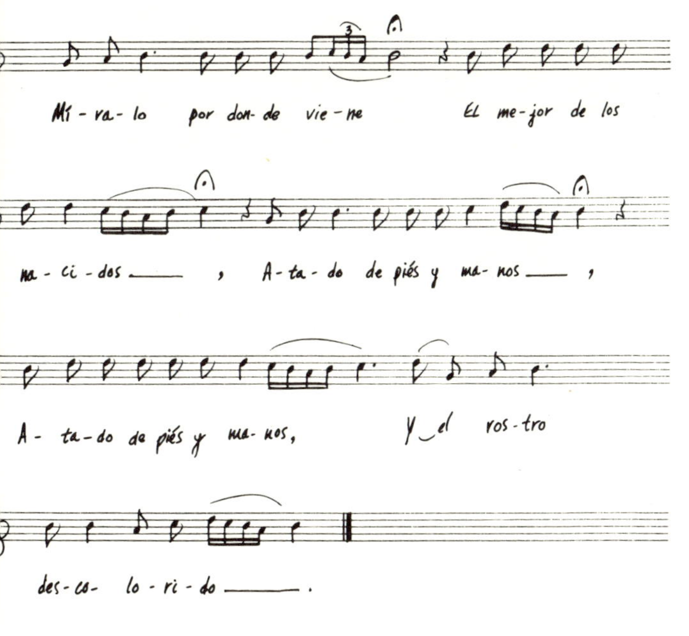

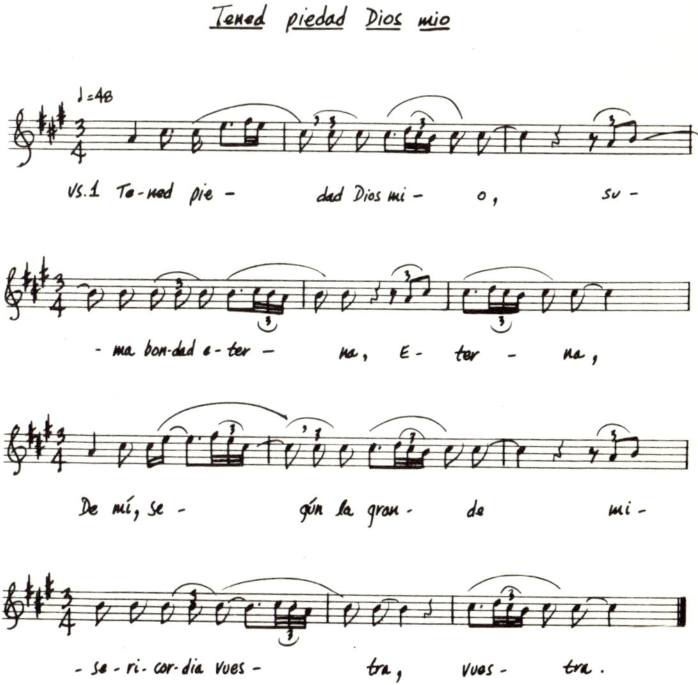

There is one essential difference in the melodic structure. The Spanish saeta that Larrea had shown me rises to a note like rising to a reciting tone in Gregorian chant, comes to a cadence on the note above, and returns to the reciting tone. This New Mexican alabado does the same thing except that it cadences on the note *below* the reciting tone and then returns to the reciting tone. "*A la muerte, pecador*" (Rael 1951: 122–23, 151) is another New Mexican alabado somewhat alike in melodic structure.

I talked again with Infante Galán. During our visit, he sang a saeta that he had collected in a little village near Seville. He called it a "saeta primitiva," and believed it to be the type preceding the florid saetas now heard during Holy Week. It conformed to the saeta structure as outlined by Larrea, and its ornamentation was as chaste as that of the New Mexican alabado.

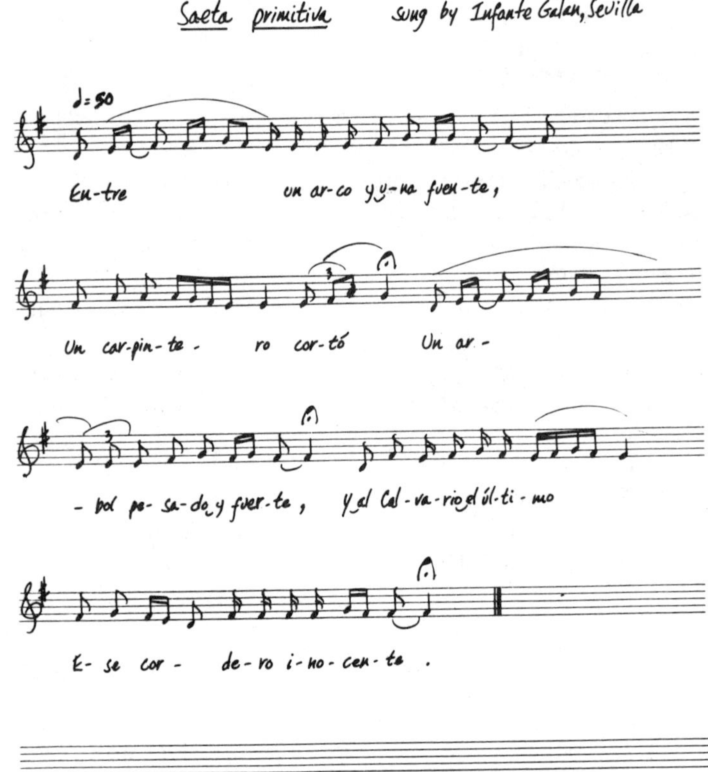

In the National Library in Madrid, I found a similar "saeta" in a nineteenth-century *cancionero* from Jérez de la Frontera, delineated as a "Canción Andaluza."

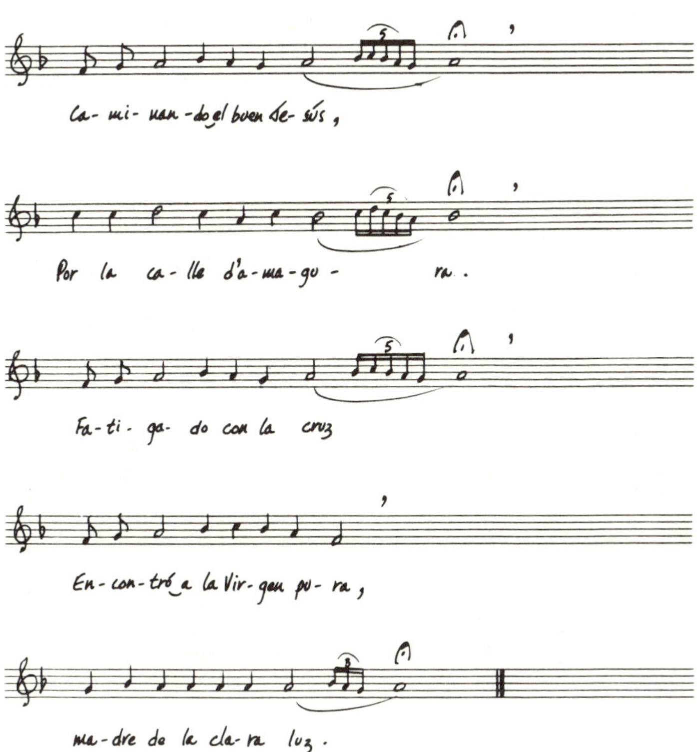

Infante Galán expressed great interest in my search and offered to help in any way possible. Arcadio de Larrea grew interested in the texts of the New Mexican alabados, and I sent him Rael's book. After studying it, he concluded that a few of them were known in Spain, but most were not. This suggested to him the possibility that they were written by missionaries outside Spain, who used the popular style of Spanish verse, *coplas* and *villancicos.* He believed that the texts of the alabados could not be earlier than the eighteenth century, with most probably dating from the nineteenth century.

There are several types of alabados other than the "saeta" type. In Cádiz, the largest southern city in Spain, priests and musicians claimed that the alabado "*Dividido el corazón*" (Rael 1951: 21–23, 139) was very much like music of their area, although I found no comparable examples. A musicologist priest from Badajoz, Extremadura, said the alabado "*Dulce esposo de mi alma*" (Rael 1951: 88–90) was similar to a type sung in his province. This would be possible since so many colonists came from the province of Extremadura. Spain's foremost authority on Spanish folk music, García Matos of the Royal Conservatory in Madrid, thought, however, that the connection was tenuous, although he said that the alabado had a distinct flavor of Extremadura and closed with an Extremenian cadence. He suggested Mexico as the probable source of the New Mexican alabados that I showed him, saying: "Your alabado has Spanish roots but it is changed. Have you thoroughly searched Mexico?" I had to admit that I had not but agreed that I definitely would have to.[2]

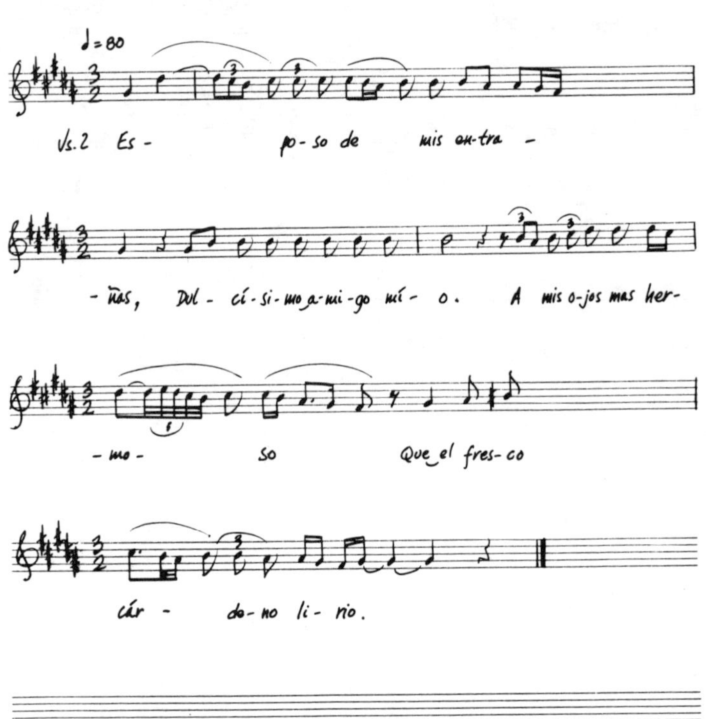

It does seem at times that there is little chance of finding specific connections with Spain or Italy or the Sephardics or anyone, anywhere. As one priest said this past summer: "Your New Mexican singers may have retained something we had long ago, but so long ago, who can ever tell, and especially with folk material which is so tenuous in its transmission." But presenting the outline of my search makes it available to others who may, possibly, add crucial pieces to the puzzle.

NOTES

1. I am grateful to Patrick Rhoads, Albuquerque, New Mexico, for preparing the musical transcriptions.

2. Matos's suggestion had been anticipated by my colleague E. Boyd in her book review of Juan B. Rael's 1965 study, *The Sources and Diffusion of the New Mexican Shepherds' Plays:* "Accidentally, at the end of the Mexican Text I, version 2, from Durango, Mexico, reproduced in full facsimile, two alabados appear (pages 439 and 442). These, with only slight variations were published by Dr. Rael in *The New Mexican Alabado* in 1951 as collected in Cerro, New Mexico and Antonite *[sic],* Colorado. This coincidence suggests that an interesting if somewhat encyclopedic study remains to be made on Mexican sources of New Mexican alabados before these are lost in both regions" (1965: 42).

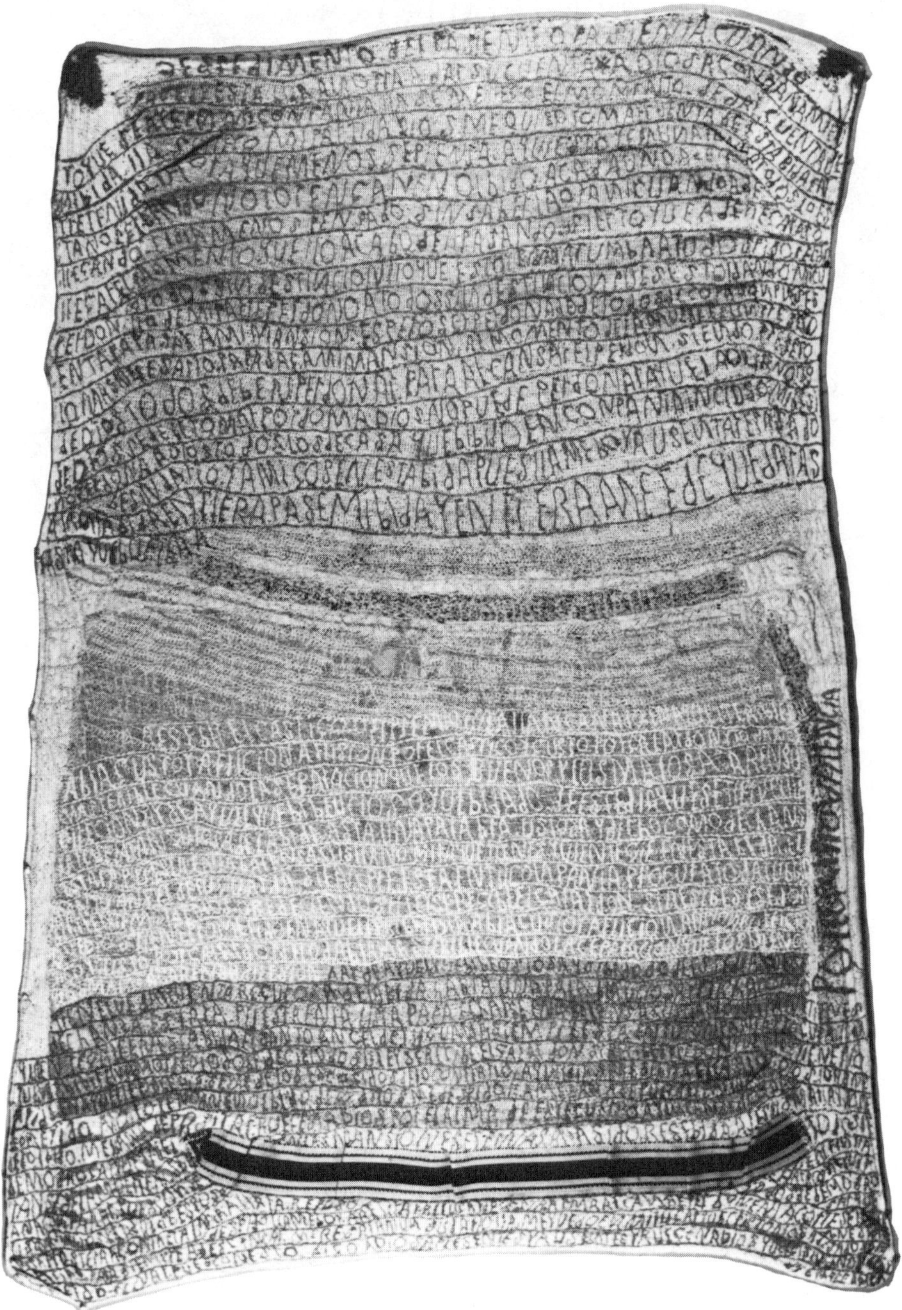

Policarpio Valencia's alabado embroidery. From the Spanish Colonial Arts Society, Inc., Collection on loan to the Museum of New Mexico, Santa Fe. Photograph by Robert Nugent, 1967. (E. Boyd Collection, New Mexico State Records Center and Archives, Santa Fe.)

THE EDITORS
E. BOYD'S WORKING NOTES ON POLICARPIO VALENCIA AND HIS ALABADO EMBROIDERY

ON JUNE 25, 1953, THOMAS A. VALDEZ left at the Museum of New Mexico in Santa Fe four embroideries by Policarpio Valencia "on approval with option of purchasing." E. Boyd examined and researched them, eventually arranging to have Valdez paid $150.00 for three of the embroideries on December 12, 1953, using three separate checks: one from the New Mexico Historical Society ($50.00) and two from the Spanish Colonial Arts Society ($52.00 and $48.00). The fourth embroidery was to be purchased in January 1954, "on condition that Mr. Valdez, who is a native of Santa Cruz, and remembers P. Valencia when he was a boy, will write down for us whatever he recalls of the old man." On January 27, 1954, a Spanish Colonial Arts Society check for $75.00 was issued to Valdez to cover the remaining embroidery and "written notes by T. Valdez on what he knew of P. V."

As curator of the Spanish colonial department of the museum, E. Boyd was instrumental in all such transactions. Her working notes on the artist and his unusual alabado embroidery are instructive and illuminating. They are transcribed below virtually as they appear (except for minor orthographic and punctuation changes) in the E. Boyd papers now housed in the New Mexico State Records Center and Archives, Santa Fe.

LOAN RECEIPT

December 12, 1953: Mr. Valdez states that these are all of the remaining embroideries by him, as they came from his "family"—(daughter or [preceding lined out] *granddaughter—but of course others owned by unknown persons may later appear. Valdez also has a chest and a "rocking chair" said to have been made by P. Valencia in his last years. He states that the son, José Carmen Valencia, lives outside of Taos and "never comes to Santa Fe," and that he is in mid-70s. This would agree with baptismal record found by Bruce Ellis at Santa Cruz—1879, for son of P. V. (check).*

. . . M. states P. V. was alcalde mayor of acequia [irrigation ditch], *a large one which ran by his land. He ran a molino* [mill] *for flour for many years. He also farmed, did wood carving, and was a J.P. (!) P. V. "used to say many philosophi-*

cal things like what he put on his embroideries, which the boys would listen to and be very impressed by him." His home at Santo Niño, about ½ way bet. highway (large vega) and Sto. Niño church, was in Santa Fe County—if he was a JP there must be some record of his commission?
January 27, 1954: Conversation with T. V. suggested that he will try to borrow a photo of P. V. from his son, if he can—for copying for museum use. 4 samplers will now be catalogued, siburized, if wool, etc. Use for article?

POLICARPIO VALENCIA

The following is an exact transcription of a typescript by Tomas Valdez:
Mr. Policarpio Valencia the Embroiderer of some of the most unique pieces of quilts, was born in the northern part of Santa Fe County in the little village of El Santo Nino, a suburb of the Old Santa Cruz Mission or as it was called them [then] *"Santa Cruz de La Cañada, in the year of Our Lord 1864. The people living around Santa Cruz were often refered as "Cañaderos."*
The parents of Mr. Valencia were Ijinio Valencia and Maria Antonia Montoya. They were of typical Spanish blood and tiller of the soil. Policarpio was raised as a hard working boy and a religious one. He had very little schooling, must of it being in spanish. He grew up a husky young man and very healthy. As he grew to manhood the task of providing for the household fell on his shoulders. He bought himself four burros. It was not exactly a purchase. All in all the price amounted to two sacks of unhusked corn and a measure of wheat. Salt being a very useful commodity and in great demands, Mr Valencia took up this kind of trade or commerce. He would load his burros with farm produce come to Santa Fe and do business with a merchant by the name of Mr Solomon Weist, with whom he became very intimate. With this load of merchandise, mostly salt, he would proceed to Taos and there do business. All this transaction will take a period of two weeks.
At the age of 24 he married a girl by the mane [sic] *of Leandra Lopez. It was an elaborate affair as was the custom. Eighteen months after a son was born. He was Christianed Jose Del Carmel. He became more more attached to his family making his commercial trips less frequent. He got himself an idea of making his living right at home by building a Flour Mill powered by the waters of the Acequia de los Herreras, of which he was the ditch boss; "Mayordomo." People from all around would come and have their grain ground and for which he would charge a fair price. There was very little money at that time. He would receive very little money. His main recompense for his services would be a certain percent of the grain being ground.*
Three years after Jose Del Carmel was born Mr &s Valencia were blessed by the birth of daughter. Unfortuantely she did not live long. She died after six months. This was a terible blow to Policarpio. As his son grew to manhood he became more dependent on him.
Mr Policarpio Valencia being a traveled man and smart in his own ways, people

from all around sought his advice. He held the attention of all who would come and chatwith him. His wise sayings or maxims were frequent in his conversation. Many of this sayings or maxims are embroidered in his quilt works in display at the New Mexico State Museum. All this embroidery work he did by candle light in the evenings after his day at the mill or in the field.
Mrs Valencia died in the year of 1925. During his last years right after the death of his wife he was elected Justice of the Peace, position he held untile he died in 1931. His son who has related the life of Mr Policarpio Valencia still resides in the Northern part of the State.

ACQUISITION DESCRIPTION (BY E. BOYD)

L.5.54-38

Material description
Embroidery by Policarpio Valencia.

Length, 173 cm. Width at top, 112 cm., at bottom, 122 cm.
Support from top to 19th line of lettering, plain weave, brown, commercial cotton cloth. Below this Valencia made cloth in his usual manner by doing solid buttonhole stitching with white and orange string. Next is a strip of commercial cotton cloth, printed in red and blue. Then another line of buttonhole stitched string fabricated by Valencia. Proceding downward the support is a large piece of very thin, commercial cotton lining material, pale beige. This cloth had many large holes in it which Valencia either patched with scraps of cotton or filled in with beige buttonholing, before he began to do any embroidery.

All around the piece Valencia made borders with white cotton string, also entirely in buttonhole stitching. The two upper corners have blue squares in them. The bottom has unnecessarily wide corners and is worked in stripes and lines of white and orange string.

Inserted across the bottom, below line 46, is a sturdy belt of commercial manufacture, machine knitted in stripes of black, tan and yellow.

The top ten and a fraction lines are worked in red string, the next six and a fraction in brown string. The next section is done in yellow string, the following in white string and the remainder in blue string. All of these were identified by Irene Emery as commercial cotton rug warps (El Palacio, 1952, V [Emery 1952]). *All of the colors have now faded to secondary shades. Down the right hand side of the work on the self-made white border is lettered: "POLICARPIO VALENCIA," reading from bottom to top. The corresponding white border was left vacant. Unlike some others made by Valencia this embroidery has no date on it. The* [text of the reflections—crossed out] *alabado* [inserted] *which* [compose—crossed out] *fills* [inserted] *the embroidery suggests that this was made in Policarpio's last years of old age, and that this may have been the last piece of needlework that he ever did. He died in 1931, at the age of 78.*

ALABADO TRANSCRIPTION

Transcription of L.5.54-38 [from the embroidery]

Line

1 *Despedimiento del pasiente ora sienta cuando /*

2 *pase de esta bida a un otra a dar su cuenta a Dios aconpa-namien- /*

3 *to que sean en mi conpania. Lla se me llego el momento de dar cuenta de /*

4 *mi bida, lla se llego mi partida. Dios me quiso tomar cuenta de esta bida en-*

5 *tretenida la ora que menos se piensa a qui estoy en una tumba todos lo es-*

6 *tan otorgando no lo tengan en olbido a cada uno a de /*

7 *llegando el dia menos pensado sin saber la ora ni cuando a de /*

8 *llegar a to /*

9 *a todos sin destinción. Llo, que estoy en esta tumba, a todos pido perdo /*

10 *perdon. Llo de mi parte perdono a todos sin destinción pues estoy dando mi cu-/*

11 *enta para pasar a mi mansion. Espero ser perdonado de todos de corazon pues es /*

12 *lo mas necesario pa pasar a mi mansion. Al momento de la muerte es un traseto / (transito?)*

13 *de Dios todos deben perdonar para alcansar el perdon siendo presente /*

14 *de Dios se debe tomar perdon a Dios: no puede perdonar aquel a quien otro /*

15 *no perdona A Dios todos los de casa que bibio en compania vicioso ni de /*

16 *besindario y amigos en esta bida pues lla me boy ausentar era dado /*

17 *a la otra bida en tiera. Pasen mi bida y en tiera me de quedaras /*

18 *asta que buelba juisio en segunda benida a ejecutar la sentencia /*

19 *que a cada uno asi lo dada en juicio particular que no ser a rebocada /*

20 *lo pero deben ser jusgados, en jusgados, en juisio particular y quedar deposi- /*

21 *tados asta el juisio unibersal, ya sonido del tronpeta, todos sean de /*

22 *lebentar debon de esten depositados, todos a dar su cuenta final, cuando todos se le- /*

23 *banten debon de esten depositados, todos sean de presentar cuerpo y alma for-*

24 *mados a resebir el castigo o el premio que allan gañado en aqual bibienda.*

25 *Abia gusto y aflición, aflisión por el castigo, y gusto por el galardon y todabia*
26 *mas resibir cuando la separación que los buenos y los malos acaben, si /*
27 *queción ay de ay del que bibe ocioso y olbidado de este dia, que se tiene que /*
28 *las cuentan cuiosa de la bida, asta una palabra osiosa, y dicho como de chansa /*
29 *estar a puesta. En cada mansa cristiano, mira que tienes quien regie en esta bida /*
30 *el santo angel de tu guarda siempre esta en su conpanía, procurator de su bida. /*
31 *Biarte en temor de Dios, obediendo su ley, se recibe el galardon. Si resibes ese don /*
32 *que Dios tiene prometido en aquel mereiste de abia gusto y aflición, afisiona por el cas- /*
33 *tigo y gusto por galardon y todabia pa este bida. E cuando la ceparacion que los buenos /*
34 *Dios mas os acaben su diresion hay de aquel bibeo diosa. Yo olbidado de este dia que se /*
35 *tiene quedar cuenta recuiosa de la bida hasta una palabra ociosa y dicha como /*
36 *de chanza estar a puesta en la lista para echarse en la balansa. Cristiano, mira que tienes /*
37 *quien te gille esta bida, el santo angel de tu guarda, siempre esta en tu conpanía, procurato de /*
38 *tu bida. Bibir en temor de Dios, obediendo su ley, se recibe el galardon. Si recibe d'ese don que Dios tiene pro- /*
39 *metido, en aquel terible dia seras de los escogidos. De lo contrario aquel dia se recibia el castigo. Dios lo tiene /*
40 *prometido. No yo tengan en olbido de toditos me despido lla me ban a sepultar y en la tiera /*
41 *del olbido me ban al depositar. Ruegen a Dios por el alma de este cuerpo aqui tendido, que- /*

(left side) 42 *demos rosario que en el /*
43 *transe de la muerte nos be- /*
44 *an aconpañar. Pues con Je- /*
45 *sus y Maria y José su dulce esposo /*
46 *en las mansiones eternas alla sido resebida a Jesus, Maria y José /*
(center, above belt insert [line 46]*)*

(right side) 47 *todos de /*
48 *enfinita. /*
49 *Para concluir, /*

50 *todos debemos ro- /*
51 *gar que /*
(center, below belt)
52 *en la prostera agonia el alma allar a reposo /*
53 *despido lla me boy a retirar al lugar de esta alma alcanse perdon en la corte selestial, /*
54 *mi destino para siempre a descansar, merejar a un sudario, lla me quedo en mi lugar que Cristo nos a dejado. Para /*
55 *recuerdo final, pues, con este, digo adios a presentes y ausentes y ruegen a Dios que en su reino ejiste por /*
56 *siempre. Amen. /*

In 1967, University of New Mexico folklorist Rubén Cobos submitted an expert transcription of "Adios, acompañamiento," which he addressed "Para mi amiga E. Boyd." In his notes Cobos identifies the alabado as a *despedimiento* or first-person farewell in which "the deceased warns us to keep the laws of Catholicism and reminds us that in the day of judgment even a word said in jest will be recorded against us and will merit due punishment." He points out various New Mexicanisms in the text and cites a similar despedimiento in Juan B. Rael's *The New Mexican* Alabado, a single version collected in Manassa, Colorado (1951: 133–35).[1]

NOTE

1. In his recent discussion of the despedimiento, folklorist John Donald Robb notes that "Cobos in one of his articles in [the Santa Fe paper] *El Nuevo Mexicano* ["El Folklore Nuevo Mexicano," 4 May 1950] expresses the conviction that at least one of the *despedimentos [sic], Adiós Acompañamiento . . .*, was brought from Spain in the seventeenth century" (Robb 1980: 710). Robb presents texts, translations, and musical transcriptions of five such songs (1980: 710–16). Alice Corbin Henderson has published the text and translation of a similar alabado, which she copied "from a small *Penitente* copy-book, much worn from use" (1937: 85, 98–107).

KATE PECK KENT

SPANISH, NAVAJO, OR PUEBLO? A GUIDE TO THE IDENTIFICATION OF NINETEENTH-CENTURY SOUTHWESTERN TEXTILES

NINETEENTH-CENTURY TEXTILES of the Spanish people of the Rio Grande valley, the Navajo Indians, and the Pueblo Indians share many characteristics of design and technique. While most are easily recognized as the product of one or another of these three weaving traditions, every large collection of Southwestern textiles inevitably will contain a few puzzling pieces that have been incorrectly identified or that seem to defy precise classification. This essay sets forth criteria that may be used to help establish the cultural origin of such textiles and illustrates the way in which these criteria have been applied to the identification of several anomalous pieces in the collection of the School of American Research in Santa Fe, New Mexico. These criteria are intended as guides for museum curators and others charged with the documentation of Southwestern textile collections.[1]

The essential characteristics of form, technique, and design that distinguish Navajo from Pueblo textiles were quite well established by the fourth decade of the twentieth century. Navajo weaving in particular had commanded the attention of scholars and public alike beginning with Washington Matthews's "Navajo Weavers" in 1884. In his classic study *Navajo Weaving* (1949), which first appeared in 1934, Charles Avery Amsden summarizes the evolution of the art from its inception in the late seventeenth century through the early twentieth century and links changes in style to the historical experiences of the Navajo people. Gladys Reichard's *Spider Woman* (1934) and *Navajo Shepherd and Weaver* (1936) give us very lively accounts of weaving and its place in the lives of Navajo women. Finally, in a series of pamphlets written during the late 1930s and later collected and published in book form in 1948, Harry P. Mera describes the basic types of Navajo textiles such as the "chief" blanket, woman's dress, and so on. Many of his illustrations are of blankets in the School of American Research collections. Because his book continues to serve as a reference for museum curators, several of his misidentifications have been corrected here.

Although they represent products of the truly indigenous, pre-Spanish, weaving tradition in the Southwest and are the actual source from which the Navajo learned their art, Pueblo textiles have never attracted intensive scholarly or popular attention. The leaflets by Frederic H. Douglas published by the Denver, Colorado, Art Museum (1939*a*–1940*c*) remain the best descriptive summary of historic Pueblo weaving, delineating the range of forms and distinguishing, insofar as possible, between the work of the various Pueblo villages. In an unpublished manuscript on an Acoma blanket, probably written during the early 1950s, Douglas (n.d.*a*) also comments on the problem of differentiating certain Pueblo and Navajo striped blankets: "There may be variations in selvage, tassels, and perhaps inner details of weaving. But if so I know of no studies which have made these points clear." Analysis of hundreds of Southwestern textiles in American museums and private collections since his note was written has shown that there are indeed diagnostic differences in these and other features.[2]

Weaving by the Spanish in the Rio Grande valley simply was not singled out for study in any serious way before the 1960s except by Mera, whose investigations into the art began in 1910. His analysis of the Alfred I. Barton collection of Southwestern textiles, which includes almost fifty Rio Grande Spanish pieces, was not published until 1949. Between 1947 and 1951, he prepared a slender volume, "Spanish-American Blanketry: Its Relationship to Aboriginal Weaving in the South West," for the School of American Research, but it was never published. However, Mera shared his knowledge and enthusiasm for the subject with E. Boyd, who subsequently designed and put into operation (1967–1969) a project that led to the collection of data on over one thousand blankets in American museums (Kent 1980: 77). E. Boyd's own *Popular Arts of Spanish New Mexico* contains a valuable summary chapter on "Textiles and Costume" (1974: 171–245). Finally, recognizing the historic importance of Spanish weaving in the Southwest, the Museum of International Folk Art in Santa Fe published *Spanish Textile Tradition of New Mexico and Colorado* (Nestor 1979). With this, the last of the three traditions was adequately documented in print.

Those of us privileged to work with Mera, Douglas, and E. Boyd learned the importance of paying attention to detail—for example, to look for clues about the date or cultural origin of a textile in such minutiae as the direction of twist in a spun yarn or the construction of the selvage. Such an analytical approach is not an end in itself, of course, but it is absolutely necessary in order to place a piece in proper historical perspective. Before discussing the documentation of Navajo, Pueblo, and Rio Grande Spanish textiles, however, a brief review of the historical interaction between these three peoples will help to illuminate the evolution of historic Southwestern weaving, a subject that has been discussed at length elsewhere (for example, Kent 1976; Wheat 1976*b*).

HISTORIC LINKS BETWEEN THE THREE SOUTHWESTERN WEAVING TRADITIONS

The Pueblo people were dressed in cotton clothing of their own manufacture when the Spanish entered the Southwest in the early sixteenth century (Kent 1957, 1982). The most basic article of wearing apparel was the shoulder blanket or *manta.* Patterned in several different ways, these were woven on the vertical loom in sizes designed to fit men, women, or children. Mantas were rectangular in shape, the greater dimension paralleling the wefts, and often had decorative borders along the top and bottom edges. Women wore one manta as a shoulder robe and one as a dress, folded about the body under the left arm, fastened on the right shoulder and belted at the waist. Men wore sleeveless or sleeved shirts, breechcloths, and, at least in ceremonies, kilts. Belts were woven on a narrow waist loom.

With the advent of Spanish settlers in 1598, sheep were introduced, and wool soon replaced cotton in many traditional Pueblo articles of clothing, although tools, weaving techniques, and textile forms remained the same. The influence of the Spanish was undoubtedly much stronger on the New Mexico Pueblos than on the remote Hopi; however, certain items probably were adopted in all the villages before the Pueblo Revolt of 1680. These would include wool, wool cards, indigo dye and the technology for its use, knitting with needles as a replacement for the hand-looping of footwear, weaving weft-faced sarapes, and the Moki pattern.

A *sarape* is a blanket that differs from traditional Pueblo shoulder blankets in shape. Its greater dimension is measured along the *warps,* that is, it is longer than it is wide. Many of the earliest sarapes are patterned by narrow brown or black, indigo blue, and white stripes (Fig. 1). Striped blankets of this kind are usually spoken of as "Moki-patterned," *Moki* being a designation formerly used for the Hopi. Early dealers in Southwestern weaving assumed that the Pueblo Indians, more specifically the Hopi, should be credited with originating the design and weaving most such blankets, and the term is still used to describe the pattern. Although pieces of wool blankets in this design have been found in an early eighteenth-century Hopi site at Walpi, it is probable that most Moki-patterned blankets were actually woven by the Spanish or the Navajos.

Judging from the nineteenth-century evidence, other Spanish influences had differential effects on the textile industries of the New Mexico Pueblos. Zuni shows the closest links to Spanish work, both in certain selvage treatments and in the presence of a Spanish floral motif in its embroidery. This motif also appears on embroidered textiles from Jémez, Acoma, and Laguna (Mera 1943: 16). European-style drawn work and crochet have been used historically as openwork decoration on white commercial cotton cloth shirts

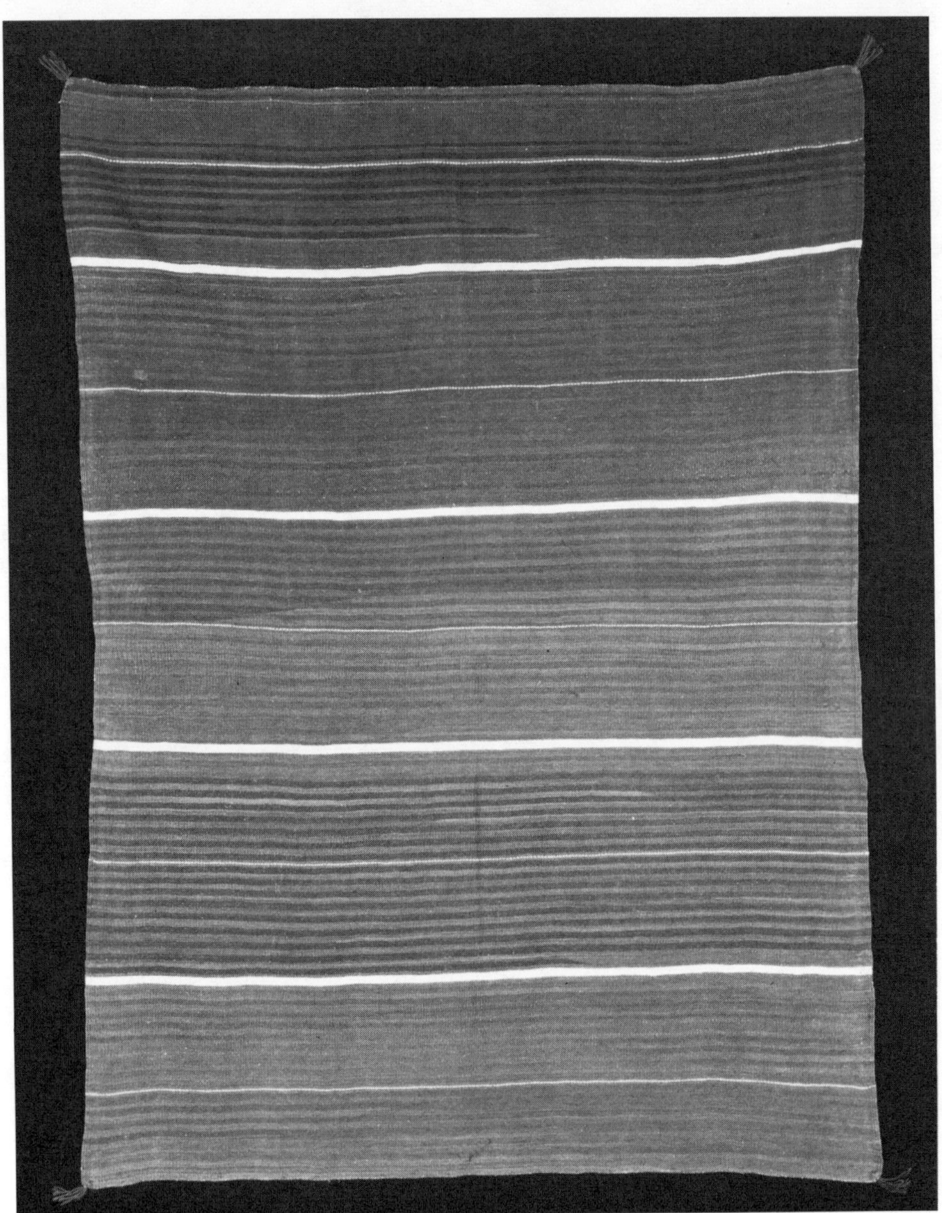

FIGURE 1
Moki-patterned blanket, probably Zuni. (IAF T.104. Courtesy School of American Research.)

at Sandia and Isleta. Interestingly, some of the design motifs duplicate those found on white cotton weft-warp openwork fabrics from pre-Spanish Mogollon and Hohokam sites. Crochet was also adopted by several Tewa Pueblos for the manufacture of openwork dance shirts and leggings formerly made by finger techniques. In short, while the Pueblos took over various techniques and new materials from the Spanish, they kept their own design system and traditional textile forms.

Spanish settlers utilized the products of Pueblo looms, taking mantas and other articles first as tribute (1600s) and later in trade (Minge 1979: 10–18). However, no Pueblo influence of any kind is reflected in the Spanish treadle-loom fabrics. Likewise, the colcha embroidery of Spanish women differs totally from Pueblo embroidery in design and stitch.

The Navajos learned to weave from the Pueblos in the last half of the seventeenth century, adopting the wide vertical loom and the belt loom and producing mantas, breechcloths, shirts, and belts, all of which must have been virtually identical with those of their Pueblo instructors. The Navajo fibers and dyes were the same as those already in use by the Pueblos. There is little doubt that, in addition to weaving clothing for themselves, the Navajo produced sarapes, many patterned by narrow blue, brown, and white stripes, for trade with the Spanish. Because they are so alike in technique and form, eighteenth- and early nineteenth-century textiles of the Pueblos and Navajos are often difficult to differentiate. Navajo and Zuni weaving have most in common, suggesting that weavers from Zuni may have been the first to teach their skills to the Navajos.

There had been trade contacts between the seventeenth-century Pueblos and the Navajos, but these were probably too casual to have led to the transfer of weaving skills. These were more likely to have been taught by captives taken during Navajo raids on Pueblo villages or by Pueblo individuals who had voluntarily left their homes and moved into Navajo communities to escape Spanish rule. Still, it is remarkable that the Navajos, like the Spanish, did not adopt the Pueblo technique of embroidery or any of the Pueblo design motifs. Early Navajo mantas and blankets were decorated with design motifs drawn from their own basketry patterns (Fig. 2).

FIGURE 2
Navajo wool manta with woven patterned border. (IAF T.355. Courtesy School of American Research.)

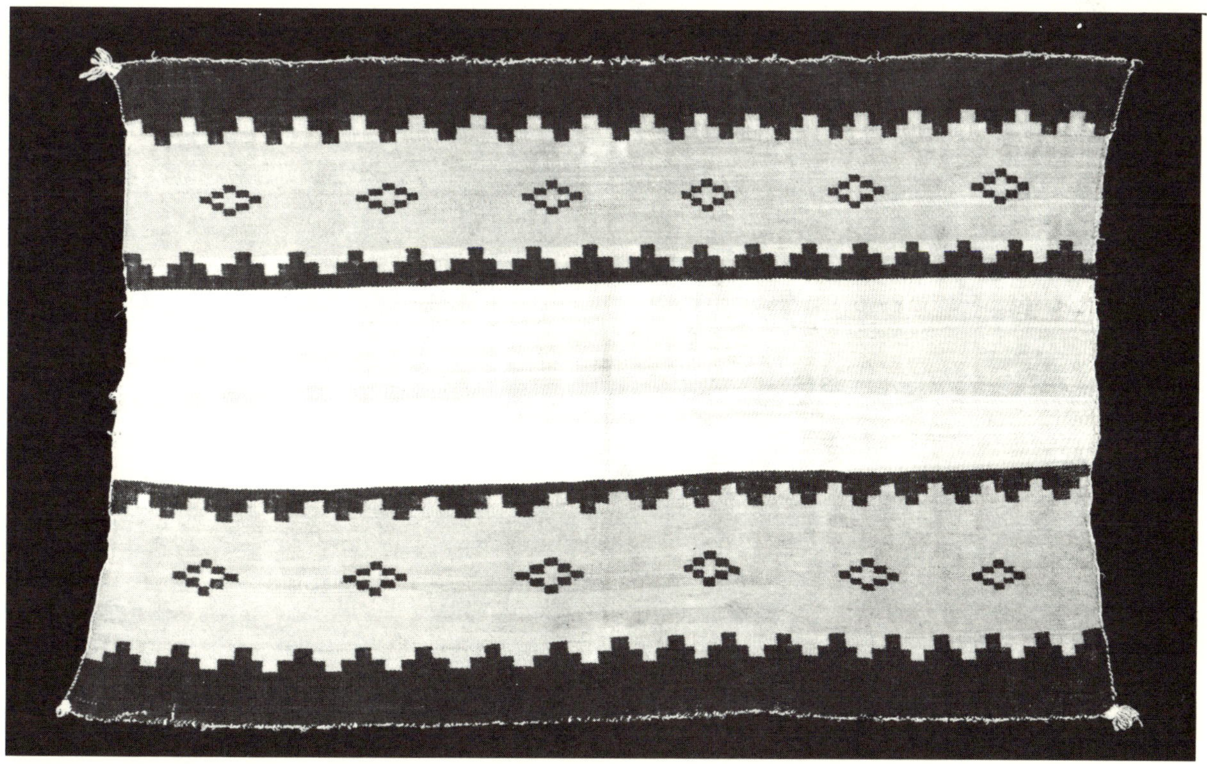

Spanish documents from the early eighteenth century speak of the quantity and high quality of Navajo blankets (Hill 1940). Throughout the century they were much in demand by the colonists for their own use and as trade items to be sent south to New Spain. Navajo blankets were also traded to Pueblo, Ute, and Plains Indians throughout the eighteenth and the first half of the nineteenth centuries (McNitt 1962: 35–36). The ready market for their work must have led Navajo women to increase their annual production.

Navajo-Spanish contacts were not based solely on trade, however. The Navajos raided Spanish settlements, as they did Pueblo villages, and were subject to reprisals. These hostilities were especially severe between about 1800 and 1870, and both sides took captives. Captive Navajos entered Spanish households as servants, as did Navajo children who had been purchased, usually from Utes. The girls and women helped with domestic tasks, including weaving. They are said to have done this on the vertical loom familiar to them, producing the blankets called "slave blankets" that combined the technical and artistic features of Navajo and Spanish weaving.[3] The presence of these Navajo weavers in Spanish households may help to account for the appearance of Navajo-style terraced figures and for the design distribution on some treadle-loom blankets of the early and middle nineteenth century (Fig. 3).

Mexican blanket designs, particularly from Saltillo, were introduced into the Rio Grande valley in the early 1800s or before, and their distinctive designs strongly influenced local Spanish weavers. Dominant characteristics of the Saltillo design system include a central serrate or diamond figure; borders (sometimes fancy side borders and simple stripes along both ends); often vertical zigzag striping of the background; and small "floating" elements. Some of these small figures, such as the hourglass and serrate diamond, were "extracted" from the large center diamond (Jeter and Juelke 1978). Backgrounds filled by tiny "dots and dashes" appear on Saltillo blankets, probably through Oaxacan influence (Bowen 1979: 97). With their internment by the Anglo-Americans at Bosque Redondo in New Mexico (1863–1868), Navajo women were exposed to Rio Grande Spanish blankets patterned after Mexican Saltillos, and serrate figures soon largely replaced the classic Navajo terraced designs (Fig. 4).

Because the three groups borrowed design ideas, fibers, dyes, and technical processes from one another, certain textiles of the Navajos, Pueblos, and Spanish are very much alike and may pose problems of identification for museum curators. Most difficulties center on the recognition of sarapes, but there are a number of traditional items of Pueblo and Navajo clothing that are apt to be assigned to the wrong group. These include the type of manta known as the "maiden shawl" (white with indigo blue and red twill weave borders; Fig. 5), the woman's black wool manta with indigo blue diamond twill borders (Fig. 6), wool mantas with woven patterns in the bor-

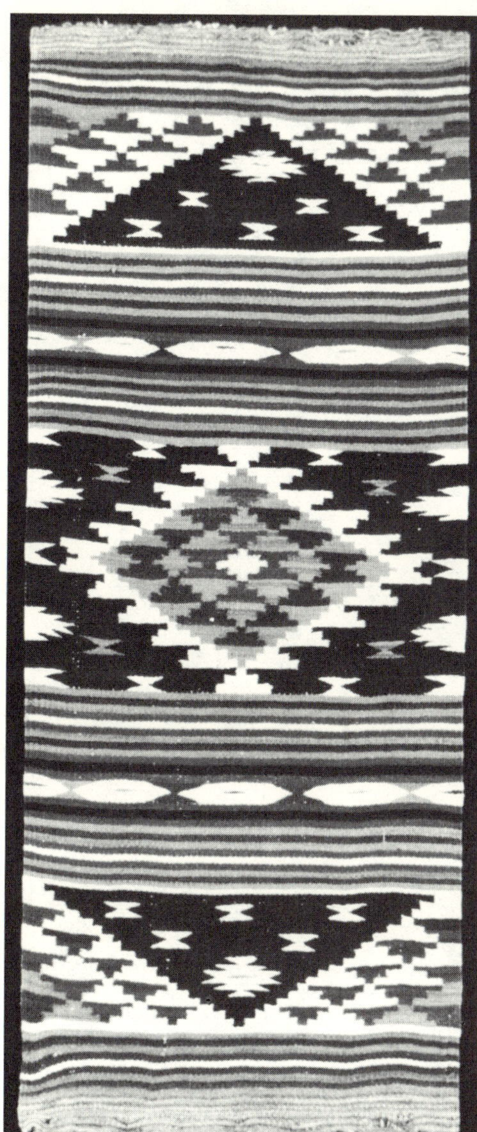

FIGURE 3
Servant blanket, woven in Abiquiú about 1875. (Museum of New Mexico Collection at the Museum of International Folk Art, Santa Fe. Gift of the Historical Society of New Mexico, A.5.57.10. Photo courtesy Museum of International Folk Art.)

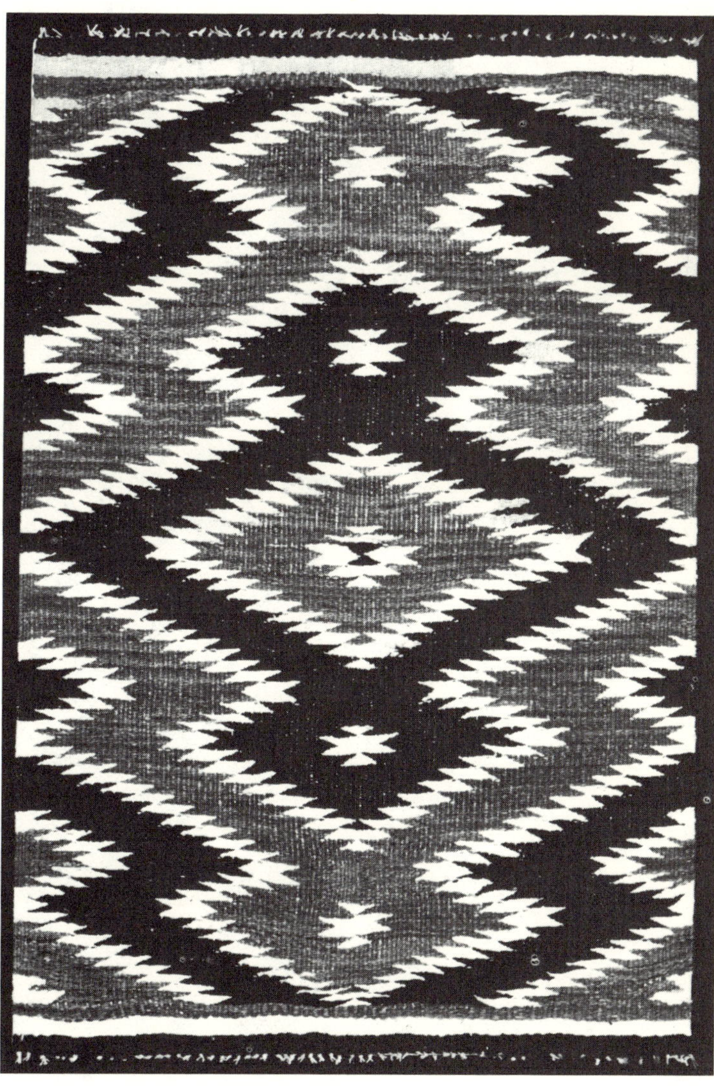

FIGURE 4
Rio Grande blanket showing Saltillo influence. (IAF T.319. Courtesy School of American Research.)

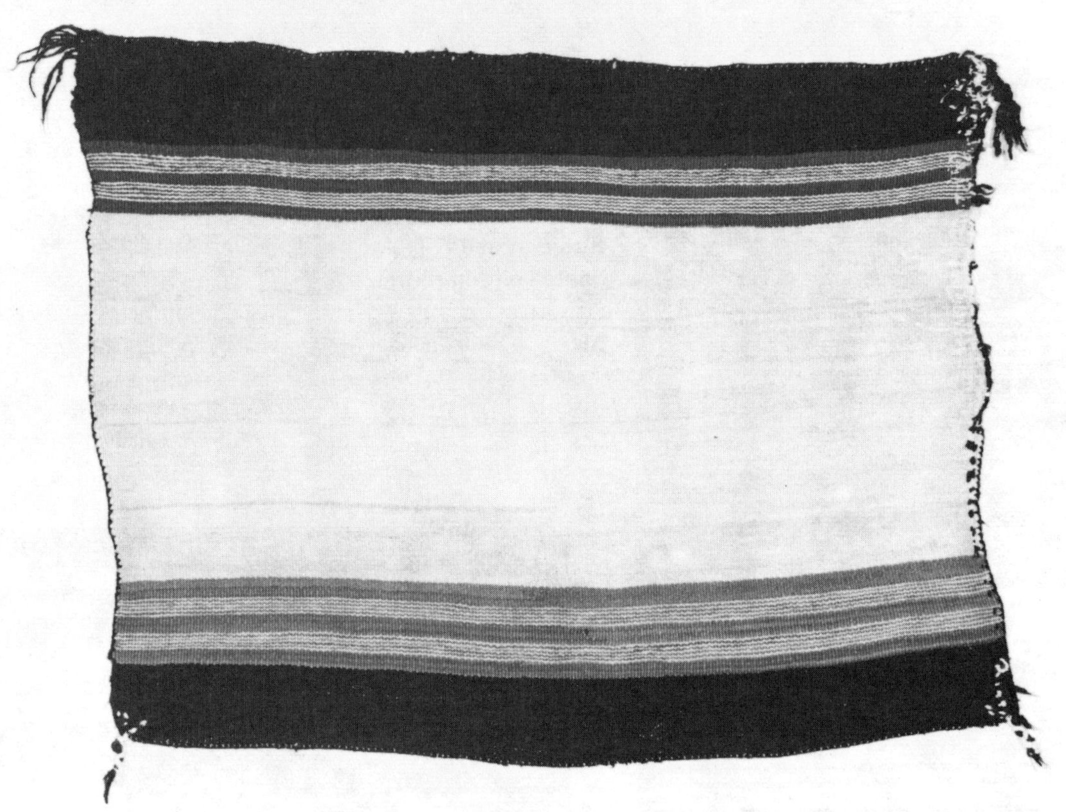

FIGURE 5
Navajo-woven "maiden shawl." (IAF T.358. Courtesy School of American Research.)

FIGURE 6
Navajo black wool manta with blue diamond twill borders. (IAF T.707. Courtesy School of American Research.)

ders (Fig. 2), wool shirts, and Navajo-style warp-float belts (red, green, and white). In the case of the wide-loom fabrics, distinctions can be made on the basis of weave technicalities and design characteristics (discussed later for blankets), but I know of no reliable diagnostic differences between Navajo-style belts woven by Navajos and those of Pueblo manufacture.

CRITERIA FOR DIFFERENTIATING NINETEENTH-CENTURY SPANISH, NAVAJO, AND PUEBLO SARAPES

Sarapes are plain weave, weft-faced, or tapestry. *Weft-faced* means that the wefts outnumber the warps per unit of measurement and are compacted so as to completely cover the warps. *Tapestry weave* is also weft-faced, but wefts do not pass from edge to edge of the web. Instead, each different color of weft weaves back and forth in its own restricted area, so that patterns of color blocks are produced. While essentially the same in technique, there are many internal differences between sarapes of the Spanish, Navajos, and Pueblos.

Some of the differences relate directly to the type of looms used. Pueblos and Navajos wove single-width blankets on the indigenous vertical loom, the warp sets controlled by a string-loop heddle and a shed rod that were manipulated by hand, and the weft beaten down with a long wooden, sword-shaped batten. The Spanish, however, wove on the flat treadle loom of European derivation. Heddles were hung from above and were controlled by foot treadles, freeing the hands to manipulate the weft. Warps were passed between the dents of a reed, which spaced them and was used to beat the weft into place.

Until wide reeds were introduced into the Southwest, probably in the late 1880s, flat looms were narrow (Fisher 1979*b*: 194–95). Cloth woven on them measured between twenty-two and thirty inches in width. Two matching widths, woven separately, were sewed together to make the sarape, or a sarape might be woven double width on the loom (Fig. 7*a* and *b*). In that case, a double layer of cloth was woven, joined only by a common weft along one edge. When removed from the loom and opened out, it was as wide as the two-piece blanket. A double-woven blanket is readily recognized by the presence of a ridge formed by one or more pairs of warps at its exact center.

While the width of a fabric was constrained by the structure of the treadle loom and its reed, the length was not. Treadle looms were used to weave yard goods of whatever length the weaver wished (Boyd 1974: 182; Fisher 1979*b*: 193, 1979*c*: 144–45). Rio Grande blankets, probably reflecting this potential, tend to be long and narrow in shape. In 85 percent of the sixty-four blankets that have been measured, the length is more than 1.5 times the width, and most of them are between 1.5 and 1.85 times longer than they are wide.

Navajo blankets, on the other hand, tend to be wider in relation to length.

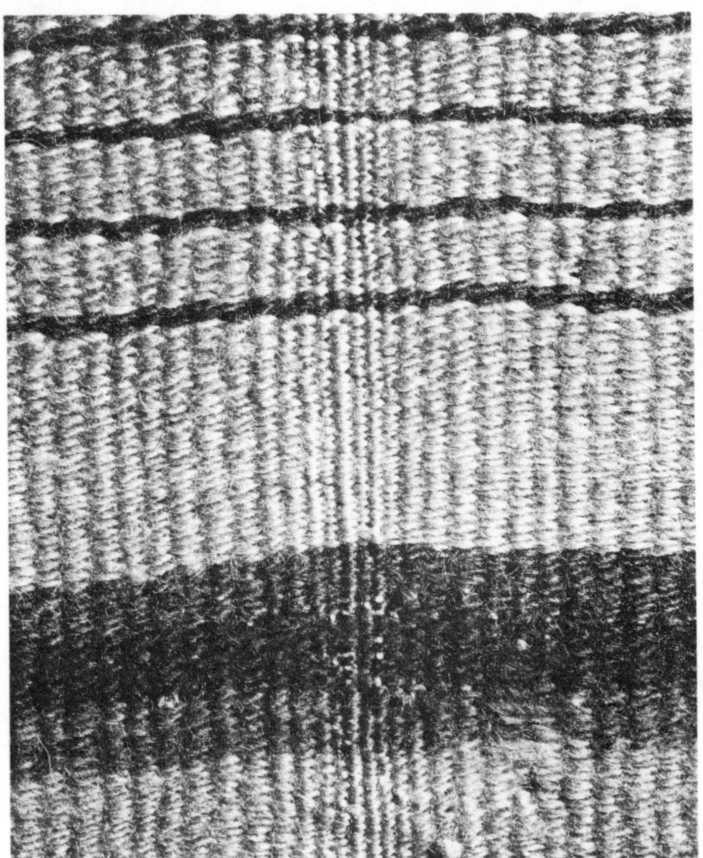

FIGURE 7
a. Paired warps at the center of a double-woven Rio Grande blanket. (Photo courtesy Museum of International Folk Art.)

b. Center seam of a Rio Grande blanket woven as two separate pieces. (Photo courtesy Museum of International Folk Art.)

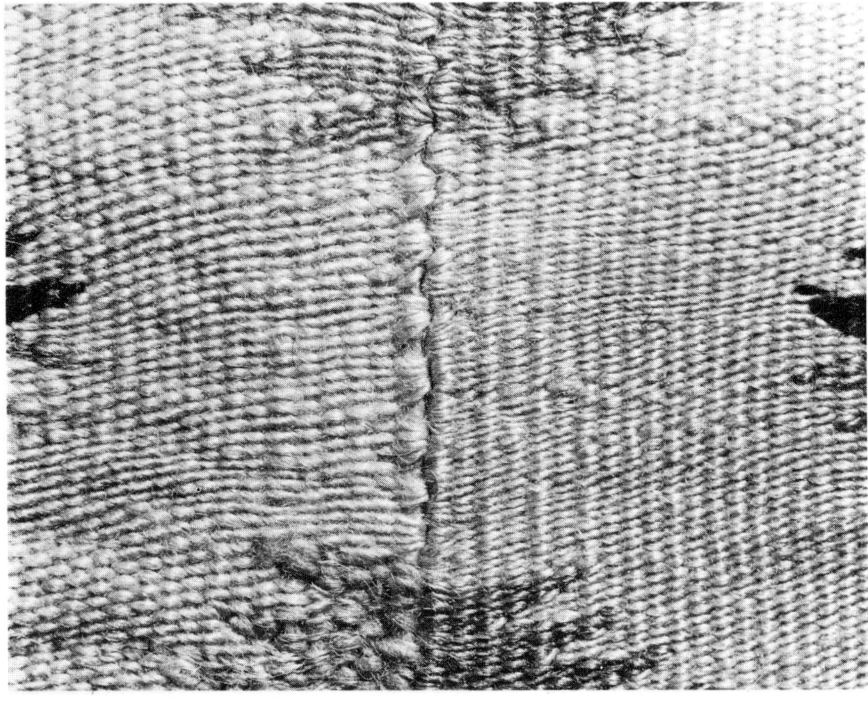

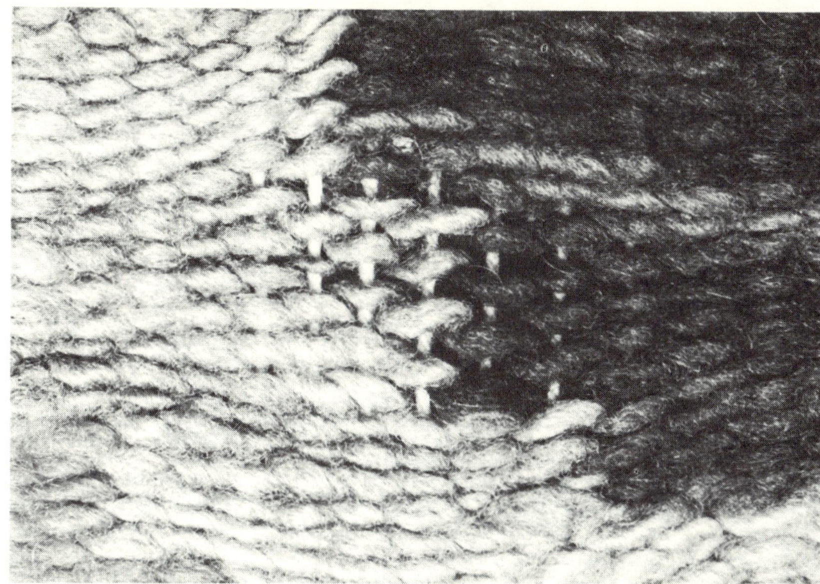

FIGURE 7
c. Interlocked wefts in a Navajo blanket. (Photo by Deborah Flynn. Courtesy School of American Research.)

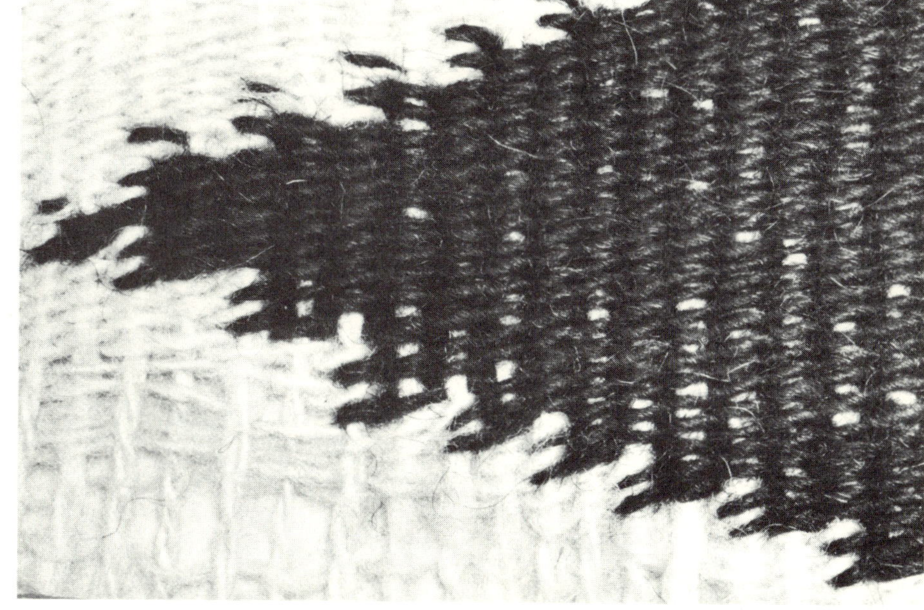

d. Dovetailed wefts in a Rio Grande blanket. (Photo by Deborah Flynn. Courtesy School of American Research.)

Of eighty-nine blankets measured, only 47 percent were more than 1.5 times longer than wide. The length of most was between 1.3 and 1.5 times the width.

Douglas (1940*c*: 177) held that blankets woven at Zuni are even wider and tend toward a square shape. I have measurements for only twenty-five blankets that I would call Zuni on grounds other than shape. Only six (24 percent) are over 1.5 times longer than wide. In the other nineteen, the length ranges from 1.12 to 1.49 times the width. Douglas's contention seems to be based on fact, but the actual distinction in proportions between Navajo and Zuni blankets is not very pronounced.

The length of the warp on a vertical loom is limited to the distance between the upper and lower bars to which the cloth and yarn beams are secured. In Navajo looms, this must conform to the length of the vertical side bars of the loom frame. As a loom cannot be higher than the distance from floor to ceiling, from five to eight feet is a realistic, practical height for a loom set up in the house or kiva, as among the Pueblos. The width may be as great as the length of the loom beams; it is not determined by a commercial reed of set size. Proportions of Navajo/Pueblo blankets thus reflect not only the structure of their looms but probably also the original, traditional shape of each group's mantas.

When a treadle-loom fabric is finished, it is cut from the loom, and the warp ends are knotted together to form a fringe at each end of the piece or run back into the fabric. There are no warp selvage cords along the ends, nor are there extra weft selvage cords. The outer warps at each edge of the blanket are simply handled in pairs. The warp of Navajo/Pueblo blankets, on the other hand, is a continuous yarn, passing between extra selvage cords that are twisted about each other between each loop of the warp. These cords are actually run in during the warping process; in the finished blanket, they are seen as warp selvage cords. Navajo/Pueblo blankets also have twisted yarns along both weft edges (Fig. 8*a*). These yarns were hung at each side of the warp set before weaving commenced and were twisted between wefts during weaving. The presence of twisted yarn selvages along warp and weft edges is an important factor distinguishing Navajo/Pueblo blankets from Spanish ones. Occasionally, however, Zuni blankets lack selvage yarns, and sometimes two or more edge warps are paired in the Spanish fashion (Fig. 8*b*). Sometimes too the Zuni weaver cut and tied his warp ends into a fringe, or knotted extra strings to the warp loops to make a fringe (Fig. 9).

Normally the Navajos used two strands in their selvages, each strand containing either two or three single-ply yarns twisted together. Pueblo weavers preferred to use three strands in a selvage, each strand containing two single-ply yarns. Sometimes the Pueblos, like the Navajos, did use two-ply strands. The Zuni might use either the Navajo or the Pueblo system, being more apt to use three strands in traditional mantas and two strands in sarapes.

Navajo women habitually tied the ends of their selvage yarns tightly together at the blanket corners, often causing the corner to roll in on itself, and ran in extra lengths of yarn at the corners to augment the small tassel formed by selvage-yarn ends. Pueblo men usually knotted warp and weft selvage ends separately or tied or braided them together beginning some distance from the fabric corner, thus leaving it open (Fig. 8*a*). They sometimes added a tassel to the selvage ends.

Although all three groups wove tapestry blankets, they tended to select different ways of handling the lines along which adjoining wefts meet (Fig.

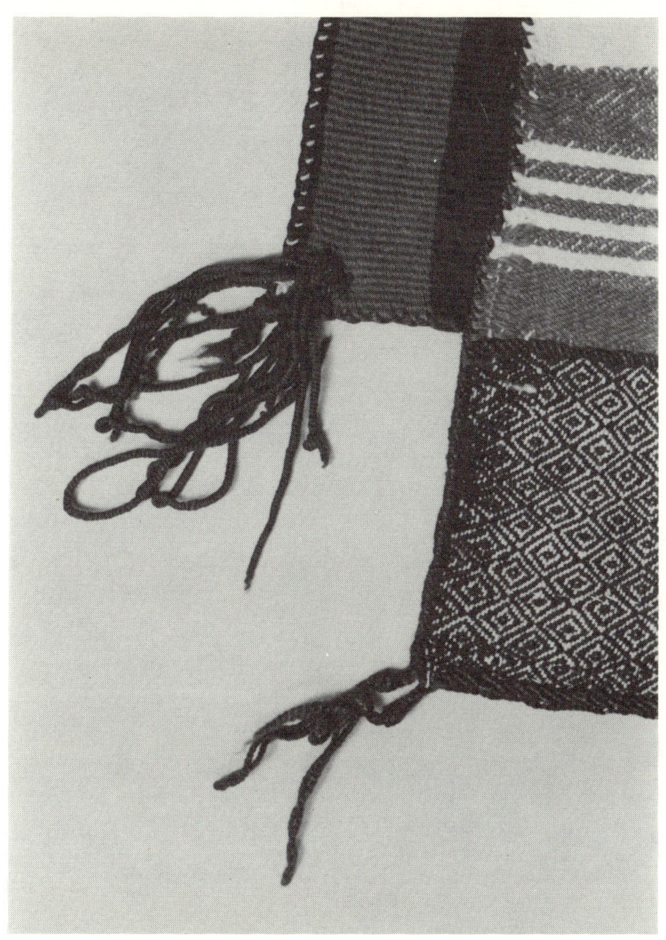

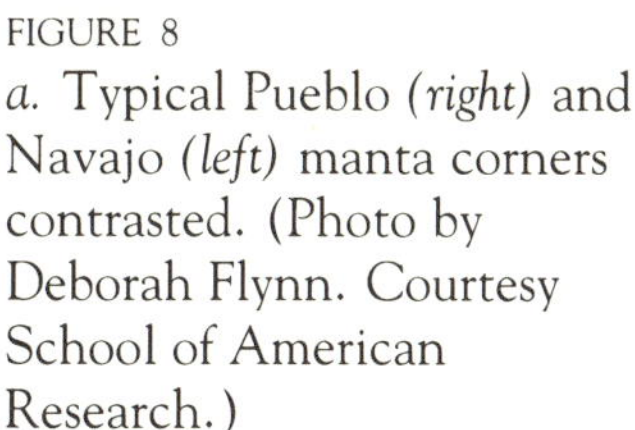

FIGURE 8

a. Typical Pueblo *(right)* and Navajo *(left)* manta corners contrasted. (Photo by Deborah Flynn. Courtesy School of American Research.)

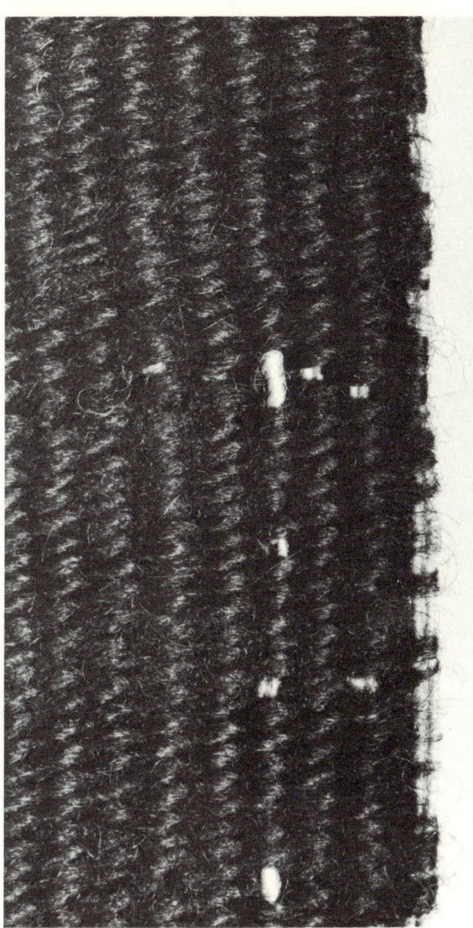

b. Zuni blanket edge with paired warps. (Photo by Deborah Flynn. Courtesy School of American Research.)

7*c* and *d*). This may be done in one of three ways: There may be no structural connection between adjoining wefts so that a slit is left in the fabric; adjoining wefts may interlock about each other between warps; or adjoining wefts may be dovetailed or passed about a common warp (Fisher 1979*a*: 203–6). If the wefts meet along a diagonal line, they are usually not structurally joined by Southwestern weavers. If, however, wefts meet along a vertical or nearly vertical line, they must be structurally connected in order to prevent the formation of a slit in the fabric. (Slit tapestry, or *kelim*, a decorative technique popular in some parts of the world, was not favored by his-

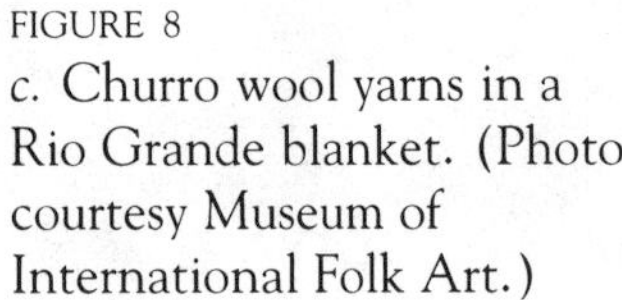

FIGURE 8
c. Churro wool yarns in a Rio Grande blanket. (Photo courtesy Museum of International Folk Art.)

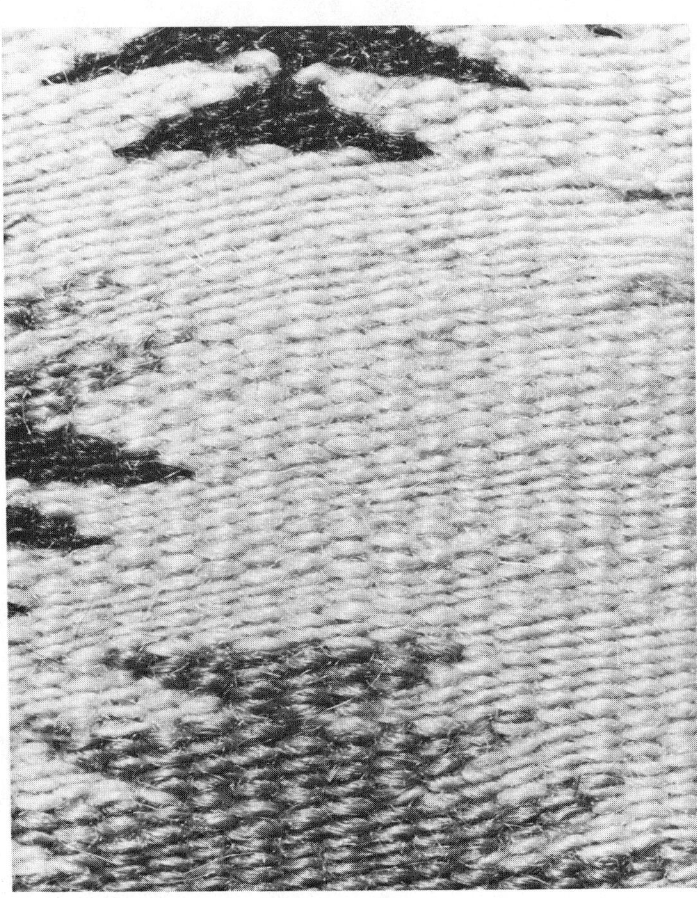

d. Rambouillet-merino wool yarns in a Rio Grande blanket. (Photo courtesy Museum of International Folk Art.)

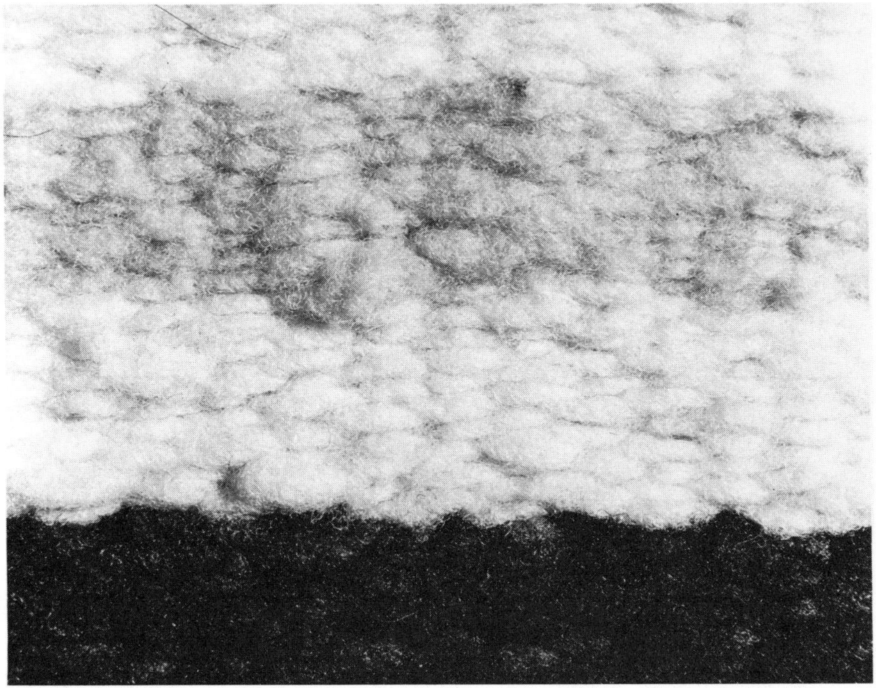

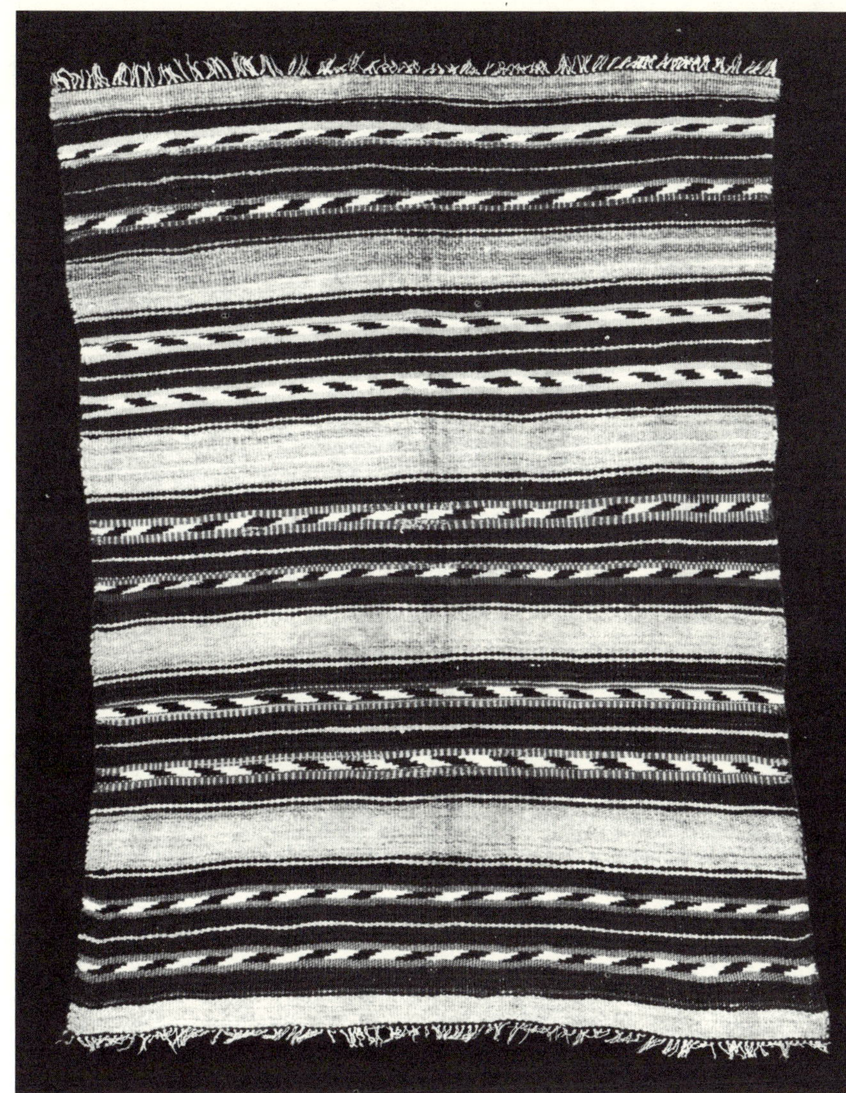

FIGURE 9
Zuni blanket with fringed ends. (IAF T.77. Courtesy School of American Research.)

toric Southwestern weavers.) Rio Grande weavers usually elected to dovetail alternate wefts around a single warp. The interlocking of wefts between warps is rare on Rio Grande blankets. Navajo and Pueblo weavers sometimes used dovetailing but more often chose to interlock wefts between warps. Thus the type of structural connection used may furnish at least a hint as to the ethnic origin of a blanket's weaver.

Another weave technicality, the "lazy line," usually indicates that a blanket is Navajo-woven. A lazy line is a diagonal break in the fabric that occurs if it has been woven in sections. The break marks the line along which the independently woven sections meet. It is technically the same as the diagonal line or slit between two colors of weft in tapestry weave, but lazy lines are found within a single color block. Although weaving a blanket in sections is the usual Navajo practice, not all Navajo blankets have lazy lines, and some Zuni ones do,[4] so the presence of lazy lines is a criterion that must be applied with caution.

Two idiosyncratic Zuni weaving practices of interest to curators working with the identification of Southwestern textiles were recorded by Leslie Spier in 1916. He described ways of inserting wefts that would produce distinctive edge features and noted that, in weaving black wool twill mantas, the weft was carried on *two* separate stick bobbins rather than one, as is usually recorded (1924: 185). The first bobbin was carried through the shed from right to left and the weft battened down; the second bobbin was inserted in the next shed, again from right to left. The two then succeeded one another, left to right, in the next two sheds. This means the first bobbin would deliver picks 1-3-5-etc., and the second picks 2-4-6-etc. The alternating of weft yarns would show at the manta's edges. Spier also describes blanket weaving in which "a length of weft slightly greater than the width of warps is broken from the ball of yarn. This is carried through the shed with the fingers and picked very slack for about a foot at a time. The surplus weft at the edges is turned back into the fell" (1924: 187).[5]

Until the 1880s the most common material used in weaving by Spanish, Navajos, and Pueblos alike was hand-spun wool yarn (Fig. 8*c*). The wool was that of the *churro,* the sheep of the common people of Spain brought to the New World in the sixteenth century. Churro fibers are long, silky, straight, and relatively free from oil, making them ideal for processing by the hand methods used in the Southwest. In 1859, however, Rambouillet-merino sheep with their crimped, oily fleece were introduced into New Mexico (Fig. 8*d*). Their wool was difficult to clean and spin and resisted dye. As a result, the quality of blankets made from hand-spun wool yarns and dyed locally deteriorated in the last quarter of the nineteenth century. My impression is that noticeably crimped hand-spun yarns appear in many Rio Grande Spanish and "servant blankets" woven between 1870 and 1885, but they are not prevalent in Navajo/Pueblo work until the late nineteenth and early twentieth centuries (Fisher and Wheat 1979: 197–98).

Rio Grande weavers used two-ply hand-spun yarns (Z-spun plied S) for warp, and Z-spun single-ply yarns for weft (Fig. 7*d*). Navajo/Pueblo weavers preferred single-ply Z-spun yarns for both warp and weft (Fig. 8*b*), although occasionally two-ply warps are found in a servant blanket. A Z-spun yarn is one in which the individual fibers trend in the direction of the center bar of the letter Z if the yarn is held in a vertical position (/). Rio Grande blanket warp yarns were spun with such a twist, but two such yarns were then joined, or plied, with an S-twist, the individual yarns both trending in the direction of the center bar of the letter S (\).

According to Douglas (n.d.*a*), Pueblo wool blankets are noticeably smoother and more even in diameter than Navajo yarns because Pueblo spinners rubbed the yarn with a corn cob during spinning, a subtle distinction that I am not able to verify. Matilda Coxe Stevenson (n.d.) recorded the use of a corn cob in this manner at Zuni in 1879, and it has been noted recently for the Hopis.

Spanish blankets woven from hand-spun wool yarns had a yarn count of five to seven warps and twenty-five to fifty wefts to the inch. In the late 1880s, wide reeds with closely spaced metal dents were imported into the Southwest. With the use of these new reeds and commercial cotton string warps, the warp count increased to six to eleven per inch (Fisher 1979*b*: 194–95). Navajo blankets were much more tightly woven, with warps numbering six to twelve and wefts twenty to one hundred to the inch.

Pueblo blankets were more loosely woven than either Navajo or Spanish, with warp counts ranging from three to five and weft counts from ten to twenty to the inch (Wheat 1979: 31). The openness of Pueblo plain-weave wool sarapes probably marks a carry-over from their prehistoric and historic plain-weave cotton mantas, in which the warp-weft count tends to be square (that is, an equal number of warps and wefts to the inch) so that both elements can be seen in the finished piece, although neither is strongly predominant visually. Historic Pueblo twill weaves also have a lower warp-weft count and tend to be more open than Navajo twill weaves.

Yarns raveled from commercially woven wool cloth, usually red in color, supplemented hand-spun yarn in the early and middle nineteenth century. The variations in weight, direction of twist, and dye color among raveled yarns furnishes a guide to dating blankets.[6]

Raveled yarns were used sparingly by the Spanish, in figures only. The Navajos, however, wove them into both figures and ground. Navajo women (ca. 1865–1875) even devised ways of utilizing wool flannel cloth that defied raveling into separate yarns for weaving. They recarded fibers from such cloth and spun them into yarn, often combining red fibers with their own white wool to produce a pink yarn. Sometimes too they cut the cloth into very thin strips that could be woven into a blanket as wefts. One does find a few Pueblo blankets with cloth strips, raveled yarns, or recarded yarns in them. For the most part, however, the Pueblos raveled commercial cloth to get materials for embroidery and, until the late nineteenth century, for belts (Douglas 1935–1938). The Navajos may also have used raveled yarns in belts. The use of cloth strips and recarded yarns is not characteristic of Spanish work, carded pink having been identified in only one Rio Grande blanket (Nestor 1979: pl. 51).

Commercial three-ply yarns dyed with natural dyes were imported into the Southwest prior to about 1860. These were utilized by the Spanish in the same manner as raveled yarn, that is, to make spots of color in blanket patterns. Such yarns are also found in colcha embroidery. The Navajos wove the yarns into both figure and ground, and the Pueblos employed them principally in embroidery.

Synthetic-dyed commercial yarns were introduced after 1860. The earliest of these were three-ply (1860–8175), but those used since about 1875 are four-ply. Cotton string also became available to weavers by 1880 and was used for warp. These commercial materials had virtually replaced hand-spun wool in Spanish blankets by the late nineteenth century and were widely used by the Navajos from 1880 to 1900. Commercial yarns appear in Pueblo belts and embroidery in place of hand-spun or raveled yarns before the turn of the century, and they have gradually supplanted hand-spun native cotton and wool in other traditional textiles since that time.

The analysis of color in Southwestern textiles has barely begun, so there are more questions than answers about the sources of the natural dyes used prior to the introduction of synthetics (Saltzman and Fisher 1979: 212–16). Natural tones of wool supplied all three groups, with white, black, brown, and various gray and tan shades produced by carding white and dark wool fibers together. Some Zuni blankets (Fig. 9) contain distinctive silvery gray or tan yarns from sheep raised by them in the late nineteenth century.[7]

From 1600 to 1880 (and, indeed, to a certain extent into the twentieth century as well) all groups used vegetal indigo imported from Europe or Mexico. All extracted yellow from local plants and also produced green by over-dyeing yellow yarn with indigo. The rich reddish tan and golden colors found in Spanish blankets have been popularly called brazilwood, logwood, or mountain mahogany, but tests of several specimens have not identified any of these substances. A reddish-brown plant dye of unknown origin has been found on early eighteenth-century Hopi textiles (Kent 1979), and red yarns in a blanket from Abiquiú (Fig. 3) test for a madderlike dye. The plum color so popular on Spanish blankets from the San Luis Valley of southern Colorado, called chokecherry by E. Boyd (1974: 209), has proved to be a synthetic rather than a natural dye.

Red yarns raveled from commercial cloth, as well as early three-ply and four-ply red factory-spun yarns were dyed with lac or cochineal. Both are insect dyes, the former from the Old World, the latter from the New. Cochineal may have been imported from New Spain and later from Mexico into the Southwest for use in dyeing locally spun yarn. However, red hand-spun yarns have been identified in only one Spanish blanket (Nestor 1979: pl. 22), and none are found in Navajo weaving. Acoma alone among the Pueblos was credited in the eighteenth century with using cochineal.[8]

Synthetic-dyed yarns and cloth appear in the Southwest by 1860. Shortly afterward, these dyes were packaged and marketed for use on hand-spun yarns. There is a marked difference between the dye colors and color combinations found in Spanish blankets (and servant blankets) of the last half of the nineteenth century and the colors used in Navajo/Pueblo blankets (Fig. 10). The

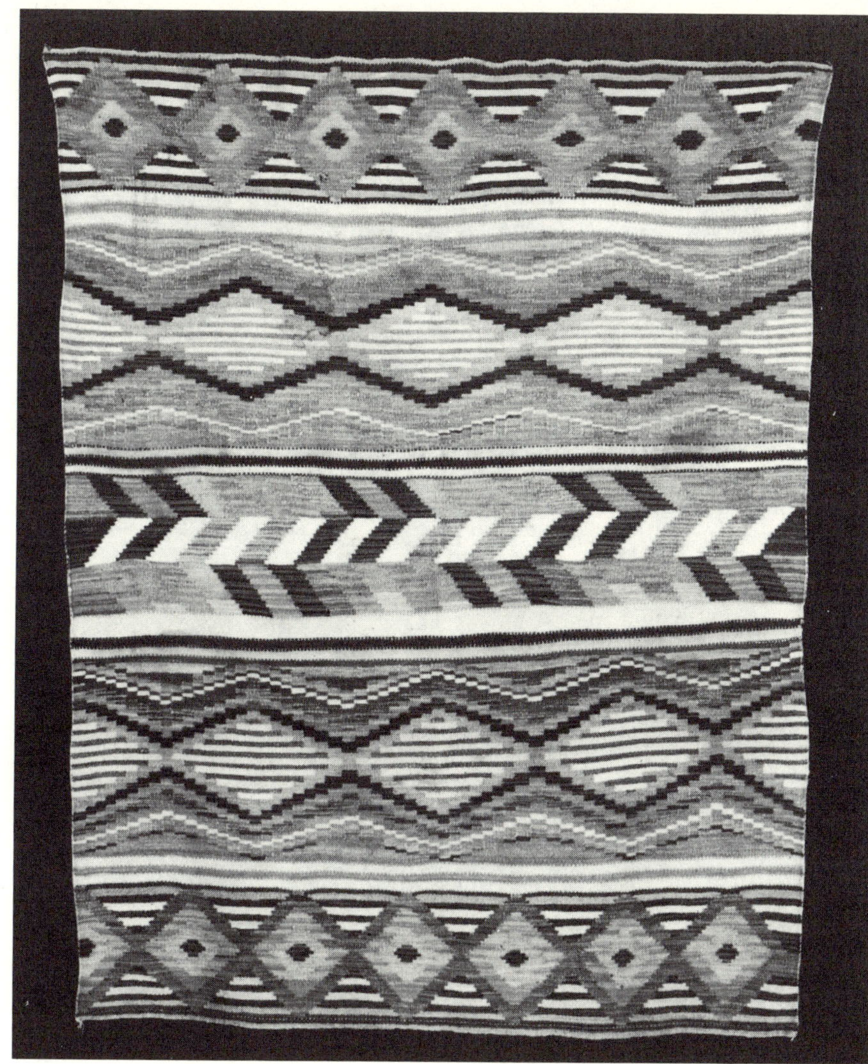

FIGURE 10
Servant blanket showing mix of the following colors: white, blue, light green, orange, cerise, pomegranate, magenta, lavender, violet, and purple. (IAF T.343. Courtesy School of American Research.)

Spanish combined a variety of lavender, pink, red, orange, and blue tones in a way foreign to Indian weavers. It is possible that the synthetic dyes available in the Rio Grande valley were not the same kind supplied to the Navajo traders by Wells and Richardson of Burlington, Vermont. It seems more likely, however, that colors were being selected according to different aesthetic principles.

During historic contacts among Navajos, Spanish, and Pueblos, there was an exchange of pattern ideas between the three groups, particularly the Moki pattern, Navajo terraced figures, and the Saltillo system. Each of the three peoples had its distinctive way of rendering a given pattern. The differences are sometimes very subtle, but when combined with other criteria they do help in identifying a piece. For example, the Moki pattern in its classic Pueblo form consisted of very narrow alternating brown and indigo blue stripes grouped into wide zones marked off from one another by a narrow white stripe (Fig. 1). Navajo Moki pattern blankets are essentially the same but may show more variety in the size of the stripes. From about 1860 on, Navajo and some Pueblo weavers often superimposed terraced and later serrate designs on the striped background. In Spanish examples of the Moki pattern, the stripes are generally wider than Pueblo ones and may contain repeats of small figures (Fig. 11).

Navajo-style terraced figures appear in many Rio Grande blankets of the 1830s and 1840s. Often they are placed according to the Navajo system of distribution: a large central figure and a quarter of that figure in each blanket corner. Since the blankets are treadle-loom products, however, there is little possibility of identifying them as Navajo, unless one considers them servant blankets (Fig. 3). Similarly, Navajo blankets incorporating Saltillo motifs can be distinguished quite readily on the basis of the colors used, weave construction, and certain ways of handling motifs—for example, placing quarters of the central figure at each corner and floating a few small elements on the surface, although not to the extent that the whole background is filled with them.

In summary, the criteria used for distinguishing between Spanish, Navajo, and Pueblo nineteenth-century blankets include size and shape of the blanket; selvage systems; corner finishes; structural weft joins in tapestry; lazy lines; types of yarns and the uses made of them; dyes; yarn counts; and pattern differences. These are presented in the appendix, which is intended as a checklist for curators and students. Cotton sarapes have not been discussed or included because they are so rare that most of us will never be faced with identifying them.[9]

THE CRITERIA APPLIED TO PROBLEM TEXTILES IN THE SCHOOL OF AMERICAN RESEARCH COLLECTIONS

Examples of the application of these criteria to six categories of textiles in the School of American Research collections follow. While most problems of identification have been satisfactorily resolved, there is still room for argument about some of the pieces, especially the "slave blankets."

1. *Black wool mantas with indigo blue borders*

Black wool mantas with indigo blue borders (Fig. 6), worn by women as a dress folded about the body and belted at the waist and sometimes as a shawl, were traditional in all the Pueblos. These mantas are so much alike in construction that they seem to have been woven according to a set formula. Warps are natural brown or black yarns, manta centers two/two diagonal twill in natural brown or black dyed wool. In nineteenth-century examples, the dye is almost certainly native black. There are borders of indigo blue diamond twill, five to seven inches deep, along both long edges.

These mantas were constructed by stringing four heddles for diamond twill,

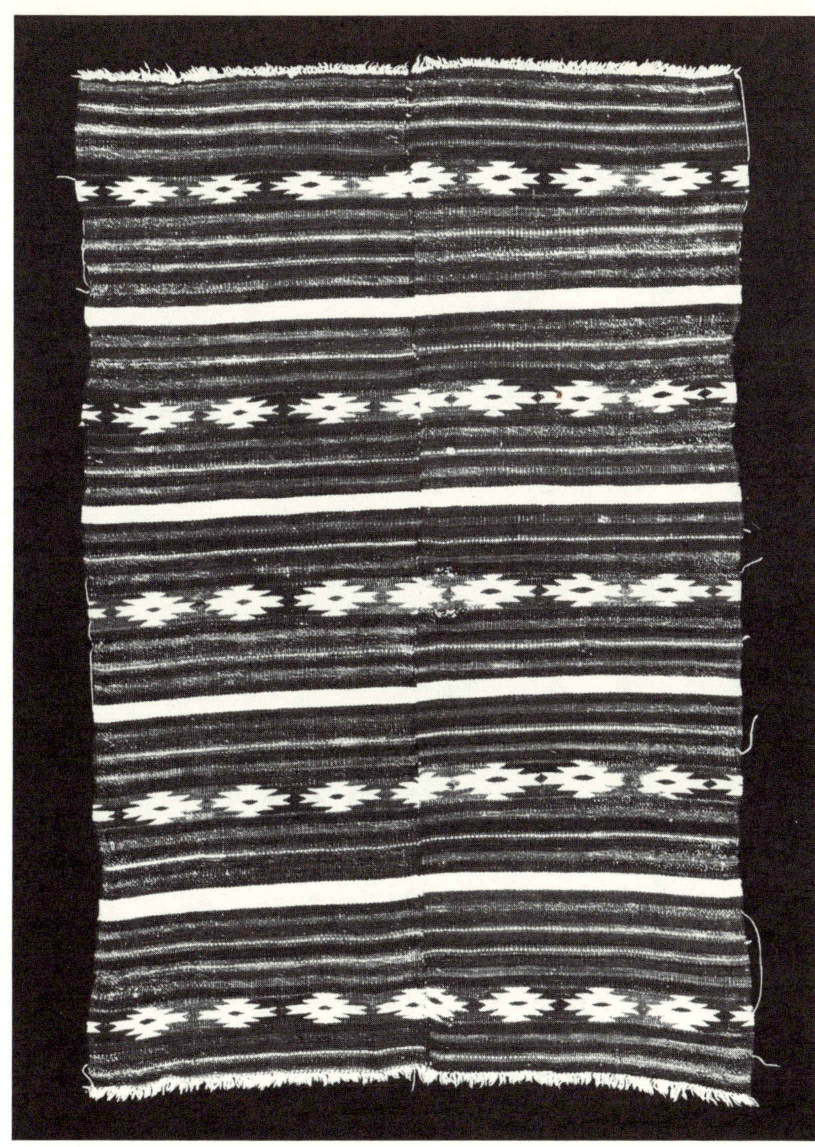

FIGURE 11
Rio Grande Moki-patterned blanket. (IAF T.445. Courtesy School of American Research.)

weaving one border, reversing the warp set on the loom and weaving the second border. Heddles were then restrung for diagonal twill and the center completed. The procedure left unused lengths of selvage yarns at each edge of the web where the diagonal twill met the inner edge of the upper border. These yarns were knotted or braided together to make small tassels. Both warp and weft selvages consist of three two-ply yarns. Selvage yarns are knotted at the corners in such a fashion as to leave corners open. A two-ply indigo blue yarn was run in just inside each warp selvage before weaving commenced as a binder to keep the warps in proper position. A similar binding yarn was inserted at the inner edge of each diamond twill border, between diamond and diagonal twill. Yarn counts are almost square, ranging from sixteen to twenty-eight warps and sixteen to twenty-five wefts to the inch.

The School of American Research owns eight examples of such mantas. Six conform to the formula just outlined, but two depart from it in several respects (T-354, T-707). T-707 was collected at Tesuque in 1964 (Fig. 6); the other was a gift with no collection data recorded. Yarn counts of the two are fifteen warps/thirty wefts and twenty-one warps/forty-two wefts to the inch, respectively. This means that there are two wefts to each warp, much too high a count to be Pueblo work.

T-354 has blue borders, but these are woven in reversed twill, as is the body of the manta. There are no binding yarns inside the warp selvages, and the binding along the inner edges of the blue borders is made by twining in two indigo yarns. There are many lazy lines in the center portion of the manta, leading to irregularities in the twill ribs. Warp selvages consist of two three-ply yarns, and corners are tightly tied, both Navajo characteristics.

The Tesuque manta has the traditional diamond twill borders, although the diamonds are unusually large. There are lazy lines. One warp binding yarn is omitted, and one appears within a diamond twill border rather than between it and the diagonal twill center. Warp selvages consist of two three-ply yarns, weft selvages of two two-ply yarns.

All these irregularities suggest a non-Pueblo origin for both mantas and leave little doubt that they should be considered Navajo-made, woven by Navajo women for their own use or for trade with the Pueblos. Wheat (1976*a:* 10, 15) records that the Navajos called their mantas "blue borders"; they were worn Pueblo-fashion as one-piece dresses until the late 1700s when Navajo women began wearing two-piece wool dresses. Some Navajos continued to use the blue-bordered manta as a shawl until late in the nineteenth century. Amsden pictures a Navajo man wearing what appears to be such a manta at Fort Defiance in 1873 (1949: pl. 82).

2. *Wool mantas with woven border patterns*

There is a class of wool mantas characterized by solid-color centers and (usually) outer warp borders but with decorative inner borders or bands patterned by woven designs of the type found on Navajo dresses (Fig. 2). The manta centers may be plain weave but are more often diagonal twill in brown, indigo blue, recarded pink, or red. Outer borders are most commonly indigo blue, often diamond twill. The mantas are strongly Navajo, not only in design but also in construction details.

In spite of their obvious Navajo character, these mantas are generally misidentified in older museum collections and early publications. Of the eleven examples in the School of American Research collection, five have been catalogued "Pueblo dress." Mera illustrates six from the Alfred I. Barton collection in his chapter on Pueblo weaving (1949: 6–13), and Amsden shows one collected by Gov. W. F. M. Arny in 1872 (1949: pl. 87*b*). This one and several other mantas in the collection of the Smithsonian Institution's

National Museum of Natural History are credited to Zuni Pueblo. James (1920) illustrates three: one (Fig. 29) is correctly identified as Navajo; the two others (Figs. 30 and 31) are called Zuni.

The confusion over these mantas arose because most were collected from the Pueblos and because they were worn as dresses or shawls by Pueblo women (mainly at Acoma and Zuni) between about 1850 and 1880. In point of fact, however, these mantas were traded to the Pueblos by their Navajo makers. It seems to me that they are to be thought of as the Navajo equivalent to the extraordinarily handsome dark wool Pueblo mantas with the heavily embroidered borders. The Navajos, not having adopted embroidery or the Pueblo design system, embellished the mantas with their own woven patterns.

3. *The "maiden shawl"*

An important traditional garment of Pueblo women is the white shoulder blanket with blue and red borders commonly called the "maiden shawl," worn by women as "best" clothes as well as in certain ceremonies and by men in most major ceremonies (Fig. 5). Early examples were of wool, with white diagonal twill weave centers and diamond twill indigo blue borders. Red inner borders were added as raveled and commercially dyed machine-spun yarns became available, probably in the early 1800s. Sometime after 1850, cotton replaced wool as warps and wefts in the center section of mantas to be used in ceremonies. All-wool mantas, often indifferently woven in plain weave and generally of a size to fit small girls, were still made as secular garments.

Many of these in museum collections show technical characteristics that mark them as Navajo-made. I had always assumed that they were woven specifically for trade to the Pueblos, but recently I learned that the Navajo claimed to have worn them in Yeibechai ceremonies hanging over the chest with the colored borders in vertical position.[10] Apparently, then, the white manta was once traditional for the Navajos as well as for the Pueblos.

4. *Zuni sarapes*

Because of their mix of Navajo, Pueblo, and Spanish features, Zuni sarapes have been especially prone to faulty identification (Figs. 1 and 9). A summary of the variety of technical characteristics they may exhibit illustrates the problems they present:

Selvages: two two-ply yarns, two three-ply yarns, three two-ply yarns, fringes along the warp edges, or paired warps at the weft edges and no extra yarns. Edges may give evidence of the use of two bobbins or of weaving in separate lengths of weft yarn.

Corners: usually open.

Shape: tend to be very broad in relation to length.

Yarns: hand-spun, single-ply, Z-spun wool warps. Often they are brown or dark gray in color. Wefts are single-ply hand-spun, frequently very soft and thick. Late nineteenth-century sarapes in the collections of the American Museum of Natural History, New York City, and in the National Museum of

Natural History have wefts that look more like loose roving than spun yarn. This is probably the kind of weftage Spier described as "a soft, fluffy native yarn, fully a quarter inch in diameter" (1924: 187).
Yarn counts: tend to be low, the weave being loose and open: five to eight warps and thirteen to twenty-seven wefts per inch.
Lazy lines: lacking in most sarapes, but appearing occasionally in some others.
Patterns: Moki pattern, and also banded patterns in which colored stripes alternate (often) with silvery gray or tan solid bands. Navajo-type designs are frequently used.

Seven of the sarapes in the School of American Research collections are almost certainly Zuni-woven. Only one of the seven (T-309), a blanket collected at Zuni, is credited to that pueblo. Two are the Moki-patterned blankets discussed later (T-104, T-641). Two are illustrated by Mera as Navajo (1948: T-77, pl. 71 [Fig. 9 here]; T-323, pl. 53), and the remaining two (T-620, T-626) are catalogued as Navajo.

Amsden illustrates as Navajo three blankets that should be classified as Zuni (1949: pls. 46, 47, 77). None has weft selvage yarns, and two have fringed warp ends. Amsden's figure captions indicate that he felt these pieces to be Pueblo in character, but that he called them Navajo because two were collected and so identified by Washington Matthews and one was collected by an army officer at Bosque Redondo, New Mexico, when Navajo captives were quartered there. Amsden's uncertainty illustrates the fact that criteria that have been validated in recent years by intensive studies of Southwestern textile collections were more in the nature of unverified, almost intuitive "hunches" in the 1930s and 1940s.

5. *Blankets combining Spanish and Navajo weave technicalities, patterns, and dye colors.*

Blankets woven on the vertical loom of the Navajos but showing strong Spanish influences have been called "slave blankets" in the literature. I am not certain where the term originated, but writing in 1934 Amsden noted: "This term is popular in Santa Fe, particularly among dealers who neglect no opportunity to add color and romance to the history of their wares. Of its authenticity one finds it difficult to judge" (1949: 89, fn. 11). Unfortunately, the term has become so firmly embedded in the mythology that surrounds the art of Navajo weaving that it probably cannot be discarded. Perhaps the suggestion that it be modified to "servant blanket" will be accepted in time (Stoller 1979*a*), but even so we are left with some problems of definition. Exactly what is a slave or servant blanket?

Until recently, Mera's definition is the one that has been most generally accepted: "The term 'slave blanket' is used to designate a class of Southwestern blanketry in which there is a curious blending of Navajo upright loom technique and design with dyes and minor decorative motifs typical of those used by the Spanish colonists" (1948: 21). He accounts for the "curious blending" on the basis of the "reliable tradition" that such blankets were woven by Navajo captives in Spanish households and that, while the women used the vertical loom familiar to them, they had access only to the dyes used by the Spanish in the Rio Grande valley. They were also exposed to Spanish blanket designs, some of which they reproduced.

Mera illustrates his discussion with seven examples, five of which are from the collection of the School of American Research (pl. 18, T-342; pl. 19, T-189; pl. 20, T-21; pl. 22, T-343; pl. 23, T-333). One of these (T-333; Fig. 12) and several others in the collection have since been classified sim-

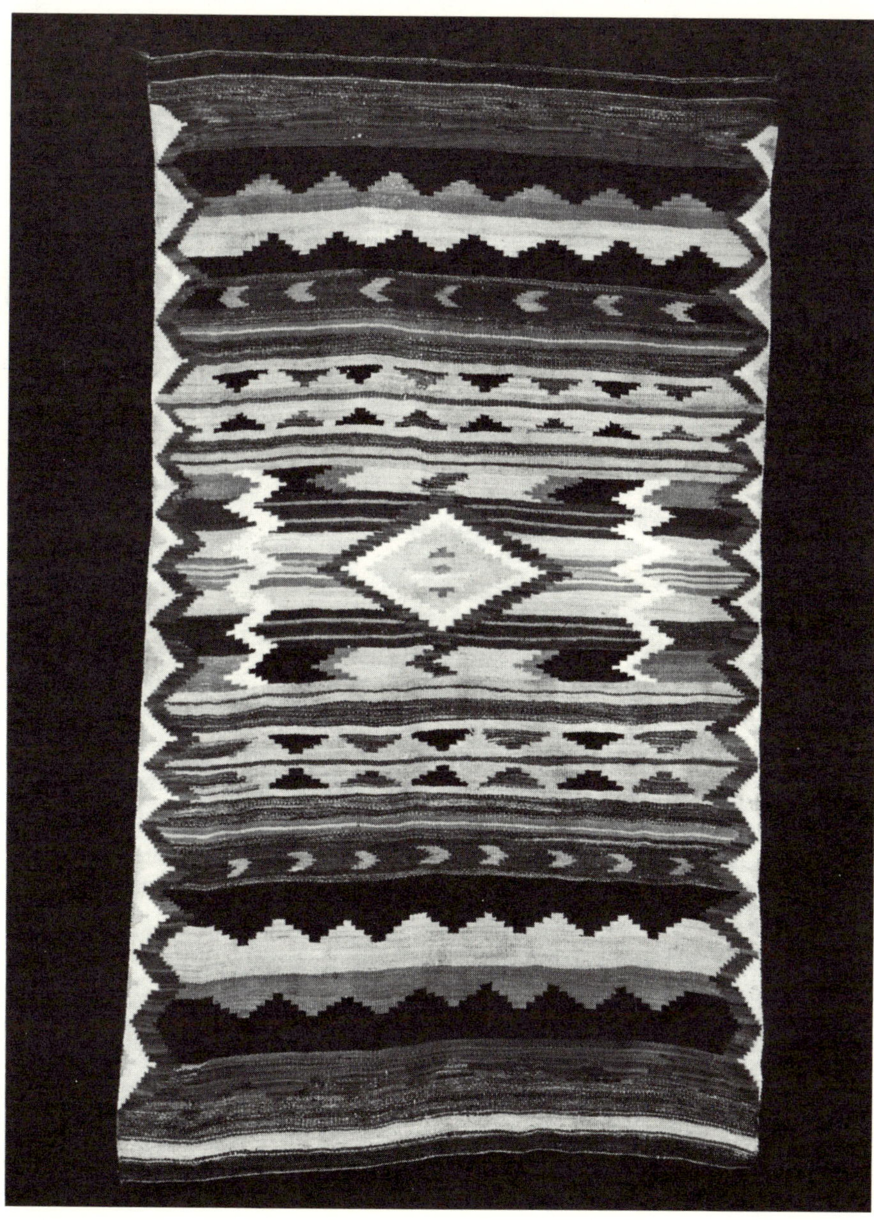

FIGURE 12
A possible servant blanket patterned in white, vermilion, orange, lavender, green, blue, brown, and gray. (IAF T.333. Courtesy School of American Research.)

ply as "Old Rio Grande" by Wheat (School of American Research catalogue notations). The fact that Mera and Wheat could disagree so markedly about these blankets points up one of the problems inherent in Mera's definition. How much Spanish influence, and what kind, must a blanket show if it is to be called a slave or servant blanket? Certainly a minimum requirement is having been woven on an upright loom. This is usually easy to determine, but in some cases (T-333, for example), there is room for argument.

I would agree with Mera that T-333 was woven on a wide upright loom. It is a single width, too wide to have been woven on the Spanish loom with the narrow reed and probably too early in date (ca. 1870–1880) to have been woven on the treadle loom after the introduction of the wider reed in the 1880s. There is only one lazy line, but wefts are so unevenly battened that the weave does not resemble that done on a treadle loom. Different colors of weft interlock where they meet, a Navajo trait. Warps are continuous, not cut and fringed or turned back into the web. Because all selvages have been restored, we have lost the valuable clues the original selvages could have provided. The proportions are Spanish, as are the yarn count (seven warps and thirty-one wefts per inch), the two-ply warp, and the range of dye colors. Wheat sees the pattern as Old Rio Grande. To me (and apparently to Mera) it appears to combine Navajo and Spanish features: the center diamond and fancy side borders being Spanish, while the terraced (rather than serrate) lines of the figures are Navajo. The two wide, patterned bands at the ends look like Navajo dress border designs to me, and the narrower bands of small repeated terraced triangles that flank the wide central area also look Navajo.

There can be lack of agreement, then, on whether a blanket, on the basis of internal physical characteristics, is to be called a servant blanket. In addition, we have no way of determining whether its weaver actually was a servant. Data recently published by the Museum of International Folk Art (Nestor 1979) raise issues that make the traditional definition even more ambiguous.

The museum has documentation on four sarapes that actually were woven by Navajo servants. One is simply described as "striped." One is a wedge weave from the San Luis Valley of southern Colorado that was woven on a vertical loom in 1876. It exhibits a typical Spanish color system (Nestor 1979: pl. 2) and is a classic example of Mera's "slave blanket." The third is a child's blanket woven in Abiquiú in 1875 (Fig. 3), and the fourth is a Moki-patterned blanket from the San Luis Valley dating from the 1870s (Stoller 1979: 44). The latter two were woven on treadle looms. The Moki-patterned piece is called a servant blanket only because the weaver is known, for it has none of the physical characteristics attributed to this class of textiles by Mera's definition. The Abiquiú blanket does combine Navajo-type terraced elements and pattern distribution with Spanish design motifs and dyes, and the colored wefts interlock where they meet, but it does not conform to the definition since it is a treadle-loom product.

The firm documentation of the Abiquiú and Moki-patterned blankets makes it clear that some Navajo women servants did use the Spanish-type loom rather than the vertical loom. Perhaps many other treadle-loom blankets, both Moki-patterned and with Navajo-style designs, woven in the early and middle nineteenth century should be thought of as servant blankets (see Bowen 1979: 123). It is logical to suppose that all capable members of a household would have been pressed into service to produce the thousands of blankets that were traded south from the Rio Grande valley to Mexico or west over the Old Spanish Trail to California between 1800 and 1875.

In the light of this new evidence, it is obvious that, if we continue to use the term *servant blanket,* we must redefine it to include two classes of blankets that are not alike in their physical characteristics: first, treadle-loom blankets known or presumed to have been woven by Navajo servants that may combine Navajo design elements with Spanish design elements and dyes; and second, vertical-loom blankets known or presumed to have been woven by Navajo servants that show strong Spanish influence in weave technicalities, design, and dye color. In my opinion, museum curators would be well advised to drop the terms *slave* and *servant* entirely and to identify a piece on the basis of its physical characteristics as a "Rio Grande Spanish treadle-loom blanket showing strong Navajo influence" or a "Navajo vertical-loom blanket showing strong Spanish influence." Further description could then include statements about the weaver's known or presumed social status.

6. *Moki-patterned blankets*

Problems may arise in the identification of Moki-patterned blankets since they were made by all three groups using the same materials: natural white and black/brown wool and indigo-dyed yarns. Misidentification of blankets in this category is quite common but can usually be corrected with assurance if all the criteria discussed in this essay are meticulously applied.

A blanket in the School of American Research collection (T-104, 1850–1865; Fig. 1) may serve as an example. Originally catalogued as Hopi (?) in 1930, it is illustrated as Navajo in an article by Wolf (1978: fig. 7*b*), and a notation by him in the catalogue suggests that it might be a servant blanket. Wheat's 1974 notes on the collection list it as Zuni. The confusion about its origin arose from its mix of Navajo, Pueblo, and Spanish characteristics, a list of which follows:

Proportions: length 1.45 times the width (Navajo or Pueblo).
Single width: woven on an upright loom (Navajo or Pueblo).
Continuous warps: woven on an upright loom (Navajo or Pueblo).
Yarn count: ten warps and forty-nine wefts per inch (Navajo).
Lazy lines: very few, scarcely recognizable (Zuni or Navajo, though Navajo might be expected to contain more of these).

Yarns: warps—single-ply (Navajo or Pueblo); wefts—single-ply (Navajo, Pueblo, or Spanish.)
Warp selvages: original warp edges missing; restored.
Corners: restored.
Weft selvages: no extra selvage yarns. The warps at both edges are grouped three-two-two from the outer edge in. This gives a ridged effect to the blanket edges. Lack of selvage yarns and multiple pairs of edge warps is Zuni or Rio Grande Spanish, although the ridged effect on this blanket is not characteristic of the latter.
Pattern: Narrow alternating blue and brown stripes (Pueblo).

Considering all the criteria, it becomes obvious that Spanish manufacture can be ruled out. The multiple pairing of edge warps might be seen as Spanish influence on a Navajo servant, but in point of fact such a treatment of blanket edges is extremely rare for the Navajos. Wheat's identification of the piece as Zuni is probably the correct analysis. Because it contains multiple pairs of edge warps, a second blanket in the collection (T-641) has also been reclassified from Navajo to Zuni, in spite of the essentially Navajo design, yarn count, and other structural features.

NOTES

1. The criteria discussed in this article are those applied to the analysis of the School of American Research collections, a task carried out under a 1980–1981 National Endowment for the Arts grant. I wish to thank the school's president, Douglas W. Schwartz, for his understanding and support of my research, and the collections manager, Barbara Stanislawski, for her cheerful, competent assistance. I am particularly indebted to Joe Ben Wheat, of the University of Colorado Museum, for sharing his fund of knowledge about Southwestern textiles with me and to Nora Fisher, Museum of International Folk Art, Santa Fe, for stimulating discussions on problems of textile identification, in particular those surrounding the elusive "slave blanket." I greatly appreciate the courteous assistance rendered me by the staffs of the following museums that made collections available for my study: American Museum of Natural History, Denver Art Museum, Denver Museum of Natural History, Heard Museum, Maxwell Museum of Anthropology, Milwaukee Public Museum, Museum of New Mexico, Museum of Northern Arizona, Peabody Museum at Harvard University, National Museum of Natural History, and the Wheelright Museum.

2. Most of the new findings have been published in recent papers by Joe Ben Wheat (1977, 1979). He presents additional criteria for the identification of textiles and clarifies, corroborates, or corrects criteria used by earlier scholars.

3. Stoller's discussion (1979*a*) of the state of Navajos living in late nineteenth-century Spanish homes in southern Colorado makes it abundantly clear that they were neither considered slaves in the Old World sense of the word nor treated as such. Often they were adopted into the family. The term *slave* with its somewhat sensational connotations has been softened, therefore, to *servant* in Nestor 1979.

4. The absence of lazy lines in Pueblo textiles, with the exception noted for Zuni, is due to the fact that Pueblo weavers normally preferred to carry each pick of weft from edge to edge of the web rather than to weave the weft back and forth in a limited portion of the web.

5. I have recorded only one example of a Zuni manta woven in the way described by Spier, but I have found no examples of the second treatment on Zuni or on any other Pueblo blankets.

6. Wheat (1979: 199–200) gives a clear summary of different types of raveled yarns.

7. Personal communication from Joe Ben Wheat.

8. Ibid.

9. However, curators should know about the existence of cotton sarapes. Bowen (1979: 140–43) discusses the seven (possibly eight) hand-spun cotton Spanish blankets woven on the treadle loom, probably in the southern Rio Grande valley villages between 1820 and 1850. Three are illustrated. Wheat (1976*a:* 11, 24) describes and illustrates a Navajo cotton sarape that he dates between 1775 and 1825. Most writers on Navajo textiles have either claimed that the Navajos did not weave cotton or have neglected to mention it. Wheat remarks: "How many pieces of early historic cotton fabrics now in museums or private collections, attributed to Pueblo weavers, are, in fact, products of Navajo looms is not known" (1976*a:* 11). Attributing hand-spun cotton sarapes to the Pueblos would indeed be an error. To my knowledge, the Pueblos reserved that material for certain articles of traditional attire and wove their sarapes strictly from wool.

10. Personal communication from Joe Ben Wheat.

APPENDIX

Criteria for Distinguishing Nineteenth-Century Spanish, Navajo, and Pueblo Sarapes (1800–ca. 1880)

	SPANISH	NAVAJO	PUEBLO
SIZE, SHAPE	1800–1880: 2 widths sewn together. Double-woven with paired warps at center. Double widths: 43″–60″ Lengths: 67″–103″ Lengths average 1.5–1.85 times widths. Late 1880s to present: Single width due to introduction of wide reed.	Single width. Widths: 30″–53″ Lengths: 44″–80″ Lengths average 1.3–1.5 times widths.	Single width. Zuni blankets: Widths: 29″–56″ Lengths: 44″–72″ Lengths average 1.23–1.49 times widths.
EDGES	Warp ends cut, knotted into fringe. Weft: no extra selvage cords; edge warps paired; sometimes more than one pair at each edge. (Recent restorations often include warp and weft selvage cords.)	Warp and weft: extra selvage cords normally present. Two 2-ply or two 3-ply cords normal; sometimes three 3-ply cords. Warps continuous. Warp fringe sometimes added, especially on Germantown blankets, 1885–1895.	Warp and weft: extra selvage cords usually present. Two 2-ply or three 2-ply cords normal. Latter is more common and is almost always present on traditional items. Warps continuous. Zuni sometimes used two 3-ply selvage cords, sometimes paired or tripled edge warps, sometimes cut and knotted warp ends into fringes, or added yarns to make warp fringes.

CORNERS	No special treatment, except that recent restorations may include adding corner tassel.	Selvage yarns tightly knotted. Extra yarns run through corner to make tassel. Closed corners.	Warp and weft selvage yarn ends knotted separately, or knotted or braided together commencing at some distance from fabric. Open corners.
LAZY LINES	Not present.	Common, although not always present.	Rare, but occasionally found, especially on Zuni blankets.
TAPESTRY JOINS	No structural connections between wefts meeting along diagonal lines.	No structural connections between wefts meeting along diagonal lines.	No structural connections between wefts meeting along diagonal lines.
	Wefts meeting along a vertical line are usually dovetailed.	Wefts meeting along a vertical line are either dovetailed or more commonly interlocked between warps.	Wefts meeting along a vertical line are usually interlocked between warps.
HAND-SPUN WOOL YARNS	1800–1860: Churro wool: soft, silky, straight, long staple fibers. Easy to spin and dye. 1860–1880s: Rambouillet-merino wool gradually increases. Crimped, oily; hard to clean, spin, and dye. Yarn quality decreases.	Same as Spanish but crimped yarns seem to appear somewhat later than in Spanish textiles.	Same as Navajo.
HAND-SPUN COTTON YARNS	Early 1800s: Blankets woven of cotton in the southern Rio Grande valley.	1700s: Navajo said to grow and weave cotton. One cotton blanket on record, 1775–1825.	A.D. 600–1500s: Cotton grown and woven into clothing by indigenous people of the Southwest. Used by Pueblos in many traditional items of clothing until present.

COMMERCIAL COTTON STRING	1880 on: Used for warps.	1880–1900: Used for warps in belts and blankets.	Used for warps and in belts and some mantas increasingly since 1880. Cotton batting replaces native cotton in early 1900s for weft.
RAVELED WOOL YARNS	Used sparingly in figures.	Used in figures and ground (red most common).	Used in embroidery and belts (red most common).
COMBED PINK	Found in one blanket only.	Fairly common, 1870s.	Selvages (Hopi). Some in Zuni blankets.
STRIPS OF COMMERCIAL CLOTH	Not found.	1870s, not unusual.	Some in Zuni blankets.
COMMERCIAL YARNS	1800–1860: 3-ply dyed with natural dyes. Used in figures and for embroidery. 1860–1875: 3-ply dyed with synthetic dyes. Used as wefts. 1875–present: 4-ply dyed with synthetic dyes gradually replaces hand-spun.	1850–1860s: 3-ply used in figures and ground. 1860–1900: 3-ply and 4-ply yarns dyed with synthetic dyes used in increasing amounts.	Probably used at Zuni. Zuni like Navajo.
YARN COUNT (per inch)	Early: 5–7 warps 25–50 wefts (hand-spun) Late 1880s: 6–11 warps (often cotton) 30–40 wefts (hand-spun) 50 wefts (commercial)	Plain weave: 6–12 warps 20–100 wefts Twill weave (two mantas): 15 warps/30 wefts 21 warps/42 wefts	Plain weave: 3–5 warps 10–20 wefts Twill weave (mantas): 16–28 warps 16–25 wefts

COLOR	Natural wool tones: white, black, brown, carded grays, and tans.	Same as Spanish.	Same as Spanish and Navajo. Zuni blankets have distinctive silvery gray and tan.
	1600–1870:		
	Indigo imported, along with technology of use.	Same as Spanish.	Same as Spanish and Navajo.
	Vegetal yellow from local plants.	Same as Spanish.	Same as Spanish and Navajo.
	Vegetal green made by combining yellow and indigo.	Same as Spanish.	Same as Spanish and Navajo.
	Reddish-tans vegetal. Formerly called "Brazil," "Logwood," and madder. Not so far found on Navajo and Pueblo hand-spun yarn.	Possibly like Pueblos.	Vegetal reddish-brown found in belts and embroidery, early 18th-century Hopi.
	Cochineal red on raveled yarns, one hand-spun yarn, and commercial yarns.	Cochineal raveled yarns and commercial yarns.	Cochineal raveled yarns and commercial yarns. Cochineal dye, Acoma.
	Lac, increasingly identified as used on commercial yarns.	Lac, raveled yarns.	Lac, raveled, and *possibly* hand-spun.
	1860 on:		
	Chemical dyes on hand-spun yarns. Different selection of colors from Navajo and Pueblos.	Chemical dyes on hand-spun yarns.	Same as Navajos. Hopis revive vegetal dyes in 1930s.
PATTERNS	Narrow brown, white, or indigo stripes; Moki pattern but usually with wider stripes and small design elements within stripes.	Moki pattern, probably from late 1600s on. Used as a background for other designs, mid-19th-century on.	Moki pattern, from Spanish in 1600s. Zuni used stripes as background like the Navajos.
	Tan, gold, and reddish stripes added to above by early 1800s.		
	Other stripe and band patterns.	Other stripe and band patterns.	Other stripe and band patterns.
	Brown monocolor everyday blankets; white wedding blankets(?).		Monocolor blankets: Zuni, black; Isleta, indigo.
	Some stepped figures and Navajo-style design distributions, ca. 1800–1840.	Stepped or terraced figures, late 18th century on. Center figure and quarters of it in corners.	Design systems follow Navajo trend, especially at Zuni.
	Saltillo system, 1800–1880.	Saltillo system, 1860s on.	

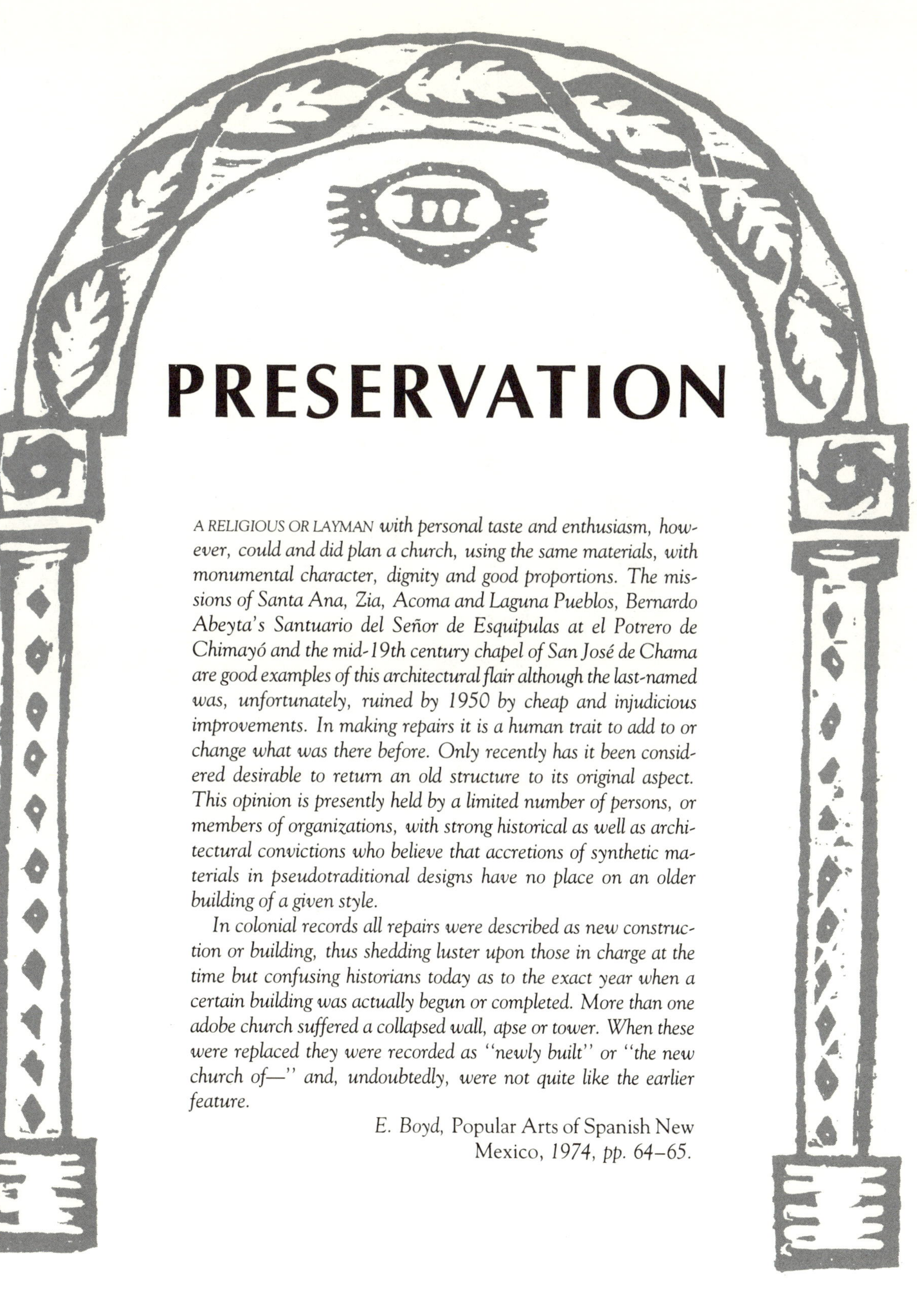

PRESERVATION

A RELIGIOUS OR LAYMAN *with personal taste and enthusiasm, however, could and did plan a church, using the same materials, with monumental character, dignity and good proportions. The missions of Santa Ana, Zia, Acoma and Laguna Pueblos, Bernardo Abeyta's Santuario del Señor de Esquipulas at el Potrero de Chimayó and the mid-19th century chapel of San José de Chama are good examples of this architectural flair although the last-named was, unfortunately, ruined by 1950 by cheap and injudicious improvements. In making repairs it is a human trait to add to or change what was there before. Only recently has it been considered desirable to return an old structure to its original aspect. This opinion is presently held by a limited number of persons, or members of organizations, with strong historical as well as architectural convictions who believe that accretions of synthetic materials in pseudotraditional designs have no place on an older building of a given style.*

In colonial records all repairs were described as new construction or building, thus shedding luster upon those in charge at the time but confusing historians today as to the exact year when a certain building was actually begun or completed. More than one adobe church suffered a collapsed wall, apse or tower. When these were replaced they were recorded as "newly built" or "the new church of—" and, undoubtedly, were not quite like the earlier feature.

E. *Boyd,* Popular Arts of Spanish New Mexico, *1974, pp. 64–65.*

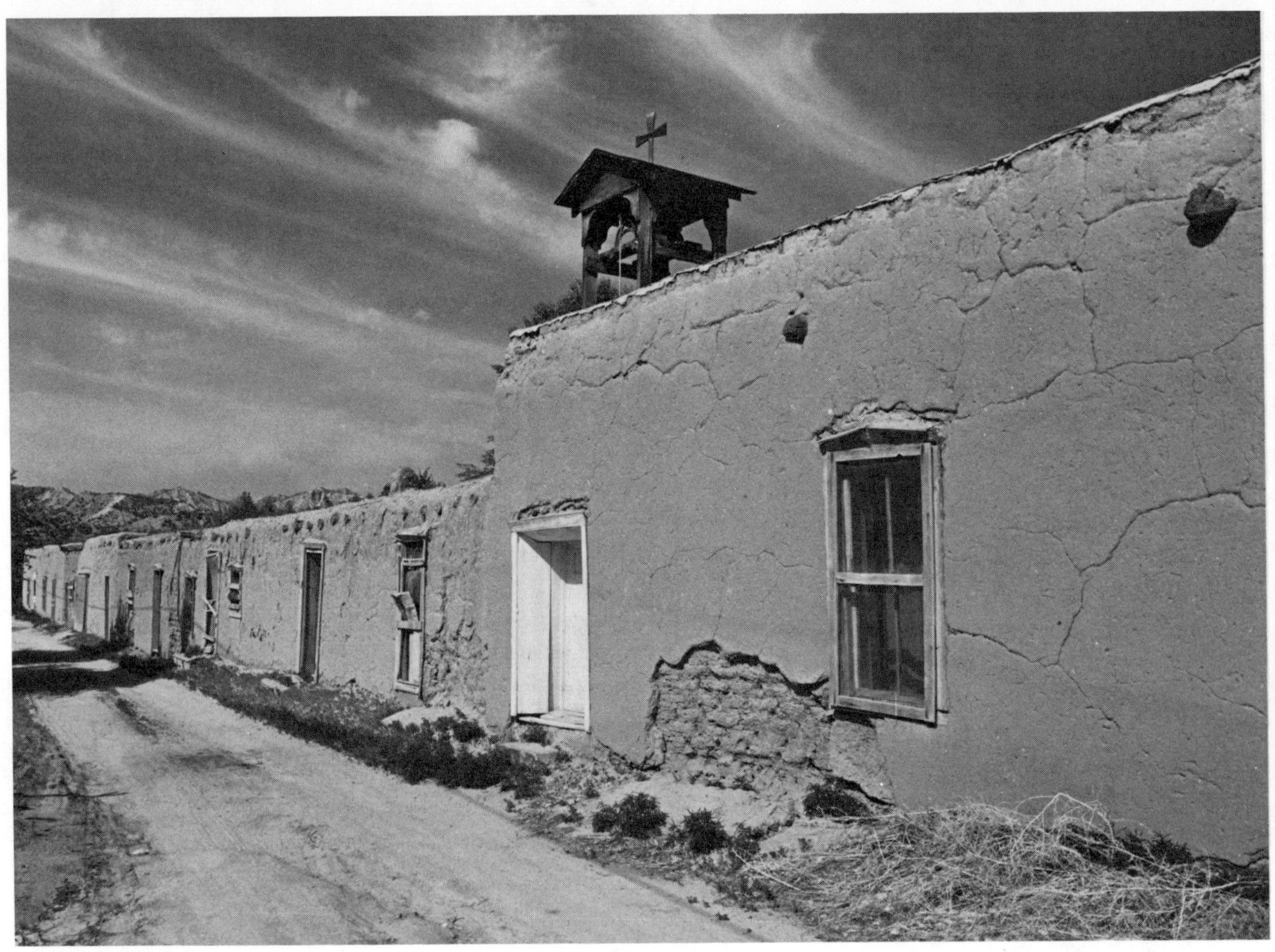

FIGURE 1
This photograph of the Oratorio de San Buenaventura, taken before the Spanish Colonial Arts Society restoration efforts in the 1960s, shows clearly how time and weather erode adobe-plastered structures. The view is to the south and includes the facades of the row of eighteenth century rooms. Wooden trim around doors and windows is of more recent origin, dating probably from the last half of the nineteenth century. (Historic Preservation Bureau, New Mexico State Planning Office, Santa Fe.)

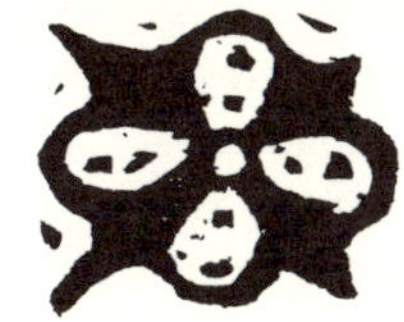

SAMUEL LARCOMBE

PLAZA DEL CERRO, CHIMAYÓ, NEW MEXICO: AN OLD PLACE NOT QUITE ON THE HIGHWAY

FEW OF THE PILGRIMS who trek to El Santuario de Chimayó and certainly fewer of the many year-round visitors looking for the village's famous weavings, apples, and chilis are aware that they pass by the site of Chimayó's beginnings, the quiet and time-worn Plaza del Cerro. This remarkable and singular survival of colonial days is a place of great historical and architectural significance. The fully enclosed plaza nestles, half hidden by trees, but a few hundred feet from the intersection of state highways 4 and 76.

Formerly a center of some consequence, in these late years of the twentieth century Plaza del Cerro shows its age and neglect all too clearly. When conducting research on the Santuario and the village of Chimayó in the early 1950s,[1] Stephen F. de Borhegyi lamented:

> Highways are made for speed and there is little hope that cars will stop in the small towns for much merchandise or large-scale business. In spite of the . . . highway now in construction between Santa Cruz, Chimayo and Truchas, it can be expected that the little villages with their old plazas will probably remain for awhile as tourist attractions, even though they have already lost their original function. Once they protected the little community against an austere and sometimes hostile world. The houses were turned inwards on the plaza like so many adobe barriers against their environmental and human enemies, and thus kept alive the flame of community living for many decades. In the exposed and open villages along the road the flame is dying, and along with it is dying the centuries-old cultural heritage of the Hispanic Southwest. (1954*b*: 29)

Fortunately, since the time of Borhegyi's research, historians and villagers have joined together to document, preserve and restore portions of the old plaza. E. Boyd championed these efforts, working for more than twenty years to make others aware of the plaza's importance and to enlist their help in its repair. Her descriptive history of Plaza del Cerro and planning recommendations in the 1971 preservation plan for New Mexico are exemplary. Her description and history follow in full:

> Originally, the Plaza del Cerro was a square enclosed by contiguous adobe

buildings. The only entrance ways were two or possibly three alleys, one on the south side, and one or two on the north, wide enough to admit only animals and people on foot, and therefore easily defensible. The fortified colonial plaza plan is shown better here than in any other plaza extant in New Mexico. This general pattern still exists, although access to the plaza was made easier by the construction through it from west to east of the county road from Santa Cruz in the 19th century. Also running through the plaza is the *acequia madre,* or main irrigation ditch, which lies parallel to the Santa Cruz road at its southern edge; it dates from the plaza's early period. The west side of Plaza del Cerro consists mainly of one-story adobe houses, many abandoned and in dilapidated condition. Also located in this block of dwellings is the Oratorio of San Buenaventura. The other three sides of the plaza are for the most part still occupied. Many of the houses on these sides have gabled roofs which form attics. Some of the buildings have been modernized with newer windows, doors, and sheet metal roofs, but these alterations are from the 19th and early 20th centuries, and represent the rural architecture common to the area at that time. The San Buenaventura Chapel underwent stabilization in 1953, and was replastered in 1969. Although it is now surrounded by a barn, the original *torreón,* or defensive watch tower, still stands south of the plaza in good condition. The central ground, which was once held communally, is divided by fences and planted in fruit trees and small garden plots. In some of these plots the Chimayó chili is grown, for which the area is famous. A few of the fruit trees in and around the plaza are wild plum, indigenous to the region and predating Spanish settlement.

The rural modernization practices which followed the close of World War II, and changed so many of New Mexico's villages, have left the Plaza del Cerro untouched. A sense of the past is clear, not only in the appearance of the simple adobe rooms, but in the ambience of the plaza's daily activities.

Although records of land deeds or disputes over lands in Chimayó go back to 1714 and settlement may have begun as much as two decades earlier, the first clear references to the actual paraje de Tzimayó come in the 1740's, by which time it is thought that the plaza of San Buenaventura (now the Plaza del Cerro) was built as an entity. No records are known, however, which give the dates of its construction. A will made in 1752 was dated at San Buenaventura de Chimayó, and the earliest existing marriage record of a couple who were residents of el puesto de San Buenaventura de Chimallo was made by Fray Andres Garcia at Santa Cruz church, within whose jurisdiction Chimayo then was, on September 1, 1767. At about this time the plaza had twenty-two families.

Fray Atanasio Dominguez in his report on New Mexico Missions in 1776 noted Chimayó as lying some two leagues east northeast of Santa Cruz: "a large settlement of many ranches in good lands and more orchards than there are at La Villa de la Cañada. Near Chimayó to the south are some ranches with different place names but they are so small that they are included here. There are two small mills" [Adams and Chávez 1956: 83]. In 1776 the village had seventy-one families of 367 persons whose focal point was the Plaza del Cerro.

The area produced fine crops of fruit and chili in addition to the staple corn and frijóles, and the weaving of blankets and other wool textiles flour-

> ished there as it did in other parts of Spanish New Mexico. Many of the village's families have five or six generations of weavers behind them.
>
> Between 1813 and 1816 the Santuario de Nuestro Señor de Esquipulas was built just down the road from the plaza, bringing in many pilgrims and greatly augmenting the economic standing of the plaza. Another chapel near the Santuario, built in the 1860's, further stimulated business and other activity. Also, by this time the San Luis Valley in Colorado had been settled, and Chimayó had a good trade with towns there, exchanging fruit and chili for wheat and potatoes. Before the new Santa Fe-Taos highway was built in 1917, following the Rio Grande Canyon, travel from Santa Fe to Taos used the Chimayó-Las Truchas-Penasco route whenever weather permitted, making Chimayó a stop on a major road.
>
> Around 1900, commercial dealers in curios of Santa Fe and Albuquerque, noting that weaving was active in Chimayó, introduced commercial looms and yarns to the weavers, and quickly made up designs for them to copy. This wholesale production kept the residents in moderate prosperity until the depression of the 1930's, and helps explain the variety of architectural styles visible in the plaza ranging from the18th century until the end of the 1920's, when modernization abruptly ended. Now, with the increasing numbers of out-of-state visitors to the area, the whole region of mountain villages is assuming a new sort of prominence. The Plaza del Cerro, still essentially unchanged from former times, and of great significance because of its layout and architecture, offers these modern visitors a chance to observe an example of 18th century village planning. Few places in the southwest remain from this period in such entirety. (Anonymous 1971: 79–81)

The most successful preservation effort in the plaza to date involves the Oratorio de San Buenaventura. This chapel lies on the plaza's west side, near the northern edge of a row of seven single-story, eighteenth-century adobe rooms, several of them near ruin. The structure most probably dates from the eighteenth century, possibly even to the plaza's initial construction. Dates of 1873, written inside on the vigas and roof boards, seem to refer to the oratorio's late nineteenth-century re-roofing.

Long known as the Ortega family chapel, the oratorio was given to the Catholic church at Santa Cruz following Bonifacia Ortega's death in the spring of 1953. David Ortega recalls a further complication, however. While in Santa Fe on business during the late 1970s, he found a document in the State Land Office which described the oratorio site as mere open space, not granted to anyone. Petitions were filed to have the building legally granted to the church. Finally the parish was able to purchase it for a token fifty dollars.

When it was given to the church in the 1950s, the Oratorio de San Buenaventura was placed in the custody of women in the Confraternity of Our Lady of Carmel. According to E. Boyd:

> At a meeting of the Spanish Colonial Art Society's Board of Trustees in the

> fall of 1954, it was voted that the Society should pay for needed materials to put on a new roof, if the Confraternity would coöperate and provide for the labor. The President of the Confraternity, Mrs. Elena Vigil of Cundiyó, her husband, Mr. Norberto Vigil, and Mr. Josué Trujillo of Santa Cruz, were most effective in their coöperation. Mrs. Vigil convinced her members that the proffered repairs, to be made in a way that did not alter the old character of the chapel, were more desirable than to remodel it with cement and a tin roof. By her efforts the cost of the labor, which was one-third of the total, was paid from the funds of the Confraternity; a carpenter-builder [Merejildo Jaramillo] was engaged; Mr. Vigil made a gift of his time and truck and hauled all of the materials needed from Santa Fe and Española to Chimayó, and the work began. (1955: 99–100)

A decade later, the Spanish Colonial Arts Society again sponsored complete replastering work. Still later, the society funded cement footings and another replastering job. In all these efforts, the Ortega family participated enthusiastically.

According to her field notes, E. Boyd visited the Plaza del Cerro and carefully surveyed the chapel's contents in 1952. Even at that time, she noted

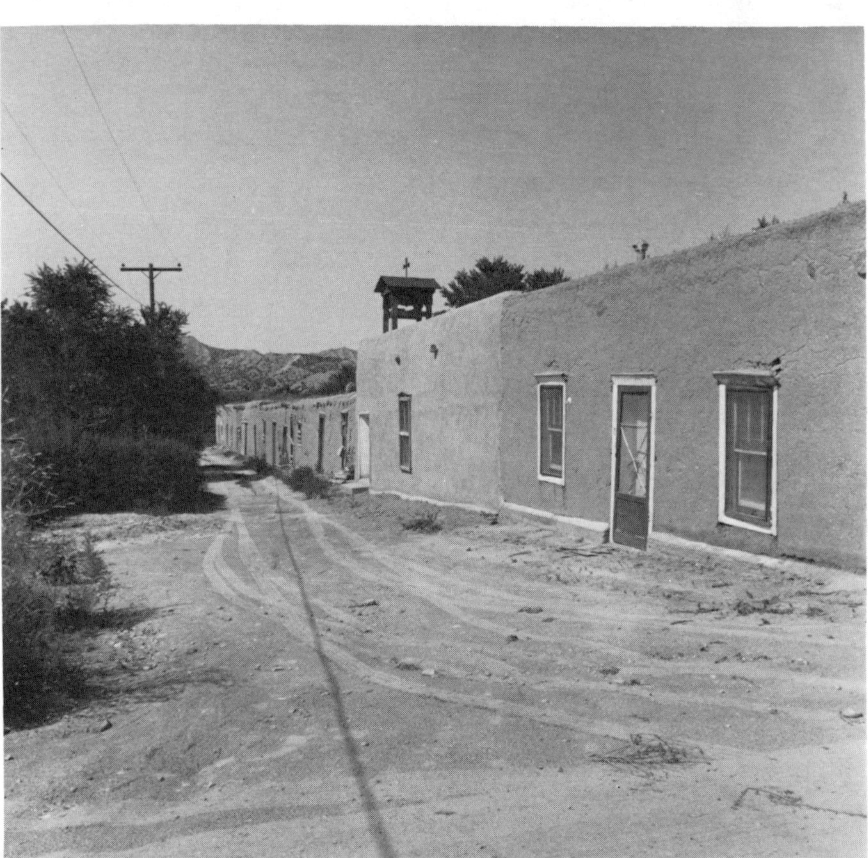

FIGURE 2
Plaza del Cerro and oratorio, 1970. (Photo Collections, No. 49291, Museum of New Mexico.)

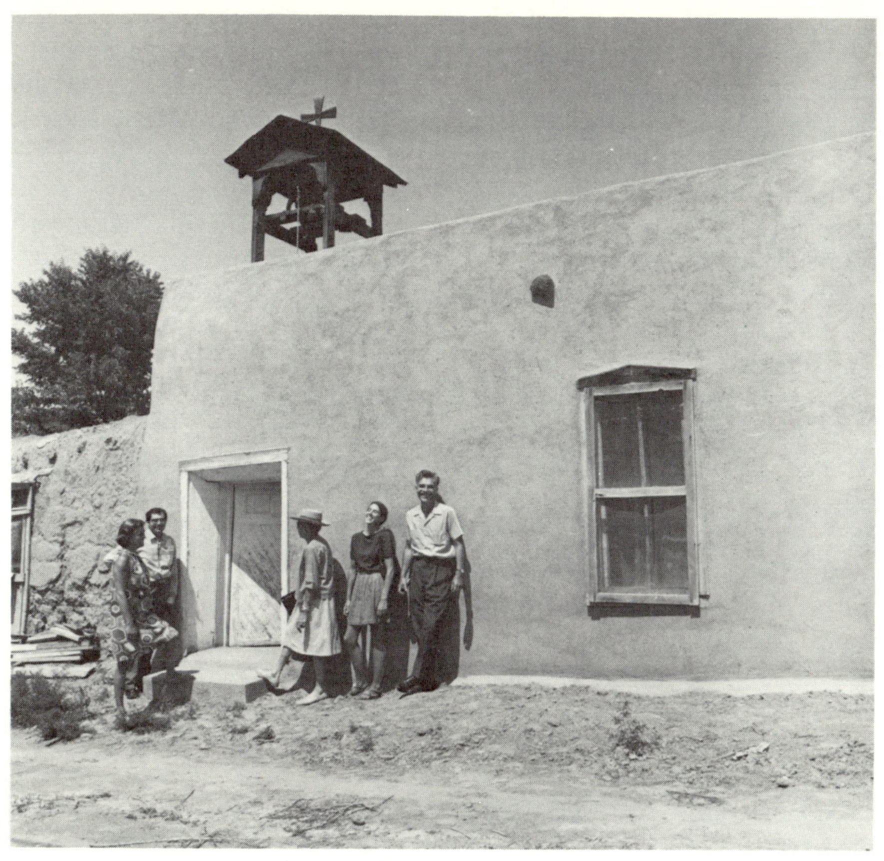

FIGURE 3
Left to right: Ann Vedder, David Ortega, E. Boyd, unidentified woman, and Alan C. Vedder outside the oratorio, 1970. (Photo Collections, No. 49289, Museum of New Mexico.)

the importance of finding a way to preserve it. When recommending the oratorio for the State Register of Cultural Properties in 1969, she wrote that "the interior of the Ortega or San Buenaventura chapel is unspoiled and contains a fine, small altarscreen of the first half of the 19th century." In the same application form, she expressed her concern for the chapel's future, in spite of its recent repairs:

> As the Santa Cruz parish is operated by the Fathers of the Holy Family, all sent from Spain, and they have no use for the Oratorio of San Buenaventura, they do not contribute to its preservation and are unlikely to do so. Its survival depends at present entirely on private interests. The formerly private, or family chapels of the Spanish and Mexican periods in New Mexico have disappeared (building and contents) more completely than have public churches and missions. The Ortega chapel of San Buenaventura is, therefore, of particular interest and should be preserved.[2]

Today, the Ortega family still holds the key to the chapel door and still sees to its day-to-day maintenance. The roofing work of 1954 has kept out the rain for almost thirty years, and the exterior and mud plaster appear to be in good condition. Although church authorities do not permit ceremonies in the oratorio, the structure is well-venerated and continually visited. In 1982, the poster and brochure for the Feria Artesana sponsored by the Albuquerque Museum featured a full-color reproduction of the reredos in the Oratorio de San Buenaventura.[3]

In recent months, I visited with Arturo Jaramillo and David Ortega, both prominent citizens of Chimayó who are devoted supporters of the plaza's preservation. Each owns parts of the plaza, and each shared with me some of their memories of plaza life.

Restauranteur Jaramillo recalled that his last visit with E. Boyd came after he bought the room adjacent to the oratorio on its north side. He said that he had asked her for advice on preserving and restoring it and remembered that she drew several quick sketches of possibilities, including one of a fireplace. He had purchased the adjacent room to keep the oratorio safe from deterioration, although, sadly, in the past few years, vandals have broken into this room and severely damaged it.

He recollected that E. Boyd was a friend of his grandfather, Merejildo Jaramillo, a carpenter, weaver, and farmer who as a young man had helped with the oratorio's earlier stabilizations. Arturo Jaramillo said that in his own youth all the rooms of the plaza, except for the row south of the oratorio, were occupied, and that the plaza was well-tended and full of flowers and vegetables in the warm months.

As we talked, he recalled his childhood, emphasizing that among the nicest moments of his growing-up years were the walks down the road to the oratorio for May devotions. He and the other children would sit by the chapel among the lilacs and *rosas de castillo* (Castilian roses) in the evening while prayers were recited in honor of the Virgin. As late as the Maytimes of the 1940s, these services were held once or twice a week.

Weaver David Ortega, speaking with me and his mother Virginia in the living room of her home beside the plaza, asked her to think back to the early years of this century and to describe the plaza as it was then. She thought that in the 1890s the rooms along the north side were sheltered from the summer sun by portals running along their southern walls. She was emphatic in her praise of how clean the residents kept their property and remembered yearly replastering work. All the plaza was occupied; neat gardens filled the interior space. Each house had its own frontage and back lot, although the land remained unfenced. In the summer time, residents slept out on their patios. None of the doors had locks, since, "in the old days there was no crime."

Some time before 1910, the first three houses in Chimayó were modernized with pitch roofs clad with metal. Soon afterward, Victor Ortega's house and general store on the plaza's southside was re-roofed similarly. This store served as the village post office for some years.

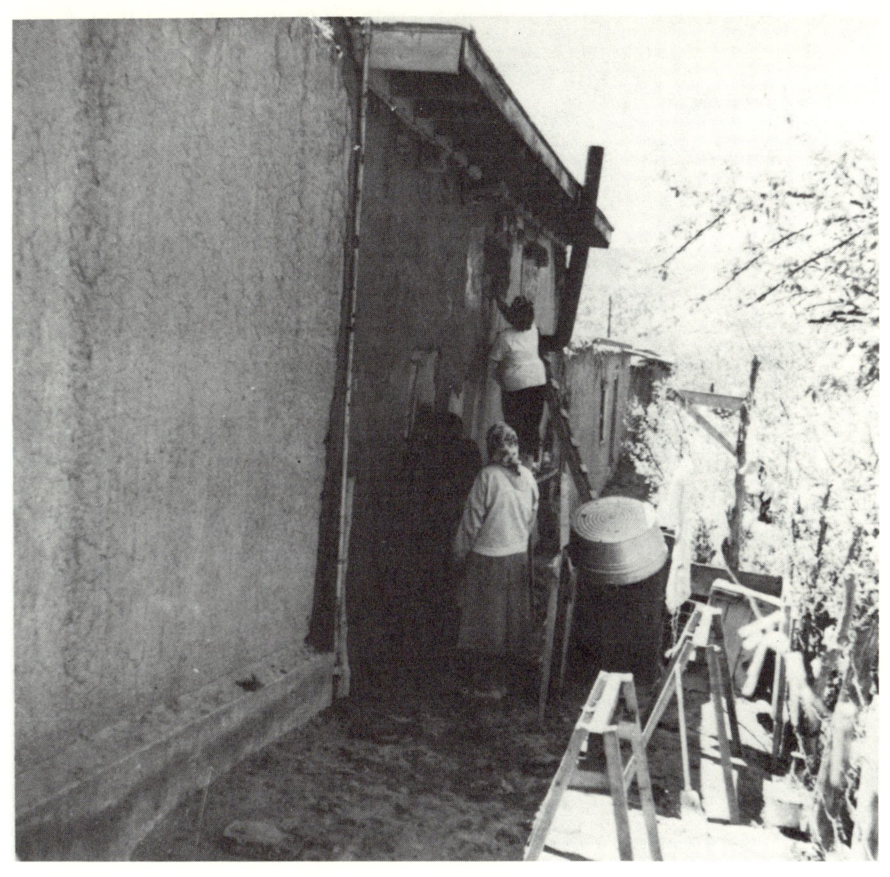

FIGURE 4
Replastering the rear of the Oratorio de San Buenaventura, 1963. Photo by David Ortega. (Photo Collections, No. 8951, Museum of New Mexico.)

Virginia Ortega recalled that the oratorio was in continual use for masses, *velorios* (wakes), meditations, and public meetings. The plaza itself, as she noted, was still the center of the whole valley. One of its rooms once served as a small *sala de baile* or dance hall.

In those days, the men enjoyed exchanging local political gossip. Whenever they gathered to talk, the first question asked was likely to be, "what's new in the precinct?"

Small circuses came occasionally to the plaza, bringing clowns, wire-walkers, and tumblers. Gypsies *(las turcas)* also visited, asking the residents for food and drink.

Especially during winter time, families made formal visits to their relatives in the evenings. After the evening meal, they would discuss issues of mutual interest. Visitors always were received warmly.

During harvest season, neighbors helped each other with cutting wheat and tying chilis. Most of what they ate they raised themselves, buying only salt and sugar.

Each year men of the plaza went out to gather *amole* (yucca root) for soap.

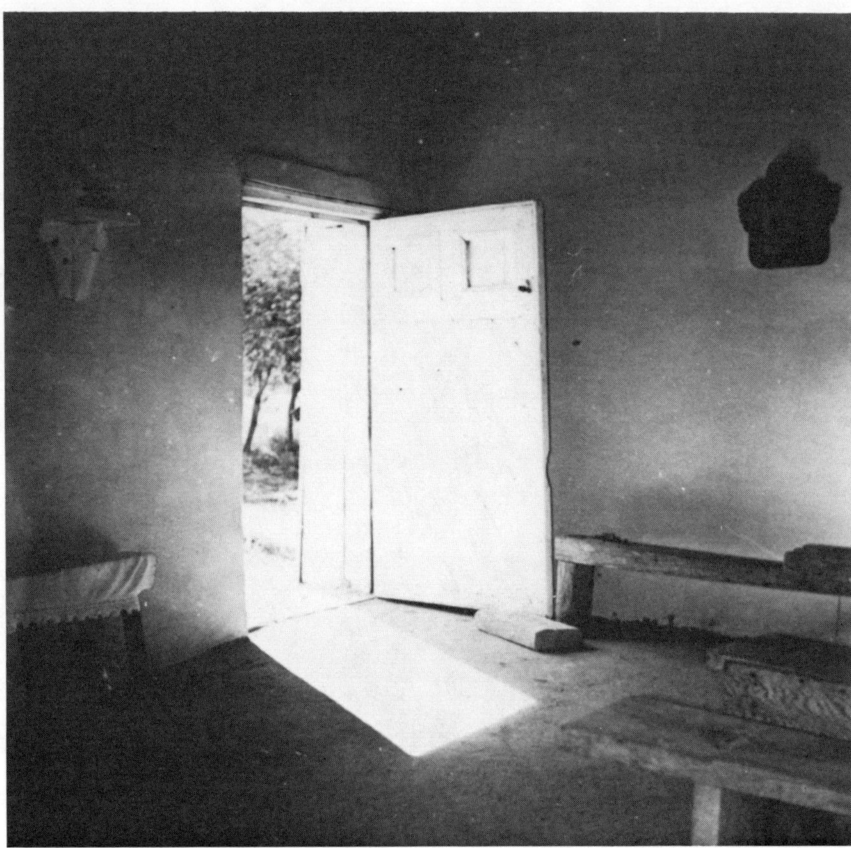

FIGURE 5
Door to the oratorio, October 1971. Photo by Melinda Bell. (Photo Collections, No. 53310, Museum of New Mexico.)

The women would gather at the acequia behind the plaza to wash curtains, bedspreads, furniture coverings, and various linens. Apparently this was a formal annual event.

In those days, young bachelors asked for their brides by letter or had a commission of neighbors call on the prospective bride's parents. By custom, the parents had eight days in which to answer. If they rejected his suit, they sent him a pumpkin, from which comes the saying "*le dieron la calabaza,*" he was given the pumpkin (see, for example, Lucero-White Lea 1953: 214).

Although the entire Plaza del Cerro has been listed on the National Register of Historic Places since 1971, and although men like Arturo Jaramillo and David Ortega have been steadfast in their efforts to see its buildings repaired and restored, its future is uncertain at best. Even as resourceful a person as E. Boyd could accomplish little more than the work on the Oratorio. Ortega has restored a suite of rooms belonging to him on the north side with good sense and success. Jaramillo made a fine gesture when he bought and repaired the room next to the chapel, only to see it vandalized. But, given the site configuration and importance, much more is needed.

Part of the difficulty lies in the fact that the plaza is owned, section by section, by different people, only a very few of whom actually live there. Indeed, some do not live even in Chimayó. For a good many years, there have been efforts to organize the plaza's owners into a preservation group. Once, a well-meaning outsider made a gesture to have the owners all deed their property to a non-profit trust in return for funds to enable a comprehensive program of research, repair, and restoration. The idea was unusual and soon rejected.

Temporary-looking protective roofs have been laid over most of the eighteenth century rooms along the oratorio row. These are commendable first steps. On the other hand, a house has just been built within the plaza itself—most unfortunate from a purist's point of view. Several portions of the plaza are vacant, and vacancy nearly always means decay.

I should like to end this essay on a cheerful note, but instead must make a plea. The days of amole gathering and May devotions may have faded from Plaza del Cerro for good, but cannot we who value the evidence and lessons of the past contrive to keep the plaza itself from disappearing? Private and public funds have been spent in New Mexico on preservation projects far less

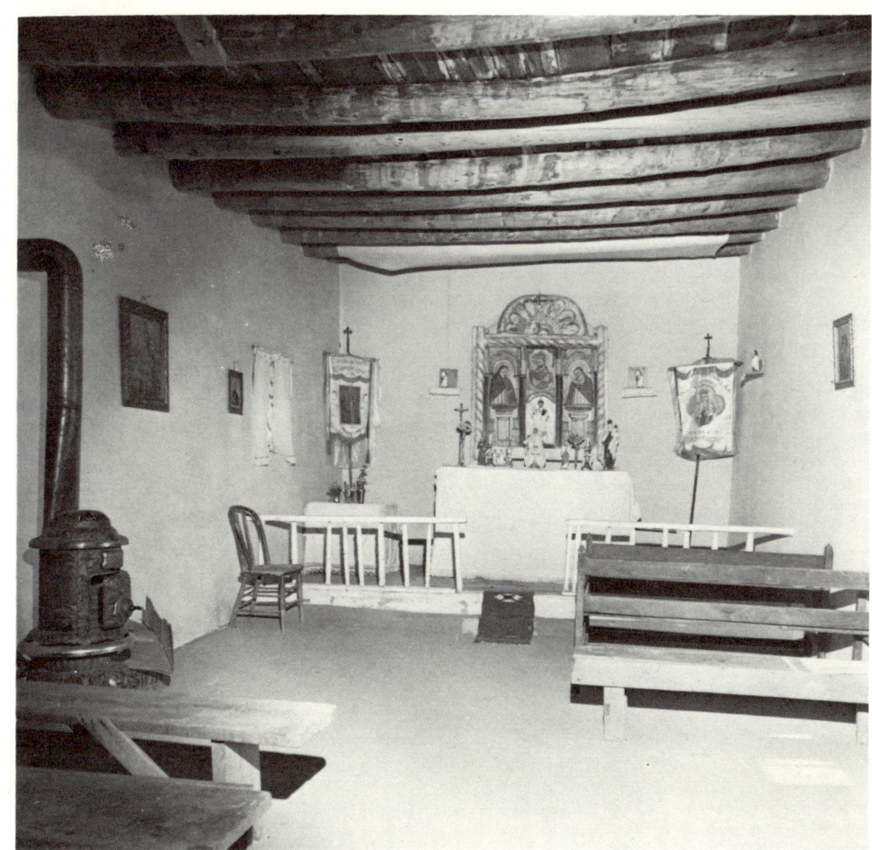

FIGURE 6
Interior of the Oratorio de San Buenaventura, 1970. (Photo Collections, No. 49297, Museum of New Mexico.)

important. Yes, this old place not quite on the highway presents us with some extraordinary challenges, but let us meet them. E. Boyd's own 1971 recommendations still can guide that effort:

> In drawing up a plan for the preservation of this important property the guiding principle has been that to reestablish its appearance in conformity with any one period or style would be wrong. Its long history of occupation has naturally involved structural changes and a host of minor alterations, but these are simply results of the requirements of the families who have lived and worked there. Instead of erasing these changes, it seems much wiser to let them offer visible evidence of the plaza's continuous use and adjustment down through the years.
>
> . . . By repairing, stabilizing, and restoring the 18th century and neoclassic survivals, and retaining the later homes with their hard plaster and metal roofs, it would be possible to exhibit a continuous visual record of the development and decline of Plaza del Cerro over a period of 200 years or more. Any future agreements between funding agencies and property owners anticipating preservation projects should include provisions guaranteeing the historic integrity of the properties involved and requiring professional supervision of planning and execution. (Anonymous 1971: 81, 86)

NOTES

1. Most material on Chimayó focuses on the pilgrims and the weavers, for example: Walter 1916, de Huff 1931, Hurt 1934, Casey 1936, Trumbo 1947, Borhegyi 1953, 1954*a,* Newhall 1962, and Scott 1964. However, field workers on the 1935 Tewa Basin Study described the vigorous trade in agriculture and weaving traditionally enjoyed by "the people of Chimayo . . . go-getters [who are] very proud of the fact that the *Chimayosos* never loaf, and of the fact that the products of this pleasant valley have been justly famous among the natives of New Mexico since the reconquest . . . and among the natives of Colorado and Arizona since before the coming of the railroad" (Weigle 1975: 85–86). This study, like Borhegyi's (1954*b*), is detailed in its socioeconomic dimensions.

2. Records in the Historic Preservation Bureau, New Mexico State Planning Office, Santa Fe.

3. According to a story in the *Albuquerque Journal* (17 March 1982), Bill Strickfaden recently completed a scale model of the Oratorio de San Buenaventura. It was painted by his wife Mary. This three-dimensional documentation can serve in its own way as an introduction to the chapel's special importance to many kinds of people today.

MARTA WEIGLE

THE FIRST TWENTY-FIVE YEARS OF THE SPANISH COLONIAL ARTS SOCIETY

The objects of this corporation are and shall be as follows: To encourage and promote generally in New Mexico and elsewhere Spanish Colonial Art; to preserve and revive the Spanish Colonial art of every character, to perpetuate and disseminate Spanish Colonial art in all its phases and manifestations; to promote and maintain suitable facilities and properties for the preservation of Spanish Colonial art and to that end to purchase, lease, or otherwise acquire real estate or personal property for the housing of collections of Spanish Colonial art; to educate the public generally and the members of this corporation especially in the importance of Spanish Colonial art in the civilization of New Mexico and elsewhere, present, past and future, and in the various phases of earlier art as well as its modern development in every branch of the same; to promote, conduct and maintain a school or schools for the teaching of Spanish Colonial art and its development from the earliest possible material and information available for that purpose to the present time; to provide for and cause the delivering and holding of lectures, exhibitions, public meetings, entertainments, classes and conferences calculated directly or indirectly to cause interest in or the advancement of Spanish Colonial art; to print, publish, distribute and sell (not for profit) magazines, articles, pamphlets and reports for the dissemination of knowledge concerning Spanish Colonial art throughout the world; to acquire, preserve and protect places, property, both real and personal, things and articles relating to or exemplifying or representing Spanish Colonial art, and to provide for the custody thereof; to restore places, things, buildings and property, both real and personal, relating to or exemplifying Spanish Colonial art.

—State Corporation Commission of New Mexico,
from Certificate of Incorporation No. 15923,
October 29, 1929.

THE CERTIFICATE OF INCORPORATION for the Spanish Colonial Arts Society, which Mary Austin, Frank G. Applegate, Francis I. Proctor, George M. Bloom, Frank E. Mera, Margretta A. Dietrich, Mrs. A. S. Alvord, John

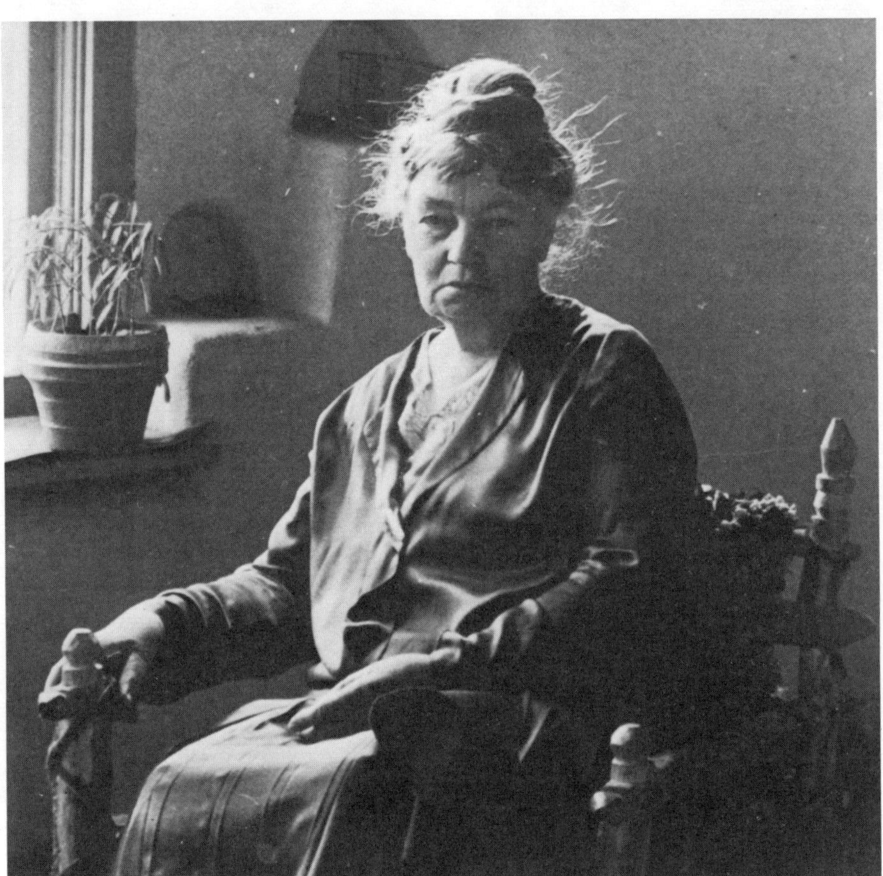

FIGURE 1
Mary Austin, 1932. Photograph by Will Connell. (Photo Collections, No. 16754, Museum of New Mexico.)

Gaw Meem, John D. De Huff, and notary public Miriam C. Bauer signed on October 15, 1929, was not the first such filed with the State Corporation Commission of New Mexico. On January 15, 1913, seventy-two signatories—among them Archbishop J. B. Pitaval, L. Bradford Prince, Amado Chaves, Albert B. Fall, Benjamin M. Read, Bronson M. Cutting, José D. Sena, Camilo Padilla, Venceslao Jaramillo, T. D. Burns, Antonio Lucero, and Felix Martínez—witnessed a certificate of incorporation for the Society for the Preservation of Spanish Antiquities in New Mexico. Its object was stated succinctly: "the protection and preservation of churches, buildings, landmarks, places and articles of historic interest connected with the Spanish and Mexican occupation of New Mexico."[1] L. Bradford Prince served as statutory agent and president, presumably using the unheralded group in his fight to preserve the integrity of the Historical Society of New Mexico and its collections from what he saw as encroachment by Edgar Lee Hewett, the Archaeological Institute of America, and its School of American Archaeology (Stensvaag 1980: 301–2).

The earlier society left few traces, and it was not until the mid-twenties when writer Mary Austin and painter-sculptor Frank G. Applegate, neighbors along Santa Fe's Camino del Monte Sol, began to examine and discuss the bultos that Applegate had started to collect along with Indian pottery. According to Austin, who dates her own interest in Spanish arts from 1918, when she was hired by the Carnegie Foundation "to make a survey of the Spanish population of Taos County" for its Americanization study:

> We rapidly grew interested in all the old and almost dishabilitated arts of New Mexico, touched with a profound regret for their disappearance. In collecting old pieces, Frank had often recourse to native workmen for repairs, and by this means we came to realize that the capacity for handcraft, of a fine and satisfying quality, though overlaid by modern American neglect, had not completely disintegrated. We began to discuss the possibility of reviving it. (Austin 1932*b:* 214; also see Austin 1932*a:* 339–40)

Although seriously ill, Austin "secured financial backing from my friend, Mrs. Elon [Blanche Ferry] Hooker [of New York City], and at a meeting at the home of Miss Manderfield (one of the Oteros) a society for the revival of Spanish Colonial Arts was launched."[2] Austin claims that she first used the term *Spanish Colonial* in her own writing and credits *Santa Fe New Mexican* editor E. Dana Johnson with popularizing it at her insistence, so that "Spanish Colonial Art became a recognized subject of interested comment in the Press" (1932*b:* 214; 1932*a:* 358).

The fledgling organization, which until 1929 was often designated "the Society for the Revival of the Spanish-Colonial Arts," "did little more than broadcast a list of examples of such crafts as might be profitable to revive and to offer prizes for new work that conformed most exactly to the old models." Local citizens promised money if "the proper article was presented" (Anonymous n.d.*b*). The first exhibition was held in conjunction with the annual art exhibit, chaired by Mary R. Van Stone, at the Fine Arts Museum during the 1926 Santa Fe Fiesta (Anonymous 1926: 97). Of the fifteen entries, those by Celso Gallegos, a carver in wood and stone from Agua Fria, proved most popular. Applegate later brought him sixty "round silver dollars, and the old man was so overcome that he wept and tried to kiss Frank, which, in view of Frank's great length of limb, was not easily managed" (Austin 1932*b:* 214).[3]

The 1927 Fiesta exhibition at the New (Fine Arts) Museum was greatly expanded, with prizes awarded for blanket weaving, handmade furniture, figure carving, a tin nicho, braided rugs, hooked rugs, and crochet. Santa Fe County school superintendent Nina Otero-Warren also arranged to have rural schoolchildren's work exhibited (Anonymous 1927). By the 1928 Fiesta, there was a Spanish colonial arts and crafts exhibition in the reception room of the museum and a Spanish Market under the museum portal, with Mrs. Gerald (Ina Sizer) Cassidy in charge of the market and Mary Austin heading "Spanish Participation" (Anonymous 1928*a:* 7, 1928*b*).

J. M. Ramírez took charge of the Spanish Market in 1929, with Benigno

Muñiz overseeing "Spanish Participation." The society had by then supplied the Normal School at El Rito with "examples of good old blanket designs [and] photographs of other good models of furniture and woodcraft," and the school's weaving instructor, Ramon Jaramillo, won first prize "for a blanket of commercial yarn woven in an old design." The news release noted that the society paid out $764.00, and "native workers" netted some $300–$400 in private sales—"most of it, of course . . . spent in having a good time at fiesta, as was right and desirable, [but] where there was a surplus . . . the society took pains to ascertain that most of it was spent in outfitting the children for school in Santa Fe shops." This sort of patronage was consistent with the two stated aims of the society: "to preserve to New Mexico many of its ancient arts and crafts, but also to provide the means [advice, instruction, tools, materials, models] by which the native Spanish speaking population can utilize its spare hours in gainful employment" (Anonymous n.d.*b*).[4]

By the time of its incorporation in October 1929, the society had begun to assemble under Applegate's direction "a permanent collection of the best examples of the old work, and, as we had the means, to collect them and place them on exhibition in the rooms of the Historical Society in the Old Palace." One of the earliest and most important pieces was a retablo which church members wished to sell from the Llano Quemado chapel near Ranchos de Taos. Applegate "was notified . . . and went up immediately, arriving a little in advance of the curio dealers, and secured it for $500" in 1928 (Austin 1932*b*: 215); it was installed in the Museum of New Mexico in 1929. Applegate wrote the label, which mistakenly attributes the piece to Miguel Aragón rather than to his father, José Rafael Aragón (ca. 1796–1862) (Boyd 1946: 43, 1974: 402, 403; Wroth 1979: 54–58, 71).[5] Other additions to the collection were either purchased or donated. Mary Cabot Wheelwright was especially generous in her donations to the society.

The Santuario at Chimayó was the next important purchase arranged by members of the Society for the Revival of Spanish Arts. María de los Angeles Cháves, granddaughter of the chapel's builder, Bernardo Abeyta, inherited the property from her mother, Carmen Abeyta de Cháves. Financial hardships and a reduced number of pilgrims forced the three remaining members of the Cháves family to begin dismantling the chapel in 1929. Alice Corbin Henderson's obituary for *Santa Fe New Mexican* editor E. Dana Johnson recounts the subsequent events:

> Gustave Baumann phoned a friend one day to say that he had discovered that the beautiful old church and its furnishings were being sold piecemeal; the small Santiago on horseback was in the hands of one curio-dealer, and the historic carved doors were being bargained for by another. What could be done about it? The answer was, of course, "Tell Dana Johnson," and Dana came out with a spread that carried to the Atlantic coast, where Mary Austin, lecturing at Yale, with Dana's article in hand, interested the anonymous donor who bought and restored the building to the Catholic Church. (Henderson 1938: 123)

Austin recalled that, after Applegate's letter to her in New Haven, "I was able to find a Catholic benefactor who made possible the purchase of the building and its content, to be held in trust by the Church for worship and as a religious museum, intact, and no alterations to be made in it without our consent. At the ceremony of reconsecration, Frank and I felt very close to each other" (Austin 1932*b:* 215, also see Austin 1932*a:* 359). According to Elizabeth Willis De Huff (1931: 39), both the Society for the Revival of

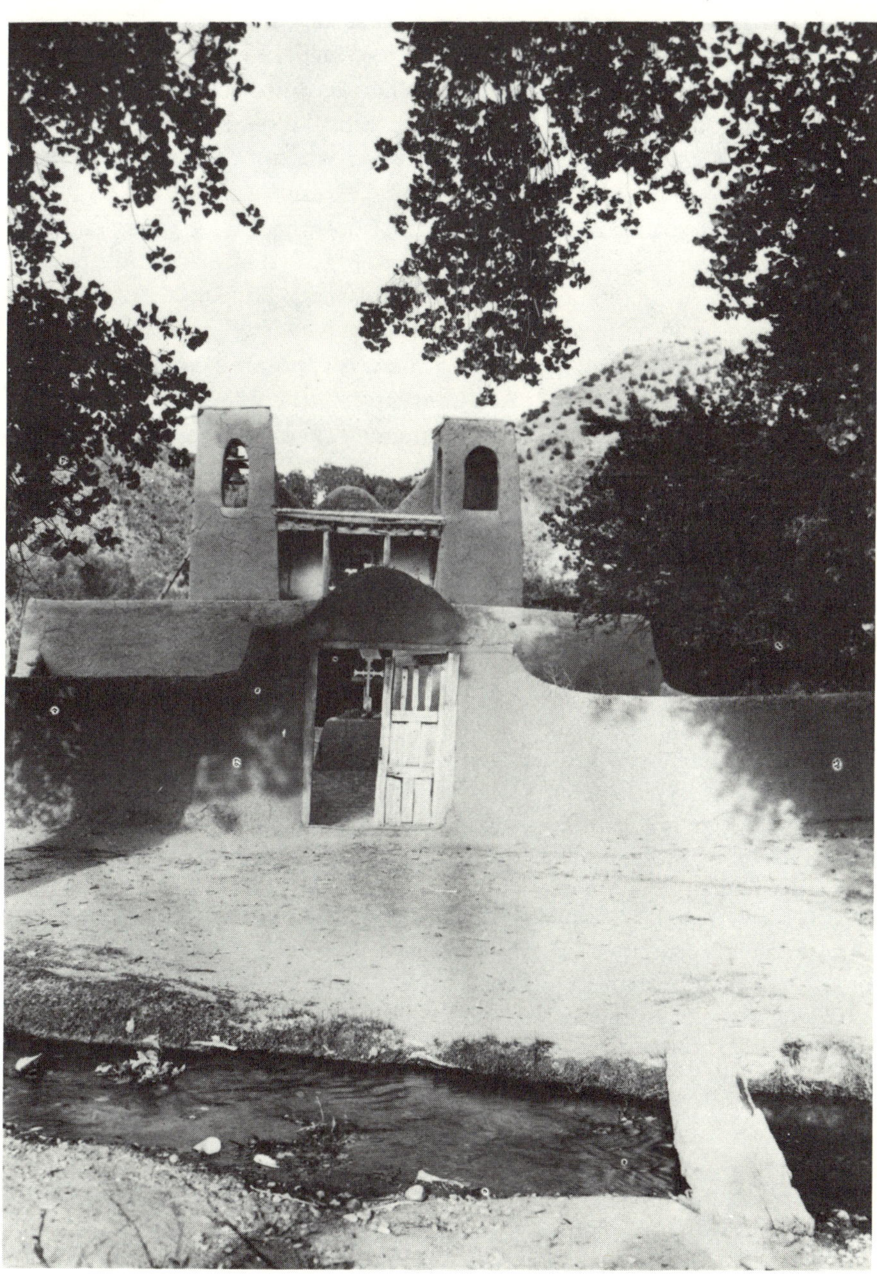

FIGURE 2
The Santuario at El Potrero (Chimayó) before the Spanish Colonial Arts Society purchased it in 1929. (Dorothy Woodward Collection, New Mexico State Records Center and Archives, Santa Fe.)

Spanish Colonial Arts and the Society for the Restoration and Preservation of Spanish Missions of New Meico, which had largely overlapping memberships, were involved, and the benefactor was a Yale alumnus who gave them six thousand dollars.[6] This check was delivered to Don José Cháves "by Archbishop Albert T. Daeger at the archepiscopal residence in the presence of a group of interested people on October 15th 1929" (Borhegyi 1956: 17), the same day that the certificate of incorporation for the Spanish Colonial Arts Society was signed.

The board of trustees of the newly incorporated society included Mary Austin, Frank G. Applegate, Francis I. Proctor, George M. Bloom, Frank E. Mera, Margretta A. Dietrich, Mrs. A. S. Alvord, John Gaw Meem, Mary Cabot Wheelwright, Martha E. White, Mrs. Elon Hooker, Sen. Bronson M. Cutting, Mrs. Datus Myers, Mrs. Thomas E. (Leonora S.) Curtin, Sheldon Parsons, Benigno Muñiz, Andrew Dasburg, Archbishop A. T. Daeger, Alice Corbin Henderson, Herman Schweizer, and John D. De Huff. At its first meeting on November 25, 1929, Austin was elected chairman, Applegate, vice-chairman; Myers, secretary; and De Huff, treasurer. Dasburg was to chair the Committee on a Permanent Collection, with Wheelwright, Schweizer, and Gustave Baumann also serving. Applegate was appointed curator. Mera, Applegate, and Meem were to act as a committee "to confer with the New Mexico Historical Society in order that some method of co-operation might be worked out."

Outgoing treasurer Applegate turned over a check for $1,017.33 to De Huff, who deposited it in the First National Bank of Santa Fe on December 13, 1929. Two funds were set up initially—a general fund ($82.33) for miscellaneous expenses and prizes and a dramatic fund ($935.00) to pay for research and prizes related to New Mexican Spanish folk dramas, Mary Austin's favorite project. This had been announced in the 1929 broadsheet:

> Mrs. Austin . . . will lecture at Yale and the University of California during 1929 on Folk Drama in the United States. . . . She will bring back with her all necessary specifications for recreating the traditional "Corrales" or street theatres which were in use in Spain at the time New Mexico was settled. Mrs. Austin thinks such a theatre with a moveable stage and proper lightings and accessories could be established at Santa Fe, for about $1,000.00 distributed over several years, and the program of the Spanish Arts society includes giving to Santa Fe an opportunity to add this unusual feature to its attractions. Such a theatre need not be confined solely to Spanish plays but would provide a suitable setting for the many amusing Indian comedies which have never been offered to the public, and any type of outdoor performance, anywhere in the city.

Austin reiterated this plan at a board meeting of May 19, 1930. At a second such meeting, on October 8 of that year, she "reported on her work in reviving the Spanish drama and in organizing a theater, beginning with puppets. Her idea is to create a show that the Spanish people can copy, that can travel around to schools and other meeting places."[7]

Despite the size of the dramatic fund and Austin's enthusiasm for native folk drama,[8] relatively few transactions are noted between March 28, 1930, when Arthur L. Campa, Spanish teacher and folklorist at the University of New Mexico, was paid five dollars for "services," and October 6, 1934, when Leonora S. Curtin was reimbursed for the fifty dollars she had advanced Campa "for his work in collecting ancient Spanish New Mexican songs."[9] Except for the tin processional torch and cross bought from the Old Santa Fe Trading Post by Applegate out of the dramatic fund in October 1930, disbursals were entirely at the discretion of Mary Austin, whose brief notes, directing De Huff to pay her book and music bills, typing bills, and bills for Harriet V. Noble's transcription of Spanish manuscripts reveal few specifics about the projects. The Reverend Father Peter Kuppers was paid twenty dollars on June 3, 1931,[10] and Pedro M. Ruelas received ten dollars for a puppet show on September 9 of that year. Most of the disbursements, totaling $675.67, went to Campa, who was presumably working on folk drama when Austin wrote De Huff on June 15, 1931, to withdraw $125.00 from Sen. Bronson M. Cutting's $500 contribution to pay Campa, "as he expects to start at his work at once."[11] Later work by both Campa and Aureliano Armendáriz, a musician from La Mesilla, New Mexico, who was paid $55.04 in 1933, undoubtedly involved the collection of Hispanic folk songs.[12] Austin's interest in such endeavors seems not to have been shared by other members of the board, most of whom devoted more energy to the cultivation and preservation of the visual rather than the verbal folk arts.

This cultivation was made possible by a confidential gift from wealthy newspaper publisher Cyrus McCormick, Jr., of Chicago and Santa Fe. In January 1930, treasurer John De Huff received a letter on McCormick's Chicago stationery:

> I am enclosing for you check from Mr. Cyrus McCormick Jr. for $175.00 with which you are to open a new account for the Spanish Arts Association. This account is to be in favor of the Field Worker in the Spanish Arts, who is yet to be appointed, and will cover salary, transportation and other necessary incidentals to the work. Mr. Frank Applegate will communicate with you very shortly about who is to be employed and whose credentials he is investigating. Make the account separate, as you have done with the Dramatic Department. Similar check will reach you each month from Mr. McCormick's office for 1930.[13]

Until May of that year, Applegate himself acted as an unpaid field worker, initiating what was to become an important association with Paul Bernat of Emile Bernat & Sons Company of Jamaica Plain, Massachusetts. At first, Applegate "arranged . . . to secure yarn at jobbers' prices and will then supply yarn to independent weavers in Chimayo and pay them for the work of weaving. In this way, he believes, blankets of good design and color can be secured."[14] Later, he and his successors worked with the company to develop yarns of suitable texture and color.

The position of field worker and its accompanying chores were taken over by Preston E. McCrossen as of May 1, 1930, at a salary of seventy-five dollars a month. Together with his wife, Helen Cramp McCrossen, he also operated the society's newly opened shop, The Spanish Arts, in Room 39 of the Sena Plaza (at a rent of fifty dollars monthly). This outlet was to provide a year-round market for "revival" Hispanic handwork of all kinds, and Applegate at least hoped it would obviate the prizes presented during the annual Santa Fe Fiesta.[15] Nevertheless, throughout the four years of its operation, shop employees administered the Fiesta activities on behalf of the society, and the annual Spanish Market continued as an important vehicle of Anglo patronage. An unsuccessful attempt to include Spanish cookery among the crafts for which prizes were offered was made in 1930,[16] but for the most part prizes were awarded annually for blankets, rugs, embroidery, furniture, wood carvings, and iron- and tinwork.

The McCrossens were weavers, and records indicate that they carried on a lively interchange both with Paul Bernat and with the craftspeople who wove, crocheted, stitched, or otherwise worked with fabrics. In June 1930, Bernat urged Applegate to "attach 'Colonial' to the name of your store [since] actually the arts are not true Spanish as their place of origin is not Spain and also they have dissimilarities," pointing out that "from the commercial Standpoint my arguments are much more telling for in leaving it Spanish one is throwing away all the sales value in the widespread interest and publicity of the Southwest and also the talking point in another American Colonial art type." He added:

> I am not sure that I would make "Chimayo" the name for the weavings. All the commercial work is branded with atht *[sic]* name and there will ensue a good deal of confusion if you ever go into wholesale work. Your weavings would go out as Chimayo and if somebody comes along with ordinary pieces, they can foist them on the store as Chimayo, and use the very same label as you. If you could hit on a catchy name for your various products, you could then add the Chimayo to the weaves, Colcha to the embroidery and so on. For the name you could go far afield but perhaps it would be best to take some name that has a distinct application to New Mexico and preferably its cultural history. If you were to adopt either Spanish Colonial or Southwest Colonial Arts you could work out an artistic letterhead design and apply this to all your products and then add Chimayo weave, Colcha embroidery or whatever the craft might be.[17]

Although The Spanish Arts shop never changed its name and adapted only a photograph of a colcha on its letterhead, Bernat shortly commended Applegate for adopting "the name of 'Spanish Colonial,' instead of Chimayo [because], as I wrote in the previous letter, if you get an attractive name such as this, you can use it on everything."[18]

Paul Bernat was also interested in the neckties that Preston McCrossen apparently encouraged. He promised to show the gift one from McCrossen to his friends in order to "get you some orders" and asked for a short article

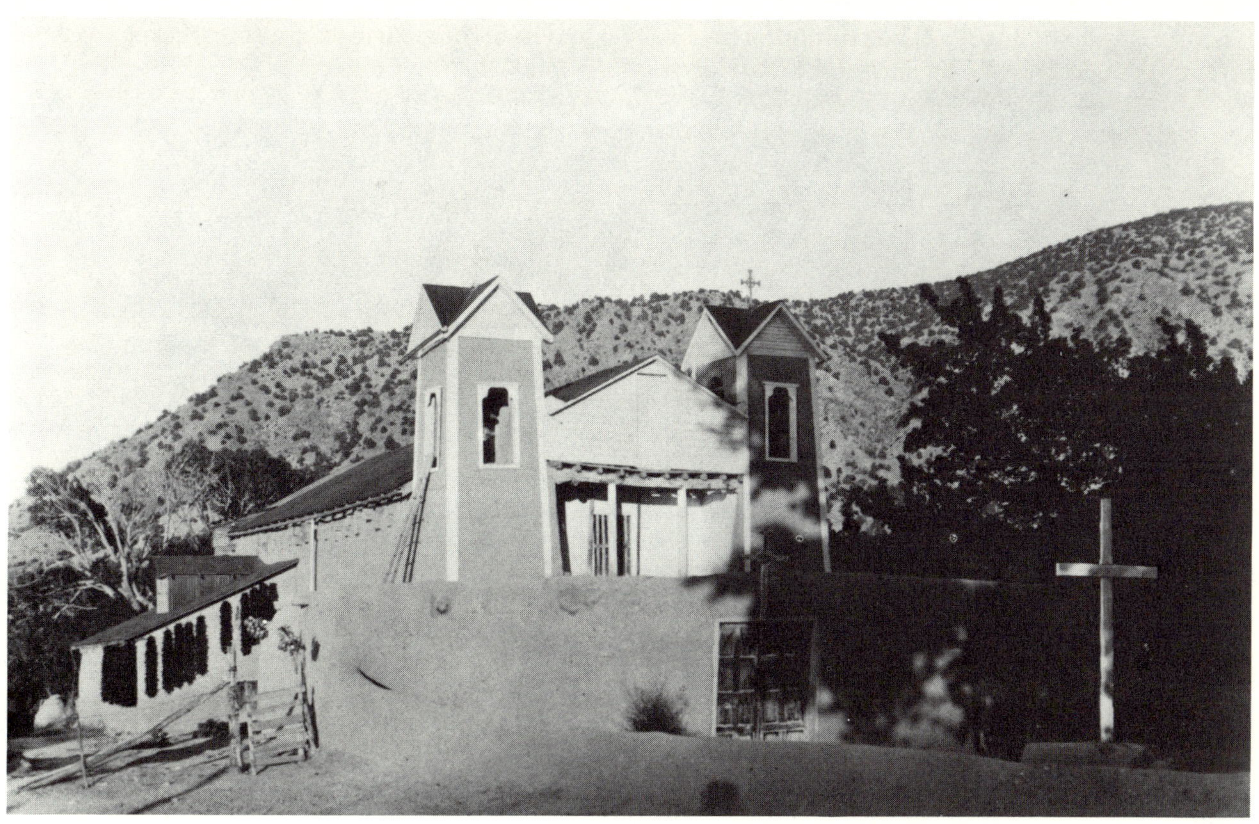

FIGURE 3
The Santuario sometime after 1929. (Department of Development Collection, New Mexico State Records Center and Archives, Santa Fe.)

on the ties for *The Handicrafter*, "a bi-monthly magazine devoted to handicrafts."[19] A later letter notes: "I appreciate your position with reference to the neckties . . . and I believe you are right in considering it an error to write an article on them. Everybody that has seen the ties considers them very natty looking and I think a market of wide scope is possible. I hope that I shall be able to develop some outlets for you and I shall look into it when I return to Boston."[20]

In September 1930, Pedro J. Lemos of Stanford University visited Santa Fe, lunched with the McCrossens, and purchased lanterns, a lazy susan, a "family tree" carving, and other items at The Spanish Arts shop. Lemos also asked Helen McCrossen to write an article "on the revival of the Spanish handicrafts in and around Santa Fe" for *The School Arts Magazine*, which he edited.[21] McCrossen's article appeared in March 1931, featuring wood

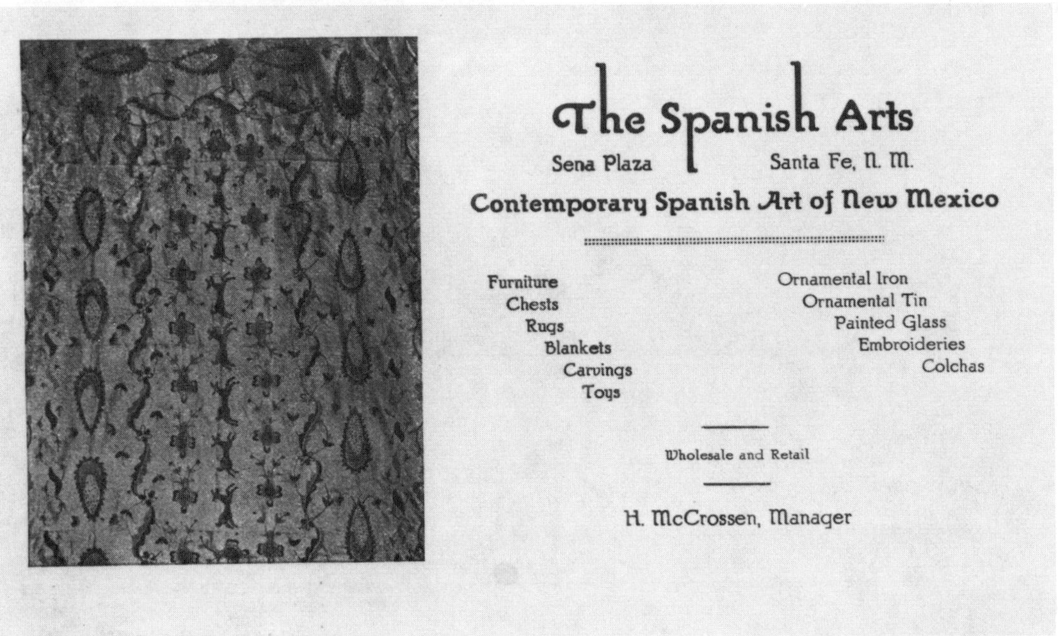

FIGURE 4
Letterhead. (Papers of the Spanish Colonial Arts Society, New Mexico State Records Center and Archives, Santa Fe.)

carvings by Celso Gallegos and José Dolores López of Córdova, New Mexico (on López, see Boyd 1974: 467–71; Briggs 1980), the revival of tinwork, blankets, and women's rag rugs.

To further such "revived" handicrafts, the Spanish Colonial Arts Society cooperated with public-school officials to encourage student crafts. Mamie Meadors was paid eight dollars from the general fund to award prizes to schoolchildren in May 1930.[22] Between May and November 1930, Santa Fe County school superintendent Nina Otero-Warren supplied The Spanish Arts shop with various pieces made by rural schoolchildren, for which "a commission should be charged by you . . . 25% is not excessive." She added: "I would like very much to get together with you in order to determine what articles can be loaned by you for our Arts and Crafts exhibit to be taken around to our schools."[23]

On November 26, 1930, Taos County school superintendent Ernest Lyckman gratefully acknowledged receipt of Bernat yarn samples and a sample blanket but admitted:

> As you know this is the first year of weaving for our students and so far, they have made nothing which you could probably sell to an advantage. However, they are making excellent progress and before the term is over I hope to bring you some worthwhile pieces of work. Your suggestions have been much appreciated.

A handwritten letter from Lyckman's successor, Wesley Freeburg, is more optimistic:

> I understand that you sometimes display for sale articles produced by the industrial arts departments in various school *[sic]*. We have a strong industrial arts department in weaving and wood carving and would like very much to find a market for it. If you can handle this for us will you please write me with details of your proposition.[24]

However, the Spanish-American Normal School at El Rito, headed by John V. Conway, was by far the most active supplier of blankets, wood carvings, and furniture. In 1931, for example, teacher Charles E. Brown noted Conway's support for photographs of student pieces because "Mr. Rockey when he heard of it wanted to take the album with a specmin *[sic]* or two of the work to an exhibit in Idaho next week."[25]

Besides the annual Santa Fe Fiesta displays,[26] there are few exhibits noted in extant documents. In late September 1930, Paul Bernat's company took a booth in the Craftsmen's Work Exhibit of the Women's Educational & Industrial Union in Boston and invited The Spanish Arts to exhibit "Indian blankets" (rather than "regular weaving," which might have offered unfair competition to Eastern weavers), neckties, "other things you are producing . . . [and] a little jewelry if you are doing it."[27] Chicago, where Fred and Lucy Leighton's Indian Trading Post was a strong outlet, seems to have offered the strongest support, perhaps through Cyrus McCormick's instigation.

In March 1931, the Leightons sponsored an ecclesiastical show, primarily of Celso Gallegos's santos, tin lanterns, and candlesticks. Apparently they also told Helen McCrossen about the upcoming American Folk Art Exhibit in Chicago, and she addressed a letter of inquiry to Raymond O'Neil of the Walden Book Shop and Gallery. He assured her that the planned exhibit "must certainly include a representative exhibition of Spanish Arts."[28] However, no furniture was shown in the January 1932 exhibit, to which carvings by José Dolores Lópoz and Celso Gallegos, Chimayó mats, rag rugs, mirrors, wall sconces, bookends, hinges, hearth brooms, colchas, and various other items were sent. In O'Neil's final accounting, The Spanish Arts was owed only $31.50 ($47.25 less commission) for one hearth broom, one Gallegos rosary, one pair of wall sconces with mirror by Sandoval, one Saint George, five pairs of sconces, a single sconce, one mirror sconce, a head on root by Gallegos, a box by López, and one burro pantalla.[29] Such dismal figures confirm William Wroth's observation of the Hispanic crafts revival in the early 1920s through the late 1930s:

> During this period, in spite of the enthusiasm of the wealthy Anglo patrons in northern New Mexico, Hispanic crafts never "caught on" nationally in the way the Indian crafts did. Interest was fairly well limited to the Southwest and southern California, the areas in which the adobe hacienda revival was taking place. The major interest in Hispanic crafts was as furnishings for these comfortable Southwestern-style adobe homes. These crafts were not, as were the Indian, viewed as valuable art objects in themselves purchased with an eye for speculation. (1977: 6)

Because it could not attract significant outside notice, The Spanish Arts shop began to decline, particularly after Cyrus McCormick's monthly donations ceased in December 1931. By that time, the McCrossens no longer managed the shop's operations for the society. They had earlier undertaken to pay the fifteen-dollar rent on Room 38 of the Sena Plaza "for the display of the McCrossen weavings," and Preston McCrossen received his final seventy-five-dollar salary in November.[30] Nellie G. Dunton took over in December at a salary of sixty dollars a month. She too was interested in textiles, having made "a collection of drawings of old designs taken from embroidered bedspreads and other old Spanish textiles . . . to assist the native women doing modern hand work."[31]

Despite Dunton's meticulous management and Mrs. Field's donating a prize "for the best monthly contribution,"[32] the shop did not prosper. In July 1933, treasurer John D. De Huff advised Mary Austin that "the shop has slumped terribly during the past few months":

> At the present rate of progress, the shop can run only three more months. If the income there doesn't pick up smartly, we should either close it out Sept. 30, or else turn it over *in toto* to Mrs. Dunton and let her run it on her own responsibility. The shop hasn't even paid the rental since February.[33]

The Spanish Arts shop was officially closed on October 10, 1933. Leonora F. Curtin's Native Market, which opened on Palace Avenue on June 16, 1934, soon took its place as a vehicle for the encouragement and popularization of New Mexican Hispanic crafts (Coan 1935; Mauzy 1936: 67–68; Nestor 1971: 18).[34]

Although The Spanish Arts shop had been a major society concern from 1930 until 1933, the board did not neglect the corporate aims of collection and preservation, work begun by Frank G. Applegate. His death on February 13, 1931, galvanized society members to arrange to purchase his collection from his widow, Alta B. Applegate. A committee reported:

> Of the collection of bultos and Santos retablos there are thirty-eight pieces valued at $1,500.00, an altar piece from a morada valued at $500.00, a three-parted panel of the Creation valued at $1,500.00. There are also a number of articles of furniture with which Mrs. Applegate does not wish to part at present, but the refusal of which she is willing to give to the Society.
>
> At a meeting of the organization at which this report was read, it was decided that the altar piece and the Creation panel might be brought in for us by some of the friends of the Society whom Mrs. Austin will see individually. As regards the collection of Santos, it was thought that the amount might be raised by small contributions. It was decided to appoint a committee to have charge of the business of raising this sum of money . . . of which Mrs. Austin will be chairman.[35]

In all, twelve hundred dollars was to be raised to purchase this collection; only five hundred of this amount was forthcoming, however.[36]

Mary Cabot Wheelwright proved another important benefactor to the society. Like other items in the permanent collections, her gifts and loans were "placed with the New Mexico Historical Society in their rooms at the old Palace for exhibition."[37] Among Wheelwright's donations was a Garden of Eden wood carving by José Dolores López (Anonymous 1932). In November 1933, she also arranged for the society to purchase a valuable colcha depicting Holy Week activities of the Penitente Brotherhood from Wayne Graves of Taos County.[38]

All society activities virtually came to a standstill after Austin's death on August 13, 1934. In August 1936, treasurer De Huff consolidated remaining monies from the dramatic, field workers', and permanent collection funds into the general fund, and converted $650.00 to a certificate of time deposit, leaving $109.42 in a checking account.[39] However, Leonora F. Curtin spearheaded an attempt to revive the society in 1938.

Some forty interested persons gathered at Curtin's Acequia Madre house on February 10, 1938. Pres. Mary Cabot Wheelwright was absent, so the vice-president, Kenneth M. Chapman, presided and explained the society's purposes and history. Harry P. Mera chided the society for allowing the Taylor Museum in Colorado Springs, Colorado, to acquire "the best collection of Santos ever made . . . [because] the Society's inability to carry on was definitely the lack of funds, the problem never having been formulated, and there was never sufficient background for constructive work." Nina Otero-Warren suggested a society committee that would "ask the clergy to prevent the sale of Santos from the Churches," while both Mrs. Chapman and Reginald Fisher discussed the needs for exhibition space in the Museum of New Mexico.[40]

Vocational schools and training were also explained by Carmen Espinosa, Nina Otero-Warren, R. P. Sweeney, and Leonora F. Curtin. The latter spoke eloquently "on the present day condition, the preservation, revival, and adaption of crafts to modern uses":

> She told of founding the Native Market during the depression, to save some of the people from its demoralizing effects and at the same time to save for New Mexico an artistic tradition that was here.
>
> "I learned from the Spanish-Colonial Arts Society, through its pioneering shop in the Sena Plaza, that guidance for craftsmen was needed and I hoped with help to provide such guidance for one craft at a time," she said. "But the Spanish Arts Shop closed and soon came Mr. Sewell, head of the new department of vocational education who said the government would provide the training, but what was needed was an outlet for the work—a market." This outlet was provided in the Native Market, where Miss Curtin pointed out, it is stressed that crafts can and should remain household arts and it is not necessary to cater to a large-scale demand.
>
> Miss Curtin closed her remarks with stress on the need for assistance in every field and from every viewpoint: for the preservation of self respect of the

> craftsmen through stimulated appreciation of cultural background; for the reclamation of higher citizenship status among the underprivileged; for access to good examples of art and craftsmanship; for a wider recognition of the value of hand work; among teachers for technical knowledge; for encouragement of individual enterprise among the native people; for the development of many more salable products utilizing native talents; for a wider understanding of New Mexico's Spanish-Colonial art and traditions, for museum specimens and facilities. She offered the services of the Native Market's facilities at all times to the society.[41]

Committees were appointed, and annual dues set at one dollar. Alice Corbin Henderson moved "that the Spanish Colonial Arts Society should be affiliated with interested Societies of the local Spanish people," an offer that Ina Sizer Cassidy seconded and that "Mrs. Ortiz accepted for the Sociedad Folklórica; Mrs. Gilbert . . . for the Lulacs."[42] Twenty-one persons joined in February 1938, prompting Curtin to write Wheelwright:

> There seemed to be so much work crying for attention, that I took it upon myself to find out what caliber of interest and enthusiasm might be lying dormant in the town. The response is magnificent. To my surprise, there is quite a number of people willing, really eager, to work. The diversity of individual interest, of course, raises a problem as to how the energy may best be utilized and at an executive committee meeting last night which lasted until late, it proved quite impossible to reach a definite decision as to the future course to be taken, there being so many angles and kinds of activity to consider.[43]

The energies of the revised society were not mobilized until the summer, however. A memorandum from Edgar Lee Hewett noted that space in the Old Palace would soon become available and that "the Museum of New Mexico will welcome the help of the Spanish Colonial Arts Society in providing the public with a permanent exhibit of the finest examples obtainable of authentic New Mexico Colonial furnishings, antiques, and specimens of early weaving, handicrafts, etc." If the society proved organized enough "that there is reasonable promise of its continuance for fifty years," and if Leonora F. Curtin were to head it, "the Museum will undertake the care and fumigation of specimens and it will endeavor to provide the part time services of a curator for the listing and cataloguing of material."[44] A meeting of the board of trustees "for the purpose of discussing and taking action on a special exhibition of Spanish Colonial Arts" was called at Mrs. Thomas E. (Leonora S. M.) Curtin's on August 5, 1938. The accession agreement with the Museum of New Mexico was signed on August 25, the day after completion of two thousand pamphlets, written by Paul Horgan, that described the special exhibit and advertised society memberships. Only four memberships are recorded after its publication.[45]

The society was not as successful in placing the other tangible legacy from founders Applegate and Austin: a jointly authored manuscript entitled "Spanish Colonial Arts." According to Austin, she had encouraged Applegate to undertake three projects: the native tales book, a book on Spanish arts, and the story of the house "as it had evolved in New Mexico."

> Always I have been gifted—or plagued—by a kind of fore-knowing which makes me vaguely aware of the future progress of events, and along in the Fall of 1930 I began to be distressed with the presentiment that something was to intervene in the work of that book [on Spanish arts]. So I insisted on Frank's committing to paper all that he had learned about the technique of the Spanish arts. I did not imagine that anything would happen to Frank, who was apparently so hale and strong; I thought it much more likely that it would happen to me. (Austin 1932*b*: 216–17)

In her autobiography, Austin notes only that she and Applegate "laid [the book] out and shaped it into a design" and that she had to set their notes aside following Frank's death: "Life has gone somewhat heavily since, but I know that when I am at the work at last I shall be reassured" (1932*a*: 367). She put the "final touches" on the manuscript three days before her own death on August 13, 1934.[46] Her niece Mary Hunter wrote De Huff on August 30 to thank him for the society's flowers:

> The work of the Society was one of Mary Austin's deepest interests. The day before her death she told me how much she hoped the publication of the book on Spanish Colonial art by her and Frank Applegate would help your work. You have my warmest gratitude and my hope that you will call on me if I can be of any service.[47]

Austin had first contacted Yale University Press about publishing the manuscript and then Houghton Mifflin Company, which returned it after her death. Several months later, T. M. Pearce of the English department, University of New Mexico, met with Roger Scaife, a Houghton Mifflin vice-president, who "advised that the material on history be separated from the material dealing with the arts and crafts." Society records show that Pearce was paid forty dollars in 1937 and ten dollars in 1939 for his work on this ill-fated revision, which was rejected by Houghton Mifflin, the University of New Mexico Press, and, in 1939, by Walter Goodwin of Santa Fe's Rydal Press. "As late as 1941, the matter was still under discussion" at the Laboratory of Anthropology in Santa Fe.[48]

In his foreword to the revised manuscript, Pearce acknowledges help from Alice Corbin Henderson, the late Sen. Bronson M. Cutting, Mary Cabot Wheelwright, and Alta B. Applegate, as well as grants from the Spanish Colonial Arts Society and the American Council of Learned Societies, which "made possible the complete illustration of the text, furnishing the finest collection of photographs of the Southwestern Spanish Arts in existence [as] the work of Ansel Adams, done in the life time of Mr. Applegate, made possible the excellent reproductions here."[49] The specific photographs for the original manuscript were eventually turned over to Mrs. Thomas Wood Stevens, but Alta Applegate later sent Pearce "a package of several score additional pictures made at the same time and doubtless under similar conditions."[50] Many of the pictures were taken in The Spanish Arts shop, and Pearce later recalled too "Ansel Adams and his piano playing along with the picture taking," presumably at the Applegates' residence.[51]

Extant records indicate that the Spanish Colonial Arts Society was largely dormant from the late 1930s through the 1940s. During the New Deal, many of its functions were taken over by federally funded art projects and state vocational-training programs.[52] Bank statements throughout the war years show an unchanging balance of $730.97, with many mailings going unopened. In September 1949, Ina Sizer Cassidy wrote secretary George M. Bloom that: "As there are some matters coming up for consideration of the members of the Spanish Colonial Arts Society we feel that a meeting of the Society should be called before too long."[53] No further records of these "matters" presently exist, and the Spanish Colonial Arts Society was not reorganized and revitalized until 1951, when E. Boyd proved as dynamic a figure as her founding predecessors, Mary Austin and Frank G. Applegate.

In many respects the history of the Spanish Colonial Arts Society parallels that of the New Mexico Association on Indian Affairs, begun in 1923 and later called the Southwestern Association on Indian Affairs, with its annual Indian Market, and the related Pueblo Pottery Fund, incorporated as the Indian Arts Fund in 1925. Austin was also instrumental in the latter's development, "particularly in 1928 when the permanent cooperative agreement was perfected between the Indian Arts Fund and the newly incorporated Laboratory of Anthropology, an institution which was planned to extend the field of southwestern research beyond that covered by the fund" (Anonymous 1944: 59, 60; also see Austin 1932*a*: 360–62; Weigle and Fiore 1982: 19–20). However, while it certainly generated a notable local constituency in Santa Fe, the Spanish Colonial Arts Society never enjoyed statewide and national support as the various Indian groups did. It was not clearly connected with an academic discipline like anthropology or archaeology, and its association with the Museum of New Mexico was never as secure as that between the Indian Arts Fund and the Laboratory of Anthropology, which opened in 1931 (Toulouse 1981). Nevertheless, the legacy of revival crafts, the Santuario at Chimayó, and the nucleus of the collection now housed in the Museum of International Folk Art, opened at Santa Fe in 1953 (Sellars and Langlois 1978), endures as a tribute to all whose vision and energies launched the Spanish Colonial Arts Society, guided its activities, and kept its potential alive through very trying times in the late 1930s and 1940s.

NOTES

1. The letterhead of the Society for the Preservation of Spanish Antiquities, Santa Fe, lists: L. Bradford Prince, president; Archbishop J. B. Pitaval, honorary president;

Benjamin M. Read, secretary; Felix Martínez, vice-president; Bronson M. Cutting, vice-president; and Antonio Lucero, treasurer. In addition to the five general officers, the board of governors included F. W. Clancy, R. L. Baca, J. Wight Giddings, O. N. Marron, Nestor Montoya, A. J. Loomis, Filadelfo Baca, G. W. Pritchard, J. H. Grist, Camilo Padilla, B. C. Hernandez, G. Volney Howard, José D. Sena, R. E. Twitchell, and W. G. Turley. From the Papers of the Spanish Colonial Arts Society (hereafter PSCAS), New Mexico State Records Center and Archives, Santa Fe.

2. An undated [1929] broadsheet, "Spanish-Colonial Arts Commences 5th Year of Activity," notes that Austin was helped by Mr. and Mrs. Frank G. Applegate, Mrs. A. T. *[sic]* Alvord, Sheldon Parsons, Mr. and Mrs. Datus Myers, Mr. and Mrs. Kenneth M. Chapman, Sen. Bronson M. Cutting, Mrs. Asplund, Mrs. Fenyas, Mrs. Thomas E. (Leonora S.) Curtin, Nina [Otero-] Warren, Dr. and Mrs. Frank E. Mera, "and others." A Spanish Colonial Arts Society pamphlet from the early 1950s claims that the 1925 group founded by Austin and Applegate was supported by Ruth Laughlin Alexander, Mr. and Mrs. A. S. Alvord, George M. Bloom, Mr. and Mrs. Gerald Cassidy, Kenneth M. Chapman, Mrs. Thomas E. Curtin, Sen. Bronson M. Cutting, Andrew Dasburg, Mr. and Mrs. John D. De Huff, Mrs. Charles (Margretta A.) Dietrich, Mrs. Lois Field, Mrs. William Field, Alice Corbin Henderson, Wayne L. Mauzy, Mr. and Mrs. Cyrus McCormick, George McCrossen, Preston McCrossen, Mr. and Mrs. John Gaw Meem, Frank E. Mera, Alice Clark Myers, Leonora F. Curtin Paloheimo, Sheldon Parsons, Francis I. Proctor, Marie Robinson, H. Cady Wells, Mary Cabot Wheelwright, "and others sensitive to Spanish culture."

3. For more on Gallegos, see, for example, Boyd 1974: 431, 433, 435; Briggs 1980: 64, 226; and Stevens 1974. Canceled checks from August 1926 include ones for twenty dollars to Louisa López, ten dollars to Anastasia Gonzáles, five dollars to Angela Arias, five dollars to Juanita M. López, three dollars to Emilia M. Casados, twelve dollars to Concepción Garcia, thirteen dollars to Mrs. Marina Martínez, and twenty dollars to Damacio Cruz.

4. For a discussion of Anglo-American and Hispano upper-middle- and upper-class patronage of the revival of selected Hispanic handcrafts, see Briggs 1980: 50–52 and Wroth 1977.

5. This altarpiece is the first entry in the 1950s pamphlet, "Hand List of the Collection of the Spanish Colonial Arts Society, Inc." Of the 140 items collected as of May 1954, 35 (altarpiece, bultos, retablos, textiles, miscellaneous objects) are starred to indicate their being "from collection of original Spanish Colonial Arts Society."

6. According to the newspaper account of the garden ceremony, Mary Austin was joined by Paul A. F. Walter, Dan Kelly, and John Gaw Meem. With Carlos Vierra and others, Meem had been active in the missions-restoration project. Austin announced "that in the future the work of the Spanish Colonial Arts organization and that for the preservation of the old missions is to be combined and one body will be incorporated for the joint work"; *Santa Fe New Mexican,* 15 October 1929, p. 2. A photograph in Kelly (1972: opposite 192) shows Meem delivering the deed to Daeger with Walter, Kelly, Applegate, Baumann, Proctor, Austin, Mrs. John Robinson of Sunmount, Alice Corbin Henderson, Dana Johnson, Marcos Chávez, Judge Charles Fahy, José Cháves, Victor Ortega, Bishop Espelage, and Father Salvatore Gene of Santa Cruz in attendance.

7. Minutes, 8 October 1930, PSCAS. According to minutes from the meeting of 25 September 1931, Austin had decided to include folklore and folk dramas "in a series of supplementary readers to be used in schools where there are Spanish-speaking children. Volunteers are wanted to assist in the work of translating the material. The money arising from the sale of these books is to be devoted to the work of the society." She also reported "that the Penasco high school was awarded a prize this year for the presentation of a Spanish drama."

8. See, for example, Austin 1927, 1933, and 1934. Austin claims: "That acting talent is native to the Spanish-speaking in the Southwest is easily observable wherever they can be found in the relation of speaker and audience. Listen to George Armijo interpreting in the legislature, watch José Sena conducting a religious procession, or the local reader at the village tienda dispensing the news to those of his neighbors who are too poor to buy a paper, or could, perhaps, not read it if they did, and you will see that the impulse which gave life to the 'siglo de oro' is not yet decayed" (1928: 574).

9. Curtin to De Huff, Santa Fe, 29 September 1934, PSCAS.

10. The Reverend Kuppers was at Chaperito, New Mexico, when he wrote "The Penitentes and the Literary Digest" for *The Southwestern Catholic,* 17 September 1921, p. 62.

11. Austin to De Huff, Santa Fe, 15 June 1931, PSCAS. In a letter to Mrs. Preston McCrossin *[sic]* dated 25 April 1931 (PSCAS), Austin remarked: "Senator Cutting has just told me that he would like to put the work which has been done at the University in Spanish Folklore and Literature under my direction. He wants me to take charge of Mr. Campa who has been doing the work and to disburse the funds." No reason is given for this request. Campa's published works in the early 1930s include 1930, 1933, 1934*a,* and 1934*b.* For an overview summary of his life's work, see Campa 1979.

12. Aureliano Armendáriz, who later headed the folklore section of the Federal Music Project in New Mexico, was Campa's assistant during a field trip to collect songs in northern New Mexico in the summer of 1932; Stark 1973: preface.

13. Mary Austen *[sic]* per CMcCJr. to John David DeHoff *[sic],* 17 January 1930, PSCAS. This monthly donation to the field workers' fund continued for two years, through December 1931.

14. Minutes, 19 May 1930, PSCAS. Bernat remained the primary supplier of yarns for four years, but some materials were also obtained from Horner Brothers Woolen Mills, Eaton Rapids, Michigan; J. H. Clasgens Company, Manufacturers of Woolen and Merino Yarn, New Richmond, Ohio; and Thomas Young, Inc., Manufacturers, Importers and Originators of Unusual Linens, 42 White Street, New York City. In 1933, Diamont Tints & Dyes, Wells and Richardson Company, Inc., Burlington, Vermont, quoted prices on the "Old Navajo Dyes" that they had been selling to Indian traders in Arizona and New Mexico for some forty years.

15. Ibid. According to an anonymous report (1930: 106): "The object of both the Spanish Arts Shop and the Fiesta prizes are to stimulate the production of such things as were made by the early Spanish people in New Mexico. . . . Mary Austin and Frank Applegate and a number of others have worked faithfully for the revival of these handicrafts, and with great wisdom, encouraging the people not only to copy old designs but to create new ones in the same spirit of originality *and play* as did their ancestors."

16. Handicrafts were exhibited in the Governors' Palace, cooked items at the Spanish Folk Market near the DeVargas Hotel, with prizes covering "dishes based on cornmeal, on beans, and chile, as well as sweets . . . all under expert supervision"; Anonymous 1930: 106. Ruth Barker was in charge of prizes, but "due to delays and misunderstandings—and the rain of the last afternoon—no prizes were awarded"; Minutes, 19 May and 8 October 1930, PSCAS.
17. Bernat to Applegate, 1 June 1930, PSCAS. Bernat also claims that "so much of the interest in these arts revolves about the fact that they were developed in U.S. territory and are out growt *[sic]* of Spanish art like the American Colonial is of English, Dutch etc. . . ." He observes: "I appreciate the pride of the natives in their early Spanish origin; but then they are going on a wrong track to my mind. The New Englanders of Mayflower descent are just as proud of their English origin and the fact that they are the first settlers, yet they do not howl about their arts being English in style type; rather taking credit in their American colonial period. Of course there exists one salient difference—these New Englanders are the ins and apt to consider America themselves; while the Spanish in New Mexico have been relegated to the background and feel their rights are usurped so the attitude might be psychological defiance."
18. Bernat to Applegate, 11 June 1930, PSCAS. Bernat also suggests: "In all probability you could get a great deal of inspiration from the real Spanish work as well as the Spanish Colonial. No doubt, some of the books on Spanish Art can supply a good deal of design that is attractive. Have you thought of the possibility of using peasant material." His examples are Scandinavian, "Roumanian, Czecho-Slavakian, and even that of countries like England and Spain," as well as France. Bernat was clearly influential, as Mary Austin later wrote Helen McCrossen: "I think the idea for a folder of Spanish Colonial Arts is excelent *[sic]*, and there is enough money in the treasury to spend the amount you mentioned, but I think the name Colonial should by no means be omitted. Frank was always insistent that this shall not be called Spanish Arts, but New Mexican Colonial Arts"; Austin to Mrs. Preston McCrossin *[sic]*, 25 April 1931, PSCAS.
19. Bernat to Preston McCrossen, 29 July 1930, PSCAS.
20. Bernat to Preston McCrossen, 15 August 1930, PSCAS. Either McCrossen had decided that the neckties were not truly Spanish colonial or he had encouraged them as part of his own weaving interests, not the society's.
21. Lemos to Mr. and Mrs. McCrossen, 22 September 1930, PSCAS.
22. Check No. 4, to Miss Mamie Meadors, 10 May 1930, PSCAS.
23. Otero-Warren to Helen McCrossen, 10 November 1930, PSCAS. There are miscellaneous receipts in the files for one table, one tin candelabra, six stone animals (lion, elephant, porcupine and three bears), oxen and wagon by Daniel Quintana, Cundiyo baby chair, ten bone heads, eleven rubber animals, one carreta from Chupadero, one picture from Cundiyo, three stone animals, as well as six tin sconces, six candlesticks, a wooden picture frame, and a towel (tie) rack from "the schools of Cundiyo & Canada De Los Alamos."
24. Lyckman to Helen McCrossen, 26 November 1930; Freeburg to Spanish Arts Shop, 8 October 1931, PSCAS.
25. Brown to Helen McCrossen, 29 April 1931, PSCAS. Brown also wanted pictures of the furniture so he could make an album and "use it to sell things next year."
26. In September 1931, the Harwood Foundation of Taos sponsored a crafts exhibit

with Mrs. B. C. Harwood footing the bill from her personal account. There were entries from Santa Fe, with at least two sales—mats by Gallegos and a tin sconce by Manuel Griego. Blanche C. Grant to Helen McCrossen, 2 September and 11 September 1931; Mrs. M. Tallmadge to Helen McCrossen, 17 September 1931, PSCAS.

27. Bernat to Applegate, 11 June 1930; Bernat to Preston McCrossen, 19 September 1930, PSCAS.

28. O'Neil to Helen McCrossen, 7 July 1931, PSCAS. In a later letter he notes: "I have written twice to the Indian Arts Fund, from whom I am expecting an exhibit and have had no reply. Can you inform me immediately whether this organization is still in existence, or if not, to whom I might send for an Indian collection?"; O'Neil to Helen McCrossen, 27 October 1931, PSCAS.

29. O'Neil to Spanish Arts, 4 July 1932, PSCAS. The only other exhibit recorded was "at Folklore Festival, St. Louis in May 34 of Old Spanish Embroidery Designs with embroideries"; Nellie G. Dunton, item 10 on the "Data Blank Volume 31 American Art Annual," 16 November 1934, PSCAS.

30. McCrossen to De Huff, 27 October 1931, PSCAS. The Spanish Arts shop began to rent Room 38 and Room 39 on 16 April 1931. They ceased to pay the $65.00 monthly in November, but Room 39's rent was then raised to $55.00. It was not decreased until October 1932, after which the society paid $35.02 monthly through September 1933.

31. Minutes, 19 May 1930, PSCAS. In November 1934, Dunton reported that the society's "Collection of Spanish dramas & folklore at Laboratory of Ethnology and Old Spanish Embroidery Designs—can only be consulted there"; "Data Blank–American Art Annual." Her book, *The Spanish-Colonial Ornament* (1935), is a portfolio of forty plates (twenty in color) and text. Like Helen McCrossen, she too contributed to *School Arts Magazine* (1942). Dunton, who first came to Taos in 1920 with her artist husband, W. Herbert Dunton, had divorced and moved to Santa Fe in 1928 (Weigle and Fiore 1982: 202).

32. Austin to De Huff, 17 April 1933, PSCAS.

33. De Huff to Austin, 8 July 1933, PSCAS. De Huff itemized 1933 shop repayments to the society as: January, $72.61; February, $41.53; March, $28.58; April, $14.83; May, nil; June, nil; July, $1.81.

34. Early in 1934 Mary Austin asked the financial status of the Spanish Colonial Arts Society's general fund because "Miss Curtain *[sic]* wants me to offer some music prizes for the opening of her shop which is to be an important occasion"; Austin to De Huff, 31 January 1934, PSCAS.

35. McCrossen to Mrs. A. H. Schmidt, 16 July 1931, PSCAS. Also see Austin 1932*b*: 217–18.

36. De Huff to Austin, 9 September 1932; Austin to De Huff, 13 September 1932, PSCAS. A promissory note for the remaining $700.00 was issued at this time. Alta B. Applegate had received $350.00 on March 22, 1933, and the remainder on October 12, 1933 (check No. 144). Fifteen retablos, twenty bultos, and "1 bordado (piece of embroidery)" were thereby purchased by the society; De Huff to Charles Fahy, 21 January 1933, PSCAS.

37. A. B. Applegate to Austin, 12 March 1931, PSCAS. Curator Hester Jones wrote letters acknowledging the receipt of two paintings on buffalo skin (8 April 1931) and six blankets (25 October 1933) for these loaned exhibits, and curator Paul Reiter thanked Mary Austin for volunteering to write colcha and weaving labels (3 February 1934). Ten colchas, four blankets, three "rebosas," two altarcloths, and a hooked blanket from the Applegate collection are recorded; Jones to Austin, 9 February 1934, PSCAS. A three-page, typed, itemized loan receipt (MNM-ACC ART-1938 Nos. 127-75) is dated 25 August 1938 and signed by Frances Urban, PSCAS.

38. Wheelwright to Graves, 14 November 1933; Dunton to De Huff, 18 November 1933; counter check dated 12 March 1934, PSCAS. Austin wrote two cryptic letters to De Huff on the subject: (1) "Please credit the enclosed to the permanent Collection Fund. It's for a penitente Colcha Mary Wheelwright dug up" (3 November 1933); and (2) "Please deposit the enclosed [B. M. Cutting $25.00] to whatever fund you drew from to pay for the colcha" (28 November 1933), PSCAS. According to an unidentified newspaper clipping in the PSCAS: "The [colcha's] body is white wool with a border of points of brown wool enclosing small blue crosses; inside of this is another border of the variety of cactus known as cholly. In the middle space is a carefully worked-out design of a Penitente crucifixion. The Cristo is on the cross surrounded by a whipping procession with cantador and resador and Penitentes whipping themselves with bloody flagils. At one side is a presentation of a morada in brown and over it a moon and star. . . . The purchase of this interesting example was made possible by Mrs. Albert Sims, Miss Amelia Hollenback and Senator Bronson Cutting."

39. De Huff to Wheelwright and Curtin, 30 September 1936, PSCAS.

40. Unsigned minutes of the society meeting at Curtin's, 10 February 1938, PSCAS. Those attending included Leonora F. Curtin, Sheldon Parsons, Mrs. Venceslao (Cleofas M.) Jaramillo, Harry P. Mera, Mrs. James Goodwin, R. P. Sweeney, Hester Jones, Henrietta Harris, Mrs. Henry S. A. (Ruth Laughlin) Alexander, Carmen Espinosa, Mr. and Mrs. Ernest Knee, Datus Myers, Alice Corbin Henderson, Dr. and Mrs. Reginald Fisher, Mrs. R. Hunter Clarkson, Concha Ortiz y Pino, Mr. and Mrs. John Gaw Meem, Wayne L. Mauzy, Lloyd Moyland, Mr. and Mrs. George M. Bloom, Mrs. Carlos (Fabiola Cabeza de Baca) Gilbert, John D. De Huff, Mrs. Manuel Sanchez, Nina Otero-Warren, Mrs. Jesse L. (Aileen) Nusbaum, Helen Dorman, Mrs. I. H. Rapp, Mr. and Mrs. Albert Schmidt, Mrs. John Lowe, Paul Reiter, Mrs. Alfredo Ortiz, Mr. and Mrs. Kenneth M. Chapman, Mrs. Gerald (Ina Sizer) Cassidy, Mrs. William (Jeanette) Lumpkins, Mrs. Charles H. (Margretta A.) Dietrich, Mrs. Wilbur Wiswall, Nell Ruth Roughton, and Scudder Mekeel. Curtin also sent letters to University of New Mexico professors George P. Hammond, Dorothy Woodward, F. M. Kercheville, Lansing Bloom, and Arthur L. Campa, all of whom expressed interest but were unable to attend.

41. The first quotation is from the minutes (PSCAS), the second from the newspaper adaptation of those minutes, "Spanish Colonial Arts to Be Preserved According to Plans of 40 Persons at the Curtin's," *Santa Fe New Mexican,* 11 February 1938, p. 2. For more on Curtin and the Native Market, see Nestor 1971.

42. Minutes, 10 February 1938, PSCAS. Sheldon Parsons headed the exhibitions and loans committee; Mrs. Clarkson, music and drama; Mrs. Alexander, publicity; Dr. Harry P. Mera, collection and preservation of material; Mrs. Dietrich, membership, finance, and organization; Miss Curtin, modern crafts and adaptations; and John Gaw Meem, preservation of monuments and architecture. For more on La Sociedad Folklórica de Santa Fe, see the account by its founder (in 1935), Cleofas M. Jaramillo (1955: 173–77).

43. Curtin to Wheelwright (Sutton Island, Maine), 18 February 1938, PSCAS.
44. "Dr. Hewett says," memorandum, 15 June 1938, PSCAS.
45. Kenneth M. Chapman to the Trustees, postcard, 25 July 1938; MNM-ACC Art-1938 Nos. 127–75, 25 August 1938; invoice, Rydal Press, 998 Canyon Road, Santa Fe, to Spanish Colonial Arts Society c/o John De Huff, Treasurer, 24 August 1938. Dues for 1938 are recorded in a "Money Receipts" book and show later contributions and dues from Brice H. Sewall (20 August 1938), H. Cady Wells (26 August 1938), Mrs. Florence McCormick (10 September 1938), and Mrs. Neil Cowham (10 February 1939). All PSCAS.
46. T. M. Pearce, editorial foreword to the revised manuscript, "Spanish Colonial Arts," by Frank Applegate and Mary Austin (n.d.: 51); archive 255, box 1, Special Collections, Zimmerman Library, University of New Mexico, Albuquerque.
47. Hunter to De Huff, 30 August 1934, PSCAS.
48. Pearce, memo to archive 255, Special Collections, Zimmerman Library, 18 October 1976. The revised manuscript, which this memo accompanies, is in three parts: The Colonizing, five chapters on the history of Spanish New Mexico; The Arts and Crafts, nine chapters on leatherwork, chests, intrusive chests, ironwork, tincraft, weaving, furniture, embroidery, and religious art; and illustrations of miscellaneous objects, tinware, chests, textiles, furniture, santos retablos, bultos, churches, and church furniture. A second table of contents listing fifteen "mixed" chapters also accompanies this manuscript. The original manuscript was sent to the Huntington Library, San Marino, California, with Austin's literary papers. According to E. Boyd (in a letter to Pearce): "When the proposed publication did not materialize copies of the mss. were in the hands of Ina Cassidy (I believe she still has hers), Dr. Kenneth Chapman, you—and who else? Dr. Chapman, a past President and Director of the Board of the Spanish Colonial Society, turned over his copy to me some years ago as I am, of necessity, curator of their collections as well as of the Spanish Colonial material in this museum"; 22 April 1965, PSCAS. About 1970, Boyd showed me this copy, together with illustrations. My brief notes indicate only that the manuscript contained 143 pages and that the pagination on references to the Penitente Brotherhood does not jibe with Pearce's revised manuscript. E. Boyd's copy has since disappeared.
49. Pearce, editorial foreword, p. 5. Records in the society's ledger show only that Adams was paid twenty-five dollars for five photographs, 13 October 1930, PSCAS.
50. Pearce to Boyd, 29 April 1965, PSCAS. These additional photographs were turned over to the society in 1965, through the efforts of Richard B. Stark, Sallie Wagner, and E. Boyd; Pearce to Wagner, 31 March 1965, and Boyd to Pearce, 22 April 1965, PSCAS.
51. Pearce to Boyd, 29 April 1965, PSCAS. Ansel Adams wrote a note dated only "Wednesday" to "Mrs McCrosky" [*sic,* although he apologizes: "I blush with shame that I do not know if your name is McCrossen or McCrosky"]: "Thank you and your husband for all your assistance with the photographs; I have some very nice things—the carved tree came out exceedingly well." Also see the note on Adams and the Austin–Applegate manuscript in Pearce 1979: 217–18.
52. During the first full year of the New Mexico Federal Writers' Project, for example, Aurora Lucero-White (later Lea) began what state director Ina Sizer Cassidy de-

scribed in an 16 August 1936 letter to national director Henry G. Alsberg as: "a book on the native plays and old Spanish customs of New Mexico. Included . . . will be her M.A. thesis which was prepared in 1934 ["Coloquios de 'Los Pastores' de Las Vegas," New Mexico Normal (Highlands) University, 1932]. These plays will be published in Spanish and English." It was to have been entitled "Spanish Life and Customs of New Mexico—Yesterday and Today." Alice Corbin Henderson, then an NMFWP editor, encouraged its publication and brought it to the attention of Ira Rich Kent, managing editor of Houghton Mifflin Company, in 1937. Ina Sizer Cassidy had earlier secured assurances "that the Spanish Colonial Arts Association will sponsor this, if we can find a publisher, who will assume the cost of publication. This book, as you know, will be a slow selling book, but will be long in demand, especially in the West"; Cassidy to Alsberg, 19 February 1937, Record Group No. 69, National Archives, Washington, D.C. Both Houghton Mifflin and Santa Fe's Rydal Press rejected the manuscript, portions of which were incorporated into her post-Project volumes (Lucero-White 1940*a,* 1940*b,* 1941, 1947, 1953). For more on Cassidy, Henderson, Lucero-White, and the NMFWP, see Weigle and Fiore 1982: 50–57 and Weigle with Powell 1982.

53. Cassidy to Bloom, 21 September 1949, PSCAS.

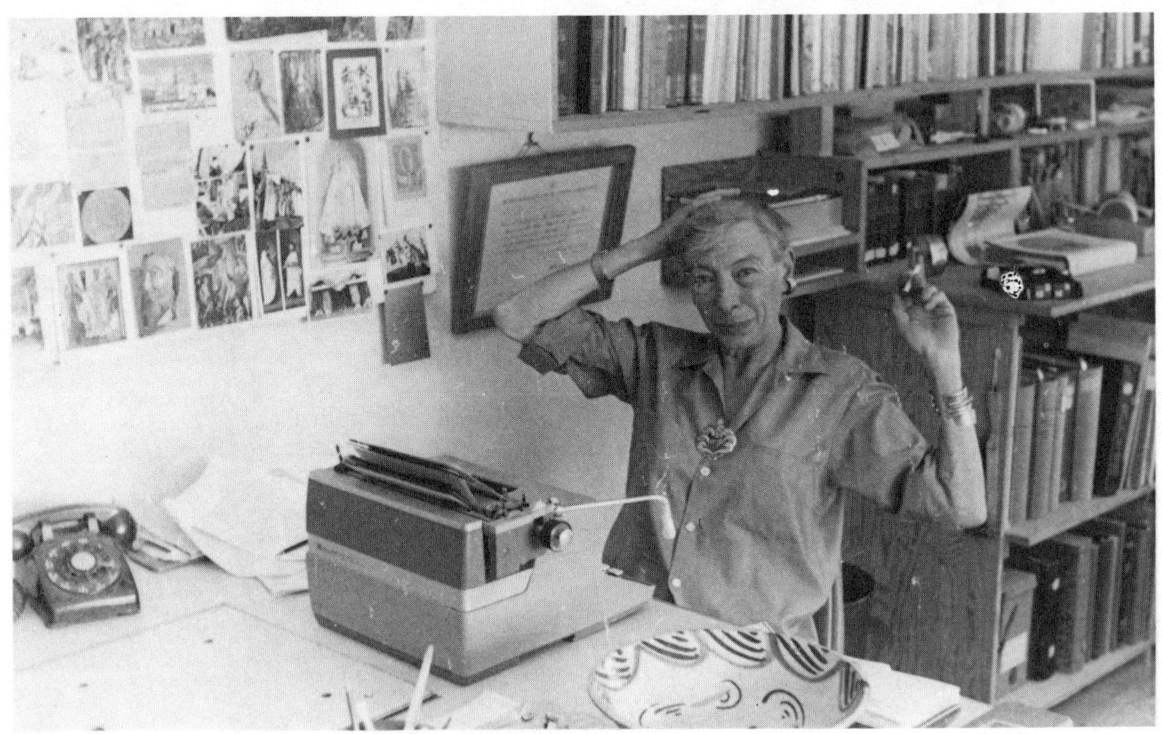

FIGURE 1
E. Boyd in her office at the Museum of International Folk Art, Santa Fe. (Photograph by Richard B. Stark.)

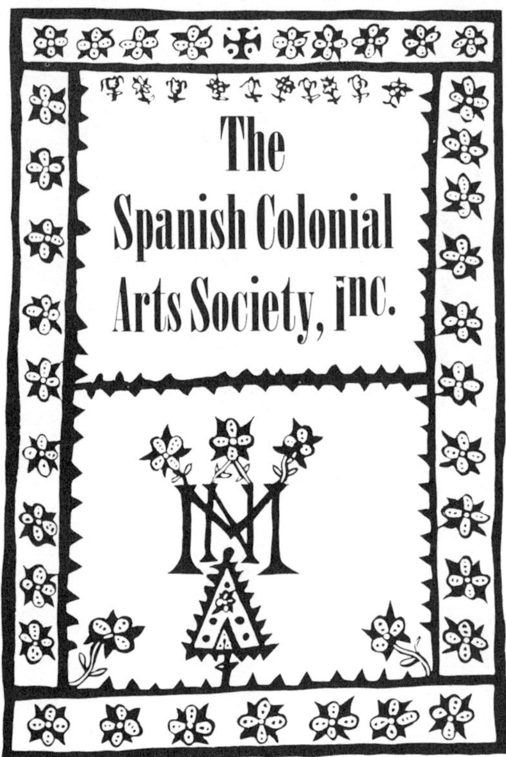

FIGURE 2
From the cover of the membership solicitation leaflet, n.d.

ANN VEDDER

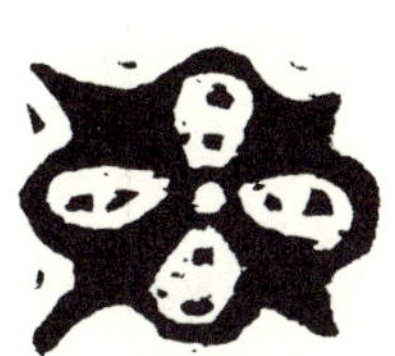

HISTORY OF THE SPANISH COLONIAL ARTS SOCIETY, INC., 1951–1981

THE SPANISH COLONIAL ARTS SOCIETY was originally founded in 1925 by the late Mrs. Mary Austin and Mr. Frank G. Applegate. . . .

The Society was active for many years, but after the deaths of Mrs. Austin and Mr. Applegate, and because of the distractions of World War II, it was inactive until early in 1952. The Society was reactivated at that time because the Museum of New Mexico had recently established a Department of Spanish Colonial Art with its own Curator. A small group of the original members, together with other interested persons, felt that there was a real need for an active and energetic group to promote the aims set out by the original Society, to collect more material and to arrange for the safekeeping and display of the material already in the Society's collection. People often forget that the Museum of New Mexico, like all other museums which are operated with public funds, receives very limited appropriations for the purchase of exhibition material. Instead, such funds are supplied by the Museum's friends, in our case the Society. By the purchase of unique examples which might otherwise have been removed from this region, or simply destroyed in the path of progress, the Society has saved, and is now saving, many rare items which can never be duplicated. . . .

The revival of the Spanish Colonial Arts Society is a movement of importance not only in the history of folk art in New Mexico, but in the entire United States. The Southwest, whose history antedates that of our eastern coast, might be called the birthplace of American Colonial art. The Society is the only active, private organization still engaged in collecting material for preservation and exhibition in the State of New Mexico. Much of the material has already gone out of the State into the hands of Museums or private collectors.

—E. Boyd, leaflet soliciting memberships, n.d.

THE FOUNDATIONS FOR THE REACTIVATION of the Spanish Colonial Arts Society were laid in 1951 with the creation of a Spanish colonial arts department in the Museum of New Mexico at Santa Fe. The artist and collector Cady Wells (1904–1954) was instrumental in the department's creation. He donated his santo collection with the stipulation that E. Boyd be named curator, a position she held for the remainder of her life (Robertson and Nestor 1976: 141–42). Within a year of her appointment, E. Boyd began work to revitalize the society, a task in which she received enthusiastic support and even donations of objects as early as 1952.[1]

The first official revitalization and reorganization meeting was held on February 14, 1952. After Mrs. Gerald Cassidy read the minutes of the last meeting in 1938, a nominating committee proposed a slate of officers. Lois Field was elected temporary president.[2] At the February 18 meeting, George Roy was assigned the task of working on the bylaws, and plans were initiated for a membership drive (annual dues then being two dollars); both of these matters were further discussed on February 25. On March 28, 1952, Lois Field resigned as president, and E. Boyd was appointed to fill the vacancy for the remainder of the interim period. In addition, a committee was appointed to approve purchases by the society and to receive gifts to its collection. Other meetings were held on April 4 and June 2.

Permanent officers, led by president Wayne L. Mauzy and a sixteen-member board of trustees, were elected at a general membership meeting on June 16, 1952. The purchasing committee was then asked also to serve as a publications committee to work on informative pamphlets. This committee consisted of E. Boyd, Cornelia G. Thompson, Mrs. Joseph C. McKibbin, and Mrs. Y. A. Paloheimo.

A resolution was adopted at the September 25, 1952, meeting that the society "undertake to furnish and install the contents of an old New Mexican house and outbuildings from Spanish Colonial collections." The house was to be owned by either the Museum of International Folk Art or the International Folk Art Foundation; the land would be purchased by the Museum of New Mexico. Among those primarily interested in this project were Leonora S. Curtin and Mr. and Mrs. Y. A. Paloheimo. These plans never materialized, and at the next meeting on February 16, 1953, it was agreed to defer action on raising funds for such a building project. (It is noteworthy, however, that serious consideration was given to a comprehensive cultural exhibit even before the paperwork was completed for reorganizing the society.)

On February 18, 1953, members of the original society and temporary officers of the reorganized society met to agree on the general purposes of the new organization. To comply with various legal requirements, a meeting of those who had been board members of the Spanish Colonial Arts Society in 1938 was called. A notice announcing the meeting was published on May 6 and 7, 1953; the meeting itself was held on May 16. Present were board members Mrs. Thomas E. (Leonora S.) Curtin, Andrew Dasburg, Margretta A. Dietrich (who was appointed temporary secretary), John Gaw Meem, Frank E. Mera, Mrs. Datus Myers, and Mary Cabot Wheelwright (who was appointed temporary chairman). Four motions were duly made, seconded, and passed: to take immediate steps to reactivate the society; to admit to active membership seventy-two additional individuals as listed in the minutes; to call a special meeting to elect a new board of trustees or to fill vacancies on the present board, to revise the bylaws, and to consider such other business as might properly come before the meeting; and to accept the resignations of all present board members effective upon the election of a new board of trustees. At the special meeting of May 27, Wayne L. Mauzy was reelected president, sixteen trustees were elected, the amended bylaws were adopted, and a consolidation of the society's two bank accounts, one of which had been in existence since the 1930s, was approved.

To further formalize this organizational structure, a meeting was held on August 25, 1953, to submit a contract to the School of American Research providing for the loan of the society's collection. Such an agreement was executed on April 21, 1954. This agreement was subsequently terminated by mutual consent, and a new loan agreement between the society and the Museum of New Mexico was signed on May 4, 1961, for a period ending October 30, 1979, a date coinciding with the end of the then corporate existence of the society, which had been incorporated in 1929 with a term of fifty years.

By May 1954, the society's trustees had authorized and E. Boyd had produced an attractive pamphlet entitled *Hand List of the Collection of the Spanish Colonial Arts Society, Inc.*, a twenty-page publication, now out of print, which sold for one dollar. The pamphlet describes an important altar screen from Llano Quemado, a painting on tanned hide, twenty bultos, twenty-one retablos, seventeen textiles, thirty-eight pieces of tinwork, seven metal objects, four recent wood carvings, and seven miscellaneous items. Fifteen objects are illustrated with black-and-white photographs. Of the total listed in the pamphlet, only thirty-five items were from the original collection; the remainder had all been acquired through gifts and purchases during a two-year period, a tribute to the efforts and enthusiasm of E. Boyd.[3]

At the same time, E. Boyd also produced a four-page illustrated leaflet to accompany the *Hand List* and to encourage membership in the society. Her text, portions of which are excerpted in the epigraph to this essay, presents a concise history of the society from 1925 to 1954 and reiterates its purpose. Unfortunately, this leaflet too is out of print.

In September 1954, the Museum of New Mexico, the Spanish Colonial Arts Society, and the Taylor Museum of the Colorado Springs, Colorado, Fine Arts Center sponsored a three-day roundtable on Spanish colonial materials at the Museum of International Folk Art in Santa Fe. By all reports, this initial conference was very successful, and another roundtable was held in Santa Barbara, California, in 1957.

The society also became involved in another aspect of Spanish colonial culture in September 1954, when its trustees agreed to contribute funds for materials to repair the roof at the Oratorio de San Buenaventura on the old Plaza del Cerro at Chimayó, New Mexico—a project thoroughly documented by E. Boyd in various memoranda, in her 1955 curator's report to the society, and in an April 1955 article for *El Palacio* (Boyd 1955; also see Boyd 1974: 32). This private chapel belonged for generations to the Ortega family (hence, it is often referred to as the Ortega Chapel), until the spring of 1953 when Srta. Bonifacia Ortega died and in her will left the oratory to the Archdiocese of Santa Fe. It was placed in the custody of women in the Confraternity of Our Lady of Carmel.

This small oratorio is one of the few surviving examples of a private chapel left in New Mexico. It has a mud floor, old ceiling, wooden chandelier, and handcarved railing and benches. A handsome small altar screen by José Rafael Aragón stands behind the altar table, which once held several excellent small bultos, including a rare one of San Buenaventura. Unfortunately, the small, rare bulto of San Buenaventura, a bulto of San Antonio, and the small tower bell were stolen in September 1971 and have never been recovered.

By 1954, the roof of the oratorio was in such a state of deterioration that the interior furnishings, including the Aragón altar screen, were endangered. Some four tons of dirt, which had been piled on the roof since its last renovation in 1873, were threatening to destroy the walls and vigas. The Spanish Colonial Arts Society offered to provide materials if the confraternity would cooperate by providing for the labor. This arrangement was accepted, and E. Boyd convinced the persons involved that repairs should be made without altering the old character of the chapel. The respected and experienced builder was Merejildo Jaramillo, grandfather of Arturo Jaramillo. He removed the heavy load of dirt, built up the front (east) wall with layers of adobe and a cement cap, laid new stringers and boards with a good slope to the west, and put on heavy-grade tar paper instead of dirt. The inside and outside of the chapel were replastered, screens and windows were repaired, and a new wooden belfry was made. Upon completion of the project in November 1954, members of the confraternity expressed their sincere gratitude to the society.

The society again assisted in the maintenance of the oratorio in 1963, when it provided funds for adobe plaster for the two exterior walls. In 1969 additional funds were voted for replastering and adding cement footings.

Further interest in conservation projects is evident from the society's records. In 1956, a small sum was donated to a project in Ojo Caliente to rebuild an abandoned church as a community center and historical landmark. During the same year, the society expressed its willingness to co-sponsor, to the extent of its ability, any project undertaken in connection with restoration of the old Chimayó Plaza as a living museum. It also offered to aid Fray Angélico Chávez in the restoration of La Conquistadora Chapel in St. Francis Cathedral, Santa Fe.

E. Boyd and Alan C. Vedder were consultants on the Conquistadora Chapel project in 1956–1957. Chávez's research indicated that the altar screen was of the eighteenth century and had been brought from Mexico to Santa Fe for the bulto of La Conquistadora, who fits perfectly into the nicho (1948: 19–

20, 37–45). The altar screen had been overpainted before and, unfortunately, was overpainted again in garish colors rather than being restored. Substantiation of the possibility of restoration occurred when a carpenter working on the altar screen gave the two consultants seven pieces of "leftover" wood. Vedder removed the then white oil paint to find Mexican *estofado* (gilding) underneath on six of the seven pieces. Perhaps one day this altar screen can be restored so it can be seen as it was originally rather than with the white oil paint of three decades ago or with the garish oil-paint colors of today.

On another occasion when E. Boyd and Vedder stopped at La Conquistadora Chapel to check on the restoration, they received a further surprise. They asked the whereabouts of a stone sarcophagus that had been in the west wall. A brown-robed Franciscan showed them where it had been placed for protection. He opened the lid, and both E. Boyd and Vedder exclaimed, "Indigo blue!," when they saw the blue material on each side of the divided stone. The Franciscan pulled a scissors from beneath his robe and snipped a piece of cloth from each side. These pieces are now framed under glass in the Museum of New Mexico, providing visual proof that the Franciscans wore blue robes in New Mexico during the eighteenth and nineteenth centuries, as E. Boyd had always maintained (1974: 222). These swatches are from materials familiar to the New Mexican santeros of the classical period, who painted indigo blue robes on the San Antonio and San Francisco santos.

In an effort to generate income to finance its various projects, the society published an illustrated thirty-two-page pamphlet, *El Santuario de Chimayo,* in 1956. Two articles from *El Palacio,* Stephen F. de Borhegyi's "The Miraculous Shrines of Our Lord of Esquípulas in Guatemala and Chimayó, New Mexico" (1953) and E. Boyd's "Señor Santiago de Chimayo" (1956), were combined as a detailed guide to the shrine and its history. This booklet was well received and has been reprinted numerous times.

Through its curator E. Boyd, the society also continued to make good progress in augmenting its collection through gifts and purchases.[4] An important addition in 1956 was the gift of twenty-four pieces of South American silver from Mrs. Henry Lyman, a cousin of Mary Cabot Wheelwright. In 1958, when a trader trusted by the society learned that an important painting on tanned buffalo hide depicting the crucifixion with mourning figures and cup-bearing angel was for sale from a morada in Alcalde, he approached the society, which indicated its interest in the right of first refusal. This valuable object was beyond the society's cash resources, but E. Boyd and Alan C. Vedder approached three individuals for funds for this specific purchase. Their help, plus general society funds, made possible the acquisition of this early eighteenth-century New Mexican painting, which is regarded as a prototype for later santos.

Late in 1961, the society received from Ruth Catlin a gift of 3.2 acres of land in Santa Fe adjacent to St. John's College. Discussion immediately ensued about using the site for reproductions of authentic Spanish colonial buildings that could house the varied collection of the society. According to the records of the society, this planned facility was not to duplicate any existing museum exhibits in Santa Fe. However, on February 12, 1962, the director of the Museum of New Mexico wrote the president of the Spanish Colonial Arts Society that its museum plan was in conflict with the state museum's plans for the Palace of the Governors. The letter further stated that the museum's published plans were to include room- and building-replica displays of a chapel, gristmill, homes, and shops, as well as other replica units around and in the expanded palace patio. The letter indicated that such displays would be installed as soon as possible and would bring out of storage the bulk of the collections in the museum's custody, including materials then covered by long-term loan agreements such as that in effect between the museum and the Spanish Colonial Arts Society. Naturally, this letter totally discouraged the society, although the museum did not proceed with its plans.

During the late 1960s and 1970s, Y. A. Paloheimo kept the society informed about plans and progress on a museum at the Paloheimo ranch at La Cienega, just south of Santa Fe. Through the devoted efforts of Mr. and Mrs. Y. A. Paloheimo, an outstanding living museum now exists there at El Rancho de las Golondrinas (Jordan and Cooke 1977).

The society received another very important gift in 1962, a collection of textiles from Mr. and Mrs. John Gaw Meem: thirty-two Rio Grande blankets made in the nineteenth century and two *jergas* (floor coverings). The Meems acquired this collection in February 1939. In her 1962 curator's report to the society,[5] E. Boyd stated: "The collection was selected by the late Dr. Harry P. Mera for the purpose of illustrating as completely as possible the development of New Mexican Spanish weaving, the usage of design elements, vegetable dyes and weaving techniques through the classic period and into the era of innovations in dyes and designs resulting from first Mexican and, later, eastern American commercial imports. The collection was catalogued and appraised by the late Mr. James MacMillan from whose trading shop most of the examples were selected."

A committee on education and research was appointed in 1964 under the chairmanship of Lois Field. This committee was to keep members informed about activities in the general field of Spanish colonial art. The 1964 newsletter of the society mentioned two long-range projects, both involving members. Alan C. Vedder in 1961 had installed two and one-half New Mexican period rooms in the American Museum in Britain at Bath, England, the first permanent New Mexican exhibit in the world. E. Boyd installed an eighteenth-century New Mexican room in 1963 at the Smithsonian Institution in Washington, D.C. The Bath installation is still on display. Vedder also collected folk-art prototypes in Spain in 1961 and 1963 for the society and for the International Folk Art Foundation.

In 1965, the society agreed to sponsor a Native Spanish Market during the two days of August that coincided with the Indian Market. This represented a revival of the Spanish markets held under society auspices prior to the mid-1930s. Eighteen exhibitors attended the 1965 Native Spanish Market, held on the Plaza under the portal of the First National Bank of Santa Fe. Due to scheduling problems that could not be resolved in time, there was no market in 1966, though it was resumed in 1967. By 1971, the Indian Market had become so large that the Spanish Market dates were moved to an earlier weekend in August. Since that year, the market has been held under the portal at the Palace of the Governors and is now an annual event during the last weekend in July. It has grown considerably over the years. In 1981, there were forty-three exhibitors plus eleven of their children who showed in a special children's category. Cash prizes and ribbons are awarded at the market, and the society often makes purchases for its collection from among the exhibits. In recent years, Spanish New Mexican music has enlivened the festivities.

Since the revival of the market, members of the society, especially its curators E. Boyd and Alan C. Vedder, have worked diligently with exhibitors and other craftsmen to develop their interests and skills in traditional Spanish colonial crafts. The result has been an improvement in those crafts and an expansion in their types. For example, encouragement by the society has introduced furniture makers into the market, as well as persons doing straw appliqued work, ironwork, and traditional Spanish jewelry. Traditional contemporary weaving now encompasses a much greater use of natural dyes, better quality work, and documentation of methods and materials used. A few excellent pieces of ikat dyeing have been exhibited in the market in recent years. In keeping with the society's stated purposes, all the crafts must be traditional. Innovations are not discouraged, but, since there are many other avenues and outlets for nontraditional and contemporary crafts, the society has felt it proper to adhere quite strictly to its stated purposes.

Two more publications were undertaken by the society. James Webb Young provided a new foreword to Kate Chapman and Dorothy N. Stewart's charming forty-page pamphlet, *Adobe Notes, or How to Keep the Weather Out with Just Plain Mud.* Illustrated with linoleum cuts and printed in 1930 on Spud Johnson's famous Laughing Horse Press in Taos, New Mexico, the booklet was reprinted in 1966 in the style of the valuable original. In 1972, the society copyrighted and published *El leon y el grillito: The Lion & The Cricket,* a sixteen-page (3½-inch-by-5-inch) booklet containing a facsimile of a popular nineteenth-century Spanish fable told by C. S. Suarez and an English translation. It was planned for bilingual education programs, and efforts were made to promote it through educators and legislators.

Since September 30, 1974, when E. Boyd died, numerous gifts to the society have been received in her memory. Some of these funds have been applied to the publication of this book, a project of which she most certainly would have approved. The Spanish Colonial Arts Society remained a primary interest until her death, and her devotion to Spanish colonial art left a great legacy to that field.

The 1975 annual meeting noted with sorrow not only the loss of E. Boyd but also that of Norma Fiske Day, who left a bequest to the society that included fifty-three important New Mexican retablos. Other devoted members of the society who have contributed significantly to its collection over the years through gifts and bequests include Eleanor Bedell, H. M. Berg, Mrs. Gerald Cassidy, Kenneth M. Chapman, Margretta A. Dietrich, Lois Field, Byron Harvey III, Rebecca S. James, Mr. and Mrs. John Gaw Meem, Frank E. Mera, Mr. and Mrs. Y. A. Paloheimo, Cornelia G. Thompson, Cady Wells, Mary Cabot Wheelwright, and Amelia Elizabeth White.

In 1977, work was completed on amendments to the certificate of incorporation and amended bylaws of the society. The society's purposes and objectives remained the same. The primary changes in the certificate were to correct the name of the society to correspond with that in general use and, most important, to provide for the perpetual existence of the corporation. In addition, the certificate was updated in line with changes in tax and corporate law. The bylaws were updated, clarified, brought in line with current laws, and made to provide for unforeseeable future circumstances. These amendments to the certificate of incorporation and the amended bylaws were approved at a general membership meeting on May 25, 1977, and subsequently were filed.

Efforts of the committee formed in 1975 to negotiate a new long-term loan with the Museum of New Mexico continued in earnest during the next two years. Various meetings were held with the board of the society for guidance, and numerous sessions took place with the committee representing the museum. The final agreement, signed by the society and the museum on November 1, 1979, provides for the care and preservation of the collection, procedures for adding to it, an annual report from the museum, and appropriate credit lines when objects are used publicly. It requires approval by the society's executive committee for loans of items outside the Santa Fe facilities of the Museum of New Mexico.

One of the main items of discussion in the negotiations was the duration of the agreement. The society consistently insisted on a short-term contract, while the museum wanted a long-term agreement. In initial negotiations the museum offered virtually a perpetual loan agreement. This was in no way satisfactory to the society, which is a separate, private, nonprofit organization dedicated to the purposes set forth in its corporate papers and in its publications. Negotiations continued, and finally a twenty-year loan agreement was reached, but with important provisions as to termination.[6]

These termination provisions are most important to the society and to its future. If and when it is possible to develop sources of funding sufficient to build or purchase a building and to adequately endow it, the society would be able to use its collection three years after such plans were finalized. It would then be possible to have comprehensive exhibits of New Mexican Spanish colonial art on continuous display for the enjoyment and education of New Mexicans and tourists alike, as well as for students and scholars. The society's collection is well suited to such overall cultural themes, as the appended inventory and comments illustrate.

New projects undertaken by the society in 1980 and 1981 include the so-called *Viejos* Project to record the oral traditions and history of the Spanish in northern New Mexico. A committee has been appointed to pursue this idea. This book itself represents a major new project of the society. The board of directors approved it early in 1981, and the membership voted to contribute financial support and to act as the tax-deductible recipient of funds designated for this memorial to E. Boyd. Her research, acumen, and enthusiasm truly provided impetus, inspiration, and a firm foundation for the society's second quarter-century.

NOTES

1. Donors in 1952 include Eleanor Bedell, Mrs. Gerald Cassidy, Norma Fiske Day, Cornelia G. Thompson, Cady Wells, Mary Cabot Wheelwright, and Amelia Elizabeth White, all individuals who later became substantial patrons of the society through their gifts and bequests.

2. It is of interest to note that almost thirty years later, in 1979, Lois Field's son William Field became president of the society. The list of presidents reads: Lois Field (February–March 1952), E. Boyd (March–June 1952), Wayne L. Mauzy (June 1952–May 1957), Erik K. Reed (May 1957–May 1962), no president for various administrative reasons (May 1962–May 1964), Sallie Wagner (May 1964–May 1967), George Roy (May 1967–May 1971), Samuel Larcombe (May 1971–May 1972), Mrs. Walter L. Goodwin, Jr. (May 1972–May 1977), Don J. Madtson (May 1977–November 1979), and William Field (November 1979 to the present).

3. Information about the current inventory of the society's collection is appended to this essay.

4. The importance of the Spanish Colonial Arts Society, Inc., in providing a vehicle for tax-deductible gifts can hardly be overemphasized. It has saved for New Mexico numerous objects that would have gone out of state or would otherwise have disappeared from public view. Equally important, however, is the fact that the society usually has been able to make purchases without extended delays, which are often unacceptable to traders and result in the objects being sold elsewhere. There has been little or no money for collecting provided by the Museum of New Mexico, and other supportive organizations usually require board approval coincident with their meeting schedules. The society tries to fill the gap and assure that an important object is not lost due to lack of funds or delayed approval of purchase. As in the early 1950s, however, acquisitions still require approval by those individuals so designated by the society's board of directors.

5. As society curator, E. Boyd presented thorough annual reports, not only record-

ing and acknowledging gifts and purchases but also giving background on the objects from both scholarly and human-interest viewpoints.
6. Termination provisions are set forth in section V of the agreement. The first paragraph of that section provides not only for termination for cause, but also for termination for any reason and without cause by either party with at least three years' notice before the termination date, which cannot be less than ten years after the effective date of the agreement. Paragraph 2 provides: "Notwithstanding the provisions of paragraph 1 of this Section, should the SCAS (the Society) present to the Museum a substantial plan whereby the SCAS will be able to provide, operate and maintain a facility in New Mexico for the housing and exhibition of the entire Collection, this Agreement may be terminated upon a minimum of three years' notice."

INVENTORY SUMMARY OF THE SPANISH COLONIAL ARTS SOCIETY, INC. COLLECTION (Through L.5.81-3; as of October 1981)

The following inventory was prepared from the society's own accession books. The number of objects and books totals 1,354.

1. Altar screen by José Rafael Aragón

2. Six paintings on hides

3. 223 retablos and other paintings:
136 New Mexican retablos by the following santeros:

Miera y Pacheco	1	"Quill Pen"	8
"18th-century Novice"	3	"Santo Niño"	4
"Laguna"	3	"A. J."	7
Fresquis	15	Gonzáles	1
Molleno	20	J. B. Ortega	4
José Aragón	18	Unidentified (pre-1900)	12
"Dot-Dash"	2	Celso Gallegos	7
Rafael Aragón	29	Other 20th century	2

87 others:

Mexican oils on tin or copper	42
Other Mexican or South American oils	24
Mexican engravings, lithographs, etc.	9
Spanish	3
Other European	7
U.S.–"Anglo"	2

4. 147 bultos:
117 New Mexican bultos by the following santeros:

Garcia	1	J. R. Velasquez	5

Fresquis	5	J. B. Ortega	9
Molleno	3	J. D. López	2
José Aragón	1	Celso Gallegos	15
Rafael Aragón	6	Unidentified	39
"Chubby Cheeks"	2	Recent 20th century	14
"Santo Niño"	8	Orlando Romero 3	
"A. J."	4	A. Martínez 2	
Gonzáles	1	L. Salazar 2	
Herrera	1	One each: Barela, M. A. Chávez, S. Córdova, B. López, Gloria López, S. López, Luis Tapia	
"Arroyo Hondo"	1		

30 others:

Mexican	11	Philippine	4
Spanish	9	Puerto Rican	3
Guatemalan	3		

5. 146 textiles:
   115 New Mexican:
   14 colchas (of which 7 are catalogued as fragments)
   15 jergas (of which 4 are catalogued as fragments)
   47 Rio Grande blankets (the Mera collection accounts for 32)
   10 other embroidery
   29 other textile items

   33 others:

Mexican	24	Chinese	3
Spanish	5	German	1

6. 74 pieces of tin, most of which are New Mexican. Eight are contemporary.
   18 frames with prints, lithographs, engravings, etc.
   15 frames, including those with mirrors
   17 sconces
   10 nichos
   4 boxes
   4 crosses
   4 chandeliers
   2 other

7. 17 New Mexican straw appliqued items
   15 crosses, of which 3 are contemporary
   1 box
   1 pair of sconces (contemporary)

8. 99 books; particularly valuable is a complete 14-volume set of publications of the Quivira Society.

9. 28 New Mexican architectural features
   8 doors, one of which is Mexican

14 vigas and beams
3 window frames and shutters
3 other

10. 68 pieces of furniture
55 are New Mexican:

11 chests
4 chest stands
10 chairs
2 *trasteros* (cupboards)
7 benches
3 *andas* (carrying platforms) and *carretas* (carts)
5 tables
2 daybeds
6 *repisas* (hanging shelves)
5 other

13 others:

Mexican	5	Guatemalan	1
Chinese	4	Bolivian	1
Spanish	1	Midwestern U.S.	1

11. 545 "miscellaneous" objects that do not fall into any of the above classifications. These can be categorized as follows: household, 177; agricultural, 52; tools, 34; lighting, 49; smaller architectural features, 6; containers, 11; tobacco flasks, 10; religious, 51*; musical instruments, 11; horse trappings, 22; military and ceremonial, 18; jewelry, 33; South American silver, 33; and other, 38.

*In addition to the specific category "religious," several other categories contain church and/or Penitente objects: South American silver, lighting, architectural features, and musical instruments.

COMMENTS ON THE COLLECTION OF THE SPANISH COLONIAL ARTS SOCIETY, INC.

The José Rafael Aragón altar screen and the six paintings on hide are extremely valuable and important items. The altar screen, purchased about 1928, was from the old church of Nuestra Señora del Carmen at Llano Quemado, just south of Ranchos de Taos. Frank G. Applegate noted: "When purchased this reredos had been removed from its setting and had been replaced by a gaudy one made by the village carpenter who had made much use of milled mouldings. In this purchase there was no question of vandalism on the part of the buyer. It was sold by the committee in charge of the church building." This altar screen has been on exhibit at the Palace of the Governors for many years. The society's paintings on hide are of the eighteenth century and, except for one, are possibly as early as 1693. Many paintings on hide were listed in the inventories of New Mexican churches by Fray Francisco Atanasio Domínguez in 1776 (Adams and Chávez 1956), and his way of describing them leaves the impression that they were already old.

In the New Mexican retablo category, four eighteenth-century works—a dated (1780) retablo by Miera y Pacheco and three retablos by the "Laguna" santero—are of prime importance. Most of the others are from the nineteenth century; they are in good condition and are excellent and representative examples of both santero and subject. There is a good variety of subjects, including not only popular New Mexican saints but also those not usually depicted in the state.

There is a reasonably good representation of nineteenth-century works in the New Mexican bulto category. The society hopes that future gifts and, to the extent possible, purchases can augment this segment of the collection. Presently the works of Celso Gallegos (1860–1943) are particularly well represented. This is probably due to E. Boyd's appreciation of his work and to the fact that his bultos were more available for purchase during the society's active years since 1952 than were those by early and mid-nineteenth-century santeros.

The society has a very strong position in the textile area. Its collection of Rio Grande blankets (in large part due to the Mera collection generously donated by the Meems), jergas, and colchas is extremely fine. The blankets and colchas are well diversified in age and type.

Likewise, the society's tin collection is an excellent one. Note especially the four chandeliers, at least half the number of authentic old ones known to exist. Although not large, the society's straw-work collection is very adequate for exhibition purposes. Its New Mexican furniture collection has variety as well as some excellent pieces. Further gifts in these categories would be most welcome. Tin, textiles, furniture, and straw work are extremely important in rounding out a collection and in making possible comprehensive exhibits.

A review of the miscellaneous category shows areas of considerable strength, which are also most important from an overall cultural aspect. Note the large number of household and agricultural implements, tools, lighting devices, and so on, which adds background and meaning to the more obviously artistic objects like santos, textiles, and furniture of the colonial period in New Mexico.

Many of the non–New Mexican items were gifts, and many, especially from Mexico and Spain, were acquired because they were prototypes for objects made locally. In addition, some were imported into New Mexico during the nineteenth century, for example, the Chinese export chests and the rawhide chests that came from Mexico.

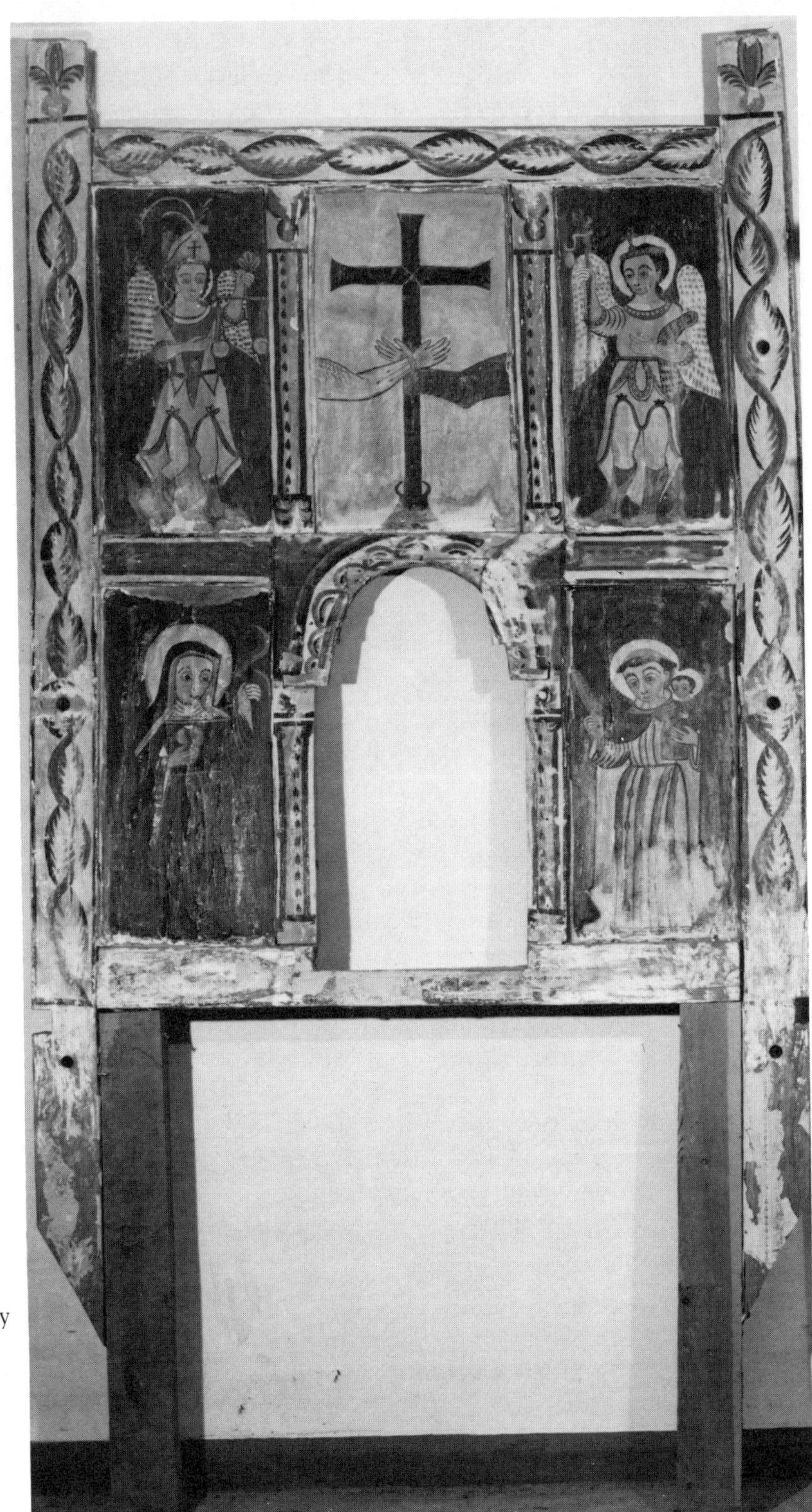

FIGURE 1
Vadito morada altar screen before conservation. Photo by Art Taylor. (Collection of the International Folk Art Foundation, Museum of International Folk Art, Museum of New Mexico, Santa Fe.)

ALAN C. VEDDER

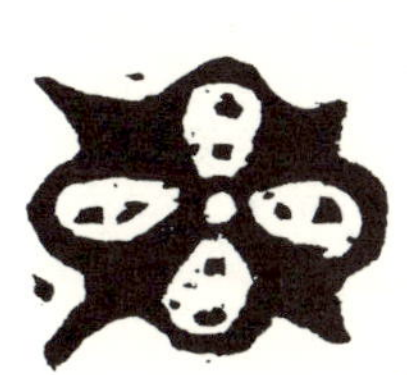

CONSERVATION OF AN ALTAR SCREEN FROM A PENITENTE BROTHERHOOD MORADA

IN 1960, AS PART OF OUR UNSTINTING EFFORTS to augment the Museum of New Mexico's collection of Spanish colonial folk art and to further public awareness and appreciation of this unique and little-known regional art through comprehensive exhibitions, E. Boyd and I pursued a lead regarding an altar screen made by José Rafael Aragón. One of her large circle of friends informed her that an altar screen in a morada at Vadito, New Mexico, was to be sold by the Penitente Brothers to pay for materials being used by the villagers of Vadito to build their new church. The implication was that a trader knew about this and was, or would be, negotiating for it. The friend made arrangements for E. Boyd and me to meet with the Brothers at Vadito as soon as possible, for it was obvious that the screen was to be sold and would not remain in situ, as she and I always preferred.

On our visit there, we were taken directly to the morada, which had no windows and just one door. Fortunately, the Spanish Colonial Arts Society had received one of the Polaroid Corporation's latest cameras on indefinite loan (at that time, it was against company policy to give away cameras). With the morada door open, there was just enough light for me to take a number of photographs of the altar screen.

E. Boyd and I were immediately interested in this comparatively small piece, which measures three meters thirty centimeters in height, including the lunette, and one meter sixty-three centimeters in width. It was painted by José Rafael Aragón, an important nineteenth-century santero who died in January 1862.[1] The morada at Vadito was built ten years later, in 1872. According to oral reports, the altar screen was sent to Vadito from Chimayó as a gift to the Brotherhood from two pious women. It was probably made some time after 1830, as it is in Aragón's mature style.

E. Boyd asked the Brothers if they knew the significance of the Franciscan coat of arms in the upper central panel, showing the bare arm of Jesus crossed by Saint Francis's arm clothed in indigo blue cloth before a large cross. They had no idea and obviously had not thought about it.

After studying the altar screen and agreeing that we wanted to save it for

New Mexico if we could find the money to purchase it, we accompanied the Brothers to the new Catholic church that the villagers were constructing, contributing their labor as in the old days. We were surprised to see that the ceiling was a rounded arch, not the flat roof typical in New Mexico. We asked the men how they learned to do such a ceiling. Raymundo Romero, who appeared to be the leader of the group, said he had read about it in a book, thus showing once again the ingenuity of Spanish New Mexicans in adopting outside influences.

Upon returning to Santa Fe, E. Boyd prepared a request to purchase the altar screen for twelve hundred dollars. She submitted it, together with the Polaroid prints, to the International Folk Art Foundation. The foundation agreed and acquired the piece in October 1960.

The entire altar screen is of native pine, hand-hewn, with five beveled panels and a central nicho on the lower tier. The old legs had been cut down and new props nailed to the frame. Its condition was poor, and, at that stage, if it were not protected, important losses easily could have occurred (Fig. 1).

There were almost total losses in the cartouches on the frame, where only dots of dark paint remained, although once there had been many words, perhaps including the painter's name, the date, and so on. The reason for this loss was that at some time several layers of wallpaper had been put on the lower cross bar, and still later much of it had been pulled off, probably to see what was underneath. Wallpaper came in with the railroad in the 1880s and was quickly put to use by the New Mexicans.[2]

The lunette, on which is painted God the Father, can be slipped out of the grooves in the two uprights. It was badly warped convexly because of its unusually thin wood, which was painted and gessoed only on one side. There was much water damage, and a large amount of gesso had fallen off, some of it in large pieces. Fortunately, the gesso loss was mostly from the background, but it had also occurred straight across the middle of God's right hand, below the nose, through the ermine cloak and on top of the cross. However, God's left hand, which looks slightly awkward, is completely original.

In addition to losses on the borders surrounding the five santo panels, there were some losses on the tops, sides, and bottoms of the panels themselves, which were covered with stains and a dirty film. The most disconcerting problem was that each panel had been covered with cloth that had been gessoed and painted. This is most unusual. The joins and frame of the arched nicho were also covered with cloth before gessoing and painting. Thus, when the wood dried and shrank, considerable buckling and loosening of the cloth took place, a condition shown in Figure 3.

Besides protecting the altar in our storage, our first action was to gesso the losses on the lunette, particularly to keep any more from falling off and to secure in many places the original remaining gesso that had risen from the backing. This was done by running more gesso underneath to adhere

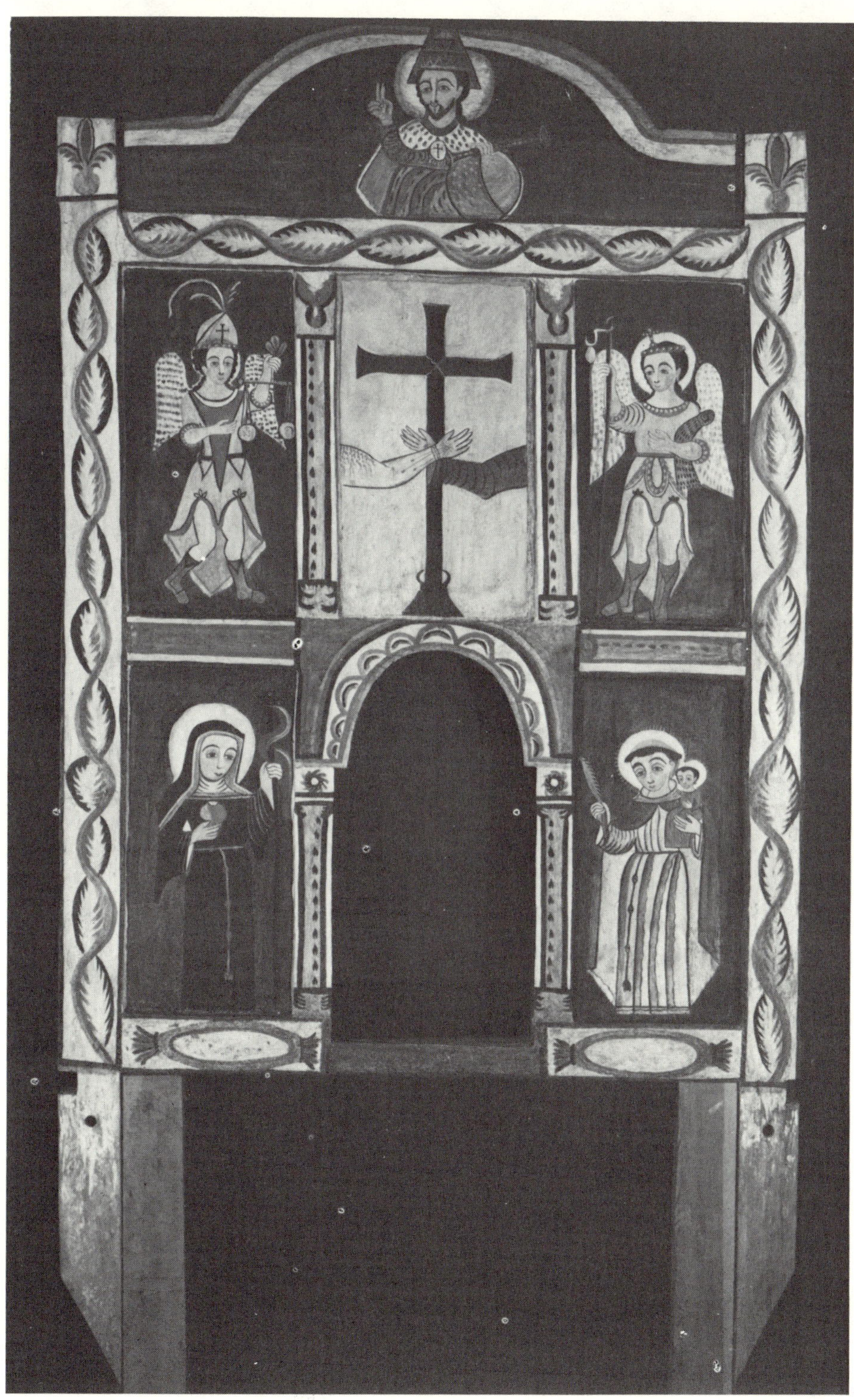

FIGURE 2
After conservation.

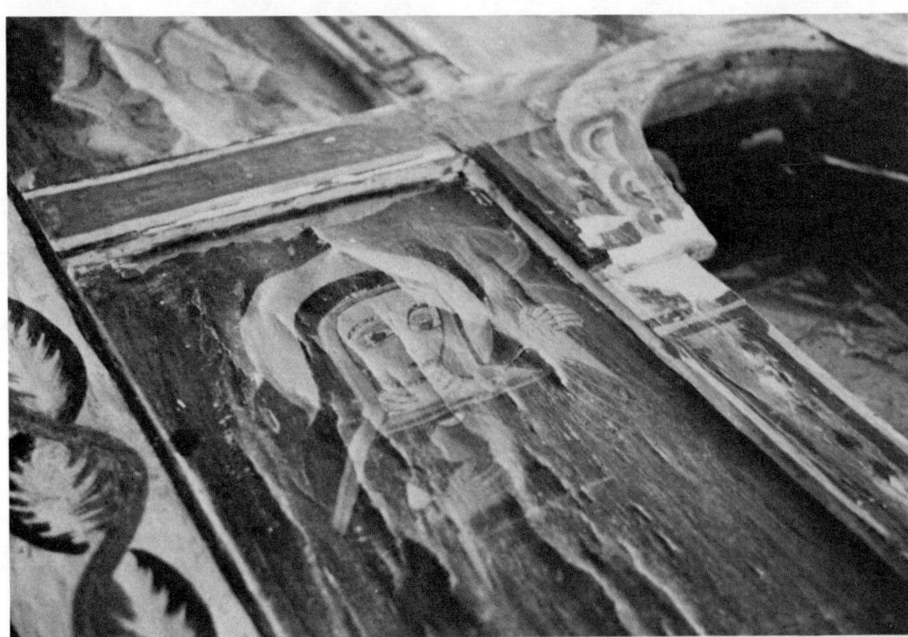

FIGURE 3
Saint Gertrude the Great, lower left panel, before conservation.

the old gesso to the wood in order to keep as much as possible of the original. As so often happens, because of work pressures the lunette was then put in storage. When it was finally returned to my laboratory for further conservation eighteen years later, the new gesso was still solidly attached to the pine, indicating that the wood had stabilized before it left the morada and that I had added sufficient rabbit glue to the commercial gesso. Conservation through this stage is shown in Figure 4.

At this point I once again worked on the lunette. After cleaning the original paint, inpainting was done on the losses to the background and border; then losses on the face and dress were restored. No imagination was required since all the lines were indicated, except below the nose where the mouth and part of the beard were missing. Doing appropriate lines to restore these areas was possible after examining other retablos of bearded saints by Aragón in the museum collections. To stabilize it further, the lunette was waxed with Plenderleith Formula (Plenderleith and Cursiter 1934) and, when dry, polished with a brush to help keep dirt and dust from adhering.

After the lunette was finished on July 11, 1978, the main part of the altar screen was moved into the laboratory and placed on a large table with the top end about six inches higher than the bottom. Before starting conservation, I discussed with several conservators the best way to handle the buckling and raising from the wood of the gessoed cloth (Fig. 3).

One possibility was to remove the cloth completely and then put it down flat. It was suggested that one could start by trying to remove the cloth with a thin palette knife and, if that did not work, by using other methods such as water and xylene or water and toluene. One would first use mulberry paper to cover the panels and then would put wax on top before removing the cloth. I also did an experiment with another conservator on one of the bubbles on the Franciscan panel, first waxing that section of the panel, injecting D8 Beva with a small hypodermic needle, and then using a hot iron to flatten the raised part. Weights were then placed on top. After considering these possibilities, I decided instead to wax the raised areas and then to inject liquid gesso with rabbit glue added into the space between the raised cloth and the wood in order to soften the material, which I would then slowly flatten to the wood by pressing on silicone-release paper.

After going to several drugstores, I obtained a number of syringes with a three-cubic-centimeter capacity and a twenty-two-gauge, 1½-inch needle, for use in those areas where the cloth was not broken. At a feed and grain store, I purchased two syringes that had nine- to sixteen-gauge needles, used for horses. When it was not necessary to pierce the cloth in order to insert the gesso, these larger needles were more satisfactory, as they were much easier to clean.

The first sections I worked on were the uprights and the top horizontal board, where there were some raised and loose gesso spots. There were also large round holes in each outer upright, where dowels had been put at some time to fasten the altar screen to a wall. These were covered with cloth and gessoed, as were the gesso losses on the borders. After cleaning these areas, inpainting was done on the new gesso and these sections waxed with the Plenderleith Formula.

The top central panel with the Franciscan coat of arms had somewhat fewer raised pieces than the others and was the first to be conserved. The initial step was to wax the raised parts. Rabbit glue and water were added to the commercial gesso, and the mixture was heated in a double boiler. When

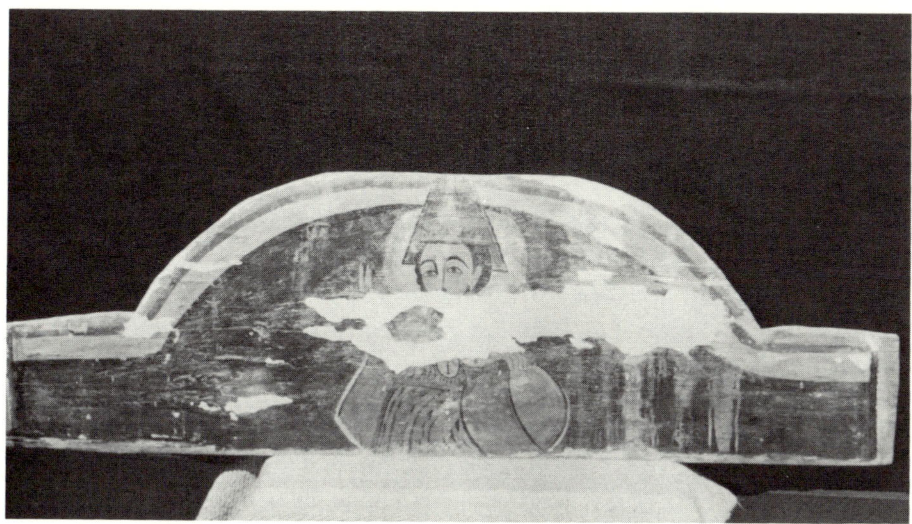

FIGURE 4
God the Father, lunette, partially conserved.

the consistency was correct, the gesso mixture was sucked into the syringe and then injected into the smaller bubbles. It was possible to guess how much was needed to soften the area in order to flatten it with silicone-release paper without having any gesso come through the cloth and paint. Silicone-release paper was the most satisfactory method of putting down the cloth without taking off the original paint. The larger raised strips, some as long as two feet, were filled with gesso and flattened when soft with silicone-release paper over which weights were placed. Bags filled with sand inside plastic containers covered with muslin served as weights. On top of these were placed bricks covered with muslin. This was done to keep the cloth attached to the wood until it dried, as the wood was so uneven due to being hand-hewn, adzed, split, and so forth. After the entire cloth was completely reattached to its backing, the losses, mostly around the edges, were filled with gesso, and the paint was cleaned with acetone. Then I inpainted the new gessoed areas, as well as a few spots of original gesso where the paint had worn off.

The upper left panel with Saint Michael the Archangel was conserved next, as it seemed to have less damage in important spots than the panels of the other three saints. Adhering the buckling to the wood went smoothly, losing practically none of the original paint, only a speck here and there. Again, some losses of gesso on the edges were taken care of. While cleaning this panel I found that Aragón did overpaint several times: the hair on the top of the head showed through the helmet, the wings were made smaller than the original ones, and the chin was changed. Such overpainting is not common with New Mexican santeros. I recall only one place where José Rafael Aragón overpainted for a correction on the main altar screen at Santa Cruz Church, which is twenty-four feet high and twenty feet wide.

Actually, I did not work exclusively on any one section until it was completed. On most santos, I have found that the best way to make sure that the finished conservation would be balanced is to conserve different areas at the same time. At various stages, I worked on the painted columns and on the arch of the nicho, which was damaged considerably.[3]

The most difficult problem with the upper right panel of Saint Raphael the Archangel was the long raised section of cloth running down the central portion of the figure itself. This buckling had spread out in several places. This area was waxed, and the next day gesso was injected slowly into the top raised spot and allowed to run down. This was possible because the support for the altar screen was six inches lower at the bottom than at the top. Gradually, when the cloth and gesso had absorbed some moisture, the material was put down onto the wood backing by light pressure on the silicone-release paper; then more gesso was inserted and the process repeated, with the result that there was seldom any excess gesso to be removed. Sandbags and muslin-covered bricks were put on top as weights.

Of interest is the object held in Saint Raphael's left hand, which is sup-

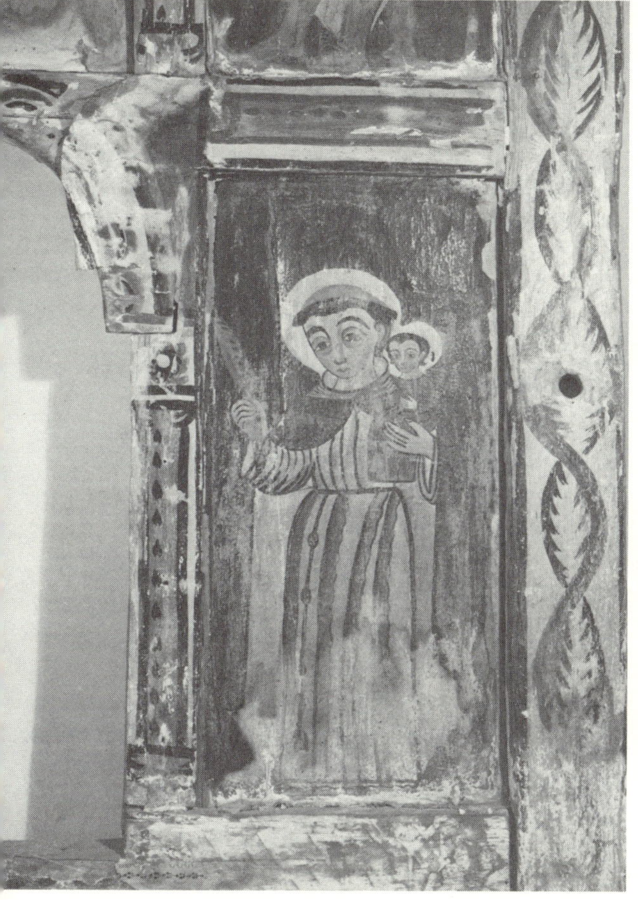

FIGURE 5
Saint Anthony of Padua, lower right panel, before conservation.

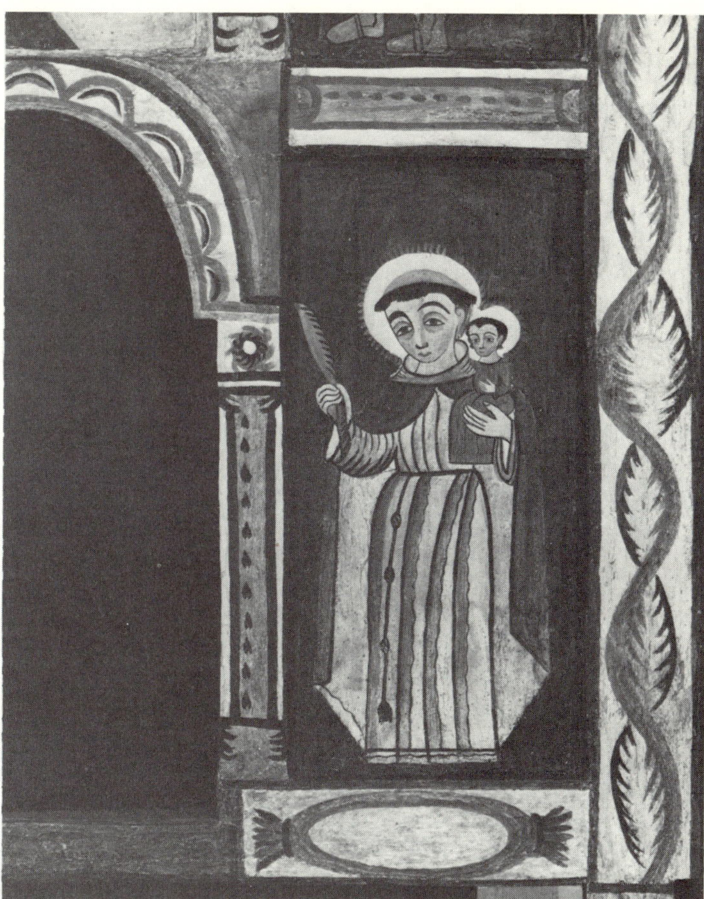

FIGURE 6
After conservation.

posed to be a fish, his main attribute. However, it appears more like an eel. Before dams were built on the Rio Grande, eels came up the river in late winter or early spring. This migration was important to New Mexicans, since the supply of food was usually low at that time of year and the eels supplied needed protein. Recognition of this coincidence undoubtedly influenced the santeros to regard the eel as important. Thus, in this altar screen and in a number of other New Mexican retablos of Saint Raphael, the fish he holds looks more like an eel.[4]

The large board behind Saint Anthony of Padua in the lower right had pulled away from the main upright on the outside, so there was actually an empty space of almost one-half inch down the panel (Fig. 5). An aged pine molding was glued the length of the panel and then gessoed. Raised areas were put down and the panel cleaned. Fortunately, the water damage on the lower half of Saint Anthony's robe was eliminated by the use of acetone and by some inpainting. Figure 6 shows this panel after conservation was completed.

The lower left panel of Saint Gertrude the Great was the one that had suffered the greatest damage due to wood shrinkage. About one-third of the cloth was raised, including large areas on the face (Fig. 3). I purposely worked on this panel last, since it was the most difficult and I wished to benefit from my experience in securing the raised cloth on the other panels. A number of raised sections were quite broad; therefore it was a very slow process to work the gesso toward the center and lower parts of the raised areas. In this case, due to the gap at the top of the painting (Fig. 3), I could use the larger horse hypodermic needle to insert the substantial amount of gesso required without injuring any cloth or the remaining original paint. It was gratifying that this gesso-injection method worked out so well, and I believe it was more successful than any of the other possible methods, such as removing the entire cloth and replacing it, would have been.

Conservation of the rest of the altar screen was comparatively simple. Although there were large losses, particularly under the nicho and in the cartouches, there was no design that could not be replaced, except for the missing words in the cartouches. These losses were only gessoed since this altar screen is in a museum and there is little chance that anyone would try to paint in some statement (see Fig. 2).[5]

While working on this altar screen, I constantly removed modern and even hand-forged nails, which had been added over the years. No nails were used in the original construction, as it was made by mortise and tenon with dowels, and the panels, like the lunette, were grooved. I secured the tenons with Elmer's Glue-All to tighten the entire structure.

Much mud was removed, as well as just plain dirt (some plastic wood, candle wax, flakes of splattered paint, and even a dead caterpillar that had started to spin a cocoon), especially from the arch. The top of the right upright was split and had to be glued and clamped overnight so that the lunette would slip down properly and remain stable. The sides of the altar screen, as well as some of the back, were waxed. Numerous times when I waxed sections, a small flower design would appear while the area was still moist with turpentine and would disappear when it dried. This indicated that the santero had used a cloth with a floral pattern.

When I began this conservation project, I was not sure whether the sides and top crosspiece should be cleaned. After working on the altar screen for some time, I realized that the panels of the saints would have to be cleaned to remove large areas of water stain and to bring out certain details. I finally decided that the cleaned sides and top crosspiece would add an interesting and contrasting border to the dark backgrounds of the panels and would also make the altar screen look more as it had when it was first painted. The dark brown backgrounds have many gold mica flakes in them, which showed up after cleaning. This micaceous background must have been most effective in candlelight. José Rafael Aragón and at least one other santero often added these flakes to dark brown backgrounds of their retablos.

At each stage and completion of the entire conservation project, I waxed the altar screen with Plenderleith Formula on the front, on all sides, and on most of the back. In my opinion, this step not only counteracts the dryness caused by the use of chemical cleaning agents but also assures protection against the natural and sometimes harsh elements of aging. Over a period of more than twenty-five years, I have not seen that this wax formula has affected the color or darkened any painted object to any noticeable degree.

During the entire period during which I worked on the main part of the altar screen—from July 1978 to the middle of February 1979—I took black-and-white and color photographs of the various stages. I also kept a daily record of exactly what I did. The conserved altar screen (Fig. 2) is now in good condition and would be an important addition to any exhibition of New Mexican Spanish colonial art.[6]

NOTES

1. For a biography of José Rafael Aragón (ca. 1796–1862), see Wroth 1979: 54–58, and 1982: 129–31, and for an account of Aragón's work, see Boyd 1974: 392–407 and Wroth 1982: 132–59. Aragón was first buried in Córdova, New Mexico, where he died. The next day, however, his remains were exhumed and taken to Santa Cruz Church, Santa Cruz, New Mexico, where a large gathering attended a second burial mass. According to the Book of Burials in the Archives of the Archdiocese of Santa Fe, Aragón's remains were then reburied in Our Lady of Carmel Chapel at the Santa Cruz Church. Aragón is known to have painted at least three of the five altar screens that were in the Santa Cruz Church during the early twentieth century; the three there today were done by him.
2. This is not the only altar screen to have been damaged by the addition of wallpaper. Note particularly the altar screen at Rosario Chapel in Santa Fe, which I conserved in 1974–75.
3. Janet Adams was a most helpful volunteer, who spent much time gessoing large areas and removing small sections of wallpaper from the cartouches, which had been so severely damaged. She also did some inpainting and cleaning.
4. Personal communication (letter) from the late Robert Jones of Embudo, New Mexico, 24 August 1981.
5. On the altar screen at Rosario Chapel I added wording where it was missing in the cartouches, having been told that if I did not someone else would. At least then I could control what was painted.
6. This altar screen can be compared with another by José Rafael Aragón, which is in the church at Córdova, New Mexico. There are similar designs, such as intertwining red and blue vines on both the horizontals and the verticals between the panels of saints and a similar treatment of the pillars on either side of the nicho. The painting of faces and clothing is also similar (see Briggs 1980: 25).

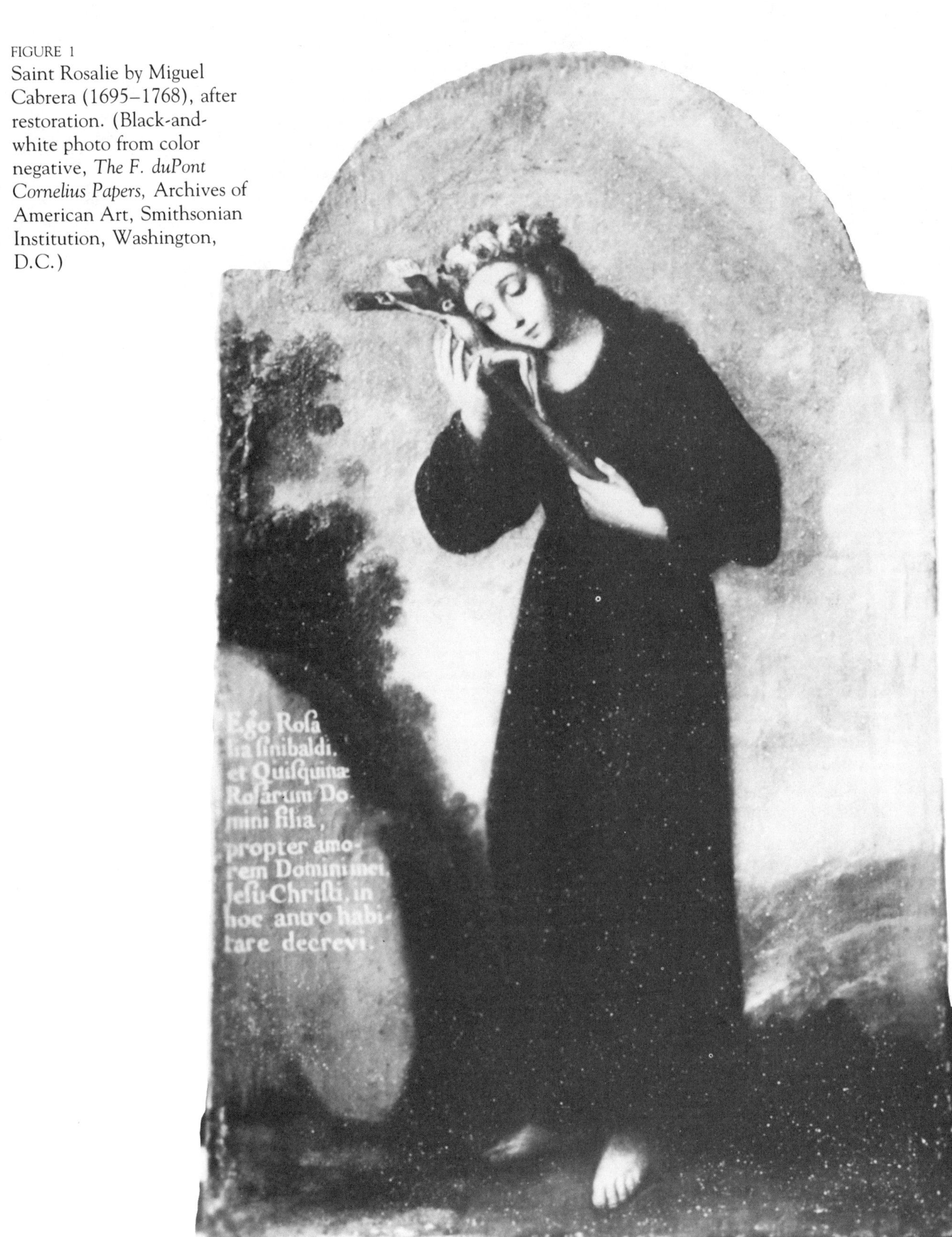

FIGURE 1
Saint Rosalie by Miguel Cabrera (1695–1768), after restoration. (Black-and-white photo from color negative, *The F. duPont Cornelius Papers,* Archives of American Art, Smithsonian Institution, Washington, D.C.)

F. DUPONT CORNELIUS

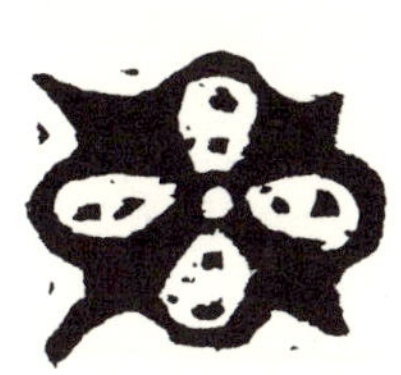

RESTORATION NOTES ON CERTAIN SPANISH COLONIAL PAINTINGS IN SANTA FE

SANTA FE, NEW MEXICO, HAS BEEN FORTUNATE that individuals of E. Boyd's caliber have concerned themselves with the preservation and conservation of its rich heritage. Through my friendship with E. Boyd and my familiarity with the work of restoring many Spanish colonial paintings, I was asked to restore several early religious paintings now in the Santa Fe Cathedral of Saint Francis of Assisi and the Chapel of San Miguel at Santa Fe. The present restoration notes are by way of humble addenda to E. Boyd's superbly researched and documented *Popular Arts of Spanish New Mexico* (1974).

It is apparent that the Roman Catholic church has long recognized the value of graphic representations for the propagation of its faith. It is no less obvious that paintings have been retouched, repainted, obliterated, and otherwise altered by means of various layers of paint. This has often been done by well-intentioned, if unskilled, persons, and certainly the second version is never as good as the original, for no artist would ever attempt to redo or alter another artist's creation in such a wholesale manner.

Nevertheless, when a big church festival was due, it was a common practice to brighten up dull and dirty paintings by applying various oils and varnishes, to say nothing of onion juice or raw potato. In some cases, as at San Miguel Chapel, this was carried to the point of complete repainting.

In the past, little was known, and in many cases less cared, about how a picture could be best and most honestly preserved. Nowadays the sincere and skilled conservator has as his or her prime intent the revelation and preservation of as much as is possible of the original artist's work in a form as near as possible to the way the artist left it, with due allowances for age. The conservator will paint only in the actual areas of loss and will never cover up any original work.

During the middle period of Edwin V. Byrne's term as eighth archbishop of Santa Fe (1943–1963), a major restoration of the Lady Chapel of La Conquistadora was undertaken in the Santa Fe Cathedral. According to an anonymous publication at the time of the cathedral's rededication on October 2, 1968:

> Since [the old Lady Chapel of La Conquistadora] was in very poor condition, it was decided to restore it in the authentic Spanish Colonial style proper to Santa Fe and New Mexico. A new ceiling of split cedar was placed over the original carved round beams and corbels of 1717. The old walls were replastered over their wavy outlines. As a most fitting completion, the two remaining sections of the old adobe parish's high altar, which had been serving as side altars in the lateral naves, were placed on each other and painted in traditional colors and gold leaf, to form an authentic Spanish Colonial reredos and throne for La Conquistadora. Afterwards, unfortunately, the pastor installed stained-glass windows which not only clash with the carefully restored architecture but make the chapel dark and gloomy as well. (Anonymous n.d.*a:* 50)

The new, excessively ornate reredos houses six paintings: Saint Gertrude, Abbess, in the upper left and Saint Rosalie in the upper right, both from the north transept; and the lower section from the south nave with four saints—Saint Bernard of Clairvaux, a bearded hermit who is probably Saint Augustine, a Franciscan lay brother, and Saint Anthony the hermit. When all these arrived in my studio late in 1975, they were so dark that even their subject matter was unrecognizable.[1]

All the paintings were in much the same condition.[2] They carried extensive spatters of very hard white paint, undoubtedly resulting from various renovations of their surroundings. In some cases, brushed white or other paint had slipped over from the molding around the picture. Attempts had been made from time to time to cover the spatters and freshen them up, all of which resulted in innumerable layers of nonoriginal darkened overpaint. Each painting was further coated with a disfiguring surface film and with a heavy layer of greasy grime.

Artistically and historically, the most delicate gem of these features Saint Rosalie (Fig. 1). This painting and its companion piece, Saint Gertrude, are round-topped pictures measuring approximately 29 by 17½ inches each, painted in oil on rough linen, sacklike canvas that, prior to painting, was glued flat to the front of sturdy stretchers in the same manner as the San Miguel Chapel paintings. On both these paintings, some parts of the painted image extend to the extreme edge, even in the case of the inscription on Saint Rosalie. On the reverse of the stretcher of Saint Gertrude is written in ink "EVANGELIO"; on Saint Rosalie's stretcher the word "EPISTOLA" appears. These notations would indicate that the paintings were probably by the same hand, intended as a pair, and painted very early.

My treatment was to remove the unnecessary layers of repainting and the discolored surface film and grime with various solvents. I sometimes had to resort to a surgeon's scalpel, which made the cleaning an unbelievably tedious job. Underneath the spatters, the original paint remained in remarka-

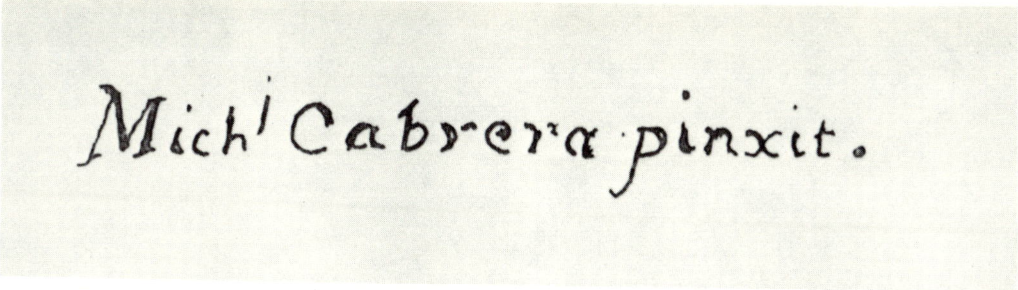

FIGURE 2
Signature facsimile of Miguel Cabrera from the portrait of Saint Rosalie. *(The F. duPont Cornelius Papers,* Archives of American Art, Smithsonian Institution, Washington, D.C.)

bly fresh condition, requiring almost no treatment beyond filling a few voids and applying a protective surface film.

The long job of removing the layers of overpaint on Saint Rosalie had its reward when on the lower left margin I uncovered the complete, undamaged signature of Mexican painter Miguel Cabrera (1695–1768), followed by the word "pinxit" (Fig. 2). The signature itself is 2½ inches long and 3/16 inches tall, located ⅝ of an inch from the lower left edge and 1¼ inches up from the bottom. Although in all printed matter Cabrera is spoken of as "Miguel Cabrera," in all facsimiles he is "Mich^{l} Cabrera," just as on this painting of Saint Rosalie.[3]

Miguel Cabrera was born in Oaxaca, Mexico, in 1695. There is a record of his christening, but his parents are unknown. He moved to Mexico City in 1719 and eventually became Mexico's most famous and most prolific painter as well as her best portraitist (Kubler and Soria 1959: 315). The first picture unquestionably by him, the image of Fray Toribio de Nuestra Señora, was dated 1740, so we would date the Conquistadora painting (or paintings?) soon after 1740.

The altarpiece paintings from Santa Fe's Chapel of San Miguel are most likely about the same age but are more simply painted than those in the cathedral's Our Lady Chapel. San Miguel underwent major restoration in 1955 (Boyd 1974: 46–48, 52–57, 63, 65; also see Kubler 1939; Stubbs and Ellis 1955). I was pleased to be asked to restore the four altarpiece paintings, and unless otherwise noted the following material comes from my January 28, 1957, report on this project.

All four pictures—Saint Louis, Saint Francis, Christ in a Niche, and Saint Michael—were completely covered over with extremely hard and durable paint; not even a small area of the original was visible. This overpainting may have been done in the late 1860s during a refurbishing of the chapel.[4] Probably no one with a knowledge of cleaning paintings was available, although there was apparently no dearth of eager "house and sign painters." Certainly a person or persons of no artistic ability applied the mid-nineteenth-century repaint to these four pictures.

In the two ovals (Saint Louis, size 32⅜ by 24½ inches; and Saint Francis,

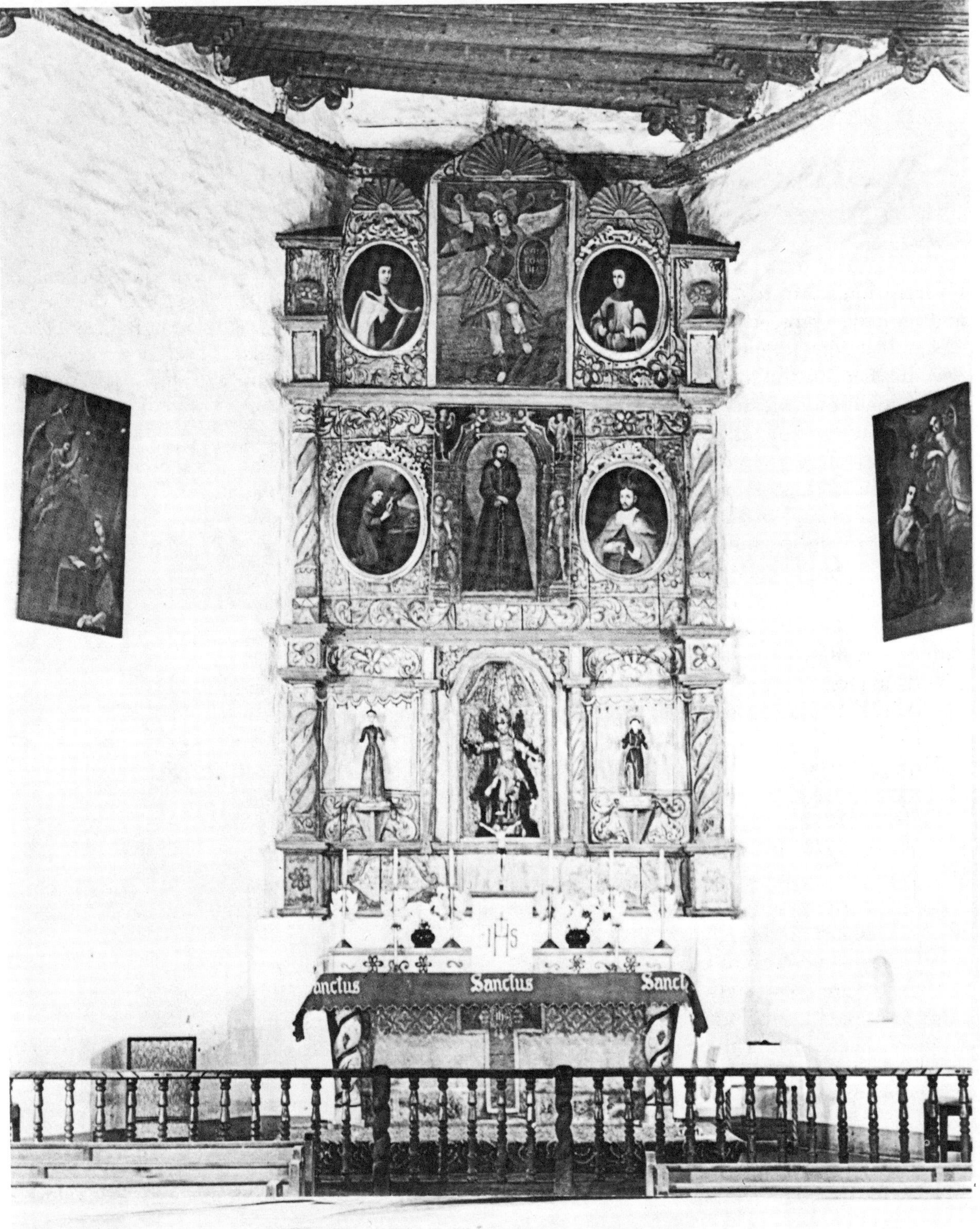
Sanctus

size 33 by 25½ inches), the painter followed, in general, the original design of the figure but changed all the colors and added backgrounds and other details of his own invention. In an 1881 photograph of the reredos (Kubler 1940: pl. 151), architecture can be seen behind Saint Louis. Also, only one set of ovals is evident where there are now two sets (Fig. 3; also see Boyd 1974: 63).

I reported my preliminary examination of Saint Louis (Fig. 4) in a letter to Brother Francis, who was in charge of the 1955 restoration. I found what "appears to be a relatively undamaged (for its age) and very nearly complete painting. The oval portrait appears to be a repainting over an original of exactly the same design and subject. In the background of the original, there would not seem to have been any architecture. The only question is how difficult it may be to remove the heavy overpaint. Due to the condition of the fabric support and poor attachment of the paint to the fabric, the painting must be relined with new linen canvas prior to cleaning" (February 14, 1955).

In the Saint Louis repainting, besides the Gothic architectural background, the overpainter had added a black beard and much black hair and reduced the crown to a coronet. The removal of this later paint was greatly aided by

FIGURE 3 *(left)*
Reredos of San Miguel. (Black-and-white photo from color postcard, *The F. duPont Cornelius Papers,* Archives of American Art, Smithsonian Institution, Washington, D.C.)

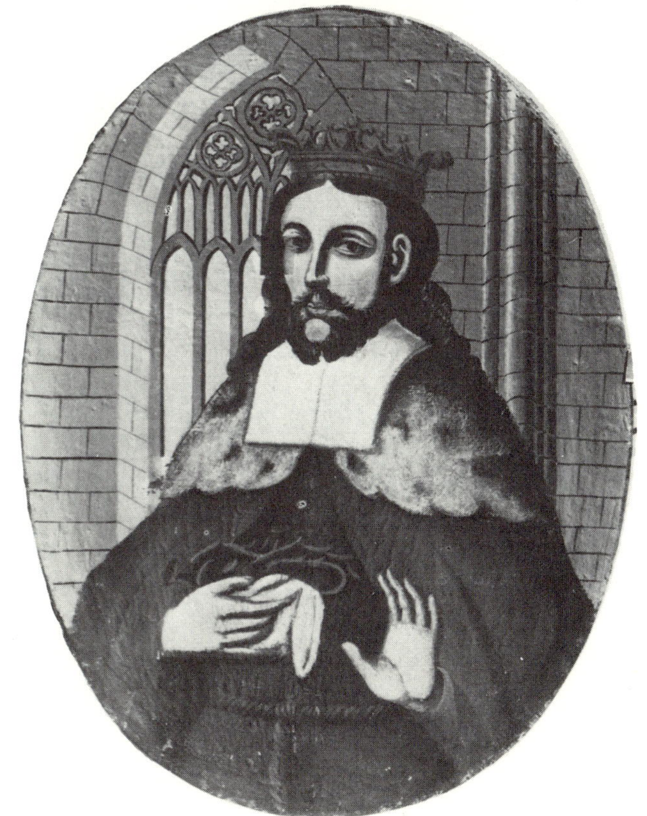

FIGURE 4
Saint Louis, after initial examination. (Photo from negative; *The F. duPont Cornelius Papers,* Archives of American Art, Smithsonian Institution, Washington, D.C.)

the presence of a very heavy coat of varnish on the original, which had not been removed prior to the repainting. The overpaint, not affected by any safe solvent, was removed with a surgeon's scalpel, minute chip by chip. The layers separated at the level of the varnish, which was later removed in the ordinary manner with solvents. The original painted surface was found to be in almost perfect condition and required very little further treatment beyond the application of a nonyellowing surface film. During restoration, I wrote to Brother Francis on March 24, 1955: "He is showing up to be a handsome critter. All fooling aside, I can hardly wait to finish him and get him back in the church to see what he looks like. A complete royal crown *with arches* was obliterated by the 'house paint' and now shows up. The background is perfectly plain. The whole picture has dignity and oomph."

The oval of Saint Francis had been treated in much the same manner. The head was increased considerably in size, and a beard was added to a formerly clean-shaven face. The color of the robe was changed from gray to brown, in keeping with color then used, and a background was added. There had been a loss or burn about the size of a hand near the lower edge of the oval. In the removal of the overpaint, and so on, I followed the same procedure that I had used with Saint Louis. As with the latter, the original paint was underlaid by a thin coat of calcium carbonate, which would have been available wherever limestone was found.

The fabric support of the ovals appeared to be crude jute sacking glued directly to the stretcher. In both cases, the width had been increased by sewing a narrow piece to the right edge. On Saint Louis, the addition was of much finer weave than the major portion; on Saint Francis, the addition was like the rest. In both ovals, there were double rows of eighth-inch holes about one inch apart, which could be accounted for if the fabric had formerly been part of a sack. Prior to the painting, these holes had been covered with paper (of high-grade rag content) on the paint side of the canvas and then the painting done on top of it all. Unfortunately, the paper in this case could not be removed for further investigation of clues to date and origin.[5]

In the case of the two rectangular images (Christ in a Niche and Saint Michael), the fabric was quite different. In both pictures, it was comparable to high-grade linen woven purposely as a painting support. It was much heavier, and there was no evidence of holes covered by paper as in the ovals. There was also no evidence of the originals (as we now consider them) having been done over earlier worn-out paintings. The Saint Michael had selvage at each side, but I am led to believe that the original had been 62⅜ inches (or more) by 40½ inches. It had been cut down into the painted area at both top and bottom, possibly an inch at the bottom and several inches at the top. The 1860s version was painted at this reduced size of 60 inches high and 38 inches wide.

When found, the "Christ in a Niche" (Fig. 5) appeared to be nothing

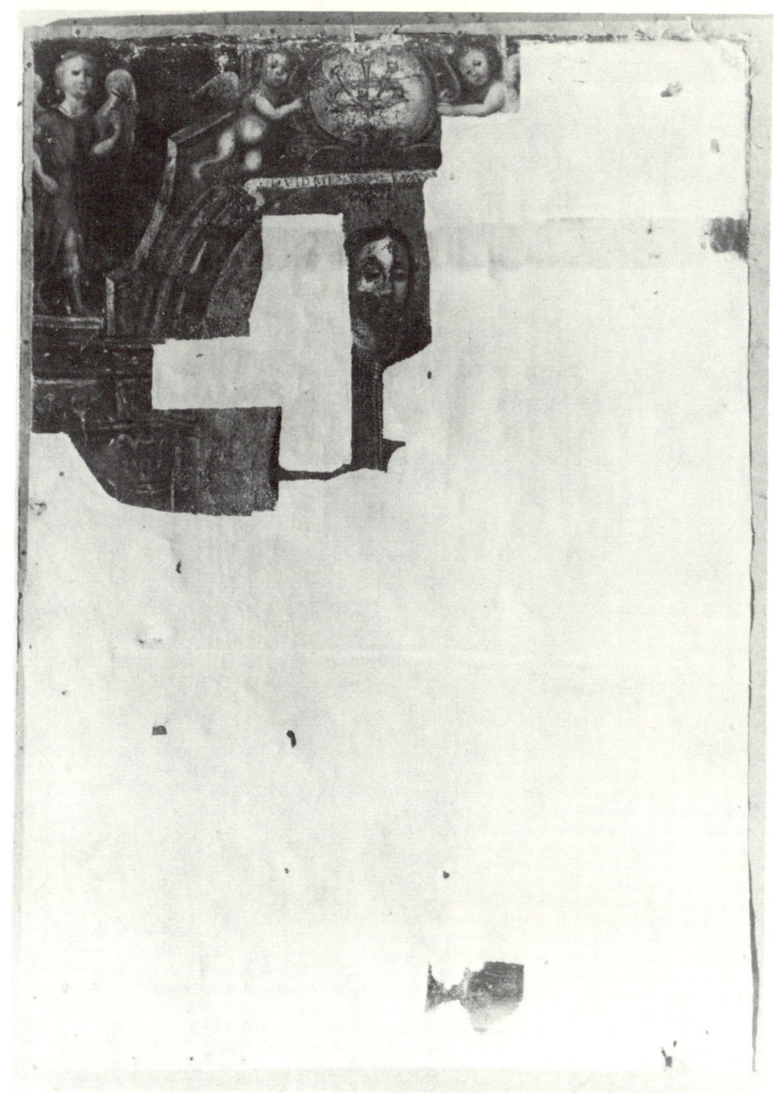

FIGURE 5
Christ in a Niche, during restoration. (Photo from negative; *The F. duPont Cornelius Papers,* Archives of American Art, Smithsonian Institution, Washington, D.C.)

more than a stiff fabric covering for a niche in the reredos. It had been cut down all around, several inches at the left and the bottom with less at the top and the right. In most cases, cutting had infringed on the design. The picture had been reduced in size to 58⅜ by 41 inches in order to fit it into the niche and then had been flatly covered by innumerable layers of house paint in various colors. The flat overpaint was removed mechanically and with solvents. The solvents, although they just barely softened the tough old house paint, did penetrate it sufficiently to soften the varnish layer between the original and the overpaint to the extent that, by working in limited areas and with lightning speed, one could remove the overpaint almost intact before the solvent affected the more delicate original. Fortunately, the paint losses in the original, although numerous, were minute and scattered so that, when individually replaced, the whole gave a very fair idea of the original. In my letter accompanying the restored painting's return to San Miguel, I wrote: "The results were extraordinary, almost better than could be hoped for. This is even more noticeable when considered in its relation to the reredos both as to color and design, and to the other paintings on it. It could not possibly have been done for any other position or any other church. It fits too well where it now is. It is mounted at the full size of the painted surface which remained" (November 7, 1955).

The condition of Saint Michael (Fig. 6) was slightly different. Upon my preliminary inspection, I noted in an April 20, 1955, letter to Brother Francis: "There does not appear to be any varnish between the original and

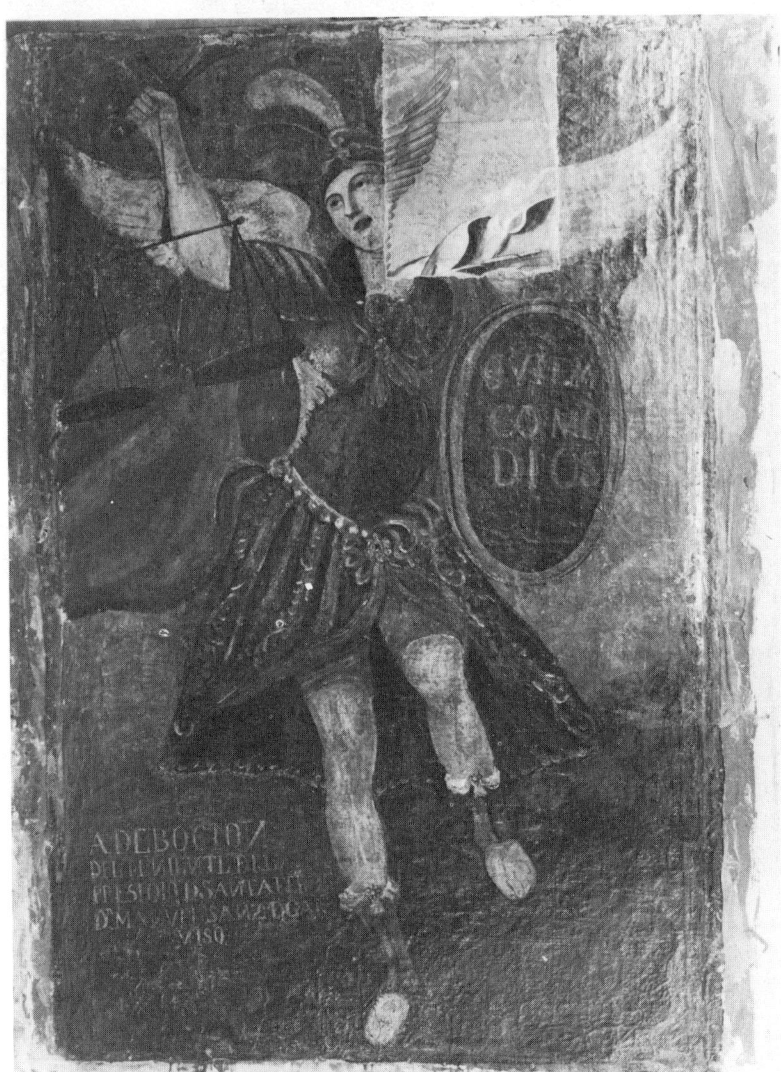

FIGURE 6
Saint Michael, during restoration. (Photo from negative; *The F. duPont Cornelius Papers,* Archives of American Art, Smithsonian Institution, Washington, D.C.)

the overpaint and hence the two layers of paint are much more firmly attached to one another, and will be more difficult to separate. The painting seems at one time to have been slightly larger than its present stretcher. The fabric has paint all the way to the edge, even where it is wrapped around the edge of the stretcher. This on the edge is original design and for the most part is quite different from the adjacent paint and design on the front. The overpainting is much more complete than is St. Francis, or was St. Louis, and leaves no trace of the original showing on the front."

The task of paint removal from the Saint Michael was indeed much more difficult. I found by August 2, 1955, that some of the overpaint was as hard as flint, while there were other small areas of soft substance. There was nothing consistent about it, and because there was no varnish between the two versions I could not resort to piecemeal chipping. The top version was done with paint very similar to baked-on automobile enamel. No regular solvent or ordinary paint remover touched it. I later found that the strongest commercial paint remover, used to strip down autos before repainting and ordinarily *never under any conditions* to be used on works of art, was the only thing possible tc use. There was a highly critical point reached where the top version was softened sufficiently for removal and before the much more fragile original was harmed. Only very small areas could be treated at a time, and lightning speed was again necessary. The ground layer on which the painting was done was composed of a very thin layer of brownish earth pigment in oil.

During further inspection I reported to Brother Francis that "I removed a 1" x 1" area of overpaint from the lower right edge, in the shadow and uncovered what could be taken for bright flame and rock. Another 1" x 1" area removed, top edge center, shows original bright red rather than blue sky. A third 1" x 1" removal of overpaint on the calf of St. Michael's leg shows a line directly following the outline of his leg, but no adjoining mountains or blue sky exist here. The above three areas lead me to believe the person who did the overpaint probably followed pretty closely the design of the figure itself (as in St. Francis and St. Louis) but let his imagination go wild when it came to putting in the scenery."

Along the left edge there was a complete loss of paint and ground down to the fabric, probably due to a water drip. Assuming the Saint Michael and the Christ paintings were hung above the other prior to the 1860s redoing, there may be some relation between the loss noted at the left side of Saint Michael and the fact that a fairly large portion of the edge to the left of the Christ is missing. Might it have been due to damage resulting from the same water drip? The loss was several inches wide at the top, diminishing to almost nothing at the inscription.

The restoration process required a year and a half. On August 2, 1955, Brother Francis was informed that "St. Michael will turn out to be an entirely different figure, *but will be a Saint Michael,* never the less. The scale of the figure seems to be larger." I also attempted to answer some questions posed by Brother Lewis in his 1957 pamphlet: "From all I can find there appear to be two versions of this subject, i.e. St. Michael by Raphael now owned by the Louvre. One is quite small and was painted about 1509. The other is on fabric and is about 9 feet x 5 feet. The later is almost exactly the same as the repainted version I am presently removing. The large Louvre version was done about 1518." E. Boyd has since identified the painting's "Mexican prototype, a picture of St. Michael by Cristobal Villalpando (1648–1714), now in the Wadsworth Atheneum, Hartford, Connecticut" (1974: 103, figs. 73 and 74).

On further observation I deduced that the scales Saint Michael is carrying must have been added later than the original as they are more crudely painted. The fact that the hand already grips the sword with vigor while the line of the crude scales is just run up to the fingers with no sign of being firmly held is indicative. The fact that the painting over which these scales are painted is complete also supports this assumption.

A translation of the inscription reads: "By the Devotion of the Commandant of the Presidio of Santa Fe, Don Manuel Saenz De Garvisu" (Boyd 1974: 103). It is interesting to note that this inscription had at one time been obscured by a pastelike paint found on no other area of the original picture. Could it be that when the reredos was given in 1798 by Don Antonio José Ortiz, the thought of competition was not to be tolerated and so the de Garvisu inscription was obliterated?[6]

Again in reply to Brother Lewis's questions about Saint Michael, I stated: "The original over which the 1865 work was done by Brother Gelasian appears without question to be of *far higher artistic value* than the 1865 version. From what has been uncovered to date, the two versions are very different in conception although both are, or appear to be, one central figure with lesser goings-on in the landscape background. No evidence was uncovered during restoration to indicate the authorship, but the only thing I am sure of is that the original appears to have been done by someone who had considerable ability." My speculations—"As to the age of the original, I would say that the original must be at least 100 years older, or more, than the overpainting"—were confirmed when E. Boyd identified the unknown painter as Captain Bernardo de Miera y Pacheco, a professional soldier and cartographer born in Spain who moved with his family from El Paso, Texas, to Santa Fe about 1754 (Boyd 1974: 98). Her identification makes it virtually certain that at least this picture and probably the other three were among the eight "not very large oil paintings on canvas of saints" mentioned by Fray Francisco Atanasio Domínguez in his visitation report of 1776 (Adams and Chávez 1956: 38).

NOTES

1. A seventh painting, which arrived at the same time, was the tabernacle door, Agnus Dei, measuring only 13¾ by 8½ inches, tempera on wood with joints and grain running horizontally. These would seem to indicate that it had been one of a series in a long predella (altar step or platform) from an altarpiece that was considerably older than the other paintings. Prior to painting, the joints between the several boards in this picture were covered with strips of high-grade rag paper to present an uninterrupted surface for painting. Quite prevalent in early colonial days, this practice was sometimes extended to covering holes in canvas, as was done on some of the paintings at San Miguel Chapel, to which the Conquistadora paintings may have some relation.

2. A report describing construction of the present assembled reredos mentions former fire damage to one of the original altarpieces. I found no evidence whatever of any fire damage to any of the seven paintings treated.

3. Note that the facsimile of Cabrera's true signature on the center reproduction (Mantecón and Aquino 1958: 33) matches precisely the one found on the Saint Rosalie painting, except the latter lacks a date.

4. In a 1957 San Miguel Chapel pamphlet, Brother Lewis claims that Brother Gelasian repainted several of the paintings in 1865. According to E. Boyd, the Saint Michael painting was overpainted "by an amateur using household enamel paints, and in the color scheme of a Neapolitan wine garden. In the annals of the Christian Brothers, whose order has had the custody of the chapel for over a century, it is noted that one of their number had painted the overlayer in 1869 in thanksgiving for his improved health, and had then left the order. When he took to sign painting later is not known" (1974: 104).

5. The practice of covering blemishes in painting supports with paper prior to painting was, it seems, quite common. This was probably due to the scarcity of good fabric in out-of-the-way places. Such covered holes are found in any number of Spanish colonial paintings in the Museum of New Mexico's collections. In one such case the paper was removed from an obscure position and cleaned of paint to reveal considerable printing, which may some time lead to a date or origin.

6. E. Boyd later wrote: "A silent witness to human vanity was exposed by Mr. Cornelius, who found that an opaque layer of resinous substance covering the inscription at the bottom of the canvas was laid on before it had been completely repainted. All the pictures had hung on the adobe walls of the sanctuary until 1798 when a new hand-hewn and painted altar screen was presented by Don Antonio José Ortiz, whose name as donor was painted in the two cartouches on the screen (p. 61 & 44-45). Although this was designed as a setting for the pictures on canvas one suspects that the name of the earlier donor was discreetly painted out at this time. This would account for the fact that the inscription is in better condition than other parts of the canvas, since it was sealed away from dust and light for 158 years before being cleaned—and only 40 years after being painted—while the rest of the canvas was exposed to damage from dust, light and water for 111 years before it was repainted in 1869" (1974: 104, 106).

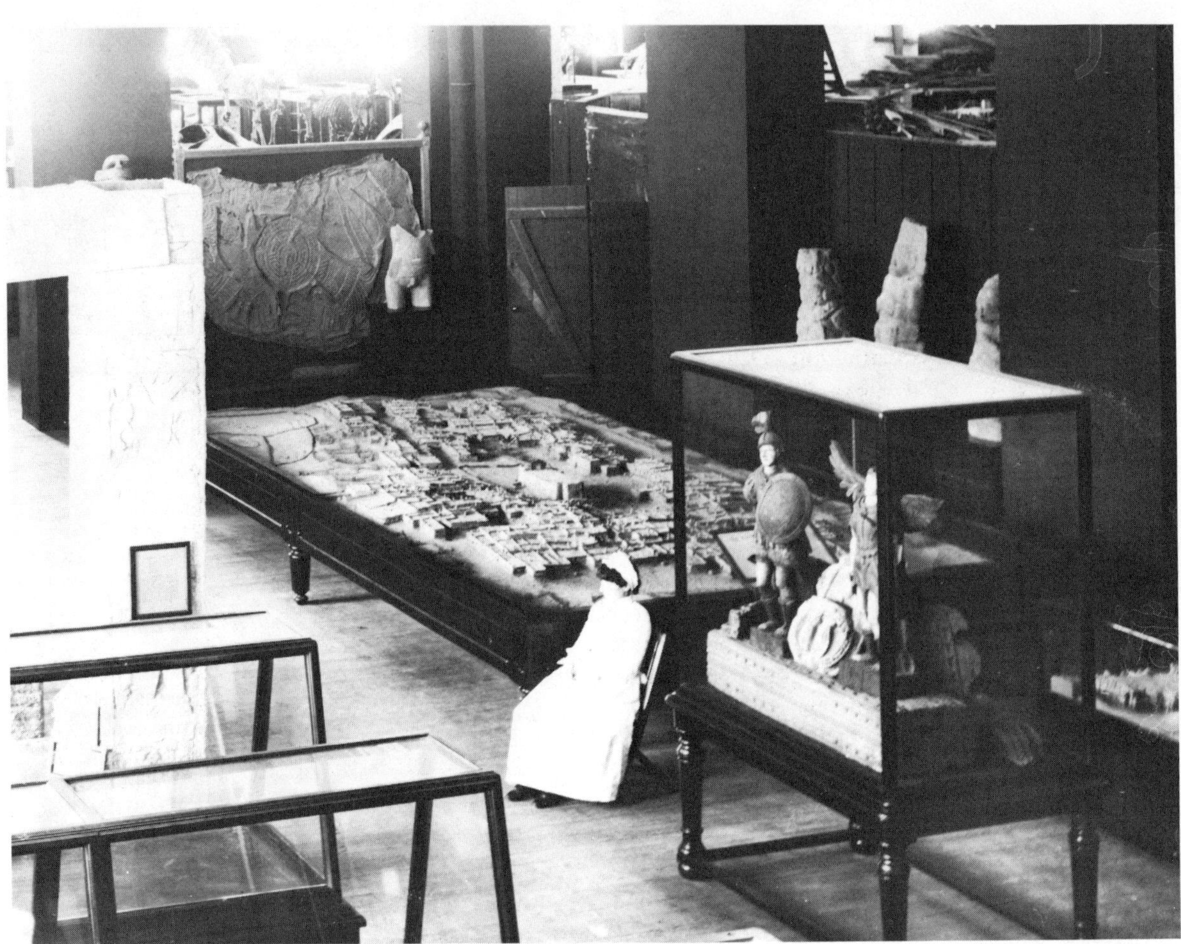

FIGURE 1
Arts and Industries Building,
Smithsonian Institution,
1898.

RICHARD E. AHLBORN
HARRY R. RUBENSTEIN

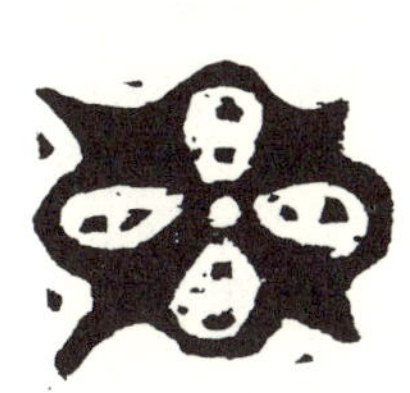

SMITHSONIAN SANTOS: COLLECTING AND THE COLLECTION

IN TWO PERIODS (1879–1904 AND 1961–1969) extending over nearly a century, the Smithsonian Institution has collected fifty-six Roman Catholic images or santos as well as other ethnographic materials closely related to Hispanic culture in New Mexico. Incidental acquisition characterized the first period, from 1879 to 1904. Some ethnologists confused santos with the fast-arriving bulk of artifacts made by native Americans. Although santos attracted these collectors' curiosity, the images were seldom incorporated into scholarly publications but instead were displayed as curios of Indian mission churches (Fig. 1).

Several events after 1960 provided an impetus to intentional collecting, research and display of santos. The Library of Congress transferred two santos to the Smithsonian as part of an artifact collection in 1961. Shortly thereafter, anthropologist Clifford Evans suggested to cultural historian C. Malcolm Watkins, both Smithsonian curators, that he engage E. Boyd, curator at the Museum of New Mexico in Santa Fe, to examine the institution's Hispanic Southwest materials for display in a colonial New Mexico room setting for the new Museum of History and Technology, then being built. Next door, in the Natural History Museum, ethnologist John C. Ewers had created a display containing santos, "Christianity and Pueblo Culture," which an electrical fire destroyed in 1965. That same year, as a new curator with special interest in Hispanic New Mexico material culture, Richard E. Ahlborn began to consolidate and collect santos for the Cultural History division. Thus a second period of santo collecting ensued from 1961 to 1969. With the reduction of public funds, the increasing cost and scarcity of santos, and a need to research, conserve, and publish the collection, collecting reached a plateau in 1969.

We regard the New Mexican santo, like the Pennsylvania German *fraktur*, as one of the few true folk or ethnic arts to have flourished in this nation. The roots of traditional Hispanic religious imagery tap the subsoil of Roman Christianity, draw sustenance from Near Eastern design and medieval European iconology, and flower throughout the Spanish colonial empire. There, santos provided foundation for affective faith and social values in an entire frontier population. Santos, as painted banners or as polychromed statuettes, led processions of conquest across the Americas; as miniatures on medals or in reliquaries, they identified the religious and cultural commitment of priests and laity; as figures rendered in ink on paper, in repoussé silver plates, in painted stucco, and glazed ceramics, santos formed an idealized, advocate population symbolizing the needs and hopes of spirits sorely tested in life.

In the frontier conditions of New Mexico, the manufacture of santos is no less impressive than their strength of style and evocative power. Traditional smaller santos, as in this collection, function as domestic and personal devotional aids rather than as church imagery or decoration. Therefore, they must first meet the criteria of identifiability rather than stylistic integrity. New Mexican santos perform a primary social function as devotional aids. Moreover, they are considered a symbolic community whose members intercede with God on behalf of the Hispanic population and who serve as supportive friends to devout individuals.

THE SANTO CATALOGUE

The fifty-six santos in the Smithsonian's collection have been grouped chronologically by the date of Smithsonian acquisition (accession number), numbered sequentially, and identified by subject, Spanish name, and form.[1] The forms are "painted on panel" *(retablos),* "painted relief panel," "painted on hide," and "carved in wood" *(bultos).* Each identification is followed by its institutional catalogue and negative numbers, sizes in centimeters, description, condition,[2] and history. Reference notes are set in parentheses and are keyed to the bibliography at the back of this book.

Form-Frequency Chart of Smithsonian Santos:

Painted relief panel (1)
Painting on hide (4/3)
Sculpture in wood (12/11)
Painting on panel (39/34)

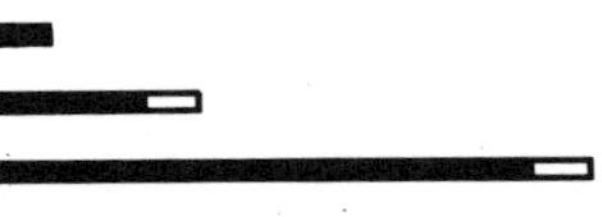

The typical retablo is split, adzed, and sawn from a log, often of pine, to produce a rectangle. The proportions of retablos are seldom based on the colonial *vara* stick of eighty-four centimeters (one-third vara = twenty-eight centimeters; one-quarter vara = twenty-one centimeters; one-sixth vara = fourteen centimeters). Specific size ratios reoccur: eight retablos at about fifteen by twenty-four centimeters, six at about twenty by twenty-eight (one-quarter by one-third vara), and five at about twenty-four by thirty-five. With one exception, the grain runs vertically. Six of the thirty-nine retablos in the Smithsonian collection display a distinct sloping toward each side; another six reveal beveled upper edges, probably to reduce checking or cracking. The surface and sides are prepared with gesso, a paste of water, powdered gypsum, and, at times, animal glue. Pigments of earth, vegetal, and insect colors, generally suspended in water, are used to render the image. Many retablos are finished with a resinous varnish known to yellow. Motifs borrowed from imported prints depicting specific altar arrangements recur in retablos as pulled-back drapery, pedestals, floor patterns, and flanking, flower-like ornaments called *floreros*.

Paintings on tanned hide are rare (fifty-seven known) in comparison with retablos. Furthermore, their material origin has resisted analysis. Nevertheless, colonial inventories list about 115 paintings on buffalo or elk hide (Espinosa 1960: 96). Equally rare (about fifty; Boyd 1974: 152–54) are panels of painted, gesso relief (Fig. 10).

Sculptures (bultos) are made up of sawn and knife-carved pieces joined with glue, gesso, pegs, and flexible sleeves and thongs, the latter for the articulated members of Cristo figures. This collection has no hollow-skirted bultos, but gesso-soaked cloth appears on four out of twelve of them. The bare wood surfaces are treated like retablos and are gessoed and painted. Unpainted carvings are more recent (1915–1975) craft revivals, produced largely for the tourist market (Briggs 1980).

Coincidentally, the four most popular subjects noted by Steele (1974: 198) are repeated in the Smithsonian collection: Jesus crucified, Saint Anthony, Saint Joseph, and a Marian advocation noted in Steele's list as Dolores and as Guadalupe on the Smithsonian's. Of the fourteen next most popular saints listed by Steele, thirteen are represented in the Smithsonian collection. The collection contains thirty-four subjects and a representation of the most well-identified image makers.

The six most frequently identified santo makers and their working dates are:

"Franciscan B," 1725–1740
Pedro Antonio Fresquís of Las Trampas, New Mexico (also called the Truchas master), 1785–1831
Molleno, the "Chili Painter," 1804–1854?
José Aragón of Spain, 1820–1835
José Rafael Aragón of Córdova, New Mexico, 1826–1855
"Santo Niño Santero," 1830?–1850?
José Benito Ortega of Mora area, New Mexico, 1880s–1907

These identifications are based on specific groups of stylistic traits as recognized by E. Boyd. Her contributions to this field are substantial, but certain traits within a group appear to us to have been used by several santo makers, suggesting that they drew their selection of traits from a common cultural pool or that new regroupings of traits may lead to the identification of additional or fewer santo makers.

EARLY COLLECTING: 1879–1904

Stevenson Expedition: Accession 9899

In 1879, Congress transferred anthropological field work previously under the Department of the Interior to the Smithsonian Institution. To continue this area of research, the Bureau of Ethnology (renamed the Bureau of American Ethnology, the BAE, in 1892) was established under the directorship of John Wesley Powell (Judd 1967: 3). In the first of a series of ethnological expeditions, Powell sent a party led by James Stevenson to collect data and artifacts among the Pueblo Indians of New Mexico and Arizona. Accompanying Stevenson were his wife, Matilda Coxe Stevenson, photographer J. K. Hillers, and Frank Hamilton Cushing. Spencer Baird, secretary of the Smithsonian, assigned Cushing the responsibility of studying a single Indian village or pueblo and of reporting directly to him. Originally intending to spend three months at Zuni, Cushing remained there for four years.

Considerable public concern existed over the ransacking of Southwestern ethnological complexes by treasure hunters and European collectors and over the disappearance of traditional cultures through contact with Euro-American civilization. The Stevenson expedition was to demonstrate the scientific claim of the United States to the area when it began to amass artifactual evidence of traditional Pueblo life. From 1879 until 1881, the Stevensons shipped back to Washington literally thousands of objects from Southwestern pueblos that could be conserved for future studies, somewhat recalling the shipment of native treasures to Spain shortly after 1500 (Hinsley 1981: 194–95; J. Stevenson 1883: 429).

While Cushing began his investigations at Zuni, the Stevensons established a trading operation for Indian artifacts. Certain pieces they obtained from what they believed to be abandoned remains inside the defunct Spanish mission site. Cushing discovered that the Zunis considered the mission and its contents to possess religious significance and disassociated himself from collecting materials from the site (Kessell 1980: 210). He wrote that "a party of Americans [the Stevensons] who accompanied me to Zuñi desecrated the beautiful antique shrine of the church, carrying away 'Our Lady of Guadalupe of the Sacred Heart,' the guardian angels, and some of the painted bas-reliefs attached to the frame of the altar" (Cushing 1896: 337).

It was well known that Cushing and the Stevensons did not get along. Years later, Matilda Coxe Stevenson defended their actions, insisting that permission had been obtained from civil and religious leaders to take the material to the "great house" (National Museum) in Washington (M. C. Stevenson 1904*b*: 16–17). Of this material two relief fragments and the sculpture figures (bultos) of archangels Michael and Raphael from the altar screen were catalogued into the institution's collection.

1.

Saint Michael, *San Miguel*, carved in wood
Cat. No. 41,910 (shield, 41,911); Neg. No. 42706
Sizes: Figure—H. 104 cm.; W. 40 cm.; D. 20 cm.
Shield—H. 32 cm.; W. 22 cm; D. 5.6 cm.
Description: Made from one log carved in the round and finished with a one-centimeter-wide chisel. Standing figure with tilted head, black hair falling below wings. Flesh and fabrics colored throughout. Brown iris with black outline. Unfinished left shoulder socket. Costume: White morion with black, white, and red feathers; oval, white shield with red and gold border and black Roman letters, "QUIS UT DEUS" (Boyd 1974: 103); long red cape with a white border and an oval clasp; white cuirass with red lines and broad fringe straps; white fringed tunic with brocaded, red swirls; black shorts with white border; black, toeless boots with white frontal welt and cloth tops. Material analysis indicated red of lead and madder, flesh hues of earth color and gesso white, black of carbon and umber, unidentified blue and white, yellow of orpiment, dark brown of a red earth and carbon, and gold leaf from the shield. Ungessoed top and sides of base; burnished flesh areas; pegs used to join horizontal sections of wings and to attach wings, shield, and left forearm to figure.

Condition: Missing right arm, which presumably held sword; wings missing, except lower right section; vertical crack filled with original gesso; later candle scorches and paint losses.
History: The subject of archangels as guardians of the faith was popular on the frontier. This figure, along with No. 2, has been illustrated and documented by E. Boyd (1974: 100–101). It was made about 1775 by Spanish-born Capt. Bernardo Miera y Pacheco for the mission at Zuni. The captain's Continental background enabled him to create an image relatively close to late Renaissance stylization of a Roman soldier's light, colorful costume.

2.
Saint Raphael, *San Rafael,* carved in wood
Cat. No. 41,912 (wings, 41,915); Neg. No. 42,706A
Size (estim. from card): H. 92 cm.; W. 60 cm.; D. 20 cm.
Description: Based on photograph, construction repeats that in No. 1. One log carved in the round with attached attributes; wings made in horizontal sections. Standing figure with right arm lowered, left raised, right foot turned out. Flesh tones only; outlined iris. Rosette on headband and cape clasp. Long cape; long-sleeved tunic, cut up over knees; vest with scalloped waist and wide cincture; footgear like No. 1, but without welt. The illustration in Figure 2 comes from Matilda Coxe Stevenson's *Zuñi and the Zunians* (1881: 10), perhaps the first published representation of a New Mexico santo.
Condition: Before loss in 1965 fire, the upper section of left wing, most of the polychrome on the wings and costume, and the attributes were missing. A vertical crack runs entirely through this figure as through its mate, Saint Michael, suggesting that both were cut from one log.
History: Boyd (1974: 115) suggests that the ecclesiastic visitor Fray Francisco Atanasio Domínguez in 1776 (Adams and Chávez 1956) misnamed one of the Zuni mission images "de bulto medianos y nuevos" as "S. Gabriel." The archangel Raphael was popular with Franciscan missionaries as a protector of the weak. Accepting Boyd's identification, the missing attributes would be a fish in the lowered hand and a staff with a water gourd in the left (Roig 1950: 236). Curiously these positions were reversed by artist-explorer Miera y Pacheco (see No. 1, History) in paintings of the subject (Boyd 1974: 112, 114). The figure appears more awkward and less detailed than the Saint Michael, perhaps the result of a first or hurried effort, the maker's tiredness, or even the employment of an assistant image maker.

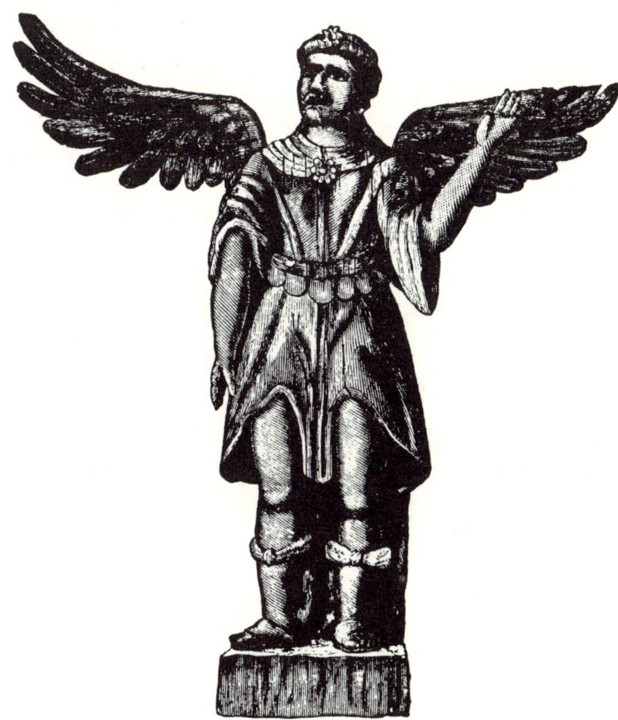

FIGURE 2
Saint Raphael. (From M. C. Stevenson 1881: 10.)

George Brown Goode: Accession 25819

The next santo, a retablo, was purchased for the Smithsonian in 1895 by its assistant secretary, George Brown Goode. Goode began his association with the institution in 1873, when he was invited to organize the ichthyological specimens; in 1881, he was appointed assistant director of the new Arts and Industries Building. While he continued his studies in natural history, his administrative responsibilities expanded. From 1887 until his death in

1896, Goode served as assistant secretary of the institution.

Among his many contributions were the promotion of historical collections and studies within the museum. He emphasized its role as an institution for public education as well as for scholarly research. Goode took particular interest in international expositions and was influential in widening their focus from commercial topics to include educational and scientific displays. He successfully supervised the installation of Smithsonian exhibits at the Philadelphia Centennial Exposition of 1876, as well as later institution displays in the United States and abroad.

The traveling that Goode undertook in connection with his work presented opportunities to add to the museum's collections. He obtained objects in a wide range of fields from musical instruments to ecclesiastic art (Langley 1901: 41–61; Lindsay 1965: 127–40). During the installation of the Smithsonian exhibits at the Atlanta Exposition of 1895, Goode purchased a New Mexico retablo for six dollars from a José Haut. For many years Goode kept the panel in his office, and it was not until 1907 that it was finally incorporated into the general collections (Smithsonian accession records).

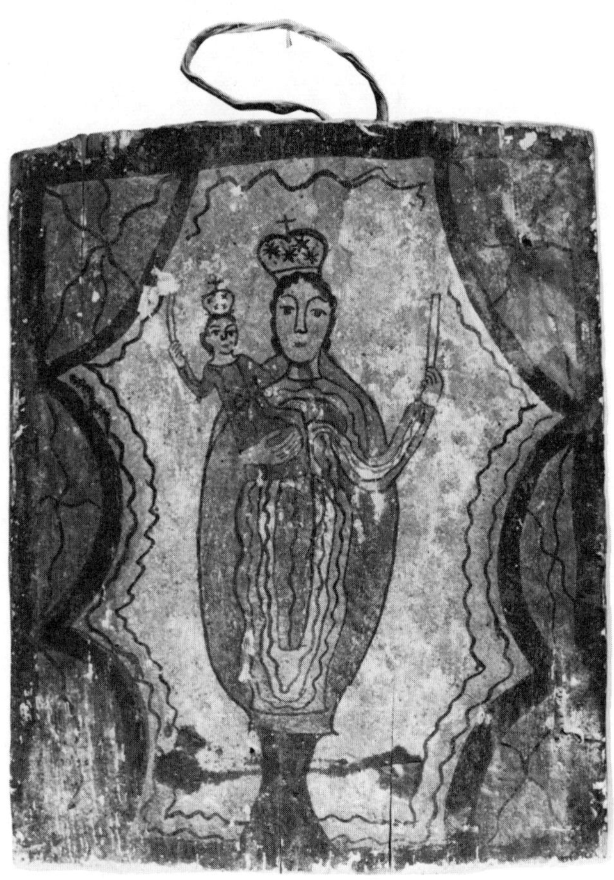

FIGURE 3
Virgin Mary with Infant Jesus. (Catalogue no. 3.)

3.
Virgin Mary with Infant Jesus, *Nuestra Señora y el Santo Niño,* painted on panel
Cat. No.: 211,876; Neg. No. 72-5076
Size: H. 30.3 cm.; W. 23.6 cm.; D. 1.5 cm.
Description: Rectangle; black border with lateral light blue drapery arches and wavy black and red lines. Female figure stands on black, concave pedestal with child in right arm; both hold burning candles and wear bulbous, star-filled crowns. The Mary figure wears a cape, a red and white robe with blue front panel (scapular?); the child is in red. (Fig. 3)
Condition: Good; cleaned and waxed by E. Boyd and Alan C. Vedder, 1968.
History: The Marian advocation cannot be positively identified, although an attached label reads "Our Lady of Carmel . . . eighteenth century" and claims that it was collected at "Mission Church at Jemez . . . by Jose Haut." Boyd identified the maker as José Benito Ortega.[3] This work closely resembles contemporary (1880–1920) painted panels from northwestern Mexico.

Jesse Walter Fewkes: Accession 31785

The museum obtained additional New Mexico Hispanic material in 1897 from the Bureau of American Ethnology survey of Indian sites conducted by Jesse Walter Fewkes. While the collection acquired during the survey focused on Pueblo Indian pottery and other technological items, Fewkes picked up random examples of regional Catholic artifacts (Smithsonian Institution 1898: 20, 36). With a doctorate in marine biology, Fewkes became interested in the Southwest while returning from a collecting trip in 1887 along the southern California coast for the Museum of Comparative Zoology at Harvard University. Passing through Arizona and New Mexico, he had his first glimpse of Pueblo culture. Fascinated by what he saw, Fewkes later returned to record Hopi songs on wax cylinders. When Frank Hamilton Cushing became ill in 1889, Fewkes replaced him as leader of the Hemenway Southwestern Archaeological Expedition—a privately funded research project that was halted in 1894 with the death of Mary Hemenway, its benefactor. In 1895, Fewkes joined the BAE staff and under its auspices continued his studies, eventually rising to the position of bureau chief (Hough 1932: 261–67; Judd 1967: 26–29).

4.

The Sacred Heart of Jesus, *La Sagrada Corazón de Jesús,* painted on panel
Cat. No. 176,385; Neg. No. 37356, upper right
Size (estim. from photo): H. 17 cm.; W. 12.5 cm.
Description (from photo): Hexagon in pine. Central heart, probably in red with black outlines, with flames coming from top, and marked with three long triangles, possibly representing the nails used in the crucifixion of Jesus. Pulled-back drapes indicated by dark (black?) lines along sides and upper edges. Double border at bottom, with (later?) inscription, "Sagrada Corazón."
Condition: Abrasions and gesso losses on edges; painted splotches above border; broken fiber hanging loop; destroyed in 1965 fire.
History: Collected at Jémez; dated about 1825 to 1850. This simplified version lacks the crown of thorns. Its small size suggests domestic rather than church usage.

5.

The Crucifixion of Jesus, *El crucifijo,* painted on panel
Cat. No. 176,399; Neg. No. 37356, lower right
Size: H. 27.5 cm.; W. 20 cm.; D. 1.2 cm.
Description: Horizontal rectangle with stepped crest, in pine. Corpus rendered in delicate black lines; eyes open; feet crossed with transparent ankle. Outlined loincloth washed in gray, tied on figure's left. Red marking suggests blood from wounds. Cross, painted black, extends to base. Black border with red liner, except in crest shadowed with red. Below, red lines represent pulled-backed drapery, and red washes with black lines represent fleur-de-lis-like *floreros.* Gesso provides white for background, drapery, and corpus. (Fig. 4)
Condition: Allover fading; scattered gesso losses.
History: Collected at the Hispanic village of San Ysidro, just south of the Indian pueblo of Jémez. This treatment of the major subject of Christian missionary art resembles works made after 1820 (Boyd 1974: 94; Steele 1974: 38) by Pedro Antonio Fresquís, or perhaps by a follower working after 1840. However, Boyd suggested that it was an (Hispanicized?) Indian product, made as late as 1870 (1961:13).

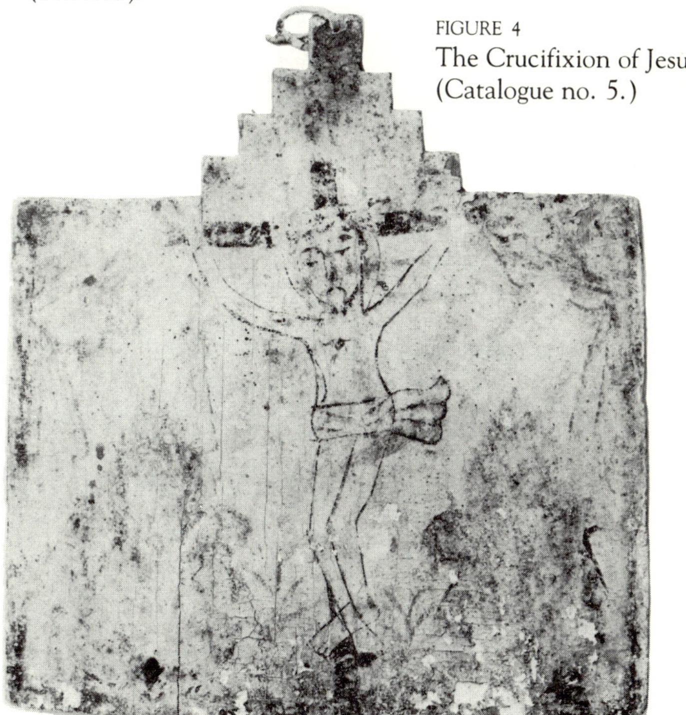

FIGURE 4
The Crucifixion of Jesus. (Catalogue no. 5.)

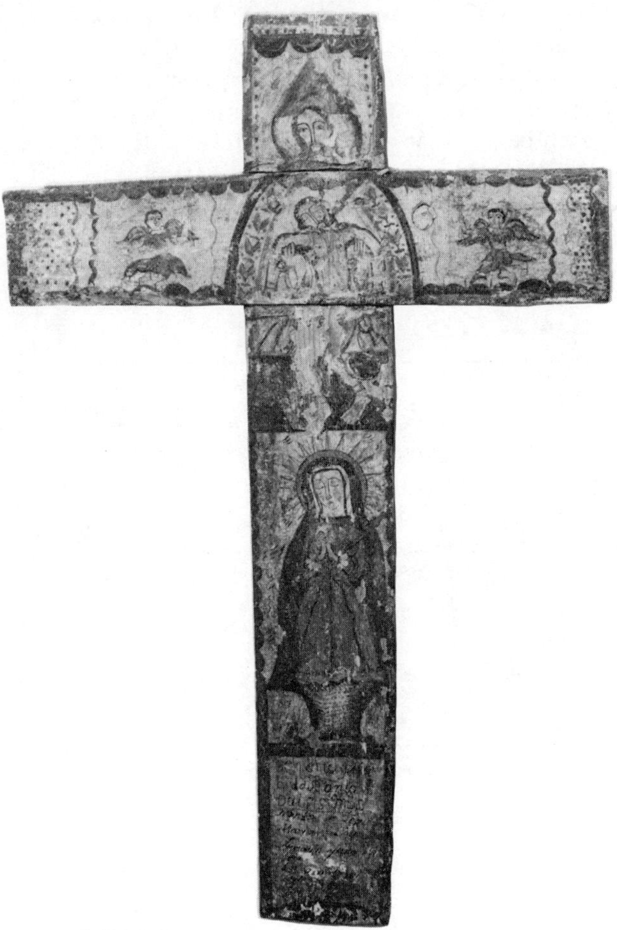

FIGURE 5
Cross. (Catalogue no. 6.)

6.
Cross, *La cruz,* painted on panel
Cat. No. 176,400; Neg. No. 37356C
Size (estim. from photo): H. 76 cm.; W. 49 cm.
Description (from photo): A Latin cross made from two boards notched into one another. Depicted are God the Father wearing a triangular nimbus and a cape with floral decorations, holding the corpse of his Son under the arms with legs dangling into the lower register. The Holy Ghost (dove) is floating above and, below, the Virgin Mary as Our Lady of Sorrows with halo, dagger in breast, is posed on a concave pedestal. Each crossarm displays a cross-bearing, wide-skirted angel, dot-filled drapery, serpentine lines, and scallops. In the lowest register is an imperfect Spanish inscription:

> Bendito y Alabado sean los Dulsísimos nombres de Jesus Maria y Jose, Joaquin y Ana [?la hora de muerte, rogad por mi alma] (Blessed and praised be the most precious names of Jesus, Mary and Joseph, Joaquin and Anna. [?At the hour of my death, pray for my soul]) (Fig. 6)

Dark border with sgrafitto, serpentine line, and scallops. (Fig. 5)
Condition: Gesso losses especially on corpus and base; destroyed in 1965 fire.
History: A masterpiece created by Pedro Antonio Fresquís, the inscription and design of this object suggest a personalized commission based on an elaborate engraving of intense, late medieval style.

7.
Saint Anthony of Padua and the Infant Jesus, *San Antonio de Padua y el Santo Niño,* painted on hide
Cat. No. 176,401; Neg. No. 72-5095
Size: H. 52 cm.; W. 39.5 cm.; D. 0.5 cm.
Description: Rectangle of hide formed by two pieces sewn together with fiber and painted. Dark lines indicate standing figure with halo, who wears robe with cord and holds the child in its right arm. Scalloped border lines have red, blue, and yellow tones; quarter-circles in upper corners flank a central rosette. The blue area along top and sides suggests a niche. Double dark lines indicate a tile floor.
Condition: Extensive fading with surface losses, torn edges, and oil stain. Edges cut down from original.

History: Collected at Indian pueblo of Tesuque. Boyd (1961: 2) identifies it as the work of "Franciscan B," early 1700s. These painted hides draw heavily on the style of seventeenth-century popular European woodcuts and missionary fresco paintings in Mexico.

8.

Saint Anthony of Padua and the Infant Jesus, *San Antonio de Padua y el Santo Niño,* painted on hide
Cat. No. 176,402; Neg. No. 76-9347
Size: H. 118 cm.; W. 67 cm.; D. 0.1 cm.
Description: Rectangle of hide. Standing figure outlined in brown with white halo wears grayish robe with knotted cord and holds a green stalk of purple lilies and a naked child on a long swaddling cloth, pointed halo on child. Angular white clouds are set in an indigo blue sky; pear-shaped green trees appear amid rounded hills. Below the figure, there are an outlined, open book and a white ribbon inscribed "S. ANTONIO . . . ." Brown bands reinforce the entire border and the edges of the robe. (Fig. 7)
Condition: Faded colors; pitted surface with small holes; tears along edge. Cleaned for bicentennial exhibition, "A Nation of Nations," and illustrated in its catalogue.
History: Collected at Santo Domingo Pueblo. Boyd (1961: 1) identifies style as that of "Franciscan F" in "the first years of the reconquest, 1693–1710." The book on the ground is probably the rules of the Franciscan order.

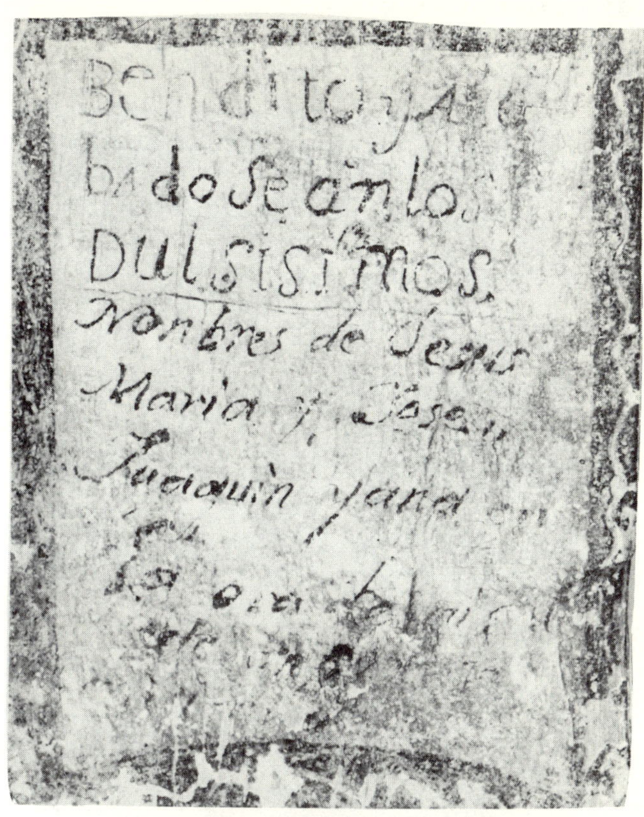

FIGURE 6 *(above)*
Close-up of cross inscription.
(Catalogue no. 6.)

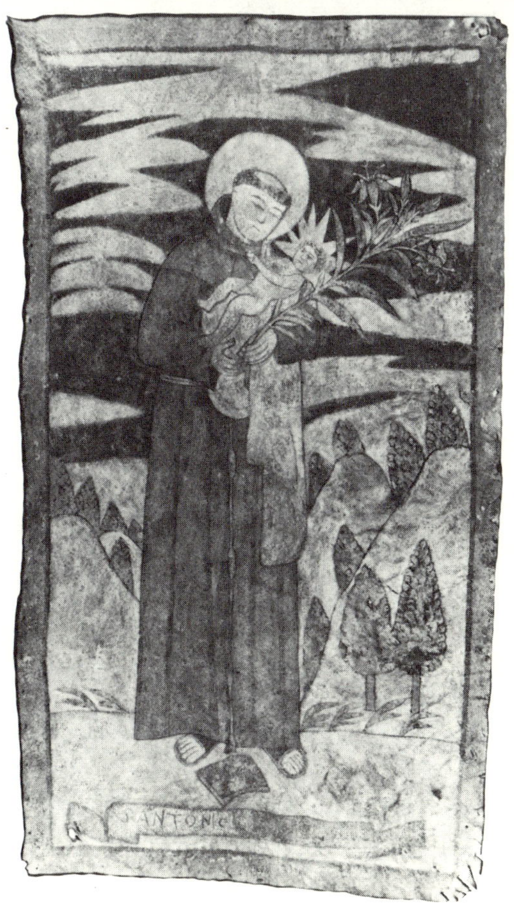

FIGURE 7
Saint Anthony of Padua.
(Catalogue no. 8.)

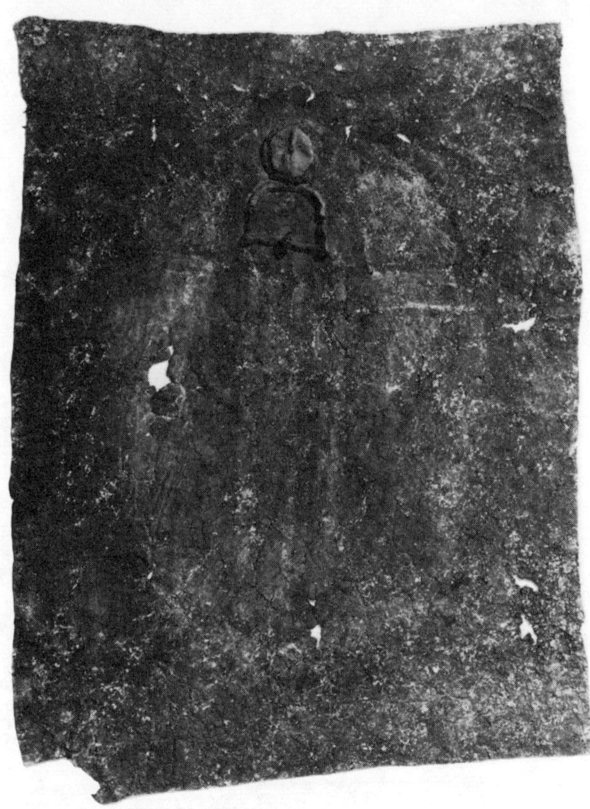

FIGURE 8
Virgin Mary (?). (Catalogue no. 9.)

9.

Virgin Mary(?), painted on hide
Cat. No. 176,403; Neg. No. 72-5094
Size: H. 69 cm.; W. 51 cm.; D. 1.8 cm. (with head)
Description: Rectangle of hide, mounted with sewn-on rawhide pieces worked into a relief head, cordlike shoulders and arms, and clawlike, juxtaposed hands. Surfaces entirely painted (in oils?). Pink face with circular eyes; lower figure in red robe with three white, vertical stripes; dark, upturned arcs (moon or angel wings?) at feet. Background of yellow and red; oval aura of yellows, blue, and white with yellow zigzags; halo of a yellow arch. (Fig. 8)
Condition: Overall cracked and darkened colors, holes, and oval abrasions.
History: An ethnographic specimen collected at "Rio Grande, N.M.," probably the village near Santa Fe rather than the one near El Paso, Texas. Boyd states (1961: 2), "apparently of Indian origin," and later "probably fetish; ex votos attached . . . at Tesuque Pueblo" (1974: 143), thus, perhaps, not a real Hispanic santo. However, elements of Catholic iconography are present throughout the painting.

10.

Virgin Mary as Our Lady of Guadalupe, *Nuestra Señora de Guadalupe,* painted on hide
Cat. No. 176,404; Neg. No. 43373D
Size (estim. from photo): H. 75 cm.; W. 35 cm.
Description (from photo): Rectangle made of two pieces of hide, painted with figure standing on upturned moon supported by winged angel's head, wearing robe and cloak, surrounded by spikelike radiance; hands clasped in prayer. Above, a six-point star and an eight-point star in both scalloped, quarter rondels in upper corners. Double border of bands and short bars. (Fig. 9)
Condition: Soiled, torn edges; destroyed in 1965 fire.
History: Collected at Peñasco, a Hispanic village. In Fig. 9, shown appropriately displayed on a crossarm, the subject of Mexico's holy patroness was promoted by Franciscan missionaries into New Mexico, using design of original "miraculous" painting. Boyd (1961: 2) noted that it was "painted with indigo and water soluable dyes" by "Franciscan B."

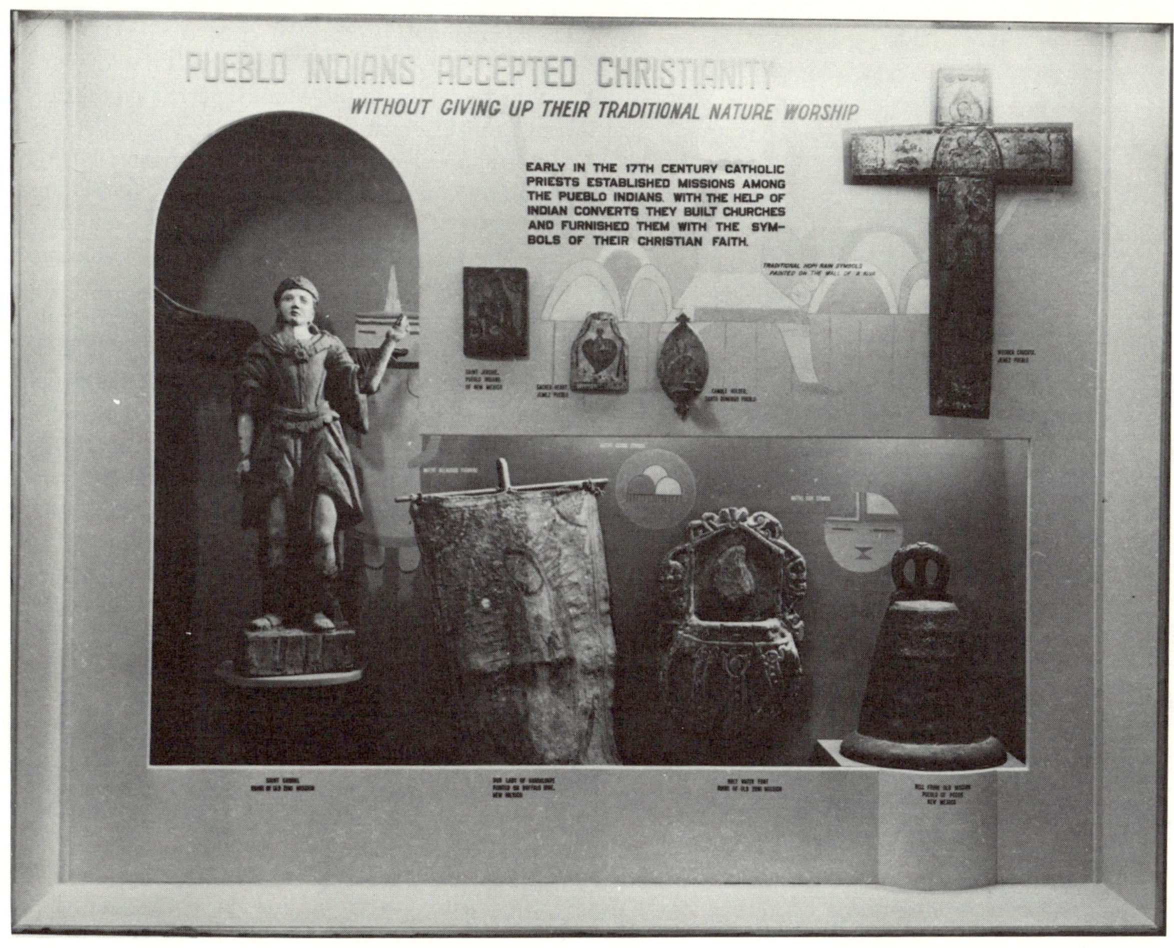

FIGURE 9
Virgin Mary as Our Lady of Guadalupe, second from left. (Catalogue no. 10.)

11.
Virgin Mary as Our Lady of Sorrows, *Nuestra Señora de los Dolores,* painted relief panel
Cat. No. 176,405; Neg. No. 72-5087
Size: H. 78.5 cm.; W. 45.6 cm.; D. 4.8 cm.
Description: Oblong, octagonal panel; pegged-on moldings; carved-relief head, and white scroll-ended shell in crest, blue above and red below. Moldings painted red, with black and white bands at angles. Standing figure of built-up gesso: seven swords (sorrows, *dolores)* radiating from breast; sunburst halo; red robe; blue cloak with crosshatched scallops. White background with red-and-black bushes at base. (Fig. 10)
Condition: Missing molding at top and base, gesso losses throughout; cleaned and stabilized by Alan C. Vedder in 1968.
History: Collected at Jémez. Similar to Saint Joseph relief panel illustrated in Boyd (1974: fig. 114). The subject refers to Mary's various sufferings as mother of Jesus. The number of her "sorrows" theologically shifted over the centuries; one or seven are common in New Mexico.

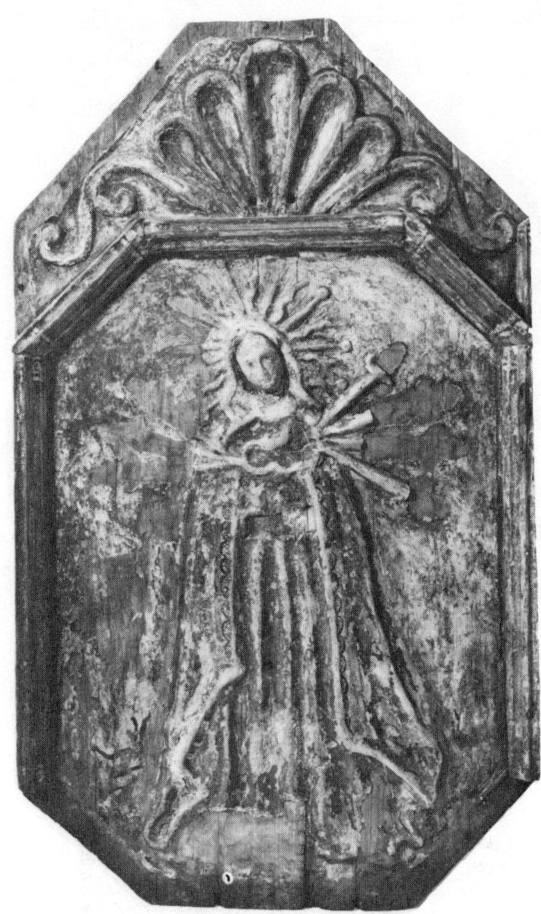

FIGURE 10
Virgin Mary as Our Lady of Sorrows. (Catalogue no. 11.)

Emile Granier Purchase: Accession 34005

In 1898, the Bureau of American Ethnology, using the secretary's reserve funds, purchased the personal collection of Emile Granier. The collection was contained in eight boxes and consisted largely of native American material from the Great Plains and Rocky Mountain regions. Granier had obtained the material in the vicinity of Rawlins, Wyoming, where he spent summers operating a gold mine.

Preferring winters in Paris to those in Wyoming, Granier returned to his native France each fall, passing through Washington. During his annual stopovers in the capital, Granier established personal contact with Otis T. Mason, first curator of ethnology at the National Museum. When Granier eventually sought to dispose of his collection, he offered it to the Smithsonian.

Within the Granier collection was a single retablo of unknown historical origin (Smithsonian accession records).

12.

Virgin Mary as Our Lady of Guadalupe, *Nuestra Señora de Guadalupe,* painted on panel
Cat. No. 200,826; Neg. No. 76130
Size: H. 43.1 cm.; W. 30 cm.; D. 1.6 cm.
Description: Rectangle with shell crest of five black and red lobes. Standing figure in dark blue cape with yellow stars, yellow crown, and red robe; below, dark crescent and red, winged angel. Framelike border, with dash and serpentine fillers, broken by her red-and-black, scalloped, oval aura, with interspace fillers of black, red, and yellow dots and blossoms. (Fig. 11)
Condition: Candle scorches on robe; cleaned and waxed at Smithsonian, 1970 (preconservation Neg. No. 73539).
History: Once-attached paper label misnames subject as "Our Lady of Light," locates source as "ruins of the old pueblo Cochiti," and claims that it was "placed there by Padre Jesus Maria Ortiz in 1698." However, the overall design and brushwork recall an anonymous image maker named "A. J." by Boyd,

who dates his work about 1820 (1974: 366, 378).

Father Nöel Dumarest Purchase: Accession 40071

Father Nöel Dumarest was born in 1868 in Lyons, France. There and in Rennes, he studied for the priesthood, receiving ordination in 1893. As part of the continuing influx of French priests into New Mexico following American occupation in 1846, the archdiocesan headquarters in Baltimore, Maryland assigned Father Dumarest in 1894 to Peña Blanca. From there, he visited the nearby pueblos of Cochiti, Santo Domingo, and San Felipe, as well as other Hispanic and Anglo villages in the region. Shortly thereafter, he was given increasing responsibilities for the pueblos under his jurisdiction (Dumarest 1919: 139–40).

It was during his assignment at Peña Blanca that Father Dumarest began a collection of Indian and Hispanic artifacts that he would eventually offer to sell to the Smithsonian Institution. Correspondence with the Bureau of American Ethnology began in 1897 when Father Dumarest initiated an offer to provide information on Pueblo Indian customs. Father Dumarest eventually came to fear that he would be forced to leave if the Indians discovered that he was divulging tribal secrets, but, nevertheless, in 1898 he sent his ethnological collection of ninety artifacts to the Smithsonian for appraisal and, he hoped, for sale. His brother Michael was to handle the final transaction. Father Dumarest requested a minimum of $350 for the collection, "a kind of museum of secret Indian relics," which had taken him years of intense effort and personal risk to obtain, but received only $100 from the Smithsonian (Smithsonian accession records).

Included in the 1898 collection were eight retablos, six of which are still at the Smithsonian. It is possible that they were taken from Pueblo missions or Hispanic village churches, or bartered from private homes of the local Hispanic population, since, after the 1850s, retablos were being replaced with more naturalistic representations such as imported chromolithographs (Lange 1974: 51–64).

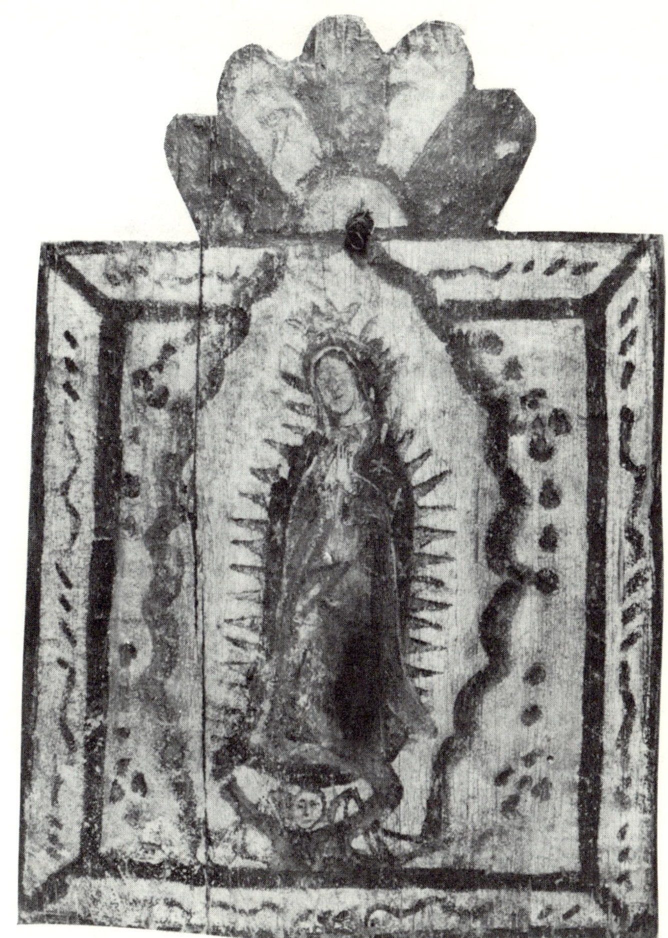

FIGURE 11
Virgin Mary as Our Lady of Guadalupe. (Catalogue no. 12.)

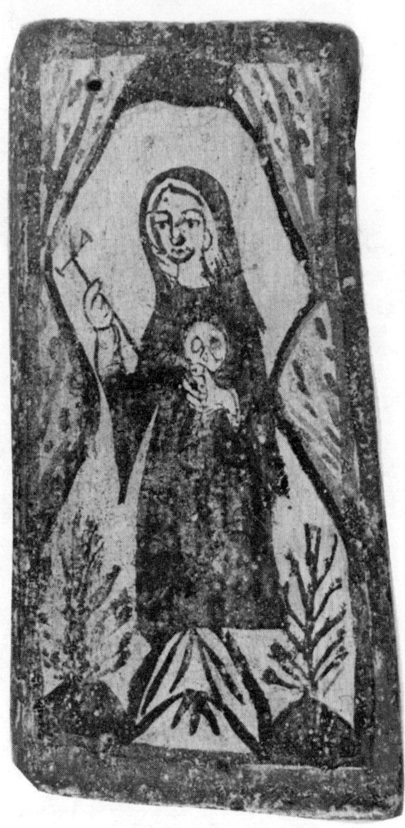

FIGURE 12
Saint Rita of Cascia.
(Catalogue no. 13.)

13.
Saint Rita of Cascia, *Santa Rita de Casia,* painted on panel
Cat. No. 219,160; Neg. No. 69995
Size (estim. from photo): H. 16 cm.; W. 8 cm.
Description (from color slide): Irregular rectangle. Figure in black habit holds cross in right hand, skull in left; stands on outlined mound flanked by a solid mound with tree. Black and red borders; light drapery with black outline and folds, black and red dashes. (Fig. 12)
Condition: Good, after cleaning about 1967; stolen from exhibit in 1971.
History: The subject, an Italian Augustinian nun of the early 1400s, bears ecstatic mark on her forehead from Jesus' crown of thorns (Roig 1950: 237; Steele 1974: 195).

14.
Saint Rita of Cascia, *Santa Rita de Casia,* painted on panel
Cat. No. 219,161; Neg. No. 82-2408
Size: H. 15.5 cm.; W. 7.5 cm.; D. 1.2 cm.
Description: Irregular rectangle reflecting exact form and design of No. 13: red border, yellow drapes with black outline, figure in black flanked by tree in red and black.
Condition: Uncleaned.
History: The mirror shapes and identical designs of Nos. 13 and 14 suggest that the panels were mass-produced, having been split from a single board and painted with the same subject, probably about 1830.

15.
Saint Raymond Nonnatus, *San Ramón Nonato,* painted on panel
Cat. No. 219,162; Neg. No. 72-5091
Size: H. 27.3 cm.; W. 18.9 cm.; D. 1.2 cm.
Description: Rectangle with bearded figure in halo and religious habit, red cloak, and white robe. The figure holds a monstrance in right hand and a palm frond with three crowns in the left.
Condition: Very dark, numerous gesso losses.
History: Subject was a thirteenth-century Spanish Mercedarian cardinal born by cesarian section and credited with ransoming and preaching to Christian captives of the Moors in Africa (Steele 1974: 191).

The crowns on the palm frond symbolize chastity, eloquence, and martyrdom, which he never underwent (Roig 1950: 236). This object is in the style of José Aragón (Boyd 1974: 360–75).

16.
Saint Jerome, *San Gerónimo,* painted on panel
Cat. No. 219,163; Neg. No. 37356, upper left
Size (estim. from photo): H. 20 cm.; W. 15 cm.
Description (from photo): Rectangle with multiple border. There is a stylized trumpet in the upper right corner; a humanized lion's head in the lower left. Naked figure on left knee wears a long cloak and holds a cross. (Fig. 13)
Condition: Good; destroyed in the 1965 fire.
History: Subject is a late fourth-century cardinal and doctor of the church. He is revising and translating the Bible while inspired by the trumpet of God's voice. Living as a hermit, he appears on barren rocks with his symbolic guardian lion. The face and brushwork suggest the style of José Aragón.

17.
Saint Anthony of Padua and the Infant Jesus, *San Antonio de Padua y el Santo Niño,* painted on panel
Cat. No. 219,164; Neg. No. 37356A, left
Size: H. 19 cm.; W. 16.7 cm.; D. 1.5 cm.
Description: Rectangle with no border but wide red drapery at top and sides. A standing figure in a dark blue habit with sgraffito knotted belt holds a child in a red gown in both arms; there is an original thong loop through the top and back.
Condition: Fair, uncleaned.
History: Unidentified maker, probably working about 1820 to 1850.

18.
Saint Philip of Jesus, *San Felipe de Jesús,* painted on panel
Cat. No. 219,165; Neg. No. 82-2407
Size: H. 25.8 cm.; W. 22 cm.; D. 1.5 cm.
Description: Rectangle. A standing figure with extended arms wears a black habit and a sgraffito belt; behind him, crossed lances with heads are placed in upper corners. There are multiple borders of blue, red, and white with red and black dots within black wavy lines. (Fig. 14)

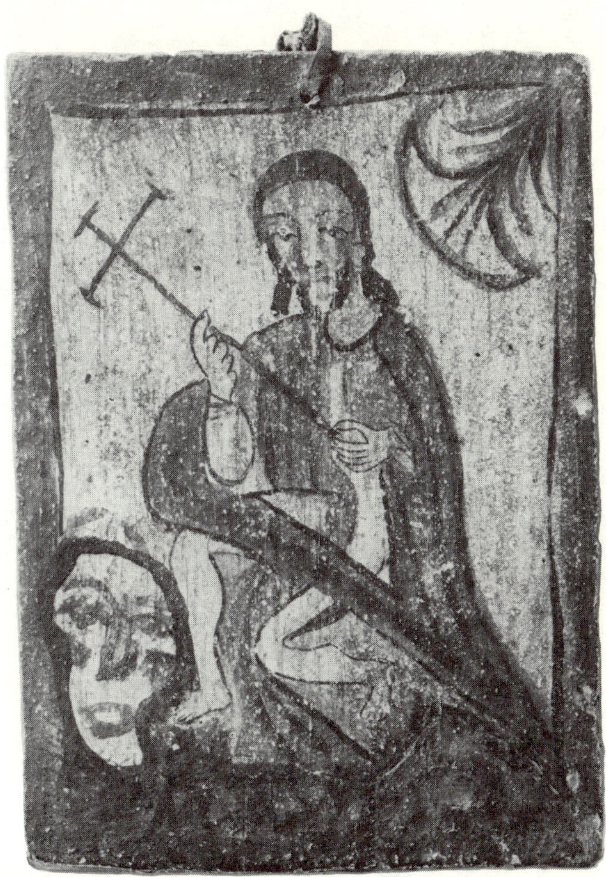

FIGURE 13
Saint Jerome. (Catalogue no. 16.)

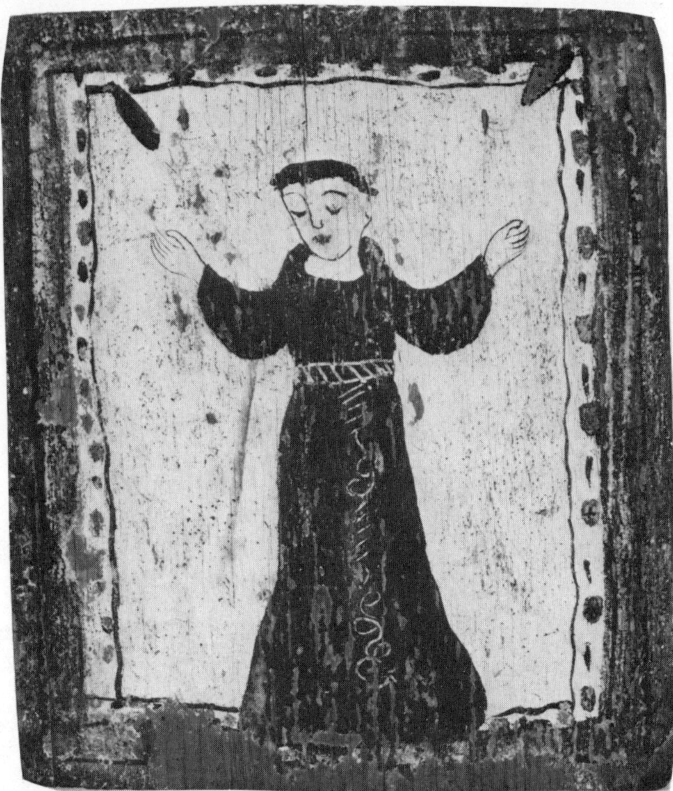

FIGURE 14 *(above)*
Saint Philip of Jesus. (Catalogue no. 18.)

FIGURE 15
Saint Joseph and the Infant Jesus. (Catalogue no. 19.)

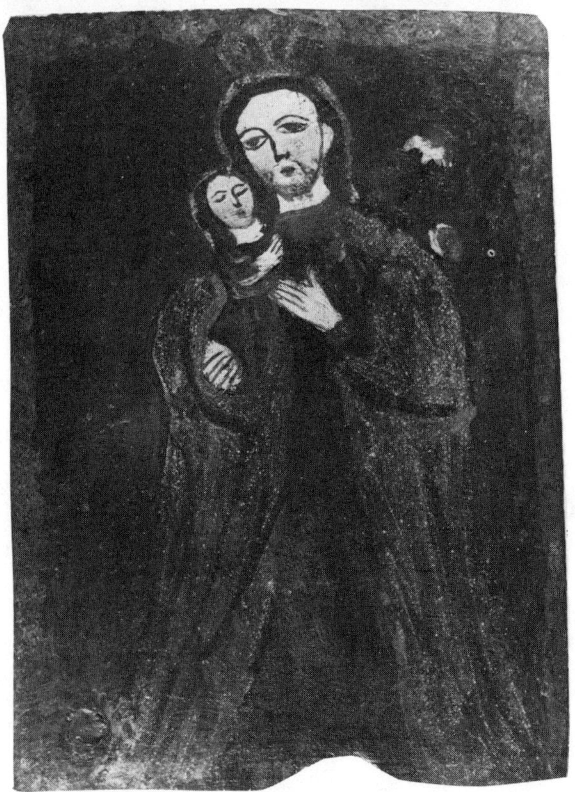

Condition: Good; gesso losses and faded lance shafts.
History: Subject is a sixteenth-century Mexican Franciscan martyred in Japan by means of lances and crucifixion (Steele 1974: 184; Wilder 1943: pl. 56). The style shares traits of Fresquís and José Aragón and probably dates from between 1815 and 1835.

19.
Saint Joseph and the Infant Jesus, *San José y el Santo Niño,* painted on panel
Cat. No. 219,166; Neg. No. 72-5089
Size: H. 33.7 cm.; W. 24.6 cm.; D. 2 cm.
Description: Rectangle with white border. Standing figure in yellow crown, green robe, red collar and cuff, yellow cloak with orange and green lines cradles a red-gowned child in its right arm; its left arm supports a green staff with red and white blossoms. (Fig. 15)
Condition: Candle damage at base; cleaned and waxed by Alan C. Vedder, 1969.
History: With infant, Joseph is depicted as the foster-father of Jesus. Boyd credits this retablo to the "18th-century Novice," working about 1775.[4]

20.
Virgin Mary as Our Lady of Guadalupe, *Nuestra Señora de Guadalupe,* painted on panel
Cat. No. 219,167; Neg. No. 72-5090
Size: H. 50 cm.; W. 27.8 cm.; D. 2 cm.
Description: Rectangle with border band, leaf motifs, and clouds that surround a standing figure, crowned with a pointed radiance, hands over breast in prayer; the figure wears a starred blue cloak and a red gown. A winged angel with raised arms is at its feet.
Condition: Darkened varnish; overcleaned areas at base.
History: Shares stylistic elements with the work of Molleno and the "Quill Pen Santero," dating the piece between 1815 and 1835 (Boyd 1974: 350, 388–89).

Matilda Coxe Stevenson: Accession 43829

In the years following the first BAE expedition, Matilda Coxe Stevenson continued her interest in

Southwestern ethnology. She assisted her husband on his research trips and established herself as a leading ethnologist in her own right. When James Stevenson died in 1888, Powell appointed his widow to the bureau's staff. Although her relationship with Powell was often strained, she remained with the bureau, where she pursued her investigations of Pueblo culture (Judd 1967: 56–57).

Stevenson's years of field work in New Mexico also led to the acquisition of large collections of Southwestern material for the National Museum. Among the thousands of Indian-associated artifacts were a few Hispanic pieces that had attracted her interest. One of those was a wooden carving of Saint Acatius. According to Stevenson, she obtained the santo in 1904 from the wife of a former leader of a penitent brotherhood, near Jémez Springs at Goattown. The woman's husband had carried the saint in religious ceremonies from the time of his youth until his death (M. C. Stevenson 1904*a*).

21.

Saint Acatius (or Achatius), *San Acacio,* painted on panel

Cat. No. 234,748; Neg. Nos. 82-673 and 82-676, reverse

Size: Cross—H. 45.5 cm.; W. 28.6 cm.; D. 1 cm. Bracket—H. 5.2 cm.; W. 3.7 cm.; D. 3 cm. Corpus—H. 25.3 cm.; W. 5.6 cm.; D. 4 cm.

Description: Four pieces of wood: (1) cross of two lap-notched lathes; white ground with red florals; red edges and front with black dashes; cutout ends, two with silver-leaf bands; at top, white plaque fragment with black letters; (2) concave, white bracket with yellow, angular designs, held to cross by two pegs; (3) bearded figure in white shirt, black jacket, knee breeches, slippers, and white hose; silver-leaf trim; pink undercoating. Smithsonian test (CAL Report 3133, 1978) indicates that the leaf has been "gilded" with a solution of chrome yellow in resin medium (gamboge?); glue in the arm sockets was colophony (abietic anyhdride). There are attachments of cloth and beads of glass and bone. (Fig. 16)

Condition: Missing are plaque, nails in hands, gesso at ankles, front of left foot, and both arms. Extensive gesso losses on cross, later blackened. Cleaned at Smithsonian, 1978.

History: Collected near Jémez. Subject is a legendary, second-century Roman commander who was crucified with his Christian legions in Armenia (Boyd 1974: 231; Steele 1974: 180). Shown in late eighteenth-century dress, the bulto dates between 1810 to 1840.

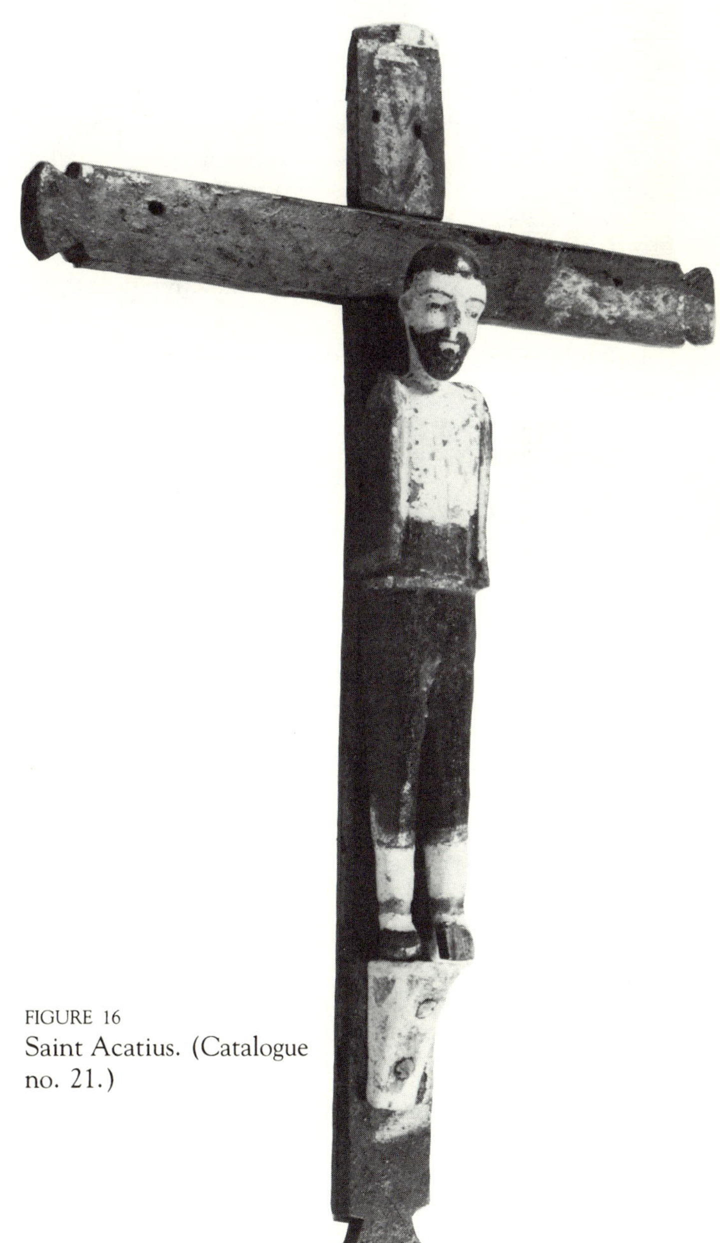

FIGURE 16
Saint Acatius. (Catalogue no. 21.)

LATER COLLECTING: 1961–1969

Joseph M. Toner Bequest: Accession 235052

The organization, acquisition, study, and display of santos were revived at the Smithsonian by the early 1960s, after a half-century lull. Collecting activity was reestablished in 1961 with the transfer of a box of miscellaneous objects from the Library of Congress's Toner Collection. Since the original gift to the Library in 1896, the material had been shifted around to various storage areas and had remained unstudied. The assortment of objects transferred ranged from a pair of English silver spectacles to Hispanic American retablos (Smithsonian accession records).

Joseph M. Toner, in addition to being a leading figure within the country's medical community, was a tireless collector and a generous donor of historical material and data. He initiated donations to the Library of Congress in 1882 and added to his gifts until his death in 1896; in all, he contributed nearly fifty thousand printed and manuscript items. Listed in his final bequest were those objects remaining in his bookcase and his safe. Presumably among these things were the two religious panels now in the Smithsonian's collection.

Unfortunately, Toner's private papers do not indicate how he obtained these pieces. He had corresponded with doctors and researchers throughout the country, including New Mexico. Perhaps the retablos were sent as a gift to Toner, who was a devout Catholic. He also made trips to the West beginning in 1871, when he joined a group of doctors attending the first American Medical Association meeting in San Francisco, California. This group of western travelers held periodic reunions, and at one of these Toner presented a paper on North American Indian medical practices. The doctor, it seems, enjoyed a knowledge of and a curiosity about Indian culture and other Southwestern topics (W. J. Bell 1973: 1–24).

22.
The Crucifixion of Jesus, *El crucifijo,* painted on panel
Cat. No. 389,412; Neg. No. 69985
Size: H. 20.3 cm.; W. 15.9 cm.; D. 1.8 cm.
Description: Rectangle, with light blue border and black lines; in upper corners, red and blue drapery with black outlines. In lower corners, floreros of trees in wide-lipped urns in black, red, and blue. Black-outlined figure on solid black cross; "INRI" plaque; wounds in red; lace-edged loincloth *(sendal)* and angular tie on right (Boyd 1961: 12). (Fig. 17)
Condition: Good; cleaned by Boyd, 1968.
History: Made in the style of José Aragón (Boyd 1969: 13). Design and technique related to Spanish Romanesque.

23.
Virgin Mary as Our Lady of San Juan de los Lagos, *Nuestra Señora de San Juan de los Lagos,* painted on panel
Cat. No. 398,413; Neg. No. 69993
Size: H. 24 cm.; W. 14.9 cm.; D. 1.7 cm.
Description: Rectangle in white, red, and black color scheme. At top, swags of drapery; below, three-banded altar with two tall candles. Figure kneeling(?), hands in prayer with cross; concentric halos; sgraffito stars on black cloak; red robe; red lips, dots on cheeks, lines over eyes. (Fig. 18)
Condition: Some paint losses; yellowed varnish.
History: Subject based on sculptured and dressed image in the Mexican village of San Juan de los Lagos, but this folk version lacks the crown, pedestal, and elaborate dress of the original. Boyd's 1961 report dates this retablo about 1850, but in her 1968 letter to Ahlborn, suggests that it may be a work of José Ortega, made after 1880.

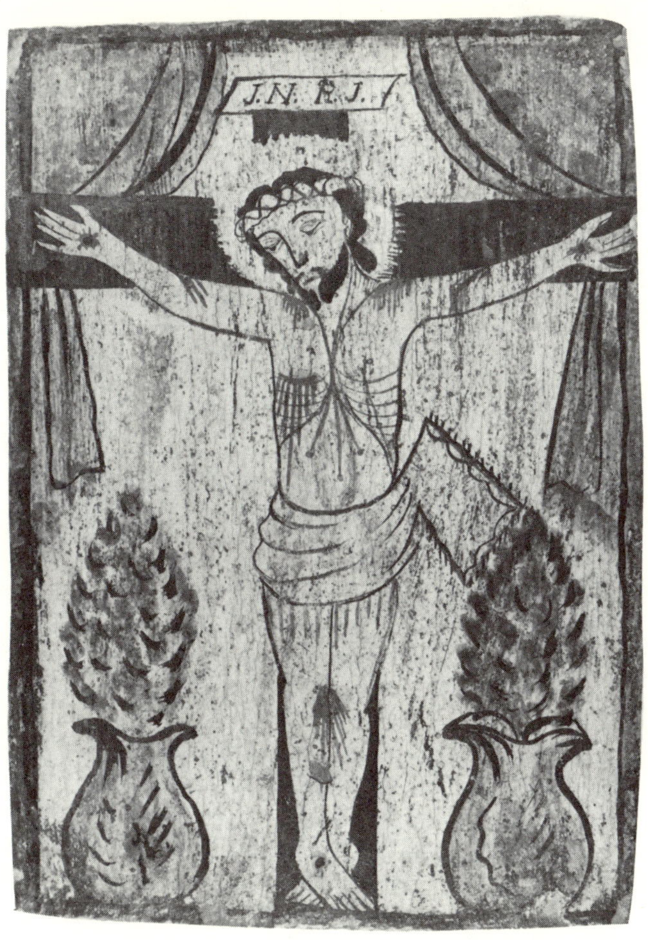

FIGURE 17
The Crucifixion of Jesus.
(Catalogue no. 22.)

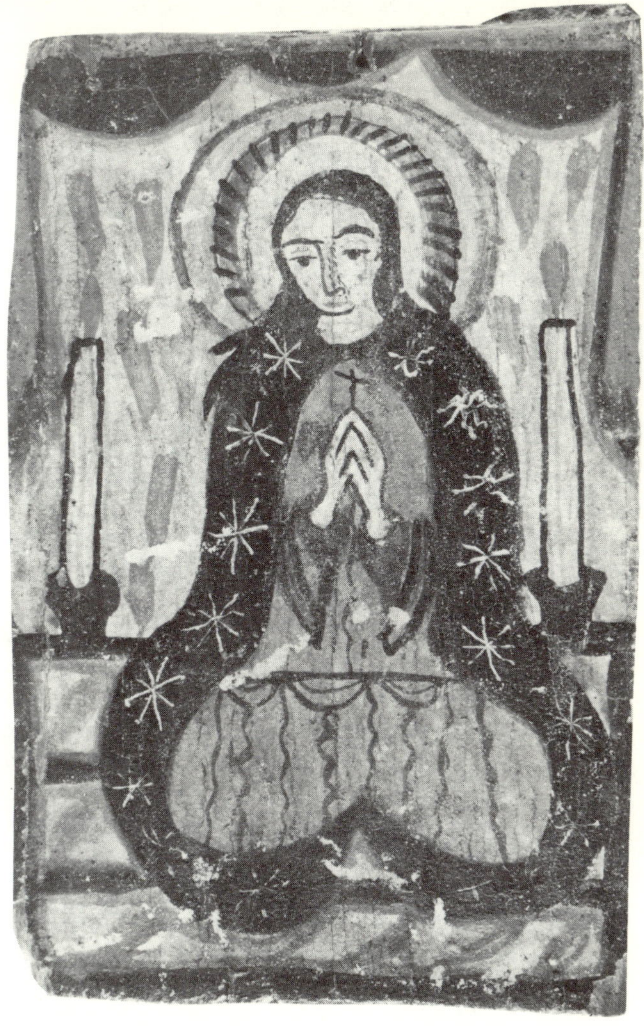

FIGURE 18
Virgin Mary as Our Lady of San Juan de los Lagos.
(Catalogue no. 23.)

José Mondragón Commission: Accession 268275

During Boyd's review of the Smithsonian's Hispanic material in 1961, she suggested that the museum supplement its collection with contemporary pieces. One of the craftsmen she recommended to Curator C. Malcolm Watkins was José Mondragón. Mondragón and his wife, Alice, began their careers as wood carvers in Córdova, New Mexico, around 1959. Their work primarily consists of hand-carved, unpainted pieces, which they sell at their shop in nearby Chimayó and at craft fairs (Briggs 1980: 99–100). Watkins and his wife, Joan, first visited Mondragón's shop in 1962, and in 1966 Watkins commissioned him to create a subject of his choice for the institution.

24.

Death Cart, *La carreta de la muerte,* carving in wood
Cat. No. 67.8; Neg. No. 82-675
Size: Figure—H. 54.5 cm.; W. 15 cm.; D. 26.5 cm. Cart—H. 31 cm.; W. (axle) 60 cm.; L. (bed) 70.5 cm.; L. (tongue) 63 cm.
Description: Seated skeletal figure, carved and sanded from seven pieces of aspen, holds bow and arrow; white, braided horsehair wig attached with Elmer's Glue-All. Rectangular cart bed, bench, tongue, and solid wheels sawed from pine; notched front and rear bed boards; separate axle pins. Screw holes in cart covered with wood putty.
Condition: Mint.
History: Subject is a traditional cult image of the Catholic penitent brotherhood, Los Hermanos de Luz. It was chosen by the artisan for sale to institutions and tourists due to their interest in romanticized aspects of Hispanic culture and the higher price brought by larger pieces. Thus, this figure represents a twentieth-century functional shift from a folk survival to a popular and commercial revival. Illustrated in Ahlborn (1967).

Mrs. William C. F. Robards Purchase and Donation: Accession 269937

In 1966, the museum secured a major collection of retablos from Mrs. William C. F. Robards. Under the agreement of the acquisition, the museum purchased five panels and received seventeen additional pieces as donations. The collection had originally been assembled by Col. Daniel Burns Dyer and passed down to family members, eventually ending up in the possession of Mrs. Robards, the colonel's great-niece.

Colonel Dyer was a nineteenth-century western entrepreneur. Raised in Kansas and Missouri, his careers included such diverse occupations as Indian trader and Indian agent for the Cheyenne and Arapaho, first mayor of Guthrie during the land-rush days in Oklahoma, and later urban developer, operating in Kansas City, Missouri, and Augusta, Georgia. His wealth permitted him to participate in the frenzy of collecting, which occupied so many turn-of-the-century capitalists. He assembled a collection of over sixty thousand Indian artifacts, which he exhibited at the 1893 Chicago World's Fair and at the 1895 Atlanta Exposition (*Augusta Chronicle,* December 23, 1912). His home in Kansas City was an eclectic assemblage of antiques from around the world, including a series of retablos, two of which hung in the living room ("The House of a Thousand Antiques," *Kansas City Star,* October 8, 1911).

Robards Purchase

25.

Saint Raphael, *San Rafael,* painted on panel
Cat. No. 67.787; Neg. No. 69988
Size: H. 21.5 cm.; W. 14.5 cm.; D. 1.5 cm.
Description: Rectangle with border outlined in black and pink; areas filled in red. A winged figure wears blue chest armor with long rounded straps, a short red tunic, and a red cape; the lowered left hand holds a fish; the raised right hand supports a staff with gourd. The black, scrolled base is inscribed "SS. RAFAEL." (Fig. 19)
Condition: Good; crazed surface under resinous varnish.
History: Painted in the later (1840–1855) style of Molleno. This archangel carries a fish, whose scales cured the blindness of Tobias's father (Roig 1950: 235–36). The inscription is an abbreviation of "Señor San Rafael" (Lord Saint Raphael). Sale price, $250.

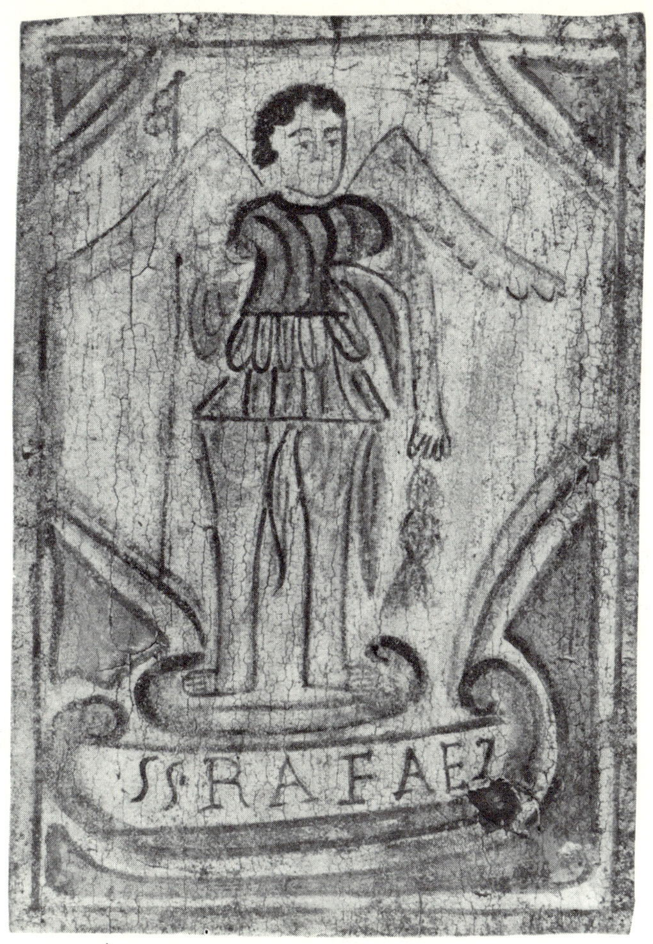

FIGURE 19
Saint Raphael. (Catalogue no. 25.)

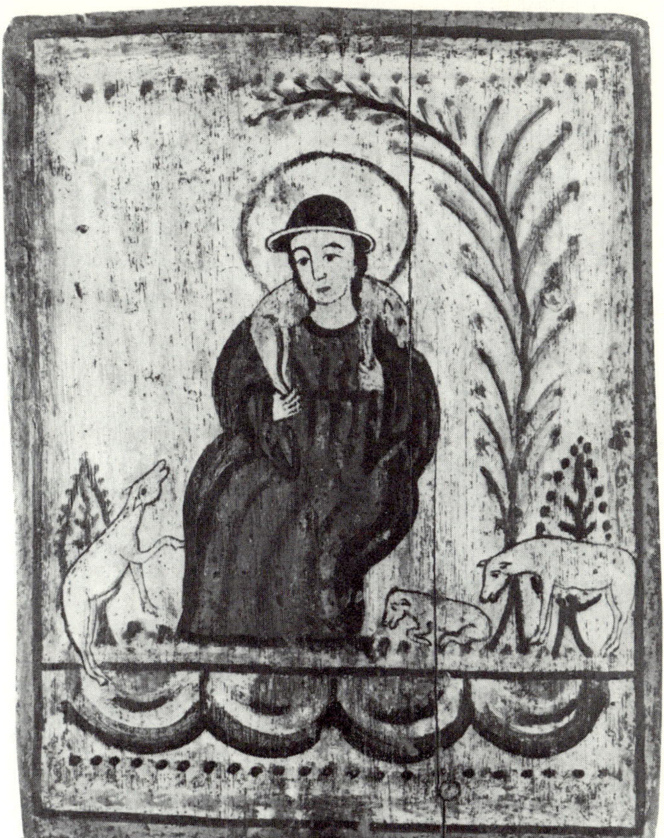

FIGURE 20
Virgin Mary as the Good Shepherdess. (Catalogue no. 26.)

26.
Virgin Mary as the Good Shepherdess, *La Buena Pastora,* painted on panel
Cat. No. 67.788; Neg. No. 76035
Size: H. 34.2 cm.; W. 26.3 cm.; W. 2.1 cm.
Description: Rectangle with seated figure under halo and arching branch wearing brimmed, domed hat, red dress, and blue cape, holding lamb over her shoulders. Below, lambs and bushes at each side. Red, black, and pink border with red dots across the top, lower section with four scallops outlined in black and blue with red centers and black dots below. (Fig. 20)
Condition: Vertical candle damage in lower center.
History: Subject was popular by 1700s throughout Spanish America, with similar designs produced in Peru and Mexico. This panel displays stylistic elements of José Aragón. Sale price, $300.

27.
Saint Ignatius of Loyola, *San Ignacio de Loyola,* painted on panel
Cat. No. 67.789; Neg. No. 77682
Size: H. 13.2 cm.; W. 10.4 cm.; D. 1.4 cm.
Description: Rectangle with relief frame. Bald, beard-

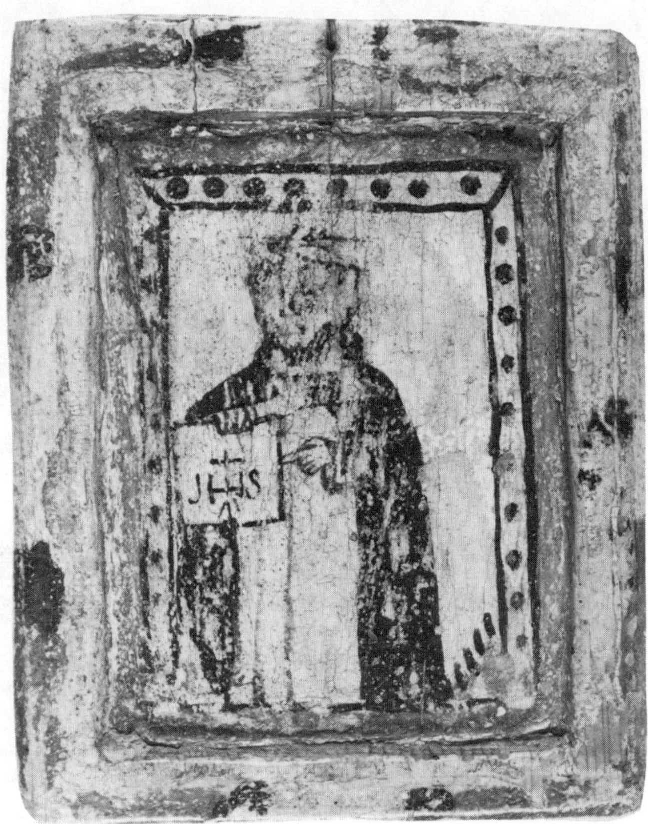

FIGURE 21
Saint Ignatius of Loyola.
(Catalogue no. 27.)

ed figure dressed in black cassock over white robe holds in right hand a plaque with the IHS-monogram cross and three nails of crucifixion; bordered in orange with black outlines and dots, red and white with red and black bands on relief frame. (Fig. 21)
Condition: Gesso and paint losses; cleaned at Smithsonian, 1971.
History: In 1762, Governor del Valle, commissioned the Castrense stone altar screen, which includes an image of Saint Ignatius (ca. 1491–1556), founder of the Order of Jesus, the Jesuits (Roig 1950: 133; Steele 1974: 186). The governor's wife, Ignacia, may have influenced the selection of a Jesuit subject in Franciscan New Mexico. The small size of this panel made it a personal, portable item. Sale price, $300.

28.
Saint Anthony of Padua and the Infant Jesus, *San Antonio de Padua y el Santo Niño,* painted on panel
Cat. No. 67.790; Neg. No. 69982
Size: H. 36.8 cm.; W. 22.7 cm.; D. 1.4 cm.
Description: Rectangle of standing figure in dark blue robe; sgraffito lines mark folds and knotted cord. Right hand holds child wearing red gown; left holds a palm frond. The red and black borders are incised with wavy lines, and the background is composed of horizontal red and white bands, blue sky, and sketchy trees; there is a crosshatched curtain in upper left corner. Single-width lines throughout.
Condition: Vertical cracks repaired. Gesso losses over surface.
History: The rendition displays the sgraffito, halo, and two-branch bush of Fresquís, as well as the hand and floor motifs of Molleno, placing the work around 1825. Illustrated in Ahlborn (1970: 8). Sale price, $350.

29.
The Crucifixion of Jesus, *El crucifijo,* painted on panel
Cat. No. 67.791; Neg. No. 69983
Size: H. 57.9 cm.; W. 36.1 cm.; D. 2.3 cm.
Description: Rectangle with solid black background; corpus drawn in fine black lines with wider red lines of blood; closed eyes with gray outlines, halo with sgraffito and black lines, crown of thorns, and loincloth with lobed knot on left. Brown cross with yellow "INRI" plaque; nimbus with red swags and four winged angel heads in red and black. Two floreros of trees and pedestals, drawn in red and sgraffito lines. Brown border with red and white bands and black lines.
Condition: Largely cleaned and waxed by Alan C. Vedder, 1971; candle scorches at lower right; gesso buckling and losses.
History: Identified by Boyd (1968 letter to Ahlborn) as early work (1790–1810) of Pedro Antonio Fresquís. Illustrated by Ahlborn (1970: 7) and Boyd (1974: 336). It is nearly identical to another retablo in the collection of the Hispanic Society of America,

New York City (Espinosa: pl. 30). The design and controlled intensity recall Eastern Orthodox icons, as well as eighteenth-century European engravings. Sale price, $400.

Robards Donation

30.

Saint Stanislaus Kostka, *San Estanislao Kostka,* painted on panel

Cat. No. 67.792; Neg. No. 69986

Size: H. 37.7 cm.; W. 28.4 cm.; D. 2 cm.

Description: Convex rectangle of pine. Figure of a haloed youth wearing a white scapular and surplice, a black hood, and a cassock, holding a flaming crucifix with a bluish, bloodied corpus. Yellow-brown background, with red and black borders. Two holes at the top for the hanging thong.

Condition: Cleaned and waxed about 1970 by Alan C. Vedder; gesso losses along base; original resinous varnish.

History: The subject may be the wellborn Polish runaway who studied in Vienna and died a Jesuit novice in Rome in 1568 (Roig 1950: 97; Steele 1974: 184). In any case, it has been attributed to Rafael Aragón's style (Boyd: inscription on reverse). This uncommon New Mexico theme was used by Rafael Aragón on his 1834–1838 altar screen at San Antonio Chapel in Córdova, New Mexico (Wroth 1979: 65). Illustrated by Ahlborn (1970: 9).

31.

Saint Francis of Xavier, *San Francisco Javier,* painted on panel

Cat. No. 67.793; Neg. No. 72-804

Size: H. 15.2 cm.; W. 13.5 cm.; D. 1.8 cm.

Description: Rectangle of pine. Striding, bearded figure in black biretta, robe, and cape, outlined in yellow; pink halo; crucifix in right hand, red palm frond in left. Bands of blue suggest a tile floor; borders of blue and red with wavy blue and sgraffito lines. (Fig. 22)

Condition: Vertical cracks; cleaned by Alan C. Vedder, 1969.

History: Another Spanish Jesuit, a rare subject in New Mexico, probably originally promoted there by a prominent citizen and perhaps admired for his overseas (Asian) work as a missionary (Roig 1950: 116; Steele 1974: 185). The wavy, fine, sgraffito lines and the ground treatment are stylistic traits of Pedro Antonio Fresquís (Boyd: 1968 letter to Ahlborn).

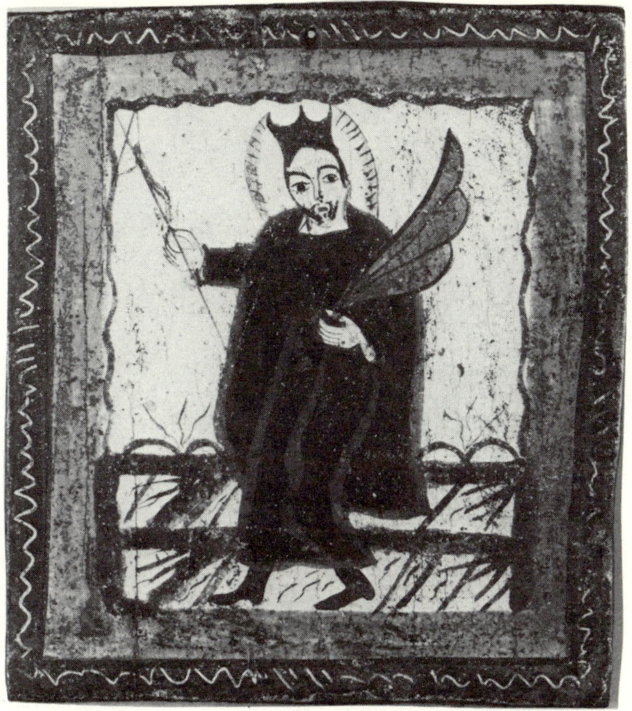

FIGURE 22
Saint Francis of Xavier. (Catalogue no. 31.)

32.

Saint John of Nepomuk, *San Juan Nepomuceno,* painted on panel

Cat. No. 67.794; Neg. No. 69990

Size: H. 17.7 cm.; W. 11.2 cm.; D. 0.8 cm.

Description: Rectangle of standing, bearded figure with pink halo, dressed in a biretta, white surplice with red and yellow stripes, black cape, and cassock. Holds yellow cross with red flames with both hands, black frond in left. Red lining in cape; red curtain tied back on right. (Fig. 23)

Condition: Fair, with gesso losses on left.

History: Subject is the Bohemian priest and confessor to the queen of King Wenceslaus, who had him

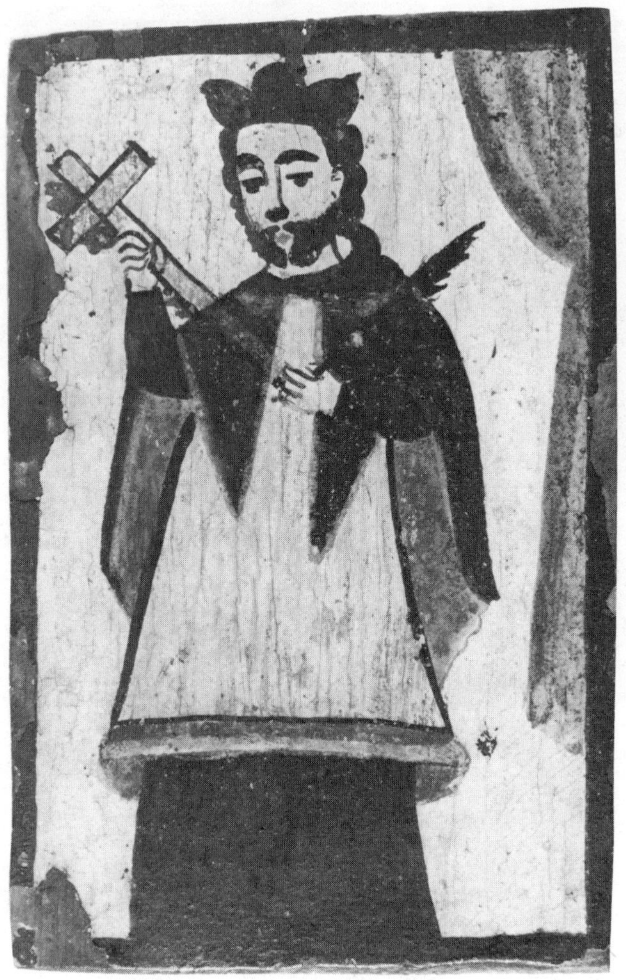

FIGURE 23
Saint John of Nepomuk. (Catalogue no. 32.)

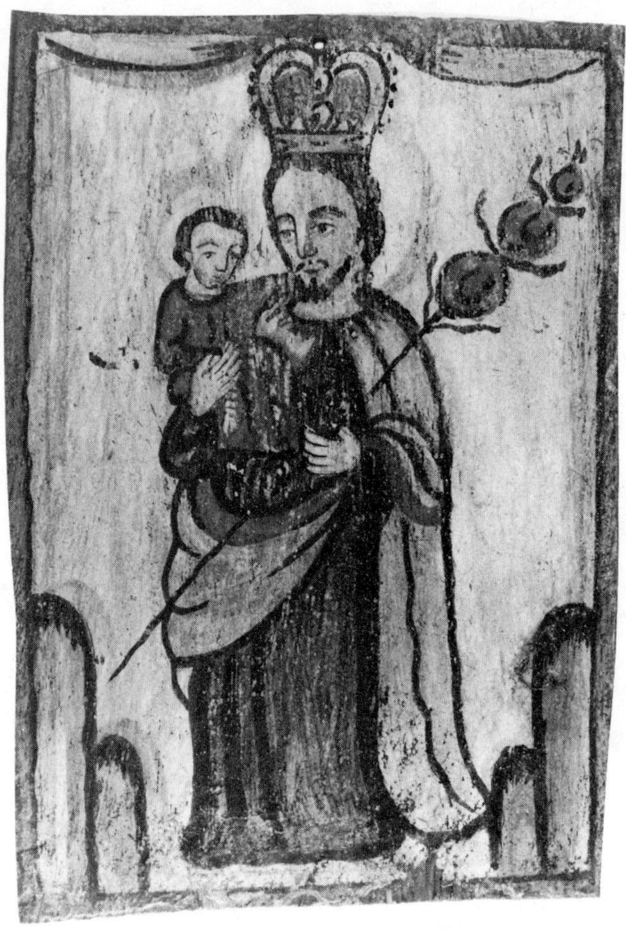

FIGURE 24
Saint Joseph and the Infant Jesus. (Catalogue no. 33.)

drowned, supposedly for not revealing confessional secrets. His silence endeared him to the New Mexican brotherhood of penitents. The retablo reveals traits of the school of Rafael Aragón (Boyd: 1968 letter to Ahlborn).

33.

Saint Joseph and the Infant Jesus, *San José y el Santo Niño,* painted on panel
Cat. No. 67.795; Neg. No. 69998
Size: H. 29 cm.; W. 19.4 cm.; D. 1.3 cm.

Description: Rectangle with bearded, standing figure with large crown, wearing white cloak with red lining and blue robe and holding staff with three red, bulbous blossoms in left hand and child in red gown in right arm; both figures with pale halos; soft shadows on nose and around eyes. Red border with upper swags of pink drapery and lower corner fillers with black outlines, all outlined in pale blue. (Fig. 24)
Condition: Good; check at bottom.
History: This retablo displays brushwork, colors, and

crown used by José Rafael Aragón (Boyd 1969: 15).

34.

Saint John of Nepomuk, *San Juan Nepomuceno*, painted on panel
Cat. No. 67.796; Neg. No. 72-5688
Size: H. 28.8 cm.; W. 21 cm.; D. 1 cm.
Description: Rectangle with standing, bearded figure in pink halo; dressed like No. 32 in biretta, surplice, and cassock, but in brown cape with black stars and pink lining; holds branch in left hand and stares at cross in right. Framing oval divided into brown and red halves; four-petal red blossoms with blue leaves in each corner. (Fig. 25)
Condition: Good, with some paint losses.
History: See No. 32 for subject. The corner fillers, dark colors, and drawing style identify this as a retablo by Molleno. Flowing leaves, reinforcing the wavy lines around the oval, provide an intense focus on the simple, central figure. This oval composition demonstrates how traditional print sources firmly established a basis for later folk stylization at its best.

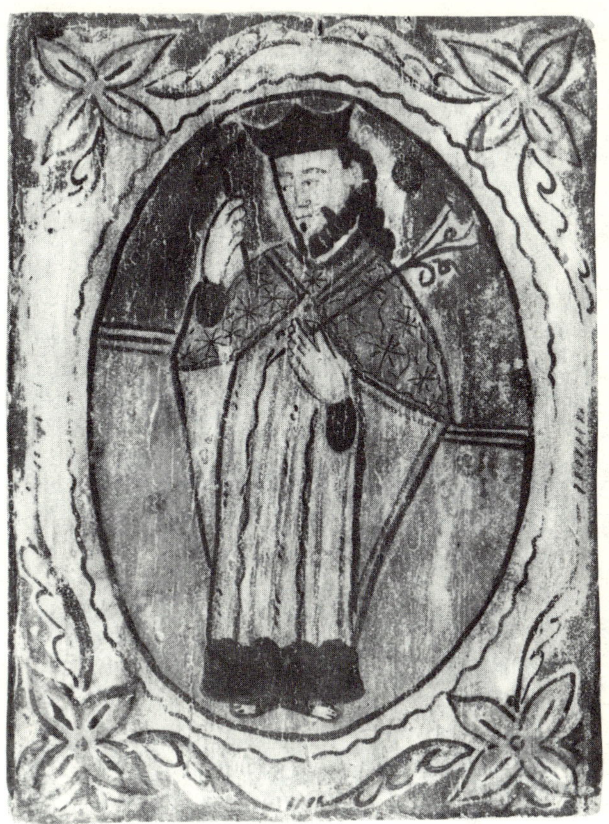

FIGURE 25
Saint John of Nepomuk. (Catalogue no. 34.)

35.

The Annunciation, *La anunciación*, painted on panel
Cat. No. 67.797; Neg. No. 69984
Size: H. 33 cm.; W. 20.4 cm.; D. 1.2
Description: Rectangle of pine; painted black border. At top, red, white, yellow, and pink drapery swags; central bell form with dark outline; descending spread-winged dove (Holy Spirit), black-outlined pink rays, and loops of wide red ribbons. To the left, a profile figure of Gabriel the archangel with left leg bent, right hand raised, and left holding a flowering branch; Gabriel is wearing a green cape, high-cut red tunic, and black boots. To the right, a kneeling figure (Virgin Mary) appears. She wears a white gown and darker shawl with red lining and points to Gabriel with her left hand and to some object (a book?) on a prayer stand with her right. On the stand, vertically banded in red, white, and brown, lies a vase that awaits the angel's branch. Similar banding, crosshatching, and plaid squares suggest carpet and tiles. At the bottom, a blue oval reserve, outlined in red, contains an illegible inscription. (Fig. 26)
Condition: Uneven, yellowed varnish, perhaps from attempt to clean; gesso losses near the dove and along the bottom, damaging banded and inscribed areas.
History: Steele records no known example of this subject among New Mexico santos (1974: 174). While design elements suggest Rafael Aragón, the finer drawing recalls the work of the "Santo Niño Santero" (Boyd 1974: 376–77). The panel may have been flipped prior to being gessoed, as the slight beveling cut into top and bottom appears on back.

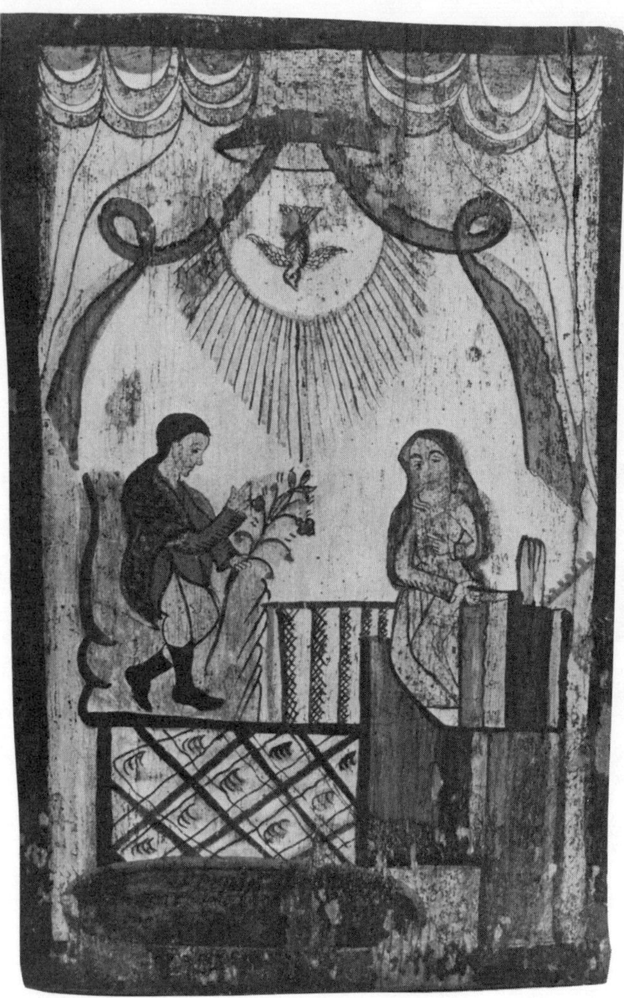

FIGURE 26
The Annunciation. (Catalogue no. 35.)

36.

Saint Anthony of Padua with the Infant Jesus, *San Antonio de Padua y el Santo Niño,* painted on panel
Cat. No. 67.798; Neg. No. 72-10959
Size: H. 46 cm.; W. 27 cm.; D. 2.4 cm.
Description: Rectangle of pine with semicircular crest outlined in red, with eight red and black blossoms. Crosshatched arch in crest; lobed drapery in upper corners with fringed, tied-back drapery below. Red-and-black color scheme throughout, except for figure in dark blue Franciscan habit with sgraffito knotted cord. Standing figure holds "feather" frond in left hand; a child in a gown with a scalloped collar in the right. Both figures have halos. Scalloped border at sides and base; floor rhomboids; tadpolelike (ermine tails?) background fillers. (Fig. 27)
Condition: Good; cleaned at Smithsonian, 1974. (Photo shows cleaning in progress.)
History: Boyd identified Pedro Antonio Fresquís as the maker of this object, which has been displayed since 1976 in "A Nation of Nations" bicentennial exhibit at the National Museum of American History.[5]

37.

Sudarium or Veil of Veronica, *El sudario,* painted on panel
Cat. No. 67.799; Neg. No. 69994
Size: H. 10.6 cm.; W. 8 cm.; D. 1.5 cm.
Description: Rectangle with attached hanger peg cut from pine; red border. Bearded head of Jesus with long hair, red streaks for blood; bluish band with red dots and sgraffito for crown of thorns; shadowed eyes and nose.
Condition: Good; cleaned at Smithsonian.
History: The legendary subject was a cloth used to wipe sweat (Latin *sudare* = "to sweat") from Jesus' "divine face," *el divino rostro,* another term for the cloth. This panel was small enough to serve as a portable "true icon" *(Vera icon* = Veronica). Stylistic details repeat those of Rafael Aragón. Illustrated by Ahlborn (1970).

38.

Saint Isidore the Worker, *San Isidro Labrador,* painted on panel
Cat. No. 67.800; Neg. No. 76129
Size: H. 17 cm.; W. 14.2 cm.; D. 1.7 cm.
Description: Rectangle of pine, with grain ending at sides. Color scheme throughout is red-and-black on white, except for blue jacket of plowman. Narrow borders with wider scallop-and-dot border above. In upper left, angel in sash appears above cross on (altar?) before which a haloed, bearded figure in coat prays, hat at his side. In lower right, stands a small plowman with prod, in domed hat and knee breeches; plow pulled by a team of oxen with dark

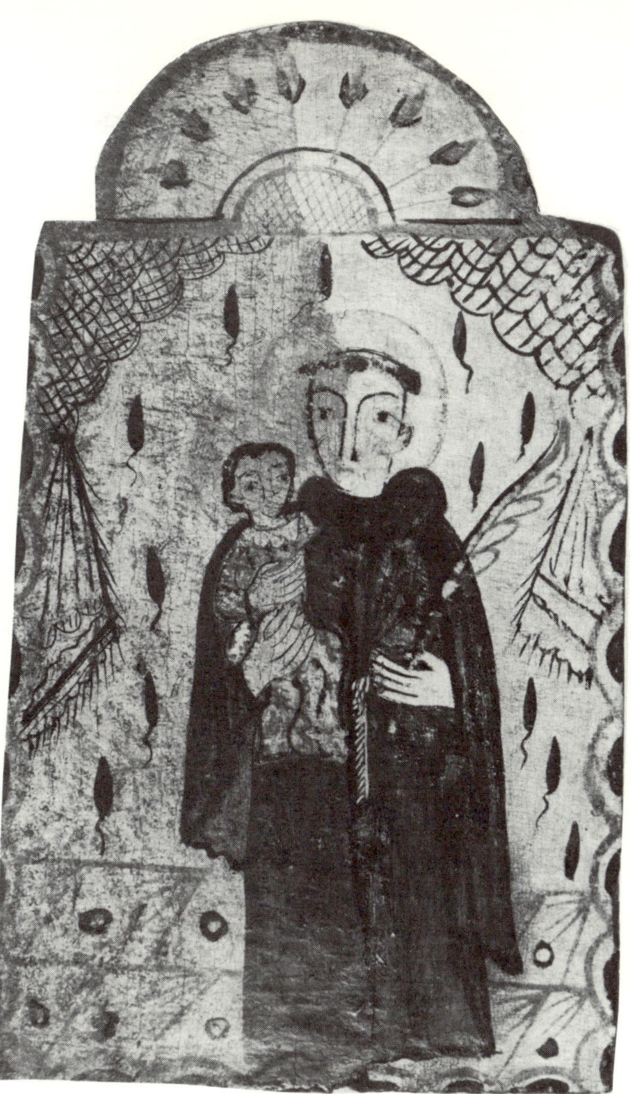

FIGURE 27
Saint Anthony of Padua with the Infant Jesus. (Catalogue no. 36.)

FIGURE 28 *(right)*
Saint Isidore the Worker. (Catalogue no. 38.)

foreheads, horns tied to yoke, trudging along furrows. (Fig. 28)
Condition: Allover gesso losses; cleaned and waxed at Smithsonian, 1970.
History: The subject lived in Madrid and died in 1130; his devotions were facilitated when God sent an angelic plowman to free him from labor demanded by the harsh landlord (Roig 1950: 142–43; Steele 1974: 187). New Mexico folklore and religion reflected the popular Spanish theme of class struggle between peasant and manor lord. Painted in the style of José Aragón.[6]

39.
Saint Theresa of Avila, *Santa Teresa de Ávila,* painted on panel
Cat. No. 67.801; Neg. No. 82-2406
Size (from files): H. 19.1 cm.; W. 13.3 cm.; D. 1.3 cm.
Description (from photo): Rectangle with haloed figure wearing habit of dark cloak and a light hood and robe, holding a crosier with banner inscribed, as on her breast, "IHS" between cross and three nails. Radiance in upper left corner; slashes and bars along ground. Inscription at base, "SANTA TERESA [DE] JESUS." (Fig. 29)
Condition: Good, with candle scorch at bottom; stolen from museum exhibition, 1971.
History: Saint Theresa, a noblewoman of Avila,

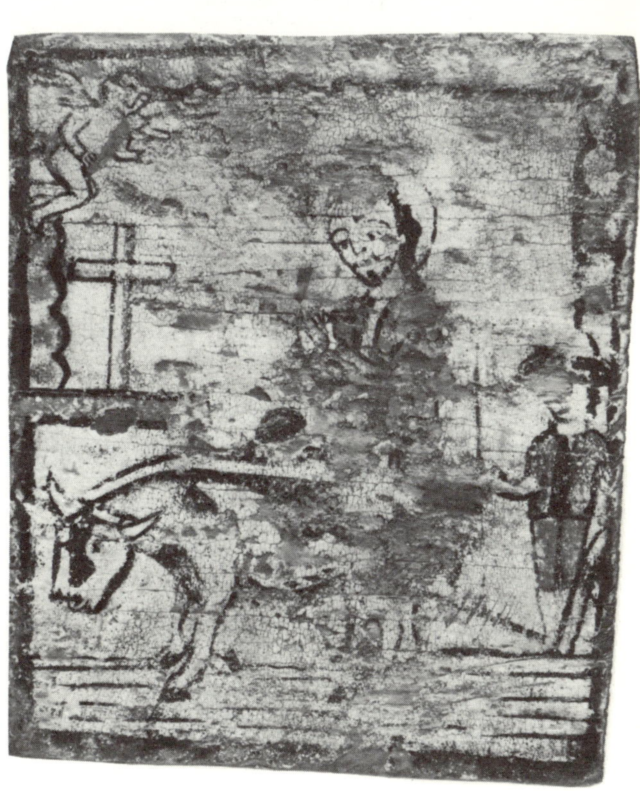

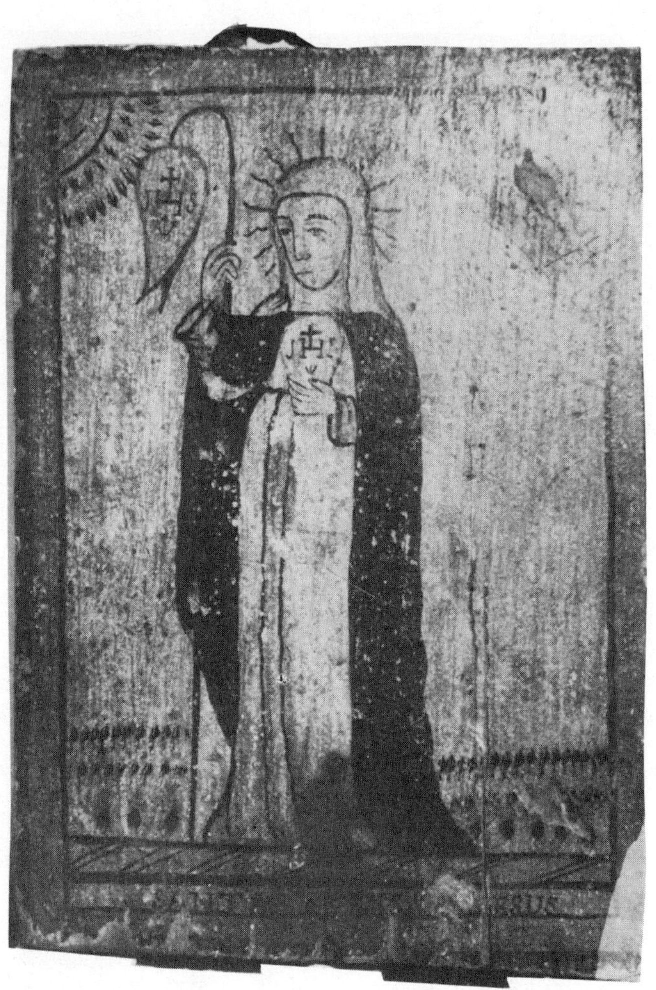

FIGURE 29
Saint Theresa of Avila. (Catalogue no. 39.)

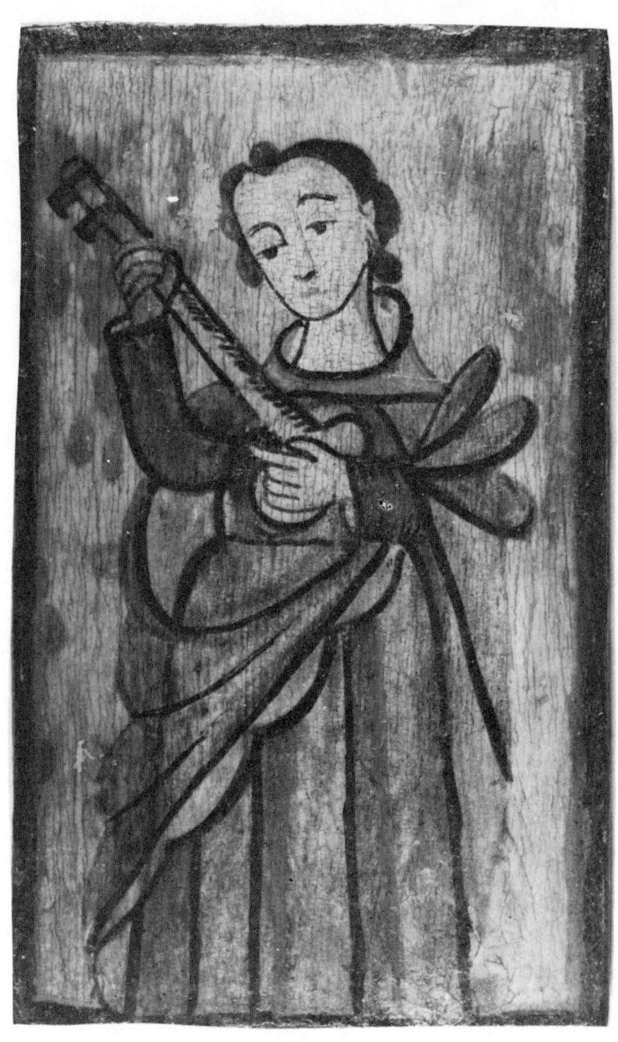

FIGURE 30
Saint Peter. (Catalogue no. 40.)

Spain, reformed the Discalced Carmelite Order. Founding thirty-two convents and producing ascetic, mystical literature, she was canonized in 1622 (Roig 1950: 255–57; Steele 1974: 196). Radiance suggested her divine inspiration. In painting this, José Aragón neglected to darken the hood of her order.

40.
Saint Peter, *San Pedro,* painted on panel
Cat. No. 67.802; Neg. No. 82-672

Size: H. 23 cm.; W. 13.4 cm.; D. 1.8 cm.
Description: Rectangle with standing figure of a young man wearing a green robe with black and red stripes and a blue, translucent cloak with red (yellowed by overvarnish) lining and collar, holding an enormous key. Red and black borders. (Fig. 30)
Condition: Good; panel cleaned, inpainted, and wax-impregnated by Peter Michaels, 1967 (report on file).
History: Apostle and first pope, Peter is popularly credited with holding the key to the gate of heaven,

but he is seldom seen as young as shown here. This object recalls the hasty work of Rafael Aragón.

41.

Saint Raphael, *San Rafael,* painted on panel
Cat. No. 67.803; Neg. No. 72-2370
Size: H. 35.2 cm.; W. 24.2 cm.; D. 3 cm.
Description: Rectangle with chiseled-out center, leaving a one-piece relief "frame." Dark blue border with bands at top and bottom of frame; inner borders of light blue, black, and red. Standing figure, with red-tipped blue wings, wears black boots and a pink tunic cut long in back with red, scalloped openings and scroll medallion at front. The angel carries a crook with water gourd in left hand and raises troutlike fish on loop in right. (Fig. 31)
Condition: Fair; gesso losses along base. Cleaned and waxed at Smithsonian, 1972.
History: Identified by Boyd as the work of José Aragón.[7]

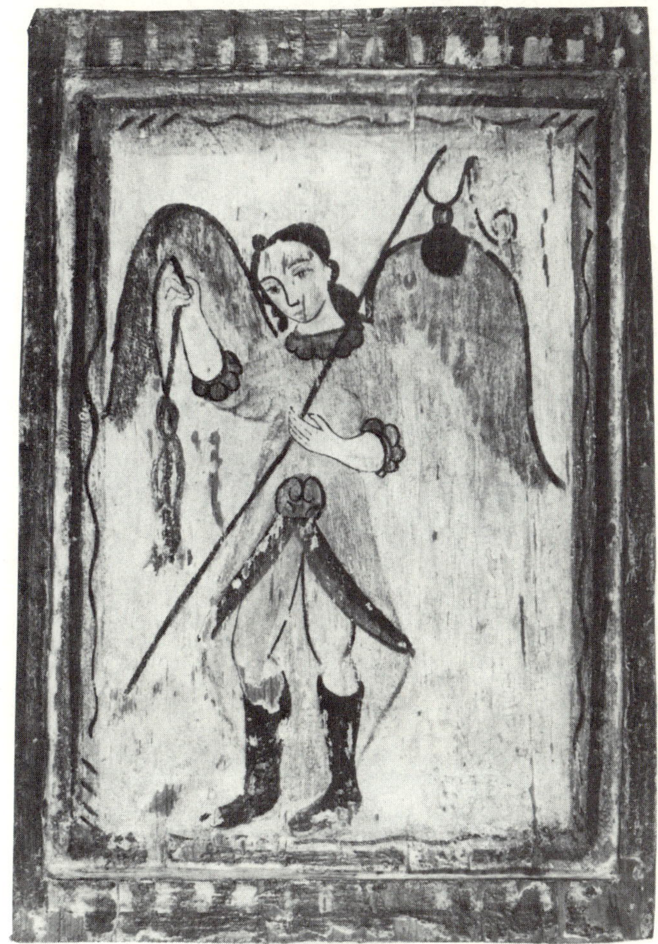

FIGURE 31
Saint Raphael. (Catalogue no. 41.)

42.

Saint John of Nepomuk, *San Juan Nepomuceno,* painted on panel
Cat. No. 67.804; Neg. No. 72-5092
Size: H. 23.4 cm.; W. 14.8 cm.; D. 1.6 cm.
Description: Rectangle of pine with black, white, and red borders. Standing, bearded figure with red halo, dressed in black biretta, brown cape with black collar and red lining, and black cassock with white scapular; holds black cross in raised right hand, a black frond in the left. (Fig. 32)
Condition: Good, except cupping of gesso on face; previously cleaned.
History: See No. 32 for subject. Done in style of "Santo Niño Santero" (Boyd 1969: 17).

43.

Saint Raymond Nonnatus, *San Ramón Nonato,* painted on panel
Cat. No. 67.805; Neg. No. 69997
Size: H. 25.4 cm.; W. 17.4 cm.; D. 1.6 cm.
Description: Rectangle of pine; widely beveled edges with yellow, red, and brown borders. Pink curtains with dark fringe and folds. Bearded figure with halo stands on a concave pedestal of yellow, blue, red, and brown; wears yellow cloak with pink lining over a white robe; raises yellow and red monstrance in right hand and holds a branch with three crowns in the left. Hanging leather loop runs through top level. (Fig. 33)
Condition: Good.
History: See No. 15 for subject. The fine lines, casual brushwork, droopy shoulders and facial treatment suggest one of the styles which E. Boyd attributed to the "Quill Pen Santero," working after 1830 (Boyd 1969: 16, 1974: 388–89).

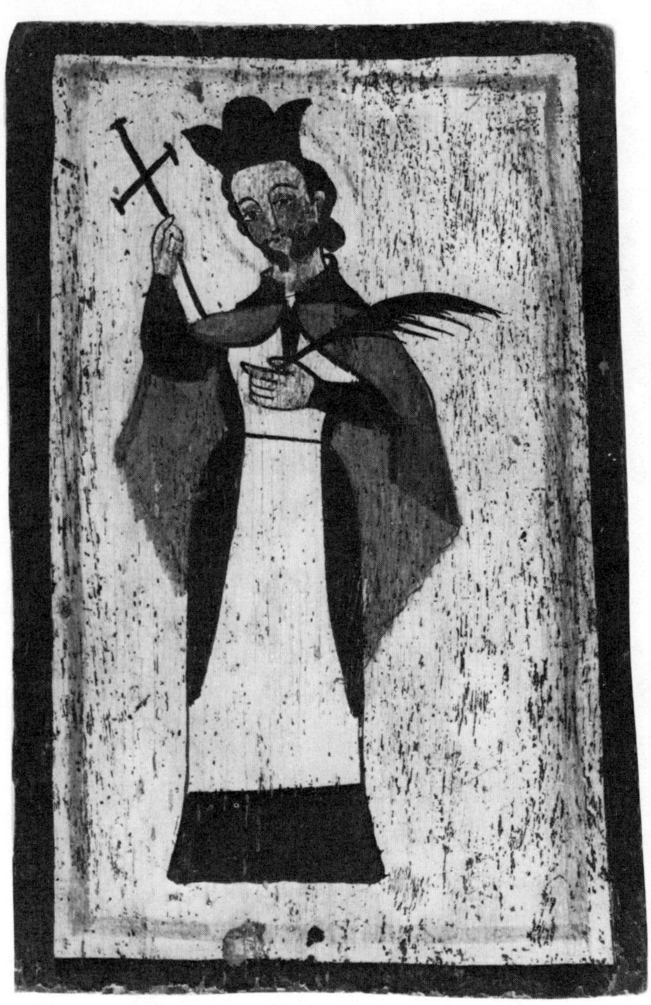

FIGURE 32
Saint John of Nepomuk.
(Catalogue no. 42.)

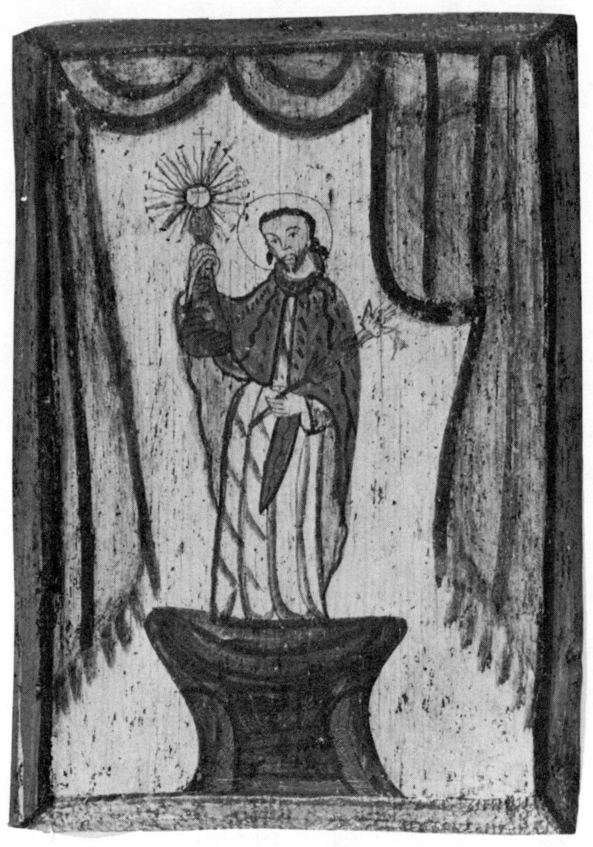

FIGURE 33
Saint Raymond Nonnatus.
(Catalogue no. 43.)

44.

Infant Jesus as Holy Child of Atocha, *El Santo Niño de Atocha,* painted on panel
Cat No. 67.806; Neg. No. 69992
Size: H. 25.1 cm.; W. 16 cm.; D. 1.4 cm.
Description: Convex rectangle of pine with black border. Swagged and tied-back drapery in black, red, white, and blue. Standing child in blue, square-crown hat with wide brim and red feather; wearing a blue cape with red collar and lining; a red belt; a white gown with black and red dots. The right hand holds a black bag with red objects; the left places crook on back of snake.
Condition: Good.
History: Disguised in pilgrim garb, except for stylish Flemish hat of the early 1600s, the infant Jesus was said to have comforted and fed prisoners of the Moors at Atocha, a Madrid suburb (Boyd 1946: 126–27). The work is typical of Rafael Aragón, illustrated by Ahlborn (1970: cover).

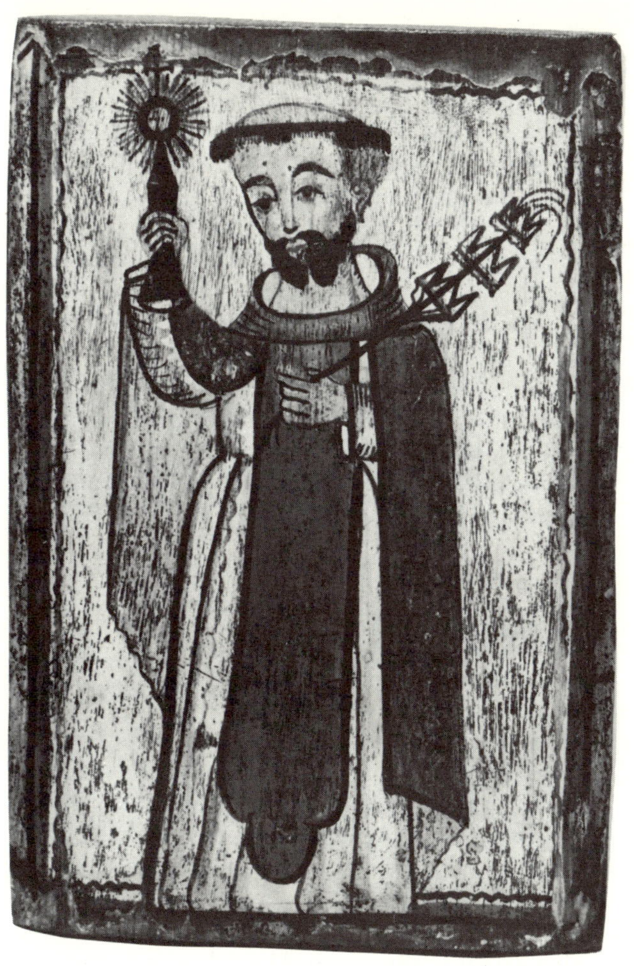

FIGURE 34
Saint Raymond Nonnatus.
(Catalogue no. 45.)

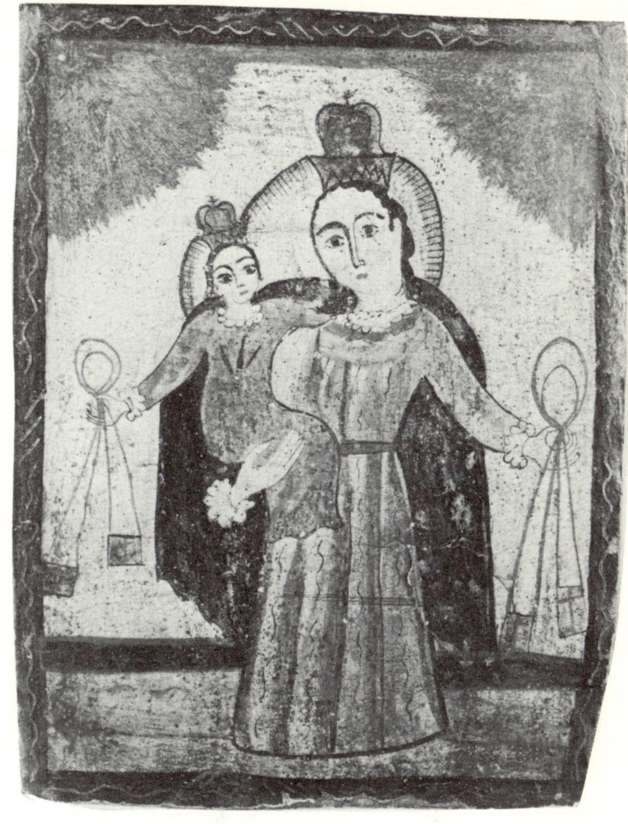

FIGURE 35
Virgin Mary as Our Lady of Mount Carmel. (Catalogue no. 46.)

45.
Saint Raymond Nonnatus, *San Ramón Nonato,* painted on panel
Cat. No. 67.807; Neg. No. 72-803
Size: H. 23.4 cm.; W. 15.4 cm.; D. 1.6 cm.
Description: Rectangle of pine with beveled sides; borders of yellow, black, and red with inner wavy line. Bearded, tonsured figure standing in brown cloak with pink lining and blue collar, white robe, and red scapular raises black and red monstrance in right hand and holds triple-crowned branch in the left. Red scroll outlines ear; washed-in shadows. (Fig. 34)
Condition: Fair, gesso losses on cloak, beard, and along top and base.
History: See No. 15 for subject. An example of Rafael Aragón at his full powers, about 1835.

46.
Virgin Mary as Our Lady of Mount Carmel, *Nuestra Señora del Carmén,* painted on panel
Cat. No. 67.808; Neg. No. 72-802
Size: H. 25 cm.; W. 19.2 cm.; D. 2.1 cm.
Description: Convex rectangle of cedar (?). Black border with wavy sgraffito lines; red radiance in up-

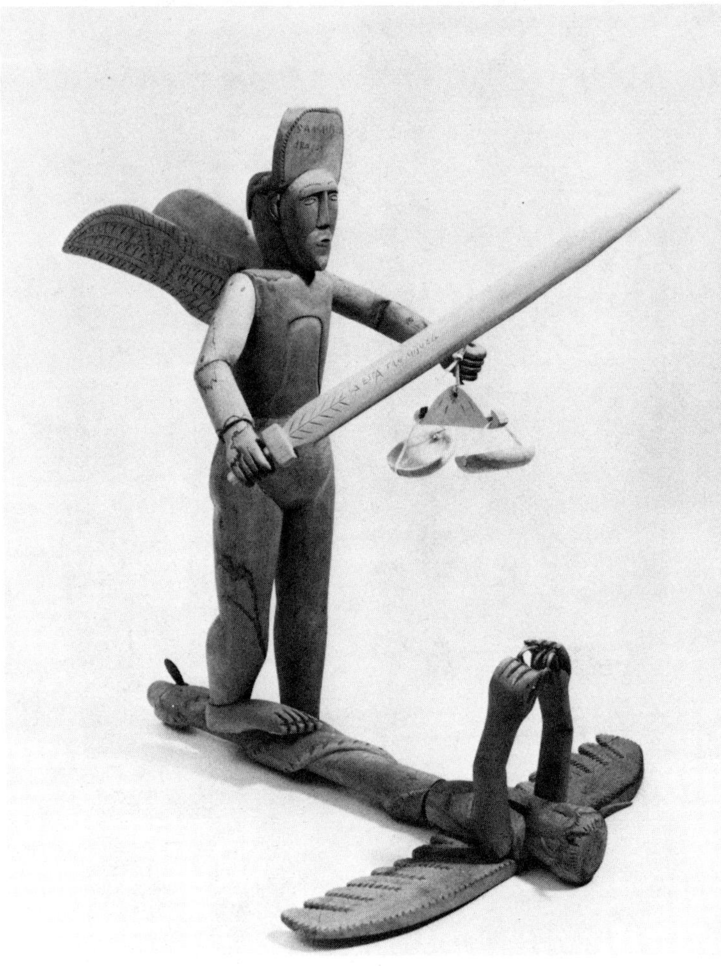

FIGURE 36
Saint Michael and the Devil. (Catalogue no. 47.)

per corners. Standing figure in yellow robe with scalloped openings and blue cloak holds child (infant Jesus) dressed in red gown in right hand. Both have halos and domed crowns, and both hold blue phylacteries with red crosses in opposing hands. Blue, black, and red bands on the robe and along the ground. (Fig. 35)
Condition: Good; yellowed original resinous varnish.
History: Devotion to the subject, which originated at a shrine in northwest Israel and was spread by Carmelite nuns and monks to medieval Spain, reaching New Mexico by 1760 (Boyd 1974: 442; Steele 1974: 174). In addition to this panel, Pedro Fresquís produced a more sophisticated version, suggesting a wide range of patronage and motivation in his long career (Boyd, 1974: 327 ff. and pl. 17).

Brooklyn Museum Gallery Shop Purchase: Accession 276185

The Smithsonian purchased a santo by George López from the Gallery Shop of New York City's Brooklyn Museum in 1967. Under the direction of Carl Fox, the shop was obtaining choice examples of folk art. In November 1955, he received from Córdova, New Mexico, a carving by López of "San Michael and the devil" for seventy-five dollars, as recorded in a letter.[8] The sword and scales that Saint Michael originally held had been lost, but, immediately following the institution's acquisition, López replaced the missing parts (Smithsonian accession records).

47.
Saint Michael and the Devil, *San Miguel y el diablo,* carved in wood
Cat. Nos. 276185.1–276185.5; Neg. No. 72-10333
Size: Michael—H. 71.5 cm.; W. 32.6 cm.; D. 51 cm. Devil—H. 21.5 cm.; W. 52.5 cm.; L. 65 cm.
Description: Parts carved freehand with knife in aspen, sanded and glued. Standing figure places right foot on cedar-tongued serpent-tail of the bearded, winged, and horned devil, whose clawed hands reach up. Right hand of the angel raises a long sword inscribed "LA ESPA[DA DE] SAN MijuEL"; left

hand holds a balance beam with two pans hung by thongs; the backward-projecting wings have been carved with a cross; the crestlike headgear is inscribed "SAN MigueL y dRAGUN." Chip carving on serpent, crest, hair, and wings; wire nail holes pegged with wood. Large pegs join devil's two-part body together and attach the wings to Saint Michael. Signed in pencil and ink on devil's wing, "George J Lopez–Cordova N Mex."
Condition: Water stains on figures; lighter toned sword and balance. (Fig. 36)
History: The subject combines two appearances of the devil as an anthropomorphic demon and as a serpent, both subdued here by God's steward (see No. 1).

Apolonio D. Martínez Commission: Accession 277996

Curator Ahlborn continued the practice of strengthening the collection through the commissioning of pieces directly from craftsmen. In 1967, he requested Apolonio D. Martínez of Chimayó, New Mexico, to carve a subject of his choice for ninety dollars. Martínez, admiring a calendar scene in his workshop, chose "The Flight into Egypt." The carvings by Mondragón, López, and Martínez were shown in the Watkins display "American Folk Craft Survivals," arranged to coincide with the first Smithsonian Folklife Festival (1968).

48.
The Flight into Egypt, *La Huida al Egipto,* carved in wood
Cat. No. 277996.1; Neg. No. 78-19064
Size: H. 37.6 cm.; W. (base) 51.3 cm.; and D. (base) 28 cm.
Description: Rectangular base of pine; parts hand-carved with knife from aspen and sanded. Tanned leather halter. Standing figure at left of man (Saint Joseph) in a robe holding a staff. Central figure of woman (Virgin Mary) in cloak, holding child (infant Jesus), seated sideways on donkey, lead by striding winged figure in jacket. Parts attached with Elmer's Glue-All.
Condition: Mint.
History: The traditional scene shows the Holy Family fleeing Bethlehem, lead by an angel. Martínez used a Protestant calendar as his source for santos, which he began carving, as he told Ahlborn, after retiring in 1960 as a carpenter at age sixty-five; he died in 1976. Illustrated in Briggs (1980: 104).

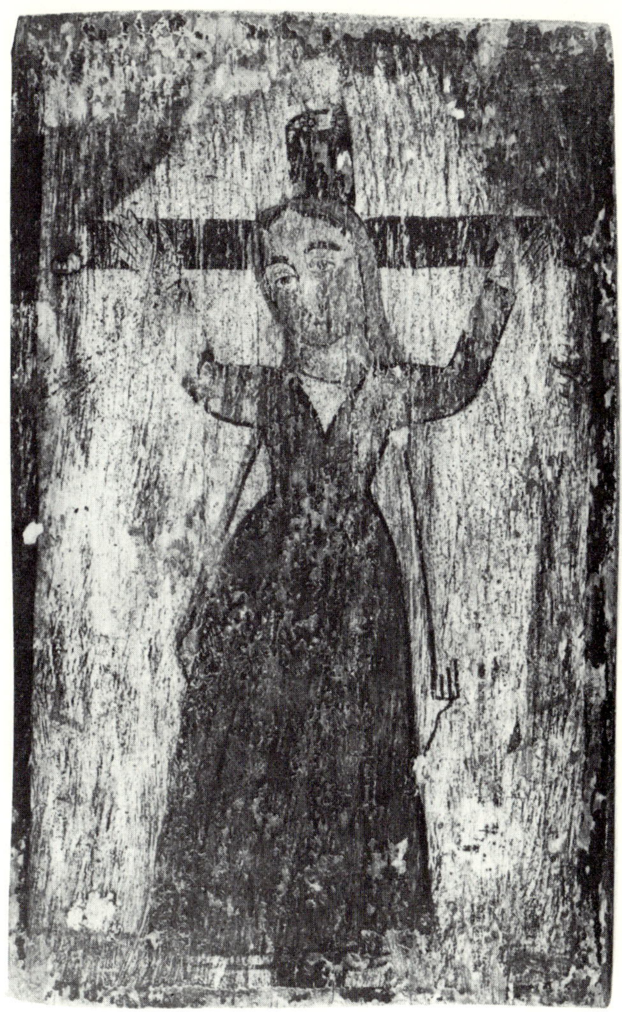

FIGURE 37
Saint Liberata. (Catalogue no. 52.)

May D & F Company Purchase: Accession 280129

The expansion of the santo collection encouraged curatorial plans for a display to accompany the New Mexico colonial room created by Boyd in 1964 in the Hall of Everyday Life in the American Past (removed in 1981). Boyd and Alan C. Vedder of the Museum of New Mexico had secured furnishings for the room, which made the Smithsonian aware of its continuing need to acquire other traditional Hispanic cultural materials.

An unusual opportunity arose in 1968 when the May D & F Company of Denver gathered together several collections of santos and related material for an exhibit and sale. The store offered museums and universities first choice of the over 750 artifacts presented. The majority of the pieces had been acquired by Nolie Mumey who had practiced medicine in northern New Mexico around 1920. After forty years of collecting, Mumey sold his collection to Morton May, grandson of the founder of the May Company (B. Kelly 1968: 39).

Boyd reviewed the objects for the store, helped prepare the catalogue, and presented a lecture in conjunction with the sale. She also advised the Smithsonian on its purchases, which totaled just under forty-five hundred dollars. Important acquisitions included two bultos by Molleno, a death cart, and other Penitente Brotherhood objects.

49.
Crucifix, *El crucifijo,* carved in wood
Cat. No. 280129.1 (old 69.82); Neg. No. 70048
Size: Cross—H. 79.2 cm.; W. 45.7 cm.; D. 2.8 cm. Corpus—H. 43 cm.; W. 33 cm.; D. 11 cm.
Description: Cross, shaped by knife from three sticks attached at intersection and painted black with two red bands on each end; curved "INRI" plaque set in deep notch. Emaciated corpus made up of separate pieces: drooping head set with gesso-built crown of thorns and beard; arms, legs, and torso show painted and built-up wounds. Loincloth of gesso-soaked fabric draped over carved knot peg and painted; hands and feet pegged to cross.
Condition: Poor, with major repairs on head, shoulder, and lower torso; cracked right arm and left foot; gesso losses.
History: Attributed to Molleno by Boyd. Sale price, $720. Illustrated by Ahlborn (1970: 13).

50.
Saint Joseph, *San José,* carved in wood
Cat. No. 280129.2 (old 69.83); Neg. No. 70058
Size: H. (overall) 56.7 cm.; W. (base) 21.5 cm.; D. (base) 12 cm.
Description: Standing, bearded figure on a 3.2-centimeters-high rectangular base holds hands out; wears green robe with black stripes painted over orange ground and heavy white cloak of gesso-soaked cloth, painted yellow and black with black and red blossoms. Holes in left hand and front left of base.
Condition: Poor; extensive repainting, gesso losses, and surface abrasions.
History: Flowering staff missing from right hand went into hole in base; hole in left hand once held figure of infant Jesus. Attributed in sale catalogue to the "Santo Niño Santero." Sale price, $465. Illustrated by Ahlborn (1970: 13).

51.
The Nazarene Jesus, *Jesús nazareno,* carved in wood
Cat. No. 280129.3 (old 69.84); Neg. No. 70057
Size: H. (overall) 58.7 cm.; W. (base) 25.3 cm.; D. (base) 12 cm.
Description: Standing, bearded figure nailed to back slat, which is notched and nailed into 2.3-centimeters-high, rectangular base with beveled upper edges and red border on white surface. Figure displays "crown" of painted, braided cord and real thorns; thongs articulate lower arms; eight other parts attached by glue. Body extensively bloodied by red splashes; varnished above the neck and wrists. Printed cotton cloth glued around hips, above left knee.
History: Wire nails along upper sides of base may

have secured long garment. Holes in each hand suggest attachment to column, a typical position for the flagellation of Jesus. Such figures are familiar in churches and meeting halls *(moradas)* of local Penitente Brotherhoods. Style recalls work of José Benito Ortega about 1900, as shown by Boyd (1974: 417, 419). Sale price, $385. Illustrated by Ahlborn (1970: 11).

52.

Saint Liberata, *Santa Librada,* painted on panel
Cat. No. 280129.5 (old 69.86); Neg. No. 72-5093
Size: H. 35.5 cm.; W. 21.6 cm.; D. 2.3 cm.
Description: Convex rectangle with black border; tied-back, red curtains; and a black cross extending into basal border. Crucified figure of a woman with darkened lower face in knee-length blue shawl and long red dress. Old cigar paper seals on top and left end of cross. Inscriptions on reverse read, "St Liberata . . . By Miguel ARAGON SHUPE Taos N Mex." (Fig. 37)
Condition: Yellowed varnish; allover gesso losses; uncleaned.
History: Also known as Kummernis and Wilgefortis, the subject is an apocryphal Portuguese princess who grew a beard, thwarting her father's wishes to marry her off to his advantage; he then executed her (Steele 1974: 194). The simple, rapid style is that of Rafael Aragón. Apparently this object passed through the hands of dealer Elmer Shupe, formerly located south of Taos, prior to the 1968 sale. Sale price, $185.

53.

Death Cart, *La carreta del muerte,* carved in wood
Cat. No. 280129.13 (old 69.94); Neg. No. 70050
Size: H. (overall) 109 cm.; W. (axle) 63 cm.; D. (railing) 69 cm. Cart—H. (bed to railing) 29 cm.; W. (bed) 38 cm.; D. (bed) 62 cm. Wheel—H. (diam.) 44 cm.; D. 4.5 cm. Figure—H. (torso with neck) 45 cm.; W. (hip) 15 cm.; D. (torso) 9 cm. Head—H. 16 cm.; W. 14 cm.; D. 13 cm.; arm—L. (upper) 21.5 cm.; L. (forearm) 12 cm.; L. (hand) 8 cm.; leg—L. (thigh) 29 cm.; L. (lower) 21.5 cm.; L. (foot) 12 cm.
Description: Sawn cart members with traces of gray, green, and white; railing with overlapping rabbit-joint corners set on peg-end posts; wheel with large wooden washer, iron sleeve, and axle pin. Round-head iron screws hold seat to railing and the frame to the bed. Seated, hand-carved skeletal figure with braided horsehair wig and articulated joints. At knee, nail through round tenon and open mortise; at hips, tied-off thong (replacement) goes through leg, into hip, then angles out and across back and in again; at shoulder, same in-out thong passage as hip. Pegs used to set neck onto shoulder, hands into wrist, and ankles into feet. Cloth on upper arms, across shoulder, and down spine, under first layer of gesso, with red marks for blood. Second gesso layer, on head with black eyebrows, red and black eyes, red cheeks, and yellow skin. Hands hold wooden arrow and bow with thong string. Necklace of string with black lacquered wood; "rosary" of ivory and glass beads in 1–3–1 sequence and struck aluminum medal inscribed, "St. Roch Protect Us," and "St. Hubert Pray for Us."
Condition: Fair; gesso and paint losses.
History: Used by the local penitent brotherhood, the subject is often given the Spanish synonym for death, Doña Sebastiana (Steele 1974: 197). As in Picasso's *Guërnica,* the open mouth silently screams out the horror of death's extinction. Sale price, $1,450. Boyd (1974: 413) illustrated and noted the cart as the creation of José Benito Ortega. Also illustrated in Ahlborn (1970: 10).

54.

Jesus Entombed, *El santo entierro,* carved in wood
Cat. No. 280129.14 (old 69.95); Neg. No. 70053
Size: Figure—H. 64 cm.; W. (hips) 11 cm.; D. 10 cm. Head—H. 9 cm.; W. 7 cm.; D. 6.5 cm.; torso—H. 26 cm.; W. (shoulder without arms) 12 cm.; D. (hips) 5.4 cm.; feet—H. (length) 9.2 cm.; W. 4.6 cm. Casket—H. 18 cm.; W. 78.7 cm.; D. 29 cm.
Description: Casket of five sawn boards with end battens used to line up arched lid of openwork lattice (one replaced) decoratively notched and secured by cleated nails and thongs. Thongs in bottom tie corpus down and allow casket to be hung. Bearded corpus with machine-sewn human-hair wig is made up of ten carved pieces of wood pegged and glued together; arms are articulated at the shoulder by a thong (same as No. 53) and at elbows with a sleeve of commercial cotton cloth. Blue emphasizes wounds

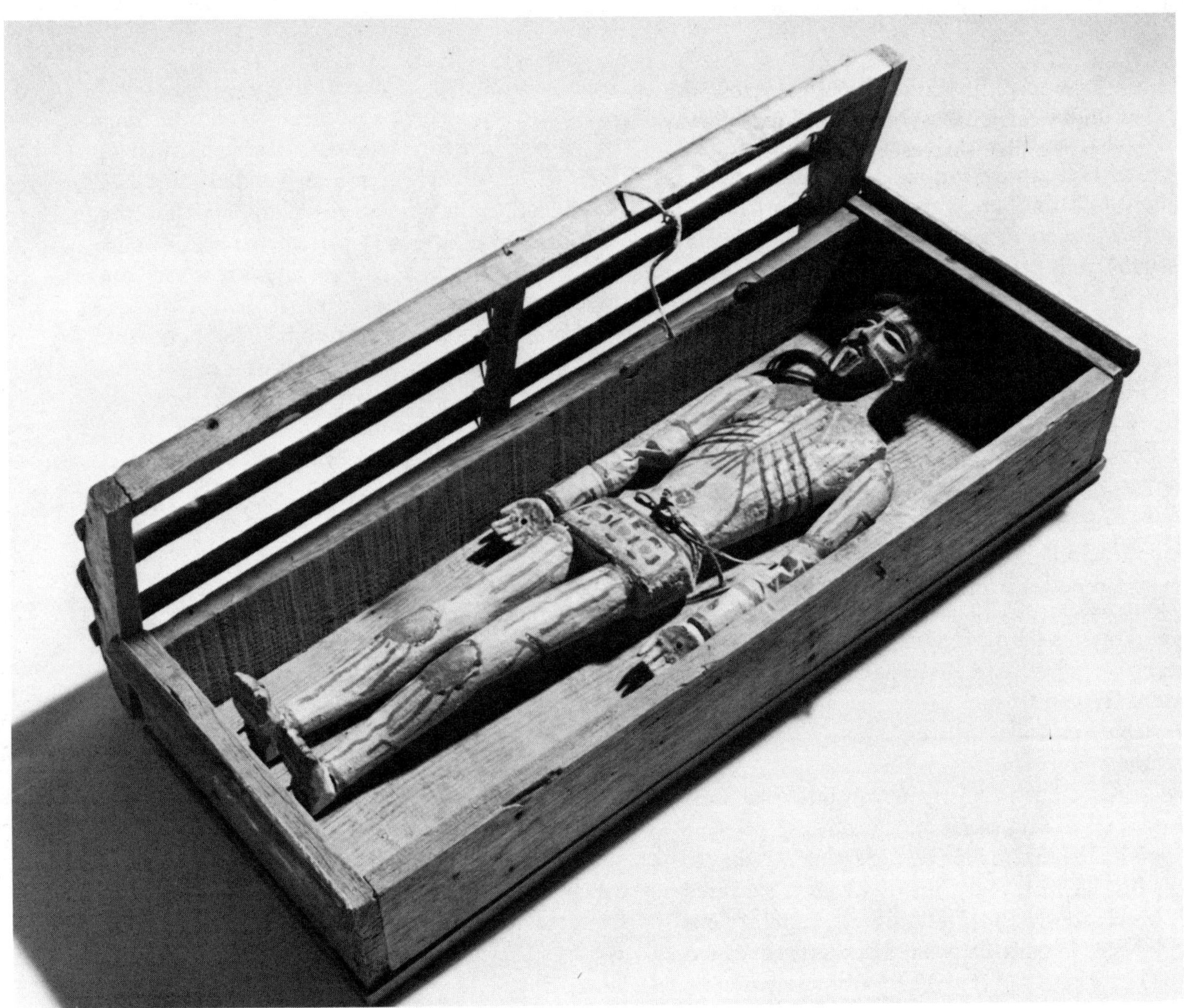

FIGURE 38
Jesus Entombed. (Catalogue no. 54.)

and ribs; red wound patterns all over body; yellow on head and loincloth block, with red and green circles and black and green borders. (Fig. 38)
Condition: Good; dirty toes; repair above spear wound in chest.
History: Both New Mexican churches and moradas display such figures, which are removed and posed in moments of the Passion. This figure reveals a hole in each hand and nail and wood fragments in the feet, suggesting that it was attached to a base in order to stand at a column with hands bound, or to be crucified. It is a fine example of José Benito Ortega's vivid style: bright colors, crescent eyes, hairy brows, and patterned bleeding. Sale price, $725.

55.
Saint Acatius, *San Acacio,* painted on wood
Cat. No. 280129.17 (old 69.98); Neg. No. 69987
Size: H. 20.1 cm.; W. 14.2 cm.; D. 1.7 cm.
Description: Rectangle, beveled on four surface edges, with black and red borders and brown tied-back

drapery. Figure crucified on black-outlined cross with shadow lines wears a crown of thorns, a red cutaway coat with long blue sleeves, black knee breeches, white hose, and black shoes. At the side, there is a drum with pink heads and five lances. (Fig. 39)
Condition: Fair; allover gesso losses.
History: See No. 21 for subject. The panel shares stylistic traits of both José and Rafael Aragón. Sale price, $135.

John Gordon Gallery Purchase: Accession 285781

The most recent acquisition of a santo was the purchase of a figure of a flagellated Jesus. In 1969 the John Gordon Gallery of New York City offered the Nazarene Jesus for fifteen hundred dollars. The mid-nineteenth-century image filled a major gap in the Smithsonian's bulto collection in the "classic" santo era, about 1800 to 1850.

56.

Jesus the Nazarene, *Jesús nazareno,* carved in wood
Cat. No. 285781.1; Neg. No. 82-674
Size: H. 102.5 cm.; W. (hips) 16.5 cm.; D. 20.6 cm. Head—H. 14.2 cm.; W. 8.6 cm.; D. 9.3 cm.; arms—L. (forearm) 26 cm.; L. (upper) 18 cm.; legs—L. 55 cm.; L. (feet) 13.5 cm.
Description: Bearded figure of ten parts with arms articulated at shoulder by wedged-in thong and at elbow by nailed-on, tanned-leather sleeve; ankles bound by tanned leather. Wounds in red; nipples and ribs in blue; yellow (varnish?) on head, lower arms, and legs. Loincloth of sized (cotton?) fabric, painted blue and black, covers joining of legs to torso. Wrists tied together by hemp cord; fiber set into wound on palm. (Fig. 40)
Condition: Good; cracks in chest, hip, and ankles.
History: The red soles of the feet suggest that the figure was placed in a casket after crucifixion (see No. 54), as well as being stood at a column (see No. 51) after flagellation and mocking. The rapidity of painting and the yellowed extremities indicate that the figure was dressed on occasion for altar display or processional use. Done in the style of Rafael Aragón (Boyd 1974: cover, fig. 207).

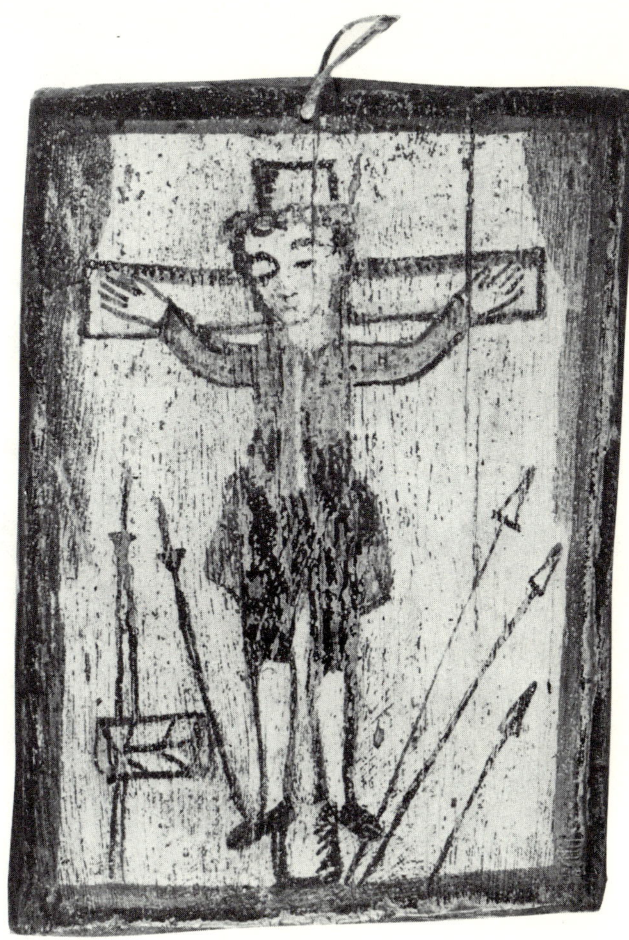

FIGURE 39
Saint Acatius. (Catalogue no. 55.)

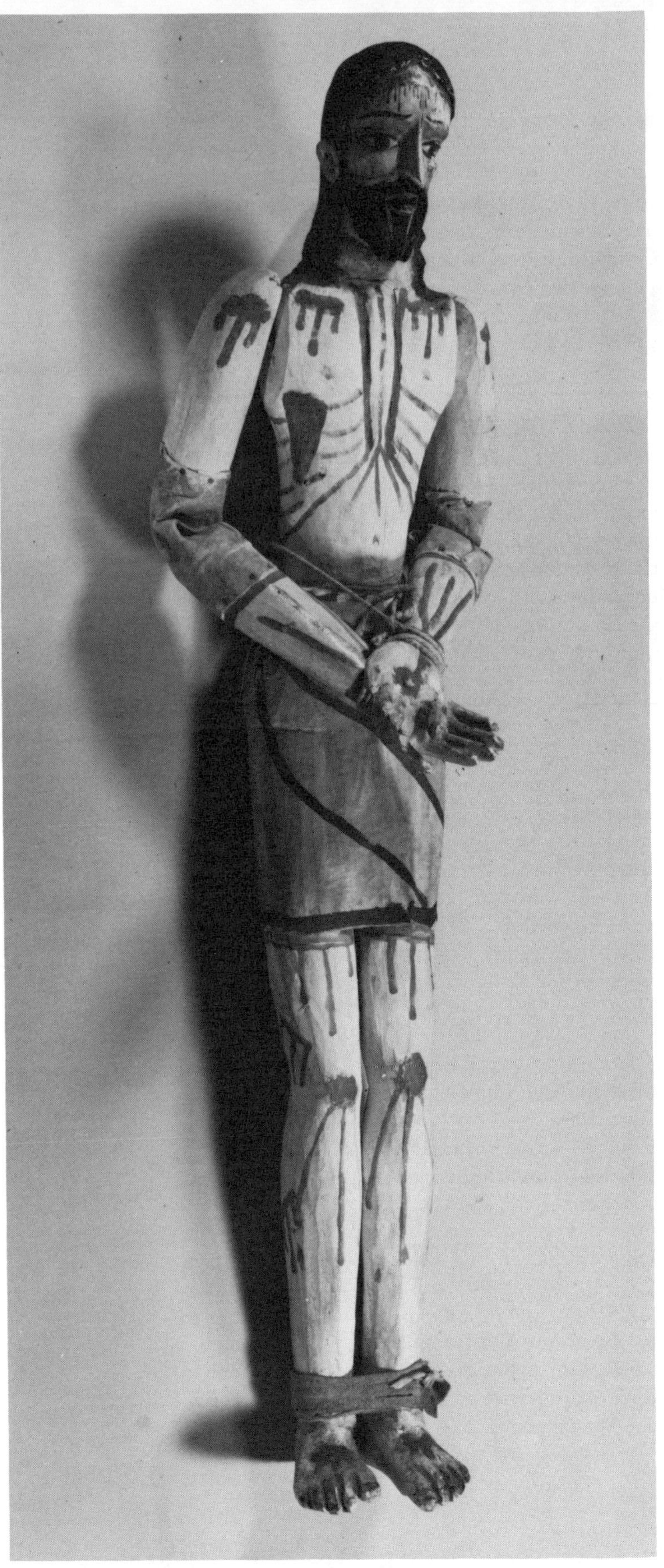

FIGURE 40
Jesus the Nazarene. (Catalogue no. 56.)

NOTES

1. Unfortunately, a sculpture, a painted hide, and five panels have been burnt or stolen (1965–1968), leaving a count of only forty-nine objects.

2. Scientific analysis of santo materials and their conservation began at the Smithsonian in the 1960s. Dorothy M. Briggs meticulously cleaned and stabilized the surface of nearly a dozen santos before her retirement in 1981. Similarly, identification of samples taken from santos has continued to the present. Through the conscientious work of Martha Goodway, Conservation Analytical Laboratory Report 4090 provided "hard" and some yet-to-be-confirmed data on materials sampled from bultos Nos. 1, 50, and 56. CAL Report 3133 described analysis by Peter Waldstein and conservation by Walter Angst on bulto No. 21.

3. Boyd to Ahlborn, 15 January 1968, personal files of recipient. Copy in E. Boyd Collection, New Mexico State Records Center and Archives, Santa Fe.

4. Ibid.

5. Ibid.

6. Ibid.

7. Ibid.

8. López to Fox, 27 November 1955, Smithsonian Collection, accession files.

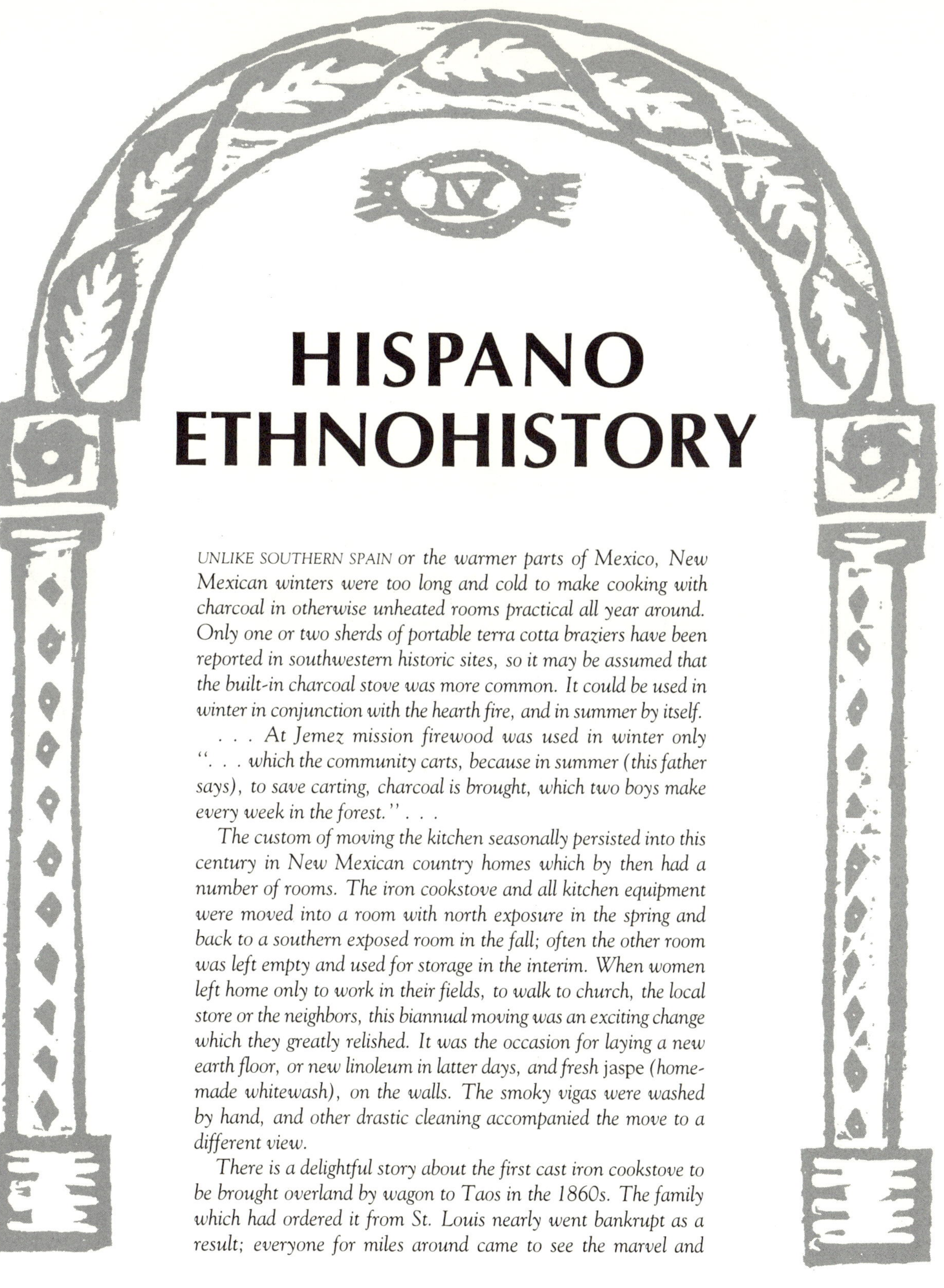

HISPANO ETHNOHISTORY

UNLIKE SOUTHERN SPAIN *or the warmer parts of Mexico, New Mexican winters were too long and cold to make cooking with charcoal in otherwise unheated rooms practical all year around. Only one or two sherds of portable terra cotta braziers have been reported in southwestern historic sites, so it may be assumed that the built-in charcoal stove was more common. It could be used in winter in conjunction with the hearth fire, and in summer by itself.*

. . . At Jemez mission firewood was used in winter only ". . . which the community carts, because in summer (this father says), to save carting, charcoal is brought, which two boys make every week in the forest." . . .

The custom of moving the kitchen seasonally persisted into this century in New Mexican country homes which by then had a number of rooms. The iron cookstove and all kitchen equipment were moved into a room with north exposure in the spring and back to a southern exposed room in the fall; often the other room was left empty and used for storage in the interim. When women left home only to work in their fields, to walk to church, the local store or the neighbors, this biannual moving was an exciting change which they greatly relished. It was the occasion for laying a new earth floor, or new linoleum in latter days, and fresh jaspe *(home-made whitewash), on the walls. The smoky vigas were washed by hand, and other drastic cleaning accompanied the move to a different view.*

There is a delightful story about the first cast iron cookstove to be brought overland by wagon to Taos in the 1860s. The family which had ordered it from St. Louis nearly went bankrupt as a result; everyone for miles around came to see the marvel and

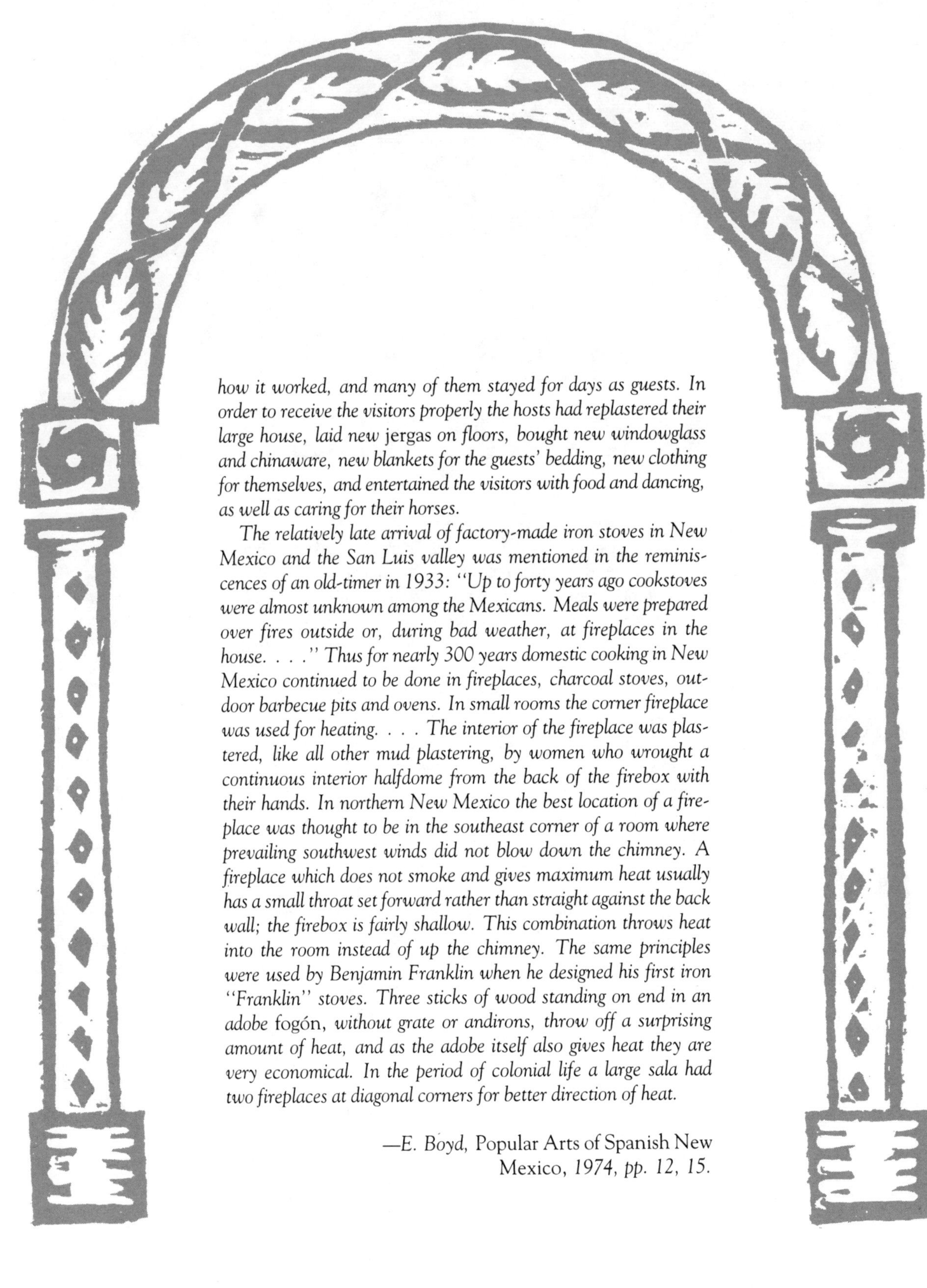

how it worked, and many of them stayed for days as guests. In order to receive the visitors properly the hosts had replastered their large house, laid new jergas *on floors, bought new windowglass and chinaware, new blankets for the guests' bedding, new clothing for themselves, and entertained the visitors with food and dancing, as well as caring for their horses.*

The relatively late arrival of factory-made iron stoves in New Mexico and the San Luis valley was mentioned in the reminiscences of an old-timer in 1933: "Up to forty years ago cookstoves were almost unknown among the Mexicans. Meals were prepared over fires outside or, during bad weather, at fireplaces in the house. . . ." Thus for nearly 300 years domestic cooking in New Mexico continued to be done in fireplaces, charcoal stoves, outdoor barbecue pits and ovens. In small rooms the corner fireplace was used for heating. . . . The interior of the fireplace was plastered, like all other mud plastering, by women who wrought a continuous interior halfdome from the back of the firebox with their hands. In northern New Mexico the best location of a fireplace was thought to be in the southeast corner of a room where prevailing southwest winds did not blow down the chimney. A fireplace which does not smoke and gives maximum heat usually has a small throat set forward rather than straight against the back wall; the firebox is fairly shallow. This combination throws heat into the room instead of up the chimney. The same principles were used by Benjamin Franklin when he designed his first iron "Franklin" stoves. Three sticks of wood standing on end in an adobe fogón, *without grate or andirons, throw off a surprising amount of heat, and as the adobe itself also gives heat they are very economical. In the period of colonial life a large* sala *had two fireplaces at diagonal corners for better direction of heat.*

—*E. Boyd,* Popular Arts of Spanish New Mexico, *1974, pp. 12, 15.*

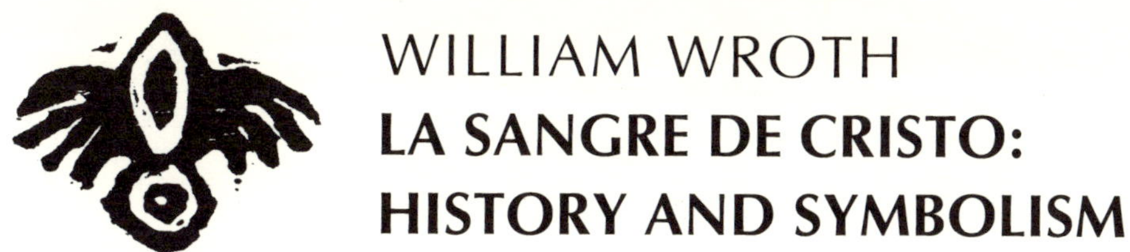

WILLIAM WROTH

LA SANGRE DE CRISTO: HISTORY AND SYMBOLISM

SANGRE DE CRISTO is today the commonly accepted designation for the eastern spur of the Rocky Mountains ranging from southern Colorado to Santa Fe, New Mexico. What is the source of this provocative Spanish name? In this essay, I will explore popular legends and historic references to the Sangre de Cristo Mountains and examine the symbolism of the name in the Hispanic cultural ambience of northern New Mexico.[1]

> As practically everyone knows, the phrase *Sangre de Cristo* translates as "Blood of Christ" and derives from the ruddy light that some sunsets spread across the western slopes. (Lavender 1980: 10)

"Practically everyone"—both popular and scholarly writers to this present day—has accepted and perpetuated this romanticized tradition for the naming of the mountains.[2] It is often said that the name derives from a legend of the early colonial period. With his dying breath—so the legend goes—"Padre Juan," a Franciscan missionary martyred in the 1680 Pueblo Rebellion, prophesied the eventual triumph of Christianity over the paganism of the Indians. His prophesy was accorded a heavenly response with the sudden appearance of the "crimson stain" upon the mountains, which terrified the rebellious Indians and ever after reminded them of Christ's triumphal sacrifice:

> My body only has thou killed
> Blood of Christ o'er mountains spread
> Shall preach to you when I am dead.
> (True 1917: 4; also see Hallenbeck and Williams 1938: 89–96)

In fact, the mountain range in New Mexico did not receive the name Sangre de Cristo until the late nineteenth century. It was not named by the early colonial missionaries or by the Spanish explorers, but rather by late-arriving Anglo-American promoters. Prior to this time, the range was called the *Sierra Madre* ("Mother Range") by the Spanish; in English it was most often known simply as the Rocky Mountains.

The place-name *Sangre de Cristo,* however, does date to the colonial period,

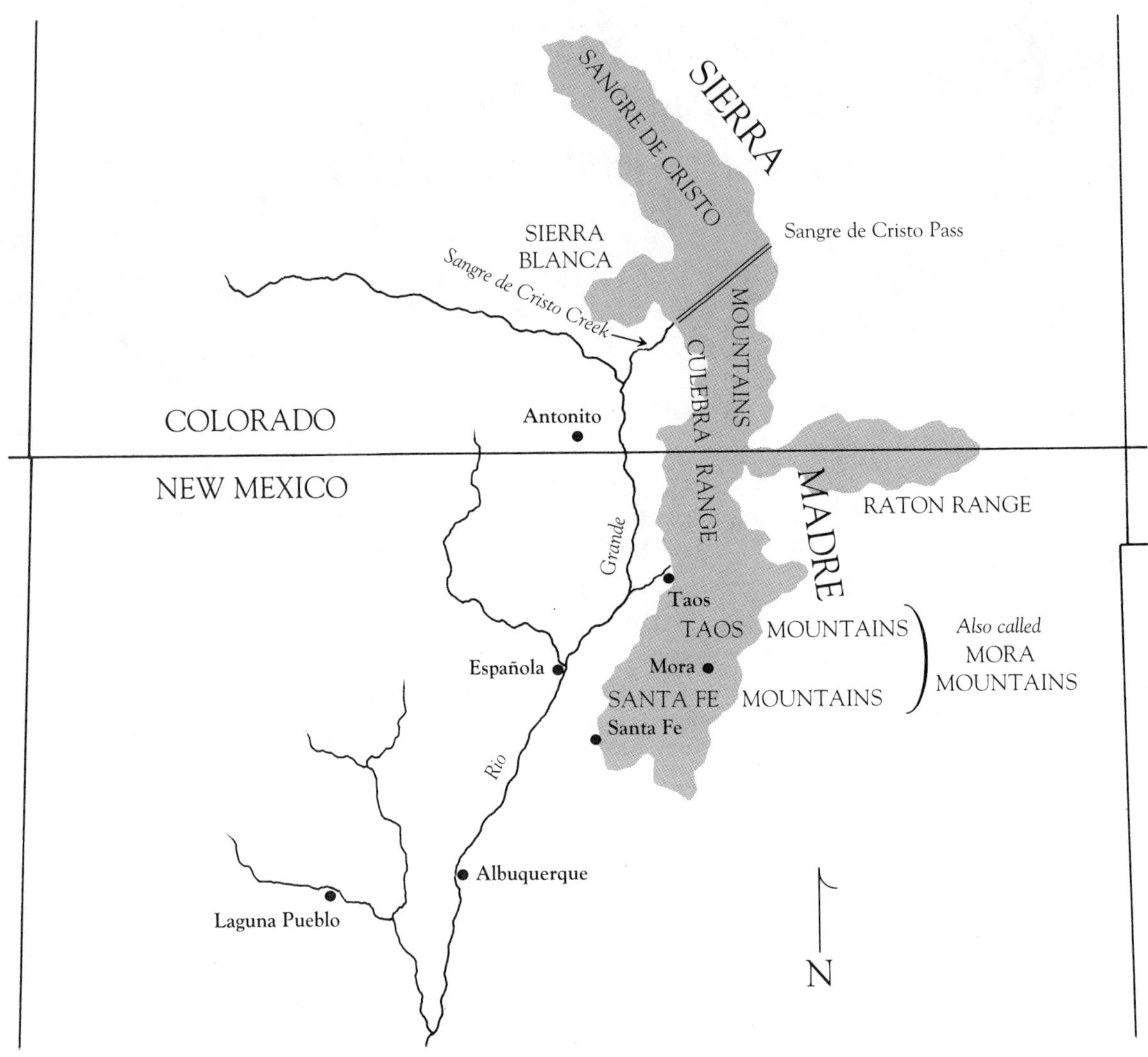

Map of the Sangre de Cristo Range
with some of the terms used between 1850 and 1880.

but as the name for a body of water not for mountains. Eighteenth-century Spanish explorers, possibly Don Antonio de Valverde Cosio and his expedition of 1719, named a creek on the northern frontier *El Río de la Sangre de Cristo.*[3] This small watercourse, still bearing its original name today, finds its source in the Rocky Mountains of southern Colorado, flows southwestward into the San Luis Valley through Fort Garland, into the Rio Trinchera, and thence into the Rio Grande. The creek is named on the 1779 map of Gov. Juan Bautista de Anza and on the Mascaro map of 1782, which is based on Anza's map. It is also mentioned by Anza as "the stream and arroyo of la Sangre de Cristo" in his account of the successful campaign against the Comanches in 1779.[4]

The name was soon used to designate the pass through the Rocky Mountains at this point, where it followed the creek to the summit and then passed to the south of Sheep Mountain, descending into the Huerfano valley in the east. By 1818, the mountains surrounding this pass were known as *la sierra de la Sangre de Cristo,* in distinction from *la Sierra Blanca,* the spur of the range extending to the west.[5] Between 1816 and 1819, the Spanish attempted to fortify the Sangre de Cristo pass against the threatened invasion of the Americans allied with the Pawnees and other Plains tribes. *El puesto* (outpost) *de la Sangre de Cristo* was built by Gov. Facundo Melgares, probably in 1819, a few miles east of the pass. It was attacked by the Pawnees in 1819 and abandoned by 1821.[6]

By 1844, the name Sangre de Cristo was given to the land grant ceded by Gov. Manuel Armijo to Narciso Beaubien and Stephen Luis Lee. The Sangre de Cristo grant encompassed a vast area extending from the Sierra Blanca just north of the Sangre de Cristo River, south beyond present-day Costilla, New Mexico, west to the Rio Grande and east to the Sierra de la Sangre de Cristo. This area had some reputation for gold placers as early as the 1830s, for according to Josiah Gregg: "at a point called Sangre de Cristo, considerably north of Taos (above the 37th degree of latitude) . . . a very rich placer has been discovered"(1933: 112). Later accounts questioned the richness of this placer, but a gold camp named Sangre de Cristo on Cottonwood Creek near Crestone, Colorado, still appeared on the Wheeler survey maps of 1873–1876.[7]

After the American occupation of New Mexico in 1846, the careful observations of government explorers, geographers, and cartographers from the first reports of 1846–1850 through the Hayden and Wheeler surveys of the 1870s, recorded the name Sangre de Cristo for the Rocky Mountain range in Colorado, but for its continuation in New Mexico, they either used local Spanish terms, often translated into English—Culebra range, Taos Mountains, Moro (= Mora) Mountains, Sierra Chimayon, and Santa Fe range—or they continued to designate the range simply as the Sierra Madre or the Rocky Mountains.[8]

Most government, promotional, and popular writings through the 1880s and into the 1890s used these terms. In his *Illustrated New Mexico,* William G. Ritch carefully describes the range: "In the northern part of the Territory the Culebra range looms up to the east into the Raton spur, and to the South is known, according to proximity to local towns, as Taos, Mora and Santa Fe Mountains" (1885: 31).

Ernest Ingersoll located the southern end of the Sangre de Cristo range with Trinchera peak in southern Colorado and described the watercourses of the Taos valley as issuing forth from the Culebra range (1885: 68, 110). The highly romanticized account of Susan E. Wallace speaks not of the Sangre de Cristo, but of the Santa Fe range and the Rocky Mountains (1888: 48, 77).

The careful descriptions of towns and counties found in the official publications of the New Mexico Bureau of Immigration mention only the local ranges, such as the Taos and Santa Fe mountains, well into the 1890s. The Sangre de Cristo range is mentioned only in descriptions of the mountains at the Colorado border (Anonymous 1894: 127). Adolph Bandelier in *The Gilded Man* does not mention the Sangre de Cristo but describes "the massive chain of the Sierra Madre" and the "wild Sierra de la Truchas" (1893: 232, 290). Many other accounts could be cited from this period in which the name Sangre de Cristo is notably absent (for example, Anonymous 1883: 22).

The coming of the railroads brought major changes to life in the untamed West, making remote areas immediately accessible to large numbers of curious travelers from the eastern states. Due to the rugged terrain of the Rocky Mountains, northern New Mexico was not easily reached; laying track was a slow, arduous and expensive process throughout the 1870s with bitter competition between the two major lines—the Denver and Rio Grande and the Atchison, Topeka and Santa Fe. Among the surveys made to determine the best routes into New Mexico was one by Lieutenant E. H. Ruffner for the United States Army in 1874–1875. Lieutenant Ruffner considered possible routes through the mountains, beginning at the termination points of the railroads in eastern Colorado. In his careful surveying, he viewed the overall system of mountains, passes and valleys from Pueblo, termination point of the Denver and Rio Grande, over the Sangre de Cristo pass, south to Santa Fe and thence westward to Fort Wingate. Rather than naming all the local ranges separately, Ruffner saw the southern Rocky Mountain range as a whole: "The north and south line of the Sangre de Cristo range presents an almost unbroken front from the Arkansas River canon to Santa Fe" (Ruffner 1876: 15).[9] This description of the Sangre de Cristo range extending all the way to Santa Fe is also seen on Ruffner's map of the region published two years later in a revised version of his report (Ruffner 1878).

By 1880, the Denver and Rio Grande Railroad had reached southward into New Mexico, making Taos, Santa Fe, and many other sites easily reachable. Publicists for the railroad wrote and distributed a series of effusive promotional booklets extolling for the benefit of tourists and speculators the glories to be seen along the route, among which was the dramatic Sangre de Cristo range. They claimed that between Antonito, Colorado, and Santa Fe, the tourist "is seldom out of sight of the Sangre de Cristo mountains, one of the grandest of all the Rocky Mountain ranges, running parallel with his course at the east side of the park; and there are many far-reaching and magnificent views of the park, and beautiful glimpses of the Taos Valley" (Anonymous 1881: 88–89, also 85).[10]

It seems likely that, perhaps following the usage of Ruffner in his 1878 map, the railroad publicists in Denver had extended the name Sangre de Cristo southward from the Colorado range into New Mexico for the benefit of their passengers. The rail passenger with leisure to view the passing landscape would be well aware that the mountains from north of Sierra Blanca all the way south to Santa Fe were one continuous range. An early traveler on the Denver and Rio Grande was Lt. John G. Bourke who in April 1881 traveled the route from Denver to Antonito and on south into New Mexico, disembarking at Española, where he continued by stage to Santa Fe. Crossing the Rio Grande at Española, Bourke described the mountains: "In front of us, as we crossed the river, the Sangre de Cristo uplifted its snowcapped summit to form a background in relieving contrast with the front of the picture which was a monotonous succession of red sand and dry mesas" (in Bloom 1935: 298).

The legend of the naming of the range by early colonial settlers and friars, so popular in twentieth-century writings, seems also to derive from the promotional publications of the Denver and Rio Grande Railroad. A book issued by the railroad in 1896 titled *Slopes of the Sangre de Cristo* gives this explanation for the origin of the name:

> Many, indeed, who have long lived under the shadows of Colorado's mighty peaks, are not familiar with the fact that the Sangre de Cristo is a title which the Spanish pioneers more than three hundred years ago gave to the entire Rocky Mountain range from Yucatan to British America. (Anonymous 1896)[11]

The name Sangre de Cristo, promoted by the Coloradan publicists for the Denver and Rio Grande Railroad, gradually came into use by popular writers, who were often out-of-staters, in the 1890s. The name was readily adopted by American journalists, who were fascinated with the penitential brotherhoods of the Hispanic mountain villages of New Mexico, Los Hermanos de Nuestro Padre Jesús Nazareno (popularly known as the Penitentes). The highly colored journalistic accounts reveled in creating for the benefit of readers in "the States" an atmosphere of mystery and barbarism in describing the "primitive" rituals of the Penitentes. The Blood of Christ was a central concept in the activities of the Brothers, so it was indeed appropriate—and opportune for the journalists—that these ritual activities should take place in the "Sangre de Cristo" mountains, stronghold of the still medieval

Hispanic Catholic culture in which religious observances focused upon the suffering and crucifixion of Christ.

A rather heavily dramatized account, which by its appearance in *Harper's Weekly* brought national attention to the Penitentes, was D. J. Flynn's article on Holy Week celebrations at Ranchos de Taos in 1894. Flynn left Denver on Tuesday morning of Holy Week on a Denver and Rio Grande train, disembarking at Tres Piedras and proceeding by wagon the thirty-five miles to Taos. The following day he continued the four miles to Ranchos de Taos and wrote: "The road to Ranchos de Taos led along the foothills of the Sangre de Cristo range" (Flynn 1894: 489).

While mentions of the Sangre de Cristo range in New Mexico are few and far between in the 1880s and 1890s, the name soon became current in both official and popular writings of the early twentieth century. The 1901 *Report of the Governor of New Mexico to the Secretary of the Interior* describes the physical setting of Santa Fe County: "The main range of the Rockies or the Sangre de Cristo Range on the east and the Valles and Jemez Mountains beyond the Rio Grande on the west, shelter this favored locality from violent winds." This description is clearly an interpolation, with the intentional addition of "Sangre de Cristo Range," into an earlier version found in an 1894 Bureau of Immigration publication: "On the eastern boundary the main range of the Rockies protect the plains from violent winds, while on the West the Jemez and Valle Mountains perform the same office" (Anonymous 1894: 162).

By 1918, popular writers such as Clara D. True could, with authority, restate the myth of the early colonial naming of the mountains and add the romance of the "luminous rose color"—the "crimson stain"—of sunset:

> The name "Sangre de Cristo" literally, "Blood of Christ" was bestowed upon the spur of the Rockies to the north of Santa Fe, extending into Colorado, by the early Spanish missionaries on account of the peculiar luminous rose color which so often tints the range in the evening. (1917: 1)

By the mid-1920s, this imagery was so well known that Willa Cather could weave it into her narrative in *Death Comes for the Archbishop* with no explanation necessary: "A fine sunset, Father. See how red the mountains are growing; Sangre de Cristo" (1927: 310).

In the early decades of the twentieth century, the legend of the Sangre de Cristo was perfectly in keeping with what the newly arriving Anglo-Americans expected of their "Land of Enchantment," and it has persisted as literary folklore, although not without its seed of truth, to the present day.

> The water here is most noxious, but I discovered a little spring of excellent water which I named Sangre de Cristo. (Fray Andrés García, Laguna Pueblo, March 15, 1773)[12]

Although late in coming to the New Mexico mountain range, the name Sangre de Cristo does have profound significance in Hispanic Catholic tradition as the designation for a watercourse and is quite appropriate for the mountains where the water finds its source. It is especially apt in arid New Mexico where water plays such an obvious and crucial role in the maintenance of life, making human settlement possible in an unhospitable environment.

Just as water makes mundane life possible, the Blood of Christ in Catholic dogma is considered the source of eternal life, the life of the spirit. In the sacrament of the Eucharist, the celebrant drinks the consecrated wine to partake of the eternal life offered by Christ through his supreme sacrifice for man: "Whoso eateth my flesh and drinketh my blood, hath eternal life; and I will raise him up at the last day" (John 6:54). The Eucharist is based on the words Christ spoke at the Last Supper: "And he took the cup and gave thanks and gave it to them, saying, Drink ye all of it; for this is my blood of the New Testament, which is shed for many for the remission of sins" (Matt. 26:27–28). The Blood of Christ thus has a central role in traditional Catholic doctrine and ritual.

In many Hispanic cultural areas, the emphasis on Christ's suffering and crucifixion, which arose in the European Middle Ages, has continued to the present day. In New Mexico, Los Hermanos de Nuestro Padre Jesús Nazareno have perpetuated this emphasis on Christ's suffering, and within the practices of the Brotherhood the term *Sangre de Cristo* obviously has great significance. Brothers pledge themselves to the remembrance of the Blood of Christ or designate themselves as "slaves of the Blood of Christ" *(esclavos de la Sangre de Cristo)*. Some local brotherhoods were named after the Blood of Christ, for instance: la Santa Hermandad de la Sangre de Nuestro Señor Jesucristo in Abiquiú and el Fondo de la Sangre de Cristo in Río Chiquito.[13]

The central image of Christian worship since the Middle Ages, the three-dimensional representation of the crucified Christ, is popularly called in New Mexico, among other terms, *La Sangre de Cristo.*[14] Traditional hymns of the Brotherhood—the alabados—often refer to the Blood of Christ (Rael 1951: 212, 254):

Venir, pecadores,
Venir con su cruz,
a adorar la sangre
del dulce Jesús
(Come sinners,
Come with your cross
to adore the blood
of sweet Jesus)

Oh, Sangre de mi Jesús!
Oh, remedio universal
libranos de todo mal
nos ser vertida en la cruz!
(O, Blood of my Jesus
O, Universal remedy
Free us from all evil
by being shed upon the cross!)

In the secular realm the word *sangría,* derivative of *sangre,* has meanings analogous to the sacred signification of blood, for, among other meanings, it refers to a secondary irrigation ditch used to bring water to fields and gardens. This meaning is common in New Mexican usage.[15] Just as the circulation of the blood animates the human body, sustaining its life, so the circulation of water from the *acequia madre,* the "mother ditch," through the system of secondary channels, sustains vegetal life in the fields, providing the basis of human sustenance. This symbolism is especially poignant in New Mexico where the vital green of freshly sprouted fields and the airy blossoms of fruit trees, watered by sangrías, contrast dramatically with the dry severity of the brown and red mesas surrounding them.

The sangrías of New Mexico and the mountain streams that feed them serve another function in traditional Christian practice. Every year on June 24, the feast day of Saint John the Baptist, pious villagers perform a ritual ablution, a sort of annual renewal of baptism, by plunging themselves into the cold running water. This practice, of course, is not limited to New Mexico, being widespread and ancient in Christian tradition. Through this observance we may see the qualitative differences between the symbolism of water and blood.

Water in the sacrament of baptism serves as a purificatory element, preparing the soul to live a good life on earth and purifying the soul to receive divine life—salvation attained through participation in the Holy Communion of the Eucharist. While both are liquids, blood is clearly the more potent substance; thus in the Eucharist it is represented by wine rather than by water. Wine, with its alcoholic content, has a transformational symbolism, while water is neutral and purificatory. Wine's red color in contrast to the transparency of water extends this symbolism.

The ritual ablution on the feast day of Saint John the Baptist reenacts the sacrament of baptism, preparing the soul for human life. The role of Saint John the Baptist parallels this symbolism. It is he who prepares the way for Christ prior to His coming, making "straight the way of the Lord" and baptizing those willing to convert to a virtuous life while awaiting the coming of Christ: "therefore am I come, baptizing with water," but Jesus who "is preferred before me," "baptizeth with the Holy Ghost" (John 1:23, 30,31,33).

This symbolism is elaborated by the coincidence of the feast of Saint John the Baptist with the summer solstice, when the days again begin to get shorter. The feast of Saint John the Baptist inaugurates the second half of the solar year (June 22–December 22). The limitative and decreasing cycle of the second half of the year corresponds to the cycle of human life with its inevitable conclusion. The birth of Christ, on the other hand, inaugurates the expansive cycle of the first half of the year (December 22–June 22) in which the hours of sunlight gradually increase. This cycle corresponds to the divine life offered by Christ. Saint John the Baptist confirms this remarkable difference between himself and Christ, between the human and the divine, with his words: "I am not the Christ . . . He must increase, but I must decrease" (John 3:28,30).

While water and blood—baptism and the Eucharist—signify qualitatively different levels in the spiritual life, they are analogous levels, for human life initiated by baptism is the precursor and microcosm of divine life. The life properly lived on earth is the foundation for salvation in the afterlife. But the level of mundane life can only be elevated to the divine realm by the mercy of heaven. In the Christian tradition, this function is given to Christ who alone is capable of redemption. This function is symbolized by his miraculous transformation of water into wine at the marriage at Cana (John 2:1–10) and by his words concerning "living water" to the woman of Samaria: "The water that I shall give him shall be in him a well of water springing up into everlasting life" (John 4:14). The miracle of blood and water flowing from his wound during the crucifixion also speaks of this power of unification that alone is Christ's. Thus, through Christ the water of baptism is transformed into the wine of the Eucharist, and finite man is given the possibility of eternal life.

It is appropriate in this context to name a stream of water Sangre de Cristo, for water sustains life on the earthly plane. This is perfectly analogous to the Blood of Christ, which simultaneously sustains all mundane life and provides the means to salvation.

NOTES

1. I would like to thank Marianne Stoller and Marc Simmons for reading and commenting on this work prior to publication.

2. One of the few exceptions is Fray Angélico Chávez (1974: 205). Also see Pearce et al. 1965: 144–45.

3. Valverde may have returned from his expedition against the Comanches via the Arkansas River and over the mountain pass where the Sangre de Cristo Creek has its source. However, Valverde's account of his return to Santa Fe is not extant (A. B. Thomas 1935: 32). Janet Lecompte also suggests that Valverde may have been the source of the place-name Sangre de Cristo (1978: 34).

4. Anza's map and his account are included in A. B. Thomas (1932), facing p. 1 and p. 136, respectively. The Mascaro map is in the Map Division of the Library of Congress; a photocopy is in the History Library of the Museum of New Mexico in Santa Fe. My thanks to Michael Weber for information concerning these maps.

5. Reference to *la sierra de la sangre de Cristo* occurs in the diary of Don José María de Arce, 1818, translated by A. B. Thomas (1929*a:* 159). Most eighteenth-century Spanish colonial sources seem to use the term *Sierra Blanca* to include both the present Sierra Blanca and the Sangre de Cristo range.

6. On the outpost of the Sangre de Cristo, see A. B. Thomas (1929*a:* 158, 1929*b:* 172, 1929–1930). The date of abandonment of the outpost is established by Jacob Fowler, who camped at the site in February 1822 and estimated that the "Remains of a Spanish fort" that he found there had been occupied "about one year back" (Coues 1970: 85). The possible location of the fort is described by Chauncey Thomas (1937).

7. U.S. Geographical Surveys West of the 100th Meridian, "Part of Southwestern Colorado, Atlas sheet No. 16 (D)."

8. For instance, a memorial to the House of Representatives in 1864 concerned with the boundary between the Territories of Colorado and New Mexico, signed by New Mexico officials T. M. Galligos *(sic)* and Francisco Salazar, speaks of land between the 37th and 38th parallels of latitude and "lying east of the Sierra Madre" (Galligos and Salazar, 1864: 1).

9. My thanks to Marianne Stoller for calling my attention to this reference.

10. This work was written by F. C. Nims, general passenger agent for the Denver and Rio Grande from 1880 to 1884. It was reprinted by the Museum of New Mexico Press in 1980.

11. This work was copyrighted and apparently written by S. K. Hooper, general passenger and ticket agent.

12. Fray Andrés García, resident friar at Laguna Pueblo, 15 March 1773, in Archives of the Archdiocese of Santa Fe (AASF), Book of Accounts 84 (box 11), Laguna Inventory.

13. The Abiquiú reference is found in AASF, Loose Documents, 1856, No. 12 (quoted in Ahlborn 1968: 129). The Río Chiquito reference occurs in the will of José Guadalupe Vigil in 1886, Taos County Records in the State of New Mexico Records Center and Archives (microfilm roll 4, frame 1048).

14. Another term for the image of Christ crucified is *la Misericordia,* the "divine mercy." This term and the symbolism of the living cross of Our Lord of Esquípulas, also popular in New Mexico, indicate the merciful and life-sustaining significance of this image.

15. Bandelier 1893: 397; Adams and Chávez 1956: 71. Domínguez notes: "Still others (fields) are irrigated from the Nambe River, which is very scanty by the time it reaches these parts, because everyone located beyond Nambe bleeds it *(le van sangrando)*" (Adams and Chávez).

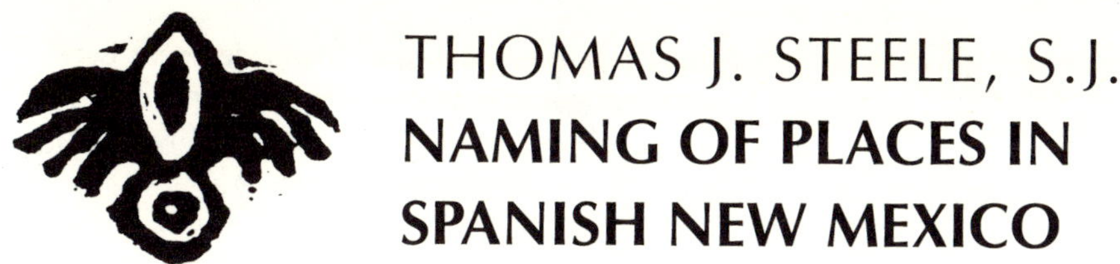

THOMAS J. STEELE, S.J.

NAMING OF PLACES IN SPANISH NEW MEXICO

FOR US TO BE HUMAN means for us to take hold of nature and do something to it that renders it no longer nature, or at least not nature in its pure form. All peoples, even the simplest, have their human strategies for dealing with the wilderness, for making a humane place of it if they are to live there. I would like in this essay to explore a very interesting strategy used in bygone years by the New Mexican Spanish: their practice of giving names to natural locations and thereby elevating them from the natural world into their Spanish cultural world.

Scholars have offered various interpretations of the vertical connection between man and God, the angels, and the saints that has been set up by the cult of the santos in New Mexico (for example, Dickey 1949: 142–43, 185–86; Mills 1967: 22–23, 58–60; Mills and Grove 1956: 34–35; Steele 1974: 45–50, 84–87, 1976: 6). The santo, the painting or statue of the holy person, is a participating expression of that person's power at the place of need and enables people to ask effectively for aid in all their hopes and fears. This study treats the horizontal effects of the same devotion to the saints and the divinity, especially as it enabled the New Mexican Spanish to gain a communal sense that they controlled the space they inhabited. They named the geographical features of the landscape, the towns in which they lived, and especially the chapels in these towns, and by so doing they incorporated hitherto profane space into the sacred cosmos of order and beauty.

The Spanish space-conception is a unique one. The Spanish established colonies in which they concentrated on taking over and Christianizing the Indians, gathering them into the Spanish society (on a lower level, of course), and exploiting them. There were very few Spanish settlements founded in vacant areas except where there were precious metals, and even then the Spanish imported Indians into the area to work the mines. Consequently, influenced by this close contact with the native population, the Spanish for the most part could and did absorb the Indians' space-conception and could derivatively enjoy their control of the space. Of course, in places the Spanish tampered with the indigenous notion of space as dominated by a center and points in each of the four sacred directions and converted this non-Euclidean pattern into completely bounded Euclidean figures by giving land grants to each of the Indian pueblos. But the pattern-setting event of the Spanish, as regards the validity of their being where they were, was some single historic event of a land grant received, a town founded, or an *entrada* accomplished. Such an event generated an imprecise but static boundary, and beyond this static frontier was a preromantic irrational space. For although the Spanish of the sixteenth to nineteenth centuries in New Mexico were essentially temporal in their approach to the total world, they did not have as yet the post-Enlightenment notion of the dynamic temporal, the process-thinking that characterized nineteenth-century Europe and America.

So, comparing the three main New Mexican peoples—Spanish, Pueblo, and Navajo—in regard to their balance of space and time, we find that the New Mexico Spanish participate in the European tendency to value time more, although they have come to put more stress on particular space than did the Europeans of the mainstream from which they derived. The Pueblo Indians, by contrast, value space more than time; they have a rigid liturgical cycle, but it has always been subordinate to spatial considerations. The Navajo Indians, the third of the peoples, are thoroughly spatial in their approach, subordinating the temporal altogether.

By examining the two Indian peoples to clarify the context within which we may understand the Spanish, we find that the Tewa Pueblo seem to symbolize their world first and foremost as a set of events in space. Their "beginning-time" as a people lies outside of profane chronology in such a way as to be more a place than a time. The beginning-time is what happened in the sacred lake of origin, at the edge of the lake, and along the trail from the lake to the places of present residence, and the main paradigms of value are located in "the Dry Food People Who Never Did Become," the sacred beings who never existed in time at all, yet who do seem to exist in space, "in the lake." The Tewa world is constituted according to these beginning-time patterns of mountains, mesas, and shrines in each of the four directions, and within that world the temporal cycle of sacred and secular offices eternally returns upon itself and keeps itself in balance (Eggan 1972: 297; Ortiz 1969: 16 and passim, 1972: 142–43). The same remarks might be made, with differences that make no real difference, for any of the Pueblo peoples.

The Navajo mind, by contrast, has a "passion for geography [and a] preoccupation with locality"; "the idea of unrestricted motion progressing through space with only a peripheral reference to time as a significant feature of Navajo verbs" (Wyman 1962: 78).[1] The Navajos above all wish to integrate terrestrial with celestial space. They seek to validate the places they inhabit by having them appear among the pattern-setting events of the beginning-time—which, as with the Pueblos, is not historical time. Instead, for the Navajos, the beginning-time marks stages on the journeys of the whole people out of the emergence place or of the hero of some curing myth to places of illness and subsequent health, even of death and subsequent resurrection. The Navajo sandpainting seems to be the core of each major section of each curing ritual. A feature of each sandpainting is a location symbol, identifying the place of this event (the patient's present stage of being restored to health) with the place of the exemplary event (in the *agon* of the beginning-time hero). Contrasting with the fully exfoliated Navajo geography is the simple Navajo calendar, which for ritual purposes seems to be divided into only two parts—winter and summer (Dyk 1967: 213–14; Harmon 1976; Reichard 1974: 152; 84). So with both of the New Mexico Indian groups, we find a decided priority of space over time, as we do with most if not all the other Native American peoples.

Because the Spanish came into New Mexico with their religion already formed and because they were not as space-oriented as the Pueblos or especially the Navajos, they found it impossible to employ the same means of integrating the locales in which they now lived into their scheme of things. They had come into the middle of a world of things unknown. First of all, there was no continuity with the former world they had known in Mexico, for the new foundation of 1598 was separated by hundreds of miles from the former extent of European control. Second, the various portions of the colony were separated from one another by the topographical divisions of the terrain: hills and mountains separated one river valley from the next; impassable cañons separated one segment of a valley from another.

The first phases of the problem may have, in a way, been the easiest, for the Spanish seem to have ridden piggyback on the Pueblo domination of space as they rode piggyback on the Pueblo people economically. Most of the earlier Spanish foundations were in direct connection with Pueblo towns—like the first capital of San Gabriel, which simply took over the Tewa village of Yunque, old San Juan—or developed in connection with the *encomienda* arrangements that the first governor-general, Juan de Oñate, made for his captains, giving each of them a pueblo or a part of a pueblo to govern and exploit. Up to the middle of the eighteenth century, the Pueblo Indians were the majority of the settled New Mexican population, and the space-conception depended on them.

After the colony had been resettled fifty years or so following the Pueblo Rebellion of 1680–1693—largely brought on by the abuses of the encomienda system—the organizational structure of the colony began to interact with religious and demographic factors to provide a new map of New Mexico and to demand a new Spanish method of coping with space. As Donald E. Worcester and Wendell G. Schaeffer describe the Spanish colonial structure:

> In considering Iberian colonial administration, it is necessary to emphasize a highly significant aspect—the dual nature of royal control. There were, in fact, two branches of the kings' imperial organizations, each with special fields of endeavor, but with overlapping duties. On the one hand was the branch charged

> with managing the political, military, and economic affairs of the colonies. On the other was the religious establishment, responsible for the spiritual instruction of colonist and native, the education and indoctrination necessary for the various levels of society, and the physical welfare of the sick and needy. (1971: 114)

Now whereas the Anglo-American frontier stayed roughly a thousand miles long from north to south as the expansion process moved from ocean to ocean, the frontier of New Spain widened continually as it reached northward from the City of Mexico, so that at fifteen hundred miles distance it generated an edge—a ragged arc-shaped rim of Christendom—about three thousand miles in extent, from San Francisco on the Pacific coast to Tucson to Santa Fe, New Mexico, to San Antonio, Texas, and to San Miguel de los Adáes in east Texas. Weakening with the square of the slowly traveled distance from the capital, this frontier could develop and hold only by the constant achievements of the missionaries. A few Spanish settlements had resident pastors, but most of the Franciscan friars were assigned to the pueblos and most of the Spanish who did not live in the Spanish towns lived within easy reach of the churches in the pueblos. As Herbert Eugene Bolton wrote:

> The missions served also as a means of defense to the king's dominions. . . . It is significant, too, in this connection, that the Real Hacienda, or Royal Fisc, charged the expenses for presidios and missions both to the same account, the Ramo de Guerra, or "War Fund." In a report for New Spain made in 1758 a treasury official casually remarked, "Presidios are erected and missions founded in *tierra firme* whenever it is necessary to defend conquered districts from the hostilities and invasions of warlike, barbarian tribes, and to plant and extend our Holy Faith, for which purposes *juntas de guerra y hacienda* are held." It is indeed true that appropriations for missions were usually made and that permission to found missions was usually given in councils of war and finance. (1962: 10–11)[2]

Such was the situation in New Mexico: the work with the Indians, who formed the majority of the fighting force that enabled the colony to survive the hit-and-run raids of the *Indios bárbaros,* was both the chance of survival and the motive for existence of the Spanish colony in the early eighteenth century. And Henry W. Kelly has stated the other side of the coin: "The missions were the principal factors that prompted the Crown to retain hold of this region. Economically, the province was a white elephant. . . . The importance of New Mexico lay in its missions, in the royal and ecclesiastical aspirations for the conversion of the Indian" (Kelly 1940: 368; also see Chávez 1974: 175; Reeve 1961; v.1, 113).

The Franciscans took this responsibility as seriously as men would, even men of God, who knew which side their bread was buttered on and indeed knew who provided butter and bread both. The crown, working through the Ramo de Guerra, provided the bulk of the necessities for the missions' origin and year-by-year survival (from Bolton 1962: 7–8; Kelly 1940: 350–51).

But if financing for missions to the Indians was mainly governmental, support of the Spanish parishes had to come from the parishioners. So it is no wonder that of the twenty-three sites staffed by friars in 1749, twenty were Indian pueblos and only three—Santa Fe, Santa Cruz, and Albuquerque—were Spanish towns.

But in spite of the seeming inequity, during this period most of the Spanish were well served by the friars; Kelly notes that "a slight sprinkling of Spanish *vecinos* [citizens] was scattered up and down the valley on isolated ranchos, which were under the jurisdiction of the nearest mission (1940: 361). During this period, the Spanish accounted for fewer than 40 percent of the Christian inhabitants of New Mexico, and four-fifths of the Spanish lived in the three towns staffed by parish priests. The scattered 20 percent of Spanish, a twelfth of the total population, lived near the pueblos and could be satisfied with the spare time of the friars there.

Not that there would not have been some objections. The Indians were not liable to the "stole fees" for marriages, baptisms, burials, and other priestly ministrations, but the Spanish and acculturated *genízaros* (Indian slaves purchased or captured from surrounding tribes and Christianized and Hispanicized) were. The latter groups may well have resented the fact of the *sínodos* going for the support of Indian Catholicism, for the support in some comfort of a friar whom the Spanish had to pay for whatever services he rendered them (Boyd 1974: 21–23; H. W. Kelly 1940: 364–65, 1941: 157; Revilla Gigedo 1875: 325). And when the usual situation was reversed and Tesuque Pueblo received the part-time services of Santa Fe's priest, the Spanish could hardly have agreed with the bland 1754 recital of Fray Manuel de San Juan Nepomuceno Trigo or the attitude that lay behind it:

> Two leagues from this mission is that of San Diego de Tesuqui, a *visita* of this capital. Its Indians sow for the father two *fanegas* of wheat and one *almud* of corn, but they sow it for him there in their pueblo, they eat the crop themselves. . . . They pay no parochial dues, but this does not cause the minister any discomfort, for these are paid by the settlers and soldiers. (Hackett 1937: v. 3, 465)[3]

But meantime the population was beginning to shift dramatically. A study of census figures for the latter half of the eighteenth century indicates that in New Mexico (excluding El Paso) the numbers of Spanish in the total population rose from about two-fifths to about two-thirds as the Pueblo population remained steady or even dropped, but that the ratio of Spanish in the only three towns with resident pastors dropped from four-fifths to one-third. Governor Alencaster warned the viceroy in 1805 that the censuses were carelessly done, it is true, but the trend was clear in its effects and it was clear to local observers such as Pedro Bautista Pino at the time (for example, Bancroft 1962: 278–80; H. W. Kelly 1940: 362–63; Kinnaird and Kinnaird 1979: 38–39; Revilla Gigedo 1875: 334; Stoller 1976: 29–32).[4]

The towns of Santa Fe, Santa Cruz, and Albuquerque were not shrinking, but as someone wisely remarked, a New Mexican Spanish town, like a desert plant, grows rapidly at first but gets only so big and then no bigger.

Meanwhile, the Franciscans lingered behind the times, gazing fondly in the rear-view mirror as events lurched unsteadily ahead, thinking that the future still lay with the pueblos and the conversion of the Indios bárbaros. Yet all around them the Spanish and the genízaros were streaming out of the three *villas reales* ("royal towns"—Santa Fe, Santa Cruz, and Albuquerque) and even out of newer towns that had become saturated—in search of unoccupied farmlands, exercising a sort of derivative Franciscanism in their development of the art of the santeros and their formation of the penitent Brotherhood of Our Father Jesus—and wondering where the friars were keeping themselves (Boyd 1974: 440–44).

And at this time, the only ecclesiastical change in the wind was the secularization of some of the New Mexican towns. In its wake, slowly, over the next half-century came a switching of many parish seats from the Indian pueblos to the growing Spanish towns in their vicinity—from Taos Pueblo to Fernando de Taos, from Sandía to Bernalillo, from Santo Domingo to Peña Blanca, from Picurís to Peñasco, from Pecos to San Miguel. The genízaros were settled in their own Spanish towns in such militarily sensitive areas as Tomé–Valencia, Abiquiú, and San Miguel del Vado, and in time many of these towns had their own diocesan-staffed parishes. There was no sudden changeover, for the supply of priests was dwindling and nice physical facilities were already available at the pueblos; but by 1829, by and large, the seculars were in the Spanish and genízaro towns, and the friars were still in place at the pueblos (Chávez 1957: 194).[5]

Granted the lack of priests to accompany them into the new settlements in the outlying regions of the colony, Spanish pioneers had all the more reason to make use of any available method to bring the previously uninhabited areas within the cosmos of Spanish order. With the shrinking Pueblo population and the diminishing relative area of Pueblo control, the Spanish could no longer rely on a derivative control exercised through their Indian allies and encapsulated in the Indian names of places. The Spanish had exercised this earlier mode of control in earlier years by retaining Indian place-names, though the name often underwent a certain "domestication" by being assimilated into Spanish sounds, syllables, and spellings, if not even to Spanish words. Thus the Navajo name for a certain cañon was *chahatquel,* meaning "wash" or "river," and the Spanish had heard it as *chaco,* "deserted"; the Navajo called some mountains *nazisetgo,* meaning "gopher water," and the Spanish had heard it as *nacimiento,* "nativity" (Chávez 1950*b;* Pearce 1955, 1965). Sometimes the game got played twice: the Spanish had taken *tat unge onwi,* "spotted dry place," from the Tewa Pueblos and turned it into "Tesuque," so the Tewa took "Tesuque" and turned it into *tay tsoon ghay,* "cottonwood tree place" (Pearce 1958: 218–19).[6] But at any rate, by borrowing Indian names the Spanish had achieved some sense that the place in question was rational, that it fitted in to a world of order; for the function of a name is not merely to denominate, it is also to dominate, as we can see from Adam's naming of the animals in the second chapter of Genesis.

But as the Spanish passed into areas beyond the vicinity of the pueblos, where they did not know or did not choose to adopt—or adapt—Indian place-names, they had a couple of ways of giving new names, which we may call intrinsic and extrinsic denomination. *Intrinsic denomination* is naming something according to its characteristics, which can be either descriptive, historical, or ethnographic. Examples of the descriptive mode would be Cuesta—the slope; La Ladera—again, the slope; Angostura—the narrows; Alameda—the cottonwood grove; Cieneguilla—the little marsh; Cebolleta—the little onions; and so on. The historical mode would include such site-names as Llano Quemado—burned prairie; Algodones—cotton fields; Atarque—dam; and so on. The ethnographic mode would cover animal names like Las Nutrias—the beavers; Pajarito—the little bird; Gallinas—wild turkeys; human designations such as Los Lunas, Los Garcías, Los Candelarias—all family names; and more general designations such as Bueyeros—ox-team drivers. Such intrinsic denominations would give the group bestowing and using the name a sense of comprehension of the place they inhabit, a certain comforting if limited sense of noetic control (Chávez 1950*a;* Pearce 1955: 206).

In Hispanic America, naming places by *extrinsic denomination* means either naming them for other places, such as Ranchos de Taos, Corrales de Alameda, Atrisco, or Santa Fe (named for the city in Granada),[7] or naming them for saints. This last method of naming is very common, of course, in New Mexico, and it is very pertinent to this discussion. If the new settlers of an area do not reach for the intrinsic intelligibility of a place and encapsulate it in a name, they can at least import some intelligibility from outside and bring it to bear on the place in question. In this connection, we might apply an old New Mexican proverb—"Rogar al santo hasta pasar el tranco" (Pray to the saint until you cross the threshold)—for a saint can by the proper invocation be gotten to make his or her power available at any place of need at least on a temporary basis. No matter how wild the wilderness, it can be Christianized (Hispanicized). Give a new and strange place the name of the saint, and the needed power will ideally continue to operate until the place of safety—the threshold of the house—is attained. But who indeed legitimizes the house and its threshold, if not the saint for whom the town is named? And if the town happens to be named intrinsically, not for a saint but for some characteristic the place possesses, what can give the town ultimate legitimacy—insertion into the ultimate order that is sacred time—but the saint for whom the village chapel has been named? Even the unparalleled Rev. Alex M. Darley got the notion pretty well in a casual remark in his 1893 *Passionists of the Southwest:* "Every Papal town has two names—a secular one, as this [Cenicero], and a sacred one, such as this of 'Jesus, Mary and Joseph' " (1968: 18).

The Spanish in eighteenth-century New Mexico would not, finally, have thought of their intellectual control over the hitherto unknown as being sufficient to tame it completely. They would have had an abiding awareness of their own low position in relation to the wider Spanish and Catholic world of church and empire that had their centers at Madrid and Rome and that mediated power to them through the viceroy and the archbishop in the City of Mexico. Rather than supposing after the manner of primitives that they knew all of real value that might be known, peasant societies tend to recognize their limitations, to admire from afar, without hope and probably without wish to imitate, the prodigies of the provincial and imperial capitals.

The peasant has a deep attachment to a special *pais* and even draws his descriptive name from it, and for someone else's nature or nobody's nature he has no use at all. "Aqui tenemos nuestro ombligo," he says, "it is here that we have our umbilicus"; and by "aqui" he means the village, and for him the village is centered on the church and inserted into one kind of sacred time—the solar cycle of the feast days of the saints—by the annual fiesta of the patron saint of the village (Simmons 1969:13). A town named Cebolleta or Las Nutrias or Los Lunas or Atrisco would have its chapel, and the chapel would inevitably be named by extrinsic denomination—San Antonio, San Pedro, Santa Clara, Nuestra Señora de Guadalupe. And the extrinsic nature of the name of the chapel would be its great strength, for it would summon a power from outside into a profane world and would thereby establish an intelligible center within the warm glow of which the entire community of villagers could feel secure. So in New Mexico the villages, one by one, were centered and inserted into the sacred calendar by naming the chapel and in many cases the village itself with the name of a sacred personage.

The village chapel was the ultimate focus of the people's lives, and the name of the chapel served as a designation of identity; the space of the village received its most profound and universal validation in the name of the saint. Since in contrast to the Indians, the Spanish attribute primacy to time rather than to space, the main function of the name of the saint is to tie the chapel and the village and the people into the liturgical cycle of the Roman Catholic church. "A cada capillita se le llega su fiestecita," runs an old *dicho*, "to every little chapel comes its little fiesta." Though the saying applies to many other things—"Every dog has his day" is not so much a statement *about* dogs as it is a statement *in terms of* dogs—the saying was phrased in terms of chapels because it was an evident truth. Every village would make the preparations for its annual fiesta as elaborate as its means would allow, arranging for the priest to arrive the evening before for vespers, decorating the chapel for mass the next morning as nicely as possible, preparing mammoth meals, staging a parade with *tirotea* (fireworks or shooting off guns), and concluding with a *baile* (dance); every year was an attempt to outdo the last.

In many villages, the fiesta mass would have been the only mass of the year. The rest of the year, the people would have been left to their own devices, trying their best to be Roman Catholics without a priest—no easy accomplishment. The annual fiesta would take care of the insertion of the village space into the solar cycle of the saints, but at a time different from the times of the other nearby villages. The lunar-solar cycle that brings Lent, Holy Week, and Easter each year keys the central common Christian feast, and on these holiest of days, only the parish centers would have enjoyed the full priestly rituals. For this special time of the year, each village without a priest would have had to manufacture a ceremony of its own. At first, the ceremony would have been a passion play, based on the stations of the cross (Steele 1978). As time went by, the central part, which earlier had been taken by a large statue of Jesus, might be played by one of the men of the village, for around the end of the eighteenth century or the beginning of the nineteenth, there originated the New Mexican Catholic *Cofradía de Nuestro Padre Jesús Nazareno.* The *Hermanos penitentes* kept New Mexico in the Christian-European orbit of religion and culture during an era when without them there was grave danger that the majority of the colony, or at least the vast majority of the newly converted genízaros, might have lapsed wholly into the barbarism that some accounts mention as having overtaken the residents of certain more isolated regions.[8]

The forty new Spanish village chapels licensed and built from 1800 to 1850 are impressive testimony to Spanish population growth; the figures for Penitente moradas, the private meeting places of the Cofradía de Nuestro Padre Jesús Nazareno, built before the end of that century would be vastly more impressive, but they cannot be quoted because they are unknown. The reenactment of the events of Holy Week—through passion plays or Penitente ceremonies—unites every village simultaneously with the greatest event in salvation history, for the figure of Christ is most powerful while going through the episodes of his unique temporal passion and death. For though Christ may have meant, when he said "Before Abraham came to be, I am," just about the same things that the Tewa Indians mean when they speak of "The Dry Food People Who Never Did Become," the central fact of Christianity is not the eternal existence of the Word but the fact that the divine did *become*—become flesh—in the matrix of time and died in that flesh within time.

In summary, the naming of Spanish New Mexican village chapels and some of the villages themselves was a mode of horizontal communication among the people, assuring them that they had a sure hold on centeredness, validation, and security because they were properly related to the absolute in life-giving power. They may have been living in some raw new village, recently wrested from the unbounded chaos of the outer darkness, but now the local habitation constructed a chapel and therefore possessed a sacred name, and in this name the people sensed that they could survive and that they should survive. And they did survive in the fullness of their humanity and their Christianity within a space that they and their saints had humanized.

NOTES

1. See also Astrov 1950; Reichard 1974: 19; and Witherspoon 1977: 49. Witherspoon also notes that objects at rest are divided into fifteen classifications according to their readiness to move or be moved (1977: 120–26). According to Karl W. Luckert, "By way of these round trips [in chantway myths] the Athapascan hunter mind laid claim to a southwestern homeland" (1975: 195).

2. Bernardo de Galvez wrote: "With respect to the supervision of the royal treasury, which his majesty prohibited to the late commanding general, Don Felipe de Neve, and his successors, you should not attend to it, but you shall have authority to issue the usual military warrants, pay the missionary stipends, the auditing and secretarial officials, troops in the field, and finally the extraordinary expenses which must of necessity be made for the operations of war" (1967: 30–31).

3. Fray Francisco Atanasio Domínguez noted a parallel at Jémez Pueblo in 1776 (Adams and Chávez 1956: 315).

4. Fray Angélico Chávez notes an extraordinary growth of Spanish population in many areas in the late eighteenth and early nineteenth centuries (1957: 201–10, 214–18). John L. Kessell remarks that the "priest-to-parishioner ratio had been thrown out of all proportion by the Hispano population spiral" (1979: 419); see also Oakah L. Jones (1979: 123–31, 164). Governor Alencaster is quoted in Simmons 1969: 187; Pedro Bautista Pino in Carroll and Haggard 1942: 50. Pino was named for a Franciscan martyr, San Pedro Bautista, hence, perhaps, some of his devotion to the friars.

5. The Franciscans did not leave as suddenly as Paul Horgan suggests in *Lamy of Santa Fe* (1975: 205).

6. Victor Turner and Edith Turner do a similar study of "Guadalupe" in *Image and Pilgrimage in Christian Culture* (1978: 89).

7. Atrisco is a version of Atlixco, near Pueblo; "Santa Fe de Granada" appears on some early maps of New Mexico.

8. Simmons (1968: 76), quoting Fray Juan Agustin de Morfi in the 1780s, Archivo General de la Nacion, Historia 25, "Desórdenes," fol. 132v. Raffaele Baldassarre, S.J., calls the Spanish around Conejos, Colorado, "this miserable people so unlearned and so superstitious" (1874–1875: 83). Also see Weigle 1976.

MARIANNE L. STOLLER

THREE CHURCH INVENTORIES FROM HISPANIC FRONTIER COMMUNITIES

AMONG THE DOCUMENTARY RECORDS AVAILABLE for the study of material culture in historic communities, few are more valuable than inventories. This has been shown to be particularly true for the Spanish Colonial period of northern New Mexico by the works of E. Boyd. Her culminating book, *Popular Arts of Spanish New Mexico* (1974), as well as many of her earlier articles, exhibits her skillful use of these (and other) documents in combination with the material remains of this historic period (see, for example, on church furnishings, pp. 68–76, and the section on inventories, pp. 341–65). She thus demonstrated the development of a local folk art, especially centered on religious objects, beginning in the late eighteenth century and continuing past the middle of the nineteenth. This combination of source materials has enormously increased our knowledge and understanding of the arts and crafts of the regional New Mexican version of Hispanic culture in the New World.

This essay offers three more inventories in translation. The first two are the earliest inventories made in their respective churches; the third is from one of those same churches, but a year later. These three inventories were chosen for examination because they represent nineteenth-century church furnishings in two frontier communities: San Miguel del Vado, the earliest Hispanic settlement on the Rio Pecos, about fifty miles southeast of Santa Fe; and Conejos, one of the first settlements in the San Luis Valley and site of the first church in what is now the state of Colorado, along the headwaters of the Rio Grande about 125 miles north of Santa Fe.[1]

Inventories, first and foremost, are records of what is present in a given place at a given time. For those who use them to reconstruct culture history, the (often unstated) assumption is made that those material objects documented in such inventories are instruments and symbols of other, nonmaterial aspects of the culture under study. Like archaeologists, ethnohistorians or art historians hope to deduce something about a people's way of life from the material goods they possessed. A specialized inventory, such as these church inventories, may be a window into a particular aspect of a culture. E. Boyd, José E. Espinosa (1967), and others who have used church inventories in combination with artifactual collections and a variety of other documentary sources have thus been able to reconstruct much of the religious beliefs, rituals, and values of Hispanic culture in New Mexico from the seventeenth through the nineteenth centuries in general, as well as the origins of the regional religious art that was their primary concern. Used also to interpret the religious history of the specific church inventoried, as Stephen F. de Borhegyi (1953) and E. Boyd (1974: 68–76) did for El Santuario de Chimayó, considerable insight into the pervasive attitudes and patterns of participation in religious life may be gained for the community or local area. The comparative study of such cumulative data then provides researchers with a variety of additional problems to pursue, such as the reconstruction of more generalized histories that reveal the dynamics of change in sociocultural institutions over time and space, or controlled inquiries into particular problems of change or adaptation in specific situations.

In selecting the church inventories presented here for examination, I anticipated that they would share many resemblances since they would reflect, I thought, the frontier character of their respective communities. A brief summary of the history of each of these communities and their churches will be presented, followed by their inventories and a discussion of the differences and similarities they provide and the possible reasons for these. In conclusion, I shall return to some considerations on the characteristics of inventories.

THE SETTLEMENT OF SAN MIGUEL DEL VADO

A little over twenty miles down the Rio Pecos from Pecos Pueblo, at the "place called El Vado [The Ford]," Lorenzo Márquez and fifty-one other heads of families, all from Santa Fe, were placed in possession of their new lands on November 26, 1794, by Antonio José Ortiz, principal alcalde of Santa Fe. Gov. Fernando Chacón had, the previous day, honored these people's request for the land that became the San Miguel del Vado grant. By 1803, when Pedro Bautista Pino, "Justice of the Second Note," established their individual allotments of house sites and garden lands (the remainder of the land to be reserved for others and the grazing land to be held in common), their numbers had swelled to fifty-eight families.[2] Among the original grantees were thirteen Genízaros (Hispanicized Indians), hence San Miguel has been called an Genízaro settlement by various authorities (Boyd 1971: 17–18; Cabeza de Baca 1954: 76–77; Chávez 1957: 205; Hayes, 1974: 17; Simmons 1968: 151). In the first couple of decades of settlement, other Indians, especially some Comanches but including some Pecos Pueblos, assumed Genízaro status, as Chávez phrases it, by joining the community, and others did the same through intermarriage (Chávez 1957: 205; Márquez 1973: chart 7). The original grantees were directed to live at Pecos Pueblo while they prepared homes and brought the land under cultivation; church records reveal the first statements of residence at El Vado in 1798 (according to Kessell 1979: 418) or 1799 (according to Chávez 1957: 205, 221, 232).

E. Boyd did some research on the history and architecture of San Miguel del Vado and concluded that "the plaza gives a sort of textbook course in New Mexico adobe architecture over a period of some 125 years" (1971: 26).[3] More recently, Kessell has provided rich detail on the early years of its growth; he attributes the demise of Pecos Pueblo (totally abandoned by 1838) to the establishment of this outpost of Hispanic settlers at The Ford. San Miguel became the "port of entry" from the east to Santa Fe and rapidly dominated trade with the Plains tribes (Kessell 1979: 355, 410, and the entire last chapter of this history of Pecos).

Grow San Miguel did. By 1803, its sister settlement, San José del Vado, three miles upstream, had been established (Pino allotted lands there, too; Carroll and Haggard 1942: 8). In 1820, there were 735 people, and in Gov. Antonio Narvona's census of 1827, the population was up to 2,893 with a number of smaller communities, including La Cuesta (the present-day Villanueva), founded downriver from San Miguel (Boyd 1971: 19; Carroll and Haggard 1942: 88; Chávez 1957: 205; Kessell 1979: 419; the latter figure undoubtedly included all of the settlements on the grant and not just the plaza of San Miguel itself as Boyd seemed to assume).

The opening of the Santa Fe Trail in 1822, following Mexican independence from Spain, made San Miguel a true port of entry and turned it into a virtual boom town. San Miguel was the first real settlement reached after hundreds of miles on the trail, and every known account of the trail caravans from the 1820s through the 1840s (and later, too, although the rise of Las Vegas soon diminished San Miguel's status) has something to say about it, though often in none-too-flattering words (Boyd 1971 and Kessell 1979 both quote from various accounts, and Earnshaw et al. 1973 include many more). It must have been a raw, raucous town when the caravans arrived; many accounts report the fandangos that were staged for their benefit. Often a wagon train stayed several days since the wagons were repacked to minimize the number on which customs duties would be charged when they reached Santa Fe, or the goods were shifted to mules and taken over Galisteo Mesa to intersect with the Camino Real and thence to Chihuahua, bypassing customs in Santa Fe altogether (see especially Bloom 1945 and Escudero's note in Carroll and Haggard 1942: 66). Most accounts also remark on the kindnesses of the people of San Miguel; George Wilkins Kendall, the chronicler of the Texas–Santa Fe Expedition of 1841, whose members were arrested by Mexican soldiers and spent many days in the jail at San Miguel before being marched down to Chihuahua, had particularly flattering words for the women (as opposed to the men) of the town (1966: 312).

The church at San Miguel, raised on a platform of earth and built of stone and adobes with two towers, is often mentioned in travelers' accounts and must have been the first landmark of the town they sighted. It was already started, so he said, when Fray Francisco Bragado, stationed at Pecos Pueblo, petitioned the bishop of Durango, on December 17, 1804, for a chapel license at San Miguel. He wrote on behalf of "*Los Yndios Genisaros de la nueva Poblason del Bado,*" claiming their need to have a chapel because of the day-long and dangerous journey to the mission church of Nuestra Señora de los Angeles at Pecos. The bishop granted the license on February 22, 1805, and it was endorsed by Gov. Joaquin Real Alencaster in Santa Fe by April 30 of that year.[4] El Vado was to be a *visita* of the Pecos mission. Kessell provides evidence that the building of the imposing church was not always done gladly by the citizens, but it was finished in 1811 (1979: 424–26).

With many more people at San Miguel and San José than were left at Pecos, José Cristóbal Guerrero, an Genízaro of Comanche descent who earlier had collected funds for building the church, now petitioned the bishop to have the Pecos priest, Fray Manuel García del Valle, moved to San Miguel, and on February 6, 1812, this request was granted (Chávez 1957: 74). Del Valle stayed until 1818 when Fray Francisco Bragado was reassigned. Bragado died there in early 1825 and was buried in the sanctuary of the church (Kessell 1979: 448, 452–54). Fray Juan Caballero Toril soon replaced him, and on February 28, 1828, Caballero made the church inventory included here. This inventory appears to have been Caballero's last act there for, four days later, Gov. Manuel Armijo was pushing him out of New Mexico since he was a Spaniard and the Mexican Congress, late in 1827, had ordered all Iberians out of the new republic (Chávez 1957: 98). Fray Teodoro Alcina and Fray José de Castro, both "too old and too much needed in priest-poor New Mexico" to be expelled, tended San Miguel–Pecos for the rest of 1828, the last Franciscans to do so (Kessell 1979: 454). Thereafter, secular (diocesan) priests were assigned, often journeying out from Santa Fe. In 1833, only five years after Caballero's inventory, Bishop Zubiría found the church in "very sad condition" on his visitation (Chávez 1957: 209).

In his last chapter, Kessell presents a vivid picture of the involved political and religious intrigues occurring in New Mexico over the first quarter of the nineteenth century following the beginnings of secularization of the churches and Mexican independence. He suggests that the continual prominence of Genízaros in official documents concerning San Miguel was a deliberate ploy "in order to win concessions from the church and state" (1979: 417). The use of Genízaros of Comanche origin (for example, Guerrero) was a constant reminder to political authorities of the benefits of maintaining good relations with this tribe following the peace treaty of 1785 extracted by Governor Bautista de Anza (Kessell 1979: 428–39).

Some such explanation is called for since, as Kessell (1979) and Márquez (1973) both found, the frequency with which Genízaros are mentioned is quite out of proportion with the number of them actually living at San Miguel. It is possible that the Franciscan priests were using the Genízaros as a justification for their own presence in San Miguel. Since, from their beginnings in New Mexico, the Franciscans were subsidized by the Crown of Spain to serve the Indians and not the Hispanic settlers, it behooved them to maintain their touchstone with Indians—even Hispanicized ones—even after that subsidy had dwindled and disappeared. This was their forlorn hope of retaining a hold on this mission field. No doubt, too, this explains why the facade was maintained that Pecos was the *cabecera* (parish church). Chávez emphatically states in his notation on the Caballero inventory that San Miguel "is still a chapel under Pecos mission" (1957: 98). We know, however, that from 1812 forward, the priests were actually in residence at San Miguel.

THE SETTLEMENT OF CONEJOS

In 1854, years after the last Franciscan priest in New Mexico had died, a few years after the area had become part of the United States, and three years after New Mexico had finally been assigned a bishop of its own, a small group of settlers from around Ojo Caliente established themselves on the north bank of the Rio Conejos ten miles or so upstream from its juncture with the Rio Grande. Since 1832, when a grant of land—to be known as the Guadalupe or Conejos grant—was allegedly made to a group of petitioners from El Rito above the Rio Chama who found land and water insufficient to support their families there, Hispanos had been trying to colonize the headwaters of the Rio Grande in the San Luis Valley of Colorado (Stoller 1980 briefly reviews the history of this land grant and, in 1979*b*, the history of settlement).

Throughout the Spanish Colonial period, this high, intermontane valley had been regarded as the domain of the Utes with whom colonial authorities had maintained shifting, but predominately peaceful, alliances (Jefferson et al. 1972: 4–10). Changes in the Mexican administration's policy and the increasing population spread from the Taos and lower Rio Chama areas combined to cause a deterioration of Spanish-Ute relations beginning in the 1830s (Jefferson et al. 1972: 11). Would-be colonizers on the Conejos grant were chased off by the Navajos, the Utes' new allies. Still, the long tradition of friendly interpersonal relations between Hispanos and Utes prevailed sufficiently for a small group of settlers from El Rito, under the leadership of Atanacio Trujillo, an interpreter and trader with the Utes, to establish themselves in 1849 at Rincones, a few miles east from the later Conejos plaza (according to a manuscript in the Conejos church records). With the coming of American administration, and especially the founding of a U.S. Army post, Fort Massachusetts, on the east side of the valley in 1852, colonists felt assured enough of protection from Indian raids to begin in earnest the settlement of this northernmost Hispanic frontier.

Although Conejos is often given primacy as the oldest settlement in the San Luis Valley on the western side of the Rio Grande, in fact there were several others in the general vicinity that predate it by a few years—Rincones (already mentioned), La Servilleta, Los Cerritos, and possibly San Rafael. In August 1854, twelve men came to reconnoiter an area to settle; they returned in October of that year accompanied, apparently, by their families, and by Maj. Lafayette Head who became the Ute agent for the Valley. These colonizers settled on the north bank of the Rio Conejos, calling their settlement the Plaza of Guadalupe. Finding that the region flooded badly in the spring, the settlers moved to the higher south bank in 1856; this plaza was called Conejos (C. L. Gibson 1932–1933: 349/10; Velásquez 1957).

Streams of people must have migrated north between roughly 1850 and 1860 because Charles Beaubien, the U.S. census taker, counted 1,512 people there in the latter year (Eighth U.S. Census). By then, plazas and placitas had been founded as far north on the Rio Grande as present-day Del Norte and over La Garita Mountains in the mouth of El Carnero Canyon, as well as along Rio Conejos and Rio San Antonio. Colorado was made a territory in 1861 and became a state in 1876. All of the area just described became one of the original counties with Conejos as the county seat, a distinction it still retains. By 1878, the first contingent of Anglo settlers—a Mormon colony—had arrived in the southern part of the county; Anglos had established themselves on the west bank of the Rio Grande at Del Norte six years earlier (Morgan 1950; Richmond 1973). The Utes were soon exiled from the Valley. By 1870, the population of this huge area (approximately 2.5 million acres were claimed as the Conejos grant) was up to about 2,500 people (Ninth U.S. Census).

The settlements prospered. At the foot of the San Juan Mountains, they had excellent grazing lands, and the sheep industry flourished especially after the Denver and Rio Grande Railroad reached the area at the end of the 1870s. Earlier in that decade, the opening of gold and silver mines on the western side of the San Juan Mountains turned the northern settlements into trade and transportation centers. Although there was rapidly increasing Anglo migration and preemption of grant lands in the last two decades of the century, up until the end of that time at least, the Hispano population retained political control and shared economic rewards in their areas of original settlement. Increasing land loss, decline of the sheep market, and grazing restrictions imposed with the absorption of much of the mountain land into National Forest, however, lessened their political and economic influence after the 1890s.

Conejos did not have to wait as long for a church and a priest as San Miguel del Vado did. Indeed, considering the paucity of priests to serve the more populous New Mexico villages, it is rather surprising that Bishop Jean Baptiste Lamy of Santa Fe authorized the parish on June 10, 1858, and promptly assigned a priest there. The distance of almost a hundred miles from either Abiquiú or Arroyo Hondo, the two closest parishes, may have been the main reason (Stauter 1958: 5), plus the promising prosperity of the area and the soon-to-be-realized threat of Protestant prosyletizing (see Stoller et al. 1982). In 1857 or 1858, according to a diary kept by Rev. Gabriel Ussel, one of Lamy's imported European priests, serving at Arroyo Hondo, he and Vicar-General Joseph P. Machebeuf (later the first bishop of Colorado) visited Conejos, gave the people permission to build a church, which they completed that summer, and promised a priest (Stauter 1958: 5–6; there is some confusion about the dates).

Don Vicente Saturino Montaño, Mexican-born and a member of Padre Antonio José Martínez's seminary "prep" school in Taos even though he was an ordained priest when he arrived in New Mexico in 1834, was sent to Conejos (Chávez 1957: 260, 1981: 44; Stauter 1958: 6). Montaño's main claim to fame is that he kept no church records—a fact attested to by Lamy himself when he visited there on July 22, 1860, and a proclivity that may have caused Montaño trouble before.[5] The first Conejos inventory presented here was made in December 1859 by Ussel, newly assigned as *cura* of the Taos parish whose famous Padre Martínez had been suspended from that role (six months later he would be excommunicated by Bishop Lamy; Chávez 1981: 148). A month later, Montaño had left Conejos, and newly ordained Don José Miguel Vigil became the pastor; he stayed until 1866 when Don Miguel Rolli (or Michael Rolly) was assigned (Stauter 1958: 10, 12). Rolli, like Ussel, was one of Lamy's French compatriots. Stauter says of him: "not caring to learn a third language [English] in addition to his native French and acquired Spanish, he returned to New Mexico" (1958: 12). Father Salvatore Personè of the Neapolitan Jesuits, who arrived at Conejos in December 1871 to accept the parish, was less kind about Rolli as pastor, noting that "almost no one used to go to confession to him" (Stoller et al. 1982). The Neapolitan Jesuits administered the huge parish from 1871 to 1920 when the Theatine Fathers took it over (Stauter 1958: 26).

Accounts of the first church of Our Lady of Guadalupe vary. Horgan (1975: 258–59) says the chapel was "built as a *jacal* [vertical logs chinked with mud]—open to the sky, an enclosure of walls made from slim cottonwood stakes with bindings of salt-cedar branches." Stauter (1958: 6) says it was a sixteen-by-thirty-foot jacal with four large cedar posts at the corners and smaller posts close together in between with the tops all pointed and large logs fitted over the corner posts for roof supports, the whole plastered with adobe and having a tamped earthen floor. Oral history was divided: some said it was made of cottonwood logs placed upright and plastered, while others said it was of adobe surrounded by jacal palisades (C. L. Gibson 1932–1933: 349/2). Whatever the crude structure was, Vigil immediately set his parishioners to work building a proper foundation and a large adobe church. It was built around the existing structure, which was then demolished, a custom followed for Lamy's cathedral in Santa Fe years later (Horgan 1975: 359). When Lamy again visited Conejos, on July 22, 1862, he reported that the walls were up to ten feet in height, and the structure was usable when he returned to dedicate it on the feast of Our Lady of Guadalupe, December 12,

1863 (Conejos parish records; also Stauter 1958: 10–11). It still had an earthen floor however, because in their first year there (1872), the Jesuits added a board floor to the church and sacristry (Stoller et al. 1982).

DISCUSSION OF THE INVENTORIES

Comparing the inventories of Conejos with that of San Miguel immediately raises the question of how useful it is to consider them reflective of their frontier situation. The church at San Miguel had been in existence for twenty-five years by the time it was inventoried; its structure had been complete for fourteen. The Conejos church had existed for only three years; its structure was temporary. The community of San Miguel del Vado had been established for at least twenty-eight years; Conejos for only six. Geographically, politically, and socially they were both still outposts, but to what extent do their churches reflect the frontier qualities of "rough and ready," improvisation, and making do with what is at hand?

As a reflection of a religious community, the inventory of the church of San Miguel has no more of a frontier quality, and perhaps less, than do most other churches in New Mexico for the same period. In fact, it is unusually well provided for in terms of the necessary religious accouterments for the performance of church rituals, vestments for the priests, and ornaments for the interior decoration of the building, albeit in Caballero's judgment some items are old or worn or not of the most appropriate material or refinement of appearance. Given their intertwined histories, it might be expected that San Miguel was the recipient of vestments, ornaments, and church goods from the old mission church of Pecos. This must remain a possibility, although a comparison of this inventory with Domínguez's descriptions of Pecos's possessions in 1776 does not provide any obvious correspondences (Adams and Chávez 1956: 210–11). Caballero was careful to mention those things that came from Pecos, but since he had only served at San Miguel for three years, it might be assumed that he was unaware of the origin of some of the things. The only likely possibilities are the "four oval-shaped paintings," but since he specifies neither their subjects nor technique, they cannot be definitely linked to the "Eight ordinary old oil paintings" of Domínguez's record. Some of the venerations are the same—Jesus of Nazareth, Saint Anthony, Our Lady of Sorrows, and Our Lady of Guadalupe—but whereas these are represented in paintings at Pecos, they are three-dimensional images at San Miguel and, of course, are among the most popular venerations in all of the nineteenth-century Hispanic communities of New Mexico. It is known that the treasured image of the patroness of Pecos, Our Lady of Porciúncula of the Angels, was entrusted by the departing Pueblo Indians to the new settlers of the Spanish village of Pecos (Adams and Chávez 1956: 210, n. 3; Hayes 1974: 18). Perhaps Spanish Pecos inherited other things, too, and since Pecos Pueblo still had some inhabitants in 1828, its church's possessions were probably still kept there as the above painting clearly was.

The inventory probably reflects the contact this outpost community had with the United States via the Santa Fe Trail. The number of mirrors, the kinds of fabrics, and the amount of metal, especially the door with iron pivots, are all materials in such scarce supply by the end of the Spanish regime that they must have been the result of trade to appear in such comparative abundance. At Conejos, the window panes and bronze and brass crucifixes also signify the Anglo-American commercial presence.

Caballero at San Miguel, unlike Domínguez at Pecos, does not specify whether paintings and statues are imported, or of oil, and so forth. There seems good reason, therefore, to assume that all the images he itemizes, except the engravings but including the altar screen, were the products of New Mexican santeros. This assumption can be further strengthened by two other kinds of evidence. Bishop Zubiría, during his visitation in 1833, scorned the local folk art (Boyd 1974: 363), and this may be why he deplored the condition of the church at San Miguel. Further, several of the Santa Fe Trail accounts and those of other visitors to San Miguel provide descriptions of the church and its decorations (for example, Bloom 1945: 51). Kendall, incarcerated at San Miguel, describes a procession apparently held to solicit divine aid in warding off an invasion by the miserable Texans who kept straggling into town. First came the priest in the procession, then two musicians flanked by children,

> then came the four men bearing the car, the patron saint in a sitting posture in front, and his head, either from being hung on a pivot or from having become loose in some way, bowing and bobbing to the multitude like the figures of Chinese mandarins in some of the tea shops. . . . On the same platform, and immediately behind the figure I have just described, stood the Virgin, dressed in Pink Satin and spangles, as stiff and inanimate as wood and wax could make her (1966: 362).

The first figure, from Kendall's description, may have been a bulto of Jesus, articulated so that it could be placed in different positions; the Virgin, of wood and wax, is undoubtedly in the local santero tradition for the gesso and tempera paint on wood could certainly look waxlike from Kendall's distance.

Caballero describes the statue of the patron saint, together with his clothing and attributes, in detail in the inventory. A bulto of San Miguel, now in the collections of the Taylor Museum in Colorado Springs, Colorado, and shown in Figure 1, is said to have come from the church of San Miguel del Vado where it stood on the main altar. It was in the Alice Bemis Taylor collection, acquired by her from the Santa Fe dealer G. L. Seligman, probably in the 1920s or 1930s. It is approximately twenty-nine inches tall, on a green base; the right arm, which held a metal sword, was broken and has been replaced at an awkward angle. The chain, affixed to the extraordinary winged devil, appears to be of commercial manufacture. It is very possible that it was a later addition; the left hand could well have held the balance scales Caballero lists. The helmet follows closely the description in the inventory, with white, blue, and green stones and a dove on top, but the plumes are missing. The figure together with the legend of San Miguel is more thoroughly described in Mitchell A. Wilder and Edgar Breitenbach (1943: pl. 28). The relative sophistication of the carving, especially in the posture and detail of clothing, may have prompted the dating of it to the eighteenth century (Taylor Museum Catalogue No. 1599). We can only wish that E. Boyd's opinion of its date and possible maker had been recorded. Certainly there is good reason to assume that this is the San Miguel of the 1828 inventory.

The Conejos inventories, in contrast to that of San Miguel, show a very sparsely furnished church—what one might expect in a new frontier community. Only the minimal necessities for celebrating Catholic rituals are present. Conspicuously absent are any paintings or statues except for the three "images of the crucified" in the 1860 inventory, and their materials—bronze and brass—demonstrate that they are not of local manufacture. It is strange indeed that no image of the Patroness, Our Lady of Guadalupe, is present. Does the newness and remoteness of the church and village explain the lack of ornaments? According to local legend, an image of Our Lady of Guadalupe was carried by the pioneers seeking a place to settle; the mule transporting the image balked, refusing to move until its owner vowed to erect a church on the spot (Pascual 1958: 1). Other folk accounts of the original settlements mention the settlers bringing images of their patrons with them (for example, the Silva diary, published by Richmond 1973).

It seems very likely that New Mexican–made retablos and bultos were carried into the San Luis Valley by the early settlers. A few have been collected there (some are in the Woodward collection, now at the Adams State College Museum, and were identified by Boyd), and a few remain in family collections. It would seem that the most logical explanation for the absence of such images in the church inventories is that they had been banned from display. Zubiría's condemnations of the local santos were apparently shared by Lamy. Chávez discusses a letter from Padre Martínez to Bishop Lamy written on March 29, 1858, complaining about the sermons of the priests at Arroyo Hondo, as well as about those of Don Eulogio Ortiz at Taos, in which the local images were derided (1981: 147). One of the priests at Arroyo Hondo at this time was Gabriel Ussel. Even if works by the New Mexican santeros had been present in the Conejos church, Ussel would not have been likely to record them.

Despite the growth of the community in Conejos after these inventories were made, and the demonstration of the people's dedication to their faith by erecting a large church, the ornamentation of it remained very sparse. Not only did the Jesuits have to add a floor twelve years later, but they also added "candlesticks, flower vases, engravings and other ornaments" to the altar. There was a statue of the Patroness, for she was carried in a procession on her feast day in 1872, but whatever the statue looked like, the Jesuit priests found it unsatisfactory for they soon purchased another from "the States" (Stoller et al. 1982).

In sum, it may be said of these inventories that they reveal more of the religious history, and of the events in ecclesiastical administration, than they do of the geographical, social, and economic statuses of their respective churches or communities. That both San Miguel and Conejos were frontier settlements does not account for their similarities or differences. That they were founded more than fifty years apart—and that those intervening years were momentous ones in Southwestern history—matters only in a general way. What does seem important is that the San Miguel church was the recipient of the Franciscan mission tradition of church building and decorations, fading though the Franciscans were. Conejos, on the other hand, reflected all the turmoil and neglect of secularization and the effects of the new order introduced by Lamy with its suppression of the arts of the native santeros. Conejos was the poorer for these changes.

ON INVENTORIES

In conclusion, I offer a few remarks on the characteristics of church inventories from Hispanic New Mexico. Many things could be pointed out about them, and they could be studied for many different purposes. Most of the observations I offer here will be readily recognized by others who have worked with these inventories, but they may be helpful to future researchers.

The purposes for which inventories were created must be considered. Very obviously, the church inventories were primarily records of identification for transaction purposes; they are documents of accountability as the responsibility for the things listed is shifted from one agency or individual to another. Although I am unaware of any directive that so specifies, it is apparent from archival sources that inventories were to be prepared by the priest who was leaving a church to be given to the priest succeeding him. They were also prepared by or for church authorities (such as the Franciscan visitors like Domínguez, or the bishops) on the occasion of their official visits to a mission or church. They may have been a sort of shopping list for such individuals, showing them what kinds of material supplies were needed and allowing them to gauge the dedication and affluence of the parishioners.

The inventories also inform us of concepts of ownership and property. Evidently, they reveal the material items that are thought of as owned by the church in a particular community and not by the ecclesiastical agency (the order or diocese) or by the particular agent (the priest). The punctiliousness with which Fray Juan Caballero had every local official sign the San Miguel inventory suggests that there was some anxiety either over ownership or over the shift in responsibility—another clue to the tensions of the times between the Franciscans and the secular priests, and between Spaniards and Mexicans. It can also be pointed out that the church building itself is not included in the inventories but that certain pieces of its architecture, such as window panes, doors, and locks, are. Again, these provide interesting glimpses into how material property was conceptualized: what is considered separable and what integral.

After examining many inventories in the archival records, it becomes apparent that there is a considerable degree of standardization in the language used for descriptive purposes as well as the overall format in which things are listed. The three inventories presented here exhibit these characteristics. In other words, the inventories are forms, and the researcher soon comes to expect to find items entered in a certain order and described in a certain way. Departures from the norm—the lack of any images in the Conejos church, for example—are likely to signal exceptional circumstances or conditions.

Finally, the language of description used in inventories provides other kinds of clues as to how people in a given cultural tradition conceptualize material qualities. What are the significant attributes by which objects are to be identified and described? Again, examination of the inventories reveals that the qualities of number, location, material of manufacture, color, and condition of wear are the attributes most commonly used. Size, in terms of specific units of measurement, is very rarely specified; its place is very commonly taken by location ("in the sacristry") and by relationship of one object to another ("on the side altar under the crucifix").[6] Form is not always used as a descriptive category, nor is the technique of manufacture. The social origin of an artifact, however, is often conscientiously recorded: an amice was given by Don Lorenzo Márquez, for example. Most rare of all is to be told who actually made the object.

The information that is missing, the questions that students from other time periods and other cultural traditions want to know, provide the challenges in cultural reconstructions that scholars like E. Boyd have shown us ways to discover and to answer.

NOTES

1. I am grateful to J. Richard Salazar for the initial translation of the San Miguel inventory. William Wroth also checked sections of it, and access to a working glossary of textile terms compiled by Joe Ben Wheat was most helpful for textile terms; I thank both of these scholars, too. The Conejos inventories were translated by Rev. Thomas J. Steele, S.J.; they are also published in both Spanish and English, with a schematic drawing of the altar vessels and extensive annotation, as Appendix A in Stoller et al. 1982. Timothy Fuller, editor of The Colorado College Studies series permitted me to use the English translation of these inventories. Years ago, Rev. A. Bonet gave me access to the Conejos Parish church records, and I am pleased to acknowledge his help.

2. Surveyor General of New Mexico, Spanish Archives of New Mexico, series I, file 119 (microfilm), New Mexico State Records Center and Archives, Santa Fe.

3. In 1973, E. Boyd also served as a consultant and adjunct professor to my class of students from The Colorado College on the Ethnohistory of the Southwest, sharing her enormous knowledge especially with the four students whom she directed in additional research on San Miguel. Earnshaw et al. (1973) is the result.

4. Archives of the Archdiocese of Santa Fe, Loose Documents, Missions (microfilm), 1828, No. 12, New Mexico State Records Center and Archives, Santa Fe.

5. Chávez (1957) lists one Vicente Saturino Montaño in his appendix of diocesan clergy and in the index, although some of the references—including one in 1849 where he was ordered to make a record, and may not have, at Isleta—are to José Vicente Montaño. In his 1981 book on Padre Martínez, Chávez says there were two Montaños, both attending Martínez's school, one name José Vicente and the other Vicente Saturino. Efforts to straighten out these identities have so far been futile.

6. Land measurements followed the same pattern of using relationship to others' plots or to natural features rather than a system of arbitrary, abstract measures. See Van Ness and Van Ness 1980: 9.

APPENDIX A

San Miguel del Vado Chapel Inventory, 1828[1]

Inventory of the articles and goods belonging to the church and sacristy of the chapel of the administration of San Miguel del Bado completed by its parish priest the Reverend Father General Fray Juan Caballero Toril, who did not find one [inventory] at the time of his arrival, which specified that which was at the chapel. This [inventory] includes that which has been added during the time of his administration and that which has been borrowed from the mission of Santa Maria de los Angeles de Pecos. It will also aid the priests who will succeed me. Completed February 28, 1828 before the Constitutional Alcalde Josef Miguel Sanchez and Tomas Sena as follows:

Goods in the Sacristy. First

One gilded chalice with the Paten and small spoon.

item—a plate with its vessels [cruets for wine and water], all of silver.

item—a silver censer with a boat of copper and a metal spoon *escanades*[2] which until now has served its good purpose.

item—a white cape adorned with lace and a silver brooch.

item—a white chasuble with silver braid, white, with its stole, maniple, chalice cloth, burse with corporals and corporals with pall.

item—a red chasuble with bottom of green velvet, flowered, trimmed with ribbons of flowered silk, stole, maniple, chalice cloth, and burse of corporals of the same [that is, all of the same color].

item—a chasuble of violet satin with bottom of *Yo.*[a], trimmed with white ribbons with stole, maniple, chalice cloth, and burse of corporals [all] of the same [color], with corporals and pall.

item—a chasuble of black velvet, extremely worn, trimmed with gold, with its stole, maniple, chalice cloth, and burse of corporals [all] of the same [color].

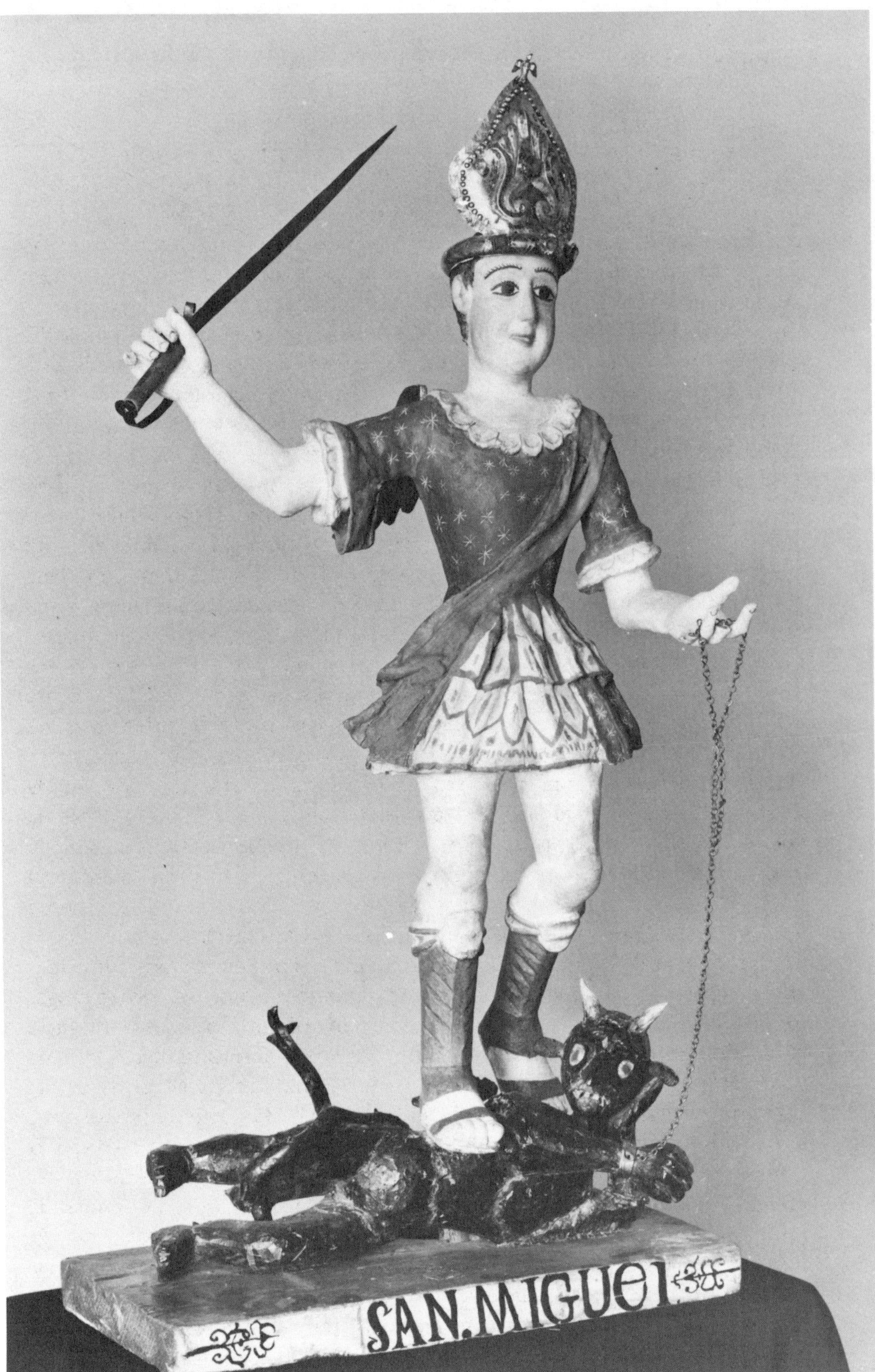

FIGURE 1
Bulto of San Miguel, patron saint of San Miguel del Vado. (Taylor Museum Collection 1599, Colorado Springs Fine Arts Center.)

item—a white satin frontal, with gold braid, rude, fringed with silk threads of various colors, and its altar-cloth of the same.

item—a frontal with its altar-cloth of various colors, old.

item—two white linen albs with their amices.

item—two white linen altar-cloths, extensively worn.

item—two *tovajias,* silver lined, both worn.

item—a violet satin altar-cloth, violet lined, and fringed with silk threads of various colors.

item—a surplice, well cared for.

item—an umbrella, very old.

item—a cincture of blue satin, laced with gold trim.

item—a small silver reliquary with its burse.

item—some scissors which were donated during my time and a firmer chisel.

item—two satin vestments belonging to San Miguel; one violet and the other the color of the sky.

item—two old *manosejos* and two purificators.

item—a wooden box for the hosts and a jar, silver-leafed, for the hosts for the laity with a smaller box for the blessed salt.

item—container for holy-water of copper with the lash [strap] of iron and *sopo* of wood.[3]

Note: that which was replaced during the time of the said Father Minister was primarily an altar-cloth of muslin batiste; an alb of fine linen with a batiste of the same; an amice of the same kind with rose colored ribbon, given by Don Lorenzo Márquez.

item—a violet frontal with its lined pall *en contencies* and trimmed with white ribbon given by Don José Maria Alarid.

item—a small white cloth for the communion rail, with its trim, given by Doña Viviana Gutíerrez.

item—a coverlet which was given by the priest to serve as a carpet during feast days.

item—a statue of Jesus of Nazareth purchased by me and the community with two tunics, one of white linen which was given by Doña Ana Maria Rendon and the other of violet satin which was given by Doña Simona Rendon along with its threaded cotton cord.

item—a Christ Child with its dress which was given by a devotee and two small crucifixes which were given by two devotees, they are situated in the two sides of the church; these have come in during my tenure.

Note: a lock which is on the vestment box, obtained with church funds, with its key, for safeguarding the vestments and holy vessels.

Continuing: The altar and nave of the church with everything which is required in it.

First—a colateral [altarscreen] of wood, painted with various colors, and in the center a small box without decorations nor paintings of any sort, with its lock and key, without doubt [of its security] for at some time the Blessed [Sacrament] may be placed in it.[4]

item—a *bulto* of San Miguel in the middle niche with its dress and the *incinas de*

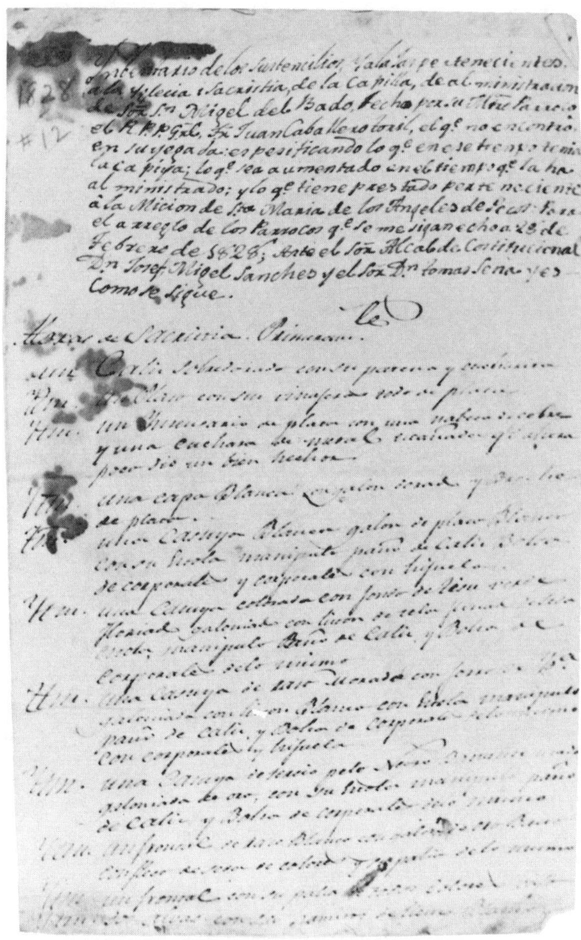

FIGURE 2
The San Miguel inventory, Archives of the Archdiocese of Santa Fe, Loose Documents, Missions, 1828, No. 12. (Photographed by Thomas J. Steele, S. J., from original document in the Archdiocese of Santa Fe, Albuquerque, New Mexico.)

balancas [equal-arm balance scale] of yellow metal and silver sword, and silver helmet adorned with stones and plume and paper beads of blue, mother of pearl, and half as long as those of the feather of the white dove. The garment is a blue satin [*soleta - coleta:* short jacket?] adorned on the collar; a silver crucifix with four crystal stones and below it a small cross of yellow metal of filigree; a small medallion which appears to be of gold; a ——— of black velvet with two stones and a shell; a string of *[Julias?]* pearls in the collar; three strings of *[Julia?]* pearls with a shell inserted; two pairs of *chapones,* half of various colors, being of glass [half of stained glass?]; a stone of crystal embossed in silver; bracelets, one of black *cancitillo* and two *sultanas,* one on each wrist fastened with a ribbon of black velvet. [See Fig. 1.]

item—four oval-shaped paintings on the sides of the retablo.

item—and, on the higher part of the colateral is a crucifix.

item—six statues; San Antonio, Our Lady of Sorrows, Our Lady of Guadalupe, San Juan Nepomuceno, Jesus of Nazareth, small, with the crucifix which is in the center of the altar table.

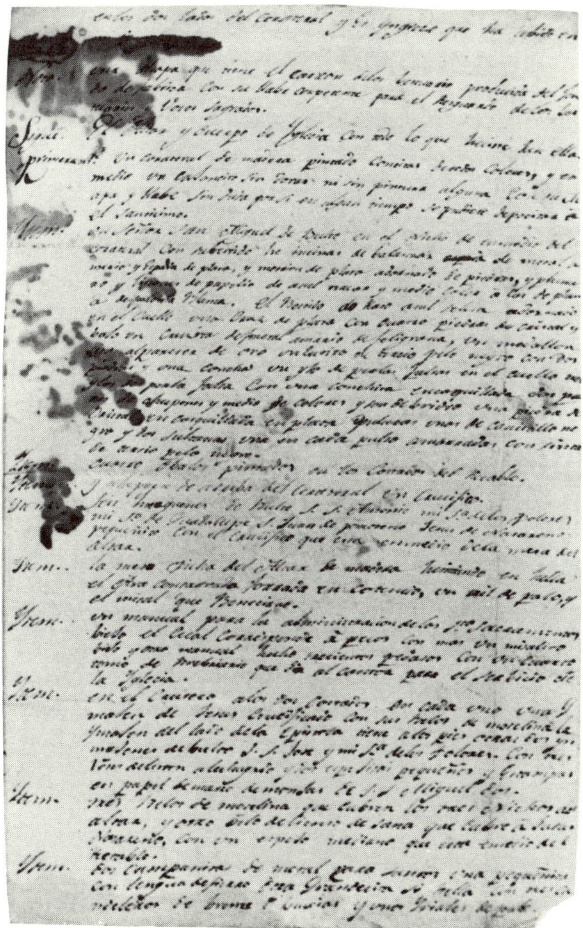

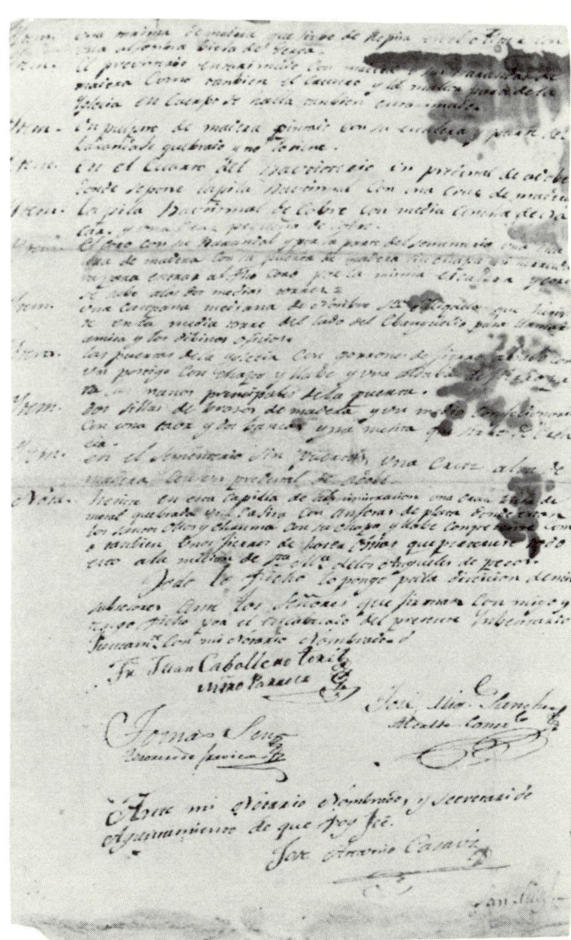

item—the said altar table of wood, containing the altarstone, consecrated, covered in cotton cloth, a wooden *tril* [stand?] and the missal which is used.

item—an old manual [handbook of rites] for the administration of the Holy Sacraments which belongs to Pecos, along with an old missalet and another manual made of three hundred pieces [loose pages?], along with a quarto volume breviary which I gave to the cantor for use in the church.

item—in the transept, on both sides, on each wall, an image of Jesus crucified with their muslin veils, and the image on the Epistle side has at its feet two other statues *[ymagenes de bulto]* of San José and Our Lady of Sorrows with three bows [?], and two small mirrors, and two engravings on the *mano de monsas* of San Miguel.

item—three veils [or curtains] of muslin which cover the altar niches, and another veil of linen *de sana*[5] which covers the Jesus of Nazareth, with a medium-sized mirror in the center of the retablo.

item—two small metal handbells for santos [that is, for specified moments of the mass] a small one with its metal clapper; another one a bit larger, with three bronze candlesticks and wax-candles and some *yriales de bale.*[6]

item—a wooden bench which serves as a shelf in the altar with an old rug for a carpet.

item—the sanctuary with its wooden floor and its wooden altar rail, as well as a wooden floored transept, with the major part of the nave also having a wooden floor.

item—a painted wooden pulpit with its circular [staircase] and its rails, part of which is broken and missing.

item—in the baptistry an adobe pedestal on which is placed the baptismal font along with a wooden cross.

item—a copper baptismal font with a half shell of mother of pearl and a small copper cross.

item—the choirloft with its rail and on the cemetery side a wooden ladder, and a wooden door, without lock nor its attachments, to enter the said choir and also with the same ladder and through the choirloft you climb to the two half towers.

item—a small bell named Señora Miquela which is in one of the half towers on the Gospel side to summon [the people] for mass and other divine offices.

item—the doors of the church with pivots of iron below and with a hinged hasp with its lock and key and a metal knocker for the main handles of the door.

item—two chairs with wooden arms and a partial confessional with a *taor* and two benches and a small table which serves as a *credencia.*[7]

item—in the cemetery, without doors, is a tall wooden cross with an adobe pedestal.

Note: There exists in this chapel of administration an old broken metal cross; a small box with silver lining where the holy oils and chrism are kept, having a lock and key for security, as well as a tool for making hosts; all this belongs to the mission of Santa Maria de los Angeles de Pecos.

All the aforesaid I list for the information of my successors, [done] before the men who sign with me and as I have said at the beginning of the present inventory, jointly with my so named notary.

Fr. Juan Caballero Toril (rubric)
Parish Priest

José Miguel Sanchez (rubric)
Alcalde Constitucional

Tomas Sena
Treasurer of the Church

Before me, notary so named, and Secretary of the Ayuntamiento, as I so swear.

José Antonio Casados

APPENDIX B

Our Lady of Guadalupe Church Inventory, Conejos, 1859

Conejos, December 18, 1859
Inventory of the items in possession of the parish
Church of Our Lady of Guadalupe of Conejos

1 complete set of white vestments —each burse with its corporals
1 complete set of violet vestments and purificators
1 green cope with white ornaments
1 multicolored antependium
1 linen amice
2 linen albs
1 linen altarcloth, with fringe [embroidered or crocheted fringe]
1 cincture
1 altarstone
2 missals
the three altarcards
1 mission chalice with its [traveling] case
3 tin candlesticks, and another one broken
cruets (1 cruet only, and the tray)
2 altar-bells
1 bell of medium size, situated on the temporary jacal
1 censer with its boat
1 mold for making hosts [or, canister for keeping unconsecrated hosts]
1 plated metal box with the holy oils in bottles
2 candlesticks and two crosses, all of wood
1 surplice

All this I received from the hands of the Priest V. S. Montaño, on this day the 18th of December, and I gave it into the case of the caretaker Don J. Mª Velásquez

Gabriel Ussel
Pastor in acting charge

Our Lady of Guadalupe Church Inventory, Conejos, 1860

Initial possessions of the parish of Our Lady of Guadalupe in
the year 1860, under the care of P. Vigil—
and it is as follows:

1 house which is made up of four rooms, with their four doors, three with locks and all with ———, and two window frames, one with fifteen panes, with its casing and shutters, the other with twelve panes and of less gl*[ace* or *glase]* than the first.
200 varas of land to the west of the church, as appears in the deed, on which the house is built.
3 images of the crucified, one of bronze which is used on the altar where Mass is said; two of brass, one of which is on the high cross and the other of which is in the place where the priest vests.
1 *jerga* carpet which is of use above the altarscreen.
2 bronze candelabra for three candles each.
1 altarstone, for offering mass in the various *placitas.*
3 altar cards
2 altarcloths
2 cruets
1 pyx for carrying the holy viaticum
6 purificators, with their cardboard container
3 *lavabos.* 1 linen surplice
3 linen amices
3 dishes of tin plate, one for the holy water and two for use as the baptismal font
1 case in which are kept the ornaments which Doña Martina donated
1 padlock which closes the door of the church, the fittings for which Don Pedro Lobato gave

All that is noted here in the year 1860 is in addition to the inventory made by Padre Gabriel Ussel in the year 1859. José Miguel Vigil

[rubric]

Everything on the list of Padre Grabriel Ussel I, José Miguel Vigil, the pastor of this parish, received, except one of the two sanctuary bells mentioned, since there was no more than one.

José Miguel Vigil
[rubric]

NOTES

1. Archives of the Archdiocese of Santa Fe, Loose Documents, Missions (1818–1829), 1828—No. 12, reel No. 54, frames 991–93, New Mexico State Records Center and Archives, Santa Fe. (See Fig. 2.)

2. Although *escanades* is the best reading of the word as written, its identification is unknown to us; possibly *acanaladas,* meaning fluted, beveled, or grooved is intended: a fluted spoon. Other words whose exact meanings are no longer known have similarly been left untranslated.

3. *Sopo* might be *cepo*—block, clasp, clamp, support, or stand for an anvil; or *soporte*—support or stand; or *hisopo*—aspergillum.
4. This should now be added to Boyd's list of wooden altar screens put up between 1780–1830 (1974: 59).
5. *cana?:* a measure used for cloth of about two English ells or ninety inches.
6. *ciriales?:* candlesticks for the large thick candles used in processions (Adams and Chávez 1956: 352).
7. This word would be literally translated as "the sideboard of an altar."

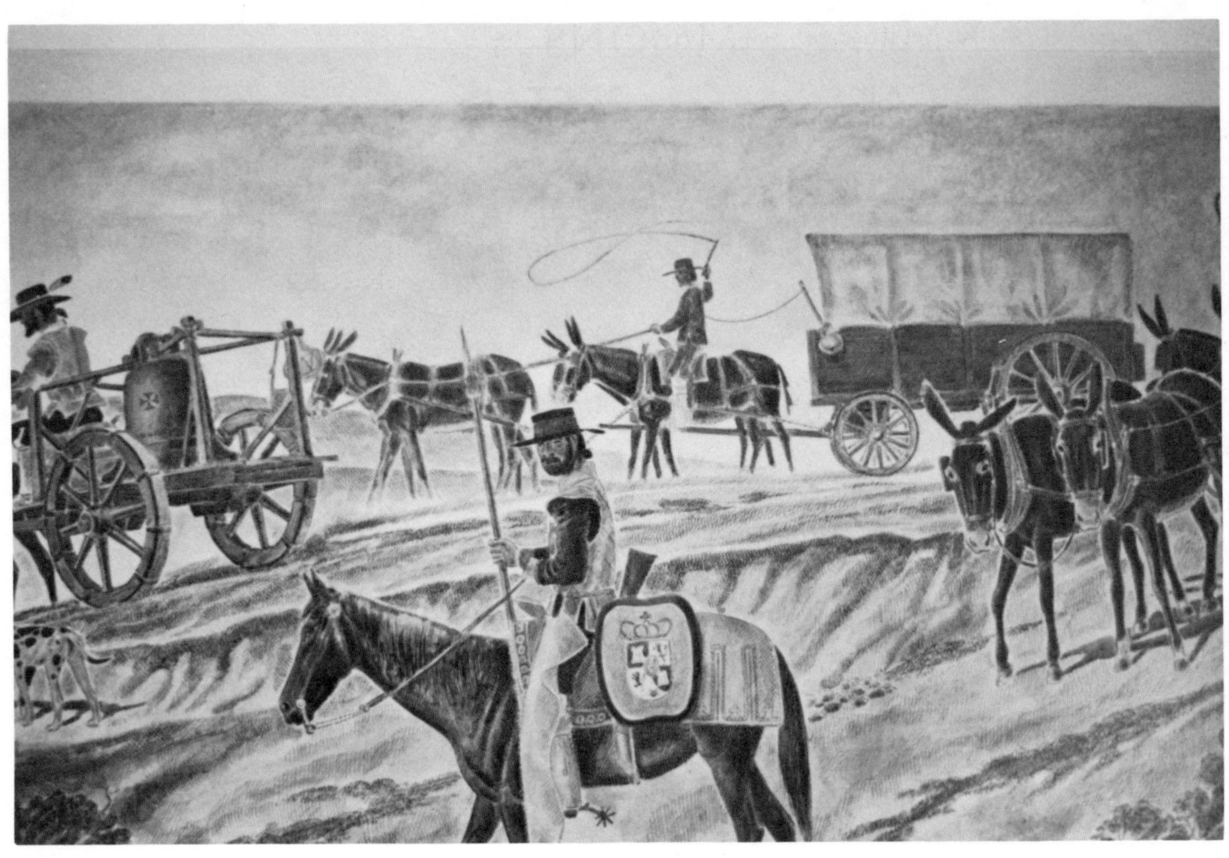

FIGURE 1
Spanish carros and carretas on the Camino Real. Drawing by José Cisneros. Collection of the Museum of New Mexico, Santa Fe.

MARC SIMMONS

CARROS Y CARRETAS: VEHICULAR TRAFFIC ON THE CAMINO REAL

THE VICEROYALTY OF NEW SPAIN was tied together during the colonial period by a vast network of trails and roads, over which passed a great volume of foot traffic as well as pack trains and cart caravans. Thoroughfares were classed, in a general way, as either *caminos de la herradura* (literally, "horseshoe roads") suitable for pedestrians and pack animals only, or *caminos de rueda* ("wheel roads"), which were passable by vehicle (Tamarón y Romeral 1958: 985).

Main highways were designated as *caminos reales,* that is, "royal roads," laid out and in theory maintained by the government. In colonial times, four of these royal roads radiated from Mexico City like the spokes of a wheel. The oldest and the first in importance was the road to the Gulf port of Veracruz by way of Puebla. A second led south from the capital through Oaxaca to Guatemala. The third crossed the mountains of the southwest to the port of Acapulco. And the fourth, the longest of all, ran northward 440 leagues (about 1,200 miles) to the frontier province of New Mexico.

The northern road was known popularly among travelers as *el camino de tierra adentro,* or "the road from the interior," because the frontier was usually spoken of as "the interior country." This vital artery extended from Mexico City, through Querétero, Zacatecas, Durango, Chihuahua, and El Paso del Norte to Santa Fe, and finally on to Taos. At various points along the main route, ancillary roads branched off and bore traffic to provinces situated to the east and the west. These tributaries included the roads to Guadalajara and Colima; to Saltillo, Monterey, and the settlements of Texas; and in the latter eighteenth century to Sonora and Alta California. Although these highways were referred to as caminos reales in their own right, they were recognized as appendages to New Mexico's camino de tierra adentro (Humboldt 1966: 462–63).

Scholars have paid considerable attention to the political, military and commercial aspects of the road to Santa Fe, but very little research has been brought to bear on the technical aspects of the wheeled vehicles used to carry freight and passengers over this route. From the founding of New Mexico by Juan de Oñate in 1598 down to Mexican independence in 1821, freight caravans seasonally traveled from southern cities to the upper Rio Grande valley. In the seventeenth century, they took the form of triennial government convoys, the famous mission-supply trains, referred to as *cuadrillas de carros.* In the following century, private contractors organized trains to carry supplies to the Santa Fe presidio, while local New Mexico merchants and ranchers formed their own protective caravans *(conductas)* to transport their products to the leading fairs and markets of the south. This freighting industry, extending over more than two centuries, made use of two principal types of wheeled conveyances: the *carro* and the *carreta.* An examination of their design, manufacture, and use can serve to illuminate a little-known aspect of Hispanic colonial technology.

Of the two, the carreta was in use for the longer period of time and is the better known, because numerous nineteenth-century visitors to the Southwest left detailed descriptions and because a number of examples have survived and are available in collections for study. Apparently, it still saw duty for purely local service in New Mexico as late as the 1890s.

In construction, the carreta was a simple cart body mounted over a few hounds (or braces), an axle, and a pair of wheels. Axles, made of cottonwood or occasionally pine, projected beyond the bed of the cart. Approximately eight inches of the axle at each end were reduced in diameter to form round journals bearing the wheels. The wheels were secured in place by linchpins, which were no more than wooden pegs inserted in holes bored near the extremities of the axle. James F. Meline, touring New Mexico in 1866, noted that carreta axles were prone to break. A plentiful supply of extras, he tells us, was loaded into the cart for any journey beyond a day, so that the carreta was frequently half-filled with them (Meline 1868: 159). His statement, no doubt, carries some exaggeration.

Cottonwood was the favored material in the making of carreta wheels. When a tree of sufficient girth could be found, the wheel would be formed from a single section of the trunk. Using no more than an ax and an adze, the wheelwright would trim the outer edges to produce as true a circle as possible. Next he reduced the thickness of the wood, tapering it toward the rim. At the center of the wheel, on both sides, he left hemispherical burrs to serve as the hubs. A hole to receive the axle was pierced through these hubs, either by boring or by using a hot iron.

It seems that in many cases the wheelwright could not find a tree large enough in diameter from which to fashion a one-piece wheel. In that event, he made three separate sections and fitted them together with wooden dowels to create a solid disc. Sometimes two crescent-shaped segments, or felloes, of wood were affixed to the core of a wheel by doweled slats, forming a rough circle and leaving open spaces on the surface of the finished wheel (Kendall 1935: v. 2, 44–45). A refinement almost never seen was "dishing," that is, construction of wheels not in one plane but as a flattened cone. A dished

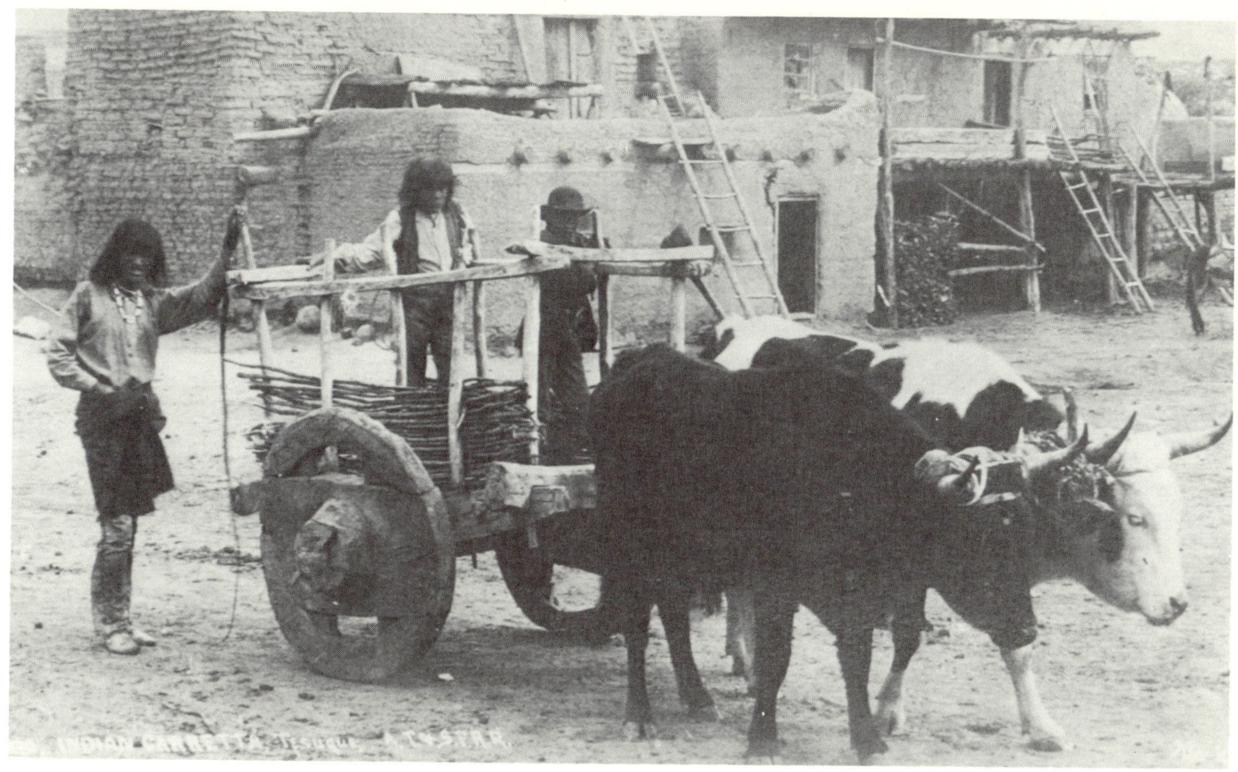

FIGURE 2
Carreta at Tesuque Pueblo, New Mexico. (Photo Collections, No. 11826, Museum of New Mexico.)

wheel is designed for strength against the sideways thrust inevitable with the swaying of heavy loads. Lacking this, the carreta in motion appeared quite unstable.[1]

Because of its density and resistance to splitting, cottonwood proved to be the best material available for the manufacture of cart wheels. Nevertheless, under the stress of hard use, most wheels soon developed cracks, a condition exacerbated by the dryness of the climate and by occasional wettings experienced in crossing streams. Many carreta wheels now in collections show evidence of patching, usually in the form of wooden mending plates nailed over a split.

In the absence of iron bushings and casings to reinforce the bearing surfaces of the axles and hubs, the hole in the wooden wheel was rapidly enlarged through wear. When this occurred, the carreta wobbled in motion and placed a greater strain on the draft animals.

To cut down on friction, the wheels were sometimes greased with buffalo tallow, but more commonly this simple maintenance practice was neglected.

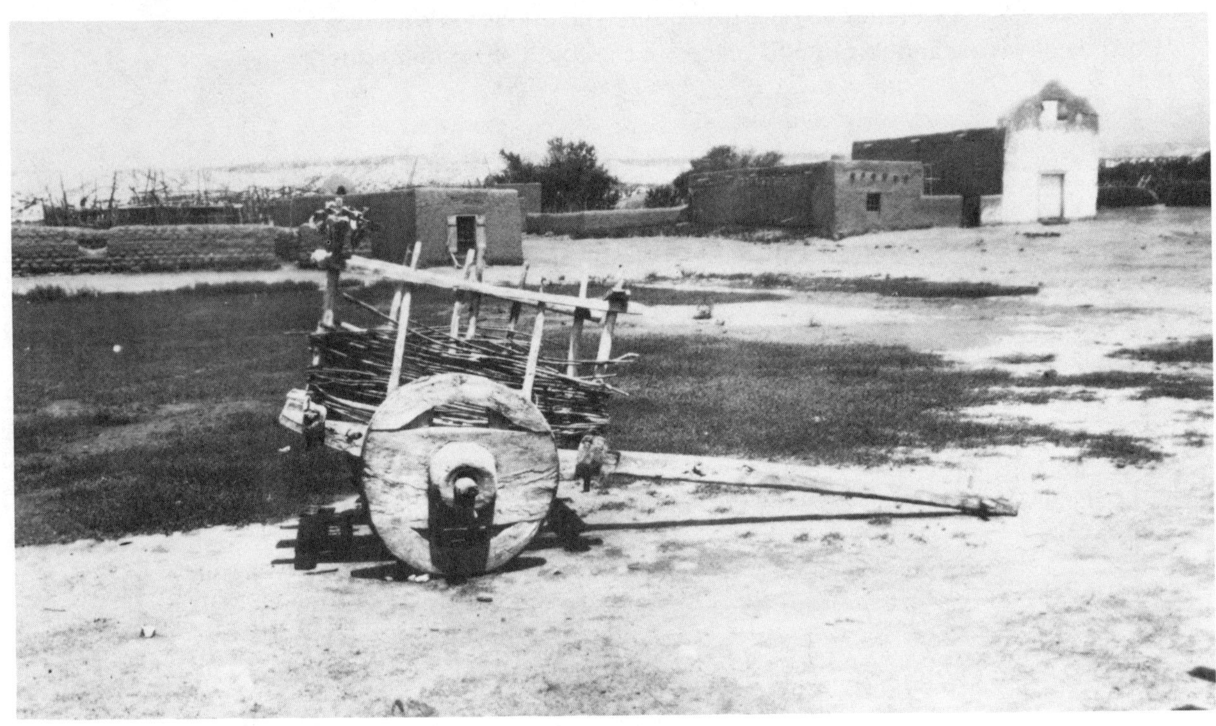

FIGURE 3
Carreta at Tesuque Pueblo, New Mexico. Photograph by Dana B. Chase. (Photo Collections, No. 11827, Museum of New Mexico.)

Americans coming over the Santa Fe Trail and encountering a train of carretas invariably spoke of the piercing noise of the wheels, describing it as a blood-curdling screech. Typical of early-day comments was that of Lt. John G. Bourke, who said of the carts: "As they rolled over the dusty roads, they squeaked a siren song which wakened the dead for five miles or more" (Bloom 1934: 298). Samuel Woodworth Cozzens added, "The genius who invented the steam-whistle must have obtained the idea from the noise made by the [carreta] wheels" (1876: 58).

Americans were always astonished that the noisy scream of the cart wheels did not irritate the New Mexicans. Indeed, there is evidence to suggest that this sound, far from displeasing the Hispanic carter and freighter, was actually music to his ears. Peasants in Spain, who employ similar vehicles, refer to them as "singing carts" and speak affectionately of the wheel's soothing, familiar song (Foster 1960: 105).

The bed of a carreta, which rested directly on the axle without benefit of springs, had a foundation composed of adzed beams joined by mortise and tenon. A center beam, running the length of the underbody, projected some ten feet beyond the front of the cart and served as the tongue. Flooring for the bed was provided by rough-hewn planks. The superstructure was merely a series of open stakes or undressed poles, each one anchored near the edge of the bed by doweling and joined and braced at the top by a railing, reinforced with rawhide.

Ordinarily the carreta was drawn by one or two yoke of oxen, but more yokes could be added if the load or terrain demanded it. The style of yoke used by carters on the Camino Real was that derived from southern Spain, the horn yoke, which was tied behind the horns with rawhide thongs. With this device the ox had to push with his head and neck, whereas with the collar yoke, which was employed in northern Spain but had not been introduced to the colonies, the animal pulled the load with his shoulders.[2]

This crude, unwieldy carreta with no iron fittings or hardware represents the sort of cart prevalent in New Mexico during the nineteenth century. But documentary evidence suggests that carretas of more skillful construction that were even furnished, at times, with iron tires and iron bushings inside the hubs had been the rule in an earlier day. For long journeys over the Camino Real, such a sophisticated and sturdy vehicle would have been necessary to withstand the hardships of the trail.[3]

The Mexican carreta was of the same fundamental design as that used for more than three thousand years by peoples of Asia Minor and southern Europe. In 1958, Soviet archaeologists uncovered several intact carts between the Caspian and Black seas, dating from about 1400 B.C., whose three-part disc wheels and axle arrangement bore a striking similarity to New Mexican carretas (Piggott 1976: 212–15). From Roman times down to the present day, carts in Spain have been made according to the traditional pattern, although variations in wheel type and body form, representing the whims of individual cartwrights, have brought about superficial stylistic differences in some regions (Foster 1960: 105–6).

The first carreta built in the Viceroyalty of New Spain, indeed, in the New World, was the handiwork of Sebastián de Aparicio who began transporting freight over the Camino Real between Veracruz and Mexico City in 1536.[4] After that year, the manufacture of carts expanded rapidly. In the last decade of the century, Juan de Oñate included a number of carretas among the vehicles making up his supply train bound from Zacatecas to colonize the upper Rio Grande valley.

In the decades before the Pueblo Revolt, it appears that several professional cartwrights settled in New Mexico and helped launch local production of carretas. Pueblo Indian labor was sometimes used in the manufacturing process. In 1660, ten new carretas were reportedly made for the governor who used them to ship assorted merchandise to the settlements in Nueva Vizcaya (Scholes 1942: 45). We can assume that these carts were built with considerable precision and strength, since they were destined for commerce on the Camino Real.

Colonial records occasionally mention citizens whose occupation is listed as carreta maker. Unfortunately the information is too thin in most cases to determine whether this represented specialized, full-time employment or whether, as seems more likely, cartwrighting was merely an adjunct of general carpentry.[5]

While it is possible to ascertain from a study of existing carretas the standard design and method of construction, nevertheless, many procedures and customs associated with the craft remain a mystery. No colonial cartwright, as far as we know, kept a journal noting the qualities he looked for in selecting proper wood for his task or outlining the steps in fabricating a cart from start to finish.

Capt. Henry Smith Turner, an officer with Gen. Stephen W. Kearny's Army of the West, provides an illuminating comment about carretas. In his diary of 1846, Turner recalled that, while traveling along the Rio Grande below Albuquerque, "We occasionally see a grove of cottonwood which is preserved with great care, as it furnishes the only material with which carts for the whole country are made. These groves are always private property" (Clarke 1966: 77). His statement lends weight to the conclusion that carreta making was an important cottage industry in Hispanic New Mexico.

Turning from carretas to the other major vehicle used for freighting on the Camino Real, the carro, we find that the data are far less voluminous. This is because carros were rapidly displaced on the northern frontier by the Conestoga and Murphy freight wagons introduced over the Santa Fe Trail. Writing in 1856, U.S. Atty. W. W. H. Davis indicates that carros, as of that time, had virtually disappeared from New Mexico's roads (1938: 81).[6] No example of this type of vehicle is owned by any museum, nor do we even have a pictorial representation of a carro from any documentary source.

What we do have are a number of sketchy and often conflicting statements that fail to present either an accurate or a complete picture of a carro. The most crucial question still to be answered is this: was it a two-wheeled vehicle, essentially a larger version of the carreta, and thus a true cart; or did it in fact have four wheels and, therefore, qualify as a wagon? In attempting to solve the problem, the word *carro* itself is of little help, for in Spain the term is used rather indiscriminately for both carts and wagons. In any case, the word *carro,* as employed in colonial New Spain, had a highly specialized meaning, since it was applied to a distinctive type of conveyance invented and produced mainly in the city of Zacatecas.

Philip Wayne Powell, who is best known for his series of meticulous studies on the northern frontier of New Spain in the sixteenth century, has come to the conclusion, based on a survey of numerous documents, that the carro actually had only two wheels (1952: 231), and most other writers have accepted his judgment. However, a review of the evidence cited by Powell suggests that the documents are not clear on the matter, and that a different interpretation could lead one to believe that carros in truth were furnished with four wheels, probably two large ones in the rear and a pair of small ones in front.[7]

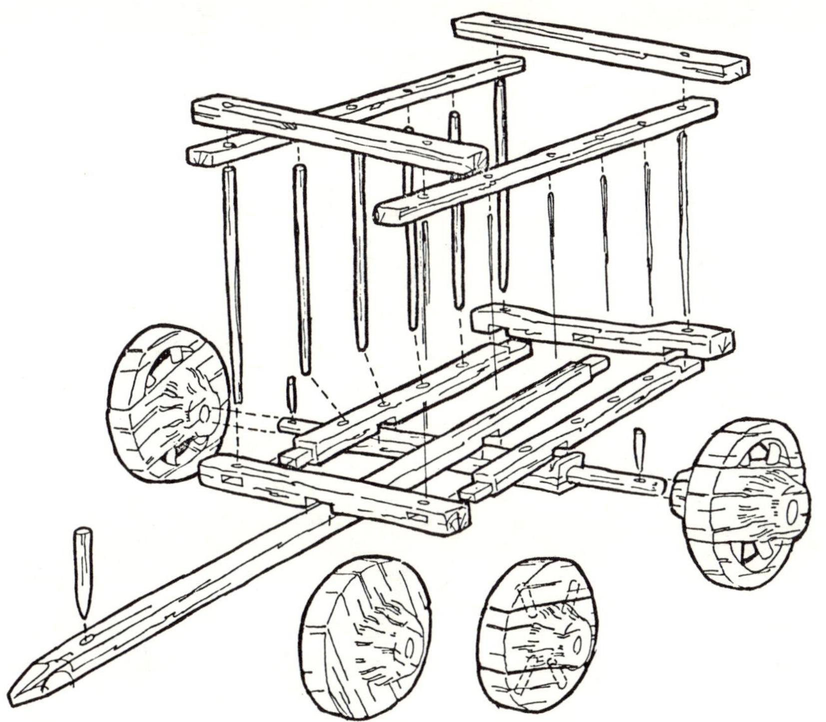

FIGURE 4
Method of assembling a carreta. Three styles of wheel are illustrated: on the cart, construction using two felloes; lower left, solid wheel made from a single section of cottonwood; lower right, solid wheel consisting of three sections doweled together. (Drawing by Louann Jordan.)

The entire issue might seem trivial, a case of splitting hairs, but for a person dealing with Spanish colonial technology and transportation it is of some interest and importance. For example, several years ago, the Education Division of the Museum of New Mexico commissioned the celebrated artist and illustrator, José Cisneros of El Paso, Texas, to prepare a panel depicting a Spanish caravan moving over the Camino Real. It bears mentioning that Cisneros, who is a lifelong student of colonial material culture, chose to show the carros with four wheels.

In other particulars, it is possible to describe the carro more precisely. France V. Scholes's study of the seventeenth-century mission-supply service includes an inventory of the cuadrilla de carros that came to New Mexico in 1631. From it, we learn that the caravan of that year comprised thirty-two carros, each pulled by eight teams of mules. Sixteen spare axles were taken, as well as a large quantity of extra spokes and felloes. The last two items offer conclusive proof that the carro was furnished with spoked wheels, rather than with solid wheels like the carreta. Further, iron tires, weighing twenty-seven pounds each, iron bushings, and iron linchpins comprise part of the inventory, confirming that the carros' running gear was comparatively sophisticated, at least for the time and place (Scholes 1930: 105–7).

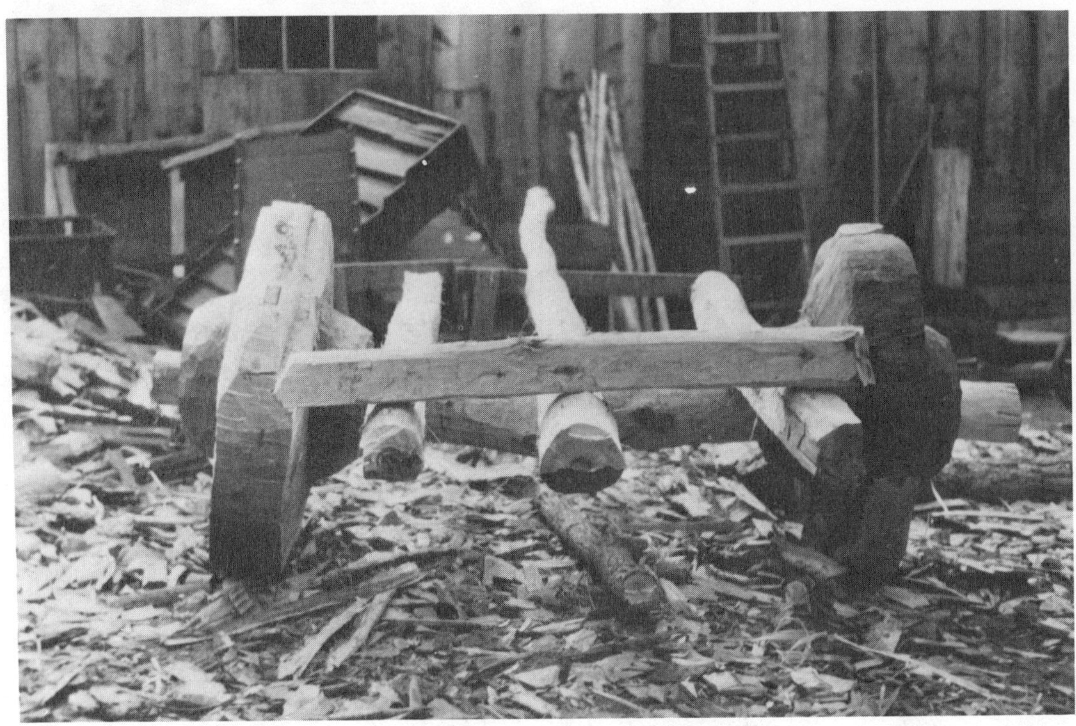

FIGURE 5
"Carreta carved for Winslow," June 1930. (Photo Collections, No. 14962, Museum of New Mexico.)

For the protection of its freight, each carro was provided with wooden wagon bows *(costillas)* that supported a cloth cover made of *jerga de Michoacán*. Fitted out in this fashion, they must have resembled the American covered wagon of a later day.[8] The legal load limit for carros operating in the mission-supply service was 160 *arrobas*, or about 2 tons. In some instances, freight transported weighed far in excess of this limit. To withstand such heavy loads, the body of the carro must have been well crafted and stout. The great weight of the cargoes is also another bit of evidence favoring four wheels on the carro.[9]

The method of harnessing the mule team to the carro is not known. The draft mules wore leather collars, lined with sheepskin, and the harness of the lead teams was embellished with eight bells (Scholes 1930: 107; West 1949: 83, 86). The subject of Spanish colonial harness remains in need of serious investigation.[10]

If the physical appearance and form of the carro are still open to question, its early history is known with somewhat greater clarity. According to sixteenth-century records, the originator of the colonial carro was a freighter named Pascual Carrasco, who created it initially to handle the transfer of heavy machinery and supplies to and from the Zacatecas silver mines. Developed in response to specific conditions on the mining frontier, in size and design this vehicle had no apparent European forerunner (Powell 1950: 240).

In time, the carro came to be used in all parts of New Spain for general transport, and its manufacture no doubt spread to other cities. But the center of carro production remained in Zacatecas. Some models were fortified to serve as rolling blockhouses, providing a defensive bastion to which travelers on open stretches along the Camino Real could rally in time of Indian attack.

Juan de Oñate, himself a native of Zacatecas, was well supplied with both carros and carretas when he set out from that place to colonize New Mexico. The official review of his expedition, conducted by a government inspector before departure, reveals that, while most of the carros were drawn by the customary mules, some in fact were pulled by oxen, up to ten yoke in number. It is also curious to note that a few of the wheels on his carretas were mounted with iron tires, suggesting that they were of the more efficient spoke type rather than the common solid wheel. Thus, while it is a general rule of thumb that carros were moved by mules and had spoked wheels and carretas used oxen under draft and were equipped with solid disc wheels, this formula was not engraved in steel (Hammond and Rey 1953: v. 1, 44–47, 139, 225–26, 266). Clearly Oñate and others after him rigged their vehicles on the basis of expediency, practicality, and economy, not according to any custom or laws associated with the business of freighting.

NOTES

1. On the construction of cart wheels in Spain, see Menéndez Pidal 1951: 75–76.
2. On the relative merits of shoulder-versus-neck yokes, see Herrera et al. 1777: 8. For a description of yoking in New Mexico, see Meline 1868: 159.
3. Two variations of the carreta, used in New Mexico, can be noted. One was the *carretón,* thought to be simply an oversized carreta. Prominent Santa Fe citizen Manuel Antonio Chaves owned such a vehicle, along with carros and carretas, as shown by a mortgage deed dated 1854 in Deed Book A (Registro), Santa Fe County Records, pp. 335–37. The second kind was a handcart, called a *carreta de mano.* On the trail between Santa Fe and Las Vegas, New Mexico, William A. Bell saw a group of Pueblo Indians using one in 1867. "Each pushed before him a little hand-cart composed of a body of wicker-work on wooden wheels, filled with grapes, the produce of their vineyards" (Bell 1870: 158). The wickerwork was undoubtedly a lattice of osiers, an arrangement frequently used on full-size carretas when transporting farm produce.
4. A detailed biography of Aparicio appears in Lummis 1929: 50–87.

5. One José Vásquez, evidently of Zacatecan origin, was listed in 1715 as a resident of Santa Cruz and a cartwright by trade (Chávez 1954*a:* 307).
6. The last references to carros in Mexico appears in the 1840s (Ringrose 1970: 38n).
7. For reference to a four-wheeled carro in New Mexico in 1680, consult Hackett 1942: v.2, 210.
8. The old term for a covered wagon was *carro encamisado* (Campa 1979: 224).
9. The average distance traveled per day by carts and wagons in 1680 was reported to be six leagues, or about fifteen miles (Hackett 1942: v.1, 40).
10. On the evolution of the harness in Europe, see White 1962: 59–61.

MYRA ELLEN JENKINS

SOME EIGHTEENTH-CENTURY NEW MEXICO WOMEN OF PROPERTY

After completing a research project about the land history of the Pueblo of Taos and the Tewa Pueblos of San Ildefonso, Santa Clara, Nambé, Tesuque, and Pojoaque under three sovereignties—Spanish, Mexican, and American—I was struck that documentary investigation reveals no information about any specific role played by women. One can only conclude that the *principales* who spoke and acted for their pueblos in land issues and adjudications before the officials and courts of all three governments presented the consensus of the Indian community, including the women. However, the records concerning the pueblos during the eighteenth century did reveal many property transactions by Spanish women in the area, and I elected therefore to present case studies of four such women. I made the acquaintance of three of them through their relationships with the Pueblos; I crossed the path of the fourth several years ago in the course of conducting research for the state engineer on acequia priorities in the area of the village of Chimayó. (She did not encroach on Pueblo land since she was far too busy encroaching on the lands of other Spanish women.)

This essay makes no pretense of being a portrayal of the general status of women in Hispanic New Mexico. However, the official Spanish archives of New Mexico show that under Spanish law and administration women did have protected property rights. Except for one, the lives of the following women are quite the opposite of the often-described stereotype of the docile, unusually refined Spanish woman, completely dominated by her husband or, if unmarried, by another close male relative. But then, stereotypes have a way of disappearing when confronted by documentation.

The records show that, on the contrary, women often actively engaged in buying, selling, and managing property. A widow had greater freedom, to be sure, but, even if there was a husband whose consent had to be secured in the signing of a property conveyance, the evidence indicates that it was often the woman who made the decision. As a matter of fact, the husbands of the women described here, again except for one, were completely overshadowed by their vigorous wives.

FRANCISCA GIGOSA

Antonio Moya, a twenty-one-year-old stonemason from Mexico City, with his seventeen-year-old wife Francisca Gigosa (de Guijosa, Aguijosa, Equijosa), joined the colonists who returned to Santa Fe with Gen. Don Diego de Vargas in 1693.[1] Nothing further is known about Antonio, except that he was dead by 1713 when his widow entered the real-estate business. Throughout the following years, Francisca bought, was granted, and sold land as far north as the Taos valley and to all indications capably managed her own affairs even after she remarried. The details of her negotiations reveal much about the property rights of those women who chose to exercise them.

On September 7, 1713, Francisca Equijosa, widow of Antonio Moya, secured a house and lot on the Santa Fe Plaza in a confusing exchange of property with Juan Paéz Hurtado, a well-known general under Vargas who also frequently served as lieutenant governor or acting governor during the decades following the reconquest.[2] Francisca also owned livestock. In early summer 1715, she petitioned Gov. Juan Ignacio Flores Mogollón for a grant to a tract of land in the Taos valley on which to pasture her sheep and goats, promising to settle it in accordance with the royal ordinances.

The petition was granted, and on October 20 Juan de la Mora Piñeda, lieutenant to the governor, placed her in possession of a grant that extended from the Rio del Pueblo on the north, to the opening of an Indian acequia on the east, to the black rocks as far as the *arroyo hondo* on the west, and to the middle road to Picurís on the south. The claim was obviously very close to, if not within, the lands used by the Taos Indians, which under Spanish colonial law were to be strictly protected from encroachment. Piñeda reported that he had carried out the act of possession in the presence of the Taos Pueblo principales to determine if they had any adverse claims, but that they had registered no objection.[3] The granting document stipulated that Francisca must settle the land within six months, but there is no evidence that she ever made any attempt to do so.

On May 19, 1716, still designated as the widow of Antonio Moya, Francisca bought property in the Villa of Santa Cruz de la Cañada, the Spanish settlement made by Vargas some twenty-five miles north of Santa Fe and the headquarters of the northern jurisdiction. Purchased from Juan Alonzo de Mondragón and his wife Sebastiana Trujillo, this property became Francisca's home for several years.[4]

Events within her Santa Cruz household abruptly brought her to the attention of the authorities. In September 1718, the Pueblo of Taos brought charges against one Andrés de la Paz, "mulatto servant of Francisca Guijosa," for mistreatment of Indian laborers. Gov. Antonio de Valverde placed his lieutenant Pedro de Villasur in charge of the investigation, which dragged on for three months with hearings both in Santa Cruz and at the Pueblo of Taos where they were conducted by alcalde mayor Miguel Tenorio de Alba.

According to the statements of the Indians, the servant, without any provocation, had verbally abused them and then had attacked one of them with a club. They at once returned to the pueblo to report the affair. The testimony at Santa Cruz showed that other settlers besides Francisca had been in the habit of bringing Taos Indian construction workers from the pueblo, a practice of dubious legality that was much frowned upon by the authorities. Finally, on December 6, Governor Valverde, after reviewing the lengthy proceedings, issued an order to return the servant, whom he had found guilty as charged, to Santa Fe for sentencing. The arresting officers reported, however, that they arrived too late, as the culprit had taken flight. Although the case was ordered to remain open, nothing further is on record about it.[5]

The identity of Andrés de la Paz, "the mulatto servant," is particularly interesting in light of the fact that two years later (on August 14, 1720) Francisca Aguijosa and her *husband* Andrés de la Paz sold their Santa Cruz property to Santiago Romero and Juana Bautista de Olibas of Santa Fe. The probable explanation is that the bellicose servant had taken the name of his master, the Andrés de la Paz whom Francisca married about this time. In her separate statement attached to the sale document in favor of Romero and his wife, Francisca indicated the apparent requirement that the husband's permission was necessary to convey real property: "I bind myself in said instrument with the permission of my husband, who is present, without his having obliged me to do so either by entreaties or threats, but that I am thus in agreement of my own free and spontaneous will in order to be able to feed and clothe my children."[6] This concluding sentence is perplexing since her children were long since grown. The eldest, Pedro Antonio Moya, husband of Ana María Domínguez, had lived in the Taos area and died there in 1716; the daughter, María Francisca, married Juan Estévan de Apodaca in Santa Fe in 1709; Lucas Miguel Moya, though as yet unmarried, was of age (Chávez 1954*a*: 240).

In the meantime, although Francisca made no attempt to comply with the terms of her Taos valley grant by occupying that property within six months, there was no official objection raised when she sold it to Baltazar Trujillo in 1725, with the conveyance again recording that the permission had been given by her husband, Andrés de la Paz.[7] Francisca died in Santa Fe on April 20, 1752 (Chávez 1954*a*: 240).

JUANA LUJAN

One of the large property owners and influential Spanish residents in the Tewa Pueblo region north of Santa Fe within the jurisdiction of the new Villa of Santa Cruz de la Cañada was Juana Lujan. Her parents, Matias Lujan and Francisca Romero, had returned to their pre-Revolt holdings in La Cañada about 1695, but whether Juana accompanied them on their return from El Paso is not known. Her first documentary appearance is in 1714 when she bought out Matias Madrid's claim to lands near San Ildefonso

Pueblo. She then had three young children—Francisco, Juan, and Luisa—who on occasion were known as Lujan but later took the name of Gómez del Castillo. When Juana made her will in 1762, she stated that she had been married to Francisco Martín according to the rites of the church, but that there had been no issue. She then named Francisco, Juan, and Luisa as her "carnal children" and heirs.[8] The identity of this Francisco Martín is a mystery, since his name never appears in the records of her various transactions. The Martín name was very common throughout the entire northern region because of the numerous branches of the influential Martín Serrano clan, and there are several contemporary Martínes bearing the Christian name of Francisco, but none that can be connected with Juana.

To complicate matters, there was no Gómez del Castillo family in New Mexico. However, members of the prominent Gómez Robledo family had held important civil and military positions before the Revolt. Andrés Gómez Robledo had been killed in the fighting at Santa Fe; the others took his orphan daughter Francisca with them in the retreat to El Paso. There she married Ignacio de Roybal and was the only Gómez Robledo who returned to Santa Fe. Since Juana and her offspring were closely identified with the household of Roybal, military leader, high sheriff of the Inquisition, and even more persistent encroacher on San Ildefonso, historian-genealogist Fray Angélico Chávez postulates that Juana's children were sired in El Paso by a Gómez Robledo who also had a Castillo family connection (1954*a*: 187). At any rate, and at the expense of the Pueblo of San Ildefonso, Juana was a highly provident mother when it came to acquiring property and goods for her unusual family. Unfortunately also for the pueblo, her sons learned her business methods all too well.

In 1702, Matias Madrid had received a grant from Gov. Pedro Rodríguez Cubero for land lying between the Pueblo of San Ildefonso on the west and the abandoned Pueblo of Jacona, which earlier that year had been granted to Ignacio de Roybal, on the east. Because of its proximity to the pueblo, the concession was of doubtful legality, but Cubero had a habit of making such questionable donations to favored settlers. San Ildefonso had objected to Madrid's presence but to no avail. On July 16, 1714, Madrid sold the tract to Juana Lujan. Juan Paéz Hurtado, acting as investigator for Gov. Juan Ignacio Flores Mogollón, validated both the deed and the Madrid grant to her the following year, in spite of the fact that, as he noted in his report, "some clauses and details necessary to its vigor and force were lacking."[9] Juana soon acquired, or had already acquired, land at La Cañada as well as another parcel at "Chama" within the boundaries of the Pueblo of San Juan. The Madrid purchase, however, became the family home and was soon known as the "Rancho de San Antonio."

For nearly three-quarters of a century, San Ildefonso was faced with constant encroachment from Juana and her sons. In 1740, Francisco Gómez del Castillo, who had married Ursula Guillén, bought a piece of land between the Pueblos of San Ildefonso and Santa Clara that had been illegally granted by Cubero to a Mateo Trujillo in 1700 and then sold and resold over the protests of both pueblos.[10] Juan, the younger son, built another house even closer to the pueblo than his mother's and appropriated other lands north and northwest of the village proper. Lujan–Gómez del Castillo livestock regularly caused damage to San Ildefonso acequias and fields.

Juana died in the summer of 1762 shortly after making her last will and testament. She listed the Rancho de San Antonio as then consisting of a twenty-four-room hacienda with nine doors, a garden, a walled orchard and stable, as well as agricultural lands.[11] The latter were, of course, irrigated by an Indian-constructed acequia. This property and the Chama piece were divided between Juan and the heirs of his older brother, Francisco, who had died two years before. Daughter Luisa did not share in the real estate since the Cañada land had been part of her dowry when she married Juan Estévan García de Noriega in 1721, but she received her portion of the large amount of personal property and other assets. There were various accounts due Juana from her trade business with merchants in El Paso and Chihuahua. She had also been a livestock owner of significant importance, with one big herd being pastured as far away as the Rio Puerco valley southwest of Albuquerque.

The story of Juana Lujan and the Pueblo of San Ildefonso has an epilogue. In February 1763, less than a year after her death, Felipe Tafoya, who held the position of Protector of the Indians, brought suit before Gov. Tomás Vélez Cachupín on behalf of the Pueblo of San Ildefonso against several Spanish encroachers who for more than a half-century had continued to trespass and to allow damage from their stock. With reference to the Gómez del Castillo clan, Tafoya contended that the Madrid grant had been invalid from the beginning and pointed out the increased encroachment, especially from Juan who had built his house so close to the village "that the cultivated lands of the aforesaid adjoin the gardens next to the said pueblo."[12] He also charged Marcos Lucero, the deceased Francisco's son-in-law who had been occupying the Trujillo purchase along with the rest of that family, with illegal purchase of a plot of land from an individual Indian and with building another house north of the pueblo.

In order that justice might be done, Tafoya requested that a league (a short three miles), the recognized minimum right of an Indian pueblo to land, be measured to the north, east, and south of San Ildefonso for the sole use of the Indians. Vélez Cachupín granted his request, and the measurement proved that all the ranchos—Juana's, Juan's, Lucero's, and most of Francisco's—were within the league. Tafoya recommended that the land be obtained for the Indians. After two years of proceedings during which the issue was referred to the *corregidor* of Chihuahua, a licensed royal attorney, it was determined that Juan would be allowed to keep the land (apparently he had secured the other half of the Rancho de San Antonio). The Indians would be compensated by being given all the land to the west of the pueblo that they needed for grazing. Lucero was ordered to vacate the property he had illegally bought, and all the settlers were ordered to herd their stock so that they would not break the acequias and destroy the fields.

Suits brought by Tafoya on behalf of San Ildefonso and Santa Clara against the Francisco Gómez del Castillo heirs, especially Marcos Lucero, continued for another twenty years. Measurements and remeasurements of their respective leagues had shown that only some 234 varas of surplus land lay between the north boundary of San Ildefonso and the south boundary of Santa Clara. Finally, on June 10, 1786, Gov. Juan Bautista de Anza decreed that Lucero and the others had only had temporary ownership of this small parcel and that it should be sold to San Ildefonso. They were allowed to keep only four milk cows and enough oxen to cultivate it until the acreage was disposed of.[13]

ANTONIA MORAGA

Somewhat older than Francisca Gigosa and Juana Lujan and most adept at securing and managing property in her own inimitable way was Antonia Moraga of Chimayó. Antonia also became embroiled in controversies that brought her before the authorities. She had at least six children, although at one time she claimed seven, all legitimate, who were often involved with her, or she with one of them, in one situation or another. There was a husband, who outlived her, but except for one incident, he seems to have played a very minor role in family affairs.

Before the Pueblo Revolt, Alonso de Moraga and Luis Martín Serrano II were neighboring landowners at Chimayó, where they had built their homes, constructed acequias, and were raising crops and grazing stock. With their large families and the other La Cañada settlers, they escaped to Santa Fe in 1680 and joined in the retreat to El Paso. Among them were Alonso's daughter Antonia and her husband Cristóbal Martín Serrano, son of Luis, and their small son, also named Cristóbal. Alonso apparently died in El Paso (Chávez 1954*a:* 79, 239). The couple, now with several children, returned during the reconquest, as did Felipe Moraga, Antonia's younger brother; Luis Martín Serrano, married to a second wife; and the rest of his family. By the spring of 1695, the Martínes were back at Chimayó, rebuilding their homes. On March 13, Felipe Moraga received a grant from Vargas to a small tract east of his former home.[14] For some reason, he did not ask for his father's "hacienda de Moraga."

At this time, Antonia and her family were apparently living on Santa Fe property formerly owned by her father and, before that, by her grandfather Diego Moraga. In 1696, she petitioned Vargas to grant to her the holdings consisting of farming lands on the *ciénega* and a torreon on the hill above them. The ciénega, which contained a number of springs, was the area east and northeast of the Palace of the Governors. Vargas acceded to her request.[15] Late in the year, she presented another petition that the ancestral hacienda de Moraga in Chimayó, west of her brother's grant, be conceded to her. She claimed that the Santa Fe holding was insufficient to support her family of seven children and her husband who was going blind, and that she was entitled to the Chimayó estate. Vargas obliged again by regranting this to her on December 10. Shortly after doing so, however, he notified her that she was to surrender the Santa Fe property since she had received other land and the land in the capital was needed for another settler. Vargas apparently granted it to a Juan del Rio, who actually was married to another Moraga, but this man returned to El Paso without occupying the land. Antonia then appealed to Vargas's successor, Pedro Rodríguez Cubero, to revalidate it to her, which he did on August 9, 1697; he also reapproved the Chimayó grant in 1699.

Antonia made no attempt to occupy the Santa Fe property, and in 1706 Gov. Antonio Cuervo y Valdés declared it vacant and granted it to the landless soldier Salvador Matias de Rivera. He was killed fighting Indians in 1712, leaving his widow, Juana Sosa Canela, in possession. Antonia sued to recover. The widow relied on the revocation of the grant by Vargas, but Antonia responded that the land she had been required to give up was not the cienega land, but another site near the new church. Acting Governor Paéz Hurtado, who consistently upheld Antonia in various suits, nullified Juana's claim on March 10, 1713, and ordered the land returned to Antonia. After some six years of peaceful occupation, the widow of the slain soldier was summarily ejected. Three years later, Antonia conveyed the property to Governor Flores Mogollón to be incorporated into the municipal commons.[16]

Nothing further was mentioned concerning Cristóbal's supposedly failing eyesight after Antonia got her Chimayó land. However, Felipe Moraga did suffer from progressive blindness. In 1703, together with her father-in-law Luis, her brother-in-law Antonio Martín ("El Tecolote"), and other family members, but not husband Cristóbal, Antonia was named in a hearing before Inquisition authorities as having taken part the previous year in occult ceremonies to cure Felipe's blindness. He testified that his wife had hired three San Juan witches to make him blind, but that his sister and the Martínes had secured the services of a more potent San Juan witch to perform the curing rites.[17] Apparently, no action was taken against anyone involved.

Thus far Antonia and her sons had been on good terms with her husband's family, but that situation soon changed. In 1703, about the same time that Felipe was being questioned by the Holy Office about the hexing matter, brother-in-law Francisco was petitioning Governor Cubero for a grant in his own name to provide for his increasing family. The tract requested was for virgin land bounded on the west by Felipe's holdings. Cubero approved a grant, but for only one-half of the area requested.[18] Several years later, blind Felipe moved to Mexico, and shortly Antonia's son Cristóbal II, with the assistance of his mother, was quarreling with his paternal uncle Francisco over ownership of his maternal uncle's land.

In April 1711, Cristóbal, claiming that he had bought out Felipe three years before, charged Francisco with trespass; the latter countered with the insistence that Felipe had permitted him to plant the disputed land as early as 1704. After much investigation of boundaries and documents, it was decided that both men had appropriated more land than they were entitled to. Cristóbal was cultivating his mother's land also. The Marqués de la Peñuela, who was governor, ruled in favor of Francisco and revalidated his grant on September 30. Peñuela was soon recalled, and Paéz Hurtado, who had been named acting governor, promptly set aside the decision. On April 20, 1712, he ruled that the land in litigation belonged to Cristóbal and ordered Francisco to drop his suit or face a two-year exile.[19]

At planting time one year later, Francisco appealed against Paéz Hurtado to the new governor, Juan Ignacio Flores Mogollón, and filed additional charges against Cristóbal. After some months, Sebastián Martín Serrano, cousin of the Chimayó Martínes and recently appointed alcalde mayor of Santa Cruz, conducted further proceedings and investigations during which Antonia appeared with more documents allegedly proving her son's claim and the extent of Moraga lands.[20]

In July 1714, the governor appointed a special commission headed by Ignacio de Roybal to determine, measure, and monument the boundaries of each litigant. The commission ruled that Antonia's title to the hacienda de Moraga was clear. Felipe's 1695 grant was adjudged to Cristóbal, including the land in controversy. Francisco's 1703 grant was revalidated, but a request for additional land was denied. To prevent further litigation, all three were fined fifty pesos each, the amount to be applied toward the building of the Santa Fe church.[21] Antonia and Cristóbal appeared to have won the day. However, this was but the first phase. The quarrel between the men continued unabated until 1738, ten years after Cristóbal's litigious mother had gone on to her reward.

While the property suit was in full tilt during the summer of 1713 and shortly after she had succeeded in dispossessing the soldier's widow, Antonia found herself and her daughter Josefa being sued for slander by María de Benavides of Chimayó, widow of the *alférez* Diego González. That issue, however, got lost in court action involving the rest of the family over the serving of a warrant. Jacinto Sánchez, alcalde mayor of the Villa of Santa Cruz, on the complaint of María, dispatched officers to Chimayó to escort Antonia into the *casas reales* for questioning. On the road, they met Antonia, accompanied by husband Cristóbal, Josefa, and the younger son, Diego, on their way to Santa Fe to take Antonia's cause before the governor. Father and son took up arms to resist the deputies after Antonia loudly announced in no uncertain terms that she had no intention of obeying an order from "un indio con calzones," a contemptuous ethnic slur at alcalde Sánchez. Cristóbal and Diego were forthwith taken to the Santa Fe guardhouse. Governor Flores Mogollón, however, for some reason saw to it that an attorney was secured for their defense. Two refused to take the case; they probably knew Antonia. The third accepted.

Cristóbal and Diego were found guilty of disobedience and disrespect to the authorities on August 7. They were each fined ten pesos, plus four additional pesos in costs for the building of the new church at Santa Cruz. The governor decreed that, if there was any repetition of the performance, they would be exiled from the jurisdiction.[22] Antonia, who was responsible for their predicament, did not even stand trial. It is to be hoped that at least she paid their fines.

The record is silent as to whether María obtained any satisfaction in her slander suit. This episode is about the only time Cristóbal the husband gets into the act. Diego appears to have inherited his mother's temper: two years later, he was tried for beating one Joseph Vásquez over the head with a cudgel in a fight involving a young lady. The charges were dropped when Diego agreed to pay the bill Vásquez owed to the Chimayó surgeon Francisco Xavier Romero.[23]

JOSEFA BUSTAMANTE

Josefa Bustamante, widow of Nicolás Ortiz III, was not so successful in managing her business affairs as were Francisca, Juana, and Antonia. When Nicolás was killed while fighting Comanches in 1769, she was undoubtedly the wealthiest woman in New Mexico. Twenty years later, she was reduced to living on the pittance from the *monte pio,* the pension fund to which she was entitled as the widow of a presidial captain.

Josefa was the daughter, or adopted daughter, of aristocratic, Spanish-born Bernardo de Bustamante y Tagle and Doña Feliciana de la Vega y Coca (Chávez 1954*a:* 150). On February 6, 1751, she became the second wife of Nicolás Ortiz III whose grandfather, Nicolás I, had come to New Mexico from Zacatecas as a colonist in 1693. Nicolás III's first wife had been Gertrudis, the daughter of the ubiquitous Juan Paéz Hurtado (Chávez 1954*a:* 249). Holding the rank of captain in the Santa Fe presidio, Nicholas III was also politically powerful. By grant and purchase he had amassed property throughout the territory, as well as in the capital where he maintained his town home. By the 1760s, through questionable "purchases," he had acquired valuable agricultural land extending some two miles along the Pojoaque–Nambé river at the expense of both small pueblos. Across the river from the much-encroached-upon Pueblo of Pojoaque, he had constructed a sizable hacienda complex of buildings that served as his country residence. He also conducted a thriving trade with merchants in Chihuahua. Called into active duty to lead an expedition against the Comanches in 1769, he was killed in an engagement at San Antonio Mountain.

In the settlement of his large estate, Josefa inherited the Santa Fe property, half the Pojoaque land, and much of the Chihuahua business. His children by Gertrudis received the remainder, with the lion's share going to the eldest,

Antonio José, who had married Josefa's sister, Rosa Bustamante.

When Gov. Pedro Fermín de Mendinueta came to pay his condolences following Nicolás's untimely death, Josefa sadly remarked that such calamities befell New Mexico because it had no sworn patron saint. To remedy the situation, she was instrumental in assisting the governor and Antonio José in reestablishing the Confraternity of Nuestra Señora del Rosario (Our Lady of the Rosary) and the annual fiesta in honor of "La Conquistadora," as the little statue of Nuestra Señora del Rosario was affectionately known (Adams and Chávez 1956: 240–41; Boyd 1974: 331). She also donated vestments for the Military Chapel (Castrense) of Our Lady of Light in Santa Fe and paintings for the mission church of Nuestra Señora de Guadalupe at Pojoaque Pueblo (Adams and Chávez 1956: 249–50; Chávez 1954*a:* 249–50).

Finding it difficult to make ends meet, she was persuaded by Antonio José to sell him the Santa Fe property. To bail out the Chihuahua business and pay her creditors, she leased and mortgaged the Pojoaque land to him in 1784. Two years later, he foreclosed and took over the land when Josefa could not redeem the mortgage.[24] By 1790, she was broke. The moral to this story might be, never trust your stepson if he is also your brother-in-law. Antonio José may have felt some twinges of conscience, for until his death in 1806 he rehabilitated every church structure in Santa Fe, but that helped Josefa not at all.

It might be argued that Josefa, who was a woman of gentility, devoted to the church and to good works, illustrates much more accurately the status of the eighteenth-century Spanish colonial woman who was the victim of a completely male-dominated society, and that the other women discussed here were exceptions. On the other hand, it seems evident that Josefa simply did not have the temperament or business sense to cope with financial matters, especially when it came to dealing with her somewhat unethical brother-in-law. However, like the others' Josefa's story tells much about social and economic conditions in New Mexico during the 1700s.

NOTES

1. Chávez 1954*a:* 240; Spanish Archives of New Mexico, Series II, No. 54c, muster roll of colonists, New Mexico State Records Center and Archives, Santa Fe. Hereafter, these documents will be cited as SANM, with proper series and document number.

2. SANM, I, No. 258.

3. Records of the Surveyor-General of New Mexico, Case 109, New Mexico State Records Center and Archives, Santa Fe. Hereafter these records are cited as SG.

4. SANM, I, No. 9.

5. SANM, II, No. 293.

6. SANM, I, No. 742.

7. SG, Case 109, Gigosa grant.

8. Juana's will is SANM, II, No. 556.
9. The original of this grant is contained in the case file of the lengthy litigation involving San Ildefonso and Spanish encroachers in 1763–1766, SANM, I, No. 1351.
10. These conveyances are not in the records, but references to their contents are in the proceedings of 1763–1766, SANM, I, No. 1351, and in proceedings before Anza in 1786, SANM, I, No. 1354.
11. SANM, II, No. 556.
12. SANM, I, No. 1351.
13. SANM, I, No. 1354.
14. The dates and details of Felipe's grant are specified in the litigation between the Moraga and Martín families, SANM, I, No. 490, No. 515; SANM, II, No. 496.
15. The grants to Antonia and the litigation with Juana Sosa Canela are incorporated into SANM, I, No. 491.
16. See Ellis 1978. Ellis's interpretation of these documents is somewhat different from mine.
17. Archivo General Nacional, Mexico, Inquisition, t. 735, ff. 306–8.
18. SANM, I, No. 501.
19. SANM, I, No. 490.
20. SANM, I, No. 501.
21. SANM, I, No. 496.
22. SANM, II, No. 197.
23. SANM, II, No. 228.
24. SANM, I, No. 120; II, No. 980.

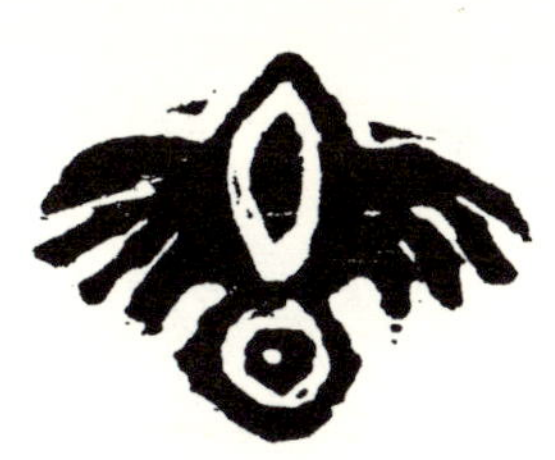

DAVID H. SNOW

A NOTE ON ENCOMIENDA ECONOMICS IN SEVENTEENTH-CENTURY NEW MEXICO

BOTH THE ROLE AND THE IMPACT of the encomienda (grants of Indians' labor and tribute) in seventeenth-century New Mexico are obscured by the notorious reputation it had gained in Mexico during the preceding century. Interestingly, much of what we do know about the operation of the encomienda stems from testimony concerning abuses of encomenderos by Spanish colonial governors. Avaricious administrators during the "troublous times" and the civil strife characteristic of the period sought to enrich themselves at the expense of resident colonists and Pueblo Indians, particularly where encomienda grants were concerned (for example, Hackett 1937; Scholes 1936, 1937, 1940: 249 ff.).

The tendency has been to project, usually unthinkingly, the abuses practiced in the name of encomienda in sixteenth-century Mexico to the conditions of frontier New Mexico nearly a century later (for example, Sauer 1980: 60, who claims that the encomienda in New Mexico was illegal; and Simmons 1979: 182). Encomienda abuse in Mexico is well documented (C. Gibson 1976: 76–77; Simpson 1950), but uncontrolled exploitation of tributaries and political misuse of the encomienda system led to reforms that, by mid-century, greatly reduced its power and significance (C. Gibson 1976: 58 ff.; Taylor 1972) as well as its excessive abuses.

Encomienda grants continued to be made as the frontier of New Spain pushed northward into New Mexico. Rooted in medieval practice, the granting of tribute privilege and the services of the tributary population (the latter prohibited in 1549 by royal decree) was an inducement by which the crown guaranteed itself a modicum of military response in the absence of a standing colonial army or militia in newly occupied land (Scholes 1935: 102). The crown granted Juan de Oñate the right to distribute encomiendas in New Mexico in 1598, as

> prescribed in article 58 of the ordinances for new discoveries and colonies, namely, that he might give in encomienda unassigned Indians, or those who might become unassigned, in the territory of Spanish settlements already es-

> tablished, for a term of two lives, and those in the newly settled territory [that is, in New Mexico] for three lives. (Hammond and Rey 1952: 509)

Oñate's successor, Pedro de Peralta, was instructed in 1609 that

> inasmuch as it has been reported that the tribute levied on the natives is excessive, and that it is collected with much vexation and trouble to them, we charge the governor to take suitable measures in this matter, proceeding in such a way as to relieve and satisfy the royal conscience. (Hammond and Rey 1952: 1088–89)

Clearly there were abuses of the encomienda in New Mexico, and it is not my purpose here to deny that Pueblo Indians might not have suffered from its demands or from the unscrupulous nature of individual encomenderos. Rather, I am concerned that the impact of the encomienda on both Indian and colonist has not been seriously examined. We have been too willing to accept willy-nilly the pernicious nature of the encomienda without questioning how it affected the structure and organization of frontier New Spain's society and economy. In this essay, I comment briefly on one significant aspect of the encomienda from the perspective of its role in Spanish colonial economy and subsistence. In addition, I have endeavored to list the known encomenderos and, where known, their tributaries during the eighty years of encomienda in New Mexico.

New Mexico in the seventeenth century, physically isolated from the center of Spain's New World hegemony, presented fundamental economic differences from sixteenth-century Mexico, and the encomienda in these circumstances differed as well. New Mexico lacked the large organized native population, the productive land base, and the resources of central Mexico. Money was only an indirect factor in the seventeenth-century New Mexican economy, in distinct contrast to the cash that sustained the local and regional Valley of Mexico economy. The frontier market system was based on a rather stable monetary value assigned to local products such as corn, wheat, pinyons, hides, and the like (Scholes 1935: 109). The system was sustained by the barter of these products usually between individuals, and their accumulation and shipment south by governors and mission personnel did nothing to stimulate local economy.

The accumulation of wealth by permanent residents in the Rio Grande colony (as opposed to transient governors and their staff) could not be effected by banking currency (or products) or by investing cash in local profit-making ventures such as cattle ranching, mining, or labor-intensive agricultural haciendas characteristic of sixteenth- and seventeenth-century Mexico. In the face of a purely subsistence economic base, the New Mexican encomienda could never become the powerful political system of a century earlier (see also Service 1954: 42–49 for a similar situation in colonial Paraguay). In New Mexico, nevertheless, the encomienda itself was a resource to be exploited, not so much by the encomendero, as by its transient governors (Scholes 1940).

As of 1601, no encomienda grants had been issued by Oñate (Hammond and Rey 1952: 641), but in 1608 interim governor Juan Martínez de Montoya is reported to have held the encomienda of Santiago de Jémez (Scholes 1944), a grant undoubtedly bestowed by Oñate. This is the only documented encomienda from the early years of the settlement. Other encomenderos from these early years, though not recorded, are known or suspected from statements made later in the century. These men and their encomiendas are listed in Table 1 of the appendix to this essay.

By 1639, the number of encomenderos was set officially at thirty-five (Scholes 1935: 79), an action that may simply have reflected the lack of additional pueblos for conversion. Many of the forty-three pueblos listed in Table 2 of the appendix were portioned into halves, thirds, quarters, and other units for encomienda purposes, presumably to accommodate the less than one hundred soldiers of the colony's first ten or so years. Visitas were given separately in encomienda, and as Pueblo population declined and reconsolidated throughout the century, some encomenderos must have found their tribute disappearing. Continued splitting of the village for encomienda tribute may have been an attempt to compensate for this since the encomienda was inherited down to the third generation.

There is little detail about the encomienda in New Mexico, and the information we have stems from miscellaneous statements and documents generally from about 1620 through the 1660s. For example, because of "certain differences and disputes" between Gov. Juan de Eulate and the custodian of the Franciscan order in New Mexico, Eulate was instructed in 1621 to remedy the fact that

> the encomenderos of those provinces and other persons have also their pastures of the said stock near the pueblos and sowed fields of the Indians whereby much damage is done them. (Bloom 1928: 368)

In reality, there seem to have been relatively few complaints about the encomienda from the religious orders. The problem addressed in Eulate's instructions presumably emanated from the Franciscans but refers to stock depredations, not to excessive tribute, collection abuses, or to illegal labor for the encomenderos. Fray Alonso de Benavides admonished the encomenderos, pointing out that

> as the encomendero is ready to receive the tribute of houses added to their pueblos, he should also be ready to lose and cease taking tribute from abandoned houses, even though the owners live in someone else's house. (Hodge et al. 1945: 170)

Benavides also petitioned the crown sometime prior to 1635 not only to exempt unconverted pueblos from encomienda but also to exempt converted pueblos from encomienda for five years following their conversion. He argued that "even before the pueblos are converted, the governor himself gives them out in encomienda without notifying the custodian or the viceroy" (Hodge et al. 1945: 171). Eulate was also warned against this procedure with regard to as yet unconverted Zuni and Moqui in 1621 (Bloom 1928: 365). Benavides pointed out furthermore that the practice referred to had the effect of damping the enthusiasm of as yet unconverted pueblos. The crown granted the exemptions in 1635 (Hodge et al. 1945: 168), but, as a result of Benavides's own missionary zeal and efforts, there were few, if any, unconverted pueblos remaining by then.

In 1638, Fray Juan de Prada, commissary-general of the Franciscan order in New Mexico, petitioned the crown not to impose additional tribute on the Pueblo Indians, taking pains to spell out his opinion that the existing tribute was sufficient (Hackett 1937: 109–11). In 1643, Custodio Covarrubias, addressing Governor Pacheco's proposal to change the tribute levies, remarked that an increase in the total amount, by assessing Pueblo individuals rather than households, would be harmful. The old levy, he noted, "was frequently very oppressive, *especially in years when the cotton crop failed*" (Scholes 1937: 91; my emphasis).

Tribute was collected, according to witnesses from Oñate's colony, as early as 1600 (Hammond and Rey 1952: 641) in the amount of about two thousand fanegas of corn, either from individuals or households or both. (A *fanega* is a little more than 2.6 bushels.) These collections were not made under the guise of encomienda but were most likely "tribute" demanded to augment a meager colonial diet in the face of disillusionment, lethargy, and starvation. These same witnesses were unable to state why Oñate had so far failed to grant encomiendas (Hammond and Rey 1952: 641). By the first quarter of the century, Benavides described encomienda tribute as a "cotton blanket, the best of which are about a yard and a half square and a fanega of corn," and he noted that this was "understood to be for each house and not for each Indian, even though many Indian families live in such houses" (Hodge et al. 1945: 170). In 1638, Fray Juan de Prada noted that the Pueblo Indians

> are apportioned among their encomenderos, whom they recognize, and each household of Indians pays to him each year, either as tax or tribute, one fanega of maize, which in that country is valued at four reales, and also a piece of cotton cloth six palms square [about 5½ feet square], which is reckoned in price at six reales. (Hackett 1937: 110)

Former governor Martínez de Baeza added the information in 1639 that "raw buffalo hide or deer skin, either of which has the same value" might be substituted for a cotton blanket (Hackett 1937: 120).

These items were, by midcentury, collected twice a year, usually in May and October, and it can be assumed that little maize was available for surplus distribution to the encomenderos until the October collection following harvest. Hides and cotton blankets, therefore, probably made up the bulk of the May collections. Buffalo hides were undoubtedly obtained in trade from Plains groups in the fall. Cotton cultivation was apparently restricted to the Rio Abajo pueblos and to the Piros (Hackett 1937: 131; Hammond and Rey 1966: 83; Scholes 1936: 48; Winship 1896: 575), and the northern and eastern peripheral pueblos of Taos and Pecos, as well as the Tewa pueblos, must have obtained the bulk of their tribute-cotton requirements in trade.

To assess the impact of these tributes on the resident Spanish population in terms of subsistence (or "wealth"), we must have some idea of the size of the tributary and recipient populations and of the number of encomenderos. Families and individuals achieved social prominence and status in the seventeenth-century Rio Grande settlement, but their importance in sociopolitical or economic affairs is not explained simply by hereditary wealth or previously ascribed status. The periodic sanctioned extraction of tribute from Pueblo encomiendas can be argued to have been a significant factor in the aggrandizement of individuals through their ability to accumulate and/or to distribute surplus to less fortunate friends and neighbors. It might also be argued that a redistribution network, following extended kinship lines or based on population clusters, may have resulted from the encomendero's ability to supply periodic surplus. Unfortunately, we lack details of daily life in the seventeenth century to substantiate these hypotheses. Marriage preferences and identification of kin groups and settlement patterns that might reflect the role of individual encomenderos and their extended kin are not readily apparent in the meager documentation for the period. Nevertheless, the fact that several governors attempted to confiscate the tribute of individual encomenderos suggests something of the economic value of the tribute.

Discounting what seem exaggerated population estimates of the Pueblo villages during the late sixteenth century, as well as those of the overzealous Benavides, I have chosen a rather perplexing document that seems to have received little attention by historians (Simmons 1979: 185; Zubrow 1974). Scholes (1929) has translated a document dated 1664 that is a list of Pueblo missions and visitas and their populations. This list is, according to its author (Fray Bartolome Márquez, secretary-general of the Indies), a copy of the original made in 1626 by Fray Geronimo de Zarate Salmeron. It is a curious document because it lists churches, conventos, and resident priests in pueblos that, according to Benavides, were not converted until the period of his own missionary efforts between 1626 and 1629, following Zarate Salmeron's departure from the province.

The population figures in Table 2, therefore, reflect either 1626 or 1664; the calculations based on them, while subject to criticism, make a significant point: the amount of tribute paid in maize per pueblo made up only a very small percent of the total yearly minimum requirements. Based on Bradfield's (1971) Hopi figures of 12 bushels of corn per person for subsistence (plus an additional 12 bushels per person for surplus), 2.6 bushels of maize per household should have little, if any, impact except over successive poor years of yield. For each pueblo, encomienda maize represented only .04 percent of the total minimum required for the population provided by Zarate Salmeron. On the other hand, the amount of maize from encomienda for the Spanish population was, in view of their small numbers, staggering. A few comments are in order with regard to the figures in Table 2.

Bradfield (1971) has calculated that 2.5 acres of corn per person are required at modern Hopi for basic subsistence needs. This translates to about twelve bushels per person per year, a figure within the range Charles Gibson (1976: 311) has estimated for each Indian's requirements in the sixteenth-century Valley of Mexico. Based on census data from the eighteenth-century pueblos, I have averaged the number of persons per Pueblo family, arriving at a mean of five. I assume that this represents no appreciably significant difference from the seventeenth century. I also assume that by "houses," the Spanish accounts refer to individual domestic family units, so that "family" equates with tributary "household." As a result, I have calculated an approximate number of households per pueblo based on Zarate Salmeron's seventeenth-century Pueblo population figures.

Obviously this is a risky procedure, and it can be suspected that social organizational differences among the forty-three pueblos listed in the Zarate Salmeron document allow for considerable variation in family or household size (in addition to possible rearrangements in household size through time). For example, in the first instance, Zarate Salmeron (Milich 1966: 64) referred to the 6 pueblos at Zuni with 300 houses, and to 5 Hopi villages with 450 houses. If the purported Zarate Salmeron figures are correct, the mean number of persons per house is, respectively, 4 at Zuni and 6.7 at Hopi. Similarly, based on a 1662 statement (Hackett 1937: 248) that one-half of the Quarai encomienda was valued at 40 pesos, or 320 reales (at 10 reales per household, or tribute unit), the number of houses at Quarai was 64. The Zarate Salmeron population figure for Quarai is 658, indicating a mean number of persons per household of 10.3. By the same method, at Picurís in 1662, the mean number of persons per household was 5.1. If they are accurate, these figures suggest significant and intriguing variations in household sizes among the pueblos.

Arriving at an estimate of the number of Spaniards is even more problematical in the absence of census data and in view of conflicting contemporary estimates. In 1600–1601, for example, estimates ranged from about 60 to 150 persons (Hammond and Rey 1952: 651, 1077), but in 1620, only 50 residents were said to live in Santa Fe (Hammond and Rey 1952: 1140; heads of household may have been implied). In 1638, an estimated 200 persons were living in Santa Fe (Hackett 1937: 108), but the number of rural inhabitants was not given. Ex-governor Martínez de Baeza claimed that there were "scarcely more than 50 inhabitants" in Santa Fe, and only ten or twelve farms of Spaniards between Senecu and Santa Fe when he was governor prior to 1639 (Hackett 1937: 119).

Based on the 1680 refugee lists, Hackett (1937: 327–28) estimated that there were approximately 2,800 non-Pueblo Indian inhabitants at the time of the Revolt. He and Scholes disagreed on the estimates, however, Hackett preferring to rely on contemporary hearsay claims for 2,500 people in the two divisions of Otermin's retreating colonists. Scholes (1935: 96), using the official count of 1,946 persons, plus the number counted as dead and missing, as well as an estimated 500 servants, arrived at a total of 2,347. In 1679, Fray Ayeta estimated that "the Spaniards and other persons of various castes, even counting those of this last relief [that is, the 46 convicts of 1677], scarcely reach the number of one hundred and seventy that can use arms" (Hackett 1937: 299). I have calculated the mean number of persons per Spanish family from the 1680 refugee lists at 7.5, which, multiplied by the number estimated in 1679 as arms-bearing or (I assume) heads of households, results in a figure of about 1,300 Spaniards. Add to this the fact that, in 1680, some 66 percent of the Spanish families had servants whose families, in turn, averaged 7.5 persons as well, the total in 1679 was in the neighborhood of 2,000 non-Pueblo inhabitants. Under normal circumstances, we can expect fewer numbers of Spaniards and servants during the preceding twenty-five years or so.

It seems evident that there were, certainly during the first fifty to seventy-five years of the settlement, few Spaniards relative to the tributary population. Even if we assume as many as 1,500 non-Pueblo inhabitants up to about 1675, encomienda tribute in maize was available each year for no less than one-half of the yearly requirements (at 12 bushels per person) for each non-Pueblo inhabitant. Francisco Gómez Robledo in 1662, for example, who inherited his father's encomiendas, could boast of 722 tribute units from encomienda (Hackett 1937: 223; Kessell 1979: 188). This represents 361 bushels of corn a year, or enough to support 30 people subsisting entirely on corn (although it was noted in 1662 that neither he nor his father had collected from Tesuque for more than forty years "because of service rendered on contract in lieu of tribute" [Kessell 1979: 186]). The 9,992.5 total bushels from all Pueblo encomiendas, shown in Table 2, is sufficient to have fed 833 Spaniards living only on corn for a year (based on Bradfield's 12 bushels per person per year at Hopi).

These data are, of course, abstractions and do not take into account a rapidly growing Spanish population and a similar decrease in Pueblo population throughout the century. These factors, plus drought, Apache raids, and forced labor by avaricious governors, must have made the initially inconsequential encomienda tribute more and more difficult to supply on demand. The growing Spanish population must have turned more and more to small-scale subsistence farming to offset this trend. In sum, it seems reasonable to suggest that encomienda initially was not the onerous burden on Pueblo Indians that it is generally assumed to have been. From the Spanish perspective, on the other hand, encomienda tribute was a potentially significant contribution to the subsistence of a small struggling colony.

APPENDIX: ENCOMIENDA IN NEW MEXICO

TABLE 1. Encomenderos in Seventeenth-Century New Mexico

Encomendero	Encomienda/share
Francisco Gómez Robledo I	Tesuque, Sandia (?), ½ Shongopavi, 2½ Taos, ½ less 20 houses Acoma, all of Pecos less 24 houses
Francisco Gómez Robledo II	Tesuque, ½ Sandia, ½ Shongopavi, 2½ Taos, ½ Abo, ½ less 20 houses Acoma, all of Pecos less 24 houses
Juan López de Ocanto	Jémez, Nambe
Domingo López de Ocanto	Jémez, Nambe; son of Juan López de Ocanto
Francisco Anaya Almazan I	½ Cuarac, ½ Picurís, La Cienega (San Marcos)
Cristóbal Anaya Almazan	½ Cuarac, ½ Picurís, La Cienega
Diego de Montoya	San Pedro
Bartolome de Montoya	San Pedro
Hernando de Hinojos	(?) Humanas
Miguel de Hinojos	Humanas; possibly son of Hernando
Júan Gomez [de Luna?]	San Lazaro
Elena Gómez	Awatobi (½?)
Geronimo de Caravajal	½ Awatobi

Felis de Caravajal	part of Senecu; brother of Geronimo
Hernan Martín Serrano I	?
Hernan Martín Serrano II	?
Andrés Hurtado	Santa Ana and "neighboring pueblos"
Juan Alonso Mondragón	Senecu
Antonio de Salas	Pojoaque
Pedro de la Cruz	Cuquina [Kwakina]
Juan de Tapia	one of 4 encomenderos of Taos
José Telles Jiron	San Felipe
Diego de Vera Perdomo	?
Diego Romero	½ Zia, ½ Cochiti, "protector of Sevilleta"
Pedro de Montoya	½ Cochiti, *escudero** for Diego Romero
Pedro Lucero de Godoy	24 houses at Pecos
Juan Martínez de Montoya	Santiago de Jémez
Thomas de Albizu	Zuni (?)
Fernando Duran y Chávez	?
Diego de Guadalajara	Sevilleta
Juan de Herrera	Santa Clara, Jémez
Asencio de Archuleta	?
Alonso Rodríguez Cisneros	⅓ Humanas; regranted from Hinojos
Juan Gonzáles Bernal	⅓ (?) Humanas
Sebastián Gonzáles Bernal	½ Humanas, father of Juan

Toribio de la Huerta	Humanas, escudero for Miguel de Hinojos
Juan Domínguez de Mendoza	Humanas, escudero for Juan Gonzáles
Juan de la Cruz	?
Pedro Duran y Chávez	Taos ?
Cristóbal Márquez	Cieneguilla (La Cienega), escudero for Anaya
Cristóbal Duran y Chávez	?, escudero

**Escuderos* were assigned as temporary trustees for encomenderos by the governors in order to continue tribute collection. I have not attempted to sort out the encomenderos temporally because of insufficient records and space. Twenty pueblos have no identified encomendero; discounting escuderos, there are twenty-eight encomenderos for whom the origin of the encomienda is not known, and the remaining eight were clearly inherited from father to son.

TABLE 2. Calculation of Seventeenth-Century Pueblo Tributary Units by Pueblo.*

Pueblo/visitas	Zarate Salmeron's Population Figure	Number of Households	Minimum Maize (in bushels) at 60/ Family a Year	Encomienda Tribute (2.6 bushels)	Peso Value
San P——— (Pedro?)	200	40	2,400	100.0	50.00
Tesuque	170	34	2,040	85.0	42.50
San Ildefonso, with 2 visitas	400	80	4,800	200.0	100.00
Santa Clara, with 1 visita	993	199	11,940	497.5	248.75
Nambe, with 1 visita	300	60	3,600	150.0	75.00
Santo Domingo, with 1 visita	850	170	10,200	425.0	212.50
San Felipe	350	70	4,200	175.0	87.50
Pecos	1,189	238	14,280	595.0	297.50
Galisteo, with 1 visita	1,000	200	12,000	500.0	250.00
San Marcos, with 1 visita	777	155	9,300	387.5	193.75
Chilili	250	50	3,000	125.0	62.50
Tajique	484	97	5,820	242.5	121.25
Cuarac (Quarai)	658	132	7,920	330.0	165.00
Abo, with 2 visitas	1,580	316	18,960	790.0	395.00
Jémez	1,860	372	22,320	930.0	465.00
Zia, with 1 visita	800	160	9,600	400.0	200.00
Sandia, with 1 visita	640	128	7,680	320.0	160.00
Isleta	750	150	9,000	375.0	187.50
Alameda	400	80	4,800	200.0	100.00
Acoma	600	120	7,200	300.0	150.00
Oraibi	1,236	247	14,820	617.5	308.75
Aguatobi, with 1 visita	900	180	10,800	450.0	225.00
Xongopavi, with 1 visita	830	166	9,960	415.0	207.50
Socorro, with 2 visitas	400	80	4,800	200.0	100.00
Picurís	564	120	6,780	300.0	141.25
Taos	600	113	7,200	282.5	150.00
Zuni	1,200	240	14,400	600.0	300.00
TOTALS:	19,981	3,997	239,820	9,992.5 (.04%)	4,996.25

*The number of families per pueblo is based on an eighteenth-century mean of five persons per household. Population figures are from Scholes (1929).

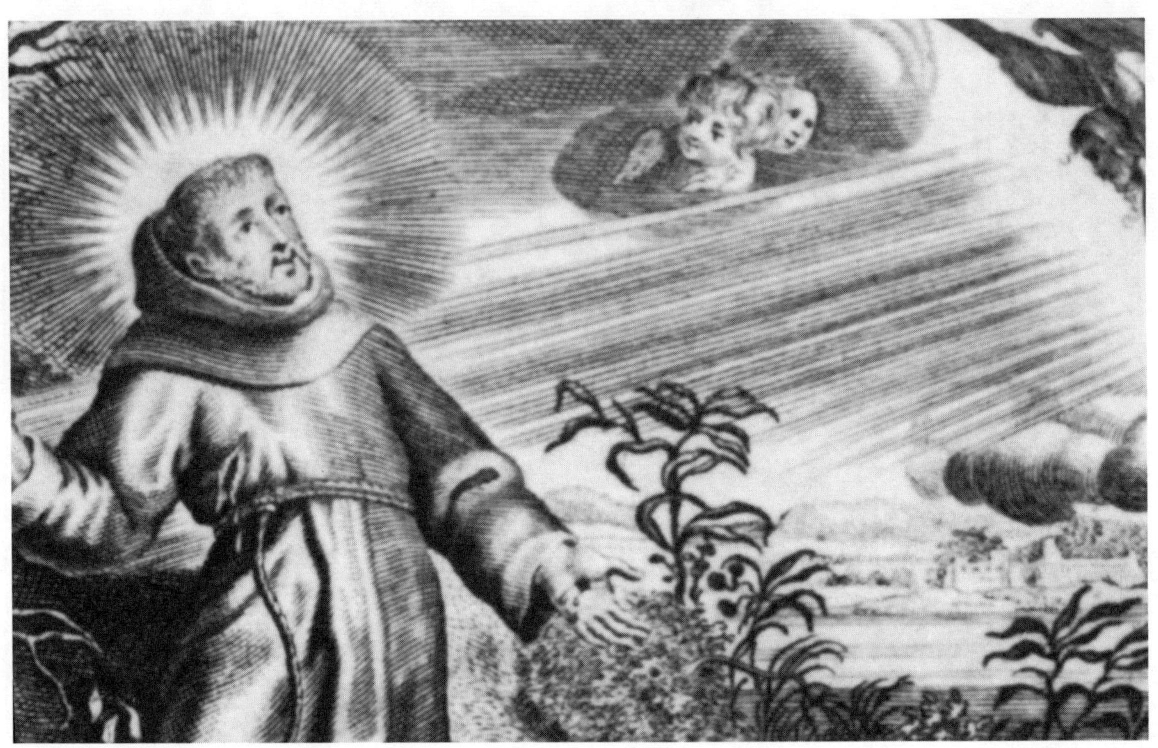

LINCOLN BUNCE SPIESS

A GROUP OF BOOKS FROM COLONIAL NEW MEXICO

In the spring of 1965, I located a group of old books of New Mexican provenance at the Franciscan-run Saint Leonard College near Dayton, Ohio.[1] The provincial librarian there at the time was Fr. Vincent Dieckmann, O.F.M., who proved most helpful and courteous as the initial inventory was made. After Father Dieckmann understood the books' potential importance for New Mexico history, he agreed to consider sending them to the Museum of New Mexico. Later that year, with approval from the Franciscan provincial, the collection was sent to Santa Fe and is now part of the holdings of the Museum of New Mexico in the Museum of International Folk Art, Santa Fe. One volume (No. 34) was kept at Saint Leonard College because of its importance to Franciscan history.

There were thirty-four items in my original inventory. Later, one of them (No. 20) was found to be part of another (No. 4), making an actual total of thirty-three books. In the list prepared for this article,[2] the numbering of the original inventory is retained with minor variation because the museum's accession list was based on that numbering.

The collection falls into two general groups: liturgical books, including four missals and several breviaries; and various works on theology, philosophy, and church history. The liturgical books are primarily eighteenth-century imprints, with one seventeenth-century missal (No. 3) and one nineteenth-century missal (No. 4). The other items include materials from the end of the fifteenth century through the eighteenth century.

The missals and breviaries are of interest not only for musical and liturgical reasons but also for their engravings. E. Boyd was particularly intrigued by these engravings and, had she time, might well have published some study of their relationship to the New Mexican santos. She wrote me:

> The Hispanic & Franciscan sections bound into some breviaries as well as big Plantin missals throw fine light on some of our cults & their santos. Strictly NOT in the Roman missals.[3]

On occasion, she pointed out to me illustrations in the breviaries that were related to specific santos and stated that the santeros clearly had access to those breviaries.

Musically, the 1728 missal (No. 2) is of particular interest because it has more music than one ordinarily finds in a missal, and its music differs considerably from that found in other missals of the period that are known to me. Of the nonliturgical books, perhaps the one with the greatest historical value is the *Decretales Domini papae Gregorii noni* (No. 9). The typographical style of the book suggests a late fifteenth-century origin, which would make it an incunabulum. The books dating from the sixteenth and seventeenth centuries (Nos. 11, 24, 26, 28, 32, 33, and 34) are also of considerable historical interest.

The condition of all the books in the collection is rather poor. Many lack title pages and so present problems of identification. Many are missing several pages at the beginning and the end. Several show water damage, and in some cases one can even feel traces of fine sand or silt on the pages, which suggests that they might have been in a flood. (One thinks of the Santo Domingo flood of the 1880s or the Peña Blanca flood of the 1920s).

The provenance of the books—from the Franciscan retreat at Peña Blanca, New Mexico, although how they came there is not known—and various details in them, as will be seen in the inventory, suggest that at least some were used in colonial New Mexico. They may even have been a part of the Santo Domingo library inventoried in 1776 by Fray Francisco Atanasio Domínguez (Adams and Chávez 1956: 220–33). Missals and breviaries are referred to in the Domínguez descriptions of individual mission churches, in each of which there is almost always at least one missal, usually described as usable or in some stage of old age. The one important variation in those descriptions is at the mission church of Santo Domingo, where there is mentioned "a new missal of our Order, which Father Zamora provided" (Adams and Chávez 1956: 134).

In the mission at San Ildefonso, separate mention is made of music for choir singers: "*Other things:* . . . a usable missal. Another very old one. Two old breviaries, which, along with the aforesaid missal and some papers with introits, etc., written in musical notes, are for the choir singers" (Adams and Chávez 1956: 67). These "papers" would be sheets of music, copied out for the choir, probably from graduals or antiphonaries; the reference to *introits* suggests antiphonary sources at least. Of course, the music could have been set down from memory and would not necessarily imply the existence of such volumes in the province.

There are many unresolved problems with this group of books,[4] and it is not my purpose here to solve the many questions that they may raise in the reader's mind. There are several potential areas of research that could result from their study, but three would be of special interest: the handwriting scattered throughout; the engravings and woodcuts and their relationship to New Mexican santos, as E. Boyd pointed out; and a detailed examination of the music in the missals, some of which may derive from the "Spanish liturgy" (see No. 2). This essay is presented in hopes that the reader may find these books useful in various areas of investigation and also because the acquisition of these books by the Museum of New Mexico was an occasion of some importance to E. Boyd, who helped catalogue the collection and criticized the 1966 version of this article.[5]

THE INVENTORY OF DECEMBER 1965

Where title pages are lacking, such information is supplied in brackets from page headings within the volume and other reliable sources.

In the commentaries, *1776* refers to the inventory of the Santo Domingo library made by Fray Francisco Anastasio Domínguez in 1776 (Adams and Chávez 1956). *1788* refers to the manuscript inventory of the same library in that year, which is preserved in the Archives of the Archdiocese of Santa Fe.[6] The 1788 manuscript is collated with the 1776 inventory in Adams and Chávez (1956).

E. Boyd's notations on the 1966 version are indicated by *E. B.* Her comments are also often found in references to information in the Museum of New Mexico accession list.

1.

MISSALE / ROMANUM / EX DECRETO SACROSANCTI / CONCILII TRIDENTINI RESTITUTUM, / PII V. PONT. MAX. JUSSU EDITUM, / ET / CLEMENTIS VIII. PRIMUM, NUNC DENUO / URBANI PAPAE OCTAVI / AUCTORITATE RECOGNITUM, / In quo MISSAE propriae de SANCTIS ad longum positae / sunt ad majorem Celebrantium commoditatem. / [Ornament: monstrance with encircling cherubs.] ANTVERPIAE, / EX TYPOGRAPHIA PLANTINIANA. / M.DCC.XI.

Description: In sexto.[7] Leather-covered boards. Pp. 1–84 missing, except for pp. 47–48. Supplemen-

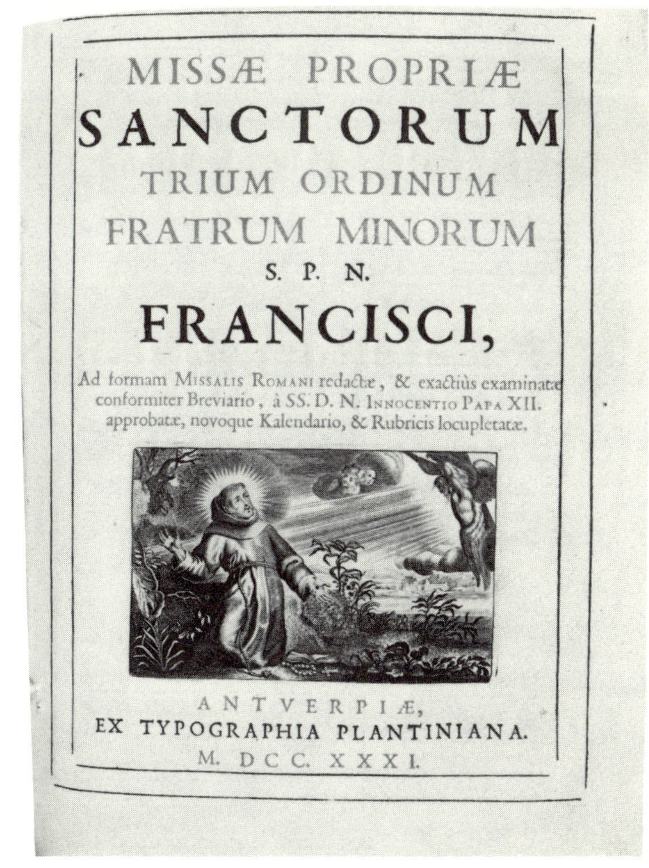
MISSÆ PROPRIÆ
SANCTORUM
TRIUM ORDINUM
FRATRUM MINORUM
S. P. N.
FRANCISCI,
Ad formam MISSALIS ROMANI redactæ, & exactiùs examinatæ conformiter Breviario, à SS. D. N. INNOCENTIO PAPA XII. approbatæ, novoque Kalendario, & Rubricis locupletatæ.

ANTVERPIÆ,
EX TYPOGRAPHIA PLANTINIANA.
M. DCC. XXXI.

FIGURE 1
Title page of Third Order missal bound with *Missale Romanum* (Inventory no. 2, Supplement no. 3), with ornament depicting Saint Francis. (A.65.51-2. Gift of St. Leonard's College Library, Dayton, Ohio, to the Museum of International Folk Art, Museum of New Mexico, Santa Fe.)

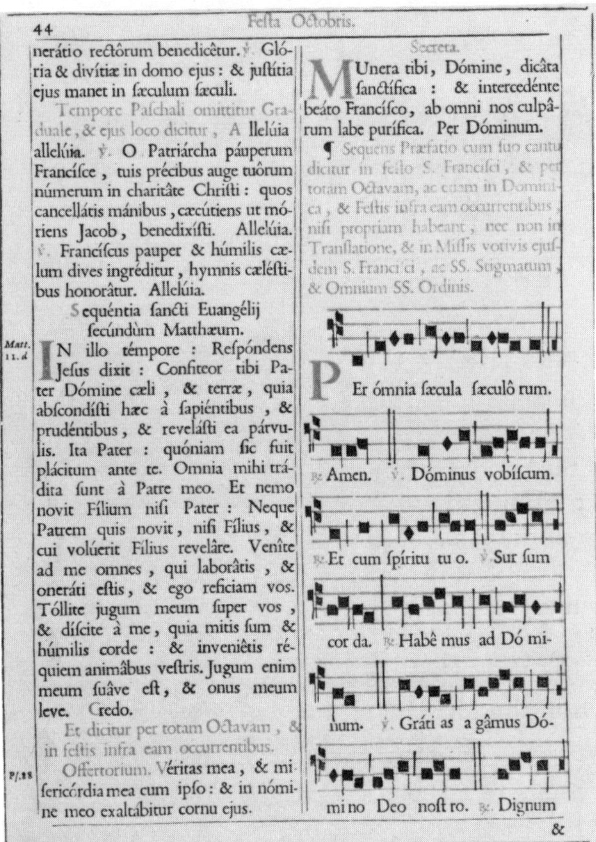

44 Festa Octobris.

nerátio rectôrum benedicêtur. ℣. Glória & divítiæ in domo ejus: & justítia ejus manet in sæculum sæculi.

Tempore Paschali omittitur Graduale, & ejus loco dicitur, Allelúia allelúia. ℣. O Patriárcha páuperum Francísce, tuis précibus auge tuôrum númerum in charitâte Christi: quos cancellátis mánibus, cæcútiens ut móriens Jacob, benedixísti. Allelúia. ℣. Francíscus pauper & húmilis cælum dives ingréditur, hymnis cæléstibus honorâtur. Allelúia.

Sequéntia sancti Evangélij secúndùm Matthæum.

Matt. 11. d IN illo témpore: Respóndens Jesus dixit: Confiteor tibi Pater Dómine cæli, & terræ, quia abscondísti hæc à sapiéntibus, & prudéntibus, & revelásti ea párvulis. Ita Pater: quóniam sic fuit plácitum ante te. Omnia mihi trádita sunt à Patre meo. Et nemo novit Filium nisi Pater: Neque Patrem quis novit, nisi Fílius, & cui volúerit Filius reveláre. Veníte ad me omnes, qui laborâtis, & oneráti estis, & ego refíciam vos. Tóllite jugum meum super vos, & díscite à me, quia mitis sum & húmilis corde: & inveniêtis réquiem animâbus vestris. Jugum enim meum suâve est, & onus meum leve. Credo.

Et dicitur per totam Octavam, & in festis infra eam occurrentibus.

Ps. 88 Offertorium. Véritas mea, & misericórdia mea cum ipso: & in nómine meo exaltábitur cornu ejus.

Secreta.

MUnera tibi, Dómine, dicâta sanctífica: & intercedénte beáto Francísco, ab omni nos culpârum labe purífica. Per Dóminum.

¶ Sequens Præfatio cum suo cantu dicitur in festo S. Francisci, & per totam Octavam, ac etiam in Dominica, & Festis infra eam occurrentibus, nisi propriam habeant, nec non in Translatione, & in Missis votivis ejusdem S. Francisci, ac SS. Stigmatum, & Omnium SS. Ordinis.

PEr ómnia sæcula sæculô rum.
℟. Amen. ℣. Dóminus vobíscum.
℟. Et cum spíritu tu o. ℣. Sur sum
cor da. ℟. Habê mus ad Dó mi-
num. ℣. Gráti as a gâmus Dó-
mi no Deo nost ro. ℟. Dignum
&

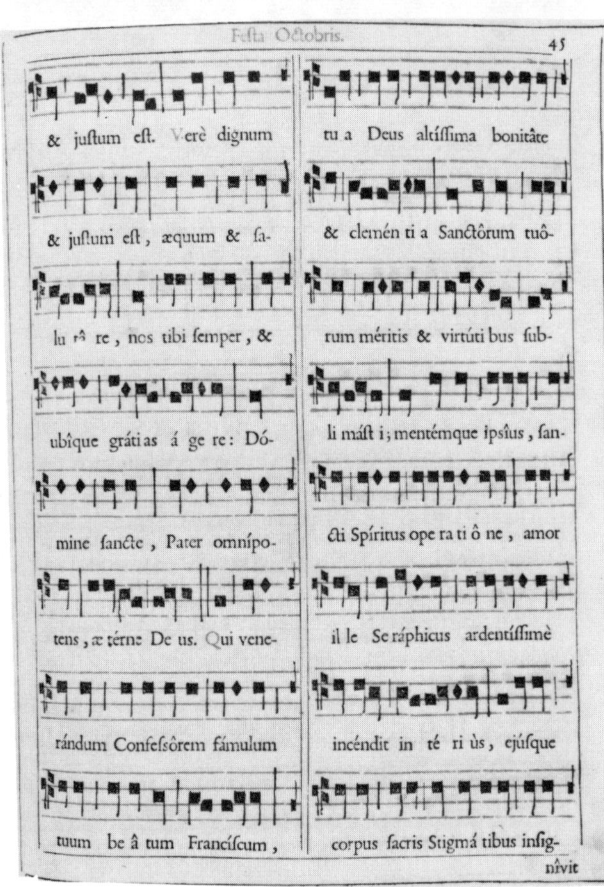

Festa Octobris. 45

& justum est. Verè dignum
& justum est, æquum & sa-
lu ta re, nos tibi semper, &
ubíque grâti as á ge re: Dómine sancte, Pater omnípo-
tens, æ térne De us. Qui vene-
rándum Confessôrem fámulum
tuum be â tum Francíscum,
tu a Deus altíssima bonitâte
& clemén ti a Sanctôrum tuôrum méritis & virtúti bus sub-
li mást i; mentémque ipsíus, sancti Spíritus ope ra ti ô ne, amor
il le Se ráphicus ardentíssimè
incéndit in té ri ùs, ejúsque
corpus sacris Stigmá tibus insig-
nîvit

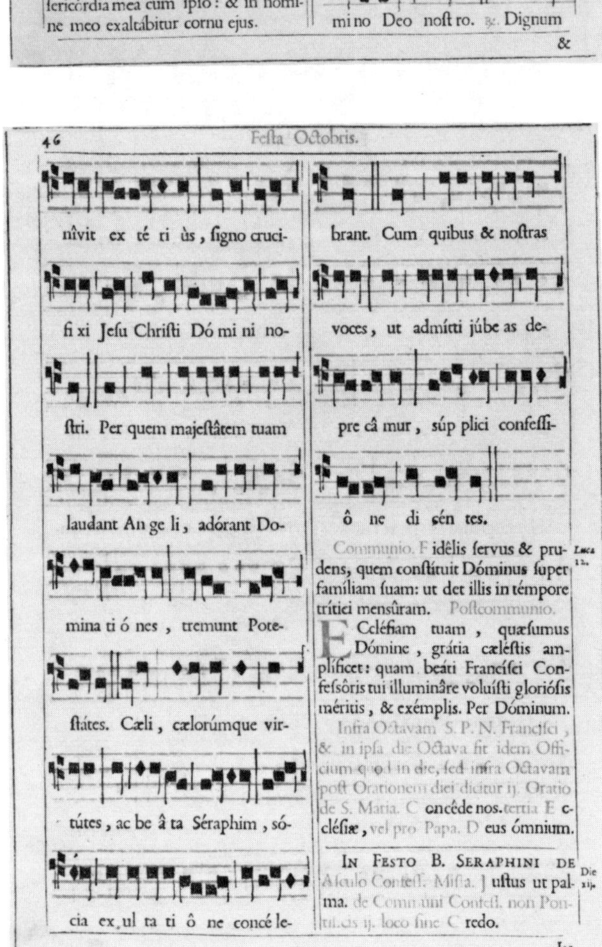

46 Festa Octobris.

nîvit ex té ri ùs, signo cruci-
fi xi Jesu Christi Dó mi ni no-
stri. Per quem majestâtem tuam
laudant An ge li, adórant Do-
mina ti ó nes, tremunt Pote-
stâtes. Cæli, cælorúmque vir-
tútes, ac be â ta Séraphim, só-
cia ex ul ta ti ô ne concé le-
brant. Cum quibus & nostras
voces, ut admítti júbe as de-
pre câ mur, súp plici confessi-
ô ne di cén tes.

Communio. Fidélis servus & prudens, quem constítuit Dóminus super famíliam suam: ut det illis in témpore trítici mensûram. Luca 12. Postcommunio.

ECclésiam tuam, quæsumus Dómine, grátia cæléstis amplíficet: quam beâti Francísci Confessôris tui illumináre voluísti gloriósis méritis, & exémplis. Per Dóminum.

Infra Octavam S. P. N. Francisci, & in ipsa die Octava fit idem Officium quod in die, sed infra Octavam post Orationem diei dicitur ij. Oratio de S. Maria. Concéde nos. tertia Ecclésiæ, vel pro Papa. Deus ómnium.

IN FESTO B. SERAPHINI DE Asculo Confess. Missa. Justus ut palma. de Communi Confess. non Pontificis ij. loco sine Credo. Die 12.

IN

FIGURE 2
Music of the Preface for the Feast of Saint Francis, October 4. Pages 44, 45, and 46 of the Third Order missal in Figure 1.

tary section with masses for Spanish saints, with separate title page: MISSAE PROPRIAE / SANCTORUM / HISPANORUM, / . . . [Engraving: Santiago on horseback, riding left to right, Moors, lances, banners, trumpeter, and so on] ANTVERPIAE, EX TYPOGRAPHIA PLANTINIANA. / M. D. CC. XI.; pp. 1–18 preserved, balance lost.

License date: Antwerp, 14 May 1710. Table of movable feasts, 1711–1750. Typography: roman, red and black. Size: 22.2 cm. x 33 cm. Museum of New Mexico accession number: A.65.51-1.

Comments: The Museum Plantin–Moretus in Antwerp has a 1711 folio missal in its holdings, but no other missal of that year's date; nor does it have the supplement for Spanish saints.

The music of the 1711 sexto missal corresponds, with minor variation, to the Gregorian of the 1961 edition of the *Missale Romanum* (Benziger Bros., New York), except that the notation of the 1711 missal uses longas, breves, and semibreves as separate notes, avoiding ligatures. This was characteristic of chant notation in the seventeenth and eighteenth centuries, in contrast to the music in modern liturgical chant books, which restores an older notation. This older notation was in use until the end of the sixteenth century and was reintroduced late in the nineteenth century in publications of the scholarly Benedictines of Solesmes.

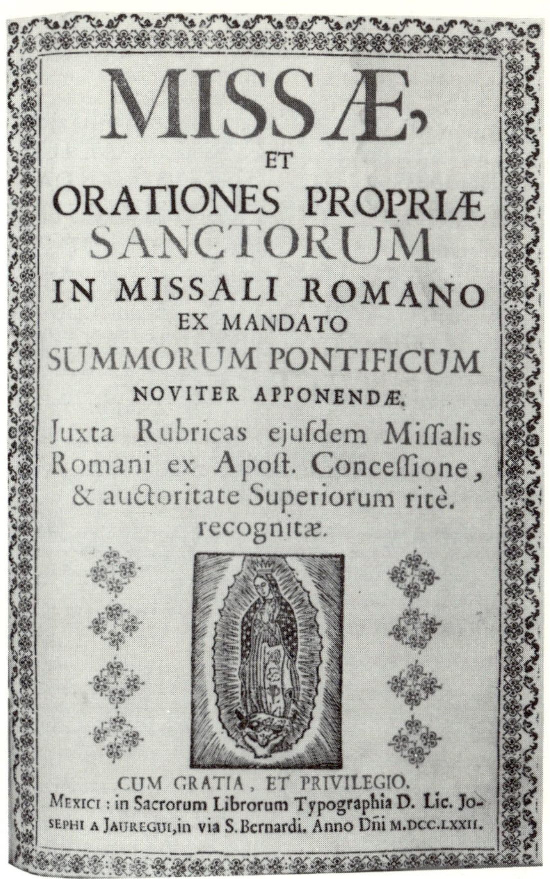
MISSÆ,
ET
ORATIONES PROPRIÆ
SANCTORUM
IN MISSALI ROMANO
EX MANDATO
SUMMORUM PONTIFICUM
NOVITER APPONENDÆ,
Juxta Rubricas ejuſdem Miſſalis Romani ex Apoſt. Conceſſione, & auctoritate Superiorum ritè. recognitæ.
CUM GRATIA, ET PRIVILEGIO.
MEXICI: in Sacrorum Librorum Typographia D. Lic. Josephi a Jauregui, in via S. Bernardi. Anno Dñi M.DCC.LXXII.

FIGURE 3
Title page of the missal bound with *Missale Romanum* (Inventory no. 2, Supplement no. 4; see Fig. 1), with ornament depicting Our Lady of Guadalupe.

2.

MISSALE / ROMANUM / EX DECRETO SACROSANCTI / CONCILII TRIDENTINI RESTITUTUM, / PII V. PONT. MAX. JUSSU EDITUM, / ET CLEMENTIS VIII. PRIMUM, NUNC DENUO / URBANI PAPAE OCTAVI / AUCTORITATE RECOGNITUM, / In quo MISSAE propriae de SANCTIS ad longum positae / sunt ad majorem Celebrantium commoditatem. / [Ornament: chalice with cherubs, angels.] ANTVERPIAE, / EX TYPOGRAPHIA PLANTINIANA. / M.DCC.XXVIII.

Description: In octavo. Tooled leather on board covers. Paging seems complete (pp. 1–632), except that at p. 293 a few leaves are inserted from a different missal to replace some missing pages. (Written on the verso of the title page are: "Sefiner / Jose Veilum / San Juan y Purisma," in bluish-purple pencil or crayon; "Fr. Juan de la Trinidad," in brownish-black ink.)

A series of supplements is bound in at the back, each separately paged: (1) Masses for Spanish Saints, 24 pages, ending with Mass for Saint James, Apostle; (2) Method of cantillating *(cantandi orationes)* in masses, vespers, and so on, 12 pages, with music; (3) MISSAE PROPRIAE / SANCTORUM / TRIUM ORDINUM / FRATRUM MINORUM / S.P.N. / FRANCISCI, / Ad formam Missalis Romani redactae . . . [Ornament: Saint Francis, etc.] ANTVERPIAE, / EX TYPOGRAPHIA PLANTINIANA. / M.DCC.XXXI. 56 pages, pp. 44–46, music of the Preface for the Feast of Saint Francis; (4) MISSAE, / ET / ORATIONES PROPRIAE / SANCTORUM / IN MISSALI ROMANO / EX MANDATO / SUMMORUM PONTIFICUM / NOVITER APPONENDAE. / . . . [Ornament: Our Lady of Guadalupe, with flowerlike designs on either side.] CUM GRATIA, ET PRIVILEGIO. / MEXICI: in Sacrorum Librorum Typographia D. Lic. Jo- / SEPHI A JAUREGUI, in via S. Bernardi. Anno Dñi M. DCC.LXXII. 36 pages, with p. 36 misprinted as "34."

The license date of the missal is Antwerp, 23 July 1728. Table of movable feasts, 1728–1767. Typography: roman, red and black. Size: 20.2 cm. x 26.3 cm. (trimmed at top?). Museum of New Mexico accession number: A.65.51-2.
Comments: The inclusion of the Mexican supplement of 1772 suggests that the volume was re-bound after that year. E. Boyd remarked that the paper backing the front cover "has ecclesiastical watermark; looks Mexican. Not original binding." This watermark is shaped like a flower of five petals.

The Museum Plantin–Moretus in Antwerp has a 1728 folio missal, but the music in the New Mexico volume is totally different from that edition. There is no melodic correspondence in such standard chants as the *Pater noster* and the *Ite missa est,* and a number of texts are given musical settings that do not normally occur with music in the Roman missal. There are other variations also in musical details: for example, the notation here is close to that of the sixteenth century and not characteristic of typical eighteenth-century missals.

The leaves inserted at p. 293 to replace missing pages are in the same notation; the paging is slightly different and somewhat larger (pages being cut to size). At the beginning of the inserted section, there is some overlapping affording some comparison; the music, at that point at least, corresponds almost exactly. Presumably the inserted leaves are from another missal of the same or similar content.

The difference in the music of this missal and the larger amount of music suggest the possibility that it may be from the "Spanish liturgy" in spite of the title, "Roman Missal."[8] (A 1689 missal at the cathedral in Santa Fe contains similar music.[9])

3.
[MISSALE ROMANUM. 1667?]
Description: In sexto. Leather-covered boards with remains of metal clasps. The volume lacks a title page and some pages of the introductory material, including the license page. Table of movable feasts, 1667–1691. Typography: roman, red and black (Plantinian?). Appended at the back are pages on different paper and with different type (varied paging), of masses for various saints: Saint Ph. Neri, Confessor; Saint Stephen, Confessor; Spanish saints; Order of Brothers Minor; and the whole is preceded by a page headed: "Missae proprium sanctorum . . . cum nonnullis Missae pro Ciuitate, et toto Regno Neapolis" (Masses belonging to the saints . . . with several masses for the city and for the whole kingdom of Naples).[10] Size: 22.2 cm. x 32 cm. Museum of New Mexico accession number: A.65.51-3.
Comments: There seems to be no corresponding missal in the collection of the Museum Plantin–Moretus. The list of known Plantinian Missals provided by the curator, Dr. L. Voet, includes missals of 1665, 1666, and 1672, but none of 1667. (The date of a missal's publication usually corresponds with the first year of the table of movable feasts, which in this case would be 1667.) Nevertheless, the style of the typography of the missal (but not of the supplementary pages), the musical notation, and the general appearance all seem to be Plantinian. The missal's musical content (except for the *Pater noster*) corresponds to No. 1 in this inventory, as to melody, chants used, and notation. (The *Pater noster* melody may be another case of Spanish liturgy source; see note 8.)

4. (and **20.**)
[MISSALE ROMANUM. 1835?]
Description: In quarto. No title page; no covers. In two pieces: (1) pp. vi–lxviii and 1–200; pp. 201–10 missing; (2) pp. 211–527 and supplement, pp. 1–116; index, four unpaged leaves; supplement for North America, pp. 1–12, plus one additional supplementary page.

Table of movable feasts, 1835–1870. Typography characteristic of the nineteenth century; probably French or Belgian. Size: 14.2 cm. x 22.4 cm.

Museum of New Mexico accession number: A. 65.51-4.
Comments: The second piece was originally inventoried as No. 20, but E. Boyd determined that it was part of No. 4 and suggested that it was of French origin.[11]

This volume contains less music than earlier missals. The *Pater noster* corresponds to that of No. 1 and to the modern *Missale Romanum* (1961). The notation is similar to liturgical publications issued from Paris and from Malines (Mechlin), Belgium, in the earlier nineteenth century. There are engravings at the end of some sections in a characteristic nineteenth-century scenic style.

The section for North America at the end of the missal is headed: "Missae foederatis Americae / septentrionalis provinciis concessae" (Masses granted to the federated provinces of North America).[12]

5.

EL SACROSANTO / Y ECUMÉNICO CONCILIO / DE TRENTO, / TRADUCIDO AL IDIOMA CASTELLANO / POR / DON IGNACIO LOPEZ DE AYALA. / AGREGASE EL TEXTO LATINO CORREGIDO SEGUN / LA EDICION *[sic]* AUTÉNTICA DE ROMA, PUBLICADA / EN 1564. / TERCERA EDICION / [Ornament: coat of arms with crown] CON PRIVILEGIO. / MADRID EN LA IMPRENTA REAL. / M. DCCLXXXVII. /
Description: In quarto. Parchment-covered cardboard covers. Preserved pages: pp. i–vii and 1–492. Typography: roman, black. Bookplate of Fray Angélico Chávez. Size: 15 cm. x 20.2 cm. Museum of New Mexico accession number: A.61.51-5.
Comments: Spanish translation, with Latin in parallel columns, of the documentary material of the *convocatoria* of the Council of Trent, sessions 1–25, 13 December 1545 to 4 December 1563. In manuscript at left, on title page: initials *LR* (see quotation in note 10). See also the comments for No. 6 in this inventory.

6.

PROMPTUARIO / DE LA / THEOLOGIA MORAL, / QUE HA COMPUESTO EL CONVENTO / de Santiago, Universidad de Pamplona, del Sagrado Orden / de Predicadores, siguiendo por la mayor parte las Doctrinas / del M. R. P. Maestro Fr. Francisco Larraga, Prior / que fuè *[sic]* de dicho Convento: / EN EL QUE SE REFORMAN. Y CORRIGEN / MUCHAS DE SUS OPINIONES; / Y SE ILLUSTRA / CON LA EXPLICACION DE VARIAS CONSTITUCIONES / de N. SS. P. Benedicto XIV. en especial de las que hablan del *Solici- / tante in Confessione: del Sigilio* de la Confession: / *del Ayuno,* &. / CORRIGIDO, *[sic]* Y ENMENDADO EN ESTA ULTIMA IMPRESION. / [Ornament: vase of flowers.][13] CON LICENCIAS, Y APROBACIONES NECESARIAS. / MADRID. Por JOACHIN IBARRA, calle de las Urosas. Año de 1765. / *A costa de la Compañia de Impresores, y Libreros del Reyno.*
Description: In octavo. Parchment covers. Preserved pages: introduction and table of contents, eight leaves plus two blank leaves; and pp. 1–591.

Writing on flyleaf and on verso of last page of index (p. 591):[14] *flyleaf,* "Algantaras" (rubric); in a second hand, "Es de Damian Figueroa / Martinez" (rubric); in a third hand, "Mauro de Figania / El dia 10 de Agosto de / 76," that is, 1776.[15] Verso of p. 591, "Es del uso de José Cosme /[16] Damian Figueroa, y / Martinez" (rubric).

Typography: roman, black. Size: 15 cm. x 20 cm. Museum of New Mexico accession number: A.65.51-6.
Comments: The work concerns church doctrine as modified by the Council of Trent. Related items in *1776:* No. 248, *Concilio Tridentino,* octavo, n.d.; No. 98, ibid., quarto; No. 181, ibid., quarto.

7.

BREVIARIUM / ROMANUM / EX DECRETO / Sacrosancti Concilii Tridentíni restitûtum, / S. PII V. Pontíficis Máximi jussu editum, / & CLEMENS VIII. primum, nun / dénuo URBANI PP. VIII. aucto- / ritate recognitum: In quo ómnia suis locis ad longam pósita sunt, pro / majóri recitantium commoditate. / PARS AUTUMNALIS. / [Ornament: papal crown with crossed keys.] MATRITI. M.DCC.LXXVII. / Apud ANTONIUM DE SANCHA, Typographum / & Bibliopolam. / Sumptibus Regiae Societatis Typographôrum Bibliopolarúmque.
Description: In duodecimo. Leather binding with remains of brass clasps; gilt 4 on spine; gilt page edges.

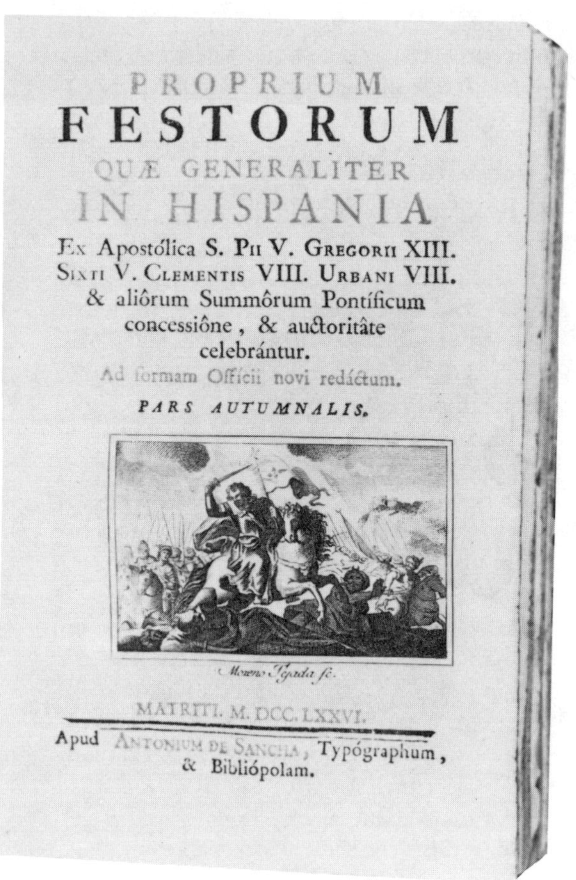

PROPRIUM
FESTORUM
QUÆ GENERALITER
IN HISPANIA
Ex Apostólica S. Pii V. Gregorii XIII. Sixti V. Clementis VIII. Urbani VIII. & aliórum Summórum Pontíficum concessióne, & auctoritáte celebrántur.
Ad formam Officii novi redáctum.
PARS AUTUMNALIS.

MATRITI. M. DCC. LXXVI.
Apud Antonium de Sancha, Typógraphum, & Bibliópolam.

FIGURE 4
Title page for feasts of Spanish saints, bound with *Breviarium Romanum* (Inventory no. 7), with ornament depicting Santiago. (A.65.51-7. Gift of St. Leonard's College Library, Dayton, Ohio, to the Museum of International Folk Art, Museum of New Mexico, Santa Fe.)

Writing on flyleaf and on verso of title page: *flyleaf*, "Es del uso del P Fr Buinaca Franc^{o}. Meriño Buinac^{a}"; *verso of title page*, "Fr. Juan Guzman" (see comments).

Supplements for the Three Orders of Saint Francis (title page partly destroyed) and for Spanish saints (separate title page, with engraving of Santiago similar to Plantinian breviaries). There are additional pages at the end, on different paper (Mexican?), with festivals for other saints.

Typography (of breviary): roman, red and black. Size: 10.5 cm. x 17 cm. Museum of New Mexico accession number: A.65.51-7.
Comments: The "Fr. Juan Guzman" might have been a "Fr. Juan Francisco Guzman," according to E. Boyd. Chávez's *Archives of the Archdiocese of Santa Fe, 1678–1900* (1957) lists a Fr. Francisco Guzman, who seems to have been active in New Mexico from 1757 to 1768; but the publication date of 1777 would seem to eliminate him as the signer in this book.[17]

Of the liturgical books I have found so far that are known to be of probable New Mexican provenance, only three are Spanish publications: the present breviary, and two breviaries in the collection of the Cathedral of Saint Francis in Santa Fe, both of which are in duodecimo and both of which were published in Madrid in 1798. The influence of the Plantinian style of printing and engraving is very noticeable in this 1777 breviary, and, were it not for the curious Spanish-style accents on the title page, it could easily be mistaken for a publication of the Plantinian Press. (The Latin form of Madrid is *Matritum*, here in the genitive, of course.)

8.
[BREVIARIUM ROMANUM. Antwerp, Plantinian Press, 1741?]
Description: In duodecimo. Buckskin-covered wood covers with rawhide thongs. Title page missing. Table of movable feasts: 1741–1779. Preserved pages: 632, many loose, but apparently none missing. Supplements: Propers of the Daily Hours for Spanish Saints (70 pages) and (ibid.) for the Saints of the Three Orders of Saint Francis (114 pages); both supplements with separate title pages, published by the Plantinian Press, Antwerp, 1738 and 1737, respectively. (For writing facing the title page of

the Three Orders of Saint Francis, see comments.)

Typography: roman, red and black. Size: 10.5 cm. x 16.4 cm. Museum of New Mexico accession number: A.65.51-8.

Comments: Facing the title page for the Three Orders of Saint Francis is, in manuscript, the text of a responsorium for Matins: "Elegi, et san[c]tificari locum istum, ut sit ibi nomen meum, et permaneant oculi mei et cor meum ibi cunctis diebus. V[ersu]s. Non fecit taliter omni nationi [rubric] et judicia sua non manifestavit eis." (And I have chosen this place to be consecrated, so that my name may be there and that my eyes may remain there, and that my heart be there for all days. Verse: He did not do this for every nation, nor did he manifest his justice to them.)

Following this, there are some lines in careless Latin; a rough translation will suffice here: "Lord, Thou who under the Blessed Virgin Mary did wish to crown us, who are present in Thy prayers, who are ordered as one with the favors of perpetual service of patron, continuously in the recital on this day, we rejoice in those lands within his sight and we are cleansed in heaven. O, Father!" (The responsorium seems to be related to Spain; the second group of lines is apparently related to the Franciscan order.)

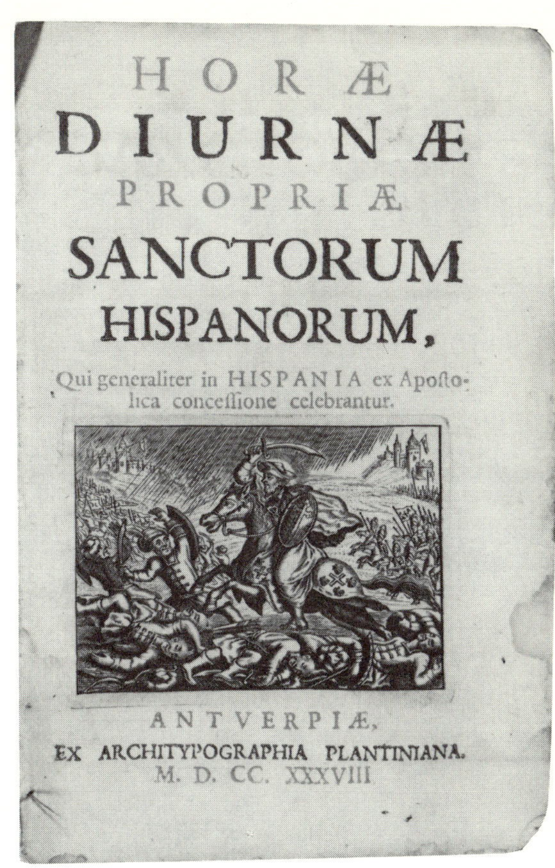

HORÆ
DIURNÆ
PROPRIÆ
SANCTORUM
HISPANORUM,
Qui generaliter in HISPANIA ex Apoſtolica conceſſione celebrantur.

ANTVERPIÆ,
EX ARCHITYPOGRAPHIA PLANTINIANA.
M. D. CC. XXXVIII

FIGURE 5
Title page for Propers of the Daily Hours for Spanish Saints, bound with breviary (Inventory no. 8), with ornament depicting Santiago. (A.65.51-8. Gift of St. Leonard's College Library, Dayton, Ohio, to the Museum of International Folk Art, Museum of New Mexico, Santa Fe.)

9.

[Decretales Domini papae Gregorii noni . . . Late fifteenth century (1498)?]

Description: In octavo. No covers, but placed in a special cloth-covered brown case (modern; No. 34 has a similar case). No title page; beginning and ending missing. Pages are numbered by folio; preserved leaves: f. lxxxii–f. cccclxxviii, with some missing leaves.

Each verso page is headed *Decretaliū*[m] *Gregorii Liber I* (through *Liber V*). The title used here is based on British Museum copies.

Two columns of text, plus a separate section in the center of each page that is a continuous and complete work in itself; the outer columns are a commentary or gloss on the material of the central section.

Many marginal manuscript notes in Latin, in a tiny hand (dark brownish ink), with typical manuscript-style abbreviations.

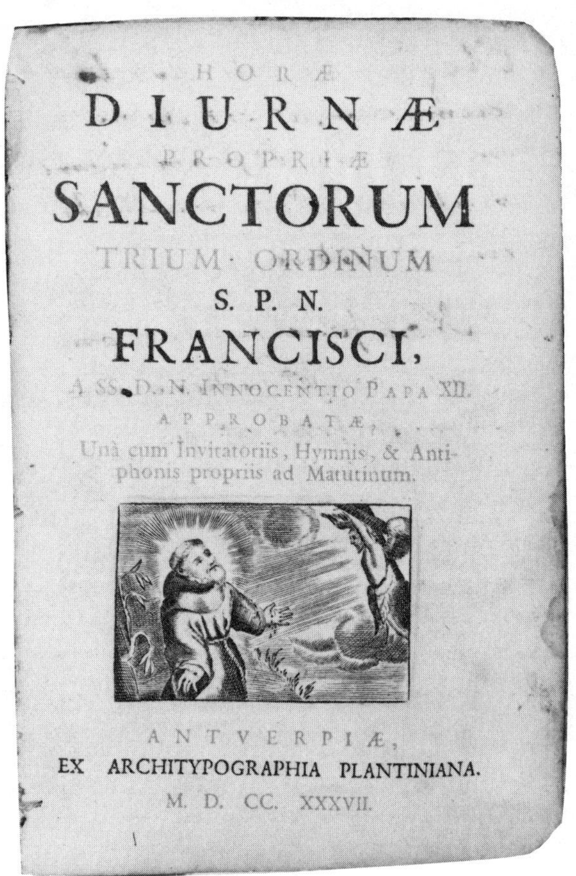

HORÆ
DIURNÆ
PROPRIÆ
SANCTORUM
TRIUM ORDINUM
S. P. N.
FRANCISCI,
A SS. D. N. INNOCENTIO PAPA XII.
APPROBATÆ,
Unà cum Invitatoriis, Hymnis, & Antiphonis propriis ad Matutinum.

ANTVERPIÆ,
EX ARCHITYPOGRAPHIA PLANTINIANA.
M. D. CC. XXXVII.

FIGURE 6
Title page for Propers of the Daily Hours for the Saints of the Third Order of Saint Francis, bound with breviary (Inventory no. 8; see Fig. 5), with ornament depicting Saint Francis.

Typography: gothic, red and black, with many abbreviations characteristic of early printing. Size: 17.3 cm. x 23.2 cm. Museum of New Mexico accession number: A.65.51-9.

Comments: The British Museum has several editions of this work, dated 1470 to 1584. The earliest octavo edition seems to be that of 1498 (Venice), listed in the *British Museum Catalogue of Fifteenth Century Books,* Part V (London, 1924), p. 313. The style of the typography of the New Mexico volume corresponds to the plate sample given (*British Museum Catalogue,* pl. 28). The 1498 octavo was published in Venice by Andreas de Torresano de Asula; 672 leaves.

Related item in *1776:* No. 124 (quarto), *Decretales,* 2 vols.

10.

[Fr. Juan de Bolaños: *Explanatio Litteralis, & Moralis in Esther.* Madrid, 1701.]

Description: In quarto. No covers or title page. Preserved pages: introductory material (incomplete), and pp. 1–536, plus supplement of fifty-eight pages, including incomplete index ending at *R.* (In Latin.)

Typography: roman, black. Size: 20.8 cm. x 29.4 cm. Museum of New Mexico accession number: A.65.51-10.

Comments: The author, title, and date are taken from the following paragraph on the first preserved page: "Vidi hunc librum: *Explanatio Litteralis, & Moralis in Esther,* aeditum per R. P. Fr. Ioannem de Bolaños, & cum his mendis suo exemplari respondet. Matriti, nona die Kalendas Iunij. Anno Domini millesimo, septuagentesimoque primo. Lic. D. Josephus Bernardus del Rio & Cordido. Corrector Generalis â Rege."

The book is badly mouse-chewed and has suffered water damage.

Related item in *1776:* No. 68 (folio), *Historia de Ester,* by Father Bolaños. In *1788:* "Fr. Juan Bolaños in Sacram Ester Historiam Comment. Liter[al] y Moral."

11.

[Fr. Francisco de Ossuna: *Ley de Amor.* Late sixteenth century or early seventeenth century?]

Description: In octavo. Remains of parchment cover with the word *Espiritual* written on it. No title page.

Preserved pages: folios li to CCiiii, with additional fragmentary leaves at end. (In Spanish.)

Typography: gothic, modified. Size: 15 cm. x 20 cm. Museum of New Mexico accession number: A.65.51-11.

Comments: When originally found at Dayton, this volume was wrapped in common brown wrapping paper with the following written on the outside: "Ley de Amor / Por el Padre Fray Francisco Ossuna." The title is confirmed by f. iv, *verso:* "Prologo del libro llamado ley de amor compuesto por el padre fray Francisco de Ossuna."

This is the fourth part of a larger work in six parts entitled *Abecedario espiritual.* Copies of that complete work in the British Museum are sixteenth-century quartos: Burgos, 1542, and Valladolid, 1551. The Bibliothèque Nationale in Paris has a quarto of 1583. Octavo editions usually appear later than quartos, hence the tentative assignment of this book to the late sixteenth or early seventeenth century.

Related item in *1776:* No. 137 (quarto), *Abecedario espiritual y ley de amor.* In *1788:* "Leyes del amor . . ."

12. / 13. / 14.

THEOLOGIA / SCHOLASTICO- / DOGMATICA / JUXTA MENTEM / DIVI THOMAE AQUINATIS, / AD USUM DISCIPULORUM EJUSDEM ANGELICI PRAECEPTORIS / ACCOMODATA PER FR. / VINCENTIUM-LUDOVICUM GOTTI / ORDINIS PRAEDICATORUM, / Sacrae Theologiae Magistrum, / & Doctorem Collegiatum, olim in Patria / Bononiensi Universitate Controversiarum Fidei Publicum Professorem, deinde / SANCTAE ROMANAE ECCLESIAE CARDINALEM. / *Editio Novissima, a mendis, quae in prioribus editionibus irrepserant, / diligenter expurgata.* [Engraving: Pope (?) with Saint Peter's (?) in background, kneeling prelate at left, standing prelate at right holding an open book.] Venetiis, / MDCCLXIII / Ex Typographia Remondiana. / SUPERIORUM PERMISSU. [From title page of Vol. 2; Vol. 1 probably 1761 or 1762.]

Description: In three large octavo volumes. Parchment covers. Vol. 1 lacks front cover and title page; title is taken from Vol. 2 (title pages of Vols. 2 and 3 correspond, including date). License page: 1761; gives date of the license for the first edition as 1726.[18] In Latin, except that the license page of Vol. 1 is in Italian.

Typography: small roman, black. Size: 23.4 cm. x 27.3 cm. Museum of New Mexico accession numbers: A.65.51-12, -13, -14.

Comments: Luigi Vincenzo Gotti (1664–1742) was an Italian theologian of the Dominican order, professor of theology at the University of Bologna, provincial of his order, and cardinal from 1728. He is said to have been highly respected and consulted by Popes Benedict XIII and Clement XII, which may account for the engraving on the title page of this work.

The first edition of the *Theologia* was published at Bologna, 1727–1735; a second edition came out in 1750. The present edition *(editio novissima)* is presumably a third, revised edition.

The title pages of both Vols. 2 and 3 have "Juan Felipe Ortiz" written on them, and the title page of Vol. 2 has, in addition, "De Jose Fran^{co}. Ruiz Arias [rubric]." The Ruíz Arias name is also on the first preserved page of Vol. 1. Chávez (1957) lists a Fr. Joaquin de Jesús Ruíz in New Mexico from 1766 to 1776; and also a secular priest, Juan Felipe Ortiz, in New Mexico from 1825 to 1845.

15.

R. P. FR. / FELICIS POTESTA / PANORMITANI, / ORDIN. MINOR. DE OBSERV. S. P. FRANCISCI, / Lectoris Jubilati, ac iteratò Ministri Provincialis, S. Officii / Consultoris, & Qualificatoris, Examinatoris Synodalis, Re- / visoris Ordinarii, & R. Monarchiae Theologi: / EXAMEN ECCLESIASTICUM / ADAUCTUM TRES COMPLECTENS TOMOS, / IN QUO UNIVERSAE MATERIAE MORALES, / *omnesque ferè excogitabiles casus conscientiae solidè, et clarè resolvuntur, cum / Denuntiationibus ad Monitoria Papae et Episcoporum, ad Edicta Inquisitorum, ac / pro Confessariis solicitantibus, Instructione Sacrae Poenitentiariae, Propositionibus / damnatis, Examine Ordinandorum, et Arte praedicandi.* / OPUS / CONFESSARIIS, PRAEDICATORIBUS. ET ORDINANDIS, / necnon cunctis Ecclesisticis per quam utile, & necessarium. / AD CALCEM OPERIS ACCESSERE PROPOSITIONES DAMNATAE / *Paschalis Quesnelli, et Decr. Sac. Congr. Rit. pluribus abhinc annis emanata.* / ET ETIAM / CONSTITUTIONES PONTIFICIAE, NON SOLUM / *in prima editione congestae, sed et aliae novissimae in hac ultimana / aditae ad Moralem Theologiam spectantes.* / [Ornament: vase with flowers.][19] SUPERIORUM PERMISSU / MATRITI. Apud Joachim Ibarra Typographum Urosarum via. MDCCLIX. /

Description: In quarto. Parchment covers. Typography: roman, black. Size: 20.2 cm. x 29.2 cm. Museum of New Mexico accession number: A.65.51-15.

Comments: This is a one-volume edition of the *Examen ecclesiasticum* by the Sicilian Felice Podestà of Palermo (Felix Potesta Panormitanus), the original edition of which was published in three volumes. The *approbatio* for the initial publication is given here as 1702. (The British Museum has an edition of three volumes of 1736, Barcelona.) The publication is an examination of the ideas of Jansenist Pasquier Quesnel (1634–1719).

16.

[Bible commentary or concordance. Seventeenth or eighteenth century.]

Description: In sexto. No covers or title page. Preserved pages: pp. 241–878; p. 241 headed "Ad Librum 3. Regum." In Latin.

Typography: roman, black. Size: 19.7 cm. x 29.7 cm. Museum of New Mexico accession number: A.65.51-16.

Comments: Unidentified (other than that it is a commentary or concordance to the Bible).

Related item in *1776:* No. 58 (folio), *Concordancias de la Biblia.* In *1788:* "Concordan. de la Biblia."

17.

[Concerning duties, privileges, regulations, and so on, of Franciscans. Eighteenth century?]

Description: In octavo. No covers or title page. Preserved pages: pp. 869–1218 (ending with *Finis*). In Latin.

Typography: roman, black, eighteenth-century style. Size: 10.6 cm. x 17.8 cm. Museum of New Mexico accession number: A.65.51-17.

Comments: This might be a work by Fr. Manuel Rodríguez. The British Museum has various works by him on the duties and privileges of Franciscans; the only one of those published in Spain is *Quaestiones regulares et caninicae* . . ., Salamanca, 1598 (quarto). A later edition or editions in octavo would be reasonable.

Related items in *1776:* No. 51 (folio), *Questiones regulares, y canonicas;* No. 168 (quarto), *Tratados del modo de corregir;* No. 185 (quarto), *Regla de nuestra religión;* No. 208 (octavo), *Exposiciones de nuestra regla,* by Fr. Martin de San José.

18.

[BREVIARIUM ROMANUM (Vol. 2) Late eighteenth century?]

Description: In octavo. Flexible leather covers. Title page missing. First preserved page begins with heading: PSALTERIUM DISPOSITUM PER HEBDOMADAM, Cum Ordinario Officij de Tempore. PARS AUTUMNALIS.

Typography: roman, red and black. Size: 14 cm. x 21.5 cm. Museum of New Mexico accession number: A.65.51-18.

Comments: This corresponds to the *Tomus alter* (Vol. 2) of the modern *Breviarium Romanum,* which includes material for Pentecost through the month of November. The corresponding location in the 1961 *Breviarium Romanum, Tomus alter,* begins on p. 29 with the following heading: "PSALTERIUM BREVIARII ROMANI PER OMNES AC SINGULOS HEBDOMADAE DIES DISPOSITUM" (The Psaltery of the Roman breviary arranged for each and every day of the week).

The volume seems to be complete, except for the missing title page and probably some introductory pages. There are no supplements for Spanish saints or for the Franciscan order.

According to the Museum of New Mexico accession list, the type is a "Turn of century type face, Mexico" (E. Boyd). There are several written inscriptions to which the accession list calls attention, such as: "El sacristan del Pueblo de Cochiti . . ." (p. 210); "Hoy 26 de 1869" (p. 261); and so on.

19.

[BREVIARIUM ROMANUM. Antwerp, Plantinian Press, c. 1730.]

Description: In octavo. No covers or title page. Preserved pages: pp. 355–638, plus supplement for Spanish saints with title page (Antverpiae, Ex Typographia Plantiniana, MDCCXXX), and a supplement for Franciscan saints with title page (partly destroyed). The Franciscan supplement is incomplete and ends at p. 96. Inserted following the supplement for Spanish saints are some additional pages, possibly of Mexican imprint, for new saints, 1728–1730.

Typography: roman, red and black. Size: 11 cm. x 19.6 cm. Museum of New Mexico accession number: A.65.51-19 (placed facing the title page for Spanish saints).

Comments: The title pages of both the Spanish and Franciscan supplements have been vandalized (probably for the engravings).

20.

See No. 4.

21.

[BREVIARIUM ROMANUM. Eighteenth century]

Description: In octavo. No covers or title page. Preserved pages: pp. 5–1004; plus supplements for Spanish saints and for Franciscan offices (separately paged but without separate title pages).

Typography: roman, red and black. Size: 13 cm. x 19.7 cm. Museum of New Mexico accession number: A.65.51-21.

Comments: Probable publisher: Antwerp, Plantinian Press.[20] The condition of the book is very poor, with the spine twisted and distorted.

22.

[BREVIARIUM ROMANUM. 1726?]

Description: In duodecimo. No covers or title page. Preserved pages begin with table of movable feasts (1726–1765), and paging is apparently complete from there to p. 1078. No supplements.

Typography: roman, red and black. Size: 9.5 cm. x 15.7 cm. Museum of New Mexico accession number: A.65.51-22.

Comments: Probable publisher: Antwerp, Plantinian Press. Condition poor, similar to that of No. 21.

23.

[BREVIARIUM ROMANUM. Late seventeenth–early eighteenth centuries.]

Description: In octavo. No covers or title page. Preserved pages: seven unpaged leaves of introductory material and pp. 1–1114. Supplements for Spanish saints and Franciscan offices, separately paged and each with separate title page (but with each title page vandalized: lower part missing).

Typography: roman, red and black. Size: 12.2 cm. x 19.2 cm. Museum of New Mexico accession number: A.65.51-23.

Comments: Probable publisher: Antwerp, Plantinian Press. The preserved portions of the title pages for Spanish saints and for Franciscan offices are typically Plantinian.

Following the main index and preceding the title page for Spanish saints is a manuscript page in Latin, largely illegible, but signed "Pater . . . Franciscus Gimenez." Chávez lists a Fray Francisco Jiménez (Ximénez), active in New Mexico from 1703 to 1708 (1957: 250). The condition of the volume is poor, similar to that of No. 21.

24.

[Concordance to the Bible in dictionary form. Sixteenth century.]

Description: In octavo. No covers or title page. Preserved pages begin with *A ante E* and end with *U ante I.* No paging, as such, except for the signatures at lower right (Bij, Biij, and so on). In Latin and Spanish (Latin to Spanish, in the manner of a dictionary).

Typography: gothic, black. Size: 15 cm. x 21.1 cm. Museum of New Mexico accession number: A.65.51-24.

Comments: E.B. confirmed the sixteenth-century type style.

A possible identification of this publication is: Fr. Diego Ximénez Arias, *Lexicon Ecclesiasticum Latinohispanicum* . . . The British Museum has two sixteenth-century editions: Salamanca, 1566, in folio; and "Apud Antoniū[m] à Maris, Braccae" (Braga, Portugal), 1569.

Related items in *1776:* No. 8 (folio), *Bocabulario* by Nebrija; No. 145 (quarto), *Lexicon Ecclesiasticum.* In *1788:* "Lexicon Eclesiastico, otro."

25.

[Homilies/Sermons. Eighteenth century?]

Description: In sexto. Cardboard covers, with canvas back. Covers have pasted-on newspaper material, the back cover having the identity of the source: "La Bandera Americana, Albuquerque, N.M., Viernes, Mayo 29, de 1903." Preserved pages: pp.

31–353. In Spanish. (Blue stamp on p. 31: "Rev. Franciscan Fathers, Pena *[sic]* Blanca, N. Mex.")
Comments: There are a number of sermon collections in *1776* (twenty-eight, in fact). The Museum of New Mexico accession list states that the woodcuts and tailpieces look very Mexican and that this might be a Mexican reprint of one such sermon publication.

In *1776*, the most likely possibilities for identification are No. 146 (quarto), *Sermones en Mexicano;* and No. 43 (folio), *Despertador cristiano,* Vol. 3, and No. 136 (quarto), *Despertador cristiano.* The *Despertador Cristiano de Sermones Doctrinales,* by José de Barzia y Zambrana, bishop of Cádiz, was one of the best-known collections of sermons in the eighteenth century. The British Museum has folio editions of this work in three volumes (Madrid, 1719, 1727).

26.

[Fr. Pedro de Ledesma: *Primera parte de la Summa, en qual [sic] se cifra y summa todo loque [sic] toca y pertenece a los Sacramentos. . .* Seventeenth century?]
Description: In octavo. No covers or title page. Preserved pages: pp. 19–574. In Spanish.

Typography: roman, black. Size: 20.8 cm. x 30 cm. Museum of New Mexico accession number: A.65.51-26.
Comments: The identification of the book is from the heading of the section following p. 414: "Addiciones a la primera parte de la summa del Padre Fray Pedro de Ledesma, de la Orden de Predicadores." The title used above is from the British Museum's 1611 folio edition.

Related items in *1776:* No. 63 (folio), Ledesma, *Moral;* No. 79 (quarto), *Morales* by Ledesma, four volumes; No. 194 (quarto), *Moral* by Ledesma. In *1788:* "1ª Parte de la Sum. Moral de Fr. Pedro de Ledesma; idem 2ª Parte de la Sum.; idem 1 Part.; idem Segunda Parte."

27.

[*Excelencias de San Joseph.* Eighteenth century?]
Description: In quarto. No covers. Identification is from a small fragment of the title page (inserted at p. 227 when examined). The title also appears as the heading of each left-hand page. Preserved pages are in two pieces: (1) pp. 79–948; (2) pp. 969–1104. In Spanish.

Typography: roman, black. Size: 20.1 cm. x 28.5 cm. Museum of New Mexico accession number: A.65.51-27.
Contents: The paper seems to be Mexican: it is thinner and whiter than the usual Continental paper of the time. The Museum of New Mexico accession list states that the watermarks in the paper are the same as for others of Mexican provenance in the archdiocesan archives in Santa Fe.

The tailpiece on p. 226 is a vase with a bouquet of flowers; the tailpiece on p. 322 is a woodcut showing gryphonlike monsters with a vase between them and Mexican-style ornaments up and down either side; the tailpiece on p. 470 is a basket of flowers (carnations?).

There is extensive water damage at the end of the first piece and the beginning of the second.

The British Museum has a French work of similar title: J. F. O. Luquet, *Des Excellences du glorieux Saint-Joseph* (Paris, 1857; duodecimo), but no Spanish work.

28.

[Fr. Domingo de Soto: *Comentarij Fratris Dominicis Soto Sego bienis, ordinis Praedicatorem, artium ac sacrae Theologiae Professoris, in Dialectam Aristotelis.* Salamanca, 1564.]
Description: In octavo, Fragments of covers (vellum/parchment). Fragment of title page (inserted at f. 9 *verso* when examined). Leaves numbered by folio; preserved folios, ff. 3–141, plus a fragment of introductory material.

Handwritten marginal notes on many pages, in Latin, in dark brown ink.

Typography: gothic, modified, black; but introductory material is roman. Size: 20.8 cm. x 29.3 cm. Museum of New Mexico accession number: A.65.51-28, placed on f. 9 *recto.*
Comments: Domingo de Soto (1494–1560) was a distinguished Spanish theologian of the Dominican order; he occupied the chair of theology at the University of Salamanca from 1552. The first edition of his *Commentaries* was published in Salamanca in 1544; the British Museum has a 1554 edition, and the Bibliothèque Nationale has one of 1583.

The title page can be restored from the preserved fragment and from other sources, as follows: "[Fratris] Dom[inicis Soto Sego bienis[21] ordi]nis Praedicatorum [, artium ac sacrae Theologiae Professoris,] Comm[entarij in Dialectam Aristotelis,] aeditio postrema . . . Cum privilegio, Salamanticae, Excudebat Andreas à Portonarijs. S. C. M. T. . . . M.D.LXIIII."

Related item in *1776:* No. 24 (folio), *Logica* by Soto. In *1788:* "Fr. Dominicus Sotus in Dialecticam."

29.
Fr. Manuel Rodriguez, Lusitano: SUMA / DE CASOS DE CONSCIENTIA, / Y OBRAS MORALES. / COMPUESTAS POR EL PADRE / *Fray Manuel Rodriguez, Lusitano de la Regular Observancia / de Nuestro Seraphico Padre San Francisco, Lector de / Theologia, y Difinidor [sic] de la Prouincia de / Sanctiago [sic]* / CONTIENE LA EXPLICACION DE LA / Bula de la Cruzada, y Addiciones *[sic]*, y el Or- / den Iudicial, / VAN EN ESTA VLTIMA IMPRE- / *sion las cosas de Tercero, y Quarto Tomo, puestas en / sus lugares, y Capitulos.* / [Ornament: crossed hands (Christ and Saint Francis?), wounds and three nails.] CON NUEVA PROROGACION. / EN VALLADOLID. / Por Francisco Fernandez de Cordoua. / Año de M.DC.XXI. / Acosta de Antonio Lopez Mercader *[sic]* de Libros. / [From the title page of Vol. 2.]
Description: In octavo. The volume has neither covers nor title page. An edition of three volumes in one; the title page of Vol. 2 follows p. 526 of the first volume (and is the source for the title-page information above); there is no separate title page for Vol. 3.

Preserved pages: Vol. 1, pp. 73–526; Vol. 2, pp. 1–436 (complete); Vol. 3, pp. 1–262, followed by an unpaged index. In Spanish. (Condition: back spine twisted.)

Typography: roman, black, with occasional abbreviations. Size: 20.7 cm. x 31 cm. Museum of New Mexico accession number: A.65.51-29.
Comments: Little seems to be known about Manuel Rodríguez beyond what can be seen in the title page information: Portuguese *(Lusitano)*, Franciscan, theologian, and a church official *(Difinidor; recte,*

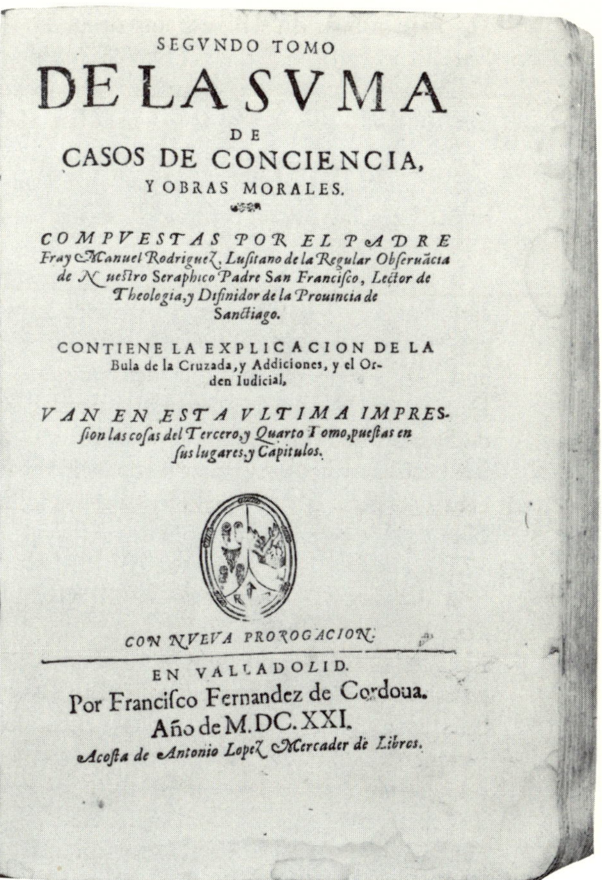

SEGVNDO TOMO
DE LA SVMA
DE
CASOS DE CONCIENCIA,
Y OBRAS MORALES.

COMPVESTAS POR EL PADRE
Fray Manuel Rodriguez, Luſitano de la Regular Obſeruācia de Nueſtro Seraphico Padre San Franciſco, Lector de Theologia, y Difinidor de la Prouincia de Sanctiago.

CONTIENE LA EXPLICACION DE LA
Bula de la Cruzada, y Addiciones, y el Orden Iudicial,

VAN EN ESTA VLTIMA IMPRESſion las coſas del Tercero, y Quarto Tomo, pueſtas en ſus lugares, y Capitulos.

CON NVEVA PROROGACION.

EN VALLADOLID.
Por Franciſco Fernandez de Cordoua.
Año de M.DC.XXI.
A coſta de Antonio Lopez Mercader de Libros.

FIGURE 7
Title page, volume 2 of Fray Manuel Rodríguez, *De La Suma* (Inventory no. 29), with ornament depicting the crossed arms of Christ and Saint Francis, the wounds, and three nails. (A.65.51-29. Gift of St. Leonard's College Library, Dayton, Ohio, to the Museum of International Folk Art, Museum of New Mexico, Santa Fe.)

Definidor) of the province of Santiago (de Compostella?).

The fourth volume mentioned in the title is probably the *Addiciones;* see below.

Related items in *1776:* No. 96 (quarto), *Explicacion de la Crusada;* No. 97 (quarto), *Addiciones.* In *1788:* "addiciones a la Explic^{n}. de la Vula de la Cruzada."

30.

Sor Maria de Jesus de Agreda: MYSTICA / CIUDAD DE DIOS / MILAGRO / DE SU OMNIPOTENCIA, / Y ABISMO DE LA GRACIA: / HISTORIA DIVINA. / Y VIDA DE LA VIRGEN, / MADRE DE DIOS, / REYNA, Y SEÑORA NUESTRA, / MARIA SANTISSIMA, / RESTAURADORA DE LA CULPA DE EVA, / Y MEDIANERA DE LA GRACIA: / MANIFESTADA / EN ESTOS ULTIMOS SIGLOS POR LA MISMA SEÑORA / A SU ESCLAVA SOR MARIA DE JESUS, / Abesada del Convento de la Inmaculada Concepcion de la Villa de AGRED[A] / de la Provincia de Burgos, de la Regular Observancia de N. P. S. Francisco, / para nueva luz del Mundo, alegria de la Iglesia Catholica, / y confianza de los mortales. / SEGUNDA PARTE. / CON LICENCIA. / EN MADRID: En la Imprenta de Causa de la VENERABLE [torn] Año de M. DCC.LXV. /

Description: In sexto. Leather covers; front cover partly torn off. Preserved pages: title page and pp. 1–943, with pages missing throughout;[22] a supplement of *Notas* (after p. 943), separately paged, pp. 1–76, ending with various licenses to print (pp. 75–76), and unpaged *Tablas* at end. In Spanish.

Typography: roman, red and black title page, otherwise roman, black. Size: 20.6 cm. x 30.5 cm. Museum of New Mexico accession number: A.65.51-30.

Comments: Mother María de Jesús de Agreda (1602–1665) was abbess of the convent of the Immaculate Conception in Agreda from 1625. *The Mystical City of God* was written before 1660 and was first published in Madrid in 1671 (according to the license and *aprobación* in the present copy; *Notas,* pp. 75–76). (An English translation was published in Chicago, 1914–1915, in four volumes.)

According to Fray Alonso de Benavides, the Franciscan who was active in New Mexico in the 1620s, Mother Agreda preached to the Indians of New Mexico, among them the Jumanos, or Jumanas, who lived in what is now west Texas, which was then part of the province of New Mexico (Forrestal and Lynch 1954: 56–62; also see Donahue 1953). Mother Agreda's interest in New Mexico and the Indians is confirmed in Zárate Salmerón's *Relaciones* (c. 1628?), sections 136–138.

31.

[Same as No. 30, but a different edition.]

Description: In sexto. Homemade buckskin covers. Lacks title page, and pages through p. 26. Preserved pages: pp. 27–943, plus *Notas* (pp. 1–76) and indexes.

Typography as in No. 30. Size: 20.3 cm. x 29.3 cm. Museum of New Mexico accession number: A.65.51-31.

Comments: On first inspection this copy seems identical with No. 30. However, there are small differences here and there. For example, the ornaments on the bottom of p. 113 in each copy are different in each. The capital letters also differ: for example, on p. 225, the capital letter of No. 30 shows a manor house, whereas that in No. 31 shows a face with flowers. It is possible that No. 31 is an older edition (perhaps even the first edition of 1671?); No. 30 may have been reset in type using No. 31 as a model.

32.

[Fr. Henrique de Villalobos: *Summa de la Theologia Moral y Canonica.* Tomo 2. Barcelona, 1632?]

Description: In octavo. Parchment covers. No title page. Preserved pages: fragmentary remains of the introductory material, pp. 1–775, and unpaged table of terms and index. Author, title, and date are from the license pages (fragmentary); license dates: Madrid, 9 June 1622; Lisbon, 22 December 1622; and Barcelona, 19 April 1632.

Typography: roman, black. Size: 20.3 cm. x 29.1 cm. Museum of New Mexico accession number: A.65.51-32.

Comments: The title also heads p. 1; and at the foot of that page is "Tomo 2." (This volume contains *Tratados* 1–41.)

Fray Enrique de Villalobos (1637–?), a Franciscan theologian, is mainly known for his *Summa* (or

Suma). The New Mexico Vol. 2 is probably from a second edition; the first edition was presumably published in 1622. Other editions exist to at least 1672 (British Museum: folio, Madrid, 1672).

Related items in *1776:* No. 1 (folio), *Teologia Moral,* Villalobos, four volumes. In *1788:* various copies of parts 1 and 2 of the *Summa.*

33.

[Fray Henrique de Villalobos: *Suma [sic] de Todas las Materias Morales.* Tomo 1. After 1660?]

Description: In sexto. No covers or title page. The title given here is from the heading of p. 1; the volume number is from the foot of the same page. Preserved pages: part of table of contents, pp. 1–730, and unpaged appendix and index.

Typography: roman, black; similar to No. 32 but lighter in appearance. Size: 20.3 cm. x 29.4 cm. Museum of New Mexico accession number: A. 65.51-33.

Comments: This is a later edition of the same work of which No. 32 is the second volume, for the *Nota,* p. 705, refers to "Bula del Papa Alexandro VII expedida en 8. de Iulio del Año 1660" (see comments for No. 32, *1788* inventory).

34.

[Fray Michael Angelus, of Naples:] CHRONOLOGIA / HISTORICO-LEGALIS / SERAPHICI ORDINIS / FRATRUM MINORUM / SANCTI PATRIS FRANCISCI / TOMVS PRIMVS, / Capitulorum omnium, & Congregationum Generalium / à primo eiusdem Ordinis exordio, vsque / ad annum M.DC.XXXIII, / AC IN IPSIS AEDITARUM CONSTITVTIONVM SERIEM, / accurata temporum apposita ratione, distinctè complectens. / HIS ANNEXA EST CVIVSCVMQVE INSTITVTI, / *sub titulo Minorum Fratrum, luculenta, suis in locis, descriptio.* / MVLTA IN SVPER ADIECTA SVNT IPSIVS ORDINIS MONIMENTA *[sic].* / Nedum Minoriticis, verum & quibuscumque Regularibus, prosicuum Opus. / [Title page is cut off here; balance from duplicate copy; see below.] [Ornament: three crosses.] [Neapoli, Ex Typographia Camilli Caualli. Anno Iubilaei M.DC.L.]

Description: In quarto. No original cover, but supplied with a modern, cloth-covered brown case, similar to that of No. 9. Lower half of title page destroyed; balance supplied from duplicate copy at Saint Leonard College Library. Preserved pages: three unpaged leaves of introductory material and pp. 1–704 (pp. 699–702 being misprinted as "399–402").

Typography: roman, red and black. Size: 20.9 cm. x 35 cm. This copy was retained at Saint Leonard College Library (along with the duplicate already in the library's collection), because of its importance to Franciscan history.

Comments: The author's name is from the first page of the introductory material, following the title page. Fray Michael Angelus of Naples seems to be unknown except for this volume. The *Chronologia* itself is very rare: there are no copies of the 1650 edition in the British Museum, the Bibliothèque Nationale, or the Library of Congress, though the British Museum has a French translation dated 1688. The only other copy of the 1650 edition so far located is the duplicate at Saint Leonard College Library.

The title page of the duplicate copy has a handsome ornamental illustration with the three crosses of Calvary framed by an elaborate, quasi-architectural "proscenium" as though one were observing the scene on a Baroque stage. (In my opinion, this ornamental illustration is a wood engraving; E. Boyd never saw the duplicate to confirm that opinion.)

Vols. 2, 3, and 4 of the *Chronologia* were published by other authors (in 1718, 1751, and 1795, respectively, according to the *Dictionnaire de Théologie Catholique,* Vol. 6, p. 827).

Related items in *1776:* No. 16 (folio), *Chronologia de N. P. San Francisco.* In *1788:* "Chronologia Historica Legalis . . ."

NOTES

1. I located this group of books after a suggestion by Fray Angélico Chávez, O.F.M. The books had at one time been held by the Franciscan fathers at Peña Blanca, New Mexico, where he was at one time a resident. (My earlier correspondence and research notes usually referred to them as "the Peña Blanca books.")

2. This version of the inventory was made at Santa Fe in December 1965; the full article was completed on March 30, 1966. It never achieved publication. However, I delivered a version relating primarily to musical and liturgical aspects of the books as a paper for the spring 1966 meeting of the Midwest Chapter of the American Musicological Society. I completed the present revision in 1981.

3. Boyd to Spiess, 13 December 1965. Author's files.

4. Apart from this present group of volumes, I should like to call attention to another book which might well have been used in colonial New Mexico. It is a small volume of seventy-eight pages containing rules for the Franciscan order and published in Mexico City in 1725: *Regla de N. S. P. San Francisco . . . por el Padre Fr. Manuel Sanchez . . . en Mexico por Joseph Bernardo de Hogal . . . 1725.* Following page 52 is a teaching manual for instruction in plainchant, *Breve Noticia del Canto Llano,* which continues to the end of the book. It is a simple, clear, and straightforward little primer on the subject and could have been used in the provincial missions. There is a copy of the *Regla* of 1725 in Zimmerman Library of the University of New Mexico in Albuquerque, although its provenance is not known to me.

5. The earlier short-title inventory was sent to Boyd for cataloguing purposes. Since the 1966 article was written after the books had been returned to New Mexico, references to information in the "Museum of New Mexico accession list" are often E's own comments. I sent her a copy of the 1966 article, and her notations on that copy are incorporated in this 1981 version.

6. Archives of the Archdiocese of Santa Fe, Loose Documents, Missions, 1680–1850, No. 1788, No. 8, "Santo Domingo."

7. The signatures are in sets of six: for example, D_1 D_2 D_3 D_4 and two blank. Signatures in sexto and in duodecimo are both found in this group of books. In the twentieth century, duodecimo still occurs, especially in some miniature musical scores, but it seems to have become simply a generic term for very small volumes.

8. Little musicological research has been published on the Spanish liturgy (Mozarabic rite) beyond a facsimile of the medieval Mozarabic Antiphonary of León, which has yet to be deciphered. Although the Roman rite was introduced into Spain in the ninth century, the Spanish liturgy continued, and as late as the early seventeenth century, polyphonic music based on the Spanish chants can be seen in works such as Sebastián de Heredia's *Magnificats* of 1618 (no modern edition to date). But there are no modern editions of Spanish chant and Spanish liturgy as there are with the Gregorian, so that research in the Spanish/Mozarabic area is difficult.

9. Boyd to Spiess, 10 May 1966; Richard B. Stark to Spiess, 10 May 1966. Author's files.

10. The Neapolitan connection of the supplementary material is curious. Spanish control of Naples ended in 1707, and used liturgical books from there may have found their way to the New World. E. Boyd claimed: "some names [in the books] . . . suggest older Spanish owners before the books came here. They certainly did send up obsolete books as well as arms & armor to the frontier"; personal communication, 13 December 1965.

11. Ibid.

12. The "federated provinces of North America" would presumably be Mexico and, until 1845–1846, its northern provinces of New Mexico and California.
13. *E. B.*: "wood cut."
14. Boyd, personal communication, 13 December 1965.
15. The *7* has the characteristic crosspiece of a seven.
16. Possibly "Cosine," but *E. B.*: "I read *Cosme.*"
17. Guzman is a fairly common Spanish name. Among others might be mentioned a scribe at the Cathedral of Mexico in the early eighteen century (Spiess and Stanford 1969: 25, No. 3).
18. The license date usually corresponds to the date of publication, but it is occasionally one year earlier, suggesting the date of Vol. 1 as either 1761 or 1762.
19. *E. B.*: "Wood cut."
20. *E. B.*: "Before 1780."
21. *Recte:*—"Fratris Dominici Soto Sego boni . . ."?
22. *E. B.*: "In blocks."

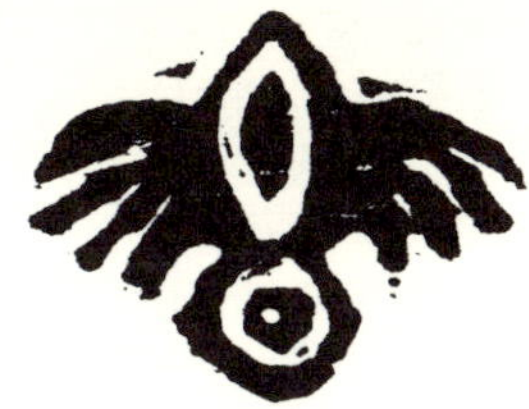

LIST OF CONTRIBUTORS

RICHARD E. AHLBORN, a cultural historian, is curator of the Division of Community Life, The National Museum of American History, Smithsonian Institution. His books include *Saints of San Xavier, The Penitente Moradas of Abiquiú, Bucaroos in Paradise* (with Howard Marshall), and an edited volume, *Man Made Mobile: Early Saddles of Western North America.* Collecting and exhibitions since 1957 have focused on Spanish American material culture.

CHARLES L. BRIGGS, an anthropologist, is an assistant professor of anthropology and sociology at Vassar College. His books include *The Wood Carvers of Córdova, New Mexico: Social Dimensions of an Artistic "Revival"* and an edited (with Marta Weigle) volume, Lorin W. Brown's *Hispano Folklife of New Mexico.*

BAINBRIDGE BUNTING had retired as professor of art at the University of New Mexico before his death in 1981. His books include *Taos Adobes, Of Earth and Timbers Made: New Mexico Architecture,* and *Early Architecture in New Mexico.*

F. DUPONT CORNELIUS is a conservator of paintings and other works of art. He was a research fellow in conservation of paintings at the Metropolitan Museum of Art, having assisted in setting up the department. He has been on the staff of the Colorado Springs Fine Arts Center, visiting conservator at the Museum of New Mexico, and conservator of the Cincinnati Museum of Art, and has worked independently in conservation on the East coast and in Colorado. He has contributed to numerous scientific publications.

BERNARD L. FONTANA, an anthropologist, is field historian at the University of Arizona Library. His books include *Papago Indian Pottery* (with William Robinson and others), *Mission San Xavier del Bac* (with Helga Teiwes-French), *Indians of Arizona: A Contemporary Perspective* (with Thomas Weaver and others), *The Material World of the Tarahumara, Tarahumara: Where Night is the Day of the Moon, Of Earth and Little Rain: The Papago Indians,* and two edited volumes, *Look to the Mountain Top* (with Robert Iacopi and Charles Jones), and *Friar Bringas Reports to the King* (with Daniel S. Matson).

MYRA ELLEN JENKINS, retired state historian and chief of the Historical Services Division of the New Mexico State Records Center and Archives, serves as a consultant on historical matters. Her books include *Guide to* and *Calendar of the Microfilm Edition of the Spanish Archives of New Mexico 1621–1821, Guide to* and *Calendar of the Microfilm Edition of the Mexican Archives of New Mexico 1821–1846, Guide* and *Calendar* (with J. Richard Salazar) *to the Microfilm Edition of the Territorial Archives of New Mexico 1846–1912,* and *A Brief History of New Mexico* (with Albert H. Schroeder).

PÁL KELEMEN studied art history at the universities of Budapest, Munich and Paris, and in 1925 traveled in Spain. On a 1932 visit to the United States, he turned from early Christian art to the art of the Americas; his *Medieval American Art* presented the ancient, *Baroque and Rococo in Latin America,* the Spanish colonial from the aesthetic standpoint. His bibliography of 136 entries also includes *El Greco Revisited, Art of the Americas: Ancient and Hispanic, Peruvian Colonial Painting,* and *Vanishing Art of the Americas.* He is Commander of the Order of Merit of Ecuador.

KATE PECK KENT was professor of anthropology at the University of Denver and is now associated with the School of American Research, Santa Fe. Her books include *Story of Navajo Weaving* and *Prehistoric Textiles of the Southwest.*

CLAUDIA LARCOMBE is a teacher in the Santa Fe public schools. She holds a master's degree in American studies from the University of New Mexico and has worked extensively with the E. Boyd Collection at the New Mexico State Records Center and Archives, Santa Fe.

SAMUEL LARCOMBE oversees alumni and community relations at St. John's College, Santa Fe. He formerly worked for the New Mexico State Planning Office.

MARGIL LYONS has assisted her husband in his field work on the Penitente Brotherhood in New Mexico and in Spain for the last twelve years.

THOMAS R. LYONS, an archeologist, recently retired as chief of the Remote Sensing Division, National Park Service/University of New Mexico operations and is engaged in private consulting practice. His books include *Remote Sensing: A Handbook for Archeologists and Cultural Resource Managers* (with T. R. Avery) and contributions to and editing of ten additional volumes on remote sensing.

HARRY R. RUBENSTEIN, a social historian, is on the technical staff of the National Museum of American History, Smithsonian Institution. This article was prepared while he was an intern on a George Washington University Fellowship to the Division of Community Life. His publications include articles in the *New Mexico Historical Review* and in Robert Kern's edited *Labor in New Mexico: Unions, Strikes, and Social History Since 1881.*

MARC SIMMONS is a historian. His books include *Spanish Government in New Mexico, Witchcraft in the Southwest: Spanish and Indian Supernaturalism on the Rio Grande, New Mexico: A History, People of the Sun: Some Out-of-Fashion Southwesterners* (with Buddy Mays), *Southwestern Colonial Ironwork: The Spanish Blacksmithing Tradition from Texas to California* (with Frank Turley), and *Albuquerque: A Narrative History.* He is currently working on a history of Hispanic agriculture in New Mexico.

DAVID H. SNOW is an archeologist with the Museum of New Mexico. His professional contributions have been devoted primarily to Spanish Colonial and Rio Grande Pueblo archeology and ethnohistory. He is currently completing a doctorate in anthropology at the University of New Mexico and supervises the Research Section of the Laboratory of Anthropology in Santa Fe.

LINCOLN BUNCE SPIESS, a musicologist, is professor emeritus of music at Washington University. His books include *Historical Musicology, A Mercedarian Antiphonary* (with E. Boyd), and *An Introduction to Certain Mexican Musical Archives* (with E. T. Stanford).

RICHARD B. STARK, formerly curator of music research at the Museum of International Folk Art, Santa Fe, is a teacher and composer. His books include *Music of the Spanish Folk Plays in New Mexico* (with T. M. Pearce and Rubén Cobos), *Juegos Infantiles Cantados en Nuevo México,* and *Music of the "Bailes" in New Mexico* (with Anita Gonzales Thomas and Reed Cooper).

THOMAS J. STEELE, S.J., is a professor of English at Regis College in Denver, Colorado. His books include *Santos and Saints: The Religious Folk Art of Hispanic New Mexico, Holy Week in Tomé: A New Mexico Passion Play,* and an edited volume (with Marianne L. Stoller and José B. Fernández), *Diary of the Jesuit Residence of Our Lady of Guadalupe Parish, Conejos, Colorado, December 1871–December 1875.*

MARIANNE L. STOLLER, a cultural anthropologist and ethnohistorian, is associate professor of anthropology at The Colorado College. She has published various articles on the Hispanic Southwest and, with Thomas J. Steele, S.J., and José B. Fernández, has edited the *Diary of the Jesuit Residence of Our Lady of Guadalupe Parish, Conejos, Colorado, December 1871–December 1875.*

ALAN C. VEDDER is a conservator of Spanish

colonial art and a consultant in that field. He is retired from the Museum of New Mexico, where he worked for two decades with E. Boyd. He has written *Furniture of Spanish New Mexico.*

ANN VEDDER is treasurer and a director of The Spanish Colonial Arts Society, Inc., and has been active in various aspects of the society for a number of years.

MARTA WEIGLE, a folklorist, is an associate professor of anthropology, English, and American studies at the University of New Mexico. Her books include *Brothers of Light, Brothers of Blood: The Penitentes of the Southwest, A Penitente Bibliography, Santa Fe and Taos: The Writer's Era, 1916–1941* (with Kyle Fiore), *Spiders & Spinsters: Women and Mythology,* and two edited volumes, *Hispanic Villages of Northern New Mexico* and Lorin W. Brown's *Hispano Folklife of New Mexico* (with Charles L. Briggs).

WILLIAM WROTH is curator of the Taylor Museum of the Colorado Springs Fine Arts Center. His books include *The Chapel of Our Lady of Talpa, Christian Images in Hispanic New Mexico,* and two edited volumes, *Hispanic Crafts of the Southwest* and *Chamisal and Peñasco: The Farm Security Administration Photographs of Russell Lee.*

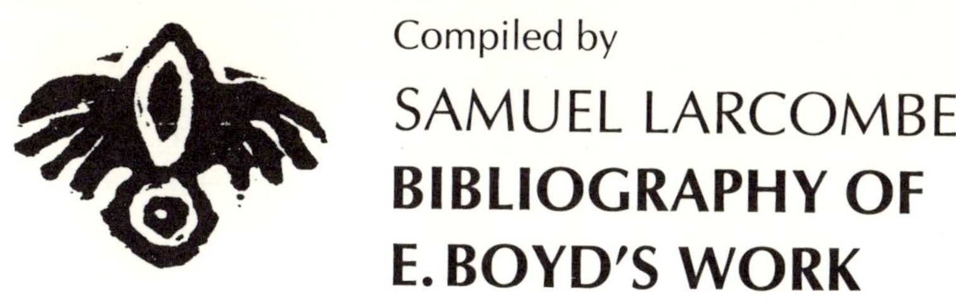

Compiled by

SAMUEL LARCOMBE

BIBLIOGRAPHY OF E. BOYD'S WORK

E. BOYD WAS A PIONEER, known as much for the rich record she left behind as for her discoveries. The following list shows how extensive her work was and how much in her debt we remain. Hers are not the last words on these subjects, but they are among the best.

Boyd's major work, *Popular Arts of Spanish New Mexico* (1974), of course stands as her single most important publication. Many of the articles she wrote found their way, usually with scholarly and stylistic improvements, into this final, monumental book. Nevertheless, *all* the earlier pamphlets, articles and reviews are identifiably and satisfyingly E.'s own. Each one resulted from the same intelligent care and command she brought to all her work. Her style is spare and direct. She saw clearly and commented candidly.

I hope scholars and lay readers alike will find this list helpful. It is substantially complete. I have tried to track down all E. Boyd's publications, but I probably missed at least a score. Some of her shorter pieces were unsigned; some may have been signed with her married names; and I simply may have overlooked a few obvious ones. I trust readers with keen memories and good libraries will help me complete this bibliography for a future edition.

Books

1946 Saints & Saint Makers of New Mexico. Santa Fe, New Mexico: Laboratory of Anthropology. (139 pages; 24 figures; appendices.)

1974 Popular Arts of Spanish New Mexico. Santa Fe: Museum of New Mexico Press. (518 pages; 231 photographs; 42 color plates; appendices; bibliography; index.)

Pamphlets

1950 The Literature of Santos. Dallas, Texas: Southern Methodist University Press. (15 pages; 2 illustrations; reprinted from *Southwest Review.*)

1951 Retablos, the Alfred I. Barton Collection. Miami Beach, Florida: Franklin Press. (Unpaged; illustrated.)

1953*a* New Mexico Santos. Santa Fe: School of American Research, Department of Spanish Colonial Art. Leaflet No. 1. (Unpaged; illustrated.)

1953*b* New Mexico Tinwork. Santa Fe: School of American Research, Department of Spanish Colonial Art. Leaflet No. 2. (Unpaged; illustrated.)

1954 (Unsigned) Hand List of the Collection of the Spanish Colonial Arts Society, Inc. May. (No publication information given;

illustrated. A four-page leaflet with the same cover design, soliciting members, was published at about the same time.)

1959 Popular Arts of Colonial New Mexico. Santa Fe, New Mexico: Museum of International Folk Art. (52 pages; illustrated.)

1962 Indigo. Santa Fe, New Mexico: Museum of International Folk Art. (Exhibition catalogue; unpaged; illustrated.)

1969 The New Mexico Santero. Santa Fe: Museum of New Mexico Press. (24 pages; illustrated; reprinted from *El Palacio* for use as an exhibition catalogue at the Museum of International Folk Art, 1969–70.)

Contributions to Books and Pamphlets

1937–1938 Portfolio of Spanish Colonial Design in New Mexico, 1938, by Workers on the Federal Art Project of New Mexico. Santa Fe, New Mexico: Division of Women's and Professional Projects, Works Progress Administration. (200 copies; E. Boyd credited for the text and renderings.)

1944 Explanatory Notes on the Religious Skin-Paintings of New Mexico. *In* Sacred Paintings on Skin. Reginald Fisher, ed. With reproductions by Martha Ann Walker and poetical interpretations by Marie Schmitt Ely. Santa Fe: Museum of New Mexico Press. August. (99 copies; unpaged; the 4 pages of notes are signed E. Boyd Hall.)

1952 Domestic Utensils of New Mexico. *In* Brand Book, Volume 7, pp. 481–508. Denver, Colorado: The Westerners, Denver Posse. (Illustrated.)

1958 Arts of the Southwest. *In* The Concise Encyclopedia of American Antiquities. Volume 2. New York: Hawthorn Books.

1963 Foreword. *In* Embroideries by Rebecca James. Rebecca James, ed. P. 3. Santa Fe, New Mexico: Museum of International Folk Art.

1965 Notes on Painted Ornaments. *In* A Mercedarian Antiphonary, by Lincoln Bunce Spiess. Pp. 25–31. Santa Fe: Museum of New Mexico Press.

1966*a* Crosses and Camposantos of New Mexico. *In* Camposantos, A Photographic Essay, by Dorothy Benrimo. Pp. 1–4. Fort Worth, Texas: Amon Carter Museum.

1966*b* Foreword and captions. *In* New Mexico Santos: How to Name Them. Illustrations by Frances Breese. Santa Fe: Museum of New Mexico Press.

1967 Santos. *In* New Catholic Encyclopedia. Vol. 12, pp. 1074–76. New York: McGraw-Hill. (Illustrated.)

1970 Introduction. *In* Aspen Art of the New Mexico Highlands, by James DeKorne. P. 7. Santa Fe: Museum of New Mexico Press.

1971 Plaza del Cerro, Chimayo. *In* Historic Preservation: A Plan for New Mexico. Merle Clark, ed. Pp. 79–86. Santa Fe: New Mexico State Planning Office. (Illustrated.)

1972 [Unspecified portions of the text.] Old Santa Fe Today, by The Historic Santa Fe Foundation. 2d ed., rev. and enlarged. Albuquerque: University of New Mexico Press.

1974 The Art of the Santero; *and* About the Santeros; *and* New Mexico Saint Names. *In* New Mexico Magazine 1975 Calendar. Pp. 1–3. Santa Fe: New Mexico Magazine.

Periodicals

1935 Southwestern Artists Annual Show. El Palacio 39 (September):53–57. (Review condensed from *Santa Fe New Mexican.*)

1943 Antiques in New Mexico. Antiques 44 (August):58–62.

1948*a* Notes in Southern California, 1948. Arts and Architecture (July):14, 16.

1948*b* [Untitled article on "Painting Toward Architecture" exhibition.] Arts and Architecture (August):6, 8, 10.

1948*c* [Untitled article on the retrospective shows of Max Beckmann and Morris Graves.] Arts and Architecture (September):6–8.

1948*d* [Untitled article on museum and gallery

exhibitions in Los Angeles.] Arts and Architecture (December):10, 12–13.

1949*a* [Untitled article on exhibitions, panel discussions, magazine articles, publications.] Arts and Architecture (February):9–12.

1949*b* [Untitled article on three exhibitions in Los Angeles.] Arts and Architecture (March):12, 14, 16.

1949*c* An Immediate Necessity. Arts and Architecture (April):16.

1949*d* New Mexico Santos. American Antiques Journal 4 (April):6–9. (Illus.)

1949*e* [Untitled article on architecture and exhibitions.] Arts and Architecture (May):14–16.

1949*f* [Untitled article on the DaVinci exhibition.] Arts and Architecture (June):11–12.

1949*g* [Untitled article on exhibitions and art news.] Arts and Architecture (July):12, 14, 16.

1949*h* A New Mexican Retablo and Its Mexican Prototype. El Palacio 56, 12 (December):355–57. (Illus.)

1950*a* The Niño Perdido Painter. El Palacio 57, 1 (January):10–12. (Illus.)

1950*b* Nuestra Señora de la Manga. El Palacio 57, 3 (March):84–87. (Illus.)

1950*c* [Untitled gallery notes.] Arts and Architecture (March):6

1950*d* Two Engravings from La Puebla, Mexico. El Palacio 57, 4 (April):114–17. (Illus.)

1950*e* The Literature of Santos. Southwest Review 35, 2 (Spring):128–40. (Illus.)

1950*f* A Tentative Identification. El Palacio 57, 6 (June):163–65. (Illus.)

1950*g* San Vicente Ferrer, a Rare Santero Subject. El Palacio 57, 7 (July):195–97. (Illus.)

1950*h* Artists of Los Angeles and Vicinity, 1950. Arts and Architecture (August):16, 42.

1950*i* Maria Hodge's "Receipts." Los Angeles County Museum Quarterly 8, 2 (Summer). (Illus.)

1950*j* Penitentes in California. El Palacio 57, 11 (November):372–73.

1950*k* Lebrun. Arts and Architecture (December).

1951*a* Preservation of the Reredos in San Jose de Laguna Mission, New Mexico. The Masterkey 25 (January-February):8–13.

1951*b* New Mexican Bultos with Hollow Skirts: How They Were Made. El Palacio 58, 5 (May):145–48. (Illus.)

1951*c* An Early New Mexican Watercolor. El Palacio 58, 6 (June):163–64. (Illus. on front cover.)

1951*d* The Source of Certain Elements in *Santero* Paintings of the Crucifixion. El Palacio 58, 8 (August):234–36.

1951*e* [Untitled article on exhibition of contemporary artists at Los Angeles County Museum.] Arts and Architecture (August).

1952*a* The Herder's Kit. El Palacio 59, 4 (April):103.

1952*b* [Signed note on the exhibit of embroideries by Rebecca James in the Palace of the Governors.] El Palacio 59, 5 (May):159.

1952*c* This Year's Spanish Colonial Art Department Accessions. El Palacio 59, 8 (August):263–64. (A staff report.)

1952*d* Representative Santos Collection Shown at Palace. El Palacio 59, 9 (September):295–96. (A staff report.)

1952*e* Mrs. Mitchell Carroll, 1868–1952. El Palacio 59, 12 (December):390–91.

1952*f* Santos of the Southwest. House and Garden (December):92–93, 165.

1952*g* Two Gift Accessions in Textiles. El Palacio 59, 12 (December):385. (A staff report.)

1953*a* (With Roland Dickey) Early New Mexican Art: *Santos.* New Mexico Quarterly 23:68–72. (Introductory note by Dickey; descriptions by Boyd.)

1953*b* New Mexican Tin Work. El Palacio 60, 2 (February):61–67. (Illus.)

1953*c* The Crucifix in *Santero* Art. El Palacio 60, 3 (March):112–15. (Illus.)

1953*d* Celso Gallegos—A Truly Spontaneous Primitive Artist. El Palacio 60, 5 (May):215. (Illus.)

1953*e* Museum Acquires Painting on Tanned Buffalo Skin. El Palacio 60, 5

(May):217–19.
1953*f* Applied Straw Work in Colonial New Mexico. Hobbies (August):90–91. (Illus.)
1953*g* Mexican Milagros. Los Angeles County Museum Quarterly 10, 2 (Summer):17–18. (Illus.)
1953*h* New Mexican Embroidered Leather Accessories. El Palacio 60, 10 (October):352–55. (Illus.)
1953*i* Santo Exhibition in Detroit. El Palacio 60, 11 (November):389.
1953*j* Museum Conservation Project at Ranchos de Taos Mission. El Palacio 60, 12 (December):414–18.
1954*a* The Vara, a Unit of Measurement. El Palacio 61, 2 (February):50–51.
1954*b* Non-Indian Ceramics in Southwestern Archaeology. Antiques (March):239–41. (Illus.)
1954*c* Spanish Colonial Lenten Exhibition in Art Gallery. El Palacio 61, 3 (March):67–69. (Illus.).
1954*d* New Mexican Spanish Textiles. El Palacio 61, 5 (May):134–37. (Illus.)
1954*e* Addendum to Paper on José E. Espinosa's Ramón Velásquez. El Palacio 61, 6 (June):190–91.
1954*f* Curator Visits Amerind Foundation and Santa Barbara. El Palacio 61, 7 (July):236–37.
1954*g* Decorated Tinware East and West: In New Mexico. Antiques (September):203–205.
1954*h* Henry Cady Wells, 1904–1954. El Palacio 61, 11 (November):374–76.
1954*i* Living with Antiques: The New Mexico Home of H. Cady Wells. Antiques (November):400–403.
1955*a* Portuguese Arts Shown during Lent in the Museum Art Gallery. El Palacio 62, 2 (February):35–42. (Illus.)
1955*b* Painting on Wood of Saint Raphael. El Palacio 62, 3 (March):67.
1955*c* Recently Installed Exhibits of the Spanish Colonial Arts Department in the Palace of the Governors. El Palacio 62, 3 (March):88–90. (Illus.)
1955*d* Repair of the Oratorio of San Buenaventura at Chimayo, Co-Sponsored by the Spanish Colonial Arts Society. El Palacio 62, 4 (April):99–101. (Illus.)
1956*a* Señor Santiago de Chimayo. El Palacio 63, 3 (March):69–72. (Illus.)
1956*b* Annual Lenten Exhibit of the Spanish Colonial Department in the Art Gallery. El Palacio 63, 4 (April):116–19. (Illus.)
1956*c* Colonial Arms Reinstated in Palace. El Palacio 63, 4 (April):119–20.
1956*d* Santos of San Ysidro Labrador. El Palacio 63, 4 (April):99–100.
1957*a* The Only Bulto of Santo Toribio. El Palacio 64, 3–4 (March-April):109–14. (Illus.)
1957*b* A Roman Missal from Santa Cruz Church. El Palacio 64, 7–8 (July-August):233–37. (Illus.)
1957*c* A Footnote on the Roman Missal from Santa Cruz Church. El Palacio 64, 9–10 (September-October):277.
1957*d* Hispanic Society of Santa Barbara Conference on Colonial Arts. El Palacio 64, 9–10 (September-October):285–87.
1957*e* Troubles at Ojo Caliente, A Frontier Post. El Palacio 64, 11–12 (November-December):347–60.
1958*a* The Use of Tobacco in Spanish New Mexico. El Palacio 65, 3 (June):103–106. (Illus.)
1958*b* Hand-Hewn Pulpit Completes New Mexico Chapel in Palace of the Governors. El Palacio 65, 4 (August):159. (Illus.)
1958*c* New Mexican Filigree Jewelry. El Palacio 65, 4 (August):151–53.
1958*d* Spanish Colonial Shield, Skin Painting, Life-Size Bulto on View. El Palacio 65, 5 (October):199–200.
1958*e* Fireplaces and Stoves in Colonial New Mexico. El Palacio 65, 6 (December):219–24. (Illus.)
1958*f* El Santo Nino de Navidad. Santa Fe Scene (20 December):6–7.
1959*a* Popular Arts of Colonial New Mexico. 10th Annual Rodeo de Santa Fe Souvenir Program, pp. 18, 45. (Illus.)
1959*b* The Oldest Known Guadalupe Imprint. El

Palacio 66, 6 (December):209–11.

1961*a* The Evolution of the "Spanish" Bridle Bit. 12th Annual Rodeo de Santa Fe Souvenir Program, pp. 6–7. (Illus.)

1961*b* A Bronze Medal of Sixteenth Century Style. El Palacio 68, 2 (Summer):124–28. (Illus.)

1961*c* Ikat Dyeing in Southwestern Textiles. El Palacio 68, 3 (Autumn):185–89. (Illus.)

1962*a* Captain Bourke's Painting of Santiago. Major Exhibitions for 1962, Bulletin 4, pp. 3–6. Joslyn Art Museum, Omaha, Nebraska. (Illus.; issued in lieu of a catalogue for the exhibit "Soldiers and Saints in Old Spain and New.")

1962*b* Colonial Silver from Latin America. El Palacio 69, 2 (Summer):119–23. (Illus.)

1963 Pesos and Pesos. 14th Annual Rodeo de Santa Fe Souvenir Program, pp. 9, 43, 45. (Illus.)

1964 Rio Grande Blankets Containing Hand Spun Cotton Yarns. El Palacio 71, 4 (Winter):22–28.

1965 New Mexico Folk Arts in Art History. El Palacio 72, 4 (Winter):10–12. (Illus.)

1966 Historic Santa Fe. 17th Annual Rodeo de Santa Fe Souvenir Program, pp. 9, 39, 41. (Illus.)

1967 The Conservation of New Mexico Santos and Other Painted and Gessoed Objects. El Palacio 74, 4 (Winter):19–34. (Illus.)

1968 Two New Mexican Retablos from the M.S.U. Art Collection. Kresge Art Center Bulletin 1, 8 (May):4–6. East Lansing: Michigan State University. (Illus.)

1969*a* The New Mexico Santero. El Palacio 76, 1 (Spring):1–24. (Illus.)

1969*b* 17th Century Medal Found in Estancia Valley. El Palacio 76, 3 (Autumn):16.

1970*a* (With Odd S. Halseth) The Laguna Santero. El Palacio 77, 3 (Autumn):19–22. (Illus.)

1970*b* (With Myra Ellen Jenkins) Fiesta House Still Stands. [Santa Fe] New Mexican, 6 September.

1971*a* The Plaza of San Miguel del Vado. El Palacio 77, 4 (Winter):17–27. (Illus.)

1971*b* The First New Mexico Imprint. The Princeton University Library Chronicle 33, 1 (Autumn):30–40.

1972 A Colonial Stone Head. El Palacio 78, 3 (September):14–20. (Illus.)

1973 Domestic Architecture in New Mexico. El Palacio 79, 3 (December):12–29. (Illus.; excerpt from *Popular Arts of Spanish New Mexico.*)

1974 The Journals of Lewis French. The Princeton University Library Chronicle 36, 1 (Autumn):63–68.

1975*a* The Conservation of New Mexico Santos and Other Painted and Gessoed Objects. El Palacio 81, 2 (Summer):11–24. (Illus.; reprint of the 1967 *El Palacio* article.)

1975*b* Portfolio of Spanish Colonial Design. El Palacio 81, 2 (Summer):1–10. (Illus.; text and renderings by E. Boyd Hall reprinted from the 1937–38 publication.)

1975*c* Colonial Horse Gear. El Palacio 81, 3 (Fall):22–24. (Illus.)

n.d. A First Visit to the Berlin Pictures. (No publication data; copy in the E. Boyd Collection, New Mexico State Records and Archives, Santa Fe.)

Book Reviews

1949*a* (Unsigned) Art as the Evolution of Visual Knowledge, by Charles Biederman. Arts and Architecture (July):17–19.

1949*b* Basic Color: An Interpretation of the Oswald Color System, by Paul Theobald. Arts and Architecture (August):9–10.

1949*c* The Materials of the Artist and Their Use in Painting, by May Doerner. Arts and Architecture (September):23.

1950 Franciscan Awatovi, by Ross Gordon Montgomery, Watson Smith, and John Otis Brew. Arts and Architecture (July):16–17.

1951 "The Santero Tradition in the San Luis Valley," by William Wallrich, in Western Folklore, Vol. X, No. 2. El Palacio 58, 7 (July):219–20.

1958*a* *Una Casa del Siglo XVIII en Mexico, La del Conde de San Bartolome de Xala,* by Manuel Romero de Terreros. El Palacio

65, 1 (February):35–37.

1958*b* The Cultivation and Weaving of Cotton in the Prehistoric Southwestern United States, by Kate Peck Kent. El Palacio 65, 2 (April):38.

1958*c* Interpreting Our Heritage, by Freeman Tilden. Landscape 7, 3 (Spring):30.

1958*d* Philippine Colonial Sculpture, by Fernando Zobel de Ayala. El Palacio 65, 6 (December):237.

1958–1959 New Mexico's Royal Road, by Max L. Moorhead. Landscape 8, 2 (Winter):31–32.

1959 Santa Fe: The Autobiography of a Southwestern Town, by Oliver La Farge. Landscape 9, 1 (Autumn):39–40.

1961*a* The Pearson Site, A Historic Indian Site in Ironbridge Reservoir, Rains County, Texas. El Palacio 68, 3 (Autumn):195–96.

1961*b* The Spanish Olive Jar, An Introductory Study, by John M. Goggin. El Palacio 68, 3 (Autumn):194–95.

1964 Treasure of the Sangre de Cristos, by Arthur L. Campa. Landscape 13, 3 (Spring):41.

1964–1965 Religious Architecture of New Mexico, by George Kubler. Landscape 14, 2 (Winter):39.

1965 The Sources and Diffusion of the Mexican Shepherds' Plays, by Juan B. Rael. El Palacio 72, 4 (Winter):41–42.

1969*a* "*Biografia de un artesano popular—El santero Andres J. Arancibia,*" by Julian Ceres Freyre, in *Cuadernos del Instituto Nacional de Antropologia,* No. 5. El Palacio 76, 2 (Summer):48.

1969*b* Los Hermanos Penitentes, by Lorayne Ann Horka-Follick. El Palacio 76, 3 (Autumn):33–34.

1970*a* American Buildings and Their Architects—The Colonial and Neo-Colonial Styles, by William Pierson, Jr. El Palacio 77, 1 (Spring):43–44.

1970*b* The Penitentes of the Southwest, by Marta Weigle. El Palacio 77, 2 (Summer):42–43.

1971 Indian Skin Paintings from the American Southwest, by Gottfried Hotz. New Mexico Historical Review 46, 3 (Summer):271–76.

1973 The Navajo Blanket, by Mary Kahlenburg and Anthony Berlant. El Palacio 78, 4 (January):37.

1974*a* Mexican American Artists, by Jacinto Quirarte. El Palacio 80, 1 (June):47.

1974*b* *Los milagros en metal y en cera de Puerto Rico,* by Teodoro Vidal. El Palacio 80, 3 (Fall):51.

Reports

Historical Society of New Mexico. Boyd contributed a piece entitled "Spanish Colonial Art" to the *Biennial Reports* of 1951–1952 (pp. 10–12); 1953–1954 (p. 12); and 1955–1956 (pp. 12–13).

School of American Research, Santa Fe, New Mexico. Boyd contributed a piece entitled "Spanish Colonial Art" to the *Annual Reports* of 1951 (pp. 36–40); 1953 (pp. 54–56); 1954 (pp. 38–40); 1955 (pp.40–41); 1956 (pp. 39–41); 1957 (pp. 20–21); and 1958 (p. 23).

Smithsonian Institution, Washington, D.C. "Report on Materials Seen in U.S.N.M. Collections Which Could Be Used in Proposed Spanish Colonial Exhibits [in the] Hall of Everyday Life in the American Past. 1961. (Typescript in the files of the Division of Community Life.)

Miscellaneous Manuscripts

All manuscripts are in the E. Boyd Collection, New Mexico State Records Center and Archives, Santa Fe.

"N.M. Santos July 74." (2 pp.; apparently written as copy for a brochure or catalogue.)

"Notes on a Fragment of Carved Stone Found on the Banks of the Little Colorado River." (8 pp.)

"Notes on the Journey of Nicolas de la Fora to New Mexico in 1766." (10 pp.)

"Remarks on *New Mexico in the 19th Century, a Pictorial History,* by A. K. Gregg, UNM Press, 1968." (3 pp.)

"Review of *American Painted Furniture 1660–1880,* by Dean Fales and Robert Bishop, and *Centuries and Styles of the American Chair 1640–1970,* by Robert Bishop." (4 pp.)

Translation of "*Cri de la Meduse*" by Henri Pastoreau. Circa 1946.

Museum Notes

In addition to the following, E. Boyd contributed unpublished notes to numerous institutions in Los Angeles, Denver, Dallas, Washington, D.C., and elsewhere.

Colorado State Historical Society, The Heritage Center, Denver, Colorado. Manuscript on the Woodard Collection of Textiles. n.d. (ca. 1954). (Ca. 35 pp.)

Museum of International Folk Art, Museum of New Mexico, Santa Fe. Accession notes on the collection.

Spanish Colonial Arts Society, Inc., Santa Fe, New Mexico. Accession notes.

Taylor Museum of the Colorado Springs Fine Arts Center, Colorado Springs, Colorado. "Comments on Taylor Museum *santos.*" April 1956. Unpublished ms. in the Taylor Museum Archives. (Comments on 100–200 pieces.)

BIBLIOGRAPHY OF SOURCES CITED

Adams, Eleanor B.
1944 Two Colonial New Mexico Libraries. New Mexico Historical Review 19:135–67.

Adams, Eleanor B., and Chávez, Fray Angélico, trans. and eds.
1956 The Missions of New Mexico, 1776: A Description by Fray Francisco Atanasio Domínguez, with Other Contemporary Documents. Albuquerque: University of New Mexico Press.

Ahlborn, Richard E.
1967 Death Cart. Smithsonian Journal of History 2, 1:74–76.
1968 The Penitente Moradas of Abiquiú. Contributions from The Museum of History and Technology Paper 63. Washington, D.C.: Smithsonian Institution Press.
1970 Saints and Brothers. Américas 22, 9:6–13.
1974 Saints of San Xavier. Tucson, Arizona: Southwestern Mission Research Center.
1975 Spanish Arts in the United States. *In* Hispanic Influences in the United States. Pp. 37–60. New York: Hispanic Institute.

Almada, Francisco R.
1952 *Diccionario de historia, geografía y biografía sonorenses.* Chihuahua, Mexico: Chihuahua.

Amsden, Charles Avery
1949 Navajo Weaving: Its Technique and Its History. 2d ed. Albuquerque: University of New Mexico Press. (First pub. 1934.)

Anonymous
1883 Berger's Tourist Guide to New Mexico. Kansas City, Missouri: Publishing House of Ramsey, Millett & Hudson.
1894 New Mexico: Its Resources, Climate, Geography, Geology, History, Statistics, Present Condition and Future Prospects. Official Publication. Santa Fe: New Mexico Bureau of Immigration.
1896 Slopes of the Sangre de Cristo: A Book of Resources and Industry of Colorado. Denver, Colorado: Published for the Passenger Department of the Denver and Rio Grande Railroad.
1926 The Santa Fe Fiesta—1926. El Palacio 21:73–100.
1927 Museum Events: Spanish Colonial Arts. El Palacio 23:337–39.
1928*a* Official Program: Santa Fe Fiesta, 30 August–1 September.
1928*b* Santa Fe Fiesta: Events at Gallup and Albuquerque. El Palacio 25:183.
1929 Valvanera. *In Enciclopedia Universal Ilustrada Europeo-Americana,* 6:853–56. Madrid and Barcelona: Espasa-Calpe, S.A.
1930 Fiesta Event: The Spanish Colonial Arts Society. El Palacio 29:105–6.
1932 Spanish Arts: Wood Carving Group. El Palacio 33:120.
1934*a* Southwestern Artists: Exhibit by Rio

Grande Painters. El Palacio 36:193–96.
1934*b* Speaking about Art: And in New Mexico. American Magazine of Art 27:608–14.
1936*a* Brilliant Water Color Show at Museum. El Palacio 40:101–102.
1936*b* Fine Examples Remain Hidden. El Palacio 41:86.
1936*c* Southwestern Artists' 1935 Eastern Exhibits. El Palacio 40:52–53.
1936*d* WPA Art Work Shown in Museum. El Palacio 40:92–94.
1940 E. Boyd (Artist). The Santa Fe New Mexican, 26 June, n. pp. (Special issue reprinted in Marta Weigle and Kyle Fiore, eds., *New Mexico Artists and Writers: A Celebration, 1940,* where this appears on p. 31. Santa Fe, New Mexico: Ancient City Press, 1982.)
1941 Fiestas in New Mexico. El Palacio 48:239–42.
1944 The Indian Arts Fund. *In* Mary Austin: A Memorial. Willard Hougland, ed. Pp. 59–61. Santa Fe, New Mexico: Laboratory of Anthropology.
1970 Santos of the Southwest: The Denver Art Museum Collection. Denver, Colorado.
1971 Historic Preservation: A Plan for New Mexico. Santa Fe: New Mexico State Planning Office.
1975 Arroyo Hondo: Penitentes, Weddings, Wakes. El Palacio 81, 1:2–19.
n.d.*a* The Santa Fe Cathedral of St. Francis of Assisi. Santa Fe, New Mexico: Schifani Brothers Printing Co.
n.d.*b* Spanish-Colonial Arts Society Commences 5th Year of Activity. Papers of the Spanish Colonial Arts Society, New Mexico State Records Center and Archives, Santa Fe.

Astrov, Margot
1950 The Concept of Motion as the Psychological Leitmotif of Navajo Life and Literature. Journal of American Folklore 63:45–56.

Austin, Mary
1927 Native Drama in Our Southwest. Nation 124:437–40.
1928 Catholic Culture in Our Southwest III: Salvaging the Old Crafts. The Commonweal 8:572–75.
1932*a* Earth Horizon. Boston and New York: Houghton Mifflin, The Riverside Press Cambridge.
1932*b* Frank Applegate. New Mexico Quarterly 2:213–18.
1933 Folk Plays of the Southwest. Theatre Arts Monthly 17:599–610.
1934 Spanish Manuscripts in the Southwest. Southwest Review 19:402–9.

Baldassarre, Raffaele, S.J.
1874–1875 *Lettere Edificanti della Provincia Napoltetana.* Vol. 1. Privately printed for the Society of Jesus. (Copy in the Regis Jesuit History Library, Regis College, Denver, Colorado.)

Bancroft, Hubert Howe
1962 History of Arizona and New Mexico, 1530–1888. Albuquerque, New Mexico: Horn & Wallace. (First pub. 1889.)

Bandelier, Adolph F. A.
1893 The Gilded Man. New York: D. Appleton.

Barker, Ruth Laughlin
1930 The Craft of Chimayó. El Palacio 28:161–73.

Barnes, Thomas C.; Naylor, Thomas H.; and Polzer, Charles W.
1981 Northern New Spain: A Research Guide. Tucson: University of Arizona Press.

Batchen, Lou Sage
1972 Las Placitas: Historical Facts and Legends. Placitas, New Mexico: Tumbleweed Press.

Bell, Whitfield J., Jr.
1973 Joseph M. Toner (1825–1896) as a Medical Historian. Bulletin of the History of Medicine 47, 1:1–24.

Bell, William A.
1870 New Tracks in North America. New York: Scribner, Welford & Co.

Bloom, Lansing B.
1928 A Glimpse of New Mexico in 1620. New

Mexico Historical Review 3:357–89.
1935 (Ed.) Bourke on the Southwest. New Mexico Historical Review 10:271–322.
1945 From Lewisburg (Pa) to California in 1849: Diary of William H. Chamberlin. New Mexico Historical Review 20:14–57.

Bolton, Herbert Eugene
1962 The Mission as a Frontier Institution in the Latin-American Colonies. El Paso: Texas Western Press. (First pub. 1917.)

Borhegyi, Stephen F. de
1953 The Miraculous Shrines of Our Lord of Esquípulas in Guatemala and Chimayó, New Mexico. El Palacio 60:83–111. (Reprinted in *El Santuario de Chimayo.* Santa Fe, New Mexico: The Spanish Colonial Arts Society, Inc., 1956.)
1954*a* The Cult of Our Lord of Esquípulas in Middle America and New Mexico. El Palacio 61:387–401.
1954*b* The Evolution of a Landscape. Landscape 4, 1:24–30.

Bowen, Dorothy Boyd
1979 Saltillo Design Systems. *In* Spanish Textile Tradition of New Mexico and Colorado. Sarah Nestor, ed. Pp. 100–23. Santa Fe: Museum of New Mexico Press, Museum of International Folk Art.

Boyd, E.
1935 Southwestern Artists Annual Show. El Palacio 39:53–57.
1946 Saints & Saint Makers of New Mexico. Santa Fe, New Mexico: Laboratory of Anthropology.
1950*a* The Literature of Santos. Dallas, Texas: Southern Methodist University Press. (First pub. in *Southwest Review* 35 [1950]:128–40.)
1950*b* Penitentes in California. El Palacio 57:372–73.
1955 Repair of the Oratorio of San Buenaventura at Chimayo. El Palacio 62:99–101.
1956 Señor Santiago de Chimayo. El Palacio 63:69–72. (Reprinted in *El Santuario de Chimayo.* Santa Fe, New Mexico: The Spanish Colonial Arts Society, Inc., 1956.)
1959 Popular Arts of Colonial New Mexico. Santa Fe, New Mexico: Museum of International Folk Art.
1961 Report on Materials Seen in U.S.N.M. Collections Which Could Be Used in Proposed Spanish Colonial Exhibits [in the] Hall of Everyday Life in the American Past. Museum of History and Technology, typescript in the files of the Division of Community Life, Smithsonian Institution, Washington, D.C.
1965 *Review of* The Sources and Diffusion of the Mexican Shepherds' Plays, by Juan B. Rael. El Palacio 72, 4:41–42.
1969 The New Mexico Santero. El Palacio 76, 1:1–24. (Also published separately by the Museum of New Mexico Press, Santa Fe, in 1969.)
1971 The Plaza of San Miguel del Vado. El Palacio 77, 4:17–27.
1974 Popular Arts of Spanish New Mexico. Santa Fe: Museum of New Mexico Press.

Bradfield, Maitland
1971 The Changing Pattern of Hopi Agriculture. Royal Anthropological Institute of Great Britain and Ireland, Occasional Paper No. 30. London.

Briggs, Charles L.
1980 The Wood Carvers of Córdova, New Mexico: Social Dimensions of an Artistic "Revival." Knoxville: University of Tennessee Press.
1981*a* "Our Strength Is the Land": The Structure of Hierarchy and Equality and the Pragmatics of Discourse in Hispano ("Spanish-American") "Talk about the Past." Ph.D. dissertation, University of Chicago.
1981*b* St. Isidore Husbandman: Meditations on a Carved Image from Córdova, New Mexico. El Palacio 87, 1:33–40.

Brown, Lorin W.; with Briggs, Charles L., and Weigle, Marta
1978 Hispano Folklife of New Mexico: The

Lorin W. Brown Federal Writers' Project Manuscripts. Albuquerque: University of New Mexico Press.

Bunting, Bainbridge
1964 Taos Adobes: Spanish Colonial and Territorial Architecture of the Taos Valley. Fort Burgwin Research Center Publication 2. Santa Fe: Museum of New Mexico Press.
1970 Las Trampas. New Mexico Architecture (September-October):37–46.
1974 Of Earth and Timbers Made: New Mexico Architecture. Photographs by Arthur Lazar. Albuquerque: University of New Mexico Press.
1976 Early Architecture in New Mexico. Albuquerque: University of New Mexico Press.

Cabeza de Baca, Fabiola
1954 We Fed Them Cactus. Albuquerque: University of New Mexico Press.

Campa, Arthur L.
1930 A Bibliography of Spanish Folk-Lore in New Mexico. University of New Mexico Bulletin, Language Series 2:3 (September). Albuquerque.
1933 The Spanish Folksong in the Southwest. University of New Mexico Bulletin, Language Series 4:1 (15 November). Albuquerque.
1934*a* Spanish Religious Folk Theatre in the Southwest (First Cycle). University of New Mexico Bulletin, Language Series 5:1 (15 February). Albuquerque.
1934*b* Spanish Religious Folk Theatre in the Southwest (Second Cycle). University of New Mexico Bulletin, Language Series 5:2 (15 June). Albuquerque.
1979 Hispanic Culture in the Southwest. Norman: University of Oklahoma Press.

Carroll, H. Bailey, and Haggard, J. Villasana, eds.
1942 Three New Mexico Chronicles. Albuquerque, New Mexico: Quivira Society.

Casey, Pearle R.
1936 Chimayó, the Ageless Village. Southwestern Lore 1:11–13.

Cassidy, Ina Sizer
1938 Art and Artists of New Mexico: E. Boyd, Painter. New Mexico Magazine (August):28.

Cather, Willa
1927 Death Comes for the Archbishop. New York: Alfred A. Knopf.

Chávez, Fray Angélico
1948 Our Lady of the Conquest. Santa Fe: Historical Society of New Mexico.
1950*a* Neo-Mexicanisms in New Mexico Place-Names. El Palacio 57:67–79.
1950*b* New Mexico Religious Place-Names Other Than Those of Saints. El Palacio 57:23–26.
1954*a* Origins of New Mexico Families: In the Spanish Colonial Period. Santa Fe: Historical Society of New Mexico.
1954*b* The Penitentes of New Mexico. New Mexico Historical Review 29:97–123.
1957 Archives of the Archdiocese of Santa Fe, 1678–1900. Publications of the Academy of American Franciscan History, Bibliographical Series, Vol. 3. Washington, D.C.: Academy of American Franciscan History.
1974 My Penitente Land. Albuquerque: University of New Mexico Press.
1981 But Time and Chance: The Story of Padre Martínez of Taos, 1793–1867. Santa Fe, New Mexico: Sunstone Press.

Christian, William A., Jr.
1981 Apparitions in Late Medieval and Renaissance Spain. Princeton, New Jersey: Princeton University Press.

Clark, Neil M.
n.d. The Weavers of Chimayo. Santa Fe, New Mexico: Vergara Printing. (First pub. in *Saturday Evening Post,* 9 May 1953.)

Clarke, Dwight L.
1966 The Original Journals of Henry Smith Turner. Norman: University of Oklahoma Press.

Coan, Mary W.
1935 Handicraft Arts Revived. New Mexico

Magazine (February):14–15, 52.

Córdova, Gilberto Benito, comp.
1972 Bibliography of Unpublished Materials Pertaining to Hispanic Culture in the New Mexico WPA Writers' Files. Santa Fe: New Mexico State Department of Education, Bilingual-Bicultural Communicative Arts Unit.

Coues, Elliot, ed.
1970 The Journal of Jacob Fowler. Lincoln: University of Nebraska Press.

Cozzens, Samuel Woodworth
1876 The Marvelous Country, or Thirty Years in Arizona and New Mexico. Boston: Lee and Shepard.

Cunningham, Helen
1937 A Layman's Review. El Palacio 43:57–65.

Cushing, Frank Hamilton
1896 Outlines of Zuñi Creation Myths. *In* Thirteenth Annual Report of the Bureau of Ethnology to the Secretary of the Smithsonian Institution, 1891–1892, by J. W. Powell, Director. Pp. 321–447. Washington, D.C.: Government Printing Office.

Darley, Alex M.
1968 The Passionists of the Southwest. Glorieta, New Mexico: Rio Grande Press. (First pub. 1893.)

Davis, W. W. H.
1938 El Gringo, or New Mexico & Her People. Santa Fe, New Mexico: Rydal Press. (First pub. 1857.)

De Huff, Elizabeth Willis
1931 The Santuario at Chimayó. New Mexico Highway Journal (June):16–17, 39.

Dewitt, Susan
1978 Historic Albuquerque Today: An Overview Survey of Historic Buildings and Districts. Albuquerque, New Mexico: Historic Landmarks Survey of Albuquerque.

Dickey, Roland F.
1949 New Mexico Village Arts. Albuquerque: University of New Mexico Press.

Donahue, William H., C.S.C.
1953 Mary of Agreda and the Southwest United States. The Americas 9:291–314.

Douglas, Frederic H.
1935–1938 Field notes on weaving in the New Mexico Pueblos. Files of the Denver Art Museum, Denver, Colorado.
1937 An Embroidered Cotton Garment from Acoma. Department of Indian Art, Material Culture Notes 1. Denver, Colorado: Denver Art Museum.
1939*a* Acoma Pueblo Weaving and Embroidery. Indian Art Department Leaflet 89. Denver, Colorado: Denver Art Museum.
1939*b* Weaving in the Tewa Pueblos. Indian Art Department Leaflet 90. Denver, Colorado: Denver Art Museum.
1939*c* Weaving of the Keres Pueblos. Indian Art Department Leaflet 91. Denver, Colorado: Denver Art Museum.
1939*d* Weaving of the Tiwa Pueblos and Jemez. Indian Art Department Leaflet 91. Denver, Colorado: Denver Art Museum.
1940*a* Main Types of Pueblo Cotton Textiles. Indian Art Department Leaflets 92–93. Denver, Colorado: Denver Art Museum.
1940*b* Main Types of Pueblo Woolen Textiles. Indian Art Department Leaflets 94–95. Denver, Colorado: Denver Art Museum.
1940*c* Weaving at Zuni Pueblo. Indian Art Department Leaflets 96–97. Denver, Colorado: Denver Art Museum.
n.d.*a* Acoma Wool Blanket. Unpublished manuscript. (Copy in files of Kate P. Kent.)
n.d.*b* Zuni Black Wool Blanket. Unpublished manuscript. (Copy in files of Kate P. Kent.)

Dumarest, Father Nöel, with preface by Stewart Culin
1919 Notes on Cochiti, New Mexico. Memoirs of the American Anthropological Association 6, 3:135–236.

Dunn, Dorothy
1968 American Indian Painting of the Southwest and Plains Areas. Albuquerque: University of New Mexico Press.

Dunton, Nellie G.
1935 The Spanish Colonial Ornament and the Motifs Depicted in the Textiles of the Period in the American Southwest. Philadelphia: H. C. Perleberg.
1942 Old Spanish Embroidery Designs. The School Arts Magazine 42:88.

Dyk, Walter, ed.
1967 Son of Old Man Hat. Lincoln: University of Nebraska Press. (First pub. 1938.)

Earnshaw, Peggy L.; Goldsmith, Galen L.; Maurer, Virginia L.; and Miles, Steven L.
1973 A Study of San Miguel del Vado. Manuscript. Colorado Springs: Department of Anthropology, The Colorado College.

Eggan, Fred
1972 Summary. *In* New Perspectives on the Pueblos. Alfonso Ortiz, ed. Pp. 287–305. Albuquerque: University of New Mexico Press.

Ellis, Bruce T.
1978 La Garita, Santa Fe's Little Spanish Fort. El Palacio 84, 2:2–20.

Emery, Irene
1952 Naming the Direction of the Twist in Yarn and Cordage. El Palacio 59:251–62.

Espinosa, José E.
1960 Saints in the Valleys: Christian Sacred Images in the History, Life and Folk Art of Spanish New Mexico. Albuquerque: University of New Mexico Press.
1967 Saints in the Valleys. Rev. ed. Albuquerque: University of New Mexico Press.

Federal Art Project of New Mexico
1937–1938 Portfolio of Spanish Colonial Design in New Mexico, 1938. Santa Fe, New Mexico: Division of Women's and Professional Projects, Works Progress Administration.

Fisher, Nora
1979*a* Fabric Structure. *In* Spanish Textile Tradition in New Mexico and Colorado. Sarah Nestor, ed. Pp. 201–6. Santa Fe: Museum of New Mexico Press, Museum of International Folk Art.
1979*b* The Treadle Loom. *In* Spanish Textile Tradition in New Mexico and Colorado. Sarah Nestor, ed. Pp. 192–95. Santa Fe: Museum of New Mexico Press, Museum of International Folk Art.
1979*c* Yardage. *In* Spanish Textile Tradition in New Mexico and Colorado. Sarah Nestor, ed. Pp. 144–45. Santa Fe: Museum of New Mexico Press, Museum of International Folk Art.

Fisher, Nora, and Wheat, Joe Ben
1979 The Materials of Southwestern Weaving. *In* Spanish Textile Tradition in New Mexico and Colorado. Sarah Nestor, ed. Pp. 196–200. Santa Fe: Museum of New Mexico Press, Museum of International Folk Art.

Fisher, Reginald
1941 Notes on the Relation of the Franciscans to the Penitentes. El Palacio 48:263–71.
1958 (Ed.) The Way of the Cross: A New Mexico Version. Designed by Ralph Douglass and printed by Frank J. Vergara. School of American Research Publication. Santa Fe, New Mexico: Graphic Printing.

Flynn, D. J.
1894 Holy Week with the Penitentes. Harper's Weekly 38:489–90.

Forrestal, Peter P., C.S.C. (trans.), and Lynch, Cyprian J., O.F.M. (ed.)
1954 Benavides Memorial of 1630. Washington, D.C.: Academy of American Franciscan History.

Forsyth, Ilene H.
1972 The Throne of Wisdom: Wood Sculptures of the Madonna in

Romanesque France. Princeton, New Jersey: Princeton University Press.

Foster, George M.
1953 *Cofradía* and *Compadrazgo* in Spain and Spanish America. Southwestern Journal of Anthropology 9:1–28.
1960 Culture and Conquest: America's Spanish Heritage. Viking Fund Publications in Anthropology No. 27. Chicago: Quadrangle Books.

French, Rachel
1962 Alamos: Sonora's City of Silver. The Smoke Signal No. 5. Tucson, Arizona: The Westerners.

Galligos, T. M., and Salazar, Francisco
1864 Boundary Line of New Mexico and Colorado. House of Representatives Miscellaneous Document No. 73. 38th Congress, 1st Session. Washington, D.C.

Galvez, Bernardo de
1967 Instructions for Governing the Interior Provinces of New Spain, 1786. New York: Arno Press. (Ed. first pub. 1951.)

Garcia Gutierrez, Canonigo Jesús
1946*a* *Ramillete de Flores Marianas, formado con el Calendario Mariano Universal y las Advocaciones de la Virgen María en Méjico.* Mexico, D.F.: Buena Prensa.
1946*b* *Santos y Beatos de America.* Mexico, D.F.: Buena Prensa.

Gettens, Rutherford J., and Turner, Evan H.
1951 The Materials and Methods of Some Religious Paintings of Nineteenth-Century New Mexico. El Palacio 68:3–16.

Gibson, Charles
1976 The Aztecs under Spanish Rule. Stanford, California: Stanford University Press.

Gibson, C. L., Jr.
1932–1933 Colorado Writers' Project, Conejos County. Manuscripts. Denver: Colorado Historical Society Library.

Giffords, Gloria Kay
1974 Mexican Folk Retablos: Masterpieces in Tin. Tucson: University of Arizona Press.

Gregg, Josiah
1933 Commerce of the Prairies: The Journal of a Santa Fe Trader. Dallas, Texas: Southwest Press. (Reprint of 1844 ed.)

Hackett, Charles Wilson, ed.
1937 Historical Documents Relating to New Mexico, Nueva Vizcaya, and Approaches Thereto, to 1773. Carnegie Institution of Washington, Publication No. 330, Vol. 3. Baltimore, Maryland: Lord Baltimore Press.
1942 Revolt of the Pueblo Indians of New Mexico and Otermin's Attempted Reconquest, 1680–1682. 2 vols. Albuquerque: University of New Mexico Press.

Hallenbeck, Cleve, and Williams, Juanita H.
1938 Legends of the Spanish Southwest. Glendale, California: Clark.

Hammond, George P., and Rey, Agapito, eds. and trans.
1953 Don Juan de Oñate, Colonizer of New Mexico, 1595–1628. 2 vols. Albuquerque: University of New Mexico Press.

Harmon, Tom
1976 While the Spiders Are Sleeping. Empire Magazine, Denver Post, 21 November, pp. 24–26.

Harper, Allan G.; Cordova, Andrew R.; and Oberg, Kalervo
1943 Man and Resources in the Middle Rio Grande Valley. Inter-Americana Studies 2. Albuquerque: University of New Mexico Press.

Hayes, Alden C.
1974 The Four Churches of Pecos. Albuquerque: University of New Mexico Press.

Hemsi, Alberto
1932–1973 *Coplas Sefardies.* Alexandria, Egypt: Edition Orientale de Musique.

Henderson, Alice Corbin
1937 Brothers of Light: The Penitentes of the Southwest. New York: Harcourt, Brace and Company.
1938 E. Dana Johnson: June 15,

1879–December 10, 1937. New Mexico Historical Review 13:120–25.

Herrera, Alonso de, with others
1777 *Agricultura general.* Madrid: Antonio Sancha.

Hewett, Edgar L., and Fisher, Reginald G.
1943 Mission Monuments of New Mexico. Handbooks of Archaeological History, Publications of the University of New Mexico and the School of American Research. Albuquerque: University of New Mexico Press.

Hill, Willard W.
1940 Some Navaho Culture Changes during Two Centuries (with a translation of the early eighteenth century Rabal Manuscript). *In* Essays in Historical Anthropology of North America, Published in Honor of John R. Swanton. Pp. 395–415. Smithsonian Miscellaneous Collections 100. Washington, D.C.: Smithsonian Institution.

Hinsley, Curtis M., Jr.
1981 Savages and Scientists: The Smithsonian Institution and the Development of American Anthropology, 1846–1910. Washington, D.C.: Smithsonian Institution Press.

Hodge, Frederick Webb; Hammond, George P.; and Rey, Agapito, eds.
1945 Fray Alonso de Benavides' Revised Memorial of 1634: With Numerous Supplementary Documents Elaborately Annotated. Coronado Cuarto Centennial Publications, 1540–1940, Vol. 4. Albuquerque: University of New Mexico Press.

Horgan, Paul
1975 Lamy of Santa Fe. New York: Farrar, Straus and Giroux.

Hough, Walter
1932 Biographic Memoir of Jesse Walter Fewkes, 1850–1930. National Academy of Sciences of the United States of America, Biographical Memoirs 15:261–67.

Humboldt, Alejandro de
1966 *Ensayo político sobre el Reino de la Nueva España.* Mexico, D.F.: Editorial Porrua.

Hurt, Amy Passmore
1934 Chimayo: The Village Time Has Blest. New Mexico Magazine (November): 10–12, 43–44.

Infante-Galán, Juan
1971 *Rocio, La Devoción Mariana de Andalucía.* Seville, Spain: Editorial Prensa Espanola, S.A.

Ingersoll, Ernest
1885 The Crest of the Continent: A Record of a Summer's Ramble in the Rocky Mountains and Beyond. Chicago: R. R. Donnelly & Sons.

James, George Wharton
1920 Indian Blankets and Their Makers. Chicago: McClurg.

Jaramillo, Cleofas M.
1941 Shadows of the Past *(Sombras del pasado).* Santa Fe, New Mexico: Seton Village Press. (Reprint, Santa Fe: Ancient City Press, 1980.)
1942 The Genuine New Mexico Tasty Recipes *(Potajes sabrosos).* Santa Fe, New Mexico: Seton Village Press. (Reprint, Santa Fe: Ancient City Press, 1981.)
1955 Romance of a Little Village Girl. San Antonio, Texas: Naylor.

Jefferson, James; Delaney, Robert W.; Thompson, George C.; and O'Neil, Floyd A., eds.
1972 The Southern Utes. Ignacio, Colorado: Southern Ute Tribes.

Jeter, James, and Juelke, Paula Marie
1978 The Saltillo Sarape: An Exhibition Organized by the Santa Barbara Museum. Santa Barbara, California: New World Arts.

Jones, Oakah L.
1979 Los Paisanos: Spanish Settlers on the Northern Frontier of New Spain. Norman: University of Oklahoma Press.

Jordan, Louann, and Cooke, St. George
1977 El Rancho de las Golondrinas: Spanish Colonial Life in New Mexico. Santa

Fe: Colonial New Mexico Historical Foundation.

Judd, Neil M.
1967 The Bureau of American Ethnology: A Partial History. Norman: University of Oklahoma Press.

Katz, Israel J.
1972 Judeo-Spanish Traditional Ballads from Jerusalem. New York: Institute of Medieval Music.

Kelemen, Pál
1951 Baroque and Rococo in Latin America. New York: Macmillan.
1954 The Significance of the Stone Retable of Cristo Rey. El Palacio 61:243–72.
1961 El Greco Revisited. New York: Macmillan.
1971 Peruvian Colonial Painting. New York: Brooklyn Museum.
1977 Vanishing Art of the Americas. New York: Walker and Company.

Kelly, Bernard
1968 World of the Santos. Empire Magazine, Denver Post, 14 April, pp. 38–39.

Kelly, Daniel T., with Chauvenet, Beatrice
1972 The Buffalo Head: A Century of Mercantile Pioneering in the Southwest. Santa Fe, New Mexico: Vergara Publishing.

Kelly, Henry W.
1940 Franciscan Missions of New Mexico, 1740–1760. New Mexico Historical Review 15:345–68.
1941 Franciscan Missions of New Mexico, 1740–1760. New Mexico Historical Review 16:41–69, 148–83.

Kendall, George Wilkins
1935 Narrative of the Texan Santa Fé Expedition. 2 vols. Austin, Texas: Steck.
1966 Across the Great Southwestern Prairies I. Ann Arbor, Michigan: University Microfilms.

Kent, Kate Peck
1957 The Cultivation and Weaving of Cotton in the Prehistoric Southwestern United States. American Philosophical Society Transactions 47:3.
1976 Pueblo and Navajo Weaving Traditions and the Western World. *In* Ethnic and Tourist Arts: Cultural Expressions from the Fourth World. Nelson H. H. Graburn, ed. Pp. 85–101. Berkeley, Los Angeles, and London: University of California Press.
1979 An Analysis of Textile Materials from Walpi Pueblo. Unpublished report submitted to Heritage Conservation and Recreation Service Interagency Archeological Services, San Francisco, California.
1980 *Review of* Spanish Textile Tradition of New Mexico and Colorado, edited by Sarah Nestor. American Indian Art Magazine (Autumn):77–80.
1982 Prehistoric Textiles of the Southwest. School of American Research Southwest Indian Art Series. Santa Fe, New Mexico: School of American Research; Albuquerque: University of New Mexico Press.

Kessell, John L.
1979 Kiva, Cross and Crown. Washington, D.C.: U.S. Department of the Interior, National Park Service.
1980 The Missions of New Mexico since 1776. Albuquerque: University of New Mexico Press.

Kinnaird, Lawrence, and Kinnaird, Lucia
1979 Secularization of Four New Mexico Missions. New Mexico Historical Review 54:35–41.

Kubler, George
1939 The Rebuilding of San Miguel at Santa Fe in 1710. Contributions of the Taylor Museum of the Colorado Springs Fine Arts Center. Colorado Springs, Colorado.
1940 The Religious Architecture of New Mexico: In the Colonial Period and since the American Occupation. Colorado Springs, Colorado: Taylor Museum.

Kubler, George, and Soria, Martin
1959 Art and Architecture in Spain and Portugal and Their American

Dominions, 1500–1800. Baltimore, Maryland: Penguin.

Kutsche, Paul, and Gallegos, Dennis
1979 Community Functions of the *Cofradía de Nuestro Padre Jesús Nazareno*. *In* The Survival of Spanish-American Villages. Paul Kutsche, ed. Pp. 91–98. The Colorado College Studies 15. Colorado Springs.

Lamb, Vic
1968 Old Cemetery. New Mexico Magazine (June-July):33.

Lange, Charles H.
1959 Cochití: A New Mexico Pueblo, Past and Present. Carbondale: Southern Illinois University Press.

Lange, Yvonne
1974 Lithography, an Agent of Technological Change in Religious Folk Art: A Thesis. Western Folklore 33:51–64.

Langley, Samuel Pierpont
1901 Memoir of George Brown Goode, 1851–1896. *In* Annual Report of the Board of Regents of the Smithsonian Institution, 1897. Part 2, pp. 41–61. Washington, D.C.: Government Printing Office.

Lavender, David
1980 The Southwest. A Regions of America Book. New York: Harper & Row.

Lecompte, Janet
1978 Pueblo, Hardscrabble, Greenhorn: The Upper Arkansas, 1832–1856. Norman: University of Oklahoma Press.

Leyba, Ely
1933 The Church of the Twelve Apostles. New Mexico Magazine (June):19–21, 47–52.

Lindsay, G. Carroll
1965 George Brown Goode. *In* Keepers of the Past. Clifford L. Lord, ed. Pp. 127–40. Chapel Hill: University of North Carolina Press.

Liuzzi, Fernando
1935 *La Lauda e i primordi della melodia italiana.* Rome.

Lucero-White (Lea), Aurora
1940*a* Folk-Dances of the Spanish-Colonials of New Mexico. Santa Fe, New Mexico: Examiner Publishing.
1940*b* New Mexico Folklore—Coloquio de los Pastores. Santa Fe, New Mexico: Santa Fe Press.
1941 The Folklore of New Mexico: Volume One, Romances, Corridos, Cuentos, Proverbios, Dichos, Adivinanzas. Santa Fe, New Mexico: Seton Village Press.
1947 Los Hispanos. New Mexico Series 1. Denver, Colorado: Sage Books.
1953 Literary Folklore of the Hispanic Southwest. San Antonio, Texas: Naylor.

Luckert, Karl W.
1975 The Navajo Hunter Tradition. Tucson: University of Arizona Press.

Lummis, Charles F.
1929 Flowers of Our Lost Romance. Boston: Houghton Mifflin.
1966 The Land of Poco Tiempo. Illus. facsimile ed. Albuquerque: University of New Mexico Press. (First pub. 1893.)

Luqui Lagleyze, Julio A.
1981 *Las iglesias de la Ciudad de la Trinidad y Puerto de Santa María de los Buenos Aires* (1536–1810). Cuadernos de Buenos Aires 57. Buenos Aires, Argentina: Municipalidad de la Ciudad de Buenos Aires.

Mantecon, Javier Castro, and Aquino, Manuel Zárate
1958 Miguel Cabrera, Oaxacan Painter of the 18th Century. Mexico: National Institute of Anthropology and History.

Márquez, Angelina V.
1973 San Migeul del Vado. Manuscript. Colorado Springs: Department of Anthropology, The Colorado College.

Matthews, Washington
1884 Navajo Weavers. *In* Third Annual Report of the Bureau of Ethnology to the Secretary of the Smithsonian Institution, 1881–1882, by J. W. Powell, Director. Pp. 371–91.

Washington, D.C.: Government Printing Office.

Mauzy, Wayne L.
1936 Santa Fe's Native Market. El Palacio 40:64–72.

Mayfield, Harriet
1925 Devout People Enact Sacred Drama Every Year in Quaint Town. Los Angeles Sunday Times, 31 May, sec. 2-a, p. 2.

McCrossen, Helen Cramp
1931 Native Crafts in New Mexico. The School Arts Magazine 30:456–58.

McDonald, William F.
1969 Federal Relief Administration and the Arts: The Origins and Administrative History of the Arts Projects of the Works Progress Administration. Columbus: Ohio State University Press.

McNitt, Frank
1962 The Indian Traders. Norman: University of Oklahoma Press.

Meline, James F.
1868 Two Thousand Miles on Horseback, Santa Fé and Back. New York: Hurd and Houghton.

Menéndez Pidal, Gonzalo
1951 *Los caminos de la historía de España.* Madrid: Ediciones Cultura Hispanica.

Mera, Harry P.
1943 Pueblo Indian Embroidery. Santa Fe, New Mexico: Laboratory of Anthropology.
1947–1951 Spanish-American Blanketry: Its Relationship to Aboriginal Weaving in the South West. Unpublished manuscript. Santa Fe, New Mexico: School of American Research.
1948 Navajo Textile Arts. Santa Fe, New Mexico: Laboratory of Anthropology.
1949 The Alfred I. Barton Collection of Southwestern Textiles. Santa Fe, New Mexico: San Vicente Foundation, Inc.

Miles, Carlotta
1962 Almada of Alamos: The Diary of Don Bartolomé. Tucson: Arizona Silhouettes.

Milich, Alicia Ronstadt
1966 Relaciones, by Zarate Salmeron. Albuquerque, New Mexico: Horn & Wallace Publishers.

Mills, George
1967 The People of the Saints. Colorado Springs, Colorado: The Taylor Museum of the Colorado Springs Fine Arts Center.

Mills, George, and Grove, Richard
1956 Lucifer and the Crucifer: The Enigma of the Penitentes. Colorado Springs, Colorado: Taylor Museum.

Minge, Ward Alan
1979 *Efectos del país:* A History of Weaving along the Rio Grande. *In* Spanish Textile Tradition of New Mexico and Colorado. Sarah Nestor, ed. Pp. 8–28. Santa Fe: Museum of New Mexico Press, Museum of International Folk Art.

Minton, Charles Ethrige
1973 Juan of Santo Niño: An Authentic Account of Pioneer Life in New Mexico, 1863–1864. Santa Fe, New Mexico: Sunstone Press.

Morgan, Nicholas G.
1950 Mormon Colonization in the San Luis Valley. Colorado Magazine 27:269–93.

Nestor, Sarah
1971 The Native Market of the Spanish New Mexican Craftsmen: Santa Fe, 1933–1940. Santa Fe: Colonial New Mexico Historical Foundation.
1979 (Ed.) Spanish Textile Tradition of New Mexico and Colorado. Museum of International Folk Art. Santa Fe: Museum of New Mexico Press.

Newhall, Nancy
1962 Sanctuary in Adobe. American Heritage 13, 3:68–75.

Ortiz, Alfonso
1969 The Tewa World: Space, Time, Being, and Becoming in a Pueblo Society. Chicago: University of Chicago Press.
1972 Ritual Drama and the Pueblo World View. *In* New Perspectives on the Pueblos. Alfonso Ortiz, ed. Pp. 135–61. Albuquerque: University of

New Mexico Press.
1981 The Pueblo Revolt of 1680: In Commemoration. *In* Ceremony of Brotherhood. Rudolfo A. Anaya and Simon J. Ortiz, eds. Pp. 7–17. Albuquerque, New Mexico: Academia.

Otero (-Warren), Nina
1936 Old Spain in Our Southwest. New York: Harcourt, Brace and Company.

Parsons, Elsie Clews
1926 Tewa Tales. Memoirs of the American Folk-Lore Society 19. New York: G. E. Stechert.

Pascual, Michael, C.R.
1958 History of Our Lady of Guadalupe Church. Ledger News (Antonito, Colorado), 24 April, p. 1.

Pearce, T. M.
1955 Spanish Place Name Patterns in the Southwest. Names 3:201–209.
1958 New Mexico Place Name Dictionary: A Polyglot in Six Languages. Names 6:217–25.
1979 (Ed.) Literary America, 1903–1934: The Mary Austin Letters. Contributions in Women's Studies No. 5. Westport, Connecticut: Greenwood Press.

Pearce, T. M., with Cassidy, Ina Sizer, and Pearce, Helen S., eds.
1965 New Mexico Place Names: A Geographical Dictionary. Albuquerque: University of New Mexico Press.

Pérez Alonso, Alejandro
1971 *Historia de la Real Abadía-Santuario de Nuestra Señora de Valvanera en la Rioja.* Gijón, Spain: Tipo-Offset La Industria.

Piggott, Stuart
1976 The Beginnings of Wheeled Transport. *In* Avenues to Antiquity: Readings from *Scientific American.* Brian M. Fagan, ed. Pp. 212–20. San Francisco, California: W. H. Freeman. (First pub. July 1968.)

Plenderleith, H. J., and Cursiter, Stanley
1934 The Problem of Lining Adhesives for Paintings: Wax Adhesives. Technical Studies in the Field of Fine Arts 3, 2:90–115.

Powell, Philip Wayne
1950 The Forty-Niners of Sixteenth Century Mexico. Pacific Historical Review 19:235–49.
1952 Soldiers, Indians and Silver. Berkeley: University of California Press.

Rael, Juan B.
1951 The New Mexican *Alabado.* With Transcription of Music by Eleanor Hague. Stanford University Publications, University Series, Language and Literature, Vol. 9, No. 3. Stanford, California.

Reeve, Frank D.
1961 History of New Mexico. New York: Lewis Historical Publishing.

Reichard, Gladys
1934 Spider Woman: A Story of Navajo Weavers and Chanters. New York: Macmillan.
1936 Navajo Shepherd and Weaver. New York: J. J. Augustin.
1974 Navaho Religion. Princeton, New Jersey: Princeton University Press.

Revilla Gigedo, Juan Vicente Guemez Pacheco de Padilla Hocasitas y Aguayo, Conde de
1875 *Estado de las Misiones del Nuevo Méjico en el año de 1793. Revista Católica* 1:324–26.

Richmond, Patricia J.
1973 La Loma de San José. The San Luis Valley Historian 5, 4:42–63.

Ringrose, David R.
1970 Carting in the Hispanic World: An Example of Divergent Development. Hispanic American Historical Review 50:30–51.

Ritch, William G.
1885 Illustrated New Mexico. 5th ed. Santa Fe: New Mexico Bureau of Immigration.

Robb, John Donald
1980 Hispanic Folk Music of New Mexico and the Southwest: A Self-Portrait of a People. Norman: University of Oklahoma Press.

Robertson, Edna, and Nestor, Sarah
1976 Artists of the Canyons and Caminos:

Santa Fe, the Early Years. n.p.: Peregrine Smith.

Roca, Paul
1967 Paths of the Padres through Sonora. Tucson, Arizona: Pioneers' Historical Society.

Roig, Juan Ferrando
1950 *Iconografía de los santos.* Barcelona: Ediciones Omega, S.A.

Romano-V., Octavio Ignacio
1968 The Anthropology and Sociology of the Mexican-Americans: The Distortion of Mexican-American History. El Grito 2:13–26.

Roschini, P. Gabriele M.
1964 *Diccionario Mariano.* Barcelona: Editorial Litúriga Española, S.A.

Rosnek, Carl E.
1974 E. Boyd, 1903–1974. El Palacio 80, 3:inside back cover.

Ross, P.
1935 Village of Many Blessings: A Fragment of Colonial Spain in New Mexico. Travel 64:35–37, 46.

Ruffner, E. H., Lt.
1876 Lines of Communication between Southern Colorado and Northern New Mexico. House of Representatives Executive Document No. 172. 44th Congress, 1st Session. Washington, D.C.
1878 Lines of Communication between Colorado and New Mexico. House of Representatives Executive Document No. 66. 45th Congress, 2nd Session. Washington, D.C.

Saltzman, Max, and Fisher, Nora
1979 The Dye Analysis [Saltzman] *and* Introductory Remarks [Fisher]. *In* Spanish Textile Tradition of New Mexico and Colorado. Sarah Nestor, ed. Pp. 212–20. Santa Fe: Museum of New Mexico Press, Museum of International Folk Art.

Sánchez Pérez, José A.
1943 *El culto Mariano en España.* Madrid: Consejo Superior de Investigaciones Científicas.

Sanford, Trent Elwood
1950 The Architecture of the Southwest: Indian, Spanish, American. New York: W. W. Norton.

Sauer, Carl O.
1980 Seventeenth Century North America. Berkeley, California: Turtle Island.

Scholes, France V.
1929 Documents for the History of the New Mexican Missions in the Seventeenth Century. New Mexico Historical Review 4:45–58, 195–201.
1930 The Supply Service of the New Mexico Missions in the Seventeenth Century. New Mexico Historical Review 5:93–155, 186–209, 386–404.
1935 Civil Government and Society in New Mexico in the Seventeenth Century. New Mexico Historical Review 10:71–111.
1936 Church and State in New Mexico, 1610–1650. New Mexico Historical Review 11:9–76, 145–78, 283–94, 297–349.
1940 Troublous Times in New Mexico, 1659–70. New Mexico Historical Review 15:249–68, 369–417.
1942 Troublous Times in New Mexico, 1659–1670. Historical Society of New Mexico Publications in History, Vol. 11. Albuquerque: University of New Mexico Press.
1944 Juan Martinez de Montoya, Settler and Conquistador of New Mexico. New Mexico Historical Review 19:337–42.

Scholes, France V., and Adams, Eleanor B.
1952 Inventories of Church Furnishings in Some of the New Mexico Missions, 1672. *In* Dargan Historical Essays. William M. Dabney and Josiah C. Russell, eds. Pp. 27–38. University of New Mexico Publications in History No. 4. Albuquerque: University of New Mexico Press.

Scott, Winfield Townley
1964 The Still Young Sunlight: Chimayo, New Mexico. *In* A Vanishing America. T. C. Wheeler, ed. Pp. 122–35. New

York: Holt, Rinehart and Winston.

Sellars, Judith, and Langlois, Janet
1978 Highlights of a Lively First Twenty-Five Years. El Palacio 84, 4:14–28.

Service, Elman R.
1954 Spanish-Guarani Relations in Early Colonial Paraguay. Museum of Anthropology, Anthropological Papers No. 9. Ann Arbor: University of Michigan.

Shalkop, Robert L.
1969 Arroyo Hondo: The Folk Art of a New Mexican Village. Colorado Springs, Colorado: The Taylor Museum of the Colorado Springs Fine Arts Center.

Simmons, Marc
1968 Spanish Government in New Mexico. Albuquerque: University of New Mexico Press.
1969 Settlement Patterns and Village Plans in Colonial New Mexico. Journal of the West 8:7–21.
1979 History of Pueblo-Spanish Relations to 1821. *In* Handbook of North American Indians, Vol. 9: Southwest. Alfonso Ortiz, ed. Pp. 206–23. Washington, D.C.: Smithsonian Institution Press.

Simpson, Lesley Byrd
1950 The Encomienda in New Spain: The Beginning of Spanish Mexico. Los Angeles and Berkeley: University of California Press.

Smithsonian Institution
1898 Annual Report of the Board of Regents of the Smithsonian Institution, 1897. Washington, D.C.: Government Printing Office.

Soil Conservation Service, U.S. Department of Agriculture
1937 Village Livelihood in the Upper Rio Grande Area *and* A Note on the Level of Village Livelihood in the Upper Rio Grande Area. Regional Bulletin 44, Conservation Economics Series 17. Albuquerque, New Mexico.

Spier, Leslie
1924 Zuni Weaving Technique. El Palacio 16:183–93.

Spiess, Lincoln Bunce
1964 Benavides and Church Music in New Mexico in the Early 17th Century. Journal of the American Musicological Society 17:144–56.
1965 Church Music in 17th Century New Mexico. Albuquerque: University of New Mexico Press.

Spiess, Lincoln Bunce, and Stanford, Thomas
1969 An Introduction to Certain Mexican Musical Archives. Detroit: Information Coordinators.

Stagg, Albert
1978 The Almadas and Alamos, 1783–1867. Tucson: University of Arizona Press.

Stark, Richard B.
1969 (Assisted by T. M. Pearce and Rubén Cobos) Music of the Spanish Folk Plays in New Mexico. Santa Fe: Museum of New Mexico Press.
1973 *Juegos infantiles cantados en Nuevo México.* Santa Fe: Museum of New Mexico Press.
1978*a* Dark and Light in Spanish New Mexico: Music of the *Alabados* from Cerro, New Mexico, Music of the *Bailes* from El Rancho, New Mexico. New York: New World Records, Recorded Anthology of American Music.
1978*b* (Comp. and ed., with Anita Gonzales Thomas and Reed Cooper) Music of the "Bailes" in New Mexico. Santa Fe, New Mexico: The International Folk Art Foundation.

Stauter, Patrick C.
1958 100 Years in Colorado's Oldest Parish. Denver, Colorado: St. Cajetan's Press.

Steele, Thomas J., S.J.
1974 Santos and Saints: Essays and Handbook. Albuquerque, New Mexico: Calvin Horn Publisher. (Reprinted and updated as *Santos and Saints: The Religious Folk Art of Hispanic New Mexico* [Santa Fe, New Mexico: Ancient City Press, 1982].)
1976 Holy Week in Tomé. Santa Fe, New Mexico: Sunstone Press.
1978 The Spanish Passion Play in New

Mexico and Colorado. New Mexico Historical Review 53:239–59.

Stensvaag, James T.

1980 Clio on the Frontier: The Intellectual Evolution of the Historical Society of New Mexico, 1859–1925. New Mexico Historical Review 55:293–308.

Stevens, Clifford

1974 Celso Gallegos: The Santero of San Ysidro. Viva [Sunday] section, The Santa Fe New Mexican, 13 January, p. 6.

Stevenson, James

1883 Illustrated Catalogue of the Collections Obtained from the Indians of New Mexico in 1880. *In* Second Annual Report of the Bureau of Ethnology to the Secretary of the Smithsonian Institution, 1880–1881, by J. W. Powell, Director. Pp. 423–65. Washington, D.C.: Government Printing Office.

Stevenson, Matilda Coxe

1881 Zuñi and the Zunians. Privately printed. (Copy in National Anthropological Archives, Smithsonian Institution, Washington, D.C.)

1904*a* List of Collection Made by Mrs. Stevenson in Pueblo Country, Jan., 1904 to Oct., 1904. United States National Museum, Washington, D.C., Division of Ethnographic Manuscript and Pamphlet File, Southwest, folder 852.

1904*b* The Zuñi Indians: Their Mythology, Esoteric Fraternities and Ceremonies. *In* Twenty-third Annual Report of the Bureau of American Ethnology to the Secretary of the Smithsonian Institution, 1901–1902, by J. W. Powell, Director. Pp. 1–608. Washington, D.C.: Government Printing Office.

n.d. Dress and Adornment of the Pueblo Indians. Ms. no. 20903. Bureau of American Ethnology, Washington, D.C.

Stoller, Marianne L.

1976 The Early Santeros of New Mexico: A Problem in Ethnic Identity and Artistic Tradition. Paper delivered at the American Society for Ethnohistory, Albuquerque, 9 October.

1979*a* Spanish Americans, Their Servants and Sheep: A Culture History of Weaving in Southern Colorado. *In* Spanish Textile Tradition of New Mexico and Colorado. Sarah Nestor, ed. Pp. 37–52. Santa Fe: Museum of New Mexico Press, Museum of International Folk Art.

1979*b* A Study of Nineteenth Century Hispanic Arts and Crafts in the American Southwest: Appearances and Processes. Ph.D. dissertation, University of Pennsylvania.

1980 Grants of Desperation, Lands of Speculation: Mexican Period Land Grants in Colorado. Journal of the West 19, 3:22–39.

Stoller, Marianne L.; Steele, Thomas J., S.J.: and Fernández, José B.

1982 Diary of the Jesuit Residence of Our Lady of Guadalupe Parish, Conejos, Colorado—December 1871–December 1875. The Colorado College Studies 19. Colorado Springs.

Stroessner, Robert J.

1981 Discovering a Lost Masterpiece: The Virgin of Valvanera by Miguel Cabrera. Research Center for Arts Review (University of Texas at San Antonio) 4, 1 and 2:9–10.

Stubbs, Stanley A., and Ellis, Bruce T.

1955 Archaeological Investigations at the Chapel of San Miguel and the Site of La Castrense, Santa Fe, New Mexico. Monographs of the School of American Research No. 20. Santa Fe: Laboratory of Anthropology, Museum of New Mexico.

Tamarón y Romeral, Pedro

1958 *Viajes pastorales y descripción de la Diócesis de Nueva Vizcaya. In Viajes por Norteamérica.* Manuel Ballesteros, ed. Madrid: Aguilar.

Taylor, William B.
1972 Landlord and Peasant in Colonial Oaxaca. Stanford, California: Stanford University Press.

Thomas, Alfred B.
1929*a* (Ed. and trans.) Documents Bearing upon the Northern Frontier of New Mexico, 1818–19. New Mexico Historical Review 4:146–77.
1929*b* (Ed.) The Yellowstone River, James Long, and Spanish Reaction to American Intrusion into Spanish Dominions, 1818–19. New Mexico Historical Review 4:167–77.
1929–1930 (Ed.) An Anonymous Description of New Mexico, 1818. Southwestern Historical Quarterly 33:50–74.
1932 (Ed. and trans.) Forgotten Frontiers: A Study of the Spanish Indian Policy of Don Juan Bautista de Anza, Governor of New Mexico, 1777–87. Norman: University of Oklahoma Press.
1935 (Ed. and trans.) After Coronado: Spanish Exploration of New Mexico, 1696–1727. Norman: University of Oklahoma Press.

Thomas, Chauncey
1937 The Spanish Fort in Colorado, 1819. Colorado Magazine 14:82–85.

Thorp, N[athan] Howard (Jack), with Clark, Neil M.
1941 Pardner of the Wind: Story of the Southwestern Cowboy. Caldwell, Idaho: Caxton Printers.

Toulouse, Betty
1981 Prelude: Founding the Laboratory of Anthropology *and* The Laboratory's Early Years: 1927–1947. El Palacio 87, 3:4–13.

Toussaint, Manuel
1967 Colonial Art in Mexico. Elizabeth Wilder Weismann, trans. and ed. Austin: University of Texas Press.

True, Clara D.
1917 A Legend of Sangre de Cristo. El Palacio 4:1–4.

Trumbo, Theron Marcos
1947 The Gifts of Chimayo. New Mexico Magazine (February):19, 33, 35.

Tucson Museum of Art
1976 *Imágenes hispanoamericanas.* Tucson, Arizona: Tucson Museum of Art.

Turner, Victor, and Turner, Edith
1978 Image and Pilgrimage in Christian Culture. New York: Columbia University Press.

United States Census
1860 Eighth. Household Census. Microfilm. Washington, D.C.: National Archives.
1879 Ninth. Household Census. Microfilm. Washington, D.C.: National Archives.

Van Ness, John R., and Van Ness, Christine M.
1980 Introduction. Journal of the West 19, 3:3–11.

Vargas Ugarte, Rubén
1931 *Historia del Culto María en Hispanoamérica.* Lima, Peru: La Providencia.

Vedder, Alan C.
1977 Furniture of Spanish New Mexico. Santa Fe, New Mexico: Sunstone Press.

Velásquez, Meliton
1957 Guadalupe Colony Was Founded 1854. Colorado Magazine 34:263–67.

von Wuthenau, A.
1935 The Spanish Military Chapels in Santa Fe and the Reredos of Our Lady of Light. New Mexico Historical Review 10:175–95.

Wallace, Susan E.
1888 The Land of the Pueblos. Troy, New York: Nims and Knight.

Walter, Paul A. F.
1916 A New Mexico Lourdes. El Palacio 3:3–27.

Weigle, Marta
1975 (Ed.) Hispanic Villages of Northern New Mexico: A Reprint of Volume II of The 1935 Tewa Basin Study, with Supplementary Materials. Santa Fe, New Mexico: The Lightning Tree.
1976 Brothers of Light, Brothers of Blood: The Penitentes of the Southwest. Albuquerque: University of New Mexico Press.

1980– Guadalupe Baca de Gallegos' "*Los tres*
1981 *preciosidas* (The Three Treasures)": Notes on the Tale, Its Narrator and Collector. New Mexico Folklore Record 15:31–35.

Weigle, Marta, and Fiore, Kyle
1982 Santa Fe and Taos: The Writer's Era, 1916–1941. Santa Fe, New Mexico: Ancient City Press.

Weigle, Marta, and Lyons, Thomas R.
1982 Brothers and Neighbors: The Celebration of Community in Penitente Villages. *In* Celebration: Studies in Festivity and Ritual. Victor Turner, ed. Pp. 231–51. Washington, D.C.: Smithsonian Institution Press.

Weigle, Marta, with Powell, Mary
1982 From Alice Corbin's "Lines Mumbled in Sleep" to "Eufemia's Sopapillas": Women and the Federal Writers' Project in New Mexico. New America 4, 3:54–76.

West, Robert C.
1949 The Mining Community in Northern New Spain: The Parral Mining District. Ibero-Americana 30. Berkeley: University of California Press.

Wheat, Joe Ben
1976*a* Navajo Textiles in the Fred Harvey Fine Arts Collection. *In* The Fred Harvey Fine Arts Collection. Byron Harvey, ed. Pp. 9–47. Phoenix, Arizona: The Heard Museum.
1976*b* Spanish-American and Navajo Weaving, 1600 to Now. *In* Collected Papers in Honor of Margery Ferguson Lambert. Papers of the Archaeological Society of New Mexico 3:199–226.
1977 Documentary Basis for Material Changes and Design Styles in Navajo Blanket Weaving. *In* Irene Emery Roundtable on Museum Textiles, 1976 Proceedings: Ethnographic Textiles of the Western Hemisphere. Irene Emery and Patricia Fiske eds. Pp. 420–40. Washington, D.C.: Textile Museum.
1979 Rio Grande, Pueblo, and Navajo Weavers: Cross-Cultural Influence. *In* Spanish Textile Tradition of New Mexico and Colorado. Sarah Nestor, ed. Pp. 29–36. Santa Fe: Museum of New Mexico Press, Museum of International Folk Art.

White, Lynn, Jr.
1962 Medieval Technology and Social Change. London: Oxford University Press.

Wilder, Mitchell A., with Breitenbach, Edgar
1943 Santos: The Religious Folk Art of New Mexico. Colorado Springs, Colorado: The Taylor Museum of the Colorado Springs Fine Arts Center.

Winship, George Parker
1896 The Coronado Expedition, 1540–1542. *In* Fourteenth Annual Report of the Bureau of Ethnology to the Secretary of the Smithsonian Institution, 1892–1893, by J. W. Powell, Director. Pp. 329–613. Washington, D.C.: Government Printing Office.

Witherspoon, Gary
1977 Language and Art in the Navajo Universe. Ann Arbor: University of Michigan Press.

Wolf, Arthur H.
1978 The Indian Arts Fund Collection at the School of American Research. American Indian Art 4, 1:32–37.

Woodward, Dorothy
1974 The Penitentes of New Mexico. New York: Arno Press. (Ph.D. dissertation, Yale University, 1935.)

Worcester, Donald E., and Schaeffer, Wendell G.
1971 Growth and Culture of Latin America. New York: Oxford University Press.

Workers of the Writers' Program of the Work Projects Administration in the State of New Mexico
1940 New Mexico: A Guide to the Colorful State. American Guide Series. New York: Hastings House.

Wroth, William
1977 Introduction: Hispanic Southwestern Craft Traditions in the 20th Century. *In* Hispanic Crafts of the Southwest. William Wroth, ed. Pp. 1–7.

Colorado Springs, Colorado: The Taylor Museum of the Colorado Springs Fine Arts Center.

1979 The Chapel of Our Lady of Talpa. Colorado Springs, Colorado: The Taylor Museum of the Colorado Springs Fine Arts Center.

1982 Christian Images in Hispanic New Mexico: The Taylor Museum Collection of *Santos.* Colorado Springs, Colorado: The Taylor Museum of the Colorado Springs Fine Arts Center.

Wyman, Leland C.

1962 The Windways of the Navaho. Colorado Springs, Colorado: Taylor Museum.

Zubrow, Ezra B. W.

1974 Population, Contact, and Climate in the New Mexican Pueblos. Anthropological Papers of the University of Arizona No. 24. Tucson.

INDEX